The Colossal Reader

Super-size Stories & Irresistible Information

WEST
SIDE
PUBLISHING

Contributing Writers: Tom DeMichael, Rhonda Markowitz, Lexi M. Schuh, Robert Norris, Bryant Smith, Richard Mueller, Katherine Don, Kimberly Morris, Colleen Delegan, Maya Henderson, Paul Seaburn, James Duplacey, Martin Graham, Terri Schlichenmeyer, Patricia Martinelli, Kelly Wittman, Paul Morie, Eric Peterson, Richard Knight, Jr.

Fact-checkers: Brenda Bourg, Kathryn Holcomb, Jennifer McCune, Keith Potempa, Leigh Smith

Picture credits:

Cover illustrator: Adrian Chesterman

clipart.com: 110, 114, 142, 143, 197, 225, 239, 303, 305, 319, 323, 356, 487; **iStockphoto:** 150, 167, 189; **Library of Congress:** 373; **liquidlibrary:** 194; **Shutterstock:** 245, 314, 482

Contributing illustrator: Robert Schoolcraft

Louis Weber, CEO
Publications International, Ltd.
7373 North Cicero Avenue
Lincolnwood, Illinois 60712

ISBN-13: 978-1-4127-1526-3
ISBN-10: 1-4127-1526-2

Manufactured in U.S.A.

8 7 6 5 4 3 2 1

Contents

❖ ❖ ❖ ❖

There's a First Time for Everything

❖ ❖ ❖ ❖

It's our first! Our first annual edition, that is. It's colossal (literally)! It's a veritable cornucopia of facts, stories, and nuggets of information about a plethora of subjects of every kind. It's full of tantalizing trivia for trying times—and there's something in this book to tickle the mental funny bone of just about anyone, young or otherwise.

This annual book is a gift from us, the editors of the Armchair Readers™, to you—it's truly a readers' eclectic confection that we believe will leave you fully satisfied yet still hungry for more. The focus—as you've no doubt come to expect from the Armchair Readers™—is unfocused. This volume is about anything and everything; history, sports, animals, science, entertainment, philosophy, business—you get the picture. You can open the book at any point and find something enjoyable, interesting, and unique to titillate your mind. It's an introduction to hundreds of different ideas, people, and events that may lead you to explore more deeply into these fascinating topics. You may decide to take the next step and become an expert. Or not. It's your choice. It's all there for your pleasure, and it was our pleasure to create it for you.

Some tasty hors d'oeuvres from this veritable feast for the intellectual palate:

• In the middle of World War II, Los Angeles exploded in violence during the Zoot Suit Riots, which had nothing to do with Germany or Japan.

• A library—with an opera house above it!—straddles the border of two countries.

• Superman took on the Ku Klux Klan over the radio, revealing the secrets of the organization to a country full of listeners.

• Noted physician and scientist Peter Mark Roget laid the groundwork for the camera shutter, invented a logarithm slide rule, helped create the London sewer system, and loved to collect words, which he published as the first *Roget's Thesaurus*.

- The people of Gander, Newfoundland, opened their city and their hearts to help heal the world on one of the worst days of the 21st century.

- The heir to the Winchester rifle fortune spent most of her life building and remodeling her mansion to appease the spirits that haunted her.

- The idea behind ARPANET, an ancestor of the Internet, was to create an "inter-galactic" computer network.

- How many ways can there be to *fail* to kill Fidel Castro?

And it's calorie and carbohydrate-free! As far as we know, brain expansion adds no true weight to the body, and it can only be a good thing. You can actually be exercising your brain while you're comfortably ensconced in or on your own favorite reading surface. So by all means assume the (most comfortable) position, and prepare to be thoroughly entertained and enlightened, secure in the knowledge that the editors of the Armchair Readers™ are working like busy little bees on the next annual edition—just for you.

Please enjoy,

Allen Orso
Publisher

P.S. If you have any questions, concerns, or ideas pertaining to this book, or if you would like more information about other West Side Publishing titles, please contact us at: **www.armchairreader.com.**

Out in 90 Seconds:
The Story of the Stopwatch Gang

*In the 1970s and '80s, Canada and the United States experienced
a whirlwind of unforgettable bank heists pulled by debonair
"celebrity" robbers. Even today, their story isn't over.*

In October 2005, FBI agents arrested Stephen Duffy, a successful
Florida real estate agent, during a security investigation involving passport fraud. They weren't actually looking for the man they
found. A fingerprint check showed that Duffy was, in reality, Christopher Clarkson, a fugitive from justice who was once a member
of a daring group of bank robbers known as the Stopwatch Gang.
As Stephen Duffy, he'd eluded Canadian and American authorities
for three decades. Time had finally run out for the last member of
the most notorious and resourceful group of bank robbers since the
feared Jesse James Gang of the 19th century.

Speed Demons
Speed was the essential ingredient of the Stopwatch Gang. Precision
timing and painstaking planning made the thieves so successful. No
heist ever exceeded 2 minutes; in most cases the robbers were in and
out in 90 seconds. Becoming living legends, they held up more than
100 banks throughout Canada and the United States with panache,
precision, and politeness.

The leader of the band was Patrick "Paddy" Michael Mitchell,
a Canadian Irishman who, together with his partners Stephen Reid
and Lionel Wright, netted somewhere between $8 and $15 million
in all. Reid wore a stopwatch around his neck to time the robberies
so they wouldn't exceed two minutes in duration—that's how the
gang earned its colorful sobriquet. Reid's favorite comment to his
intended victims was, "This won't take long, folks."

If they'd stuck to robbing banks, the criminals might still be enjoying the luxury of their posh Arizona hideaway; unfortunately, they
decided to branch out into drug smuggling. That's when Clarkson,
who had some expertise as a drug runner, joined the gang. Their first
attempt at smuggling cocaine into Canada, however, was a disaster,

and the group was busted. Clarkson made bail and disappeared. Though he was tried in absentia and found guilty, he would remain free all those years by stealing the identity of a four-year-old California boy, Stephen Duffy, who drowned in the family swimming pool. The fate of the other gang members during those 30 years is the stuff of which legends are made.

Creative Convicts

After they were captured, Mitchell, Reid, and Wright received heavy jail sentences. All three escaped, or as it's known in urban slang, enacted "jackrabbit parole." After recapture, Reid and Wright were sent to Canadian prisons on an inmate exchange.

Mitchell engineered two daring jackrabbit paroles and is believed to be the first fugitive ever to appear on the FBI's Ten Most Wanted List twice. He was arrested for the final time in 1994 after a solo bank heist in Mississippi and sent to Leavenworth Prison. Mitchell's requests for an exchange to Canada so that he could be near his family (he married while on the lam and had a son and two grandchildren) were continually denied by U.S. authorities, who, as Mitchell expressed it, "wanted their pound of flesh." Mitchell, known as "the gentleman bandit" due to his nonviolent approach to robbery, became a successful author and Internet blogger while incarcerated. Mitchell's blog posts were sent via snail mail to a third party who posted them in Mitchell's name on a Canadian Web site, where they became quite popular. Resultantly, his autobiography, *This Bank Robber's Life*, became a brisk seller online. Because he achieved all this while in custody since 1994, Mitchell never even knew what the Internet was like. He died from lung and brain cancer on January 14, 2007, in a North Carolina prison hospital at age 64. On January 25, his remains returned to his hometown of Ottawa, where hundreds of friends, family members, and admirers turned out for a good old-fashioned Irish wake in honor of this "gentle" bandit who loved robbing banks but never harmed a soul.

Stephen Reid, who was serving a 14-year sentence, also made good use of his time behind bars, writing a semi-fictional novel entitled *Jackrabbit Parole*. A copy of Reid's manuscript was sent to critically acclaimed Canadian poet and editor Susan Musgrave, writer-in-residence at the University of Waterloo. Susan agreed to edit Reid's novel, leading to a string of correspondence that resulted in her proposal of marriage to him. They were married in 1986, the same year that Reid's best-selling novel was published. It was Musgrave's third marriage, yet her first in the confines of a penitentiary, where the couple also spent their honeymoon. In 1987, Reid was paroled, and the couple settled down in a seaside tree house near Victoria, British Columbia, with Susan's daughter from a previous marriage, Charlotte. In 1989, the couple's daughter, Sophie, was born. It seemed like a modern fairy tale, if a little rough around the edges.

For quite some time, Stephen trod the straight and narrow. Life appeared blissful. However, as Susan's literary career continued to blossom, Reid's began to flounder. Struggling with the stress of trying to complete his second novel, Reid turned to the overriding demon in his life—heroin. He'd been addicted to the drug since his early teens and hadn't kicked the habit. This time his addiction would have dire consequences, shattering the near-idyllic family life of the ex-con and the writer.

During the process of building a new home, Reid met Allan McCallum, a recovering drug addict. On June 9, 1999, while doing heroin and cocaine, the two men became fairly strung out and decided to rob a bank—a bad idea that ended in a worse fate. A total disaster, the heist was a careless, sloppy, ill-planned attempt and very uncharacteristic for a former member of the Stopwatch Gang. The men were captured after a chase and five-hour standoff. Reid was charged with ten counts, including attempted murder for shooting at pursuing police officers. On December 22, 1999, the 49-year-old was sentenced to 18 years in prison. After serving more than eight years, Reid was granted day parole in January 2008. This allowed him freedom during the day but required him to spend his nights at a halfway house.

Speeding Along the Straight and Narrow
It seems the only member of the Stopwatch Gang to remain outside of prison and really go straight was Lionel Wright, who cut off all contact with his former cohorts. Wright is said to be working as an accountant for Correctional Service of Canada, a division of the criminal justice system. A richer irony may be hard to find.

Hearst at His Worst

Media mogul William Randolph Hearst built an empire out of sensationalism and dishonesty. Owning a large percentage of America's newspapers in the first half of the 20th century, he exemplified the notion of yellow journalism.

In the 1890s, long before the advent of broadcast television, cable, and the Internet, even before radio, America relied on the daily newspaper to deliver the news. Propped up at the breakfast table, opened and folded on the trolley car, or perused from a park bench, newspapers became the trusted source for "what's what" across the country. Publishers such as Horace Greeley and James Gordon Bennett, taking advantage of their influential powers, forged a path of biased, politically and monetarily swayed reporting that would soon be undertaken by other newspaper publishers such as Joseph Pulitzer and, especially, famed magnate William Randolph Hearst.

Wee Willie
Hearst was born in 1863 in San Francisco, the son of a successful mining entrepreneur. Even as a young lad, he knew how to stir up trouble. For example, he set off some fireworks in his bedroom one night, yelled, "Fire!" down the hallway, locked the door, and waited as the fire department came crashing through it. While attending Harvard University, he was expelled—possibly for a combination of pranks and poor grades. Inheriting his father's Comstock mining fortune in 1887, Hearst decided that publishing would be a lucrative, secure venture and took over a number of faltering newspapers, including the *San Francisco Examiner.*

All the News That's (Un)Fit to Print
In efforts to up his numbers, Hearst became something of a champion of the people. He focused on revealing corruption in the San Francisco Police Department, city hall, and at Folsom Prison. He relished reporting on lurid crimes and blazing fires, and he filled the *Examiner* with political cartoons of all sorts. One writer for the paper masqueraded as a homeless person and was admitted to the city's

hospital. When her story revealed the rampant cruelty and neglect she found there, the entire hospital staff was fired.

The number of publications under the Hearst banner grew, and he eventually built an unprecedented empire. At its height, he owned a whopping 28 newspapers and a variety of magazines; by the close of his career, he'd owned a total of 36 newspapers and multiple magazines. Among these were some of the most influential and widely read publications in the country, including the *Washington Herald,* the *Seattle Post-Intelligencer,* and the *Baltimore Post.*

Hearst's chief rival, Joseph Pulitzer, ran the *New York World,* another newspaper deeply rooted in aggressive reporting. In 1895, a strange cartoon character began appearing in Pulitzer's paper. A bald boy with a toothy smile, he was called the "Yellow Kid" (the Kid appeared in a color cartoon and sported a nightshirt of this shade). After a fierce bidding war, the popular "Yellow Kid" was moved to Hearst's *New York Journal* in 1896 and, with both papers' reputation for using their pages to stir up trouble, the concept behind their nature became known as "yellow journalism." As the years went on, so did the stories peppered with increasingly exaggerated and biased claims. Hearst often published articles colored with shades of his own prejudices and agendas—the opposite of fair news reporting.

A War, Made to Order

Hearst and Pulitzer received a lot of credit for getting America into the Spanish-American War in 1898. The accusations may be exaggerated, although their publications did keep Spain's occupation of Cuba on the front pages. An oft-told story (with questionable accuracy) has Hearst rebuffing a photographer's claim that there was no war in Cuba, stating, "You furnish the pictures—I'll furnish the war." For example, one week after America declared war on Spain, Hearst ran a front-page headline asking, "How Do You Like the *Journal*'s War?" The devastating explosion that destroyed the U.S. battleship *Maine* while it was docked in the Havana harbor was immediately blamed on Spanish terrorists, yet it is more likely that an internal fire ignited the ammunition stored onboard. The *World* and the *Journal* led the way in exacerbating patriotic sentiment before and during the five-month conflict, with Hearst actually traveling to Cuba as a reporter and filing regular stories of the carnage.

Fanning the Flames

With the war behind them, the journalistic holdings of Pulitzer and Hearst took separate paths. Pulitzer, feeling somewhat guilty about the direction his paper had taken, righted his *New York World*. It became a respected and prestigious daily, before closing in 1931. But Hearst hitched the *Journal* to the 1900 political campaign of William Jennings Bryan, a progressive Democrat who was running for president against Republican incumbent William McKinley. Hearst painted McKinley as a puppet of wealthy industrialists, with Bryan as a hero who would come to the country's rescue. Hearst papers also took shots at McKinley's running mate, Theodore Roosevelt. He was portrayed in political cartoons as an ugly, young boy in a Rough Rider hat who bullied McKinley.

Despite Hearst's efforts to defeat McKinley, the president returned to office. Prior to the inauguration in March 1900, Hearst editorials stooped to shockingly suggest that McKinley be assassinated. When fiction became fact in September of the next year, Hearst was accused of being somewhat responsible for McKinley's death through his papers' editorials. The backlash was so bad that he changed the name of the *Journal* to the more patriotic-sounding *American*.

Hearst did not limit his sensationalist provocations to American affairs. When the Japanese were victorious in the Russo-Japanese War in 1905, Hearst's papers warned their readers to beware of "the yellow menace." During the early years of World War I, Hearst's editorials had a pro-German slant, painting an anti-British picture. Between 1928 and the mid-1930s, he featured syndicated editorials by Benito Mussolini, dictator of fascist Italy. In 1930, Hearst asked a newly elected leader in Germany to write articles for him. The new columnist—Adolf Hitler—took advantage of the forum and wrote of his plans to bring Germany out of its economic woes. He also wrote of Germany's innocence in World War I and the unfair conditions of the Versailles Treaty. Hitler was ultimately fired from Hearst's stable for, among other reasons, missing too many deadlines.

At one point, Hearst's empire became a little too big for its own britches. In addition to the dozens of newspapers and magazines he owned, he added two news services, several radio stations, and a film company. Overextension and the Great Depression forced the liquidation of many of his holdings in the late 1920s.

What About *Citizen Kane*?

In 1941, a 26-year-old first-time filmmaker named Orson Welles cowrote, produced, starred in, and directed a film called *Citizen Kane*. The similarities between the title character, Charles Foster Kane, and William Randolph Hearst were hardly coincidental. The movie told of the life of a newspaper publisher famous for printing sensational stories, rampant artwork collecting, having an affair with a famous performer, and failed political aspirations—all factual occurrences from Hearst's life. Hearst was so outraged at first mention of the film's impending release, he offered RKO Pictures $800,000 to burn all prints and the master negative. When the studio refused, he barred every member of his media empire from even mentioning the film. Despite all Hearst's efforts to quell *Kane*, the film came to be regarded as possibly the greatest of all time by hordes of critics and filmgoers.

Opinions differ on whether or not Hearst ever saw *Citizen Kane*, but he wasn't without opportunity. In a chance meeting in a San Francisco elevator, Welles came face-to-face with Hearst. He offered the media magnate an invitation to see the film. Hearst silently declined and exited the elevator.

• *Leon Trotsky struggled with both Lenin and Stalin for control of the newly formed Soviet Union. Banished from Russia, Trotsky found refuge in Mexico, where he was killed by a follower of Stalin.*

• *Days after delivering his Gettysburg Address, President Abraham Lincoln was afflicted with red blotches, which were ultimately determined to be contagious, mild smallpox. Lincoln declared, "Now I have something I can give everybody."*

Syllable Secrets: Etymology

Kaleidoscope: A tube containing bits of colored glass or plastic that rearrange themselves when the tube is twisted or shaken; literal meaning is "observer of beautiful forms," coined by its inventor, Sir David Brewster (1781–1868), from Greek *kalos* (beautiful) + *eidos* (shape) + *-scope*, from *telescope*; the figurative meaning, a "constantly changing pattern," attributed to poet George Gordon, Lord Byron (1788–1824)

Love: Strong affection based on family ties or physical attraction, or a warmly enthusiastic attachment to a person, thing, or idea; derived from Old English *leof* (dear) and Latin *lubere* or *libere* (to please)

Mustard: A food condiment; originated in 1190 from Old French *moustarde*, derived from *moust* (must) and the Latin *mustum* (new wine), so called because it was originally prepared by adding the substance must to the ground seeds of the plant to make a paste

Percussion: Musical instrument(s) that creates a rhythmic beat, including, but not limited to, drums and maracas; derived from Latin *percutere* (to beat) and also *per-* (thoroughly) + *quatere* (to shake)

Halitosis: a medical condition causing bad breath; from Latin *halitus* (breath; related to *halare*, "to breathe") + Greek noun suffix *-osis*

Horoscope: A method of typecasting personalities and/or foretelling a possible future by studying the stars' position in the heavens at the time of one's birth; derivation of Greek *horoskopos* (nativity), from Greek *hora* (hour) + *skopos* (watching, in reference to the hour of birth)

December: Twelfth month of the year, formerly tenth month of the old Roman calendar; derivation of Middle English *Decembre*, from Latin *decem* (ten)

Butter: Creamy food spread; from Old English *butere*, a derivation of Greek *boutyron*, hailing from *bous* (cow) + *tyros* (cheese)

Horizon: The visual conjunction of earth or sea with the sky; from Greek *horizein* (to bound, define) derived from *horos* (boundary); also possibly akin to Latin *urvum* (curved part of a plow)

Yard: A unit of measurement equal to three feet, or 36 inches; from Old English *gierd* (twig, measure, yard); akin to Old German *gart* (stick) and Latin *hasta* (spear)

The Not-So-Sweet Story of *Candy*

A sensual tale jumped through countless legal hoops on its road to cult-classic status, making it one of the most beleaguered and scandalized pieces of fiction in contemporary history.

The saga of the novel *Candy* is legendary in the literary world. First published in 1958, the erotic story tells of Candy Christian, a sweet, innocent, but incredibly curious young girl who travels the world in search of adventure. Yet more interesting than the plot, perhaps, is the backstory surrounding the novel's writing and publishing—and publishing, and more publishing...

Let's Start at the Very Beginning

Many young American writers came out of World War II wondering what they could do with their wordy talents. Texan Terry Southern and New Yorker Mason Hoffenberg, both veterans, chose to take their GI Bill benefits and attend the Sorbonne in Paris in 1948. They became fast friends and were early examples of Beat artists such as Jack Kerouac (who was close with Southern and Hoffenberg in Paris). The duo spent evenings in jazz clubs drinking a thick, syrupy, anise-flavored liqueur called Pernod and smoking hashish. Occasionally one or the other would sell an article to a little-read literary magazine, while success and satisfaction eluded them.

Enter the Publisher

A man named Maurice Girodias ran Obelisk Press, a risqué book company in Paris that he had inherited from his father before the war. When one of France's largest publishers bought out the company in 1952, Girodias set out on his own with Olympia Press. He quickly made his mark by publishing English-language versions of forbidden erotic books by authors such as Henry Miller. In 1955, he made history by publishing Vladimir Nabokov's *Lolita,* only to see it banned by French censors. The publisher brought a lawsuit against the censors and won, earning the right to continue printing the story of a grown man who obsesses over a 12-year-old girl. Girodias also embraced many of the young American writers in Paris, including

Southern and Hoffenberg. He encouraged many female writers as well, many of whom wrote what were simply called "dirty books," or "DBs," under male pseudonyms.

Meanwhile, Hoffenberg returned to New York City—more specifically, to the bohemian neighborhood of Greenwich Village—where he acquired a dangerous affinity for heroin. Southern remained in Paris, where he got the notion to create a modern satire of Voltaire's 18th-century novel *Candide*. Southern described the outline of this novella to Girodias in a letter dated December 1956, telling of a young midwestern girl who is party to a series of erotic adventures with men from all walks of life. The publisher was quite intrigued and encouraged Southern to extend the book into a full-length novel.

Writing under the pen name Maxwell Kenton, Southern began to flesh out *Candy*, writing at least two pages every day. But the task quickly became tedious and, even with the encouragement of his wife, Carol, he began missing deadlines to his publisher. The frustrated author contacted Hoffenberg in New York City and asked him to contribute to the story. The two writers wrote and exchanged pages of *Candy* for nearly two years, continuing after Hoffenberg moved back to Europe.

Like Taking *Candy* from a Baby

Girodias paid Southern and Hoffenberg only a few hundred dollars for their finished manuscript. As soon as he printed and distributed 5,000 copies of *Candy* in France, the French vice squad confiscated them as immoral. Girodias would not be dissuaded. He merely changed the title and cover and rewrote the first few pages; the police were none the wiser. Girodias's "new" novel, *Lollipop*, was exported to England as well as peddled by local Parisian booksellers. He was back in business. The authors, however, received nothing from this "new" publication.

Southern continued to ply his craft, writing for magazines including popular titles such as *Esquire*. Hoffenberg, on the other hand, was a poet at heart who was also fighting a seesaw battle with his addiction to heroin. In 1962, Girodias reprinted *Candy* with a caveat that it was "not to be sold in the USA or the UK." At the same time, Southern, who continued to gain credibility as an author and screenwriter (working with director Stanley Kubrick on the *Dr. Strangelove* script), had renowned literary agent Sterling Lord working to publish *Candy* in the United States. The task was not easy, as Lord was representing a book the authors did not own.

A fault in international copyright laws at the time complicated matters by depriving the writers of the royalties owed them. Works written outside the United States were not protected by a U.S. copyright unless an interim copyright was filed in America. Neither Southern nor Hoffenberg (and certainly not Girodias) ever made the application, allowing dozens of unauthorized, pirate editions of *Candy* to hit bookshelves in the 1960s. The authors did not receive a dime of the hundreds of thousands of dollars that might otherwise have been owed to them.

Despite all of this, the editor in chief at G. P. Putnam's Sons Books was keenly interested in *Candy*, having fought the censorship battle by successfully publishing the best-selling American edition of *Lolita* in 1958. He signed a royalty contract with Southern and Hoffenberg (who ironically had possession of Girodias's pen to sign it) and an American hardcover edition of *Candy* appeared in May 1964.

America Likes Its *Candy*

To say the novel was a best seller is an understatement of enormous proportions. Putnam sold more than 10,000 copies in the first two days, with 14,000 copies sold in the first week. Although not without its share of decency lawsuits, *Candy* was a landmark publication. If *Lolita* had been the first nail in the coffin of print censorship in America, then *Candy* was the sound of it sealing shut.

Yet, sadly, *Candy*'s success led to the acrimonious parting of Southern and Hoffenberg as friends. Hoffenberg became envious of Southern's success; Hoffenberg's drug addiction had made him persona non grata on the book's publicity trail. As far as the public could see, Terry Southern was *the* author of the nation's number-two best seller of 1964.

A Happy Ending?

A final agreement was signed in early 1967 establishing Southern and Hoffenberg as the sole copyright owners. Maurice Girodias was allowed to keep the money he had made on the book and could negotiate publishing rights in Britain. All parties consented to legally pursue the myriad pirate editions together.

By the year's end, a movie version of *Candy* was under way, although Hollywood had yet to adjust its rules of censorship the way the literary world had done. Many wondered how the film could possibly be made. Hoffenberg had left the situation entirely, and Southern, miffed when he heard the book's famous "hunchback encounter" would not be included, left the screenplay writing to hired hand Buck Henry.

The 1968 film was ultimately a disaster; stars such as Marlon Brando, Richard Burton, Ringo Starr, James Coburn, and Walter Matthau couldn't save it. The movie may have been doomed from the start when a Swedish girl named Ewa Aulin—who spoke no English—was cast to play the pivotal all-American title role.

Southern's writing career continued to grow exponentially, as he went on to international acclaim for such highly influential books as *The Magic Christian, Blue Movie,* and *Flash and Filigree,* as well as for the scripts of some of the most emblematic films of their eras, such as *The Cincinnati Kid, Casino Royale,* and *Barbarella.* He even did some television work, writing for *Saturday Night Live* in the early '80s. By the time of his death from stomach cancer in 1995, Southern was known as a great literary satirist, lambasting Hollywood, pop culture at large, and the human libido. Hoffenberg, however, managed to write two other little-read books alongside a smattering of poetry and is mostly remembered as a shadow in the sometimes sweet, often bitter *Candy* saga.

- *Before the Spanish conquest of South America, the Incan Empire included 9 to 16 million people. It took Spanish explorers nine years to conquer the Incas.*

- *The discovery of the Piltdown Man in 1912 was considered the missing link between man and ape. In 1953, new tests proved it was a hoax.*

- *Joseph Stalin's mother sent him to a seminary in Tbilisi, Georgia, which was part of the Russian Empire, to study to become a priest. He spent much of his time, however, participating in revolutionary activities.*

Fumbling Felons

Choose Your Designated Driver Carefully

Many people drink alcoholic beverages responsibly. If they do have a little too much, most designate a capable driver. In November 2007, however, a 41-year-old man in Clio, Michigan, made a few key mistakes in his choice. Despite the fact that the man selected his son as his designated driver, the two ended up stuck in the mud where police arrested them both. What happened? His son was only 13 years old and also drunk.

He Was Only Reporting a Robbery

A man in south Texas called police to report a theft in 2007. Nothing unusual about that, right? Yet, the man told police that two masked gunmen had kicked in his door and stole 150 pounds of marijuana. He then explained to police that he was wrapping the drugs for shipment when the gunmen arrived. When police investigated the "crime," they found 15 pounds of the stuff lying on the man's floor. Not only did police charge the man with felony possession of marijuana, but he also turned out to be an illegal immigrant.

Half-Baked

After robbing two convenience stores in an hour, a man went for a third caper just a few hours later on September 30, 2007, in Delaware. The thief used a note that read, "Give me your money I'll shoot you." It was the same note used in the previous robberies. This time, however, the 25-year-old robber left his demand behind, and it just so happened to be written on the pay stub from his job at a local bakery. Along with fingerprints, the stub included the thief's full name. Bail was quickly set at $31,000.

Funny Money

In Gary, Indiana, a cafeteria worker broke up a money-counterfeiting scheme when she was handed a fake $20 bill. The culprit: a ten-year-old boy. He aroused her suspicion when he paid for lunch with the large bill, so she turned it in. Police say the boy enlisted the help of two of his friends and created the money on his home computer. In December 2005, the children faced charges of forgery and theft. The boys are the youngest counterfeiters the FBI has ever come across. Reportedly, the counterfeits were even pretty good.

How to Electrocute an Elephant

A circus elephant named Topsy became the pawn in a feud between two of the most prolific inventors of the era. The result was the first public electrocution and an act of animal cruelty that came close to sullying Thomas Edison's reputation.

In 1903, two important inventors were engaged in brisk competition to sell the merits of their respective forms of electricity. Nikola Tesla was the inventor of *alternating current* (AC), which varies in direction and magnitude as it flows. Thomas Edison, inventor of the version that maintains a constant direction, called *direct current* (DC), vigorously advocated his invention as the sensible and safe choice for illumination. He went to great lengths to discredit AC as being unsafe for public consumption. His opportunity to publicly demonstrate AC's supposed dangers came about when a popular Coney Island elephant named Topsy was condemned by her owners for killing her third handler in as many years. The aggressive act by the 3-ton, 10-foot-tall, 20-foot-long pachyderm was in retaliation for cruelly being fed a lit cigarette by an abusive handler named J. F. Blount. Topsy lifted Blount into the air and dashed him to the ground, killing him instantly and becoming a candidate for the gallows. The American Society for the Prevention of Cruelty to Animals strenuously objected to her hanging, a cue for Edison to proffer his services and suggest electrocution instead.

"A Rather Inglorious Affair"

The public event drew more than 1,500 onlookers to Coney Island's Luna Park. The elephant was first fed a ration of carrots containing 460 grams of potassium cyanide in preparation for the main event. She was then fitted with copper-lined wooden sandals and electrodes and jolted with 6,600 volts of electricity. A few sparks and Topsy was dead; one newspaper referred to it as "a rather inglorious affair."

The event was filmed, and Edison exhibited the film throughout the country, but his plan to discredit AC backfired. Topsy's execution, which mercifully took less than one minute, was a success due to the power of AC and was not a condemnation of the current as Edison had hoped.

French New Wave Cinema? *Mais Oui!*

*A group of Parisian filmmakers changed the way
the world conceived of and made movies.*

The filmmakers of *La Nouvelle Vague,* or French New Wave, in the late 1950s established the auteur theory of making movies, wherein the director is considered the ultimate creator of a film (*auteur* is French for "author"). These concepts about film initially appeared in a radical and influential magazine called *Cahiers du Cinema,* founded by critic André Bazin in the early '50s. Many of the writers in this journal put their theories into practice and began making films themselves. Admiring highly individualized American mavericks such as Orson Welles and John Ford as well as Briton Alfred Hitchcock, New Wave directors sought to mark each of their films with a personalized stamp. These movies broke new ground, turning away from traditional narrative forms that were the norm in post–World War II France. Directors such as François Truffaut, Alain Resnais, and Jean-Luc Godard thumbed their noses at what had previously passed for quality French cinema.

Although short on technical skills and money, these renegade filmmakers actually turned their shortcomings into strengths and signature characteristics. New Wave films were known for handheld cameras, on-location shooting, improvised scenes and dialogue, natural lighting, long single takes, and jarring jump-cut editing. Originally dismissed as esoteric "art films," many French New Wave efforts, such as Truffaut's *The 400 Blows* and *Shoot the Piano Player,* Godard's *Breathless* and *Une femme est une femme,* and Resnais's *Hiroshima, Mon Amour,* became international hits. Their influence, particularly the idea that a director should be free to include whatever nontraditional elements that he or she pleased, led to a fresh view of film. This can especially be seen in the "Hollywood Renaissance" of the late '60s and '70s.

The 400 Blows
Autobiographical in nature, this first feature by Truffaut tells of a troublesome 12-year-old boy, Antoine, who runs away from home

to create his own world of petty crime and fantasy, only to end up being arrested. Its impact was immediate, winning Truffaut the Best Director award at the 1959 Cannes Film Festival. The final scene of the boy's escape from detention camp is, like much of New Wave cinema, ambiguous. After running for what seems to be forever, Antoine arrives at a peaceful but desolate beach. He turns and the frame freezes—is he free or has he been recaptured? From the look on his face, it's hard to tell.

Hiroshima, Mon Amour

This 1959 feature by Alain Resnais chronicles the brief affair of a married French actress and a married Japanese architect who meet while she is filming in Japan. Their love scenes are contrasted with horrific footage of the aftermath of Hiroshima's atomic bombing. Resnais uses liberal flashbacks and repetitive phrases throughout the film, keeping viewers off balance while the lovers recall moments from the war. *Hiroshima, Mon Amour* seems to focus simultaneously on two tragedies: the couple's impossible romance and the world's political turmoil. Resnais's story of lost love and rebuilding earned Oscar nominations and won critics' awards.

Weekend

Director Jean-Luc Godard once wrote in *Cahiers du Cinema*, "A film should become a reality within itself." The seemingly endless 360-degree pan, accompanied by a Mozart piano piece, that opens *Weekend* may have been part of Godard's reality, but it hardly belongs to the average viewer's world. This 1967 film still stands as one of the more experimental New Wave offerings. The plot involves a married couple's nightmarish weekend trip to visit family. A famous scene features a ceaseless din of blaring car horns, children playing next to a car accident, and a seven-minute-long tracking shot that reveals a most surreal traffic jam. Godard left his definitive statement about the medium itself by ending *Weekend* with two title cards: "End of Cinema," followed by "End of the World."

The Brain of Roger Sperry

One of the most brilliant minds in recent history uncovered the truth behind how everyone else's mind really functions.

Roger Sperry, the neurobiologist whose research helped redefine the common understanding of the human brain, was born in Hartford, Connecticut, in 1913. Sperry attended Oberlin College in Ohio on an academic scholarship. After receiving bachelor's and master's degrees from Oberlin, he performed doctoral work at the University of Chicago, receiving his degree in 1941. Following a stint at the National Institutes of Health, Sperry accepted a professorship at California Institute of Technology (Caltech), where his most famous and revolutionary work was to take place.

The "Dumb" Side of the Brain

When Sperry started his tenure at Caltech, mainstream scientific conclusions about the human brain were much different than they are today. Previous experiments had allegedly shown that the left hemisphere of the brain fueled human capacity for written and spoken language. This gave rise to the "classic" view of the brain, in which the left hemisphere was dominant and the seat of intellect, controlling all language mechanisms and higher functions. Under the classic theory, the right hemisphere was viewed as being inferior to the left, lacking higher cognitive functions. When delivering his lecture after receiving the 1981 Nobel Prize for Medicine, Sperry joked that under the classic view, the right hemisphere was "relatively retarded."

The role of the corpus callosum, the fibrous tissue connecting the two hemispheres, was also poorly understood under this previous theory. In a cavalier display of ignorance, one neuroscience authority had even gone so far as to remark that it was there just to keep the two hemispheres from falling into each other. Most scientists believed that severing this tissue had no effect on the behavior and brain activity of the subject. Sperry's work at Caltech divulged the true role of the corpus callosum and turned conventional wisdom on its head.

Cutting Right to the Point

Sperry's studies on patients who'd undergone an operation severing the corpus callosum (as a treatment for epilepsy) found previous assumptions that the right hemisphere lacked all language skills were utterly wrong. Though unable to comprehend written language, the right hemisphere does understand spoken language and is the side that analyzes abstract meaning and physical space. Also, when tests were performed on the left brain to see if it had awareness about what was occurring in the right hemisphere during studies, it turned out to be completely unaware of them.

From these studies, called "Split-Brain" experiments, it was shown that brain functions are spread across the two hemispheres. While the left hemisphere is largely dedicated to sequential and verbal tasks such as reading and counting, the right hemisphere excels at spatial reasoning and contextual analysis of language. There is no "dumb" half and "super" half, just a delegation of duties, per se. Pop culture latched onto this idea, but in his Nobel lecture, Sperry warned that talk of purely "left-brained" or "right-brained" individuals is a gross distortion of the true state of affairs. Under normal circumstances, a healthy corpus callosum transfers information between the left and right halves, allowing the hemispheres to work closely together as a functional unit, sharing duties.

With that considered, Roger Sperry probably never took one of those "right-brained" or "left-brained" Internet quizzes.

- *Scientists say that the average human brain can easily remember no more than seven numbers in random sequence at a time.*

- *Human thumbs have their very own "control room" in the brain, separate from the control area of the other digits on the hand.*

- *The average Neanderthal had a brain that was larger than yours.*

Fast Facts

- Of the beheading device he proposed in 1789, Paris physician Joseph Guillotin stated, "My machine will take off a head in a twinkling and the victim will feel nothing but a refreshing coolness."

- An accident on the north end of Boston on January 15, 1919, flooded the area with two-and-a-half million gallons of molasses in a wave as much as 15 feet tall. Twenty-one people were killed, and 150 more were injured.

- The shortest reign of a Portuguese king was 20 minutes. When the royal family was ambushed in February 1908, the king died immediately and his heir, Luis Filipe, died 20 minutes later.

- National Bathroom Reading Week is the second week in June.

- In about 200 B.C., the Carthaginian ruler, Hannibal, defeated an enemy's navy by stuffing poisonous snakes into earthen jugs and catapulting them onto the decks of his opponent's ships.

- Maine is the only U.S. state whose name has just one syllable.

- Construction on the Great Wall of China began about 700 B.C. The wall was extended and enlarged to more than 4,000 miles over a period of 2,300 years.

- The coldest temperature ever recorded in the United States was in Prospect Creek Camp, Alaska, when the thermometer dived down to a teeth-chattering $-79.8°$ F on January 23, 1971.

- Commercial deodorant became available in 1888. Roll-on deodorant was invented in the 1950s, using technology from standard ballpoint pens.

- Thanksgiving is celebrated on the fourth Thursday in November, by decree of President Franklin Roosevelt. Thus, the earliest date that Thanksgiving can fall is November 22.

Shoot-out at Little Bohemia

*Infamous gangster John Dillinger was something of a media
darling during his long, terrorizing reign. He was also the force
behind one of the most embarrassing federal mishaps of all time.*

In an era known for its long list of public enemies, John Dillinger
and his crew stood out more like endeared celebrities than the
convicted killers and robbers they were known to be. Historians at-
tribute this strange awe to the gang's Robin Hood–like appeal during
a stressful time for the public.

Robbing the Rich

The public, demoralized by the ongoing Depression, lacked financial
and bureaucratic faith after suffering devastating losses at what they
saw to be the hands of irresponsible government and financial institutions. When the dashing, physically graceful Dillinger and his equally
charismatic crew began tearing through banks, they not only provided
an exciting and dramatic media distraction, they also destroyed banks'
potentially devastating mortgage paperwork in their wake. The masses
seemed eager to clasp onto the real-life drama and connect it to their
own plight. The public was more than willing to forgive the sins of
outlaws such as Dillinger's crew in favor of the payback they provided
to financial institutions that had ruined so many families already.

Law officials, however, weren't so keen on the criminals. J. Edgar
Hoover and his newly formed Federal Bureau of Investigation were
weary of gangsters' soft public perception and crafted a series of
hard-hitting laws meant to immobilize them. Those found guilty of
crimes such as robbing banks would now face stiffer penalties. Dillinger, one of the most prominent, popular, and evasive of the lot, was
at the top of Hoover's hit list. However, keeping the gangster in jail
and strapped with a sufficient sentence seemed like more work than
Hoover could handle.

Hiding Out

Dillinger, always hard to contain, had fled the supposedly escape-
proof county jail in Crown Point, Indiana, in March 1934. A month

and a few bank robberies later, Dillinger and company ended up hiding out in a woodsy Wisconsin lodge called Little Bohemia, so named because of the owner's Bohemian ethnic roots. Tipped off by the lodge owner's wife, Hoover and a team of federal investigators from Chicago responded with an ill-fated ambush that would go down in history as one of the greatest federal fiascoes of all time.

The Dillinger gang, including well-known characters such as Harry Pierpont and "Baby Face" Nelson, plus gang members' wives and girlfriends, had planned only a short layover at the wilderness retreat. Although owner Emil Wanatka and wife Nan had befriended an outlaw or two during the days of Prohibition, the Dillinger crew was a notch or two above the types they had known. The couple didn't share the public's glorified view of these men. So, upon discovering that their new slew of guests were members of the notorious gang, Wanatka made a bold move and confronted them. Dillinger assured him that they would be of no inconvenience and would not stay long. Apparently bank robbers are not the most trustworthy folks, because in the several days of their stay the bunch proved to be much more than an inconvenience.

Wanatka and his wife were basically held hostage at their humble hostel for the entire length of the Dillinger gang's stay. Telephone calls were monitored, lodge visitors were subject to scrutiny at both arrival and departure, and anyone, including Emil and Nan themselves, who went into town for supplies was forced to travel with a Dillinger escort. Even beside that, the sheer fear of housing sought-after sociopaths was too much for the Wanatka couple and their young son to handle. A plan for relief was soon hatched.

Knowing that any lodge departure would be surveyed closely, the Wanatkas decided to plant a note on Nan to pass to police. They would convince the gangsters that she and their ten-year-old son were merely departing for a nephew's birthday party and then would find a way to transmit their cry for help. Although Dillinger gave permission for the pair's trip, the frightened mother soon discovered "Baby Face" Nelson hot on their trail and ready to jump at the first sight of suspicious activity. Still, Nan managed to pass word to her family, who then contacted the authorities. At the birthday party for her nephew, Nan provided details that were ultimately shared with law enforcement. Officials planned a siege.

The Heat Is On

Seizing the opportunity to make an example of Dillinger and his exploits, FBI agents Hugh Clegg and Melvin Purvis plotted an ambush at the lodge under Hoover's guidance. Unfortunately for the agents and innocent bystanders, Dillinger and company were not so easily taken.

As the agents approached, the lodge's watchdogs indeed barked at the strangers, but only after a series of miscalculated gunshots did the Dillinger gang stir. Clegg and Purvis had mistakenly fired at three patrons leaving the lodge's bar. This was the first tragedy of Little Bohemia that day: One of the patrons was killed instantly, and the other two were brutally wounded. The Dillinger gang had long grown weary of the watchdogs' random yelps, but when they heard these unfortunate shots they knew their hideout had been discovered.

The ever-elusive bunch had plotted an escape plan upon their arrival at the lodge. The agents didn't have the same knowledge of the land's lay and fell victim to a nearby ditch and a wall of barbed wire. Wounded and entangled, the agents were sitting ducks. Their suspects were free to flee and take their turn at gunfire now that they had the upper hand.

Unhappy Ending

A premature and somewhat pompous notion had Hoover pledging a significant story to the press in anticipation of the planned attack. Unluckily for him, with the unintentional victims and their families involved, the story would be a hellish one. The ambush resulted in not a single loss for the Dillinger gang. On the other side were two injured law officers, two wounded bystanders, and the death of a complete innocent.

Although Purvis didn't find success on that infamous day, he would eventually have another chance. On July 22, 1934, Dillinger was shot dead by Purvis's agents outside a Chicago cinema in which the criminal "darling" had just enjoyed his very last gangster flick.

• *A dense fog carrying black coal smoke paralyzed London for four days in December 1952 and killed as many as 4,000 people.*

• *A newborn blue whale calf is almost as long as a school bus.*

FROM THE VAULTS OF HISTORY

Landlocked
Genghis Khan's Mongol empire in 13th-century Asia and part of Europe became the largest land empire in history. His grandson, Kublai Khan, expanded it even farther. But as overpowering as they were on land, the Mongols had little luck on the seas. Kublai Khan was twice rebuffed from invading Japan—partially by the weather itself. Both attacks were adversely affected by storms or, as the Japanese called it, *kamikaze,* "divine wind."

Ancient Wonder
For thousands of years, the Dogon people in the central plateau of Africa have practiced an extremely complex, star-based religion. The Dogon first possessed detailed, accurate astronomical knowledge, primarily of the Sirius binary star system, long before the invention of telescopes. They also somehow knew about Saturn's rings and Jupiter's four major moons, none of which are visible to the naked eye. According to the Dogon, their knowledge comes from the *Nommos,* amphibious beings from the Sirius star system who long ago visited Earth for the benefit of humankind.

Waste Not, Want Not
The tiny island of Nauru in the southwest Pacific Ocean based its economy solely on the export of bird droppings. For centuries, bird droppings and microorganisms on Nauru mixed together to form phosphates—a vital component in fertilizer. Contemporary mining for phosphates, however, destroyed the vegetation and soil on the island, forcing the birds away and leaving no other natural resources. Currently, all of the phosphate mines have been depleted, birds are scarce, and the island is nearing bankruptcy since its only export no longer exists and it has nothing left to trade.

Eat That Plate
A trend grew among chemists and other scientists worldwide to develop edible dinnerware. The digestible food holders are being created out of many different materials, ranging from oatmeal to wheat, organic bran to edible plastic made from corn and soybean starch, and proteins. Many of them are still under development, though a few are currently in use in a smattering of countries.

Comics Get Marvel-ous in the '60s

*The Marvel Comics team changed the face of
comic books with characters that had real flaws,
human problems, and timely quandaries.*

From the 1930s through the '50s, comic book superheroes were as
simple and straightforward as the stories they inhabited. Good was
good, and it always triumphed over evil. Superman and Batman led
honest and uncomplicated lives. But the mounting threat of atomic
weapons and the Cold War created a newly complex world that
seemed unsuited for simple comics heroes.

Enter Stan Lee.

Parents of the Modern Superhero

At only 17 years old, writer and editor Stan Lee began working for
Timely Comics in 1939. It was the beginning of what would become
known as the Golden Age of Comics. Some 22 years later, Lee was
the editor in chief at Timely's successor, Marvel.

Artist Jack Kirby joined Timely in late 1940 with writing partner
Joe Simon. Together, they created Captain America, a great icon of
patriotism, just in time for America's entry into World War II. Kirby
had an amazingly exciting style of illustrating action. He worked at a
number of comic book companies, with Simon and without. He was
again doing material for Timely (now called Atlas) in the late '50s.

Around that same time, artist Steve Ditko, an illustration school
grad, was drawing for Marvel's science fiction titles such as *Journey
Into Mystery* and *Amazing Adventures.* Ditko's work was admired
for its clean, angular appearance and style. A collaborative spirit was
brewing between Ditko, Kirby, and Lee that would change the face
of comics forever.

Changing the Paradigm

The comic industry usually focused on whatever was the rage in
films across America. If Westerns were big, the industry sold Western comics. If war was big, then war comics were on the stands. In
the early 1960s, science fiction and monsters were the "in" thing.

Marvel's publisher noticed that superhero teams were in vogue and urged Lee to put together a team for Marvel.

But Lee wanted to avoid the one-dimensional characters that until then had seemed the norm—Superman was so super, almost nothing could stop him. Batman's alter ego, Bruce Wayne, was rich and successful—if anything got really sticky, he just threw money and expensive gadgets at it. Lee thought readers could relate to superheroes with realistic, human problems.

A Fantastic Start

Working with Kirby, Lee created a comic book that he would enjoy as a reader. The characters would have shortcomings and bad habits. They would have feet of clay. They would have real relationships. And they would *not* have secret identities.

With those guidelines, Lee and Kirby introduced *Fantastic Four* in November 1961. Exposed to cosmic radiation, a group of space travelers return to Earth with strange powers. Here, Lee and Kirby used two of the biggest and most mysterious concerns of the day— radiation and space exploration—to profitable effect.

The Fantastic Four were a quirky bunch. Reed Richards could stretch his body like a rubber band. His fiancée, Sue Storm, had the gift of invisibility. Her kid brother, Johnny, could turn into a flaming, flying projectile. Pilot Ben Grimm had become enormously strong, but he had also become enormously ugly, like a walking brick wall. *Fantastic Four* was a tremendous hit at the newsstands.

Enlisting Ditko in August 1962, Lee introduced another innovative character in *Amazing Fantasy* #15. A high school science nerd named Peter Parker gets bitten by a radioactive spider and voilà—he is blessed (and cursed) with the powers of an arachnid. The Amazing Spider-Man was born, both as a character and as its own comic book.

Keeping It Up

Marvel had hit its stride, launching characters such as the shunned and brawny Incredible Hulk, the high-tech Iron Man, the mysterious Dr. Strange, the blind and acrobatic Daredevil, and the mythic Mighty Thor, among many others. Stan Lee, with Jack Kirby, Steve Ditko, and the rest of the "Marvel Bullpen," had created superheroes that seemed a bit closer to the ground than previous ones.

And comic readers across America liked that.

The Times They Are A-Changin'

1901

January 10: Oil is discovered in Beaumont, Texas, in a salt dome field called Spindletop, marking the beginning of Texas's reign as the center of the global oil industry.

January 22: After almost 64 years on the throne, Britain's Queen Victoria dies. She is succeeded by her son, Prince Albert Edward, who becomes King Edward VII.

January 30: Female prohibitionists destroy 12 saloons in Kansas.

March 2: The U.S. Congress passes the Platt Amendment, which stipulates the terms for the withdrawal of American troops stationed in Cuba since the end of the Spanish-American War and leases the naval base at Guantánamo Bay to the United States.

April 25: New York becomes the first U.S. state to require license plates on automobiles. The fee is $1.00.

May 3: The Great Fire of 1901 starts in Jacksonville, Florida, caused by a spark from a kitchen fire at a mattress factory. The fire eventually sweeps through 140 city blocks, destroying more than 2,368 buildings and leaving 10,000 people homeless.

July 2: A train in Wagner, Montana, is robbed, and the thieves get away with $65,000. Butch Cassidy and the Sundance Kid are prime suspects.

July 4: At 1,282 feet long, the world's longest bridge—crossing the St. John River at Heartland, New Brunswick, Canada—opens.

August 5: Ireland's Peter O'Connor sets the first recognized long jump world record of 24 feet, 11¾ inches, a record that stands for 20 years.

September 2: At the Minnesota State Fair, Vice President Theodore Roosevelt utters his now-famous motto: "Speak softly and carry a big stick."

October 12: President Theodore Roosevelt, after taking office on September 14 following the death of William McKinley, renames the Executive Mansion "The White House."

October 24: Annie Edson Taylor becomes the first person to survive going over Niagara Falls in a barrel.

"I'm King of the World!"

❖ ❖ ❖ ❖

*How Hollywood director James Cameron
ascended to his* Titanic *throne.*

It's rare to find a film with a title describing its own existence. There is, of course, no doubt that 1997's *Titanic* was precisely that. The brainchild of writer/director James Cameron was titanic in every sense of the word. With a $200-million budget, it became the most expensive film ever made up to that point. It stayed at the number-one spot at the box office for 15 continuous weeks—a record—and enjoyed a run of more than eight months. Raking in $600 million in American theaters and $1.8 billion in theaters worldwide, it broke U.S. and international records for the highest-grossing film in history. It garnered 14 Academy Award nominations—tying with 1950's *All About Eve* for the all-time lead in nominations. It won 11 of them, including Best Picture, Best Director, and Best Cinematography, tying with *Ben-Hur* and *Lord of the Rings: The Return of the King* for number of Oscars won. *Titanic* would lead Cameron and his crew to become international award-season royalty.

Ready to Roll

Cameron had the proper track record to take on a project of such magnitude. The filmmaker cowrote and directed blockbuster hits such as *The Terminator* (1984), *Aliens* (1986), and *True Lies* (1994). These three films grossed more than $800 million worldwide, proving that Cameron could handle big budgets and bring big results.

He began his plan to shoot a film about the supposedly unsinkable ship more than ten years before the project's eventual release. Scientists found the wreckage of the storied steamship two-and-a-half miles under the Atlantic Ocean in 1985. Cameron's concept combined a fable set in 1912, the year the RMS *Titanic* sank, with a present-day component including actual deep-sea footage of the hulking remains.

Cameron's script surrounds a search for sunken treasure from the *Titanic,* including a legendary diamond necklace. When a locked trunk thought to contain the necklace is brought up from the seabed, a sketch of a beautiful young woman named Rose is found instead. After a frantic search for her identity, the woman is found to be a 101-year-old survivor of the sinking. The crew brings her to the expedition in hopes of finding the necklace's whereabouts. Revealing her story in flashbacks, she tells about the maiden voyage of the *Titanic,* during which her engagement to a haughty suitor finally fails and she falls in love with a penniless artist named Jack. When the *Titanic* strikes an iceberg, she is left with Jack to survive in the icy arctic water. The young man succumbs to the sea, but Rose lives on. After finishing her story, she steals away to the stern of the exploration boat and drops the hunted necklace—a present worth millions from her former fiancé—into the sea. She had it all along but wishes it to rejoin the *Titanic* and her lost love. Throughout Rose's telling, the grandiose action is visually retold with larger-than-life detail and high drama.

Casting Off

A film of such ambition required the combined financing and resources of two major Hollywood studios. Paramount Pictures and 20th Century Fox partnered to bring *Titanic* to the screen.

Working closely with casting director Mali Finn to find the biggest stars in Hollywood, Cameron set out on a long mission to find what he would consider the perfect cast. Both Sean Connery and Gene Hackman were offered the role of treasure hunter Brock Lovett before it finally went to Cameron favorite Bill Paxton. (Ironically, Connery would be the one to hand Cameron the Best Picture Oscar at the awards ceremony.) Fox studios wanted a box-office guarantee such as Brad Pitt or Tom Cruise for Jack's character before Cameron landed teen heartthrob Leonardo DiCaprio. They tested Gwyneth Paltrow and Claire Danes for young Rose before deciding on Kate Winslet. Fay Wray (1933's *King Kong*) and Ann Rutherford (the Andy Hardy series and 1939's *Gone With the Wind*) both turned down the role of the older Rose, and it went to 87-year-old Gloria Stuart. Cameron didn't think Stuart looked old enough for the part, so she wore latex makeup. Oscar-winner Kathy Bates was brought on as the "Unsinkable" Molly Brown, while young stud Billy Zane would play Rose's jilted beau.

Lights, Camera...Ocean!

The company that built the *Titanic*, Harland & Wolff, provided original blueprints that had not been publicly available for years. Combined with Cameron's extensive undersea exploration of the ship, these items gave production designers, set builders, prop makers, and even costumers the ability to remake every facet of the voyage in meticulous detail. Opulent dinnerware and lavish woodwork were perfectly replicated for every shot.

Creating an environment in which Cameron could shoot his epic also involved re-creating the water surrounding the ship. Fox purchased 40 acres of waterfront land on the Pacific Coast in Baja California, Mexico. A nearly full-size replica of the *Titanic* was built in a 17-million-gallon tank, with another 5-million-gallon tank assembled for interior shots. Gigantic hydraulic pistons allowed the ship to repeatedly break apart and sink on cue. Computer graphics allowed for a seamless combination of real people and digital effects.

A Temperamental Genius

Throughout the six-month "ordeal," as Kate Winslet once called the making of the picture, Cameron continued to cement his reputation as a brilliant yet difficult and demanding director. He was well known for yelling at his cast and his crew alike, as well as for running his sets like they were some sort of "a military campaign." Cameron admitted the need for rigorous control, for which he was not at all apologetic, citing logistical and safety concerns. Filming continued even when stunt performers broke bones and extras caught colds, the flu, and kidney infections from their waterlogged activities. Cameron acknowledged that he wasn't an easygoing director on this project. He once asked, "Where does it say that good stuff comes from easy working situations? I don't think it does." When the movie was done, Cameron pocketed an estimated $115 million for his efforts.

In the Final Reel

Much of the success and appeal of a film such as *Titanic* seems to arise from contrasting forces that surround both the celluloid and authentic stories. Notions such as these made Cameron, the crew, and the *Titanic* itself kings of the cinematic world.

"Beat It" (1983)

Michael Jackson's monster 1982 album, *Thriller,* produced seven top ten hits, including "Beat It," released as a single in 1983. Featuring a searing solo (reputed to have been captured in one take) from guitar virtuoso Eddie Van Halen, the song provided a unique crossover from R&B to mainstream rock radio. A popular story suggests Van Halen might have missed the gig when he didn't believe he was actually on the phone with producer Quincy Jones. Once convinced, he agreed to do the solo for free.

"You're So Vain" (1972)

The entertainment world is jam-packed with vanity. That being the case, Carly Simon's 1972 hit, "You're So Vain," could be about almost anyone. Simon has never revealed who the subject of the song is, except to TV producer Dick Ebersole, who won the privilege in a charity auction and is sworn to secrecy. Many believe it could be Mick Jagger, whose backup vocals on the song stand out above the rest of the choir, or Warren Beatty, who has openly stated, "Let's be honest—the song was about me." Simon's husband at the time, James Taylor, is also a candidate. No matter who the subject is, he or she should be proud of the secret contribution.

"We're an American Band" (1973)

Hailing from Flint, Michigan, is about as American as one band can get. Grand Funk Railroad's ode to touring tells of poker games with blues artist Freddie King and meeting up with legendary groupie Connie Hamzy. Drummer and writer Don Brewer's inspiration came from a bar fight with fellow touring band Humble Pie over the merits of British bands versus U.S. groups. Brewer claimed, "Hey—we're an American band," and he wrote the rest of the song the next morning.

"Lost in You" (1999)

In the world of country music, Garth Brooks had no equal, selling more than 100 million albums before his semiretirement in 2000. That kind of success gives a performer the leverage to try all sorts of things like inventing a hard-rock alter ego dubbed Chris Gaines. Intended to create buzz for an upcoming movie, the long-haired, soul-patched fictional rocker released the album *The Music of Chris Gaines,* with the single "Lost in You" cracking the Top 40 pop charts. But the effort obviously wasn't enough, as the movie project fizzled and was never made.

Red Sun Rising

The Russo-Japanese War was a pivotal point of development
for post-feudal Japan and its fledgling empire, with European
nations finally having to accept the power of the East.

A mere 200 years ago, Japan was a feudal state where disputes were settled with samurai swords and the penalty for dishonor was ritual suicide. Yet, the nation saw unification under Emperor Meiji in 1869. He decided that Japan must modernize and become open to the West, which it did with a vengeance. Industry boomed, and German and British advisors arrived—the former to train the army, the latter to build a navy.

But Japan was still resource poor. The country needed coal and iron, oil and rice. It needed an empire.

Imperial Dreams

China had rice. China also had Korea. Japan wanted both, so it invaded and smashed China's primitive army and navy. However, building an empire wasn't going to be as easy as all that. Other countries had their interests, as well. To keep Japan in check, Russia, France, Germany, and Britain jumped in to gobble up areas of economic influence in China. Russia especially irritated Japan when it grabbed Manchuria, which had coal and iron mines and the naval base at Port Arthur. These were some of the spoils for which Japan had gone to war in the first place. Russia had to go.

While Russia had a huge army in Europe, it was at the other end of the 5,500-mile, single-track Trans-Siberian Railway. Only about 130,000 troops existed in the far eastern part of the country, and reinforcements would arrive slowly. Russian naval strength, mostly at Port Arthur, was comprised of old and second-rate ships. Against this, Japan had developed a fast, modern navy and 283,000 troops, with 400,000 reserves. On February 8, 1904—without a declaration of war—Japan struck.

Japanese torpedo boats attacked the Russian fleet anchored at Port Arthur, causing severe damage. The next day, after sinking two Russian ships at Chemulpo (Inchon), Korea, the Japanese First

Army began to come ashore. The general plan was to move the armies from Korea into Manchuria. From there they would split, some turning north to cut the Trans-Siberian Railroad while others simultaneously headed south to capture Port Arthur. The plan was simple, and the Russians probably should have known what to expect.

But Russia was plagued with bad leaders, bad equipment, and bad luck. As an example of the latter, only a couple of months into the war, their best admiral, Stepan Makarov, launched a series of energetic raids against the Japanese, but while returning to Port Arthur, his flagship *Petropavlovsk* sailed into a field of mines surreptitiously set by the Japanese and sank with all hands.

Leadership Nightmares

Though Russian General Aleksei Kuropatkin had a sound defensive plan that would take into account the Russian soldiers' strengths, Czar Nicholas II put the incompetent General Mikhail Alekseev in charge of the war. Alekseev ordered an immediate offensive—which went completely against Kuropatkin's well-laid defense plan. While the Japanese troops attacked north toward Mukden and Harbin, the Russian army was pulverized in a series of foolish counterattacks and fell back in disarray. It is an understatement to say things were not going well for Russia.

In the south, Japan had begun the siege of Port Arthur. Surrounded by three rings of defensive fortifications and well supplied, Port Arthur should have been able to hold out for a year. But the fortress commander was another incompetent who wasted valuable defensive time in inaction and worry. By the end of July, Japan had 80,000 troops and almost 500 guns in position around the fort.

Russian Admiral Wilgelm Vitgeft took over and tried to fight a defensive campaign in support of Port Arthur, but the czar ordered him to break out and take his fleet to Vladivostok. However, when Vitgeft tried, Admiral Heihachiro Togo's hyper-modern battleships caught him in the Yellow Sea on August 10. Vitgeft was killed and most of his ships wound up back in Port Arthur. Time was definitely running out.

Then began one of the strangest episodes in the history of naval warfare, and possibly one of the worst military decisions ever.

A Dubious Idea

Thousands of miles away, back in the Baltic Sea, lay extra elements of the Russian navy—eight battleships, eight cruisers, and nine destroyers. Someone got the none-too-brilliant idea that they should cruise around the world to save Port Arthur. On October 15, they brashly set sail under the command of another incompetent, Admiral Zinovy Rozhdestvenski.

After mistakenly attacking British fishing ships they thought were Japanese torpedo boats and nearly starting a war with Britain, the hodgepodge of new and very old Russian ships went sailing off around Africa. Around this time, on January 5, Port Arthur surrendered to Japan. Unaware of that development, the fleet continued across the Indian Ocean, plagued by mutinies, fever, rotten food, and problems finding coal.

A Day Late and a Dollar Short

On May 14, the haggard ship crews approached Tsushima island, situated between Korea and Japan. Opposing them was Togo's fleet, which was made up of 4 battleships, 8 cruisers, 21 destroyers, and 60 torpedo boats. With a six-knot speed advantage, the Japanese pulled ahead of and around the Russians, bringing all of Togo's guns to bear. The Russian vessels were quickly encircled and riddled with bullets. Only one of eight Russian cruisers and five of nine destroyers escaped intact.

Ironically, by then the land war had been over for two months, following Port Arthur's surrender. Later, through the efforts of U.S. President Theodore Roosevelt, negotiations led to the Treaty of Portsmouth on September 6, 1905, and an uneasy accord ensued.

Sign of Times to Come

Roosevelt got the Nobel Peace Prize. Japan got Port Arthur and half of Sakhalin Island, unobstructed influence in Korea, and a Russian evacuation of Manchuria. Russia got the Revolution of 1905.

For the Europeans, the East was no longer a land of quaint peasants who could not stand up to white men's guns. In the future, Japan's empire grew rapidly—until the nation started one undeclared war too many and planted the seeds of a little debacle known as World War II.

The Good Humor Man: Birth of an American Icon

A beloved slice of Americana—and its surprising controversy—is revealed.

American suburbia: laughing children, lemonade stands, sprinklers, and, of course, that ice cream truck emitting its soothing jingle.

In 1920, Harry Burt, an ice cream shop owner in small-town Ohio, invented the first ice cream confection on a stick. His store was selling a lollipop called the Jolly Boy Sucker as well as an ice cream bar covered in chocolate. Inserting a wooden stick into the ice cream bar made it "the new, clean, convenient way to eat ice cream."

Burt quickly patented his manufacturing process and started promoting the Good Humor bar, in accordance with the popular belief that one's palate affects one's mood. He then sent out a fleet of shiny white trucks, each stocked with a friendly Good Humor Man and all the ice cream bars kids could eat. By 1961, 200 Good Humor ice cream trucks wound their way through suburbia.

Not Without a Little Bad Humor

The ice cream on a stick suddenly found itself facing solid competition from other be-sticked frozen treats. First there was Citrus Products Company, champion of the frozen sucker. Then came Popsicle Corporation, home to the Popsicle. Good Humor took these companies to court, alleging that Good Humor's patent gave them exclusive rights to frozen snacks on a stick. Popsicle countered that Good Humor only owned the rights to ice cream on a stick, whereas Popsicles were flavored water. When Popsicle attempted to add milk to its recipe, a decade-long court battle ensued, centering on what precise percentage of milk constitutes ice cream, sherbet, and flavored water.

Popsicle and Good Humor have settled their differences and are now owned by the same corporation. As for the Good Humor Man, he's endangered but not extinct. Good Humor stopped making its ice cream trucks in 1976, but they are still owned by smaller distributors.

Fast Facts

- Diners Club was the first credit card that allowed a consumer to "buy now and pay later." The legendary piece of plastic was unleashed in 1950.

- The launch of the shuttle Discovery was delayed after woodpeckers pecked holes in the spacecraft's foam insulation. Decoy plastic owls, purchased at Wal-Mart, deterred the woodpeckers and solved the problem.

- Time magazine rarely deviates from the familiar red band on its covers. A black band commemorated the terrorist attacks of September 11, 2001, and a green band celebrated the environment on April 28, 2008.

- The oldest known wheel—from roughly 3500 B.C.—was found in Mesopotamia. Archaeologists disagree as to how much earlier than that the wheel was invented.

- When his housekeeper asked him for his last words, Karl Marx stated: "Go on, get out—last words are for fools who haven't said enough."

- The United States has more country music–playing radio stations than any other music format.

- Egyptian artwork from 3,000 years ago reveals Bes, the god of birth and carnal pleasures, wearing a condom-type device. The Chinese were said to have worn a silk sheath 2,000 years ago.

- The language of the Mazatecan Indians, natives of southern Mexico, is very tonal and harmonious. Conversations, therefore, can sound like whistling.

- Samuel Seymour was five years old when he was at Ford's Theater the night Abraham Lincoln was shot. He was the last survivor of that event. He died in 1956.

Beauty Is Pain

❖ ❖ ❖ ❖

For thousands of years, human beings (especially women)
have tried to change or improve their appearance by
applying cosmetics—sometimes with deadly results.

Back Then

In the old world, limited scientific knowledge prevented awareness
that many toxic and lethal chemicals were constantly being coated
on people's skin in the name of good looks. In fact,
during the second millennium
B.C., Old Kingdom Egyptians
took makeup so seriously that
they invented the science
of chemistry to produce it.
Chemists at France's Louvre
Museum and those of a leading
cosmetics manufacturer recently
analyzed ancient stores of kohl,
or *mesdemet,* a darkening agent
(black, or less commonly, green)
that Egyptians applied to both
upper and lower eyelids to protect vision from the glaring sun. (Not
incidentally, kohl also created a smolderingly sexy, "smoky" eye.) The
scientists found that kohl contained a dark sulfide of lead extracted
from a mine near the Red Sea, as well as synthetic compounds and
7–10 percent animal fat to make the mixture creamy—the same
percentage manufacturers use to this day, although modern cosmetics usually contain vegetable fat.

Cleopatra and her contemporaries also wore "lipstick" made of
carmine, obtained from crushed beetles, in a base made from ant's
eggs. Ancient Egyptians and Romans used other cosmetics containing mercury and white lead. Tattoos? Those are nothing new to either the Egyptians or the Indians. For centuries, they have used the
reddish vegetable dye *henna* to create temporary tattoo patterns on
the skin and to color hair, as well. Like the Egyptians, Hindu culture
also used kohl as eye makeup.

Pale Beauty

Women in Roman Britain used a tin-oxide cream to whiten their faces. In 1558, Queen Elizabeth I began a fad by doing the same with egg whites, vinegar, and white powdered lead, a deadly mixture that caused poisoning and, ironically, scarring. By the 1700s, black "beauty spot" patches to cover the scars became necessary accessories.

As a matter of fact, throughout Europe during the Middle Ages, the Renaissance, and up to the Industrial Revolution, having darker skin was considered a working-class no-no; light skin meant luxury because you afford to could stay inside. Therefore, upper-class people and upper-class wannabes lightened their skin—using white lead that often contained arsenic. In the 1800s, whitening the face was still one of the most common cosmetic practices. A mix of carbonate, hydroxide, and lead oxide was the norm. Unfortunately, when used repeatedly, this mixture could result in muscle paralysis or death. Yikes.

And Now?

Of course, in modern times, we've learned our lesson. Or have we? In today's nail polishes, the reproductive toxin dibutyl phthalate, known as DBP, is a common ingredient. Other ingredients in nail polishes include formaldehyde (a carcinogen) and toluene, which has been linked to birth defects. Double yikes.

In 1992, an epidemic of papular and follicular rashes broke out in Switzerland, caused by vitamin E linoleate in a new line of cosmetics. In 2000, an outbreak of skin boils infected hundreds of pedicure customers in a California salon. Most recently, phthalates have hit the radar. Phthalates are a class of chemicals added to many consumer products, notably cosmetics and scented substances such as perfumes, soaps, and lotions. Some research, however, shows that phthalates have the unfortunate distinction of causing cancer, birth defects, and sexual dysfunction. Triple yikes.

In autumn 2007, runway shows by designers from Versace to Vuitton featured a revival of the "Cleopatra" eye made famous by Elizabeth Taylor in the 1963 biopic. At the same time, the covers of various fashion magazines featured pale skin and deeply reddened lips—none of which, fortunately, are necessarily "to die for" anymore. It seems that humanity really takes the phrase "beauty is pain" to heart.

The Mystery of Montauk

Montauk, a beach community at the eastern tip of Long Island in New York State, has been deigned the Miami Beach of the mid-Atlantic. Conspiracy theorists, however, tell another tale. Has the U.S. government been hiding a secret at the former Camp Hero military base there?

In the late 1950s, Montauk was not the paradise-style resort it is today. It was an isolated seaside community boasting a lighthouse commissioned by George Washington in 1792, an abandoned military base called Camp Hero, and a huge radar tower. This tower, still standing, is the last semiautomatic ground environment radar tower still in existence and features an antenna called AN/FPS-35. During its time of air force use, the AN/FPS-35 was capable of detecting airborne objects at a distance of more than 200 miles. One of its uses was detecting potential Soviet long-distance bombers, as the Cold War was in full swing. According to conspiracy theorists, however, the antenna and Camp Hero itself had a few other tricks lurking around the premises, namely human mind control and electromagnetic field manipulation.

Vanishing Act

On October 24, 1943, the USS *Eldridge* was allegedly made invisible to human sight for a brief moment as it sat in a naval shipyard in Philadelphia. The event, which has never been factually substantiated but has been sworn as true by eyewitnesses and other believers for decades, is said to have been part of a U.S. military endeavor called the Philadelphia Experiment, or Project Rainbow. Studies in electromagnetic radiation had evidenced that manipulating energy fields and bending light around objects in certain ways could render them invisible. Since the benefits to the armed forces would be incredible, the navy supposedly forged ahead with the first experiment.

There are many offshoots to the conspiracy theory surrounding the alleged event. The crew onboard the USS *Eldridge* at the time in question are said to have suffered various mental illnesses, physical ailments, and, most notably, schizophrenia, which has been medically linked to exposure to electromagnetic radiation. Some of them supposedly disappeared along with the ship and relocated through teleportation to the naval base in Norfolk, Virginia, for a moment. Despite severely conflicting eyewitness reports and the navy's assertion that the *Eldridge* wasn't even in Philadelphia that day, many Web sites, books, a video game, and a 1984 science fiction film detail the event.

But what does this have to do with Montauk right now?

What's in the Basement?

Camp Hero was closed as an official U.S. Army base in November 1957, although the air force continued to use the radar facilities. After the air force left in 1980, the surrounding grounds were ultimately turned into a state park, which opened to the public in September 2002. Yet the camp's vast underground facility remains under tight government jurisdiction, and the AN/FPS-35 radar tower still stands. Many say there is a government lab on-site that continues the alleged teleportation, magnetic field manipulation, and mind-control experiments that originated with Project Rainbow. One reason for this belief is that two of the sailors onboard the *Eldridge* on October 24, 1943—Al Bielek and Duncan Cameron—claimed to have jumped from the ship while it was in "hyperspace" between Philadelphia and Norfolk, and landed at Camp Hero, severely disoriented.

Though Project Rainbow was branded a hoax, an urban legend continues to surround its "legacy," which is commonly known as the Montauk Project. Theorists cite experiments in electromagnetic radiation designed to produce mass schizophrenia over time and reduce a populace's resistance to governmental control, which, they believe, would explain the continual presence of the antenna. According to these suspicions, a large number of orphans, loners, and homeless people are subjected to testing in Camp Hero's basement; most supposedly die as a result. Interestingly, some conspiracy theorists believe that one outcropping of the experiments is the emergence and rapid popularity of the cell phone, which uses and produces electromagnetic and radio waves. Who knew that easier communication was really an evil government plot to turn people into mindless robots?

Strange Justice

What the Devil Is Wrong with This Fellow?

A Pennsylvania man filed a claim against "Satan and his staff," alleging that the "Prince of Darkness" had made the plaintiff's life a miserable failure. He also claimed that "Old Scratch" had "deprived him of his constitutional rights" and, since he was poor due to the devil's work, he couldn't afford the court costs. The court had to deny the claim, on a technicality, as no directions had been supplied as to the known whereabouts of Satan for U.S. marshals to serve him the papers.

From Soup to Nuts

A Florida man stopped by a chain restaurant and ordered a bowl of potato soup. Served clam chowder by mistake, the man claimed he suffered an allergic reaction and subsequent nightmares from the experience. He sued the chain for more than $55,000 for medical costs and pain and suffering. Refusing an out-of-court settlement for $1,000, he went to trial. The jury found the man 90 percent responsible for his damages and awarded him only $407 for his claim. But he wasn't finished yet—the restaurant chain also sued him to recover their legal costs.

You Just Have To Hand It To Him...

When a carpenter grabbed his circular saw one morning, he noticed a strange marking on his hand. It was *666*—the mark of the Devil! There was only one thing to do—he had to cut off his hand. Fellow workers packed the severed hand in ice and sent it with the carpenter to the hospital. A physician almost convinced him that two hands were better than one, but the carpenter insisted that the hand not be reattached. Several months later, the carpenter sued the doctor for $144,000 for listening to his demand. The jury, throwing up its hands, threw the case out.

Sometimes Life Stinks

A maintenance worker for a mobile home trailer court was asked to investigate an awful odor emanating from one of the homes. His inspection revealed a rotting, maggot-infested opossum, which he quickly removed and dumped. But it seems the smell was too much for him, and he suffered a heart attack as a result. The insurance company refused his worker's compensation claim, saying his weak heart was a preexisting condition. The jury didn't agree and awarded the man his full compensation benefit.

Nutty Nietzsche

A brilliant philosophical career was cut short when one of the world's greatest thinkers began to spiral into madness.

There were those who thought Friedrich Wilhelm Nietzsche was crazy before he actually went mad. Nietzsche's work formed the basis of existentialism, a controversial postmodern philosophical movement at a time when religious focus was petering out in intellectual circles. His writing has influenced scores of writers, artists, teachers, and leaders ever since.

The basic idea of Nietzsche's philosophy is quite simple: Human beings are responsible for the creation and meaning of their own lives. When Nietzsche proclaimed his infamous tenet "God is dead," what he meant was that people have the right to believe or not believe in the concept of God because they are responsible for the daily make-up of their own lives and minds. Although Nietzsche's life may have ended in the depths of mental depravity, this fact does not weaken the philosophies he unleashed upon the world in the areas of culture, science, morality, and religion.

A Life of Ups and Downs
Nietzsche was born October 15, 1844, in the Prussian province of Saxony. He was the oldest of three children. Tragically, his father and younger brother died within a year of each other before Nietzsche was seven. For a time it appeared the young boy was destined for a theological career, much to the approval of his mother. At the university in Bonn, he studied theology and philology (the study of how language changes over time), but after one semester Nietzsche rejected his faith and abandoned his theological studies. Needless to say, his mother was not pleased. Nietzsche continued his studies in

philology and became one of the youngest professors ever to teach the discipline at the University of Basel.

For most of his adult life, Nietzsche was quite sickly. Nevertheless, he served with Prussia as a medical orderly during the Franco-Prussian War of 1870. During this time, he contracted dysentery, diphtheria, and syphilis, the latter of which may have been a cause of his eventual mental illness. Because of these various health woes, Nietzsche had to take a number of sabbaticals, which marked the end of his career as a philologist. Some suggest that these sabbaticals also led to his emergence as a philosopher. There's nothing like being alone in a miserable physical state to make one consider the human condition.

A Genius on His Own Terms

In his immodest, candid, and at times humorous autobiography, *Ecce Homo,* Nietzsche relates in no uncertain terms that he saw in himself how the rest of humanity should be. It's possible that Nietzsche really did see himself as *Übermensch,* or superman, a philosophical idea he created in *Thus Spoke Zarathustra.*

Starting to Move Downhill

The first symptoms of serious mental illness surfaced in 1889 on a street in Turin, Italy, when Nietzsche experienced a delirium attack. The experience resulted in Nietzsche's creating a public disturbance that took two police officers to quell. After receiving a brief, puzzling, almost incoherent letter from the philosopher, Franz Overbeck, Nietzsche's closest friend, traveled to Turin and brought him home to Basel, Switzerland, placing him in the care of a psychiatric clinic. Although Nietzsche was displaying many of the signs of mental illness caused by syphilis, he also exhibited some signs that were not. The true cause of his madness is still a matter of conjecture: Did the great thinker's brain blow a fuse from an overload of mental stress, or did his little military stint, turn of patriotism, and possible indiscretion have dire consequences? Whatever the reason, the man who gave the world pause to think was, at the end, himself completely uncommunicative. Friedrich Wilhelm Nietzsche died of pneumonia on August 25, 1900, while in the care of his sister, proving yet another of his philosophical theories: We are indeed *Human, All Too Human.*

WHO KNEW?

Too Much Web Surfing
Studies suggest that Internet addiction is becoming a growing concern in the United States. One report found that one out of every eight people is "addicted" to being online. Addiction, in this case, is defined as a behavior-altering, habit-forming, compulsive, physiological need to use the Internet.

Not So Mobile
The world's largest functioning mobile phone is the Maxi Handy, which measures 6.72 feet tall by 2.72 feet wide by 1.47 feet deep. This phone was installed at the Rotmain Centre in Bayreuth, Germany, on June 7, 2004, as part of the "Einfach Mobil" (simple mobil) informational tour. Constructed of wood, polyester, and metal, the fully functional phone features a color screen and can send and receive text and multimedia messages. But just don't expect to slip it into your pocket.

Mining for Diamonds
It's finders keepers at the Crater of Diamonds State Park in Murfreesboro, Arkansas. This is the world's only diamond-producing site that's open to the public. Not only that, but visitors can keep any stones they dig up! The visitor center features exhibits and an audio/visual program that explains the area's geology. The center even offers tips on recognizing diamonds in the rough.

Against the Tide
In almost every country across the globe, the creation and selling of child pornography is illegal. Despite this, the possession of child pornography is *not* illegal in the Czech Republic. Political leaders cite as one of their primary reasons for not passing laws a fear of "entrapment," in which child porn can infiltrate innocent computers through the acceptance of unwanted spam e-mail.

Made of Stone
The Washington Monument is the world's tallest free-standing stone structure not created from just a single block of stone. The monument is composed of more than 36,000 separate blocks. It stands a whopping 555 feet tall and weighs approximately 90,854 tons! The outside is composed almost entirely of white marble, while the inside is granite.

Love Can Make You Crazy

Joan Crawford once said, "Love is a fire. But whether it is going to warm your heart or burn down your house, you can never tell." Oh, how right she was.

Love: the sweetest and sourest of the four-letter words. Sweet murmurs and soaring emotions can easily give way to angry shouts and irrepressible rage. And in some cases, burning houses, stabbings, and gunshot wounds also result. The violent outcomes of sexual jealousy are so common that they're an age-old and worldwide phenomenon. You don't have to read very far into the literature from any country from any time period, and the motivations behind the characters' violent and self-destructive acts will often boil down to one factor: love gone bad.

A complete listing of love-motivated crimes would take longer to write than all the world's romantic sonnets combined. But here's a brief rundown of some of the more famous and bizarre cases of love's sociopathic side.

Normal Folks Made Famous

- Joey Buttafuoco was once an unknown Long Island auto repair shop owner with an eye for robbing the cradle. He began an affair with 16-year-old Amy Fisher, who tried to convince him to leave his wife. Apparently Fisher, who was given the nickname "Long Island Lolita" in the press, was displeased with his refusal to do so, because on May 19, 1992, she rang the doorbell of the Buttafuocos' home and shot Joey's wife Mary Jo point-blank in the head. Mrs. Buttafuoco miraculously survived the assault and went on to identify Fisher as her attacker. Joey Buttafuoco served four months in prison for statutory rape, while Fisher served seven years for aggravated assault.

Both Fisher and Joey Buttafuoco seem to have recovered from the unfortunate event. Buttafuoco travels the talk show circuit, and Fisher wrote a book about her teenaged transgressions entitled *If I Knew Then*. They certainly know how to capitalize on a situation.

- During Thanksgiving weekend in 2002, failed real estate agent Richard McFarland of San Antonio, Texas, committed an elaborate, though badly planned, murder. His wife, Susan McFarland, intended to file for divorce. Richard, who had started shadowing her and even spying on her computer use, convinced himself that Susan was having an affair. He stole a Chevrolet Suburban, beat his wife to death, drove her in the stolen car to an abandoned farmhouse, and burned her remains. He was caught soon after and pled guilty to murder, receiving a 40-year prison sentence.

- Carolyn Warmus was a New York City elementary school teacher having an affair with her married colleague, Paul Solomon. On an ill-fated night in January 1989, Paul found his wife, Betty Jeanne Solomon, with nine bullets in her back and legs. It was later discovered that immediately after brutally murdering Betty Jeanne, Warmus met Paul for drinks and sex. While it appears that love drove Warmus to insanity, some claim that she was insane from the get-go—several ex-boyfriends have come forward with disturbing tales of obsession, stalking, and restraining orders.

- The media developed a prolonged fascination with the exploits of NASA astronaut Lisa Marie Nowak, and with good cause. In February 2007, Nowak embarked on a 900-mile drive from Houston to Orlando National Airport. Her apparent plan was to harm Colleen Shipman, who was involved with Nowak's ex-lover, navy commander William Oefelein. It was alleged that Nowak wore diapers during the drive from Houston so that she wouldn't have to stop to use the bathroom, although Nowak denied this. Even stranger is what police found in Nowak's car: latex gloves, a black wig, a BB pistol with ammunition, rubber tubing, plastic garbage bags, a two-pound drilling hammer, pepper spray, and four brown paper towels containing 69 orange pills. One shudders at the possible uses of this grab bag of fun, but luckily Nowak's assault ultimately proved harmless. She followed Shipman to her car and proceeded to tap on the window. When Shipman rolled the window down slightly, she received a dousing of pepper spray. She quickly drove off and contacted the police. Nowak awaits trial for attempted kidnapping, burglary, and battery. Nowak had previously been known as a smart, successful, and unusually caring woman. Her lawyers plan on pleading insanity, which, oddly enough, is the only part of this saga that makes sense.

Famous Folks Made Infamous

- French actor Marie Trintignant experienced a horrible bout of jealousy-propelled carnage from her rock-star boyfriend, Bertrand Cantat, during the summer of 2003. In what he described as a fit of jealousy that put him out of his mind, Cantat beat Trintignant over the head while she was filming a movie in Lithuania. He'd convinced himself that Trintignant was currently embroiled in an affair with her ex-husband, or possibly multiple affairs with multiple ex-boyfriends; she had four sons by four different men with whom she kept in contact. He was also jealous of her fictional affairs, having demanded that she stop acting in on-screen love scenes. By August 1, she was dead; pathologists liken the blows on her head to the impact of being thrown against a wall at 125 miles per hour. Cantat was charged with manslaughter and sentenced to eight years in prison. In October 2007, he was released on parole after serving four years. His early release set off an international debate about whether perpetrators of crimes of passion should be given more leniency than their more "cold and calculating" counterparts.

- When almost any American who owned a TV in the mid-1990s thinks of spousal murder, ex-football star O. J. Simpson immediately comes to mind. Sure, he was found not guilty of the crime. But *if* he had done it (which many people still believe he did, which the jury of the civil trial following the criminal case deemed so, and about which Simpson himself was prepared to speculate in a book that was ultimately canceled), the double homicide of wife Nicole Brown Simpson and her friend Ronald Goldman would certainly be a prime example of romance leading to dark exploits.

So, there you have it—astronauts, ex-football stars, real estate agents, European rockers, and East Coast schoolteachers all having one thing in common: love's revenge. These highly publicized tales of love's dark side are certainly the exception rather than the rule, but they do remind people that when a lover starts acting strange, it may be advantageous to sleep with one eye open.

Fast Facts

- The reproductive organs of the male spider are located on its legs.

- Plateau Station, Antarctica, a scientific station that operated from 1965 to 1969, is on average the coldest place on the planet. The average annual temperature there is −70° F (−56° C).

- Hewlett-Packard, started in 1939 by Stanford University grads Bill Hewlett and Dave Packard, was the first company to move into what is now known as "Silicon Valley."

- The largest known meteorite to have landed on Earth was found at Grootfontein in Namibia, southwest Africa, in 1920. The space stone is nine feet long and eight feet wide.

- The brass at Gillette thought they'd come up with a great idea. For the cost of only one million dollars, they were able to supply Mach3 razors for all welcome bags given out to delegates at the 2004 Democratic National Convention. Unfortunately, security officers worried that the razors presented a threat to attendees and promptly confiscated any that they tried to carry into the convention hall.

- As General George Patton crossed a bridge over the Rhine into Germany during World War II, he stopped in the middle and urinated into the river.

- During a battle at Spotsylvania, Virginia, during the American Civil War, Union General John Sedgwick proclaimed that Confederate sharpshooters "couldn't hit an elephant at this distance" before being fatally struck by a Confederate bullet.

- George Washington's Continental Army camped at Valley Forge, Pennsylvania, during the winter of 1777–78. More than two-thirds of the 2,000 people who perished in the camp were victims of disease.

One Big, Happy, Gourmet World

❖ ❖ ❖ ❖

Cow's tongue, escargot, chitterlings, and frog's legs: North Americans aren't strangers to strange foods. But take a quick look at these "delicacies" from around the globe for a real taste of the exotic.

- **Puffer Fish (aka Blowfish)**—This Japanese luxury with skin and internal organs that are highly toxic to humans can be delicious—if prepared correctly. If not, side effects range from light-headedness and rapid heartbeat to coma and death.

- **Putrefied Shark**—Though Iceland serves up a good *svie* (boiled sheep's head), why not go for the über-traditional *hakarl* (rotted shark meat)? The recipe is easy: Wash and gut a shark, bury it in gravel for six-to-eight weeks, then allow it to cure in the open air for another two months. Cut off the thick, brown crust, and enjoy it with the Icelandic liquor Brennivin's, or "Black Death."

- **Cobra Hearts**—The Vietnamese get a lot of press for serving tourists still-beating cobra hearts washed down with a slug of cobra blood. Variations of the dish include cobra hearts dropped in a glass of rice wine. Pair with a few strips of roasted dog meat, and *bon appetit!*

- **Monkey Brains**—Despite urban legends about certain cultures eating brains from a live, wriggling monkey locked in place, it's cooked monkey brains that many South Asian, African, and Chinese people embrace. This reputably easily digestible tissue can be made into stew and is considered a delicacy. It is also thought to cure impotence.

- **Spiders**—Spider-eating is practiced in many countries, but Cambodia draws the most attention with its meaty, hand-size tarantulas known as *a-ping*. For about ten cents per arachnid, they are served fried with salt, pepper, and a bit of garlic.

Paganini: 19th-Century Rock Star

❖ ❖ ❖ ❖

Centuries before legendary bluesman Robert Johnson allegedly "stood at the crossroads" to sell his soul to the devil in return for uncanny abilities on the guitar, there was classical Genovese violinist Niccolo Paganini. Yet "classical" doesn't quite describe the mass hysteria his prowess provoked.

A child prodigy who played the mandolin with skill by age 5, Niccolo Paganini (1782–1840) took up the violin at 7 and gave his first public concert at 12. It wasn't long before he outpaced all of his potential teachers, so he began a regimen of his own construction that often ran more than 15 hours a day. Paganini's star soon rose at the royal court of Lucca on the Italian peninsula, with successively impressive appointments by Napoleon's sister, Elisa Baciocchi, Princess of Lucca. The violinist broke with the court soon enough, however, no doubt feeling stifled. By 1813, he had become a national sensation through a series of Milanese shows.

Calling All Groupies...

In 1828, Paganini embarked on a lengthy European tour, making him the first violinist to do so without backup musicians. He also memorized lengthy programs, never referring to sheet music onstage. He would cut the strings of his violin with scissors and perform complicated pieces on the single string that remained. He could tune a string so that it produced supernatural-sounding harmonies. People flocked to his shows, women fainted, and Paganini became a very wealthy man—the 19th-century equivalent of a modern-day rock star.

It was then, as his reputation grew, that some dubbed the master *Hexensohn,* which means "witch's brat." Whispers speculated that he must have cut a deal with Lucifer, or perhaps was even the son of Satan himself. How else to explain such Paga-mania? The artist reveled in the rumors, sometimes inviting his mother to sit onstage, as if daring audience members to challenge his paternity. He took to wearing all black, often hiring a black carriage with four black horses to deliver him to theaters. But even before taking measures to accentuate it, he already presented an otherworldly appearance: Paganini was thin and pale with long black hair, a cadaverous face (major tooth loss) and eyes that rolled up inside his head as he played and swayed. He even had rock-star addictions—alcohol, women, and gambling. In fact, although he commanded the highest fees of any similar performer, he reportedly went bankrupt trying to open his own casino.

Playing to His Strengths

Research shows that Paganini may have had a genetic defect in collagen production now known as Ehlers-Danlos, resulting in joint hypermobility. He is also thought to have had Marfan's syndrome, a disorder of the connective tissue; symptoms include elongated facial features, limbs, and fingers. These disabilities were turned to his advantage: Paganini could play up to three octaves across the fret board without ever having to shift his hand.

Shunned in Death

On May 27, 1840, Paganini died in Nice, in present-day France, from larynx cancer. During his lifetime, he composed 24 caprices, a series of sonatas, and 6 violin concertos. Ironically, the reputation Paganini had so carefully cultivated literally followed him beyond death, with negative consequences. Not receiving final absolution—some say he even refused a priest who could have administered it—he was initially refused a Christian burial by the Catholic Church. Paganini's body was not buried in consecrated ground until five years after his death. One story claims his remains were stored in the family basement; a darker version has his son (by a mistress) traveling around Europe with the corpse until it was granted a decent resting place.

Whatever the case and however snubbed he was in death, the fame and intrigue of mythical proportions surrounding Paganini's life can be summed up in his quote, "I am not handsome, but when women hear me play, they come crawling to my feet."

Hey, it's not boasting if it's true.

HOW IT ALL BEGAN

Ice Cream
Ice cream dates back to first-century Romans, specifically Emperor Nero, who ordered runners to pass buckets of snow from the northern mountains down the Appian Way to the city, where it was flavored with fruit toppings before being served.

The Barber's Pole
Although not as prevalent as it once was (but still instantly recognizable), the red-and-white striped pole visible from storefront windows signifies that a barber plies his trade within. There's a gory origin for this symbol. In medieval times, barbers' services included surgery and bloodletting, as well as the trimming of hair and beards. The original poles were brass. A basin at the top was used to store leeches, and one at the bottom was used to hold any blood that flowed. To help blood flow more easily, patients held tightly to a staff, which worked much as a tourniquet does today. The barber pole itself may have originated in that staff, with the stripes acting as a visual representation of bandage strips, both blood-stained and clean.

Eavesdropping
Why is snooping on someone's conversation called "eavesdropping?" At one time, landholders weren't allowed to build right up against a property line—they had to leave room between their space and the neighbors' for the eaves on the house, as well as for water dripping from rainy weather. An "eavesdrip" was only about 24 inches, a small enough space for a curious neighbor to easily hear what went on next door—whether he or she wanted to or not.

Nag
The word *nag* derives from the Scandinavian *nagga,* which translates as "to gnaw." During the Middle Ages, many of the houses had thatched roofs. Rats and squirrels would sometimes burrow into these roofs, and late at night, people could hear them as they gnawed and chomped on the straw. In fact, the noise was annoying and would keep people awake. Now, the word serves as a perfect description of constantly being verbally gnawed at by another (the "nagger").

A House Is Not a Home . . . Unless It's Haunted: The Winchester Mystery House

It has been suggested that rich people who are unusual are called "eccentric," while poor people who are unusual are simply labeled "crazy." If there is any truth to that statement, then Sarah Winchester was one incredibly eccentric woman. She was heir to her husband's rifle fortune, but her fear of ghostly reprisals drove her to build one of the strangest homes ever—the Winchester Mystery House.

The Tale of Sarah Winchester

She was born Sarah Lockwood Pardee in New Haven, Connecticut, in 1839. At age 23, she married William Wirt Winchester, owner of the Winchester Repeating Arms Company. The Winchester rifle, with its ability to quickly load and fire as many as 15 bullets in rapid succession, became the favorite of pioneers as they crossed the growing country. As the settlers helped blaze new trails into the frontier, the Winchester protected them from bandits, wild animals, and other wilderness dangers. It would be remembered as "the gun that won the West." It also made William Winchester a very wealthy person.

In 1866, Winchester and his wife had a baby girl they named Annie, but she died when she was only a few weeks old. The infant's

death pushed Sarah into a deep depression. William developed tuberculosis and died in 1881, leaving Sarah alone at only 42 years old. She also inherited her husband's wealth and business, which provided her with an income of more than $1,000 a day.

Proving that money alone can't buy happiness, the sullen Sarah consulted a medium, who told her that her family was cursed by the souls of those killed by Winchester rifles. When Sarah asked what she could do, she was told that she must move West and build a house to soothe those spirits. But, the medium warned, construction on the house must never end—hammers and saws must work around the clock to keep the tormented souls at bay. (There is no record of what the medium was paid for such "sage" advice.)

Way Out... West

Sarah trekked across the country in 1884—no doubt *without* a deadly Winchester rifle at her side—and arrived in San Jose, California, where she quickly purchased a small farmhouse and nearly 162 acres of land. Construction began immediately, entirely without the aid of blueprints or plans. Instead, Sarah selected an area of the house as her "séance room." Each night, between midnight and 2:00 A.M., she would "receive" building instructions from the ghosts that haunted the house. In the morning, she would give the carpenters her own hand-drawn sketches of what work would be done next.

What an "Interesting" Place You Have Here

As a result, the mansion took on some unusual features. Stained-glass windows, made by the world-famous Tiffany Stained Glass company, gave views of inner walls or closets. One window was set into the floor. Twisting, turning staircases led back into themselves, or worse, nowhere at all. One set of stairs ascended straight up to the ceiling. Another had steps that rose only two inches at a time. Dozens of closets were installed, ranging in size from that of a three-bedroom apartment to literally one inch deep.

Although Sarah refused to entertain visitors, she designed the mansion to have two ballrooms. The Grand Ballroom was given rich parquet flooring, fine oak panels, and a silver chandelier with 13 candles. One evening, she threw a lavish dinner party, complete with grand golden plates, fine wine, tuxedoed musicians, and dancing far into the night. However, there was only one attendee—Sarah.

She Must Be a Triskaidekamaniac

Sarah was very fond of the number 13. Many of the windows and doors had 13 panes or panels. A number of staircases had 13 steps, and some rooms contained 13 windows. Chandeliers in the mansion had 13 candles apiece. Many of the trees planted around the landscape were arranged in groups of 13. Even one of the sink drains had 13 holes.

Not all of Sarah's eccentricities were superfluous, however. At times, she could be quite inventive: She once created a novel call box for her servants, complete with a number system and ringing bells. The mansion had a clever and intricate system of button-operated gaslights, as well as indoor toilets and showers. She even took a significant portion of her garage and installed a large oil-burning boiler that fed hot water to a rotating spout on the ceiling. As a result, Sarah invented the first car wash for the three cars she owned—a Renault, a Buick, and an extravagant Pierce-Arrow. All were chauffeur driven.

By 1906, the enormous mansion towered seven stories and had scores of rooms. The San Francisco earthquake of that year, however, caused the top three floors to collapse. They were never rebuilt, even though building and remodeling still continued around-the-clock. In fact, the earthquake trapped Sarah for more than an hour under the debris, where she yelled for her servants (and perhaps the spirits of the house) to rescue her.

The Final Count

In all, the Winchester House has 160 rooms, although it has been estimated that a total of 600 had been built, removed, revamped, or somehow changed in the 38 years of construction. It has more than 1,200 windows and some 10,000 windowpanes. There are more than 450 doorways and 900 doors, not including cabinet doors. The mansion holds 47 fireplaces and 17 chimneys, along with 5 or 6 kitchens.

There are approximately 40 bedrooms and 2 basements. It takes more than 20,000 gallons of paint to coat the entire manor—in fact, once painters complete their job, it is time to start again.

Finally on September 5, 1922, construction stopped, as Sarah Winchester passed away peacefully in her sleep.

Many say she died in "the house that guilt built."

Evil in the Ink: The Story of EC Comics

❖ ❖ ❖ ❖

Comic books were hugely popular in the 1950s. Plenty of publishers offered material that might politely be termed objectionable, but one outfit created the darkest, most unsettling comics of all—which remain influential today.

Newspaper comic strips became popular at the end of the 19th century and the beginning of the 20th, and comic books came into their current form in the mid-1930s. In the late '30s and early '40s, superheroes such as Superman, Batman, Captain America, and Wonder Woman burst onto the scene, enticing America's kids to bury their noses in colorfully illustrated worlds of action and adventure. GIs picked up the comics habit while they were overseas, and shortly after the end of World War II, comic book publishers were printing nearly 80 million copies every month.

One of these publishers was Max Gaines, who had a line of innocuous books the likes of *Tiny Tot Comics, Dandy Comics, Saddle Romances,* and *Picture Stories from the Bible*—all under the banner of Educational Comics, called "EC Comics" for short.

A New Direction

Gaines's son, William, took the reins of EC Comics in 1947, following Max's death in a freak boating accident. Bill Gaines was a soft-spoken young man with a chemistry degree. He'd never thought much about the family business, but his mother convinced him to step into his dad's shoes. With a new staff headed by editor-writer-artist Al Feldstein, Gaines developed a so-so line of romance, Western, and crime comics. Significantly, because both he and Feldstein had been fans of "spook" radio shows such as *Lights Out* and *Inner Sanctum,* horror tales began to sneak into EC's crime titles. By 1950, the company was committed to building what Gaines called the "New Trend" in comics: unusually intelligent tales of horror, science fiction, war, crime, and suspense. Gaines had changed the meaning of the *E* in EC Comics from "Educational" to "Entertaining" in 1947, and now the company really lived up to its name, introducing titles such as:

- **_Tales from the Crypt:_** The lead artist on this title was Jack Davis, whose declarative, rough-hewn style was ideal for chilling tales of gross, often rural horror and revenge—all hosted by the queasily ironic Crypt Keeper.

- **_Vault of Horror:_** Mainstay artist Johnny Craig brought a smart, crisply illustrative style to unnerving stories about cheating, murderous spouses and the gruesomely rough justice meted out by those they had betrayed. The manic Vault Keeper—his hideous open-mouthed grin burnished by ropes of saliva—introduced the tales in this title.

- **_Haunt of Fear:_** The third in the triumvirate of EC horror comics, _Haunt_ featured the artwork of Graham Ingels, a quiet man with a warped, spidery style that was perfect for sick stories about vengeful corpses, homicidal senior citizens, and awful goings-on inside mausoleums and ramshackle old houses. The "fear fables" were hosted by the wall-eyed Old Witch.

EC's horror stories became famous for O. Henry–style snap endings carried to comically absurd extremes: A chicken king who murders his partner ends up Southern fried; a fellow who renders his friend into a bar of soap gets his comeuppance when the soap clogs the shower drain and causes him to drown; a baseball star who murders another player is later gutted and dismembered, his intestines used to mark the baselines, his head used as the ball. Gaahhh!

Gaines and Feldstein brainstormed and wrote a story a day, not just for the horror titles but for a line that also included _Weird Science_ and _Weird Fantasy_, and _Shock SuspenStories_ and _Crime SuspenStories_. Another editor-writer-artist, Harvey Kurtzman, managed _Frontline Combat_ and a general adventure title, _Two-Fisted Tales_.

In addition to hiring skilled artists, Gaines paid top industry rates to top comics talent that included Wally Wood, Al Williamson, George Evans, John Severin—even the legendary Frank Frazetta. Science-fiction writer Ray Bradbury was so impressed with EC's unauthorized rip-off of his work that he arranged a deal that gave the company permission to adapt other Bradbury stories for use in the horror and sci-fi titles. EC Comics became the industry's leading innovator, not simply with literate, darkly funny stories and eye-filling artwork, but with a liberal social conscience that revealed itself in hard-hitting stories of racism, misguided patriotism, bad cops, mob violence, and other controversial issues.

A Bubbling Cauldron of Trouble

The success of Bill Gaines's EC Comics was unfortunately short-lived. A worrisome uptick in juvenile crime happened to coincide with cutthroat competition among comics publishers for rack space in the early 1950s. Companies' very survivals were at stake, and many fly-by-night outfits—and even EC—unwisely took shock to unprecedented levels. All of this, plus politicians' claims that a weakened moral fiber of American youth would encourage communism, focused a harshly negative light on the comics industry. The anti-comics bias of Bellevue child psychiatrist Dr. Fredric Wertham was expressed in his 1954 book, *Seduction of the Innocent,* a well-meaning but laughably argued study of the effects of comics on America's youth. In the course of his psychiatric work, Wertham saw only troubled youth: Those kids read comics; ergo, they had been corrupted by comics. Partly because it took parents off the hook, *Seduction of the Innocent* sold briskly and brought comics under government scrutiny. The State of New York and the U.S. Senate quickly held separate hearings investigating the purported link between comics and juvenile delinquency. In one of the worst decisions of his life, Gaines voluntarily testified to a Senate subcommittee, engaging Tennessee Democrat Estes Kefauver in a fruitless debate about the aesthetics of horror comics.

Fallout from the various investigations forced the comics industry to agree to the development of a censorship body to be called the Comics Code Authority. A stamp with the CCA seal (*A* for *approved*) appeared on the covers of comics that had been scrutinized and passed by the CCA's cadre of volunteer housewives. The symbol assured parents (and warned kids) that, henceforth, comic books would be as safe and as bland as oatmeal. It also assured the demise of Gaines's innovative and exciting line of EC Comics.

All except one.

Gaines had one title that took an anarchic, wickedly satirical look at American culture and the world. And, because Gaines had the foresight to change the format from a comic book to a magazine, it survived the purge of comics in late 1954. In fact, it can still be purchased and enjoyed today. The title? *MAD* magazine.

The Vatican Ratline

❖ ❖ ❖ ❖

*One of the most shocking stories in the aftermath of the
Holocaust was the participation of the Roman Catholic
Church, at its highest levels, in helping tens of thousands of
Nazis escape prosecution. Appropriately called "the Vatican
ratline," it had the support of high-ranking clergymen
and alleged American intelligence conspirators—and
some say even the tacit approval of the pope himself.*

Tangled as the truth has become in the mists of time and purpose-
ful confusion, we know that the ratlines (for there were several)
organized escapes for a number of marquee names of the Third
Reich. These included Adolf Eichmann (eventually captured by the
Israelis, tried, and hanged for war crimes); the infamous "Angel of
Death," Dr. Josef Mengele, whose cruel medical experiments still
revolt even the most jaded; Klaus Barbie, nicknamed the "Butcher"
(what did you have to do in *those* circles to earn such a nickname?);
and many others who slithered to freedom. They are estimated to
number around 30,000, although this figure has been disputed.

The Church Gets into the Act

While one ratline, made famous by Frederick Forsyth's 1972 thriller
novel *The Odessa File* (which was also made into a film), was run
by former SS members, most others were organized and administered by the prominent Roman Catholic lay group Intermarium,
which not only smuggled war criminals to safety but later reportedly
became the single most important source of Nazi recruits for the
U.S. Central Intelligence Agency. One of Intermarium's most active
members was a proudly anti-Semitic bishop, Dr. Alois (aka Luigi)
Hudal. An Austrian, he was concerned about what he thought were
attempts by "the Semitic race ... to set itself apart and dominate."
He also fantasized about a Jewish conspiracy to seize Rome's financial assets. As early as 1937, Hudal was publicly praising Hitler in his
book *The Foundations of National Socialism*.

   In 1943, Hudal met SS intelligence chief Josef Rauff, the devel-
oper of mobile extermination-gas vans, then stationed in Milan. The

two began setting up a network to be used as a later escape route for major Nazis (including Rauff himself, who was personally protected by Hudal until he could flee to Syria, then Chile). Two years later, Hudal mentored Otto Wachter, who had organized the Warsaw Ghetto and was a key member of Operation Reinhard, which led to the slaughter of more than two million Polish Jews. Wachter lived disguised as a monk in a Roman monastery under Hudal's personal protection until his 1949 death.

Smuggled to Safety

In 1944, Hudal attained control of the Austrian section of the Pontifical Commission of Assistance (PCA). This position allowed him and other priests to organize the escape of more big-time Nazis, including Franz Stangl, commanding officer of the Treblinka death camp—who was given cash, a Red Cross passport, and a visa to Syria. Then there was SS captain Edward Roschmann, known as the "Butcher of Riga"; Gustav Wagner, commanding officer of the Sobibor death camp; and many more who made their way to freedom. Other major clergy involved in helping the Nazis included Monsignor Karlo Petranovic; Father Edoardo Domoter, a Franciscan who personally forged Eichmann's Red Cross passport; and Croatian Franciscan Father Krunoslav Draganovic, who was later retained by the United States during the Cold War (he received a paycheck from the Pentagon).

Draganovic's highly sophisticated operation made Hudal's look positively makeshift. He had an Austrian-based priest make contact with Nazis hiding there and then get them across the border to Italy, where other priests (including Draganovic himself) would provide shelter in monasteries as false papers were processed. Once those were in place, Draganovic procured passage on ships sailing to South America. His ratline was so professional that many war criminals reached safe havens in such civilized destinations as Britain, Canada, Australia, and the United States. This was reportedly an open secret in Rome's intelligence and diplomatic circles as early as August 1945.

Coming into the Open

Who actually "discovered" the Vatican ratline is still open to debate: It might have been U.S. Army Counter Intelligence Corps agent William Gowen, serving in Rome after the war as a Nazi hunter and investigator. Or it could have been Vincent La Vista, another American counterintelligence agent, who in May 1947 forwarded a report to his superiors detailing all the Vatican-linked branches of this underground railroad.

That year, an Italian newspaper revealed Hudal's wartime activities, which resulted in a scandal. He hung onto his post until 1952, however, when the Holy See pressured him into resigning. Up until his death 11 years later, Hudal still maintained that he had done "a just thing...expected of a true Christian," snidely adding: "We do not believe in the eye for an eye of the Jew."

What About the Pope?

The question is no longer whether certain priests aided and abetted the Nazis, it's whether they did so on their own or with the knowledge, consent, and/or aid of the Vatican. Monsignor Karl Bayer, director of Caritas in Rome, admitted: "The Pope [Pius XII] did provide money for this [Nazi smuggling]; in driblets sometimes, but it did come." More financing arrived courtesy of the United States, specifically the American National Catholic Welfare Conference, which gave Hudal "substantial funds for his 'humanitarian' aid."

As for Pius XII, he was possibly neither as bad as is sometimes claimed, nor as good as he might have been. Terrified of a godless Communism, he considered the Nazis the lesser of two evils. Hitler had been pressuring him since 1942 to either embrace the Nazis or face destruction of the Church. The Vatican then became "neutral," in favor of Germany. Pius did allegedly manage to get Mussolini's forces to purposely screw up shipments of Italian Jews to concentration camps, and he might have saved thousands when he said that the Church would protect any Jew who married a Catholic. His supporters claim that while Churchill and Roosevelt spoke up, they did nothing; but Pius, although remaining silent, did something.

The Vatican's 1998 statement on the Holocaust, entitled "We Remember," claims that Pius saved "hundreds of thousands of Jewish lives," which would be difficult to prove—or disprove, for that matter.

• *By the end of World War II, Adolf Hitler's troops had established more than 15,000 concentration and death camps where more than six million Jews perished.*

The Twilight Zone

"You unlock this door with the key of imagination." With those opening words, TV viewers knew they had "just crossed over into *The Twilight Zone.*" This anthology series ran for five seasons in the early 1960s, hosted—and often written—by Rod Serling. The show was a mixture of science fiction, fantasy, and drama. In all, 134 half-hour and 17 full-hour episodes were produced, featuring some of Hollywood's biggest stars. The wily Burgess Meredith appeared as four different characters in four different episodes, including the beleaguered bookworm Henry Bemis, who finds himself the last man on Earth—left alone to read all the books he wants, until the far-sighted fellow breaks his only pair of reading glasses.

Who Wants to Be a Millionaire?

At its height, this quiz show was watched across America by millions of viewers as many as three times a week. Hosted by the friendly Regis Philbin, *Who Wants to Be a Millionaire?* became an enormous hit for ABC in 1999. The game had been hugely popular in the UK, but it had been several years since a game show had been broadcast in prime time in the United States, and the show's immense success took virtually everyone—even its producers—by surprise. The first million-dollar winner was John Carpenter, an IRS agent, who made it all the way to the top with no need to use his lifelines. When the final question came up—asking which U.S. president appeared on TV's *Laugh-In*—Carpenter finally broke down and used his Phone-a-Friend lifeline. Calling his father, he calmly stated he was only phoning to tell Pop he was about to win it all, revealing the million-dollar answer was "Richard Nixon."

Black Bart

Many people recall Mel Brooks's foul and funny film, *Blazing Saddles.* The 1974 Western spoof's memorable campfire scene rewrote nighttime in the Old West. But few, if any, can recollect the once-broadcast 1975 TV version known as *Black Bart.* The basic characters were still there, even if the actors playing them changed—Black Bart, sheriff of Rock Ridge, played by Louis Gossett, Jr.—along with a drunken gunslinger (called Reb Jordan instead of the Waco Kid) and even a slick showgirl named Belle Buzzer (filling in for Lili Von Shtupp). But the show was a washout, and the pilot program was the only one ever broadcast.

"The Gentler Sex" Robbing Banks

The U.S. Department of Justice reports that fewer than 5 percent of all bank robbers are women and that women involved in bank robberies are more likely to be accomplices than ringleaders. Statistics indicate that the average amount of money taken from any bank heist is less than $5,000, leaving psychologists to wonder if the motivating factor is love, money, or adventure.

'Til Death Do Us Part

For a short two-year period, 1932–34, Bonnie Parker and Clyde Barrow captivated the nation by posing as that generation's Romeo and Juliet—on the lam from the law. Credited with 13 murders and countless robberies, it is thought that Clyde and his "Barrow Gang" actually committed most of the crimes. Some in the gang claimed they never saw Bonnie fire a gun, even if she *was* frequently photographed brandishing weapons and self-parodying the gangster image. She also immortalized their legend by writing "The Story of Bonnie & Clyde," which she sent to the media. Their crime spree took them across several states, but the law finally caught up to them outside of Sailes, Louisiana, where the pair was killed in a gunfight.

Not quite as famous was Monica "Machine Gun Molly" Proietti from Quebec, Canada. A tiny woman of less than 100 pounds, Proietti was involved in more than 20 bank robberies during the 1960s, leading an all-male band of criminals. She was gunned down at age 27 after she and two accomplices robbed a bank and made off with $3,074.

In 2003, Naomi Betts robbed the Fifth Third Bank in Indianapolis, Indiana, and was arrested about six months later after an airing of *America's Most Wanted* on TV. During the robbery, she didn't even attempt to conceal her face.

Stand by Your Man

Accomplices of other famous bank robbers include: Etta Place, lover of Harry "The Sundance Kid" Longbaugh; Mary Katherine Haroney, aka Big Nose Kate, companion of Doc Holliday; and Kate "Ma" Barker, who shielded her sons and hid their crimes for years.

/yllable /ecret/: Etymology

Insomnia: State of not being able to sleep; from Latin *insomnis* (sleepless), which is derived from the negative *in-* + *somnus* (sleep)

Silver: White metallic element, often used for tableware, jewelry, and other decorative items; from Old English *seolfor*, and akin to Old High German *silbar* (silver) and Lithuanian *sidabras*

Awe: A state of shocked reverence; from Old Norse *agi*, and akin to Old English *ege* (awe) and Greek *achos* (pain)

Shock: To cause bodily functions to become dangerously slowed, usually due to sudden impact; from Middle French *choc*, which is derived from *choquer* (to strike against) and is probably of Germanic origin; also akin to Middle Dutch *schocken* (to jolt)

Extract: To pull forth; from Latin *extractus*, which comes from *extrahere*, which breaks down as *ex-* (out of) + *trahere* (to draw)

Hippopotamus: Very large, thick-skinned, mostly aquatic mammal originating in sub-Saharan Africa; from Greek *hippopotamus*, which is an alteration of *hippos potamios* (literally "riverine horse")

Horse: A large, solid-hoofed four-legged mammal used since prehistory as a beast of burden and for riding; from Middle English *hors;* akin to Old High German *hros* (horse)

Cult: A small group of devotees, or an offshoot from mainstream religion; from French *culte*, which is derived from Latin *cultus* (care, adoration)

Sequin: A small, sparkling metallic or plastic dish-shape or coin-shape adornment for clothing; French, from Italian *zecchino* and *zecca* (mint), which is derived from Arabic *sikkah* (die, coin)

Individual: Existing as a distinctly separate entity; derives from Middle Latin *individualis*, which comes from Latin *individuus* (indivisible) and breaks down as the negative *in-* + *dividuus* (divided)

Keeping International Order
Through Uniting the Nations

❖ ❖ ❖ ❖

Countries from around the world come together to try to work out their differences at the United Nations in New York. How did this organization start? What was the impulse that made the world strive for international cooperation?

The United Nations was officially born October 24, 1945, but it wasn't a new idea. Actually, an international peace-keeping organization was established after World War I. The 1919 Treaty of Versailles that ended that conflict created the League of Nations. American President Woodrow Wilson was one of the main backers of the League, but he couldn't win support for it from Congress, so the United States never joined its membership. When the League was unable to prevent World War II, it fell apart.

In January 1942, midway through the war, representatives from 26 nations fighting the Axis powers pledged to hold together until victory was achieved. President Franklin Roosevelt first coined the phrase *United Nations* to describe the group. The name became official when it was used in the title of *The Declaration by the United Nations.* Months earlier, Roosevelt and British Prime Minister Winston Churchill had secretly negotiated the Atlantic Charter, which set up principles for a postwar world. In the declaration, the Allies committed to follow those ideas. It also officially referred to the alliance as the United Nations Fighting Force, a rather inauspicious name for a group meant to abolish war and promote peace.

Organizing the War's Aftermath
Various configurations of Allies met in Tehran, Moscow, and Cairo throughout the war. In summer and fall 1944, representatives of four key Allied nations—the United States, the Republic of China, Great Britain, and the Soviet Union—gathered at the ten-acre Dumbar-

ton Oaks estate in Washington, D.C., to discuss and formulate the ground rules for an organization that would strive to maintain international peace and security. On April 25, 1945, San Francisco hosted representatives from 50 nations to draft a charter to that effect. On October 24, the charter was ratified by the five permanent Security Council members—those nations represented at the Dumbarton Oaks conference, with the addition of France—and endorsed by most of the additional signatories. Poland, which was invited but did not attend the conference, later signed the charter and brought the initial membership to 51 nations.

Continuing to Work Together

As of this writing, 192 member states represent virtually all recognized independent nations. The first session of the general assembly convened January 10, 1946, in the Westminster Central Hall in London under the auspices of acting Secretary-General Gladwyn Jebb, a prominent British diplomat. On February 1, Norway's Trygve Lie was chosen to be the United Nations' first secretary general.

The secretary general is appointed for a renewable five-year term; to date no secretary general has served more than two terms.

Today the United Nations is headquartered at an 18-acre site on New York's Manhattan Island. The land was purchased in 1946 through a donation from John D. Rockefeller, Jr.; even though it's physically located in New York City, it is considered international territory. It recognizes six official languages—English, Arabic, Chinese, French, Russian, and Spanish—and is comprised of six principle operating organs: the General Assembly, the Security Council, the Economic and Social Council, the Secretariat, the International Court of Justice, and the Trusteeship Council. The General Assembly operates on a one-state-one-vote system, and a two-thirds majority is required to pass many resolutions. The organization has twice been honored with the Nobel Peace Prize.

Fast Facts

- In 1898, the Royal Bank of Canada hauled a four-and-a-half-ton safe from Alaska to British Columbia to open a branch and cash in on the Klondike gold rush.

- Marlon Brando was originally slated to star in director David Lean's movie Lawrence of Arabia. When he turned it down, unknown Peter O'Toole snagged the role and began a stellar Hollywood career.

- On his deathbed in 1640, Sultan Murad IV of the Ottoman Empire ordered the execution of his brother Ibrahim so that he would not succeed Murad. Years earlier, Murad had had other brothers killed. The order to kill Ibrahim was not carried out, and he became sultan against his brother's wishes.

- The base salary of the president of the United States—$400,000 in 2008—is less than the average salary of an NFL player, which is well over $1 million.

- The first newspaper advertisement, an announcement looking for a buyer for an estate in Oyster Bay, Long Island, was published in the Boston News-Letter in 1704.

- Red is the color of mourning in South Africa. In Egypt, it's yellow. Mourners wear purple in Thailand. White symbolizes death in much of the East.

- The year 1848 is known as the year of revolution in Europe because of the number of uprisings that came in the wake of an economic depression. These revolutions included rebellions in the Rhineland, Vienna, Berlin, Milan, and Venice.

- The first computer bug was an actual moth that got caught inside a Mark II Aiken Relay Calculator, a primitive computer at Harvard University.

I Know What It's Like to Be Dead: The "Paul Is Dead" Hoax

Four lads from Liverpool were the biggest thing in pop culture for much of the 1960s. But by the end of the decade, were the Beatles really a trio?

They were bigger than Elvis...bigger than Sinatra...bigger than life. The Beatles had rewritten the book on stardom and fame, influencing not only the pop music world but also fashion, politics, and religion. Their slightest movements were reported by the media.

He Blew His Mind Out in a Car

In the fall of 1969, a Detroit radio DJ reported that Paul McCartney, "the cute Beatle," had been killed in a car crash three years earlier and been replaced by a look-alike contest winner named William Campbell. The story, which had been floating around the rumor mill, was propelled by an Eastern Michigan University student writing a review of the Beatles' latest album, *Abbey Road*. The review claimed that many clues, collected from album covers and song lyrics, proved that McCartney was deceased (although the student admitted in a radio interview that most of his thesis was pure fabrication). Of course, the media had a field day. Radio and TV stations blared the "facts" nightly, and newspapers put their best investigative reporters on the story.

And, in the End

Life magazine devoted the cover story of a November 1969 issue to revealing the truth—McCartney was very much alive. Calling the whole story "bloody stupid," Paul hinted at something more serious—while he was full of life, the Beatles were not—claiming "the Beatle thing is over." No one seemed to pick up on that clue— that the greatest band of the '60s would be DOA within six months.

FROM THE VAULTS OF HISTORY

The Grandfather of Invention
When Victor Mills invented Pampers—the first mass-marketed disposable diaper—for Procter & Gamble in the 1950s, he was not motivated by science or money, but by his granddaughter. He had found that it was a chore to wash her cloth diapers. Mills once remarked, "I just thought it was a mess."

A Victim of Poor Aim
On February 15, 1933, Mayor Anton J. Cermak of Chicago was shot in the stomach in an assassination attempt. Giuseppe Zangara's target, however, was not Cermak but was President-elect Franklin D. Roosevelt, instead. Cermak died weeks later from a combination of his injury and mistakes by his doctors. Zangara was believed delusional, and he blamed his severe stomach pain and the plight of the working people on the president and capitalists. Zangara's last words as he sat in the electric chair were, "Pusha da button!"

Just Making Sure
In the late 1800s and early 1900s, chastity must have been a big concern for married or committed couples. During that time, many inventors received patents for "security underwear" for men. These devices were meant to assure "masculine chastity." They "ensured" abstinence from sexual relations with anyone other than the person with the key to open that particular device.

Signage
Welsh mathematician Robert Recorde invented the "equal sign" in the 1500s. Prior to his invention, mathematicians would write out the words *is equal to*. Recorde chose the two parallel lines as the symbol "bicause noe 2 thynges can be moare equalle."

Long-Term Investing
Back in 1751, Britain began selling "consol bonds." These bonds were sold primarily to raise money to build up the British military and to pay other expenses. Consol bonds pay perpetual interest (around 2.5 percent) and never expire. After more than 250 years, it is now easier for Britain to continue paying the interest to those who hold the bonds than it is to buy them back.

The Heart of Gander: Canadian Hospitality on 9/11

A calamity allowed a small town in Newfoundland to demonstrate its kindness and generosity to the entire world.

We live under a crowded sky. At any given moment, there may be a quarter of a million human beings in the air, in hundreds of airplanes, flying to and from the farthest corners of the planet. There may be a thousand transatlantic flights in the sky, half of them on their way to North America. And so it was on September 11, 2001.

The 9/11 Attacks

The story is familiar by now. That morning two airliners, commandeered by terrorists, struck the twin towers of the World Trade Center in New York City; another hit the Pentagon; and a fourth went down in Pennsylvania when the passengers and crew fought back against the hijackers.

At 9:45 A.M. eastern time, with about 500 flights coming in from Europe, the U.S. Federal Aviation Administration closed U.S. airspace. But those airliners high over the Atlantic Ocean had to go somewhere—and fast—because they only had so much fuel.

Unable to Enter the United States

The flights that were not far enough away from Europe to reach a "point of no return" were ordered back to the continent, but that still left more than 225 aircraft with no place to land but Canada. Canadian Transport Minister David Collenette gave orders to shut down Canadian airports to all outgoing flights except outgoing police, military, and humanitarian flights, and to accept incoming U.S.–bound international flights. Action had to be taken immediately, because planes were coming into Canadian airspace at the rate of one or two per minute. There was a lot of sorting out to do in what the Transport Ministry called "Operation Yellow Ribbon."

Government officials in the United States and Canada didn't know what danger these incoming planes might carry, and they knew there was a very real possibility of another series of terrorist attacks—this time on the still-open Canadian cities. Therefore, planes were kept away from busy airports in Toronto, Montreal, and Ottawa. They were instead diverted to airports in the Atlantic provinces of Nova Scotia, New Brunswick, and Newfoundland and Labrador. Halifax International Airport handled 40 flights, while other planes went to Greater Moncton International, Stephenville International, and the Canadian Forces Base at Goose Bay. Transpacific flights were mostly sent to land at Vancouver International. A total of 39 flights landed at Gander International Airport in the province of Newfoundland and Labrador.

The Edge of North America

Gander is located in the northeastern part of the island of Newfoundland. The area was chosen in 1935 as the site of a Royal Canadian Air Force Base, and a town began to grow up around it. During World War II, as many as 10,000 people lived near the base, which became an important fuel stop on flights to Europe, when aircraft couldn't carry enough fuel to make it from one continent to the other in a single bound. It was the last stop out and the first stop in for airplanes crossing the Atlantic. This earned it the name: "Crossroads of the World."

After the war, the town was moved away from the expanded airport and became incorporated in 1958. Its orientation remained aeronautical, with many of its streets named for famous aviators such as Charles Lindbergh, Eddie Rickenbacker, and Chuck Yeager. Later, as improved aircraft made refueling in Gander unnecessary, the town's economy began to diversify, particularly with tourism.

Rising to the Occasion

In 2001, Gander had a population of roughly 9,000—it was about to get a great deal larger. As 39 wide-body jets began landing and filling the taxi-strips and parking aprons, thousands of crew and passengers were stuck on board, each one having to be screened before being deplaned and cleared through immigration. Not wanting to cause panic, the pilots of many of the aircraft had not told their passengers the reason for the stop. This had the unfortunate result of allowing rumor and fear to spread, so Canadian police and airport officials had to calm the jittery travelers as well as get them sorted out. Soon, Gander would have 6,600 additional mouths to feed and no word as to when U.S. airspace would reopen. What happened next has been seen by some as close to a miracle.

The town's citizens had been told of the situation, and they were waiting with food, blankets, and help. Some of those offering assistance had driven hundreds of miles from the other side of Newfoundland with stacks of sandwiches and kettles of soup. Gander had only 550 hotel rooms, so residents opened their schools, churches, and homes to the visitors, whom they called the "plane people." Even striking school bus drivers set aside their differences and bussed passengers to their temporary quarters. The phone company set up long-distance phone banks so the stranded could call home. High school students served as guides, and nurses and doctors saw to the passengers' medical needs. To help pass the time pleasantly, the visitors were given boat rides on the lake or excursions in the forest and were taken to restaurants. They were supplied with soap, deodorant, towels, tokens for doing laundry, and even underwear.

The residents of Gander opened their hearts and their homes to the stranded travelers and for three days housed, fed, and entertained them, until the interdict was lifted and the planes could continue on to U.S. airports. All across Canada people rose to the occasion.

An Honorable Legacy

On September 11, 2002, Canadian Prime Minister Jean Chretien, Transport Minister David Collenette, and U.S. Ambassador Paul Cellucci traveled to Gander to join 2,500 citizens at the airport for a memorial service to mark the first anniversary of the attacks. Chretien said, "9/11 will live long in memory as a day of terror and grief. But thanks to the countless acts of kindness and compassion done for those stranded visitors here in Gander and right across Canada, it will live forever in memory as a day of comfort and of healing." In summation he added, "You did yourselves proud, ladies and gentlemen, and you did Canada proud."

In gratitude, Lufthansa Airlines has named an airliner the *Gander/Halifax.*

And the passengers have not forgotten the kindnesses showed to them. Though the citizens of Gander neither asked for nor expected anything in return, their guests have sent cards, gifts, and donations of more than $60,000 for the town. Some have returned to vacation there and once again enjoy Canadian hospitality.

He Said, She Said

Champions keep playing until they get it right.

—*Billie Jean King*

Religion is what keeps the poor from murdering the rich.

—*Napoleon Bonaparte*

The best argument against democracy is a five-minute conversation with the average voter.

—*Winston Churchill*

When the missionaries first came to Africa, they had the Bible and we had the land. They said, "Let us pray." We closed our eyes. When we opened them, we had the Bible and they had the land.

—*Desmond Tutu*

A man in love is incomplete until he has married. Then he's finished.

—*Zsa Zsa Gabor*

You can't make up anything anymore. The world itself is a satire. All you're doing is recording it.

—*Art Buchwald*

The buck stops with the guy who signs the checks.

—*Rupert Murdoch*

A people that values its privileges above its principles soon loses both.

—*Dwight D. Eisenhower*

What is the use of a house if you haven't got a tolerable planet to put it on?

—*Henry David Thoreau*

My advice to you is get married: if you find a good wife you'll be happy; if not, you'll become a philosopher.

—*Socrates*

I have never killed a man, but I have read many obituaries with great pleasure.

—*Clarence Darrow*

I can accept failure, but I can't accept not trying.

—*Michael Jordan*

Space Dog

❖ ❖ ❖ ❖

The first occupied spacecraft did not carry a human being or even a monkey. Instead, scientists launched man's best friend.

The Space Age officially began on October 4, 1957, when the Soviet Union launched humanity's first artificial satellite, *Sputnik I*. The world sat stunned, and the space race experienced its first victory. Even more astounding was the launch of *Sputnik II* on November 3. *Sputnik II* carried the first living creature into orbit, a mongrel dog from the streets of Moscow named Laika.

A 20th-Century Dog
A three-year-old stray that weighed just 13 pounds, Laika had a calm disposition and slight stature that made her a perfect fit for the cramped capsule of *Sputnik II*. In the weeks leading up to the launch, Laika was confined to increasingly smaller cages and fed a diet of a special nutritional gel to prepare her for the journey.

 Sputnik II was a 250-pound satellite with a simple cabin, a crude life-support system, and instruments to measure Laika's vital signs. After the success of the *Sputnik I* launch, Soviet Premier Nikita Khrushchev urged scientists to launch another satellite on November 7, 1957, to mark the anniversary of the Bolshevik Revolution. Although work was in progress for the more sophisticated satellite eventually known as *Sputnik III*, it couldn't be completed in time. Sergei Korolev, head of the Soviet space program, ordered his team to design and construct *Sputnik II*. They had less than four weeks.

The First Creature in Space
The November launch astonished the world. When the Soviets announced that Laika would not survive her historic journey, the mission also ignited a debate in the West regarding the treatment of animals. Initial reports suggested that Laika survived a week in orbit, but it was revealed many years later that she only survived for roughly the first five hours. The hastily built craft's life-support system failed, and Laika perished from excess heat. Despite her tragic end, the heroic little dog paved the way for occupied spaceflight.

Fast Facts

- *The first great bank merger in U.S. history occurred in 1955 when Chase National Bank and the Bank of Manhattan amalgamated to form the Chase Manhattan Bank.*

- *A cow can drink more than 50 gallons of water every day—more than enough to fill a bathtub.*

- *America's modern interstate highway system was designed in the 1950s during the Eisenhower administration. Its primary purpose was not to enhance casual driving over long distances but to provide for the efficient movement of military vehicles if and when necessary.*

- *The final resting place of Dr. Eugene Shoemaker, a geologist, is the moon. He arranged to have his ashes placed on board the* Lunar Prospector *spacecraft that was launched on January 6, 1998.*

- *A shrieking baby's cry can reach 113 decibels. A shrieking car alarm can reach 120 decibels. Being exposed to either for half an hour per day will damage your hearing.*

- *James Brudenell, the seventh earl of Cardigan, is known for leading what came to be called "The Charge of the Light Brigade" during the Crimean War in 1854. But he also popularized the cardigan, a knitted jacket worn by his troops.*

- *Eddie Arcaro, one of the greatest jockeys in horse-racing history, lost 250 races before he won his first. Ultimately, in a career spanning 1931 to 1961, Arcaro rode 4,779 winners.*

- *The average dollar bill lasts a little less than two years before it's worn out and pulled from circulation.*

- *Tickling requires surprise. Since you can't surprise yourself, you can't tickle yourself, either.*

The Story of Braille

How do you make up your own language? Louis Braille
did it with equal parts perseverance and creativity.

Ingredients

Take Louis Braille, an inquisitive, creative boy who lost his sight
after stabbing himself in the eye with an awl. Send him on scholarship to the National Institute for Blind Youth in Paris. Expose him to
a cumbersome and slow method of reading. Now add a soldier from
the French army by the name of Charles
Barbier and his system, sonography, which
used raised dots to represent sound.
He developed this language to help
soldiers communicate in the field
without drawing attention to their
positions, but the army eventually nixed it for being too
complex.

The Mixture

These ingredients laid the basis for Braille's work. Over time,
Braille developed a system that could be recognized and understood
by passing the fingers over characters made up of an arrangement
of one to six embossed points. Braille is a system made up of rectan-
gles; each rectangle, or cell, has two columns and three rows. Each
position has a particular number assigned to it—in the left column,
moving down, the positions are numbered one, two, and three; in
the right column, moving down, the positions are four, five, and six.
Raised points at particular positions have particular meanings. For
example, points raised at positions one, three, and four represent the
letter *m*.

Because this system can be written with a stylus and a slate, the
visually impaired have a means by which they can both read and
write. Not only is that a recipe for further learning and efficient
communication, but it's also a method by which they can increase
their independence.

The Times They Are A-Changin'

1911

January 10: While flying over San Diego, California, Major Jimmie Erickson shoots the first photograph taken from an airplane.

January 18: Eugene B. Ely becomes the first pilot to land a plane on a ship when he lands safely on the deck of the USS *Pennsylvania* in San Francisco Harbor.

February 18: The first airmail delivery occurs when Henri Péquet flies 6,500 letters five miles from Allahabad to Naini Junction in India.

February 27: Charles F. Kettering's invention, the automobile self-starter, is installed in a Cadillac.

March 7: Willis S. Farnsworth patents the first coin-operated locker.

March 7: The U.S. government sends 20,000 troops to the Mexican border as a precaution in the wake of the Mexican Revolution.

April 12: Pierre Prier completes the first nonstop flight from London to Paris in three hours and 56 minutes.

May 15: The U.S. Supreme Court rules that the Standard Oil Company is in violation of the Sherman Antitrust Act and orders its breakup.

May 31: The *Titanic* is launched in Belfast, Ireland.

June 4: Gold is discovered in Indian Creek in Alaska.

June 15: The Computing-Tabulating-Recording Company, which later becomes IBM, is incorporated.

August 15: The Procter & Gamble Company of Cincinnati, Ohio, introduces Crisco hydrogenated shortening.

August 21: Leonardo da Vinci's painting *Mona Lisa* is stolen from the Louvre in Paris by Vincenzo Peruggia. It will be recovered in 1913.

December 10: Ending an 84-day trip, Calbraith Rodgers becomes the first person to cross the United States in an airplane.

December 14: Norwegian explorer Roald Amundsen becomes the first man to reach the South Pole, more than a month ahead of an expedition led by Robert F. Scott.

Early Contraception

Ever since humans realized how babies were made, they have either tried to conceive children or avoid them altogether. In earlier days, some techniques were more successful than others.

An ancient Greek gynecologist told women not wishing to have a child to jump backward seven times after intercourse. Ancient Roman women tried to avoid pregnancy by tying a pouch containing a cat's liver to their left foot or by spitting into the mouth of a frog.

What Can Women Do?

Barrier methods of contraception have included pebbles (Arabs prevented camels' impregnation this way), half a lemon, and dried elephant or crocodile dung. In 1550 B.C., a suggested concoction of ground dates, acacia tree bark, and honey applied locally was probably fairly effective, since acacia ferments into lactic acid, which disrupts a normal pH balance. In eastern Canada, one aboriginal group believed in the efficacy of women drinking a tea brewed with beaver testicles.

As early as the seventh century B.C., a member of the fennel family called *silphium* was discovered to be an extremely effective "morning-after pill." But since it only grew in a small area on the Libyan mountainside facing the Mediterranean and attempts to cultivate it elsewhere failed, silphium was extinct by the second century.

Getting the Men Involved

Men have almost always used some sort of sheath, dating back to at least 1000 B.C. The ancient Romans and the 17th-century British employed animal intestine (still available, albeit packaged), while the Egyptians and Italians preferred fabric, sometimes soaked in a spermicidal solution. Vulcanized rubber appeared around 1844.

The main responsibility for contraception still lies with women, many of whom alter their body's hormonal balance with "the pill," introduced in 1960. Meanwhile, due to lack of male interest, research into male contraceptive injections, pills and/or nasal sprays has stalled, and "the sheath" remains men's primary resource.

The Sad Saga of Sonny Liston

❖ ❖ ❖ ❖

Climbing up from utter poverty, this world heavyweight
champ found controversial success in the boxing ring
but couldn't maintain his balance on the outside.

Charles "Sonny" Liston was born the son of an impoverished share-cropper in rural Arkansas, probably on May 8, but the year of his birth is unknown. This is the first of many mysteries in the life of a complicated, impenetrable man. Though many who knew him said he was born in 1927, Liston himself claimed he was born in 1932, and contemporary documents seem to back him up. Emotionally and physically abused, young Liston was not unhappy when his miserable parents split up and his mother moved to St. Louis—in fact, he followed her there as soon as he could.

The Hard Time

Liston was only in his early teens when he made his way north, and like everyone else in his family, he was illiterate. He had his imposing build going for him, however, and this led local organized crime to recruit him as a debt collector. As long as Liston stuck to breaking knee-caps, he was to some degree under the mob's protection from law enforcement. But when he struck out on his own, robbing two gas stations and a restaurant with other youths in 1950, the police caught up to him, and he was busted. Liston pleaded guilty to two counts of robbery and two counts of larceny—he was lucky to be sentenced to concurrent prison terms that ran only five years.

In the penitentiary, a Roman Catholic priest noticed Liston's remarkable physique and urged him to take up boxing. Liston followed that advice, and after serving only two years of his time, he was paroled to a team of "handlers" who worked for St. Louis mobster John Vitale. Vitale set Liston up in the boxing world and controlled his contract for six years before selling it to Frankie Carbo and Blinky Palermo, underworld figures on the East Coast. Eventually, Liston's criminal ties would lead him all the way to the U.S. Senate, where in 1960 he testified before a subcommittee investigating organized crime's control of boxing.

The Big Time

Liston's first professional fight lasted only 33 seconds—he took out Don Smith with only one punch. His first five fights were in St. Louis, but his sixth was in Detroit. In that nationally televised bout, he won an eight-round decision against John Summerlin. The odds had been long, so the fight garnered the young upstart a lot of attention. He suffered his first professional defeat from his next opponent, when Marty Marshall broke his jaw. Nevertheless, Liston moved steadily up the ranks, and finally, at Chicago's Comiskey Park in 1962, he became the heavyweight champion of the world by knocking out Floyd Patterson in the first round.

Fighting success did not keep him out of trouble with the law, however. A total of 19 arrests and a second jail sentence made Liston an unpopular figure on the American sports scene. Many of his fights were thought to be fixed, and some considered him a puppet of the mob. Unfortunately for him, Liston's most famous moment was one of defeat: his knockout by Muhammad Ali on May 25, 1965. In one of the most famous sports photos ever taken, *Sports Illustrated* photographer Neil Leifer shot Liston sprawled on the mat with a menacing, screaming Ali towering over him. Some claim that Ali's punch was a "phantom punch" that never connected and that Liston had taken a dive because he feared the Nation of Islam.

Strange Death

On January 5, 1971, he was found dead in his Las Vegas home by his wife, Geraldine, who had been out of town. Though the coroner ruled that he had died from heart failure and lung congestion, Liston's body was in a state of decomposition, and there was much speculation that Liston had been murdered by unsavory associates.

The man who came into the world so anonymously that his birth year was not really known left it in fame, but with just as many unanswered questions.

HOW IT ALL BEGAN

E-mail
E-mail was developed by Ray Tomlinson and sent across the forerunner of the Internet—called ARPANET—in 1971. He chose the @ symbol to denote an online "address" for the sender. His first message, he has said, was likely "qwertyuiop," familiar to anyone who has ever used a keyboard (it's the top line). When Tomlinson was asked by people at the time (who clearly had no foresight) why he'd invented something that nobody seemed to want or even have any use for, he responded, "Because it seemed like a neat idea."

"In Cahoots"
When two or more people are up to no good, they're said to be "in cahoots." The phrase may well come from France, where a small cabin was called a *cahute*. If these cabins were occupied by bandits and robbers planning a heist, the name of the cottages may have become a sort of shorthand to signify what went on inside them.

The Safety Pin
The humble, but modesty-saving, safety pin has its origins in Central Europe, circa 1000 B.C.; this concoction held the pointed end within a curved wire, and while it may have been safer, it was not entirely safe itself. Straight pins, on the other hand, date back 5,000 years and were created from iron and bone by the Sumerians. Archeologists are convinced that the sewing needle is at least 10,000 years old—when fish spines were pierced at the top or the middle to receive a thread.

"Running Amok"
When a crowd of people begins to panic, it's said to "run amok" (or *amuck*). The phrase comes from the Malay word *amok,* which means "violent and out of control." It is said that this is what the excited Malaysians yelled when they encountered Europeans for the first time.

The Cold Shoulder
To be "given the cold shoulder" means to be snubbed. In days of yore, it originally referred to a shoulder of meat, often mutton, offered to a traveler. A warm meal was an indication that someone was welcome, whereas cold meat was a warning that, although you'd be fed, the householders weren't particularly enthusiastic about your being there.

"Crazed Publishers Forced Me to Read Their Drivel": Tabloid Sensationalism in the '60s

Strolling into a drugstore in the 1960s and looking at the cover of the National Enquirer *was much like slowing down to look at an auto accident—you knew you shouldn't, but you just couldn't help it. Sensational screaming headlines and gory gross-out photos laid the groundwork for today's celebrity-laden tabloids that shout improbable claims.*

The *National Enquirer* began its life in 1926 as a weekly broadsheet bankrolled by newspaper giant William Randolph Hearst, who was no stranger to sensational journalism. Yet, it was 1954 when an MIT engineering grad named Generoso Pope took over the paper and turned it into a tabloid format. Realizing that magazines such as *Confidential,* with their outrageous and sensational headlines, were a huge success, Pope patterned the *National Enquirer* after them. By the 1960s, newsstands were featuring incredible cover stories:

- "I DRILLED A HOLE IN MY HEAD FOR KICKS!"

- "MOM USES SON'S FACE FOR AN ASHTRAY"

- "MADMAN CUT UP HIS DATE AND PUT HER BODY IN HIS FREEZER"

- "I CUT OUT HER HEART AND STOMPED ON IT!"

- "STABS GIRL 55 TIMES"

- "MOM BOILED HER BABY AND ATE HER!"

- "DIGS UP WIFE'S ROTTING CORPSE AND RIPS IT APART!"

- "I WATCHED A WILD HOG EAT MY BABY!"

- "SON MURDERS DAD FOR $8"

- "KILLS SON AND FEEDS CORPSE TO PIGS!"

Love Triangle, Celebrity Style: Woody Allen, Mia Farrow, and Soon-Yi Previn

Director, actor, and screenwriter Woody Allen is famous for making movies that chronicle the bizarre trials and tribulations of his neurotic protagonists. But the very public personal saga that hit newspaper stands in the early '90s tops even the most convoluted of Allen's screenplays.

Woody Allen built a career as a respected film-maker with such movies as *Bananas, Sleeper, Manhattan,* and the Oscar-winning *Annie Hall.* His films were recognizably his own, and announcements of new projects were greeted with anticipation among critics and the public.

Setting the Stage
In 1980, Allen began a relationship with actor Mia Farrow, best known at the time for her role in the movie *Rosemary's Baby* and the TV series *Peyton Place.* Farrow already had six children, both adopted and biological, from her previous marriage to pianist Andre Previn. In 1987, Allen and Farrow had a son of their own, Satchel O'Sullivan Farrow (who later changed his name to Ronan Seamus Farrow). While she was with Allen, Mia also adopted a boy named Moses and a girl named Dylan. Allen and Farrow never married, but in 1991 Allen also adopted Dylan and Moses.

The Rising Action
Allen and Farrow spent 12 years leading what looked to be an idyllic, if somewhat peculiar, existence. The two never lived together, having residences on opposite sides of New York City's Central Park. Farrow and her roster of kids would trudge across the park, armed with sleeping bags, to spend the night on Allen's side of the green.

This all ended in 1992, when Farrow discovered nude photographs Allen had taken of her adopted daughter, Soon-Yi Previn.

It turned out Allen had been sleeping with Soon-Yi at least since her first year of college. Soon-Yi was 21 at the time of her mother's discovery, and Allen was 57.

Recognizing that Farrow was miles beyond peeved by this turn of affairs, Allen sued her for custody of their three children—Satchel, Moses, and Dylan. Farrow responded by accusing Allen of sexually abusing Dylan, who was seven years old at the time.

The press, not surprisingly, had a field day. The ensuing courtroom drama was covered daily in newspapers in the United States and around the world. It didn't hurt that the two stars of this media production didn't shy away from reporters. Allen was eager to emphatically deny the accusation of molestation, and he also revealed that he didn't regret his affair with Soon-Yi. When the story of the affair first broke, Allen responded, "It's real and happily all true."

Farrow, meanwhile, was more than open to depicting Allen as a small, sniveling, neurotic, and deeply creepy monster. Regarding Allen's relationship with their daughter Dylan, Farrow testified, "He would creep up in the morning and lay beside her bed and wait for her to wake up. . . . I was uncomfortable all along."

Resolution—Sort Of

In the end, Farrow was granted full custody of the three children. The judge wrote a 33-page decision in which he described Allen as a "self-absorbed, untrustworthy and insensitive" father. He chastised Allen for not knowing the names of his son's teachers or even which children shared which bedrooms in Farrow's apartment. A state-appointed group of specialists concluded that Allen was not guilty of molesting Dylan, although the judge deemed the report "sanitized and . . . less credible."

Allen was disappointed to lose custody of his children, but he was happy to continue his relationship with their older adoptive half-sister. Soon after the conclusion of the court battle, Soon-Yi and Allen were spotted at trendy restaurants all across Manhattan. They married in 1997 and have since adopted two children of their own. Farrow remains estranged from Soon-Yi but is more than busy with her current activities. In her 1997 memoir, Farrow compared her relationship with Allen to her childhood infection with polio: "I had unknowingly brought danger into my family and . . . I might have contaminated those that I loved the most."

Tonight We Love: The Romantic Age of Classical Music

The romantic era (1820–1900) is an important period in the development of classical music, spawning some of the world's most talented composers and bridging the gap between the European classical (1730–1820) and modernist periods (1900–2000).

Romanticism as it pertained to music in the 19th century did not simply refer to music that was soft, moody, and dreamy. The idea behind romanticism was that it strived to capture powerful emotional expression.

One important factor of the period was that talented, free-thinking composers were able to support themselves with their work. One cannot live on accolades alone, after all. Public concerts became a popular way for composers to survive while enjoying creative freedom—not having to suffer the whims of the ecclesiastical and imperial patronage long associated with classical music.

Ludwig van Beethoven (1770–1827)
Generally considered the first and most pivotal of the romantic era musicians, Beethoven is one of the most influential composers of all time. Two popular examples of his early romantic style are the *Moonlight* and *Pathétique* Sonatas. Beethoven ultimately lost his hearing, but proof of his genius lies in the fact that he continued to compose, conduct, and perform regardless. Beethoven was known as a very quarrelsome individual, but he is now believed to have suffered from bipolar disorder.

Hector Berlioz (1803–69)
A French romantic composer, Berlioz contributed greatly to the importance of the modern orchestra. He sometimes wrote music for a thousand musicians. His *Symphonie Fantastique* is considered a classic example of romantic-era composition—because of its hallucinatory, dreamlike overtones, some experts believe it was written under the influence of opium. Berlioz also provided the musical arrangement of Rouget de Lisle's "La Marseillaise," the French

national anthem. Although extremely influential in symphonic composition, his genius was not acknowledged until the early 1960s.

Franz Liszt (1811–86)

This Hungarian composer literally invented the symphonic poem. A close friend of Berlioz, Liszt was also instrumental in the popularity of his *Symphonie Fantastique*. Liszt may have been the Liberace of his time—not only an accomplished piano virtuoso, but a profound entertainer as well. His Hungarian Rhapsodies and Piano Sonata in B Minor have entered the realm of composition classics. Unfortunately, Liszt's fall down a flight of stairs led to a number of ailments and, quite possibly, his death.

Johannes Brahms (1833–97)

This German composer spent much of his life in Austria. Previously considered a bland imitator of Beethoven, he is now believed to have been a true innovator of rhythmic conception and a prime example of the late period of romanticism. Brahms is frequently labeled the most truly "classical" romantic composer. His Hungarian Dances are extremely popular, and his "Wiegenlied" is the world's most familiar lullaby, lulling children to sleep in practically every known language.

Frédéric Chopin (1810–49)

A Polish-born child prodigy, Chopin settled in Paris at age 21. Hailed by critics as one of the world's greatest composers of piano music, he was also an accomplished concert performer. His stormy romantic relationship with French writer George Sand (whose real name was Aurore Dupin) has been the subject of several novels and motion pictures. Chopin's waltzes are among the most popular piano recital pieces ever composed. Never a healthy man, he died of tuberculosis at age 39.

Peter Ilyich Tchaikovsky (1840–93)

Possibly the last of the romantic-era masters, this Russian composer was known for his brilliant orchestrations and strong melody lines. The popular song "Tonight We Love," recorded by Freddy Martin in 1941, was adapted from one of his most familiar works, the Piano Concerto No. 1 in B Flat Minor.

Fumbling Felons

It Pays to Follow the Styles

A 54-year-old man in San Francisco robbed several banks just seven days after being released from prison—for bank robbery. In February 2007, the man's probation officer took a photo of him on the day he was released. Still wearing the 1980s-style clothes and Members Only jacket in which he strode away from prison—but adding a new hairnet—the man proceeded to rob a bank. Authorities weren't able to positively identify the robber's face from the surveillance photos, but they were able to clearly distinguish his Members Only jacket, his hairnet, and the 1980s-era clothes he wore. He wasn't wasting any time, however, and robbed two more banks before police caught him. The images from the later robberies were widely distributed to police agencies—the bank robber's probation officer instantly recognized him and immediately contacted authorities with the man's name and address. The bank robber was apprehended later that night. He was identified due to the fact that he was still wearing the same clothes.

Choose Your Location Carefully

Perhaps he thought the lot was still vacant, or maybe he believed that no one would think to look for marijuana in such a place. Regardless of his reasoning, a 17-year-old male was arrested for growing nine marijuana plants in a wooded area of Ocala, Florida. Unfortunately for the teen, that wooded area belonged to the deputy chief of police. Neighbors noticed the teen acting suspiciously and asked why he was on the chief's property. He replied that he'd come from a skate park, but they didn't buy it. One neighbor went to where the teen had been spotted and found the illegal crop. The deputy chief was immediately notified.

Safety Goggles Wouldn't Have Helped

Two 19-year-olds were treated for minor burns and arrested after shoplifting gunpowder and PVC pipe from a Wal-Mart in Bayou Black, Louisiana, in July 2007. The youths had successfully gotten away from the store, but they didn't follow all the safety precautions that they should have. One of them subsequently set off the black powder when he flicked cigarette ashes near the open bottle. Following up on reports of a bang, police arrived to investigate. They found damage from an explosion in the kitchen and dining room. The duo was charged with shoplifting and possessing or making a bomb.

The Buffalo Creek Flood

In 1972, a calamitous flood roared through mining towns in West Virginia, leaving utter destruction in its wake. Company officials were slow to respond, which only made the disaster worse.

Buffalo Creek winds its way through 16 mining communities in West Virginia and empties into the Guyandotte River. As part of its mining operations, the Buffalo Mining Company, a subsidiary of Pittston Coal Company, dumped mine waste—consisting of mine dust, shale, clay, and other impurities—into Buffalo Creek. The company constructed its first impoundment dam in 1960. Six years later, it constructed a second dam upstream. By 1972, the mining company had built its third dam into the hillside near the Buffalo Creek communities.

The Precursors

A flood on Buffalo Creek should perhaps not have been much of a surprise. In 1967, the U.S. Department of the Interior warned West Virginia state officials that the Buffalo Creek dams were unstable and dangerous. This conclusion came as a result of a study of state dams conducted in response to a mine dam break that killed nearly 150 people—mostly children—in Wales in 1966.

In February 1971, the third impoundment dam on Buffalo Creek failed, but the second dam halted the water, preventing damage to the creek communities. The state cited Pittston Coal Company for violations but failed to follow up with inspections.

A Wall of Water

A few days before the fatal flood, a heavy, continuous rain fell, which is typical for the area at that time of year. By 8:00 A.M. on February 26, the water had risen to the crest of the third dam, which collapsed within five minutes. The force of the water then crushed the subsequent dams as the water gushed down the creek. A black wave—variously described as 10 to 45 feet high—gushed through the mining towns. The area of Buffalo Creek hollow was smothered with 132 million gallons of filthy wastewater in waves traveling at more than seven feet per second.

In all, the flooding left 125 people dead, more than 1,100 injured, and more than 4,000 homeless.

The Aftermath

It took only three hours for the gushing waves of mine waste to demolish the lives of the Buffalo Creek community. It would take years to recover from the disaster, if recovery happened at all.

Three separate commissions—federal, state, and citizen—each concluded that the Buffalo Mining Company blatantly disregarded standard safety practices. The Pittston Coal Company, in a statement from its New York office, declared the disaster "an act of God." Citizens responded by saying they never saw God building the dams in the first place.

West Virginia Governor Arch Moore, Jr., banned journalists from entering the disaster site, explaining that the state was already unduly harmed and did not need any bad press. He promised to build 750 public housing units. Ultimately, 17 model homes and 90 apartments were constructed. A promised community center was never built.

With the federal disaster funds, Moore attempted to build a superhighway through the Buffalo Creek hollow. West Virginia's Department of Highways condemned and purchased hundreds of lots from flood survivors. A two-lane road was constructed, but the superhighway never was. Most property was not sold back to its original owners but instead remained held by the state.

Both state and federal mine safety agencies passed laws that improved conditions in the coalfields. In 1973, the West Virginia legislature passed the Dam Control Act, which regulated dams in the state. However, funding was never appropriated to enforce the law, and in 1992, the Division of Natural Resources estimated that state was home to at least 400 hazardous dams.

• *When it comes to chilies—generally speaking—the smaller the pepper, the bigger the burn.*

• *Journalist Henry Morton Stanley, the explorer who located Dr. David Livingstone in Africa, served in both the Confederate and Union armies during the American Civil War.*

Fast Facts

- Fingerprints are unique to each individual, of course. But the same goes for tongue prints and lip prints.

- Until 1862, currency from the U.S. Mint took the form of coins. During the Civil War, the Union Congress authorized the Treasury to print the first paper money, which became known as "legal tenders" or "greenbacks" because of the green ink used.

- While working as a cook in New York during the early 1900s, Mary Mallon, who became known as "Typhoid Mary," infected at least 53 people, 3 of whom died. She was quarantined for three years, released for a short time when she promised she would no longer work as a cook, then quarantined again after she broke her promise. She was never released from her second quarantine, which lasted 23 years until her death.

- Beginning with Super Bowl XXXIV in 2000, game footballs have been marked with synthetic DNA to prevent sports-memorabilia fraud. Souvenirs from the 2000 Summer Olympics were marked with human DNA in the ink.

- A raisin dropped into a glass of a carbonated drink will float up and down continually from the bottom of the glass to the top.

- Comanche code-talkers, used in World War II by the Army Signal Corps to send encrypted messages that German troops could not break, referred to Adolf Hitler as posah-tai-vo, which means "crazy white man."

- An official balance beam in women's gymnastics is just four inches wide, less than the length of a ballpoint pen.

- In 1956, Johnny Mathis decided to record an album instead of answering an invitation to try out for the U.S. Olympic team as a high jumper. He became one of the top-selling artists of all time.

The World's First Renaissance Man?

❖ ❖ ❖ ❖

A brilliant mind 2,000 years before the Renaissance, the Greek philosopher Anaximander is one of the greatest thinkers of all time.

Anaximander was the first philosopher in history to have written down his work—perhaps that is also why he's known as such a groundbreaker. Unfortunately, even though he produced and recorded the work, for the most part it has not survived. We mostly know of Anaximander through *doxographers,* or writers who document the beliefs, thoughts, and theories of their predecessors. In Anaximander's case, Aristotle and Plato have told us most of what we know about his work.

A Long Time Ago in a Land Far Away...

Born in ancient Greece in the seventh century B.C., Anaximander came from Miletus, a city in Ionia, which is now the western coast of Turkey. This area was a cultural enclave known for its progressive views on philosophy and art—it paved the way for the brilliant artistic development of Athens in the fifth century B.C.

A true rationalist, Anaximander boldly questioned the myths, the heavens, and the existence of the gods themselves. He wanted to devise natural explanations for phenomena that had previously been assumed to be supernatural. As founder of the science of astronomy, he was credited with building the first *gnomon,* or perpendicular sundial, which he based on the early work of the Babylonians and their divisions of the days.

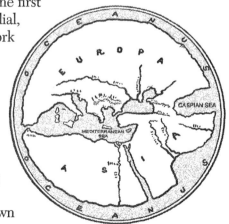

The First Map of the World

Breaking new ground in geography as well, Anaximander has also been credited as being the first cartographer to draw the entire inhabited world known to the Greeks. The map was likely circular, and a river called Ocean surrounded the land. The Mediterranean Sea appeared in the middle of the map, and the land was divided into two halves, one called *Europe* and the other, *Southern Asia*. What was assumed to be the habitable world consisted of two small strips of land to the north and south of the Mediterranean Sea.

The accomplishment of this map is far more significant than it might originally appear. Firstly, it could be used to improve navigation and trade. But secondly, and perhaps more importantly, Anaximander thought that by displaying the lay of the land, so to speak, and demonstrating which nations and people were where, he might be able to convince the Ionic city-states to form a federation to push away outside threats.

Earth Is a Tabletop

Watching the horizon, Anaximander concluded that Earth was cylindrical, its diameter being three times its height, with man living on the top. He also thought that Earth floated free in the center of the universe, unsupported by pillars or water, as had commonly been believed at the time. "Earth didn't fall," Aristotle recounted, "because it was at equal distances from the extremes and needed not move in any particular direction since it is impossible to move in opposite directions at the same time."

These were amazing and progressive ideas primarily for one simple reason: They were not based on things that Anaximander could have observed but, instead, were the result of conclusions he reached through rational thought. This is the first known example of an argument based on the principle of sufficient reason, rather than one of myth.

By boldly speculating about the universe, Anaximander molded the direction of science, physics, and philosophy. The idea that nature is ruled by laws just like those in human societies, and anything that disturbs the balance of nature does not last long, should make man pause and think... just as Anaximander did.

- *While visiting Sicily, Aeschylus, a Greek playwright, died in 456 B.C. when an eagle or vulture dropped a tortoise on his bald head, mistaking it for a rock.*

Strange Justice

He Should Have Stuck with Being a Snack Parent

Many youth league baseball coaches manage their teams with their hearts on their jersey sleeves. They live and die for their kids, so what could be worse than a losing season? How about getting sued for a losing season? One coach finished the season 0–15 and was then served with a lawsuit for $2,000 from the father of his team's catcher. The suit claimed poor coaching cost the team a trip to a tournament. A judge found the claimant was way off base and dismissed the case.

Some People Just Have No Willpower

The man's weight was nearly 310 pounds, and something had to be done. Consulting doctors, he agreed that more than 60 staples would be placed in his stomach. This would result in his food capacity being greatly reduced, and he'd be on his way to "Slim City." Returning to his recovery room after the operation, however, the man found a carton of milk in a refrigerator and downed it. The overindulgence popped his staples, sending him back to surgery. He sued the hospital for $250,000 for "extreme pain and . . . emotional distress." But, perhaps realizing he was being a bit of a pig, he dropped the suit.

Goosed Out of a Job

Many strange things can happen when starting a new job. A man tried to enter his office building on only his second day with the company when he found himself under attack by swooping wild Canadian geese. In trying to escape their wrath, he fell and broke his wrist. He sued his company, claiming they had built their offices in a dangerous "high-goose" area, complete with short grass and a pond to attract the feathered fowls. A jury found in the plaintiff's favor, awarding him more than $17,000 for his injury.

A-Wunerful, A-Wunerful

A young man paid plenty for the new high-tech sound system installed in his truck. Bass rumbling, he motored down his neighborhood streets—until a police officer arrested him for playing his loud music with the truck windows down. A judge offered the guilty offender a choice—he could pay a $100 fine or listen to four hours of polka music. He chose the polka music and can now sing "Who Stole the Kishka" with the best of the polka kings.

Oddball Beauty Pageants

Not all contests are only skin deep.

There are as many kinds of beauty pageants as there are hobbies, sports, and cultural obsessions. If you're a *Star Trek* fan, a beach bum with an artistic bent, or the proud owner of a bushy beard or moustache, these are for you.

Klingon Nation

Every year, Trekkies (or, as they prefer to be called, "Trekkers") gather in Atlanta for a *Star Trek* Convention that includes the Miss Klingon Empire Beauty Pageant. Contestants can compete as established female Klingon characters, or if they prefer, they can invent their own original characters. Contestants are judged on beauty, personality, and talent, but they are warned on the official Web site that the talent portion should not get too wild and crazy: "no flaming bat'leth twirling."

Shell Games

Hermit crabs may not be known for their beauty, but don't tell that to the organizers of the Miss Curvaceous Crustacean Beauty Pageant in Virginia Beach, Virginia. It isn't the crabs so much as their themed habitats that are judged in this annual beachfront event, and there seems to be no end to the unique ideas that contestants dream up as they surround their hermit crabs with elaborate environments. Past winners had such themes as "Hermit the Hulk," "Spider Crab," and "Beauty and the Crab."

It'll Grow on You

At the Annual World Beard and Moustache Championship, held in the past in both America and Europe, Germans usually take the top honors, but American contestants are muscling in. There may be other changes coming soon, as well: In 2003, a bearded woman became the first female to join the National Beard Registry, an Internet facial hair group, and some feel that it's only a matter of time before a bearded lady will join the men as a winner.

Nasty Nietzsche's Nazi Neighborhood: *Nueva Germania* in Paraguay

The husband was stern, commanding, and persuasive.
The wife was the sister of a world-famous philosopher.
Together, they sought to colonize a remote area of Paraguay
as the starting point for their vision of utopia.

Contrary to popular belief, the dream of a pure Aryan race was not the invention of Adolf Hitler. Four decades prior to Hitler's rise, a prominent couple envisioned a perfect world of Germanic people.

Bernhard Förster and Elisabeth Nietzsche

Herr Förster was a Berlin schoolteacher who was fired in 1883 for preaching racial hatred. He blamed the Jewish people in Europe for trying to destroy Germany and its culture through capitalistic business activities. At one point, Förster was able to collect more than 250,000 signatures on a petition demanding that Jewish immigration be halted and Jews be removed from the German stock market. It was ignored when delivered to German leader Otto von Bismarck, so Förster fostered a plan to build a superior race of Germans, traveling to South America after his dismissal from teaching. He chose Paraguay for its isolation and complete lack of Jewish people.

Fräulein Nietzsche was two years younger than her philosophizing brother, Friedrich. Before her marriage to Förster in 1885, Elisabeth was sheltered, living the good life with her mother. While she was not necessarily given to anti-Semitic beliefs before meeting Förster, she seemed to quickly embrace the vile practice.

Bringing Hatred to the New World

In March 1886, the Försters somehow convinced 14 families to pack up all they owned and travel more than 6,500 miles to where hatred could run as rampant as the jungle that surrounded them. After enduring a month-long sea voyage, the troop traveled for five days up the Parana River in a clunking steamer. Arriving in the city of Asunción, the Försters slept in its only hotel, while the other travelers bunked in drafty huts nearby. Their trek continued for another week by boat, then by horse and oxcart to the 40,000 acres of forest and farmland that Förster had purchased for a small down payment.

The Colony Collapses

Förster was convinced that fellow German anti-Semites would flock to the new fatherland he had created. He was wrong. While the Paraguayan land was fertile, it was foreign soil for German cultivation methods—they failed as farmers. Most were unable to weather such difficult travel to a land they knew nothing about. Lack of sanitation led to massive disease, and snakes were a constant concern.

Forty families made the trip to *Nueva Germania* in the first two years (minus the ten families who were smart enough to return to Germany). They could hardly fill the 40,000 acres that Förster owned. Heavily in debt, Förster left his wife at the colony in May 1889, moving back to an area near Asunción in search of more financing. Knowing that his vision had failed, Förster chose to take his own life.

What of Elisabeth?

Förster's widow inherited another crisis immediately, as her brother Friedrich became mentally ill. Returning to Europe to care for him, she took over the publishing of his writings and began to alter many of his views to embrace anti-Semitism. Following Friedrich's death in 1900, his sister released a highly edited and embellished work called *The Will to Power,* furthering her expressions of racial hatred.

Eventually, Förster-Nietzsche became a pen pal to Benito Mussolini, who dreamt of returning Rome to its ancient greatness. When Hitler took control of Germany in 1933, he embraced Elisabeth Förster-Nietzsche as a matriarchal figure. She died in 1935, and a sorrowful führer sat at the head of the casket during her funeral.

What of *Nueva Germania*?

After the end of World War II, many Nazis fled Germany and relocated to *Nueva Germania,* including Josef Mengele, the infamous concentration camp doctor. Remnants of the Förster colony remain in Paraguay, and several hundred people—including descendants of the original 14 German families—live there today. Generations of isolation, poverty, and inbreeding have left the people of *Nueva Germania* a mere curiosity in the world, instead of its masters.

ANAGRAMS

An anagram is a word or phrase that exactly reproduces the letters in another word or phrase. The most interesting of them reflect or comment on the subject of the first.

A stitch in time saves nine—This is meant as incentive.

dormitory—dirty room

debit card—bad credit

Halley's Comet—shall yet come

punishment—nine thumps

election results—lies; let's recount

Britney Spears—best PR in years

the public art galleries—large picture halls, I bet

Declaration of Independence—no finer deed, an ideal concept

Remember the Alamo—A memorable term, eh?

Eskimos—Some ski.

William Shakespeare—I'll make a wise phrase.

the earthquakes—that queer shake

Alec Guinness—genuine class

parishioners—I hire parsons.

Elvis Aaron Presley—Seen alive? Sorry, pal.

Monty Python's Flying Circus—Strongly psychotic, I'm funny.

Sherlock Holmes—heh, smells crook

Jim Morrison—Mr. Mojo Risin'

Snow White and the Seven Dwarfs—Oh, sweet DVD wins new fan's heart.

Supreme Court—Corrupt? Sue me!

Albert Einstein—ten elite brains

the Morse code—Here come dots.

What Is Mensa?

Almost everybody, it seems, has heard about Mensa—the club for really, really smart people—but nobody is sure exactly what it is. Or how to get in. Or what the standards are for membership.

More than 50,000 Americans are part of the international society called Mensa. They're just people who have scored in the top 2 percent in one of more than 200 acceptable standardized tests. (Although spokespeople won't say exactly what the magic number happens to be, the standard measurement for "very superior" intelligence is an IQ of 130 or above.) About one in 50 Americans—six million in total—qualify for Mensa membership, whether they realize it or not (you can see for yourself at www.us.mensa.org/testscores).

Currently, American Mensa's youngest member is just 3 years old, and the oldest is 103. Mensa boasts 134 local chapters that offer a variety of activities, including movie nights at a member's home and dinners out with others. The group's name, which is related to three Latin words meaning "mind," "table," and "month," would seem to suggest meeting and eating every four weeks.

Brilliant Origins

The group, originally founded in Great Britain in 1946, with the American branch beginning in 1960 in Brooklyn, New York, currently boasts 100,000 members worldwide. There don't appear to be any scary, arcane rituals involved, or any need to keep proving oneself once "inside." One of the organization's main tenets is to provide intellectual company for like-minded individuals (in America, the membership is 65 percent male, the remainder female). While the club protects members' privacy, there are some notable folks who are or were willing to be identified, including actors Geena Davis and Alan Rachins, sci-fi writer Isaac Asimov, and NASA astronaut Bill McArthur.

Our favorite members, though, are the fictional ones, both from TV shows: Lisa Simpson, Bart's long-suffering sister; and Frederick Crane, the over-therapized son of Frasier and his icy ex, Lilith.

The Hoxsey Cancer Clinics

Sick people have always sought alternatives to mainstream health and medical counsel. Some alternatives are more successful than others.

In 1924, Texan Harry Hoxsey opened his first clinic, claiming that a cure for cancer lay in herbal remedies—an internal tonic and two salves—concocted by his Quaker great-grandfather, who had seen a dying horse revived by eating certain medicinal weeds. By the 1950s, Hoxsey had clinics in 17 states, making his the largest alternative-medicine movement in American history.

Not So Fast

The American Cancer Society continues to condemn Hoxsey, while admitting that, "In some animal studies, a few of the herbs contained in the treatment showed some anti-cancer activity." Hoxsey was considered a quack, and although he was arrested more times than any other person in medical history, all charges of practicing medicine without a license were thrown out of court. Morris Fishbein, then-editor of the prestigious *Journal of the American Medical Association,* led the charge by continually filing suit against Hoxsey.

Closing Down Shop

Hoxsey, who had made his fortune in oil, claimed that Fishbein's efforts were revenge for Hoxsey's rebuff when Fishbein tried to buy the Hoxsey formulae. However, herbal treatments cannot be patented, so no company could have made significant profits from mass production. After the U.S. Food and Drug Administration banned the sale of Hoxsey treatments in 1960, Hoxsey was forced to close all of his clinics, although one was relocated to Tijuana, Mexico, where it continues to operate, using the name Bio-Medical Center.

In 1967, Hoxsey discovered that he had prostate cancer, but unfortunately neither his own medicine nor conventional surgery helped, and he died in 1974. A report by the National Institutes of Health has since urged further investigation of the Hoxsey treatments due to "several noteworthy cases of survival."

FROM THE VAULTS OF HISTORY

A Simple Name
The all-purpose lubricant WD-40 was invented by a chemist named Norm Larsen in 1953. He worked for the Rocket Chemical Company (which has since changed its name to the WD-40 Company) in San Diego, California, and he was apparently experimenting to create a formula that could prevent corrosion and displaced water from ruining an engine. The name WD-40 comes from his laboratory notes, "Water Displacement 40th attempt."

Method Chewing
Mel Blanc, one of the best character voice actors in history, could be heard in any number of cartoons at the movies or on TV. He was arguably best known as the voice of the carrot-chomping Bugs Bunny. Blanc didn't like raw carrots—at all. In fact, recording was often stopped to allow Blanc time to spit the raw carrots he chewed for the sound effects into a wastebasket before continuing with the script. He could reportedly fill several baskets with carrot pulp during a single session.

Misunderstood
Deep down, John Dillinger, the career criminal and infamous bank robber of the 1930s, was actually a romantic. Despite his hardened exterior and chosen profession, Dillinger frequently wrote long, passionate love letters to his wife and girlfriends. His letters often gushed with promises of monogamy. He regaled the recipients with claims that he was captivated by their beauty.

A Panther of a Different Color
Born in 1925 with the name Richard Henry Sellers, Peter Sellers went on to become the embodiment of the bumbling Inspector Clouseau in the successful *Pink Panther* movies. It's a good thing that he didn't star in a movie about a purple panther. Sellers had *porphyrophobia*—fear of the color purple.

Just Chilling
Staying cool on hot summer days can be hard. Do you reach for an icy, refreshing drink for relief? Perhaps you should try a leaf of cabbage like baseball great Babe Ruth. Ruth kept a cabbage leaf under his cap to keep him cool. Reportedly, he would change the leaf every two innings.

Lewis Carroll's Little Girls

❖ ❖ ❖ ❖

Maurice Chevalier famously sang "Thank Heaven for Little Girls," but it was Lewis Carroll who got the bad rap.

Charles Lutwidge Dodgson (1832–98) was the author of *Alice's Adventures in Wonderland,* although he is better known by his pen name of Lewis Carroll. Even though Alice and her fantasyland have become much beloved, Dodgson/Carroll's life and work have been tainted ever since a 1933 article suggested that his fascination with little girls hid a secret pedophilia. The truth of the matter is, of course, somewhat more complicated.

Friendly and Engaging

Dodgson was the son of a country parson, the third of 11 children. Homeschooled, he later held a professor's post in mathematics for more than 25 years at his father's alma mater, Christ Church at Oxford University. He was also a logician, a keen amateur photographer (dating from the inception of the art, circa 1856), and despite his stammer, quite a gregarious fellow. Dodgson was a gifted writer who had short stories published in 1855 and 1856. With an eye toward extra income, he had considered ideas for children's books, including a Christmas book and an instructional manual about marionettes.

In 1856, a new dean, Henry Liddell, arrived at Oxford with his wife and four children: Harry, Ina, Alice, and Edith. Dodgson originally befriended Harry, and later he would take all of the children (with their governess) on picnics and lake outings, where he told them fanciful stories and photographed them. In 1862, after 11-year-old Alice implored him to write down the story with her namesake at its center, Dodgson realized its possible commercial potential and began his masterwork.

Trouble in Paradise

There was, however, a sudden, mysterious break between Dodgson and the Liddell family in June 1863. The Liddells never spoke of it publicly, and the page that related to June 27–29, 1863, which might have shed light on the matter, was cut from Dodgson's diaries. In fact, all of Dodgson's diaries from April 18, 1858, through May 8, 1862, are missing, likely destroyed by his nieces, the heirs to his estate. The estate's executor, Dodgson's brother Wilfred, is also known to have burned quantities of personal papers after Dodgson's death.

The general assumption about the issue is that Mrs. Liddell was concerned about the amount of time Dodgson was spending in the company of little Alice. However, in 1996, after dogged research, Dodgson defender and author Karoline Leach discovered a note thought to have been written by Dodgson's niece Violet, allegedly summarizing the missing diary page. According to the letter, Mrs. Liddell had accused Dodgson of using the children as a cover for wooing their governess—and suggested that perhaps he was interested in  the Liddells' eldest daughter, Ina. Ina was tall and well-developed, 14 to Alice's 11; girls were then legally marriageable at 12, and both daughters had already spent far too much time (by the standards of the day) in the company of this adult bachelor. Tongues were probably already wagging. Then again, the authorship of the note is far from certain. Dodgson did pay the family a visit in December 1863, but the friendship would never be rekindled.

Even "curiouser"—as Alice might say—Liddell inexplicably broke college rules to allow Dodgson to stay at Christ Church, where instructors needed to have taken holy orders, despite Dodgson's rejection of the priesthood after a battle with a mysterious psychological torment in the early 1860s (the exact nature of his pain remains a mystery, as well, thanks to the disappeared diaries).

A Figment of the Imagination

Adding to the confusion, although the name "Alice" was borrowed from Liddell, Dodgson stressed that his "Alice" was entirely imaginary. Nor did Sir John Tenniel draw inspiration for his famed illustrations from Dodgson's photographs of Alice. Dodgson's own drawings for the original manuscript (then entitled *Alice's Adventures Under Ground*) bear little resemblance to the real Alice.

While Dodgson's obsession with photographing young Alice certainly seems, at the very least, somewhat kinky to modern minds, it needs to be seen through the lens of the Victorian era, when upper-class children were widely romanticized (while their poorer counterparts were most cruelly used). Dodgson became intrigued by the new art of photography because he saw in it a means to re-create a more innocent time.

The Diaries Did Him In

Dodgson was—according to Leach—effectively thrown to the Freudian wolves by Roger Lancelyn Green, editor of Dodgson's expurgated diaries. (Leach contends that between Green and Dodgson's nieces, more than half of the entries were eliminated.) Leach, in a work prepared in the United Kingdom, accused Green of concealing evidence of Dodgson's sexual interest in adult women in favor of his own Carroll construct, a wistful man-child who was a paragon of Victorian sanctity. "I suspect he had decided, at least on a subconscious level," Leach wrote, "that a soft-focus, gentle, quasi-paedophile 'Carroll' was easier for him to accept than the real, spiky, mysterious and deep Charles Dodgson."

In any case, after the immediate and extraordinary success of *Alice in Wonderland* following its publication in 1865, Dodgson became a very busy man. Even as his wealth and fame grew, he continued to teach at Christ Church until he died. He—or rather, his alter ego Lewis Carroll—published *Through the Looking Glass and What Alice Found There* in 1872; *The Hunting of the Snark* in 1876; and a two-volume novel, *Sylvie and Bruno*, in 1889 and 1893, respectively. He published mathematical papers (as Dodgson) and journeyed throughout Europe and Russia in 1867. During the 1870s, he was an active campaigner against vivisection and became a member of the Society for Psychical Research at its 1882 inception. He died suddenly of severe pneumonia in his Guildford home in January 1898.

As for Alice Liddell, she has become immortal, as generation after generation rediscover the dreamland that Carroll created for her. Charles Dodgson passed away more than a century ago, but Lewis Carroll lives on.

Fast Facts

- *The first bachelor to become president was James Buchanan. He had been engaged 37 years earlier but backed out of the wedding. His fiancée, Ann Coleman, overdosed on medication soon after.*

- *The Kentucky Derby is the oldest continually held sports event in the United States. The second oldest is the Westminster Kennel Club Dog Show.*

- *The only marsupial native to North America is the Virginia opossum.*

- *Johan Palmstruch of the Stockholm Banco introduced paper money to Europe in 1661. A better innovator than bookkeeper, he was imprisoned for life after the bank collapsed.*

- *When in operation, the Concorde was the only commercial airplane capable of breaking the sound barrier. It had a top speed of 1,345 mph (just over Mach 2).*

- *Revolutionary Fanya Kaplan attempted to kill Russian leader Vladimir Lenin in August 1918. Lenin survived, but Kaplan was executed the following next month. A bronze monument to her was erected in Moscow in 2002.*

- *Although it has not been proven, there are reports of South American anaconda snakes measuring 120 feet in length. That's longer than two average ranch homes built end-to-end.*

- *The Library of Congress was started in 1815 when President James Madison bought almost 6,500 books from former President Thomas Jefferson's library.*

- *British Admiral Horatio Nelson did not escape injury in his illustrious career. He lost sight in his right eye in 1794, and his right arm was amputated in 1797. He was mortally wounded in the Battle of Trafalgar in 1805.*

Groundbreaking Scientific Theories

Many of these scientific breakthroughs may seem glaringly obvious to modern people, but they show the fascinating evolution of knowledge. Take a trip back to when Earth was believed to be flat, and try to imagine the contemporary reactions to these cutting-edge theories.

Mineral Cures

Philippus Theophrastus Aureolus Bombastus von Hohenheim: Try saying that ten times fast! Better yet, don't: Use the name his parents gave him upon his birth in 1493, Phillip von Hohenheim, or the name he assumed for himself, which most historians now use: Paracelsus. No matter what you call him, Paracelsus pioneered the world of therapeutic medicine by treating diseases with chemical and mineral remedies—something that was virtually unheard of at the time. Back then, most physicians created their remedies from organic compounds ranging from tree bark to animal organs, from plants or plant extracts to dung. Depending on the physician, you could find any number of cures in different dosages for the same illness!

With a father who was a physician and chemist, it's no wonder that Paracelsus began studying medicine and chemistry at age 16 at the University of Basel in Switzerland. He discovered that minerals and metals could be used to treat gout and lithiasis, common diseases contracted by miners. His discovery led him to formulate ideas on the use of certain minerals as medicine. One such mineral, zinc (whose name comes from the German *zink,* meaning "pointed," due to its sharp crystalline structure), is now a common mineral found in many cold, cough, and flu remedies.

Paracelsus' knowledge of remedies came primarily from his travels to far-off places such as Russia and the Middle East. Despite this, his arrogance, his eccentric ways, and his insistence on the correctness of his theories often incurred the anger of physicians throughout Europe. In 1526, while serving as the chair of medicine at the University of Basel, Paracelsus publicly burned the school's traditional medical textbooks. Yes, he did get fired.

Before his death in 1541, Paracelsus proposed that the cause of all contagious diseases fell into two categories—natural and spiritual. He believed that the body and spirit required a balance of certain minerals and could therefore be cured of many diseases through the proper administration of minerals and chemicals in correct dosages. Paracelsus' theories paved the way for new research into cures and remedies. He is generally considered the father of toxicology.

Blood Circulation

Let's say you're a young British doctor at the turn of the 17th century, and you want to take your career to the next level. Do you (a) marry the daughter of the most important physician in the land, or (b) pioneer research and make one of the most important discoveries in human physiology? Well, if you're William Harvey, you do both!

Born in 1578, Harvey was educated at the King's College in Canterbury, Cambridge University, and the University of Padua in Italy. He returned to England around 1602 and married Elizabeth Browne in 1604. Browne just happened to be the daughter of the court physician to Queen Elizabeth I, Lancelot Browne. Not one to rest on his social achievements, Harvey soon began research- ing the flow of blood through the human body. What he found, the circulatory system, would change the way people understood human physiology.

Prior to Harvey's discovery, most people believed that food was converted into blood by the liver and then consumed as fuel by the body, more specifically, the heart. Through dissections of animals and human cadavers, Harvey quickly realized that the heart and body did not "feed" on blood, nor was blood converted from food by the liver. He discovered a series of ventricles that essentially push blood through the body with contractions (heartbeats), pumping the blood in one direction through a closed circuit of veins and arteries.

Harvey also theorized, correctly, that veins and arteries were somehow connected, but he couldn't prove it. Modern doctors now know that they're connected by capillaries, but without a compound microscope, the capillaries were too tiny to see.

In Harvey's time, claiming anything other than the commonly accepted "science" of the day was considered career suicide for any doctor. This is probably why, despite his discoveries, he waited until 1628—when he had reached the age of 50—to publish his work.

Vaccination

Remember getting vaccination shots at the doctor's office with hypodermic needles larger than you ever wanted to see? Well, you can thank an English country doctor by the name of Edward Jenner for your pain. And yes, you should thank him! Without Jenner, the world might not have discovered vaccines—medicines that help your body produce its own antibodies against such diseases as polio, mumps, and smallpox. Never heard of these diseases? Good. That probably means you never caught them—more than likely because of vaccinations you received.

Jenner was born in Gloucestershire, England, in 1749, when smallpox was a common disease that often resulted in death. With a natural interest in medicine, Jenner served as a surgeon's apprentice for nine years and later studied at St. George's Hospital in London. After his training, Jenner returned to the Gloucestershire countryside to practice medicine. After noticing that milkmaids who had caught cowpox—a milder, less dangerous disease—did not catch smallpox, he theorized that cowpox would prevent people from contracting the deadly smallpox disease.

When a milkmaid with cowpox came to him seeking medical attention, Jenner took a big gamble with his career and the life of a young boy named James Phipps. With consent from the boy's father, Jenner took liquid from the milkmaid's sores and infected Phipps with cowpox. After the boy recovered, Jenner then exposed the boy to smallpox to prove his theory. Thankfully, Phipps failed to contract the disease. His body had developed antibodies against smallpox thanks to Jenner's cowpox vaccination.

Jenner continued experimenting successfully for several years and published his findings in 1798 under the title *An Inquiry into the Causes and Effects of the Variolae Vaccinae, a Disease Known by the Name of Cow Pox.* Despite resistance to his findings, Jenner's book was soon translated into several different languages and quickly distributed all over the world. So, why did Jenner call it a vaccine? That's simple—the Latin word for cow is *vacca,* and the suffix *-ine* or *-inus* translates to "of," creating *vaccine,* "of cows." Jenner died in 1823 at age 74—but not from smallpox.

The SS *Normandie* Goes Up in Flames

❖ ❖ ❖ ❖

Luxurious liners don't always reach majestic ends.

A huge, proud vessel that cut through the sea hardly making a wave, the SS *Normandie* was a French ocean liner that many considered the finest ever built. Dedicated in 1932, it was the star of a new class of liners designed for wealthy tourists rather than poor immigrants like most of its predecessors.

Dominating the Competition

No detail was too minor in the construction, and the vessel gave new meaning to the term *luxury liner.* Upon its maiden voyage in 1935, the *Normandie* set many new seafaring standards. At a weight of more than 79,000 gross tons, it was the heaviest ship on the seas. It was also the longest, exceeding 1,000 feet. Even more impressive was its speed: During its maiden voyage, the *Normandie* averaged nearly 30 knots in its westbound journey across the Atlantic. During its return voyage, the grand liner averaged more than 30 knots.

The combination of speed and luxury made the *Normandie* the pride of France. Before transatlantic flight, ocean liners were the only means of travel from Europe to the United States. England and Italy had grand ships, including the RMS *Majestic* and the SS *Rex,* but the *Normandie* outdid its peers in terms of both size and speed. Its Art Deco interior was a marvel of design and luxury. The first-class dining room, at more than 300 feet in length and featuring a 20-foot-high bronze

entryway, was like that of no other liner in existence. The vessel boasted the work of the era's finest designers and dazzled passengers with its lavish accommodations and facilities, including both indoor and outdoor pools, a theater, and a chapel.

War Changes Everything

Despite its accolades, the *Normandie* was not destined for lengthy service. Upon arriving in New York in late August 1939, officials decided to keep the *Normandie* in harbor due to the escalation of World War II. It had just completed its 139th Atlantic crossing. After France fell to Nazi Germany in June 1940, the U.S. Maritime Commission and then the navy took custody of the ship. Hitler tried to lay claim to the liner, but the United States refused to release it. After the Japanese attack at Pearl Harbor, the U.S. War Department began converting the *Normandie* for service as a troopship, rechristening it the USS *Lafayette* in honor of the French Marquis de Lafayette, a key American ally during the Revolutionary War.

Never Work Near an Open Flame

On February 9, 1942, the final stages of the conversion process were underway when a massive fire broke out, sending billowing clouds of smoke across New York City. Unfortunately, the ship's onboard fire-protection system had been dismantled during the conversion, so fire brigades were dispatched. As the firefighters began spraying copious amounts of water at the vessel in an attempt to extinguish the raging blaze, the mighty ship listed heavily and eventually capsized.

With Pearl Harbor a fresh memory, a skittish American public initially feared that the fire was a result of Nazi sabotage, but the real cause of the blaze was an errant spark from a welding torch. Regardless of the cause, the once-majestic luxury liner lay on its side in the harbor in the inferno's aftermath. The ship was eventually set to right, but it was a total loss. The once majestic *Normandie* was ultimately sold for scrap.

• *Nobel Prize winner Nelson Mandela voted for the first time in South Africa's 1994 election. He was elected president.*

• *The scientific study of slugs is called* limacology.

Strange Justice

He Ought to Get *Some* Credit for Trying

During the 1990s, a prisoner doing time in Virginia for breaking and entering and grand larceny came up with a novel way of getting someone else to pay for his troubles. Noting that his civil rights had been abused, he sued *himself* for violating his own religious beliefs by getting drunk. Suffering from the effects of drinking too much, he maintained, he failed to exercise good judgment and had committed the acts that had led to his arrest and incarceration. The prisoner believed he was owed five million dollars for all this: three million for his wife and children for pain and suffering, and two million to make up for the salary he'd fail to earn during his 23-year sentence. Since he was behind bars, however, he had no money to pay in case the judgment went against (or would that be *for?*) him. But he had a solution: As a prisoner, he was a "ward of the state," so that meant the government should be responsible for his debts. Alas, he neither won nor lost, as the judge threw the case out of court.

Fear of Flying

An airline was found liable when a flight was too bumpy. Flying into a thunderstorm in 1995, a pilot for a large commercial jet failed to turn on the "fasten seat belt" signs, and passengers were caught by surprise in what they claimed was extremely violent turbulence. Not wearing seat belts, of course, some of the passengers were thrown from their seats, and many thought the plane was going down and that they were all going to die. Particularly traumatized, the suit claimed, were the children aboard the plane. In part, the lawsuit argued that the flight crew and those on the ground could have used radar to detect and avoid the storm. At the very least, the seat belt sign could have served as a warning. A jury granted the 13 passengers who sued a total of two million dollars for their emotional distress.

His Reputation Was at "Steak"

Who doesn't like a nice steak now and then? One man went to his local steak house, ordered a thick and juicy slab, and asked for the senior-citizen discount. There was one problem—he was only 31 years old, so the discount didn't apply. He sued the restaurant chain for age discrimination. Not only did the judge throw the claim out like a spoiled sirloin—he fined the man more than $8,500 for abusing the legal system.

Emily Dickinson:
The Belle of Amherst

❖ ❖ ❖ ❖

What caused the one-time seminary student to choose a
life of isolation? Was it a failed love affair—or something
more sinister? Will the world ever really know?

Emily Dickinson's strange, brooding, reclusive lifestyle had tongues
wagging and rumors flying in her time, and her private life remains
an enigma today. Though she penned 1,789 poems, only 9 were
published during her lifetime; her literary fame as a founder of neo-
modern American poetry came posthumously. The answer for why
she chose to shut herself away from the world may lie in her poetry.

A Secret from the World

Dickinson died at her family home in Amherst, Massachusetts, on
May 15, 1886, at the tender age of 56, after spending her entire adult
life in almost total isolation. The cause of her death was Bright's disease, a form of kidney trouble untreatable in the 19th century. With
the exception of her family and an inner circle of close correspon-
dents and visitors, her passing went unheralded—indeed, almost
unnoticed.

Seventy years passed before her immense literary contributions
received the recognition they rightfully deserved. Her unconventional staggered meter, her lack of conventional punctuation, an
idiosyncratic style, and the immersion of her deeply personal life
into many of her poems were condemned by early literary critics—
some pronounced her work "grotesque." It was not until 1955 that
"The Belle of Amherst," as she was familiarly known, became recognized as an American original. Her personal life, however, continued
to be a mystery.

A Solitary Life

Dickinson was born in 1830 into a prominent and highly political
New England family; she was the second of three children. Her
father was a Massachusetts state senator who was later elected to the
U.S. House of Representatives. Her mother was chronically ill for

most of her life. Ironically, both Emily's older brother and younger sister exhibited some of the same tendencies that led Emily to be labeled a recluse. William Austin Dickinson married Emily's most intimate friend, Susan Gilbert, and moved next door to the family homestead, where Emily and her sister Lavinia lived. "Vinnie," like her older sister, also lived at home and remained a spinster. Their puritanical and religious upbringing created very strong family ties—almost an unwillingness to completely cut the umbilical cord. It was Vinnie who discovered and helped assemble Emily's poetry for publication around the turn of the century.

Emily's withdrawal from society was not innate; in her early years she was described as sociable, friendly, even gregarious. She attended seminary but could not bring herself to sign an oath dedicating her life to Jesus. She left the seminary after a year and never returned; whether it was embarrassment over the incident or simply that she was homesick is unknown. Following her voluntary withdrawal from the school, Emily began to display the self-denying tendencies that would lead to her lifelong austerity. With the exception of brief visits to relatives, she began the reclusive lifestyle that some labeled agoraphobia. Her detractors offered darker explanations, from failed love affairs and bisexual relationships to lesbianism and an illicit relationship with her brother's wife. Only circumstantial evidence exists to give any credence to Dickinson's supposed indiscretions.

Writing from the Inside

After her stint in the seminary, Emily began the poetic foray that would eventually lead to the establishment of what is now known as the modern American style of poetry. At the time, her balladlike lyrics and halting meter were highly unconventional, yet they would eventually flourish and influence decades of modern poets. Dickinson's lyrical poetry has also become the basis for songs by such musical stalwarts as Aaron Copland, Michael Tilson Thomas, and Nick Peros. The use of common meter makes her poetry adaptable to almost any type of music, from hymns to popular ballads.

Early in her poetry-writing career, Dickinson sought the advice and approbation of literary critic and *Atlantic Monthly* writer Thomas Wentworth Higginson. He recognized the potential talent in the budding poet but attempted to tutor her in employing the more orthodox style of the romantic poetry popular at the time. Fortunately for the world, Emily rebelled at the idea and abandoned her plans to publish her poetry. Yet, the initial efforts of Higginson and editor Mabel Loomis Todd first brought Dickinson's works to the attention of the American public by publishing three heavily edited editions of her poetry between 1890 and 1896. Her poetry attained some early popularity, but it did not become well known for another 60 years. In 1955, Thomas H. Johnson, America's preeminent Dickinson scholar, published a complete edition of her poetry in her original, unorthodox style.

Still Unknown Even Today

Though Dickinson's poetry grows more popular with time, the reasons behind her voluntary exile from society remain enigmatic. Her introspective personality manifested itself early in life, and as time passed Emily developed several eccentricities: She began dressing exclusively in white and never left her family's home, though she did entertain a few visitors.

Dickinson's sexual orientation has been questioned as well. There is evidence that she had an unrequited love affair with at least one man, known only as "Master," which is how Emily addressed her correspondence. Although scholars have speculated on his identity, only Emily knew the truth. It has never been established whether or not the letters she wrote were ever sent. Emily and her sister-in-law, Susan, did exchange intimate letters, which gave rise to the rumors that they were having a lesbian relationship. According to some experts, it was not unusual behavior for women in the puritanical environment of the late 19th century to exchange intimate correspondences. But there is simply no proof that Emily ever consummated a physical relationship with anyone—man or woman.

The Personal in the Poetical

Many scholars are convinced that the answers to the paradoxical and hermitic lifestyle of Dickinson lie in the immersion of her personal life into her poetry—poetry in which she bares her innermost thoughts, almost as if revealing the answers to the many questions scholars have sought to solve. Though no definitive answers to the mystery have emerged, it may keep historians guessing forever.

Fumbling Felons

Smile!

In October 2007, a man decided to steal a camera from a store in Connecticut. His technique might have been perfect except for the surveillance camera that caught him on tape. The criminal seems to have remembered to keep his face well-hidden from that camera. Clever! The surveillance camera, however, caught the would-be thief taking a picture of himself with another display model, which he put down and left behind in the store, just before walking out with a different $400 camera in hand. Brilliant!

Don't Call Us...

A man in St. Charles, Missouri, stole a computer and printer from a driver's license facility in October 2007. The printer could be used to produce fake driver's licenses or other identification, but only with the software found on the PC. That's thinking ahead! The computer, however, was inoperable without a special key to unlock it. Summoning all his cunning, the thief called tech support two days later asking to buy the software for the make and model of the printer he'd stolen from the driver's license facility. He ingeniously used his middle name, but he provided a phone number he'd previously given to the FBI in an unrelated identity theft case.

A Quick U-Turn

A man accused of drug possession successfully eluded police after being chased from Ontario, Oregon, into the neighboring state of Idaho. Shortly after crossing the state line, however, the criminal decided to turn around and go back to Oregon. He quickly made his way to the parking lot of a Wal-Mart, where he surrendered to the authorities. He reportedly told the arresting state trooper that he had done this because he didn't want to go to jail in Idaho.

Drunk Dialing

In April 2007, a man in Germany stole a cell phone and made a clean getaway. Police decided to call the stolen phone, figuring it was worth a shot to see if they could get any information. The thief answered. The officer on the other end told him, "You've won a crate of beer," but they needed the thief's location to drop it off. He happily gave his full address. Police believe the man was drunk.

Indestructible Fidel: Assassination Plots Against Castro

❖ ❖ ❖ ❖

American intelligence agencies were very active and successful during the Cold War. But how come no one could kill the leader of Cuba?

Perhaps no human being in history has survived more assassination attempts than Fidel Castro. A popular leader who overthrew the hated Cuban dictator Fulgencio Batista in 1959, Castro had first attempted to organize the people of Cuba directly into revolution, but he was thrown into prison in 1953. He had his first brush with assassination there: Batista ordered the guards to poison Castro, but none of them would do it. In 1955, after Batista made an election promise to free political prisoners, he ordered Castro's release. But the dictator was not about to let bygones be bygones. He sent an assassin named Eutimio Guerra to get close to Castro, but the revolutionary leader was suspicious of Guerra and gave him the slip. Castro seemed to lead a charmed life, and his revolutionary army moved from town to town fighting for Cuba until it was free of Batista.

After overthrowing the dictator and liberating Cuba, Castro was wildly popular with the majority of Cubans, although he was looked on with suspicion by almost everyone else. And because he received limited support from Cuba's traditional allies, including the United States, Castro had little or no choice but to ally Cuba with the Soviet Union. After all, he was just following the age-old maxim—"The enemy of my enemy is my friend." And what an enemy he made!

Before the Bay of Pigs

Most people think that the halfhearted backing of the Bay of Pigs invasion was the starting gun for hostility between Castro and John F. Kennedy, but it was Dwight Eisenhower who set the "Kill Fidel Contest" in motion in 1960 with what ultimately became Operation

Mongoose—400 CIA agents working full-time to remove the Cuban dictator. At first, they decided to train paramilitary guerrillas to eliminate Castro in a traditional commando operation, but his immense popularity among the Cuban people made that impossible. The CIA did all the preliminary work on the Bay of Pigs. Then Eisenhower left office, and Kennedy came upon the scene.

The Bay of Pigs invasion turned out to be a fiasco, and a year and a half later the Cuban Missile Crisis almost triggered a full-scale nuclear war. America's only answer seemed to be to get rid of Fidel and try to turn Cuba back into a pliant banana republic (or in this case, sugarcane republic). But who would do it—and how?

Who's Up to the Job?

The problem was that everyone wanted to get in on the act. The U.S. government hated having a Soviet base 90 miles from Florida. Batista Cubans, who'd lost their big-moneyed businesses, wanted their privileged lives back. Anticommunists such as FBI boss J. Edgar Hoover viewed a plot to assassinate Castro as a struggle against elemental evil. American businesses that relied on sugar felt the loss of their cheap supply. The Mafia, which had owned lucrative casinos and brothels in Havana, wanted revenge. As it turned out, the Mafia had the best shot—and they had help.

The CIA, not being able to handle the job themselves, hired Mafia members to terminate Castro with extreme prejudice. In exchange, the CIA pressured the FBI to offer the Mafia a certain amount of immunity in the United States. But the Mafia got used to the new leniency, which would end if Castro were killed, so they strung the Agency along with false promises to kill Castro if the CIA would continue to protect them from the FBI. Meanwhile, President Kennedy grew impatient. Changing the name of Operation Mongoose to Operation Freedom, he sent the American intelligence community in a full-time rush to whack Fidel. But after the Bay of Pigs, intelligence planners believed that conventional measures wouldn't work, so the attempts became more strange:

- During a United Nations meeting at which Castro was present, an agent working for the CIA managed to slip a poisoned cigar into Fidel's cigar case, but someone figured it out before Castro could light up.

- Another idea was to send Castro on an acid trip by dosing his cigars with LSD. He would appear psychotic, and his sanity would be questioned. When this story finally came out, it merely gave a lot of old hippies a few laughs.

- Castro was an avid scuba diver, so the CIA sprayed the inside of a wet suit with tuberculosis germs and a fungal skin disease called Madura foot. Then they gave it to a lawyer heading to Havana to negotiate the release of Bay of Pigs prisoners. He was supposed to give the suit to Castro, but at the last minute the lawyer decided that the plot was too obvious and was an embarrassment to the United States, so he didn't take the suit with him.

- Perhaps the most famous dumb idea of all was to find out where Fidel's favorite diving spot was and prepare an exploding conch shell to kill him, but for many obvious reasons this plan was dropped as being unfeasible.

- Traditional assassination methods were also tried. Cuban exiles were sent to Havana with high-powered rifles and telescopic sights to take care of the problem with good old-fashioned lead, but none of them could get close enough to shoot Castro.

- One of Castro's guards was given a poison pen that worked like a hypodermic needle, but he was discovered before he could get close enough to inject the leader.

Not all the plots involved killing the Cuban leader. In another instance, a Castro aide was bribed to put special powder inside the dictator's boots—it contained a poison that would make his beard fall out. This never happened.

Starting in the 1970s, the CIA seemed to lose interest in these plans, and thereafter most attempts to kill the leader were carried out by Cuban exiles (with CIA funding, of course), who had made hating Castro almost a religion. Fabian Escalante, Castro's head of security, claimed that there have been 638 plots to kill Castro.

Before Fidel led a revolution, he came to the United States to try out for major league baseball. By all accounts, he was a terrific pitcher. If he had made the majors, recent history might have been very different. For one thing, a lot of amateur assassins would have had to find something better to do with their time.

🎥 Behind the Films of Our Times

Raging Bull

The compelling story of self-destructive boxer Jake La Motta earned Robert De Niro his second Academy Award (and his first for Best Actor). La Motta himself proclaimed De Niro a capable middleweight contender after training him for the movie. Costar Cathy Moriarty had never done a film before starring as victimized wife Vicki La Motta, and it earned her a Best Supporting Actress Oscar nomination. Joe Pesci played Jake's brother Joey. The *real* Joey La Motta sued director Martin Scorsese and the studio—he wasn't too pleased with Pesci's foul-mouthed portrayal.

Apollo 13

Director Ron Howard's 1995 film told the amazing story of the unlucky and unsuccessful 1970 title spaceflight to the moon. Actors Tom Hanks, Bill Paxton, and Kevin Bacon spent weeks crammed into the 48-square-foot mock-up of the Apollo spacecraft—an area smaller than the average bathroom. Just as it had in real life, the harrowing on-screen trip came to a happy ending as the haggard astronauts exited a rescue helicopter onto the recovery ship. Hanks, playing Flight Commander James Lovell, was greeted with a handshake by the ship's captain—portrayed by the *real* James Lovell.

Casablanca

The Oscar-winning screenplay for this Humphrey Bogart–Ingrid Bergman wartime tearjerker wasn't finished when the film started shooting. One point of contention was the ending. Bogart thought it important for his character, Rick Blaine, to get the girl, Bergman's Ilsa Lund, in the end. The producers apparently decided his concerns didn't amount to a hill of beans, and Ilsa left with her freedom-fighter husband, Victor Laszlo, played by Paul Henreid.

Annie Hall

Woody Allen's hilarious 1977 film about dating and love in New York City drew heavily from his own broken relationship with costar Diane Keaton, with whom he'd split up before filming started. When Allen was awarded the Best Director Oscar for *Annie Hall,* he was thousands of miles from the hoopla in Hollywood; the elusive winner was doing what he always did on Monday nights—playing clarinet with his New Orleans Jazz Band at Michael's Pub in New York City.

The Fall of the Crooked E:
Who Killed Enron?

*For a company that seemed to have everything
going its way, the end sure came quickly.*

In the 1990s, the U.S. Congress passed legislation deregulating the sale of electricity, as it had done for natural gas some years earlier. The result made it possible for energy trading companies, including Enron, to thrive. In effect, the law allowed a highly profitable market to develop between energy producers and those local governments that buy electricity—a system kept in place because of aggressive lobbying by Enron and other such firms. By the turn of the 21st century, Enron stock was trading for $80 to $90 a share.

Trouble in the Waters

All was not smooth sailing, however, for the energy giant. Its new broadband communications trading division was running into difficulties, its power project in India was behind schedule and over budget, and its role in the California power crisis of 2000–2001 was being scrutinized. Then, on August 14, 2001, CEO Jeffrey Skilling announced he was resigning after only six months in his position. He also sold off 450,000 shares of Enron stock for $33 million.

Ken Lay, the chairman at Enron, affirmed that there was "absolutely no accounting issue, no trading issue, no reserve issue, no previously unknown problem" that prompted Skilling's departure. He further asserted that there would be "no change or outlook in the performance of the company going forward." Though he did admit that falling stock prices were a factor behind Skilling's departure, Lay decided to assume the CEO position.

Don't Worry, Everything's Under Control

Enron's financial statements were so confusing because of the company's tax strategies and position-hedging, as well as its use of "related-party transactions," that Enron's leadership assumed no one would be able to analyze its finances. A particularly troubling aspect was that several of the "related-party" entities were, or had been, controlled by Enron CFO Andrew Fastow (who may or may not have realized that he was being groomed as a scapegoat).

Sound confusing? Good, then the plan worked. And if all this could confuse government regulatory agencies, think of how investors must have felt. Stock prices slowly started sliding from their highs at the beginning of 2001, but as the year went on, the tumble picked up speed. On October 22, for instance, the share price of Enron dropped $5.40 in one day to $20.65. After Enron officials started talking about such things as "share settled costless collar arrangements" and "derivative instruments which eliminated the contingent nature of restricted forward contracts," the Securities and Exchange Commission (SEC) had a quote of its own: "There is the appearance that you are hiding something."

Things Fall Apart

The landslide had begun. On October 24, Lay removed Fastow as CFO. Stock was trading at $16.41. On October 27, Enron began buying back all of its shares (valued around $3.3 billion). It financed this purchase by emptying its lines of credit at several banks.

On October 30, in response to concerns that Enron might try a further $1–2 billion refinancing due to having insufficient cash on hand, Enron's credit rating was dropped to near junk-bond status. Enron did secure an additional billion dollars, but it had to sell its valuable natural gas pipeline to do so.

Enron desperately needed either new investment or an outright buyout. On the night of November 7, Houston-based energy trader Dynegy voted to acquire Enron at a fire-sale price of $8 billion in stock. It wasn't enough.

The sale lagged, and Standard & Poor's index determined that if it didn't go through, Enron's bonds would be rated as junk. The word was out that Lay and other officials had sold off hundreds of millions of dollars of their own stock before the crisis and that Lay stood to receive $60 million dollars if the Dynegy sale went through. But the last, worst straw was that Enron employees saw their retirement accounts—largely based on Enron stock—wiped out.

By November 7, after the company announced that all the money it had borrowed (about $5 billion) had been exhausted in 50 days, Enron stock was down to $7.00 a share. The SEC filed civil fraud complaints against Arthur Andersen, Enron's auditor. And on November 28, the sky fell in: Dynegy backed out of the deal to acquire Enron, and Enron's stock hit junk-bond status. On December 2, 2001, Enron sought Chapter 11 protection as it filed for the biggest bankruptcy in U.S. history. Around 4,000 employees lost their jobs.

So Who Killed Enron?

There was blame aplenty.

- Ken Lay and Jeffrey Skilling were indicted for securities and wire fraud. Lay was convicted on 6 of 6 counts, and Skilling on 19 of 28. Skilling was sentenced to 24 years and 4 months in prison. Lay avoided prison time by dying of a heart attack before he was sentenced.

- Arthur Andersen accountants signed off on this fraud. Why? They were getting a million dollars a week for their accounting services. The firm was convicted of obstruction of justice for shredding documents related to the Enron audit and surrendered its licenses and right to practice. From a high of more than 100,000 employees, Arthur Andersen is now down to around 200. Most of them are handling lawsuits.

- Investors bought stock in a company they didn't understand for the greedy promise of quick money.

- Stock ratings companies said it was a great investment, even though they had no idea what shape Enron was in.

- Investment bankers who knew that Enron was shaky bought in for a shot at quick and easy profits. They, too, are being sued by investors.

- And we can't forget the Enron employees, some of whom knew that something was fishy yet stayed silent because they were getting paid. There were a few whistle-blowers, but the ones who knew and said nothing earned their places at the unemployment office.

Syllable Secrets: Word Histories

Ketchup: This condiment would have been unrecognizable in its earlier incarnations, especially as a fish-based sauce. But as a matter of fact, that's how it got its name. Back in 1711, the Malay name for this sauce was *kichap*, from the Chinese Amoy dialect's *koechiap*, or "brine of fish." Early English versions of the condiment included mushrooms, walnuts, cucumbers, and oysters. The modern form of the condiment began when New Englanders added tomatoes. *Catsup* (earlier *catchup*) is a failed attempt at Anglicization but is still in use in some portions of the United States.

Neocon: A 1987 abbreviation for *neo-conservative*, literally "new" conservative: An intellectual and political movement which favored political, economic, and social conservatism that arose in opposition to the perceived liberalism of the 1960s. As defined by Irving Kristol in *The Weekly Standard*, it was "hopeful...forward-looking, not nostalgic; and its general tone is cheerful.... Its 20th-century heroes tend to be TR [Theodore Roosevelt], FDR [Franklin Delano Roosevelt], and Ronald Reagan."

Hysteria: First used in 1801, this word refers to an uncontrollable sobbing or laughing, or an ongoing mental or emotional imbalance. The word comes from the Greek idea that hysteria was a condition unique to women and caused by disturbances of the uterus. The Latin term *hystericus* comes from the Greek *hysterikos*, which comes from *hystera* (womb).

Cheeseburger: Although you might think it has been around forever, the cheeseburger first became part of American folklore in 1935, when Louis Ballast of the Humpty Dumpty Barrel Drive-In in St. Louis, Missouri, applied for a patent on the concept (although other places in California and Kentucky also claimed credit for the first cheeseburger, Ballast was the only one to finish the paperwork). Alas for Ballast, the word *cheeseburger* remains in the public domain. No one can own it, and everyone can use it, much like Donald Trump's starved-for-attention attempt to trademark the phrase, "You're fired."

Idol: Hello, *American Idol*? The year 1591 called, and it wants its meaning back. *Idol* originally meant "a person so adored," from the "image of a deity as an object of [pagan] worship," circa 1250, and then Church Latin for "false god."

Make Way for Technocracy!

❖ ❖ ❖ ❖

Humankind is overstaying its welcome on the planet. But don't worry—all our problems can be solved by the right technology.

A Proposed Utopia: Techtopia

The sociopolitical movement called *technocracy* claims to have the medicine for our societal ills. Global warming, failed monetary policy—it can all be remedied. The movement began in the 1930s with the formation of the Technical Alliance, founded by technocracy pioneer Howard Scott. The basic idea is that society should not be run by politicians but according to scientific rigor and the strategic application of technology. For example, if we paid heed to the studies of ecologists and physicists, we would know exactly how much energy it takes to support the current human population, and waste would be eliminated. Technocrats propose that after the inevitable collapse of the current world order, a new world order called a *Technate* will arise.

So how will the Technate be different from the world we know now? For one thing, there will be no money. Coupons called *energy certificates* will be handed out instead. The total number of certificates will depend upon total productive capacity of the Technate, and all citizens will receive the same number. Cities will be destroyed and replaced by *urbanates,* which will be just like modern cities, only meticulously planned in an ecologically sound manner. Under this system, all citizens will enjoy the highest standard of living.

Meanwhile, in the Here and Now

Until recently, technocracy has remained a predominantly American phenomenon. Its headquarters, called Technocracy, Inc., is in Washington state. In 2006, countries on the other side of the Atlantic caught on and established the Network of European Technocrats. However, *technocracy* is often used as a generalized term to refer to those who believe specialists (particularly in the fields of technology and engineering) should run society. In this sense of the word, technocracy is a worldwide but unorganized movement.

Those Wacky TV Horror Hosts

*In the early days of television, the colorful and offbeat
hosts of horror movie shows became local celebrities.*

During the Golden Age of Television following World War II, many
stations produced their own local content. Because producing TV
shows on film was expensive, most shows were broadcast live, with
an announcer to introduce the show and read advertisements.

After *King Kong* was broadcast on TV in 1956, horror movies
exploded in popularity, and the TV "horror host" became an icon
closely associated with this era. Although many horror hosts were
local figures—sometimes weather reporters or news anchors pulling
double duty—some became known nationally.

Vampira

One of the most-loved horror hosts was Vampira. This character
was born when Maila Nurmi was discovered by a producer at the
1953 Bal Caribe Masquerade in Los Angeles. Nurmi attended the
ball wearing a slinky black dress inspired by a character in Charles
Addams's *New Yorker* cartoons. *The Vampira Show* premiered in
1953, and at the height of her fame, Vampira was known worldwide.

Zacherley, the Cool Ghoul

Another well-known horror host was John Zacherle. After playing
several characters in a TV Western, Zacherle was offered a chance to
host a horror show in Philadelphia called *Shock Theater.* This show
was gorier than its contemporaries and used elaborate props, such as
severed heads dripping blood made from chocolate syrup. He later
moved to New York City, where a *y* was added to his name.

Morgus the Magnificent

One classic horror host still on the air in the 21st century is Morgus
the Magnificent, portrayed by actor Sid Noel. Morgus debuted in
1959 on *House of Shock* in the New Orleans local television scene.
He started making new episodes after a nearly 20-year hiatus: In
October 2006, *Morgus Presents* debuted in the Crescent City.

Fast Facts

- *The chapel where Joan of Arc worshipped was the Chapelle de St. Martin de Sayssuel in Chasse, France. The chapel was moved to Marquette University in 1964. Within the chapel is the Joan of Arc Stone, on which Joan is said to have prayed, kissing the stone when she was finished. To this day, that stone feels colder to the touch than the surrounding stones.*

- *In 1985, Wilbur Snapp, the organist for minor league baseball's Clearwater Phillies in Florida, played "Three Blind Mice" to protest a call by umpire Keith O'Connor. The ump tossed him from the game.*

- *A passion for collecting fish bones inspired grocer and beekeeper Daniel David Palmer to begin studying human vertebrae and become the world's first chiropractor.*

- *Blah blah blah: The English language has more words than any other language.*

- *Steven Sasson, an engineer at Eastman Kodak, produced the first prototype digital camera. Weighing eight pounds, it took 23 seconds to capture its first image.*

- *The New York Police Department reported subway crime jumped 18 percent in the first quarter of 2005. More than a third of the felonies involved iPods being stolen.*

- *Grover Cleveland, Woodrow Wilson, Calvin Coolidge, and Dwight Eisenhower all used their middle names as their primary names. (Their first names were Stephen, Thomas, John, and David, respectively; the order of Eisenhower's birth names was later switched.)*

- *Investor, entrepreneur, and philanthropist Warren Buffett began his illustrious career by collecting and selling lost golf balls. He also worked as a paperboy for the* Washington Post.

Reno: Divorcetown, USA

Do you mark the days since your wedding with an X on a calendar, hoping for parole? If so, you might consider a visit to Reno, Nevada.

Reno has been known as the place to get a "quickie divorce" for more than a century. In the 1800s, many people sought riches in the mining, agricultural, and fur-trapping industries that spread across Nevada and California. What better place to put a town than in the path of those fortune seekers? By 1868, Reno had become an important freight and passenger center. Soon, there were plenty of restaurants, hotels, and lively entertainment venues. Good times for all? Well, not quite.

Making the Best of an Iffy Economy

Mining and agriculture were feast-or-famine industries. One minute, everyone was making stacks of money; the next, everyone was broke. To offset those low points, Reno decided to host legal brothels. The city also became the place to go for illegal gambling and quick and easy divorces. Reno law called for people seeking a divorce to reside in the town for six months and, at one point, for a full year. This was still much less time than other localities required.

"Divorce ranches" appeared overnight. These extended-stay motels gave couples a temporary place to live in order to fulfill the residency requirements. People flocked to Reno for release from their marital bondage. Enter the nickname "Sin City."

Time Is Money

When the Great Depression hit, times got hard. Remembering the cash generated from couples seeking divorces—attorney fees, hotel stays, gambling houses, restaurants, and shopping—Reno officials decided to reduce residency requirements to a mere six weeks. As a result, more than 30,000 divorces were granted in the county courthouse between 1929 and 1939. By 1940, 4.9 percent of all U.S. divorces were filed in Nevada.

To this day, Reno maintains a six-week residency requirement for divorces.

Ralph Ginzburg:
Challenging the Times

It's never easy to buck social mores. This publisher found out the hard way that some lines are better left uncrossed.

The year was 1962. John F. Kennedy, the youngest president ever elected, was in the White House. Korea was quiet. Vietnam was an unknown country half a world away. Change was in the wind.

Every generation thinks that it's the first to discover taboo—and therefore tempting—delights. They forget that iconoclasts since the dawn of civilization have been questioning values and standards accepted by the social mainstream.

The radicals of the 1960s were no exception. And though they may not have been preaching anything new, a new generation was listening. Building on the ideas spread in the 1950s by the Beat Generation, '60s radicals confronted social issues that had long been ignored. And they dared to talk about sex.

Uncovering Taboos

One of the high priests of the era's new religion was Ralph Ginzburg, author, editor, photojournalist, and publisher. He was a controversial figure whose publications about art and erotica were ruled to violate federal obscenity laws. Who was this daring man who wanted to explore topics state and federal officials considered unacceptable?

On the surface, Ginzburg was no different than many of his generation. Born on October 28, 1929, he studied journalism at the City College of New York and served as editor in chief of its downtown campus newspaper. Following his 1949 graduation, he worked at the *New York Daily Compass,* but he was drafted into the army in 1951. Ginzburg was fortunate: Instead of slogging through rice paddies during the Korean War, he was assigned to Fort Myer, Virginia, where he served as editor of the post newspaper.

Throwing Down the Gauntlet

After he was discharged from the service, Ginzburg returned to the world he knew so well. An independent thinker who spurned religious ties, he was determined to leave his mark on America's conscience. In 1958, the same year he married poet Shoshana Brown, Ginzburg published *An Unhurried View of Erotica.* In that book, Ginzburg claimed that most English literature from the year 1070 through the 1950s contained bawdy or vulgar undertones. This scholarly publication was Ginzburg's first venture into exploring an "obscene" topic.

Government standards for evaluating pornography were changing at the time, and chances are good Ginzburg's work might have escaped notice—except for one mistake he made. In 1962, he sent out a mass mailing as part of an advertising campaign for *Eros,* a new magazine he had developed. Some of these flyers, however, were addressed to people who were not all that open-minded about sex. "*Eros* is a child of its times," one circular read. "It is the magazine of sexual candor." Unfortunately for Ginzburg, not everyone was clamoring for candor.

Going Too Far

A quarterly magazine, *Eros* contained articles and pictures about love and sex. But it also served as a means for Ginzburg to challenge establishment views on obscenity. While the second issue pictured a young couple kissing passionately on the cover, inside, Ginzburg included an essay on John F. Kennedy's sex appeal. By the time the fourth—and final—issue was published, Ginzburg had become a target of the U.S. Attorney General's office, headed by Robert Kennedy—JFK's younger brother.

Whether it was public pressure over the advertising campaign or retaliation for his inclusion of the president, Ginzburg was indicted in Philadelphia in 1963 under federal obscenity laws. But although Ginzburg was taken out of the picture, that couldn't stop what had been set in motion. At roughly the same time, American "flower children" began glorifying the concept of "free love," and the country's value system was never the same again.

Although his conviction generated public sympathy and vocal support from some quarters, Ginzburg's judicial appeals fell on deaf ears. After serving eight months of a five-year term in Lewisburg Penitentiary, he returned to writing. Throughout his career, he published dozens of books and magazines, including the sexually explicit *Liaison* and erotic *Avant Garde,* before he died on July 6, 2006.

HOW IT ALL BEGAN

"Bringing Home the Bacon"

This expression is still used to denote the person in a marriage or other domestic partnership who earns the larger monetary share of household income, but it once meant exactly what it says. In the 12th century, at the church of Dunmow in Essex County, England, a certain amount of cured and salted bacon was awarded to the couple that could prove (how they proved it is not quite sure) that they had lived in greater bliss than any of their competitors. The earliest record of this contest was 1445, but evidence exists that the custom had already been in effect for at least two centuries. In the 16th century, proof of devotion was determined through questions asked by a jury of unmarried men and women. The curious pork prize continued, albeit in irregular intervals, until the late 19th century.

Groundhog Day

The practice of watching a creature's reaction to its shadow to determine whether there will be six more weeks of winter began with German farmers in the 16th century, although they didn't use a groundhog, but a badger. When German immigrants settled in the area of Punxsutawney, Pennsylvania, 300 years later, they couldn't find any badgers, but there were plenty of local groundhogs to act as stand-ins. German folklore had it that if the day was sunny and the creature was frightened enough by its shadow to dart back into the ground, there would be six more weeks of cold weather. That meant that the farmers shouldn't plant their crops yet. In more recent times, scientific studies have proven that the groundhog's accuracy in prediction over a 60-year period is only 28 percent. In other words, for every year the groundhog is correct, there are almost three years in which it is incorrect. And in truth, the only things determining a groundhog's behavior when it emerges from hibernation is how hungry and how sexually aroused it is. If the groundhog is in the mood to mate—and starving, as well—chances are it'll stick around to see if it can get either or both of those cravings satisfied. The weather, at that moment or for the next six weeks, is the least of the groundhog's worries.

The Golden Age of Piracy: 1500–1835

*The golden age of piracy spawned some of the most feared and
bloodthirsty individuals to ever sail the seven seas. Contrary
to popular belief, pirates were not only men. Women—even
pregnant women!—also competed for the illicit booty
available to any buccaneer with the daring to take it.*

Although piracy goes back to ancient times, historians consider
1500–1835 to be its golden age. These three-plus centuries of infamy
spawned some of the world's most feared cutthroats—nemeses of all
nations whose ships sailed the seven seas while engaged in exploration and commerce. These notorious buccaneers have become
legendary in the annals of high seas adventure, daring, and cruelty.

Blackbeard

Take, for example, Edward Teach, whose glisten-
ing black beard established the pseudonym
by which he became more popularly
known. Probably the best-known pirate
in history, Teach, aka Blackbeard, was
the scourge of the Caribbean and the
western Atlantic. His end came at the
hands of English Lieutenant Robert Maynard in a cove off the coast of North Carolina. Blackbeard's treasure is still rumored to
be buried somewhere on Ocracoke Island.

Captain Kidd

William Kidd was a privateer hired to rid the seas of marauders;
instead, he became a pirate himself, stealing the plunder from the
pirates he was sent to vanquish and sailing to New York with his ill-
gotten gain. His treachery did not escape the notice of authorities,
especially the powerful British East India Company, to whom the
booty belonged. Kidd was captured and sent to England in chains
where he was hanged—three times. The rope broke twice during
Kidd's execution, but the third time was the charm.

Henry Morgan

Dubbed "The King of Pirates," Henry Morgan was as much a scourge on land as he was on the high seas. Greatly feared by the Spanish, Morgan once attacked the Cuban stronghold Puerto Principe, as well as Panama's treasure city, Porto Bello. The Spanish dubbed him "Morgan the Terrible." He was probably the most ruthless of all the buccaneers. Morgan was eventually knighted and hired by the English to rid the world of piracy.

And the Rest

There were many pirates who diligently plied their trade in terror and were considered scourges in their own right, though not of the legendary status of a Henry Morgan. Some of the lesser-known pirates of the golden age were Stede Bonnet, Charles Vane, Edward England, Christopher Condent, Ben Hornigold, the dapper Black Bart, Henry Jennings, Pierre LeGrand, and Calico Jack Rackham. Calico Jack, however, was overshadowed by the exploits of his wife, the most famous of all female pirates (and there were several), Ann Bonney. Disguised as a man, Bonney fought alongside her husband and his crew, even when she was pregnant with Rackham's child. When finally captured, Bonney used her condition to plead for mercy and received a temporary stay of execution. Her fate from that point is unknown. Some believe she was ransomed by her father and returned to her native Ireland.

Life on the High Seas

Why anyone would become a pirate in the first place boggles the mind. The ships were filthy and diseased; life was harsh. Cramped quarters, rats, foul water, scurvy, weevil-infested food, dangerous weather, and backbreaking work were as much a part of buccaneer life as plundering and killing. Most pirate crews consisted of men between the ages of 17 and 27; anyone older or younger was not expected to survive. During the golden age of piracy, there were said to be more than a million noncombat deaths among the buccaneers.

Piracy abounds even today. In the Caribbean and Atlantic, many private boats are commandeered at gunpoint every year to be used in drug-smuggling activities—the fates of their owners swallowed up in the vastness of the high seas.

PALINDROMES

When you've got a word, phrase, or sentence that reads the same backward and forward, you've got a palindrome!

"Do nine men interpret nine men?" I nod.

murder for a jar of red rum

UFO tofu

goldenrod-adorned log

A man, a plan, a canoe, pasta, heros, rajahs, a coloratura, maps, snipe, percale, macaroni, a gag, a banana bag, a tan, a tag, a banana bag again (or a camel), a crepe, pins, Spam, a rut, a Rolo, cash, a jar, sore hats, a peon, a canal—Panama!

'Tis in a DeSoto sedan I sit.

A daffodil slid off Ada.

Lew, Otto has a hot towel!

Et tu, Butte?

Doc, note I dissent: a fast never prevents a fatness. I diet on cod.

Sit on a potato pan, Otis.

star comedy by Democrats

a nut for a jar of tuna

kayak salad—Alaska yak

Dennis and Edna sinned.

Rats live on no evil star.

Zeus was deified, saw Suez.

Ten animals did slam in a net.

Mr. Owl ate my metal worm.

Pull up if I pull up.

Cigar? Toss it in a can. It is so tragic.

Dalí's Muse

What makes an artist create? Different artists have different responses, but in Salvador Dalí's case, the answer is very simple.

A surrealist with a surreally long name, Salvador Domingo Felipe Jacinto Dalí y Domènech was born in 1904 in Figueres, Spain. He claimed that his given name, Salvador, indicated that he was "destined to rescue and save painting from the mediocre catastrophes of modern art." A versatile visionary, he also collaborated with other famous artists, including Man Ray, Alfred Hitchcock, Coco Chanel, Roy Disney, and Christian Dior.

Young Dalí Shows His Colors

Heavily influenced by art at an early age, Dalí attended the San Fernando Academy of Fine Arts, a private painting school in Madrid. He began to follow closely former Dadaist André Breton, who headed up the surrealist movement. When he was 22, Dalí was expelled from the San Fernando Academy for proclaiming that his teachers were idiots and that he was more qualified than those who examined him.

Shortly after his expulsion, Dalí traveled to Paris and met Pablo Picasso, whom he revered. Picasso had already heard good things about Dalí from his friend, Joan Miró, another artist who heavily influenced Dalí's early works. It was said that Dalí showed his respect by telling Picasso, "I have come to see you before visiting the Louvre." Picasso's response: "You have done right, indeed."

After several successful one-man shows, Dalí joined the surrealist movement, quickly establishing himself as its principal figure. During his time in Paris, he collaborated with Spanish-born filmmaker Luis Buñuel on the surrealist movie *Un chien andalou* (*An Andalusian Dog*), further developing his role in the movement.

Enter the Muse

In 1929, Dalí met and became infatuated with a Russian immigrant ten years his senior, Helena Dmitrievna Diakonova, also known as Gala. At that time, she was married to surrealist poet Paul Éluard. It is reported that Dalí repeatedly tried to capture Gala's attention in a number of offbeat ways: He smeared himself with goat dung, waxed the hair from his armpits and colored them blue, wore flowers on his head. How could he go wrong? She responded by becoming his lover, wife, business manager, and muse for the rest of his life. In the early '30s, Dalí started to sign his paintings with his and her names, saying, "It is mostly with your blood, Gala, that I paint my pictures."

A Surrealist Clash

In 1931, Dalí painted one of his most famous works, *The Persistence of Memory,* whose soft or melting watches debunk the assumption that time is rigid or unchangeable. *The Persistence of Memory* is still noted as one of the world's best-known surrealist works. As World War II approached, however, politics brought Dalí into conflict with some of the other predominately Marxist surrealists. In 1934, he was forced out of the surrealist group during a "trial."

This didn't deter Dalí or Gala, who continued to create a buzz wherever they went. Dalí became an international sensation, and his antics were the stuff of legend. At the 1934 New York exhibition of his works and the social "Dalí Ball," the artist arrived wearing a brassiere enclosed in a glass case. During the London International Surrealist Exhibition, he delivered his lecture wearing a deep-sea diving suit.

Political Controversy

The 1936 outbreak of the Spanish Civil War caused upheaval throughout Spanish society, but it deeply affected the predominantly left-wing art scene. Although Dalí's lifelong friend surrealist poet Federico García Lorca was murdered by right-wing forces shortly after the civil war began, Dalí later broke with the majority of the nation's artists to ally himself with General Francisco Franco. He was among the few members of Spain's cultural elite who chose to stay in the new fascist state after the Nationalist victory in 1939; others, including Pablo Picasso, chose exile over the repression of Franco's regime. Despite criticism of his political statements—which applauded Franco for establishing "clarity, truth and order" in Spain—Dalí continued to paint and followed his well-established habit of flamboyant public appearances.

Classical Dalí

After World War II broke out, Dalí and Gala moved to the United States, where they lived for eight years. During these years, Dalí began inching away from surrealism into what is known as his classical period.

Behind his famous waxed moustache, Dalí was insecure and unhappy. Gala protected him. With her tough demeanor, she was the intermediary between Dalí and the rest of the world. Dalí thanked her by making her the model for his most sensual and beautiful paintings. Critics note that Dalí's depictions of Gala are perhaps some of the most affectionate and best-loved portrayals of a middle-aged woman in Western art.

In 1948, Dalí and Gala moved back to Europe, where he continued his work, this time concentrating on science and religion. Additionally, he and Gala embarked on their largest single project, the Dalí Theatre and Museum in his hometown in Spain. The museum was built on the ruins of the Figueres theater, destroyed in the last years of the Spanish Civil War. Dalí helped envision not only the exhibits of his work, but also the reconstruction of the building itself, resulting in a surreal, eye-catching structure topped with a glittering geodesic dome.

The Persistence of Dalí

In 1982, Gala passed away, and in 1983, Dalí finished his last painting, *The Swallow's Tail*. After Gala's death, Dalí lost much of his vitality, and he died of heart failure in 1989. His body was interred in the Dalí Theatre and Museum.

Dalí's legacy, like his life, has been one of controversy. Criticized in later years for his conservative politics, over-the-top shenanigans, and willingness to endorse almost any product, Dalí remains a recognizable force in the art world. With Gala as his muse, Dalí created a body of work that is both fanciful and philosophical. And despite the cries of mediocrity and commercialization, his masterpieces speak for themselves.

• *Rembrandt painted more than 60 self-portraits, a greater number than any other prominent painter.*

The Times They Are A-Changin'

1921

January 2: Radio station KDKA in Pittsburgh, Pennsylvania, becomes the first radio station to broadcast live religious services when it airs Sunday services from Calvary Episcopal Church.

February 12: Future prime minister Winston Churchill becomes England's minister of colonization.

March 6: The police department of Sunbury, Pennsylvania, issues an order that requires women to wear their skirts at least four inches below the knee.

May 3: West Virginia becomes the first state in the nation to impose a state sales tax.

May 8: The government of Sweden abolishes capital punishment.

May 19: Congress passes the Emergency Quota Act, setting quotas for immigrants entering the United States.

June 30: President Warren G. Harding nominates former President William Howard Taft to be chief justice of the U.S. Supreme Court.

July 29: Germany's National Socialist (Nazi) Party chooses Adolf Hitler as its president.

August 3: John Macready becomes the first crop duster pilot when he drops pesticides from a plane on a farm in Troy, Ohio, to kill caterpillars.

August 10: Future president Franklin D. Roosevelt is stricken with polio while at his summer home on the Canadian island of Campobello.

October 8: The first Sweetest Day is celebrated in Cleveland, Ohio.

October 29: In college football, Centre College of Danville, Kentucky, defeats Harvard University 6–0 to end Harvard's five-year winning streak. This is the first game to be called the "upset of the century."

November 3: Striking milk drivers in New York City dump thousands of gallons of milk onto the streets.

November 23: President Harding signs the Willis Campell Act, better known as the anti-beer bill, which makes it unlawful for doctors to prescribe beer or liquor for medicinal purposes.

The Rock

❖ ❖ ❖ ❖

When people discuss famous prisons, you can bet your bottom dollar that "The Rock"—Alcatraz Island, or just Alcatraz for short—is nearly always mentioned.

For thousands of years, Alcatraz Island sat peacefully off the coast of California—until Spanish explorer Lieutenant Juan Manuel de Ayala sailed into San Francisco Bay in 1775. For a long time, the island's only inhabitants were pelicans, rocks, grass, and more pelicans. Ayala named it *Isla de los Alcatraces,* which means "Island of the Pelicans."

A Less Peaceful Future

The island evolved into a military fortress, then during the Civil War, it served as a prison for enemy soldiers, insubordinate army personnel, and Confederate sympathizers, thus beginning its long and illustrious history.

A new prison complex was built on Alcatraz Island in 1912. The U.S. Army turned Alcatraz into a 600-cell military prison—the largest reinforced-concrete building in the world. But getting food, water, and supplies to the island became too expensive for the military.

New Trends in Lockups

Before long, a new kind of criminal emerged: mobsters. The public needed a place to put these much-feared lawbreakers, and "escape-

proof" Alcatraz provided the perfect solution. In 1934, the federal government took over Alcatraz from the military and redesigned it to strike fear in the heart of any public enemy. Significantly fortified buildings, combined with the jagged rocks of Alcatraz Island and the icy waters and strong currents of San Francisco Bay, made escape from Alcatraz seem virtually impossible.

James A. Johnston was hired as warden of Alcatraz. Under his administration, prisoners received only basic necessities. When extreme discipline was warranted, prisoners were placed in a "strip cell"—a dark, steel-encased room with a hole in the floor in which the inhabitant could relieve himself. Guards controlled the ability to flush. This institution took the concept of solitary confinement to a new level. The strip cell got its name because inmates were stripped naked before entry. They were also placed on severely restricted diets. The room was kept pitch-black. A mattress was allowed at night but taken away during the daytime.

Getting Out

No prisoners were sentenced directly to Alcatraz. Instead, the facility was populated with the worst inmates from other prisons. It was not until prisoners got in trouble elsewhere in the penitentiary system that they were sent to the Rock. People tried to escape over the years, but they failed miserably—until June 11, 1962, when Frank Lee Morris, Allen West, and Clarence and John Anglin executed a clever escape plan. The complex plot involved escape holes made with crude drills fashioned from kitchen equipment, human decoys, and a rubber raft made from raincoats. After a bed check, three of the inmates were never seen again, having escaped through utility corridors and ventilation shafts to the beach. Allen West, however, failed to make his escape hole large enough by the scheduled time and was left behind. The trio's escape was officially deemed to be unsuccessful—there was no evidence that any of the three survived the attempt—but the television show *MythBusters* proved that escape was indeed possible with the materials they had at hand.

Alcatraz closed in 1963. In 1972, Congress created Golden Gate National Recreation Area, which included the island. In 1973, Alcatraz reopened as a tourist destination and is now an ecological preserve.

The Eye of the Beholder:
The Guggenheim Museum

*What happens when you need a distinctive,
uncompromising design for a groundbreaking museum?
In the 1940s, you called Frank Lloyd Wright.*

Modern art is an acquired taste. Not everyone is comfortable with
the free flow of vibrant colors and abstract swirls or the stark, feature-
less sculptures that dominate the genre. But there's a lot more to
abstract art than just splattering paint on a canvas or carving chunks
out of stone. It's about personal style and vision—creating something
that may not please everyone but is unforgettable all the same.

Setting the Stage

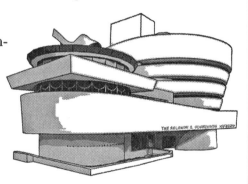

When the Guggenheim Foun-
dation in New York City
decided that it needed an
architectural maestro to
create a new home for its
collection of modern mas-
terpieces, only one man
was considered equal to the
challenge: architect Frank
Lloyd Wright, whose unique vision had produced some of the most
distinctive buildings in the United States in the 20th century. The
result was his final triumph, christened the Solomon R. Guggenheim
Museum, a building with unusual lines that make it instantly identi-
fiable, even in New York's ever-changing landscape.

Solomon Guggenheim was an industrialist who made his fortune
in copper mining. An avid art lover, he donated his vast art collection
to the foundation that bore his name before his death in 1949. His
collection included paintings by Vasily Kandinsky, Pablo Picasso, and
Georges Braque, who were noted for their daring use of color and
modern style. Together with the work of sculptors including Con-
stantin Brancusi, these works formed the heart of a multimillion-
dollar collection that continued to grow as the years passed.

Two years after its 1937 incorporation, the Guggenheim Foundation opened the Museum of Non-Objective Painting on 54th Street to house the collection of masterpieces. But the trustees dreamed of constructing a building whose exterior and interior would reflect the avant-garde art better than such a traditional site. They commissioned Wright for the job in 1943, but more than a decade passed before the dream became a reality.

Wright Makes Himself Comfortable

While Wright was initially not pleased with the Guggenheim's decision to locate the new building in New York City, he traveled the area until he found what he considered to be the most appropriate location—the museum's site on Fifth Avenue between 88th and 89th streets. The architect drew on nearby Central Park as a source of inspiration to create what he felt was an appropriately organic design.

An Astonishing Work

Although Wright did not live to see the project finished, the Guggenheim Museum fulfilled his plan to create a radical new setting for the artwork. When the museum opened in 1959, visitors were invited to start at the top of the building and follow a gently sloping curve downward. Gone were the boxlike rooms so typical of the average museum. Instead, Wright's spiral of concrete, described by some as an inverted ziggurat or a nautilus shell, drew the crowds from one exhibit space to the next. The open rotunda provided a dazzling view of different paintings on several levels at once.

Some critics dismissed Wright's work as overpowering, but the architect was pleased with the design—he felt it was an extension of the artwork itself. Unfortunately, financial constraints did not allow the building to be completed according to Wright's original concept. However, in recent years, a tower containing four exhibit galleries was finally added that more accurately reflects Wright's plan.

The Solomon R. Guggenheim Foundation celebrated its 70th anniversary in 2007. To honor the event, the museum showcased some of the original collection donated by Solomon Guggenheim—part of which had never been exhibited at the museum. Today, the building stands as a testament to the collective vision of Wright, the master architect; the Guggenheim family; and the foundation's board, which recognized that a unique art form deserved an equally unique home.

Fast Facts

- *A mother kangaroo can have two babies of different ages in her pouch at the same time. She produces different milk for each of them, depending on their age and nutritional needs.*

- *The original Hollywood Production Code of the 1930s stated that excessive kissing, illegal drugs, and indecent exposure were completely forbidden in any movie.*

- *George Welch, a flying ace and Medal of Honor recipient, claimed to have broken the sound barrier on October 1, 1947, two weeks before Chuck Yeager.*

- *Only one person has played both Major League baseball and NHL hockey. Jim Riley played baseball for St. Louis and Washington and hockey with Chicago and Detroit.*

- *The Nike swoosh was designed by Carolyn Davidson, a graphic design student at Portland State University. She was paid $35 for the famous trademark.*

- *In 1960, the USS* Triton, *a nuclear submarine, was the first vessel to circumnavigate the planet submerged. It only surfaced once during its journey, to remove a sick crew member.*

- *The Great Fire of London started in a bakery in 1666 and lasted three days. It consumed the older section of the city and destroyed 13,200 homes. Some reports state that only 16 people died.*

- *Dame Judi Dench had just eight minutes of screen time in the movie* Shakespeare in Love, *but that less-than-15-minutes-of-fame won her the Best Supporting Actress Oscar for 1998.*

- *Originally marketed as "zero proof moonshine," Mountain Dew once featured bottles with the image of a hillbilly on them. They are now collector items worth five to ten dollars.*

INSPIRE ME

Sonnet #43, *Sonnets from the Portuguese*

"How do I love thee? Let me count the ways." If this sounds familiar, it's because it is the opening line to one of the most famous love sonnets in the English language, written by Elizabeth Barrett Browning in the 1840s. The inspiration behind this sonnet was, predictably, love, and the love story of Browning and her husband is one of the enduring romantic tales of modern times.

Browning was born to a wealthy English family in 1806. She was a precocious child who published her first poem when she was 14. Unfortunately, she was also sickly and prone to bouts of depression. Although her brothers received their education at boarding schools, as a girl, Elizabeth was mostly left on her own to learn what she could. Even so, she was well-versed in both classical and modern literature. Her early life was profoundly marked by the deaths of her mother and her favorite brother, Edward. Elizabeth lived with her father until she eloped to Italy at the age of 40 with the love of her life, fellow poet Robert Browning.

Robert had read a book of Elizabeth's poems and was so affected by her work that he wrote her a moving letter, proclaiming his admiration for her. A mutual acquaintance arranged for the two to meet, and they immediately fell in love. Elizabeth wrote the love sonnet that became Sonnet #43 during the early years of their courtship.

After Elizabeth and Robert were married, Elizabeth's health rebounded. The couple lived in Italy for the remainder of Elizabeth's life. In 1849, they had a son they nicknamed Pen, and they both continued to write poetry, acting as mutual sources of guidance and inspiration. Elizabeth published *Sonnets from the Portuguese* in 1850; the title comes from Robert's endearment, for her, his *Portuguese*.

Elizabeth was successful and well-known during her lifetime, and today she is considered one of the foremost English poets of all time. During her life, she also produced a verse-novel, *Aurora Leigh,* and a series of political poems focused on the prominent social issues of the day, including child labor. Although her love sonnets were immediately popular upon publication, they have only grown in fame after their connection to Elizabeth's real-life fairy-tale love was fully appreciated. Elizabeth died in Robert's arms in 1861.

The Night *Frankenstein* Was Born

If you think the drama and anxiety in Mary Shelley's
Frankenstein *is intense, you should get a load of the lives that*
hovered in and around its creation. What a soap opera!

Born in 1797, Mary Wollstonecraft Godwin was the only child of
intellectuals Mary Wollstonecraft and William Godwin. Wollstonecraft died only 11 days after giving birth to her daughter, so young
Mary grew up with her father, to whom she became very attached.
Three years after Wollstonecraft's death, Godwin married Mary
Jane Clairmont, who brought two children into the family. Although
Mary didn't have an extensive formal education, she was tutored by
her father and given free rein in his library, which provided her with
extensive cultural knowledge.

Mary and Percy

When Mary was still a teenager, she met Percy Bysshe Shelley and
began a romantic relationship with him. Percy had been bullied
mercilessly in school and had made few friends. So he read—a lot.
Through his reading, he came up with ideas that society considered
heretical and dissident. Percy's father held a seat in Parliament that
under normal conditions would be passed on to his son. In this case,
however, Oxford University caught wind of Percy's pamphlet *The*
Necessity of Atheism and expelled him, which caused a falling-out
with his father. Shortly after that, he married a woman named
Harriet Westbrook. Percy delved deeper into radical politics,
publishing poems about atheism, vegetarianism, and free love;
giving revolutionary speeches on religion and politics; and traveling
throughout Europe.

When he made his way to the home of one of his intellectual
heroes, William Godwin, he found inspiration—as well as Godwin's
brilliant 16-year-old daughter. Against Godwin's wishes, Mary took
up with Percy. When they began their relationship, they were both
advocates of free love. Mary may have believed in it more as a
theory, because although Percy encouraged her to take other lovers,
She had little interest in pursuing anyone but Percy. Despite her

objections, Percy engaged in amorous relations with women both inside and outside of their social circle.

Enter Lord Byron

Lord George Gordon Byron was born with a clubfoot, a source of shame and embarrassment his entire life. This, however, didn't keep him from becoming a notorious poet. Byron famously ripped and roared through life—writing poems, speaking eloquently at the House of Lords, piling up debt, and burning through love affairs with both men and women. In 1816, Byron decided to leave England temporarily until the rumors about his lifestyle died down and some of his debts had been forgotten. Once he left, however, he would never return. What he expected to be a trip across Europe ended up being permanent exile from England.

A romantic associate of his, Claire Clairmont, was one of two children of Mary Jane Clairmont. When Claire's mother married Mary Wollstonecraft Godwin's father, the two—who were eight months apart in age—became close friends. Despite this, Claire became involved with Percy while Mary was pregnant with his child. At 18, after an on-and-off involvement with Percy, Claire moved on to a powerful crush on Byron. Under pretense of looking for advice on how to become a poet, Claire wrote him daily letters and eventually became his lover. When Byron left England in 1816, Claire followed, bringing Mary and Percy with her for a visit. To say the least, tensions were brewing.

The Action

It may have annoyed Byron when he saw Claire coming up the lawn to his temporary home near Lake Geneva in Switzerland. She was, after all, a speechlessly smitten teenager, and probably too desperate for Byron to take seriously (although this hadn't dissuaded him from having an affair with her). But she had in tow the daughter of William Godwin, a radical thinker whose work Byron admired, and Percy, who would soon become Byron's close friend. Claire, unbeknownst to the rest of the group, was pregnant with Byron's child.

The Year Without a Summer

Meteorological moodiness was on tap for the summer of 1816. The weather was so dank and cool that it was almost as if summer never came at all. Many nights at Byron's villa were spent inside because of the cold and rain. On one particular night, Mary, Percy, Byron, and John Polidori (Byron's physician) were reading ghost stories. Byron challenged the group to each write their own. Mary jumped to the challenge. Perhaps it was Mary's need to be accepted by the group, or her frustration with fitting into a role where she couldn't express her considerable intelligence. Perhaps she thought of it as a much-needed outlet for dealing with the strange interconnections of the group, sequestered together for so long. Or maybe she simply wanted to write, just as she had desired all her life. Or maybe, just maybe, it was the alleged rampant opium usage among the group on this rainy night.

The story Mary created started as a wisp—a few pages about a doctor who creates a monster by snatching body parts from morgues and a vaguely explained process in which these parts are fused together and animated. While the initial story was short, there was enough there for Percy to encourage her to develop it. Over the next few days, Mary completed a draft, and she finished writing *Frankenstein* the following year.

The next few years were just as drama-filled for the four characters in this soap opera. Claire had a daughter by Byron—a daughter she eventually left for him to raise, only to have him put the child in a convent where she died of typhus at age five. Mary married Percy after his first wife died; they had four children, all but one of whom died as children. Percy drowned when his boat capsized during a sudden storm in Italy six years after the summer on Lake Geneva. And just two years after that, Bryon died of a violent fever in Greece while fighting for Greek independence from the Turks.

The Finale

On January 1, 1818, the first edition of *Frankenstein* was published anonymously, with a foreword by Percy. The second edition, published in 1823, was credited to Mary Shelley, and in 1831, the first popular edition of the book was published, heavily revised by Mary. The novel became a classic despite the initial criticism it received. To this day, people around the world love to read about the sad monster who may or may not represent the feelings floating around a lavish Swiss home one stormy, bohemian night.

HOW IT ALL BEGAN

The Ballpoint Pen

John J. Loud patented the ballpoint pen in 1888, but since he used it only to mark leather, he neglected to consider its wider commercial possibilities. In later legal skirmishes over the right to claim the invention, his limited patent was ignored. And you think *you* have tough luck.

The Oldest Surviving European Dance

No, it's not the waltz—it's an Austrian-Bavarian innovation called *Schuhplattler*, or "the shoe-slapping dance." Men and women are partnered. The man lifts his feet, one at a time, to knee-height so he can slap his shoes, while the woman spins around in place. This is thought to date back to Neolithic times, or 3000 B.C. What amusements must have ensued at that moment of discovery!

Meanwhile, the earliest recorded dance poses are depicted in cave paintings at Les Trois Frères in southern France, dating back 10,000–40,000 years, where half-humans in animal costumes frolic along the walls.

The Mobile Phone

The mobile phone, or cell phone, was invented by Dr. Martin Cooper of Motorola. Its first use was in 1973 when the inventor rang up his rival, the head of research at Bell Labs. There is no available record of what was said, but it may very well have included a high-minded version of "Nyah-nyah!"

Mobile phones work because of a frequency-switching system invented in 1942 by, believe it or not, Hollywood actor Hedy Lamarr. Her patent expired before the device was used for this purpose, so she unfortunately did not receive any profits.

"Gone to Pot"

This phrase, meaning not much good for anything, doesn't refer to marijuana—honest. It actually originated in the Elizabethan era with the forerunner of beef stew, when any tidbit of meat too small for a regular portion was thrown into a big pot always boiling over the fire.

The Spindletop Gusher: When Oil Became an Industry

❖ ❖ ❖ ❖

Today, oil is a well-established industry. But a little more than 100 years ago, oil took a backseat to coal when it came to energy.

At the turn of the 20th century, most, if not all, industrial and transportation equipment ran on coal. Used only for lubrication, for lighting lamps, and sometimes for burning in stoves, oil wasn't seen as a major energy producer. The majority of America's oil was pumped, surprisingly enough, in Pennsylvania. The Seneca nation in western Pennsylvania used oil that seeped from natural springs, and corporations realized that they could refine kerosene, a liquid used for cooking and lighting, from petroleum. Kerosene was in demand at the time due to its being more abundant and easier to obtain than whale oil.

Coal Is King

Why hadn't petroleum caught on? It had to do with that old standard, the law of supply and demand. At the time, most oil rigs produced only about 50 barrels a day. There was no real indication that oil could be produced in large quantities. Coal, on the other hand, was plentiful and cheap. And gasoline? It was just a by-product of refining kerosene from oil. The internal combustion engine found in most cars today was little more than an experiment: The waste from refined kerosene made a good source of fuel for the engines. But gasoline wasn't plentiful enough to mass-market the new invention, and few people saw any real role for oil. Even so, one man believed that the world would indeed one day use oil as its major source of fuel. His name was Patillo Higgins.

Searching for a Gusher

Higgins, along with other investors, formed the Gladys City Oil Company in 1892. He was convinced that under the salt dome of Spindletop, Texas, was a large reserve of oil. After a couple of years of unsuccessful attempts and financial hardships, however, some of the partners—including Higgins—left the company. But in 1899, Higgins partnered with another man who shared his belief in Spindletop: Anthony F. Lucas.

A cable drilling tool was the industry standard for oil rigs in the 1800s. This tool lifted and dropped a wedge-shape bit into a hole, pulverizing the rock beneath. After a few drops, the debris was scooped out and the process repeated. When the team hit thicker rock layers, Lucas tried a new type of drilling system—the rotary drill. This drill used a cutting head similar in principle to modern drill bits, whereby teeth or sharp edges are rotated to cut through material. The rotary head attached to a long series of pipes connected end to end.

Eureka!

Progress continued until January 10, 1901, when the drill reached depths between 1,000 and 1,140 feet (300–348 meters), and workers suddenly had to run for their lives. It was raining pipes—tons of them! Up from the hole came a loud roar, followed by masses of steel drilling pipe shooting into the air. Shortly after, mud—the lubricant for the rotary drill—gurgled from the ground. Suddenly, the hole began to belch natural gas. Finally, the prize spewed out— black gold, Texas tea, oil. The geyser erupted more than 100 feet into the air. It took nine days to bring it under control.

Early on, Spindletop produced somewhere in the neighborhood of 80,000 barrels of oil each day. Compare that to some modern oil rigs that only produce about 100,000 barrels a day. However, the sudden abundance of oil wasn't the only reason Spindletop ushered in the modern petroleum industry. Lucas had proved that rotary drilling could cut through deep, hardened layers of rock, and that these depths could contain large pockets of petroleum oil. With that, Higgins's prediction—that the world would someday demand oil instead of coal—soon came true.

By 1904, Spindletop—an area of about one square mile—hosted 400 oil rigs. Rigs soon spread across Texas and changed the landscape forever. With oil in abundance, industry quickly shifted, making room for the internal combustion engine to be further developed, which in turn helped fuel the demand for oil to make gasoline. The modern petroleum industry had begun.

Are You Going to Eat That Jesus?

Images of religious icons, particularly Jesus and the Virgin Mary, sometimes show up in the oddest places. Some people believe they are divine. What's the story?

Sightings of religious symbols or images, called religious *simulacra*, in unexpected places are common enough that they've become incorporated into pop culture. Many of the people who discover or are involved in these sightings consider them to be miraculous events. Some also claim that the objects in which the images appear have special properties, such as bringing good luck or being immune to the ravages of time.

Jesus and Mary

For Christians, Jesus and the Virgin Mary are among the most significant religious figures, and not coincidentally, they also seem to make the most common appearances—often in food. Perhaps the quintessential sighting of a Christian religious symbol in food occurred in 1978, when a New Mexico woman named Maria Rubio was making a burrito. She noticed that a burn on the tortilla appeared to be in the shape of Jesus' head. After receiving the blessing of a priest, she built a shrine to house the tortilla and even quit her job to tend to the shrine full-time.

Islamic Words

Not surprisingly, religious sightings do not always involve Christian figures or symbols. In the Islamic world, the perception of the Arabic word for *Allah* roughly parallels the sighting of Jesus, the Virgin Mary, or other religious figures by Christians. Similarly, the objects involved sometimes have mystical properties ascribed to them. In 2006, a Kazakh farmer discovered an egg that villagers claimed had the name of Allah on its shell. After the sighting was verified by the local mosque, Bites Amantayeva, the farmer who discovered the egg, decided to keep it, saying, "We don't think it'll go bad." The name of Allah has also been sighted on fish scales, on beans, and in tomato slices.

Selling Simulacra

Sightings of religious images can have commercial as well as spiritual implications. In 1996, someone at a coffee shop in Nashville, Tennessee, discovered a cinnamon bun that bore a striking resemblance to Mother Teresa. The coffee shop parlayed the discovery into a line of merchandise, including coffee mugs and T-shirts. The merchandise was marketed with a NunBun trademark after Mother Teresa asked the shop to stop using the phrase "Immaculate Confection."

The proliferation of Internet auction sites such as eBay has created a market for these "miraculous" objects. One of the widest-known auctions occurred in 2004, when a Florida woman named Diane Duyser auctioned part of a grilled cheese sandwich she claimed bore the image of the Virgin Mary on eBay. Duyser asserted that the sandwich, which she had been storing since it was made in 1994, had never grown moldy and had brought her good luck, allowing her to win $70,000 at a casino. The sandwich was eventually purchased by another casino for $28,000.

Religious sightings—especially if they have been contrived somehow—are not always viewed in a positive light. In 1997, Nike produced several models of basketball shoes that unintentionally featured a logo that, when viewed from right to left, resembled the Arabic word for *Allah*. The Council on American-Islamic Relations (CAIR) quickly demanded an apology, and Nike had little choice but to recall the shoes. The settlement between Nike and CAIR also included Arabic training for Nike graphic designers and Nike-built playgrounds in Muslim communities.

A Scientific Explanation?

While the parties involved in sightings of religious symbols often consider them to be miraculous in nature, the prevailing scientific view is that, rather than miraculous, they are occurrences of *pareidolia,* a psychological phenomenon in which random stimuli are interpreted as being meaningful in some way. As part of its intellectual process, the mind tries to make sense of what may be unrelated images. This is the same phenomenon that psychologists credit with forming the likeness of a man in the moon or shapes in clouds. It's also what's involved when the brain creates pictures from the famous Rorschach inkblots.

Curious Classifieds

Fur coats made for ladies from their own skin.

Sheer stockings. Designed for fancy dress, but so serviceable that lots of women wear nothing else.

And now, the Superstore—unequaled in size, unmatched in variety, un-rivaled inconvenience.

We will oil your sewing machine and adjust tension in your home for $1.00.

Don't stand there and be hungry...come in and get fed up.

GE Automatic Blanket—insure sound sleep with an Authorized GE Dealer.

Open house—Body Shapers Toning Salon—free coffee & donuts

Rabbit fur coat, size medium, $45. Small hutch, $55.

Golden, ripe, boneless bananas, 39 cents a pound.

Get rid of aunts: Zap does the job in 24 hours.

Semi-Annual after-Christmas Sale

Mother's helper—peasant working conditions.

Saturday Morning 10:30 A.M. Easter Matinee. Every child laying an egg in the doorman's hand will be admitted free.

Found: dirty white dog...looks like a rat...been out awhile....Better be a reward.

Registered Miniature American Eskimos, females—$150, male—$125. Ready to go.

Will trade fire, life, automobile insurance for anything can use. Want lady with automobile.

Wanted: A boy who can take care of horses who can speak German.

Dinner Special—Turkey $2.35; Chicken or Beef $2.25; Children $2.00

For sale: a quilted high chair that can be made into a table, pottie chair, rocking horse, refrigerator, spring coat, size 8 and fur collar.

No matter what your topcoat is made of, this miracle spray will make it really repellent.

Famous Revolutionary Organizations: Where There's a Will, There's a Warrior

Since time began, people have formed organizations that espouse their political, social, cultural, or nationalistic ideas. These groups come from every walk of life, every continent, and every era. The only commonality they share is their passion for what they believe— ideas for which they will give anything, including their lives.

Carbonari
While it is unknown whether the group originally developed in France or Italy, the Carbonari, or "charcoal burners," derived their philosophy from the ideals of the French Revolution and the Enlightenment. Primarily a political organization, the Carbonari opposed absolutism and desired the establishment of a republic or, second-best, a constitutional monarchy in Italy. The society had a clearly delineated, hierarchical structure, not unlike that of the Freemasons. Like many other revolutionary organizations, the Carbonari were not averse to using violence to achieve their goals.

Black Hand
While this underground sect, whose more official name is Unification or Death, is sometimes grouped with secret societies, it is more often defined as a terrorist organization. Established in 1911 in Serbia from the remnants of the more mainstream pan-slavic organization National Defense, the Black Hand was dedicated to forming a greater Serbia. Violence was the group's primary tool. A member of the Black Hand assassinated Archduke Franz Ferdinand in 1914. The fallout from this act resulted in World War I.

The Fenians
Even before the Norman Conquest, the Irish struggled to assert their independence from English influence. In the mid-1850s, a more organized resistance to English rule began to develop in the form of the Fenian Brotherhood. The name comes from the *Fianna,*

legendary soldiers of Ireland. Although the term *Fenian* applies to the broader movement, most Fenians belonged to the Irish Republican Brotherhood—which actually originated in the United States in 1858. The revolutionary group saw armed conflict as the primary tool for achieving independence from England.

Satyagraha

Indian independence leader Mohandas Gandhi originated a philosophy of social action called *satyagraha*. It was derived, in part, from the Hindu concept of *ahimsa*, a principle of noninjury. Satyagraha further developed into a campaign of civil disobedience and nonviolent resistance as the people of India agitated for freedom from British rule. The Indian National Congress, the oldest political organization in India and a major force in the crusade to free India, adopted satyagraha under Gandhi's leadership in the 1920s. Satyagraha helped lead to the eventual independence of India in 1947 and influenced numerous other nonviolent struggles throughout the world, including the American civil rights movement of the 1960s.

Tongmenghui

Founded in Tokyo in 1905, Tongmenghui was also called the Chinese United League or the Chinese Revolutionary Alliance. Led by Sun Yat-Sen and Song Jiaoren, the secret organization was designed to unify the disparate antimonarchy forces within China. It encompassed republicans, nationalists, and socialists. In addition to governmental change, Tongmenghui also sought social revolution with the reestablishment of Chinese culture and agricultural revolution in the form of land redistribution.

The Bolsheviks

Their name derived from the Russian word for "majority," the Bolsheviks were a splinter group from the more mainstream Social Democratic Labor party. With Vladimir Lenin as their leader, the Bolshevik faction argued that the agrarian class should be the power base for the impending Marxist revolution, while their opponents (later called the *Menshevik*, or "minority," by Lenin) believed that anyone committed to Marxist ideals should be included. The more extreme view of the Bolsheviks eventually won the day; they became the ruling Communist party of Russia in March 1918.

Notable Fraternal Organizations

Fraternal organizations have been in operation, often under varying degrees of secrecy, for hundreds of years. Ancient bylaws and traditions mostly forbid women from becoming members, although many have now established sister organizations.

Freemasons

While the Freemasons' symbols of the square and the compass may be derived from the building of King Solomon's Temple in the tenth century B.C., the origins of the society itself are somewhat more modern. The organization developed among the guilds of stonemasons created during the construction of the great cathedrals of Europe in the Middle Ages. From these original professional associations came today's Masons, committed to philanthropy and ethics. Although Freemasonry includes reverence of the "Great Architect of the Universe," it is not a religion. Most lodges serve the communities in which they reside, and many are heavily involved in charity. While they don't consider themselves a secret society, Freemasons argue that they are an esoteric society with certain signs, tokens, and words that are private.

Order of DeMolay

A civic organization dedicated to helping young men grow into the responsible leaders of tomorrow, the Order of DeMolay was started by Frank Land in Kansas City, Missouri, in 1919. Membership is open to men ages 12–21, and through mentoring relationships with adults, the young men of the society focus on character and leadership skills. While it is not officially affiliated with the Freemasons, the Order developed much of its philosophy and many of its rituals from the Masonic tradition. The name of the group was chosen to honor Jacques DeMolay, the last Grand Master of the Knights Templar. Today, the Order of DeMolay has more than 1,000 chapters located around the world.

Rosicrucians

The Rosicrucians are an order that attempts to understand the connection between the soul, the body, and the higher consciousness. Many legends, both oral and written, explain aspects of Rosicrucian thought. The group seems to have roots in the mysticism of ancient Egypt and can trace its evolution through the development of Western philosophy until the group's eventual incorporation in 1915. Alchemy, specifically as applied to the transmutation of people rather than matter, has played a key role in Rosicrucian thought. Today, Rosicrucians focus on history, spirituality, and the humanities as tools for understanding the challenges confronting the people of the modern world.

Knights of Columbus

The Knights of Columbus was established in Connecticut in 1882 by Father Michael McGivney; he brought together the men of his parish to create a brotherhood of the faithful to mutually support each other and fellow Catholics. The group selected its name to honor Christopher Columbus, who had brought Christianity to the Americas. Originally envisioned as a network of social assistance in prewelfare days, the K of C, as it is known, sought to provide for widows and orphans. Since that time, the organization's ideals of charity, civic duty, and evangelism have expanded into a much broader mission. Regardless, providing insurance to the families of members still remains one of its objectives today.

P.E.O. Sisterhood

The P.E.O. (or Philanthropic Educational Organization) started as an on-campus group at Iowa Wesleyan College in 1869. The original seven members founded their association on the ideals of friendship and philanthropy. Since that time, the group has evolved into an all-female society dedicated to furthering educational opportunities for women. The organization has several scholarship and loan funds designed to advance that purpose.

- *The government-owned Indian Railways, which transports more than 16 million passengers a day, is the world's largest employer, with more than 1.6 million workers.*

Fast Facts

- In 1876, counterfeiters near Chicago attempted to steal Abraham Lincoln's corpse. They intended to hold it for ransom in order to gain the release of one of their members from jail. They attempted this twice but were stopped each time.

- The smallest adult dog on record is a Yorkshire terrier which, at two-and-a-half inches high and almost four inches long, could easily sleep in a bed the size of a paperback book.

- November 19 is World Toilet Day. It's meant to increase awareness of an individual's right to sanitation and good toilet atmosphere.

- Argan oil, which is used for flavoring foods and in cosmetics, is made by grinding nuts from the argan tree. Sometimes, though, the nuts are first processed through a goat's digestive system. These are not the nuts recommended for eating.

- In 1985, 300 people who were alive in 1910 gathered to watch Halley's Comet make its first celestial return to Earth's realm in 75 years.

- Marijuana was used in the 19th century to relieve muscle spasms. The doctor of Britain's Queen Victoria prescribed marijuana to her for the relief of menstrual cramps.

- Isaac Newton's mother pulled him out of school to help run her farm. Newton's uncle, however, saw potential and insisted the boy receive further education.

- The Recording Industry Association of America tried to sue Gertrude Walton for illegally downloading files despite the fact that the woman had died nearly two months earlier.

- In 1967, the town of St. Paul, Alberta, built the world's first UFO landing pad as a project to mark Canada's 100th birthday.

Chilly Accommodations

❖ ❖ ❖ ❖

Want to spend some vacation time at an ice hotel?
Better make reservations before spring comes,
or you'll risk having your room melt.

An ice hotel is a temporary hotel made entirely of ice and snow. Such hotels are open, logically enough, only during winter months, then they melt (which is what makes them temporary) and are reconstructed the following year. Ice hotels are white-hot destination spots whose construction is based on some of the same theories used to build igloos: Blocks of ice and compacted snow from deep drifts are cut and arranged to build a structure that can protect and house the people using it. Two of the best-known hotels can be found in Sweden and Quebec.

ICEHOTEL, Sweden

ICEHOTEL in Sweden, located in the village of Jukkasjarvi, is 200 kilometers, or 125 miles, north of the Arctic Circle. It's the first-ever hotel built entirely of ice. Because the hotel—or, *hotels,* one should say, as there is a new one every year—rests near the River Torne, there's an endless supply of clear water for construction each year.

The hotel uses 2,000 tons of ice in its construction. It covers more than 30,000 square feet. It is all ice, no kidding. The registration desk, tables, beds, chapel, art exhibition hall—all are made of ice.

So, what do you need to know before scheduling some sleep time in a hotel made of ice? First, you need to know that the temperature is kept between 15 and 24 degrees Fahrenheit. Concerned about keeping your extremities warm while spending an entire night in freezing temps? No worries—the hotel provides guests with thermal sleeping bags, and each ice bed is covered with reindeer skins. As long as you don't kick off the covers in your sleep, you should be able to stay free of frostbite for the night. A visit to the sauna in the morning is included in the price, along with a hot cup of lingonberry juice at your bedside.

Ice Hotel, Quebec

Inspired by the Swedish ICEHOTEL, designer Jacques Desbois built a similar hotel in 1996 in Sainte-Catherine-de-la-Jacques-Cartier, about 30 minutes outside of Quebec City. Quebec is a natural location for an ice hotel—the city hosts the annual Bonhomme Winter Carnival. The debut of the Ice Palace at the 1955 Winter Carnival was an early attempt at merging the pragmatic construction of igloos with the fantastical dreaminess of larger-scale ice buildings.

The Ice Hotel, Quebec, is usually made with 500 tons of ice and 15,000 tons of snow. It has 18-foot-high ceilings and theme suites, which are more numerous with each annual reconstruction. The Ice Hotel also has an Ice Bar sponsored by Absolut Vodka—a frosty delight. Guests of the Ice Hotel, Quebec, can expect ice beds similar to those at the ICEHOTEL, Sweden, but the Quebec version offers a thick foam mattress, as well as deer pelts, in addition to the requisite thermal sleeping bags. The Canadian version of the ice hotel houses two art galleries and a movie theater, which shows only "cool" movies.

Around the World

Sweden and Canada aren't the only countries to have ice hotels, of course. They can be built anywhere that's cold enough. Similar structures have been constructed in Norway, Romania, and Finland.

California's Two Valleys

*Some of the most significant real estate in California
is its valleys. Here are two: one is a natural valley,
while the other is more metaphorical.*

The San Fernando Valley in Southern California and Silicon Valley
in Northern California are like polar-opposite siblings. They're not
just on the opposite ends of the spectrum geographically but also in
terms of their industry, weather, and population. Of course, both are
still very much beholden to their Californian histories.

San Fernando

The San Fernando Valley encompasses 260 square miles in and around
the city of Los Angeles. It is bordered by the Santa Susana Mountains to the northwest, the Simi Hills to the west, the Santa Monica
Mountains to the south, the Verdugo Mountains to the east, the San
Gabriel Mountains to the northeast, and the Sierra Pelona Mountains to the north. The area was inhabited by the native Tatviam and
Tongva cultures for thousands of years before the Spanish settled
there around 1797. When the Mexican-American War ended in
1847, the land was ceded to the United States.

Secession issues seem to be a theme in the valley's life—in the
1970s and again in 2002, the residents of the city of Los Angeles
voted on a proposal to allow the San Fernando Valley to secede
and become an independent and incorporated city of its own. The
proposal came from the suburban communities of the valley, which
argued that their resources should be separated from those of Los
Angeles proper. But the city wouldn't let its suburban cousins leave:
The proposal failed both times.

The San Fernando Valley is blessed with dry, sunny weather.
Smog is a particular problem—the surrounding mountain ranges
trap it in the sunken valley—though recent environmental regulations have improved the suffocating pollution levels for residents.

Speaking of residents, they're mostly an equal percentage of
Latinos and whites. The valley has a reputation for sprawling subdi-
visions, despite the fact that there are many apartment complexes,

as well. Though a handful of valley communities have at least one in five residents living in poverty, the valley overall still has lower poverty rates than the rest of the county. Prominent aerospace-technology companies were once residents of the San Fernando Valley, but they have since moved to other locales. Currently, the motion picture industry is a predominant economic force in the area—including the multibillion-dollar pornography industry.

Silicon Valley

Like the older sister who ignores her pesky younger brother during passing periods at school, Silicon Valley sits just south of the San Francisco Bay area and seems to share with the San Fernando Valley only the name of the state in which they both exist.

Once this area was covered with orchards. The influx of various technology-related companies and research firms caused one journalist to coin the term *Silicon Valley*, and the name stuck. Since the early 1900s, believe it or not, the area has nurtured the growth of the electronics industry. It became the hub of experimentation and innovation for many industries, including radio, television, military electronics, and computers. An early radio station—the first one in the nation to carry regularly scheduled programming—was started in San Jose in 1909. Nearby Stanford University has also been a huge contributor to the evolution of industry in Silicon Valley.

The weather in Silicon Valley is moderate, quite similar to that of the Mediterranean—warm and dry. There's a growing Asian population in this area, and it's estimated that 44 percent of residents have college degrees (compared to 27 percent nationwide). People who live here are, of course, mostly employed by the area's industries—technology, computer software, and venture capitalist firms. Some of the most prominent names in business reside in Silicon Valley: Apple, Intel, and Yahoo!, among many others. The term *Silicon Valley* has entered the pop-culture lexicon as a reference to the high-tech sector in general.

- *Both Atari and Hewlett-Packard turned down Steve Jobs and Steve Wozniak when they offered the companies the opportunity to produce the Apple computer.*

Behind the Songs of Our Times

"The Sounds of Silence" (1966)

When Paul Simon first heard his song "The Sounds of Silence" on the radio, it didn't sound the way he remembered recording it. Huddled alone with singing partner Art Garfunkel and an acoustic guitar in a darkened studio, he believed the song had stood out in its stark simplicity. But this version was much different—where did the electric 12-string guitar come from, the bass, the drums? Columbia Records decided the song would be a sure hit if it were "electrified," so the original producer brought in additional musicians two years after Simon and Garfunkel had first laid down their recording. The record company was right, as the song hit number one in 1966. Over the years, the title has been presented in the singular, "The Sound of Silence," as well.

"Valley Girl" (1982)

With an unruly mop of black hair, a droopy mustache, and an overgrown soul patch, Frank Zappa was never a Top 40 teen idol. However, he was a brilliant composer, borrowing from classical, jazz, rock, doo-wop, and avant-garde genres to craft his unique style of music. With the help of his 14-year-old daughter, Moon Unit, Zappa cracked the *Billboard* Top 40 charts with 1982's "Valley Girl." His daughter provided the insipid lyrics, based on the unique teenybopper language used by rich young girls in the affluent San Fernando Valley of Los Angeles. Whether the Zappas intended it or not, the Valley accent and dialect soon became iconic.

"Stayin' Alive" (1977)

Take your pick—the sound track from the 1977 disco flick *Saturday Night Fever* produced three number-one hits for the Bee Gees. (It also included two previous Bee Gees number ones.) Brothers Barry, Robin, and Maurice Gibb lent their falsetto vocals to "Stayin' Alive" after producer Robert Stigwood remembered a song they had done years earlier called "Saturday Night." When he heard the final mix, though, Stigwood was shocked: Why had the title been changed to "Stayin' Alive"? The brothers believed that a chorus that went, "Ah—ah—ah—ah, Saturday night, Saturday night" was just too corny and common. When the song went number one, Stigwood agreed. It may never have gone number one, however, as it wasn't intended to be a single. Fans heard the song in trailers for *Saturday Night Fever* and called up their favorite radio stations demanding to hear it again.

Ed Wood: Made in Hollywood, USA

*Only in Hollywood, the land of make-believe, could Ed Wood
realize his dream of making movies; only in Hollywood
could his enthusiasm, drive, and perseverance overcome his
lack of cinematic skill. His gift was not in making movies
but in persuading people that he could make movies.*

Edward D. Wood, Jr., wrote, directed, and produced some of the
worst sci-fi and horror films of the 1950s—or any decade. Wood
had the uncanny ability to convince people to sink money into his
pictures, although doing so usually involved writing a new part in the
film for the prospective investor.

Background

Born in Poughkeepsie, New York, in 1924, young Wood quickly
found his passion. As a boy, he sat enthralled in darkened movie
theaters from open to close. Wood's mother, who wanted a daughter
rather than a son, often dressed Ed in girls' clothing, which was the
genesis of his lifelong habit of cross-dressing. He joined the Marines
at 17, later claiming to have often worn a bra and panties under his
uniform during his World War II tour of duty. After the war, Wood
settled in Hollywood to tilt at his own personal windmill.

Movies

Most notable of Wood's films was the 1953 autobiographical fantasy of cross-dressing, *Glen or Glenda?* Wood starred in it himself
but used the pseudonym Daniel Davis. His 1955 *Bride of the Monster* was a typical "mad scientist" flick, complete with laboratory
(including, literally rather than proverbially, the kitchen sink) and
a giant killer octopus. The octopus had been stolen from a prop
warehouse—the only catch was that Wood forgot to pilfer the motor
that moved the rubber tentacles, as well. *Night of the Ghouls,* shot
in 1958, was a sequel of sorts to *Bride of the Monster.*

Wood's masterpiece, however, was the 1959 epic *Plan 9 from
Outer Space.* Starting with a few minutes of silent footage, Wood
made a very silly, yet very watchable, sci-fi film. Tagged by many as

"the worst movie ever made," the film's appeal stemmed from its intense sincerity. *Plan 9* never *intentionally* winked at the camera—never mind the cardboard tombstones that fell over, the shower curtain that passed for the cockpit of an airplane, or the tiny cemetery crypt that seemed to hold more people than a taxi full of clowns.

An Oddball Acting Troupe

Each of Wood's films featured a unique cast of characters, both on- and off-screen. John "Bunny" Breckenridge was a proud homosexual who dreamed of undergoing permanent gender reassignment. Blonde, beautiful Dolores Fuller was Wood's girlfriend and confidant. White-haired eccentric Criswell had startled TV audiences with his incredible (and usually inaccurate) predictions. Kenne Duncan was known in Hollywood as the "meanest man in the movies," and many believed him to be the most lecherous, as well. Buxom, wasp-waisted Maila Nurmi made her mark on LA television by hosting a horror movie show as the gaunt and dark-haired Vampira. Hulking Tor Johnson was a professional wrestler called the "Super Swedish Angel"—his nearly unintelligible Swedish accent (and total lack of acting talent) didn't seem to bother Wood at all.

Most amazing of Wood's troupe, however, was the aging, frail Bela Lugosi. A huge theater star in Europe and a hit on Broadway in the late 1920s in the stage play *Dracula*, Lugosi naturally went on to portray the undead count in Universal's 1931 film of the same name. It was a high point that he would never again reach. He worked steadily through the 1930s and '40s, appearing (but seldom starring) in roles as gangsters, doctors (mad and sane), butlers, and servants, and he eventually became a comedic foil for the Bowery Boys in several films. By the 1950s, Lugosi was in his 70s, ravaged by an addiction to painkillers. Wood greatly admired Lugosi and gave the elderly actor friendship and a sense of being wanted once again. Too old to play the romantic leads that he once coveted, Lugosi was cast instead as a godlike character in *Glen or Glenda?* Wood continued to keep his Hungarian friend active in other films and shot footage in 1956 for a new film called *The Vampire's Tomb* in which, once again, Lugosi would rise as a blood-thirsty vampire. But Bela passed away after shooting only a few minutes of footage, some of it in his revered Count Dracula cape.

Wood Had a Plan

While Wood lost a great friend in Lugosi, his resolve was firm, and he wrote a brand-new script to incorporate the footage that Lugosi had already shot. *Grave Robbers from Outer Space* would be for Ed Wood what *Citizen Kane* was for Orson Welles: a masterpiece. Wood shot additional scenes, using local chiropractor Dr. Tom Mason as Bela's double. The fact that Mason looked nothing like Lugosi seemed to make no difference to Wood. Money problems led Wood to affiliate himself with a local Baptist church, which agreed to finance the film. As usual, parts were written into the film to accommodate the desires of the parish's would-be thespians. The church elders found the title reference to grave robbing to be in poor taste, so the film was renamed *Plan 9 from Outer Space* (though Criswell introduced the film with the original title). With a small, unpromising premiere, Wood had accomplished what he set out to do—he finished the movie as a tribute to his fallen friend.

Legacy

Consider that some people like fast-food restaurants while others prefer haute cuisine. But as long as one doesn't expect four-star fare from a fast-food hamburger, the flavor can be very palatable. Wood's work was never very good cinema, but his films *are* entertaining. They seem to improve with age—not in quality but in watchability. The more viewers get to know this eccentric film writer, producer, director, and sometimes actor, the more they can accept his work for what it is—no more, no less. Wood's films were born not from talent but from a deep passion for the movies.

- *The first high jumper to use the method of jumping headfirst to clear the bar was American Dick Fosbury. His innovative maneuver was dubbed the* Fosbury Flop.

- *Traffic lights were initially invented to control high horse-and-buggy traffic. For their first 50 years of existence, they only included red and green lights. Yellow was added in 1918.*

- *It is believed that humans wore jewelry before they wore clothes.*

The Times They Are A-Changin'

1931

January 5: Lucille Thomas becomes the first female owner of a baseball team when she purchases the Topeka team in the Western League.

January 30: Charlie Chaplin's film *City Lights* premieres at the Los Angeles Theater.

February 2: In Austria, a rocket is used to deliver mail for the first time.

February 3: The Arkansas state legislature passes a motion to pray for the soul of writer H. L. Mencken after he calls the state an "apex of moronia."

February 10: New Delhi becomes the capital of India.

February 14: The original film version of *Dracula,* starring Bela Lugosi, is released.

February 21: The first *plop-plop-fizz-fizz* is heard as Alka-Seltzer is introduced for the treatment of headaches and indigestion.

March 3: Cab Calloway records his signature song, "Minnie the Moocher," which becomes the first jazz song to sell a million copies.

March 3: Congress officially makes "The Star-Spangled Banner" the U.S. national anthem.

March 18: Schick puts the first electric shavers on the market.

March 19: The state of Nevada legalizes gambling.

March 27: Legendary baseball manager John McGraw tells reporters he doesn't think that night baseball will catch on.

May 1: Construction is completed on the Empire State Building in New York City.

October 4: Chester Gould's *Dick Tracy* comic strip makes its debut.

November 1: The Dupont company introduces the first synthetic rubber to the market.

December 10: Jane Addams becomes the first American woman to win a Nobel Prize when she is named corecipient of the Peace Prize.

Diplomacy 101

*International diplomacy is a risky business. Trying to reach
an agreement between two nations—or the leaders of two
nations—is sometimes dangerous, always difficult, and often
impossible. Here are a few of the more challenging examples.*

The job of crafting a diplomatic agreement, of bringing both sides to
the conference table, is entrusted to political leaders and diplomats.
In modern times, when there is a breakdown in international relationships, diplomatic immunity usually brings embassy staff home
safely. But it wasn't always that way.

A Brief History of Diplomacy

Certain touchy rulers in the Middle Ages, such as Attila the Hun or
the Mongol Khans of the Golden Horde, would show their displea-
sure with more "civilized" nations by holding their diplomats for
ransom or by sending said diplomats home in pieces. This seldom
prevented wars, but it certainly got the point across.

One form of diplomatic blunder that has had great consequences
can appear in the interaction between government and religion.
Roman governor Pontius Pilate was responsible for deciding between
the pardon or crucifixion of Jesus of Nazareth. Against his own judgment, he allowed the crowd to persuade him to have Jesus executed.
If Pilate had thought it over, he would have perhaps allowed Jesus
to live. After all, Jesus preached peace, not rebellion. A living Jesus
might have become a great rabbi and advanced the cause of
Judaism—but then Christianity would not have existed.

Likewise, Holy Roman Emperor Charles V could have sent Martin Luther to the stake for heresy, but due to political commitments
to Frederick of Saxony, Luther's patron, Charles allowed the renegade monk to escape. Had Luther been executed, Protestantism
might have remained a minor cult in a largely Catholic world.

But religion isn't the only stumbling block to diplomacy. In 1443,
a blunder by the Ming emperor of China changed the world forever.
Admiral Zheng's gigantic fleet had explored everywhere from China
to Africa. It was poised to explore Europe and, eventually, the

Americas. But a dispute in the Ming court caused the emperor to forbid any further voyages, break up the fleet, and finance agrarian programs instead—and for 500 years China was a land of peasant farmers, exploited by its neighbors.

World War I

"The War to End All Wars" featured some great diplomatic blunders. Preceding the war in 1908, Kaiser Wilhelm II gave an interview to the *Daily Telegraph* newspaper in an attempt to improve British-German relations. Instead, he managed to offend the British, annoy the Russians and French, and imply that the build-up of the German navy was targeted against Japan. All four of those nations would go to war against Germany six years later.

Another of the war's goofs was the Zimmerman Telegram, sent by Germany, offering a chunk of the American Southwest to Mexico for attacking the United States. However, the telegraph cable routed through London. The British read the telegram and passed it on to the enraged Americans. The telegram, coupled with the sinking of the passenger ship *Lusitania,* pushed America into the war.

But Germany's biggest diplomatic foul-up was to send the dangerous agitator Vladimir Lenin in a sealed railway car from Switzerland to St. Petersburg in an attempt to destabilize the Russian war effort. It worked far better than ever intended—Lenin became the leader of the Bolsheviks, led the Russian Revolution, and became the first head of the USSR. Germany did get its intended result of Russia pulling out of the war, but the unintended consequence of this German act came much later—28 years later—when Soviet troops marched into Berlin during the next war.

World War II

Britain and France were far less concerned about Adolf Hitler and his remilitarization of Germany than they should've been. The führer clearly intended to expand his country's borders, and he did so with little resistance. Going against the Versailles Treaty that ended World War I, Germany annexed Austria in 1938. Franco-British apathy encouraged Hitler to go further, seeking to take over a part of Czechoslovakia called the Sudetenland. To keep a lid on potential conflict, Britain and France signed the Munich Agreement with Germany, granting the territory to the Third Reich. British Prime

Minister Neville Chamberlain triumphantly returned to London, proclaiming "peace in our time." Well, peace for another 11 months, anyway, until German tanks rolled into Poland in September 1939.

France based much of its foreign policy on a chain of forts called the Maginot Line. The line was considered impregnable—until the Germans just went around the end of the chain.

Adolf Hitler allied with Benito Mussolini, who not only couldn't hold up his end of the war effort but also dragged the Germans into Africa, Yugoslavia, and Greece and weakened the Russian campaign. Finally, Hitler had to rescue Mussolini from his own troops.

Blunders in the Modern Age

After World War II, Chiang Kai-Shek's army had driven the Communists under Mao Zedong into Manchuria. They were about to destroy the Reds when American Chief of Staff George C. Marshall persuaded Chiang to enter into peace talks with the wily Mao. This gave the Reds time to regroup and retake mainland China.

When the French were losing in Vietnam, they asked President Dwight Eisenhower for help. He sent weapons and B-29 strikes, but the French effort failed. The United States somehow wound up continuing the war.

In 1962, Nikita Khrushchev called Chairman Mao an "old boot" (for his toughness), but the Chinese word for *boot* also means "prostitute." Mao thought he was being called an old whore, which started a split between China and Russia.

To defeat the Russians in Afghanistan, America armed and equipped the Taliban, including Osama bin Laden.

Diplomats still commit blunders every day; even small ones are not insignificant. When the president of Romania dined at the Pentagon in October 2003, U.S. officials put flags on the table: American—and Russian. It's an easy mistake—after all, Romania is next to Russia on the list of nations.

In another example, President George W. Bush, attempting to placate the Russians in 2007 about the construction of a U.S. missile base in the Czech Republic, invited Russian troops to be stationed there—without asking the Czechs.

Diplomacy is said to be the art of the possible. But if it's possible to win your opponents over, it's also possible to make blunders.

Fumbling Felons

Now It Can Be Told

In 2003, a jewelry heist occurred at a department store in Temecula, California. Two armed men and a getaway driver all got away—until the driver got in touch with his inner muse. In 2005, Colton Simpson published a memoir, *Inside the Crips: Life Inside L.A.'s Most Notorious Gang.* Touting its author as the mastermind, Colton's book described details uncannily similar to the actual jewelry heist. Colton discussed waiting outside while two others robbed the store and the fact that he scouted out the jewelry section two days prior. As a result of California's "Three Strikes You're Out" law, Colton received 126 years in prison for his literary spirit!

Do You Have Change for a Bill?

Since 1969, the largest U.S. bill in circulation is the $100 bill. Despite this fact, on October 6, 2007, a man walked into a Pittsburgh supermarket and attempted to pay for his purchase with a one-million-dollar bill! When the cashier refused to accept it and the store manager confiscated the bill, the customer flew into a rage. He was subsequently held in the county jail.

Sorry, Wrong Number

A man in Escatawpa, Mississippi, intended to call the local TV station after watching a news story. Angry, he apparently wanted to complain about not receiving a FEMA trailer after Hurricane Katrina. Meaning to dial 411 for the station's number, the man accidentally dialed 911. Panicking, he hung up on the dispatcher. The dispatcher, concerned, requested police to check if anyone needed assistance. When police arrived at the address from where the phone call was made, no one answered the door. Thinking the residents might be in trouble, police broke in and found the 56-year-old caller and four others in a full methamphetamine lab.

Next Time, Carry a Flashlight

A burglar broke into a German sports club around 3:00 A.M. Needing to see what he was about to steal, he turned on the first light switch he could find. That turned on the floodlights and sprinkler system for the football field outside. The groundskeeper for the sports club could see the light from his nearby home and immediately contacted the police. The man was quickly arrested.

T. S. Eliot's *The Waste Land*

Genuine poetry can communicate before it is understood.
—*T. S. Eliot*

Thomas Stearns Eliot was born in 1888 to a wealthy St. Louis, Missouri, family. He attended Harvard University and eventually settled in England, where he studied philosophy and literature. Eliot has often been described as an unusually intellectual poet, an epithet that is particularly suited—Eliot studied Latin, Greek, French, German, and Sanskrit; he was an expert on the religions and cultures of the world; and he was a philosopher and literary critic extraordinaire. Yes, that all sounds pretty intellectual. In fact, Eliot's intimidating mind may help to explain why his works often received a frigid reception from literary critics.

European Classicism via American Poet

On the other hand, perhaps people were simply perplexed by what some have perceived to have been Eliot's identity crises. In 1927, Eliot officially converted to English Anglicanism and dropped his American citizenship to become a British subject. In 1928, he described himself as a "classicist in literature, royalist in politics, and Anglo-Catholic in religion."

Universality via Specificity

Eliot may have transformed himself from a rugged American into a cross-bearing, king-hailing Brit, but through poetry he sought to express the universal beauty and tragedy of the human condition. He did this by way of intentional confusion, contradiction, irony, and obscurity. If this seems paradoxical, take heart, and read on.

Eliot's most famous poem, *The Waste Land,* is a perfect example of his delicious illusiveness. It's dense and difficult to understand. The five-part, 433-line poem was written between 1919 and 1922. Most of it was composed in Switzerland, where Eliot was "resting" after a nervous breakdown.

The poem is traditionally analyzed as an ode to the disillusionment that followed World War I. Indeed, much of *The Waste Land* contrasts the chaos and physical ugliness of modernity with the beauty and principled glory of the classical and medieval past. The poem alludes to or directly quotes such antiquated figures as Homer, Virgil, Ovid, and Dante, as well as such modern figures as Joseph Conrad, Aldous Huxley, and Walt Whitman. But the analysis of the poem as an affirmation of modern hopelessness is disputed by many scholars.

Despite the poem's references to specific people and ideas, Eliot never intended a direct relationship between signified and signifier. Rather, he hoped to use his labyrinth of layered language to evoke a feeling that is greater than the sum of his words. *The Waste Land* was not a straightforward slogan for the disillusionment of a generation. Eliot once quipped, "I may have expressed for them their own illusion of being disillusioned, but that did not form part of my intention."

Clarity via Ambiguity

So, if *The Waste Land* resists its classical interpretations, then what exactly is it about? It turns out that this question may not have an answer. Frustrated critics have accused Eliot of intentionally creating an impenetrable poem. Eliot did include notes at the end of the poem to explain his bottomless grab bag of allusions, quotes, and references. Yet, he slyly neglected to footnote many allusions, and in some cases made his explanatory notes more confusing than the citation they were meant to elucidate.

Eliot saw poetry as a tool that could partially uncover the true order of the universe. But he also knew that words are imperfect. In *The Waste Land,* Eliot resorted to surface contradiction, unexpected changes in voice, jumps in time, intentionally misplaced satire, shifts into foreign languages, and half-understood allusion, believing that these devices were ironically the only way one could achieve poetic depth and clarity. Avid fans of *The Waste Land* profess that even if they don't quite get the poem in its entirety, they value the strong feelings that its words conjure. The intent of *The Waste Land* is best described by the author himself, who once famously stated, "Poetry may make us from time to time a little more aware of the deeper, unnamed feelings which form the substratum of our being, to which we rarely penetrate."

Fast Facts

- Marilyn Monroe loved to read Tolstoy and other classic writers. In fact, while she was under contract at 20th Century Fox Studios, she was enrolled at UCLA, studying literature.

- English King George IV was so obese that it took hours for him to put on a corset. His attendants also used pulleys to place him on his horse.

- The phrase "Often a bridesmaid but never a bride" comes from an advertisement for Listerine that first appeared in 1925 and ran for more than ten years.

- Covering all the angles, journalist George Plimpton played football with the Detroit Lions and hockey with the Boston Bruins, and he sparred with boxers Archie Moore and Ray Robinson. He recounted his experience with the Lions in a book, Paper Lion, which was later made into a movie.

- In Victorian times, women's swimsuits weighed ten pounds or more when wet. They were almost always meant to be worn with a tightly laced corset beneath them.

- One of the first incidents of biological warfare occurred in the Crimean city of Caffa in A.D. 1346. The Tatars besieging it catapulted plague-infested bodies into the city.

- Charles Babbage, who created the basic design of the computer, also invented the cowcatcher, the device on a train used to remove obstacles from the tracks.

- Paper money isn't necessarily made of wood pulp. In the United States, it's 75 percent cotton and 25 percent linen.

- President George Washington died on December 14, 1799, probably due to suffocation from a swollen epiglottis. He requested that his body be laid out for three days because of a fear of premature burial.

Nixon and Mao

"If there is anything I want to do before I die,"
President Richard Nixon told Time *magazine in*
early October 1970, "it is to go to China."

By the end of 1970, President Nixon had ended the Chinese-protested Cambodian incursion and was eager to find a resolution to the Vietnam War. Ensconced in Washington, he wanted to reach out to the Chinese Communist party, which had been in power for a little more than 20 years.

At the time, there was a major gulf between the two countries: America continued to recognize the Republic of China, now splintered literally and figuratively from China and headquartered in Taiwan. Nixon had a strong reputation as an anticommunist hard-liner. The People's Republic of China considered what it called "American imperialism" to be a great threat and viewed the United States as a dangerous enemy. Chairman Mao, leader of the People's Republic of China, was also growing increasingly concerned about the Soviet Union. Border disputes and disagreement over the proper approach to communism fueled the atmosphere of mistrust. Likewise, relations between the United States and the Soviet Union consisted of fear and suspicion—it seemed a nuclear World War III could break out at any moment.

Ping-Pong Leads the Way

Elsewhere in Asia, Japan was hosting a competition that would settle, for another year at least, the burning question of which country produced the greatest ping-pong players. That's right, the 31st World Table Tennis Championship took place in April 1971 and figured into political history. The United States sent its finest table-tennis players to Japan to compete in the tournament. After a practice match, a flashy American player by the name of Glenn Cowan missed the U.S. team bus and was left at the training area with no ride. He was offered a seat on the Chinese team bus and decided that it beat walking. On the bus, Chinese player—and three-time world champion—Zhuang Zedong gave the American player a silk-screen print. Several days later, China invited the American team to mainland China, where they played some matches and toured the Great Wall. This was the most interaction the two countries had experienced since the Chinese Communist party had taken power in 1949.

Disputes over the Soviet-Chinese border, as well as Soviet support for India in a Chinese-Indian border issue, fueled the growing gulf between the communists in China and those in the Soviet Union. Recognizing the unique opportunity, the Nixon administration dispatched National Security Adviser Henry Kissinger on a secret trip to Beijing in the hopes of arranging a meeting between Nixon and Mao. The Chinese were surprised to find America reaching out to them, but concerned about potential Russian aggression and eager to resolve the Taiwan issue, they knew that better relations with the United States would be advantageous. They were unwilling, however, to make the first gesture. The question resolved itself a few months after Kissinger's journey to Beijing, when in late February 1972, Nixon became the first U.S. president to visit the People's Republic of China. This unprecedented meeting of ideological enemies stunned the world.

Only Nixon Could Go to China

Nixon went to China with the goal of opening the door for normalized relations. He was trying to negotiate an end to the Vietnam War and wanted assurances that China would not interfere. He also hoped to stem the flow of weapons and aid from the Soviets through China to Vietnam. Aware of the growing tension between China and the Soviet Union, Nixon believed that better relations with China would put the United States in an improved position to win the Cold War with the Soviet Union. In China, Mao was facing pressure from high-ranking members of the Chinese Communist party, and he saw the meeting with Nixon as a way to reaffirm his power and relevance.

Nixon's visit to China did open the door to better relations between the countries. Toward the end of the trip, a document was released that came to be known as the Shanghai Communiqué. It detailed the United States and China's shared interest in normalizing relations and made a statement that, despite the continued existence of the Republic of China in Taiwan, there was but one China.

The countries also shared sensitive intelligence regarding the Soviet Union and agreed not to use the threat of force in international relations. China made a gift to the American people of two pandas, the beloved Hsing Hsing and Ling Ling. Nixon returned the favor by giving the Chinese people two musk oxen. The pandas became the star attractions of the National Zoo in Washington, D.C. The oxen died of old age, and the U.S. government replaced them with a new pair.

Reaction at Home

Back in the United States, Nixon faced a backlash from his fellow conservatives, who favored a hard-line approach to China, especially regarding China's antagonism toward Taiwan. Nixon's secretary of state, William Rogers, had accompanied him on the China trip, but he felt snubbed by his lack of involvement in important meetings. Seeming more concerned with his image than with an improvement in relations between the two countries, Rogers began to stir things up, complaining to the press that the Shanghai Communiqué was too soft on the Taiwan issue. Despite this public-relations setback and the negative reactions from the hard-liners, most of America took a favorable view of Nixon's reaching out to China. He even drew praise from the Democratic-controlled Congress.

What started with an American ping-pong player missing a bus at the World Table Tennis Championships in Japan in 1971 was the beginning of a better relationship between two powerful and ideologically opposed nations. The wide-ranging ramifications of the famed Nixon-Mao meeting in the modern world include more than $300 billion in annual trade between the two countries and cross-cultural communication in every imaginable medium. And for the record: In the time since Nixon and Mao's meeting, a half-dozen world ping-pong champs have hailed from China, but the United States is still looking for its first.

- *The "Pig War" between the United States and Great Britain was fought over possession of the San Juan Islands off the coasts of Washington state and British Columbia. The 1859 confrontation was set off by the shooting of a pig.*

- *Fingernails grow faster than toenails.*

ſyllable ſecretſ: Word Historieſ

Wacky: Denoting "crazy" or "eccentric," this word made its debut in 1935 as a variant on late-1800s British slang *whacky*, which came from the idea of being struck sharply—or whacked—on the head once too often. *Wacko* came into being around 1975, whereas *wack*, urban slang for worthless or stupid, arrived in the late 1990s.

Pack rat: Interestingly, some believe that this word (meaning a person who can't or won't discard anything—a condition that can sometimes be a variant of an anxiety disorder), came from the North American bushy-tailed *woodrat*, a rodent that has a habit of dragging objects back to its home and packing them in. But that meaning only came into usage around 1885, whereas the use of *pack rat* for human hoarders dates to 1850. So, either the rat's name is really older than the dictionary claims, or the reference to humans was the original.

Beehive: A mound of heavily lacquered hair teased and piled atop the head was dubbed the *beehive* in 1960 (the hairstyle had been around for at least the previous two years and been called a *bouffant*, from the Middle French present participle *bouffer*, which means "to puff" or "puffed out"). Audrey Hepburn had a version in 1961's *Breakfast at Tiffany's*. The 1970s pop-rock group the B-52s sported similar hairdos (*B-52* is another slang name for the style, given its resemblance to the bulbous nose of the bomber airplane), and British singer Amy Winehouse has something of the modern equivalent.

Miniskirt: Its original creator may have been French designer André Courrèges or British fashion pioneer Mary Quant (both claim credit, but Quant is more responsible for popularizing the style), but this small garment, with its well-above-the knee hemline, was first identified in 1965.

IOU: Believe it or not, it's nothing more than the obvious pun on "I owe you," but it goes all the way back to 1618.

Hunk: In 1813, this originally meant "large piece cut off," probably from the western Flemish *hunke* ("of bread and meat"). However, in reference to an "attractive, sexually appealing man," it was first heard in 1945 (four years earlier in Australian slang).

The Spanish *Dracula*

❖ ❖ ❖ ❖

Bela Lugosi has indelibly made his stamp on the character Dracula.
But another version of the story was shot alongside the classic film.

In director Tod Browning's 1931 *Dracula*, Bela Lugosi masterfully
captured the fiendish essence of the count, a role he reprised from
Broadway. Often described as the definitive *Dracula,* the film is considered a classic largely due to Lugosi's unnerving portrayal of the
renowned vampire. Many of its fans, however, have likely missed the
Spanish-language version, shot by night on the very same set.

Parallel Pictures

Studios of the time believed international filmgoers would be cheated if
English-language films were dubbed
into other languages. Instead,
alternative-language editions
were often filmed alongside
their English-language counterparts. Traditionally, the
resulting films were of lesser
quality, due to small budgets, short
shooting schedules, and lack of big-
name talent. Yet many devotees have dubbed George Melford's
Spanish *Dracula* more artistically sound than Browning's film.

The Spanish *Dracula,* also released in 1931, featured Latin actor
Carlos Villarías and voluptuous Lupita Tovar in the female lead. The
acting chops of these actors have been questioned, but the eye-
popping expressiveness of the cast makes up for in passion what
might be lacking in technique. Also, while Browning was said to
have run a rather chaotic set, Melford had access to Browning's
dailies and could smooth over the bumps that plagued the daytime
Dracula set.

The Spanish version of *Dracula* ran nearly 30 minutes longer
than the English version due to elements Melford added at night to
perfect the concepts put forth by Browning during the day.

Strange Justice

Swept Under the Carpet
Two carpet layers were doing their job in a basement when a hot-water heater kicked on, igniting a nearby three-and-a-half gallon container of carpet adhesive and severely burning the men. Apparently, cautionary statements on the can's label such as "Flammable" and "Keep Away from Heat" meant nothing to them. They filed a lawsuit against the adhesive company, claiming the warnings on the label weren't sufficient. A jury agreed—the men received $8 million for their ignorance.

Seeking the "Plane" Truth
A prominent food company ran a promotion offering all sorts of prizes to contestants who collected points by buying the company's products. A TV commercial emphasized the magnitude of the prizes by showing a full-size fighter jet and flashing "7,000,000 points" on the screen. One clever participant accrued the 7,000,000 points and filed suit for fraud when the company refused to award the jet. A judge ruled that no "reasonable person" could believe a company would actually offer a $22 million jet in exchange for seven million points and dismissed the case.

Barefoot Book Boy Banned
A young man seeking knowledge entered an Ohio library shoeless and was turned away, as the library's policy required patrons to wear shoes. For the next four years, the man tried to enter the library barefoot only to be sent away. Fed up, library officials finally handed the man a banning for one day. He filed a lawsuit, claiming his First Amendment rights had been violated. The suit was denied—first by a federal district court and then by a court of appeals, which noted that the safety of the public, as well as the individual's feet, was at risk.

I Saw It First!
After-holiday sales often result in spirited shopping, as customers compete for bargains. Sometimes too spirited. In one case, two women grabbed the same crystal figurine bears at the same time, which turned into a fight. One of the women sued the store, saying they should have protected her from other customers. Her husband also sued, claiming loss of income, "company and consortium" due to the incident. Seeking $600,000 in damages, the couple was disappointed when the lower court and court of appeals each turned the suit down.

Rocky Marciano Retires Undefeated

*This heavyweight boxing champ achieved a
feat no one else has ever managed.*

Born on September 1, 1923, in Brockton, Massachusetts, Rocco
Francis Marchegiano was the heavyweight champion of the world
from 1952 to 1956. To this day, with 43 knockouts to his credit, he
remains the only heavyweight champion in boxing history to retire
without a defeat or a draw.

Solid as a Rock
When he was a year old, Rocky Marciano survived a near-fatal bout
of pneumonia. This was perhaps the first evidence of the strength
and resilience that led him to spend his childhood and young adulthood wrestling and playing baseball and football. He worked out on
homemade weight-lifting equipment, including a makeshift heavy
bag formed from an old mailbag that hung from a tree in his back-
yard. He dropped out of high school in tenth grade and worked as a
ditchdigger, sold shoes, and found employment at a coal company.

In 1943, Marciano was drafted into the army, where he spent two
years ferrying supplies across the English Channel to Normandy.
During his stint in the military, Marciano won the 1946 amateur
armed forces boxing tournament. He ended his amateur year with
an 11–3 record—the last time Marciano ever experienced a loss.

"Timmmberrr!"
In 1947, Marciano tried out for the Chicago Cubs baseball team but
was cut three weeks later. Subsequently, he turned professional in
the boxing ring. *Sports Illustrated* reported, "He was too short, too
light, and had no reach. . . . Rough and tough, but no finesse."

Marciano's hometown fans were believers, and they traveled in
groups to watch his fights. When Rocky had an opponent ready to
go down, they would yell, "Timmmberrr!" as they would for a falling
tree, and the audience would go wild.

Rocky catapulted to stardom in 1951, when he was pitted against
Joe Louis, his most formidable opponent and also his childhood

idol. The match, which was the last of Louis's career, was aired on national television. Marciano KO'd Louis in the eighth round—and later sobbed in Louis's dressing room after the fight.

The KO Kid

Marciano's trainer, Charley Goldman, taught Rocky his trademark technique—a short, overhand right to the jaw. This move served Marciano well when, in the 13th round against the defending heavyweight champion, lagging behind in points and struggling offensively, he suddenly KO'd Jersey Joe Walcott. The year was 1952.

Firmly established as a "marquee" fighter, Marciano went on to defend his title six times, including a first-round knockout victory in a 1953 rematch with Walcott and another knockout win over Roland La Starza later that year. With a left and a quick right to the jaw, Marciano won a decision against Ezzard Charles in 1954. But fans had a moment of panic when, in a rematch later that year, Marciano nearly lost his title in the sixth round. Charles cut Marciano's nose so badly that his corner trainer couldn't stop the bleeding. When the ring doctor considered stopping the fight, Marciano erupted against Charles and knocked him out in the eighth round. Ding!

A year later, despite organized crime enticements to throw the fight, Rocky KO'd European champion Don Cockell in an exciting nine rounds. Marciano's last fight was in Yankee Stadium on September 21, 1955. He knocked out Archie Moore in the ninth round as more than 400,000 people watched over closed-circuit television.

The Rock

Marciano spent his retirement years working as a boxing show host and commentator and making personal appearances. He died at the age of 46 when a small private plane he was riding in crashed into a tree as it attempted to land in Newton, Iowa.

Inducted into the Boxing Hall of Fame in 1990, Rocky Marciano was honored in 1999 on a commemorative U.S. postage stamp. Marciano lives on through a myriad of books, films, and of course, in the minds and hearts of fans.

And although he may not rank among the top five boxers of all time, one sportswriter summed Marciano up accurately: "If all the heavyweight champions of all time were locked together in a room, Marciano would be the only one to walk out."

Fast Facts

- *John D. Rockefeller's ambitions were to make $100,000 and live to be 100. He died 26 months shy of the century mark, but he left an estate worth $1.4 billion.*

- *On Christopher Columbus's fourth voyage to the new world, he saved the lives of his crew by convincing Jamaican natives that he made the moon disappear during a lunar eclipse in 1504.*

- *Prior to about the 1920s, underarm hair on women was generally no big deal. The invention of the safety razor and the acceptance of scantier clothing changed all that.*

- *Thanks to measurements provided by the satellite-based Global Positioning System, Mount Everest's peak has been discovered to be an additional seven feet higher than previously believed. It is now known to be 29,035 feet tall.*

- *During the "Malayan Emergency" in the 1950s—also known as the Malayan War for Independence—British forces relied on head-hunters from Borneo to track guerrilla movements.*

- *About half of us fold our toilet paper neatly or wrap it around our fingers before using it. A little more than 30 percent of us bunch it. The rest do both.*

- *Chris Klug, a snowboarder who received a new liver in 2000, is the only athlete to compete in the Olympic Games after undergoing an organ transplant.*

- *The only time in its history when the United States had five living ex-presidents was from January 2001 to June 2004. The former heads of state included Gerald Ford, Jimmy Carter, Ronald Reagan, George H. W. Bush, and Bill Clinton.*

- *Well over half of all cat owners admit to singing and dancing for the benefit of their kitties.*

Henry Ford and the Automobile Empire

Founded in 1903, the Ford Motor Company was an extremely innovative manufacturer. Henry Ford is known as the father of the modern assembly line used in mass production, and his Model T automobile revolutionized transportation in America and around the world.

Born in Dearborn, Michigan, Henry Ford developed an early dislike of farm life. Looking for a different kind of future, he took a job as an engineer with the Edison Illuminating Company in 1891. Two years later, he completed his own self-propelled vehicle, which he called the Quadricycle. Ford's second car, the 999, drove one mile in 39.4 seconds—that's 91.4 mph, a new land speed record at the time.

Unsurprisingly, the development of the 999 inspired Ford to found the Ford Motor Company.

In 1908, Ford introduced the Model T, a car that featured such innovations as the left-sided steering wheel along with an enclosed engine and transmission. The Model T's best selling points were that it was easy to drive and easy to repair. Its original price of $825 fell substantially when Ford introduced the continuous moving assembly belt in all of his plants—after that, the basic touring car cost $360. By 1912, there were 7,000 Ford dealerships in the United States; by 1918, half of all cars sold in America were Model Ts.

Payday

During this time, Ford introduced a significant change in his factories that would forever alter the American workforce: the welfare capitalism program. Ford reduced his employees' workday from nine to eight hours and doubled their salaries from $2.34 to $5.00 per day.

Though he was sharply criticized by Wall Street, Ford defended the move, claiming that not only did the $5.00 workday alleviate Ford's employee turnover problem, but it also allowed his workers to afford the cars they were building, thus boosting the economy.

World War I was a turbulent time for Ford. He was denounced by the Anti-Defamation League for owning an anti-Semitic newspaper, *The Independent.* After several libel lawsuits, he stopped its presses for good in 1927. Adolf Hitler, who was fascinated by automobiles, hung Ford's picture on his wall.

Rolling Along

By 1927, all steps in Ford's manufacturing process—from refining raw materials to final assembly of the auto—took place at the vast Rouge plant in his hometown of Dearborn, Michigan. At capacity, this plant employed more than 81,000 people and became the world's largest industrial complex. Ford's dream of producing a vehicle from scratch without reliance on foreign trade became a reality. Two years later, Henry had successful dealerships on six continents; by 1932, Ford was producing one-third of the world's cars.

In 1938, Ford turned over the running of the day-to-day business to his son, Edsel Ford. Edsel's unexpected death five years later brought Henry out of retirement until he ceded the presidency to his 28-year-old grandson Henry Ford II in 1945.

Ford died two years later, and Henry Ford II ran the company until 1982. In 1999, the company came full circle when 41-year-old William Ford, Jr., became chairman.

Little-Known Facts About Ford

• Ford was one of the early backers of the Indianapolis 500.

• Ford helped develop charcoal briquettes under his brother-in-law's name: E. G. Kingsford. Kingsford charcoal used wood scraps from the Ford auto factories to make the briquettes.

• Ford was especially close to Thomas Edison. When Edison was on his deathbed, Ford demanded that Edison's son catch his final breath in a test tube. This tube can still be found today in the Henry Ford Museum.

• Ford held 161 U.S. patents.

FROM THE VAULTS OF HISTORY

At Least There's Not a Lien on It
The Leaning Tower of Pisa is a bell tower built more than 800 years ago in Pisa, Italy. Currently, the top of the building hangs out over its base by about 16 feet! The tower's lean fluctuates seasonally, depending upon soil moisture beneath the base of the giant structure. Despite the architect's intention to build a vertical tower, it began leaning soon after construction in 1173 due to a poor foundation. There is no record of when the first tourist arrived to gawk at it.

Really Snail-Mail
The oldest message in a bottle that has ever been found spent 92 years and 229 days at sea. The bottle was released on April 25, 1914, in the Norwegian Sea northeast of the Shetland Islands of Scotland. On December 10, 2006, that same bottle was found only about a mile away from the spot where it first went into the water. It was rescued by a fisher named Mark Anderson of Bixter, a village on the Shetland Islands.

Older Than Dirt
The oldest living animal in recorded history is a clam. Nicknamed Ming, for the time period in which it was born, the clam sat in the Atlantic Ocean off the coast of Iceland. Much like the age of a tree is calculated, scientists counted the growth rings on the clam's shell to determine its age. Most clams live around 200 years if undisturbed, but Ming lived a lot longer—405 years—until a dredging team scooped it up.

Not an Easy Target
Ahmet Zogolli was elected president of Albania in 1925. He was crowned king in 1928, becoming King Zog. During his lifetime, he survived 55 assassination attempts. One 1931 effort in Vienna was thwarted when the king drew his own pistol and returned fire against the would-be assassin.

Based on a True Fake

*When movies try to depict fact, it's almost inevitable that
a little bit (or a lot) of fiction will get in the way.*

The problem with movies that claim to be based on a true story is
not the definition of *true*—it's the definition of *based on.* Movies
tend to take some parts of a particular event or story and focus on
them—thereby exaggerating their importance and relevance—while
ignoring other circumstances completely. Here are a few examples.

A Beautiful Mind
John Nash is a mathematician whose work in game theory earned
him a 1994 Nobel Prize in Economics. He attended Princeton
University and worked on his equilibrium theory. After earning a
doctorate in 1950, he continued to work on his thesis, part of which
became the Nash Equilibrium. In 1951, he was hired as a member
of the MIT mathematics faculty. In 1957, he married Alicia Lopez-
Harrison de Lardé, and shortly after that, he was admitted to a
mental hospital for schizophrenia. The couple had a son in 1959
but divorced in 1963. They became friendly again in 1970, renewed
their romantic relationship in 1994, and remarried in 2001.

But in the movie *A Beautiful Mind,* Nash is plagued by schizophrenia throughout his education at Princeton. He struggles to
maintain relationships with his classmates but flourishes as he
discovers various mathematical theories. He is also asked by the
government to decode covert Soviet messages. He gets married
and has a son but is slowly eaten up by his schizophrenia until he's
hospitalized. Through the love of his wife and his own strength of
will, however, he becomes an award-winning recluse who is happily
accepted within the hallowed halls of higher education.

One catch is that Nash's true-life delusions were auditory, not
visual. Also, while the movie portrayed John and Alicia's marriage
as a tense one, it also portrayed it as continuous. There are at least
two more important changes the movie made to Nash's life: The pen
ceremony at Princeton never really happened, and Nash never gave
a rousing yet humble speech when he received his Nobel Prize.

Catch Me If You Can

Frank Abagnale was a con artist who passed bad checks during five years in the 1960s. He impersonated a pilot, a physician, an attorney, and a teacher. Once captured, Abagnale had the dubious distinction of having 26 countries with extradition orders against him. After serving in prison for his crimes, he founded Abagnale & Associates, a legitimate company that advises businesses on fraud.

In the movie, a lonely only child deals with his wacky dad and nervous mom, but in no time, he's on his way to New York, alone and fending for himself. This is where the story takes off into fraud and impersonations, with an FBI agent chasing Abagnale around the globe. In reality, no FBI agent chased Abagnale down. *Catch Me If You Can* follows Abagnale's life, which already seems pretty exaggerated, and exaggerates it even more. In the movie, Abagnale writes $10 million in bad checks; in reality the total was only $2.5 million. And Abagnale was never on the FBI's Ten Most Wanted list.

Finding Neverland

Scottish novelist and dramatist J. M. Barrie created Peter Pan. Barrie's traumatic childhood included the death of his brother and the withdrawal of his mother, crushed by her son's death. As an adult, Barrie moved to London, where he became a journalist, then a novelist, then a playwright. He became friends with the Llewelyn Davies family, who provided the inspiration for *Peter Pan*. Eventually, after the deaths of the boys' parents, Barrie ended up providing support for the sons of the family. Barrie died of pneumonia on June 19, 1937.

In the movie *Finding Neverland*, we're treated to the moment when Barrie meets and befriends the Llewelyn Davies children and their mother. The movie weaves the lives of Barrie and the family together, and those relationships provide the inspiration for *Peter Pan*. It's a sweet story but only a sliver of the real events.

The real Barrie had many literary friends, famous ones at that, and a prolific outpouring of books and plays. When the real Barrie initially met and befriended the Llewelyn Davies children, their father was alive; in the movie, he's already dead. In the film, there are four children; in reality, there were five. Most importantly, Barrie suffered from psychogenic dwarfism—he was 4' 10" tall. In the film, Barrie is played by Johnny Depp, who is significantly taller than that.

WHO KNEW?

Domino Theory
The World Championship Domino Tournament is held annually in Andalusia, Alabama. The two-day event, usually scheduled for early July, has been going strong since 1976. Prize money has been known to total as much as $500,000.

In the Cathedral and on the Court
In 2000, the world-famous Harlem Globetrotters exhibition basketball team visited the Vatican. After a parade in Rome celebrating their 75th anniversary, the team met with Pope John Paul II and named the pontiff an honorary Globetrotter. However, no photos were released of the Pope spinning a basketball on his finger.

You've Got to Be in It to Win It
Roberto Madrazo, former presidential candidate in Mexico, was proclaimed the winner of the 2007 Berlin marathon in the 55-and-older category. His time was 2:41:12. But upon closer examination, he appeared to have ran 15 kilometers (9.5 miles) in 21 minutes—faster than humanly possible. Madrazo apparently forgot about the microchip he was wearing, which lost track of him at two checkpoints. He was disqualified two weeks later. The politician later said that he'd finished the race after the 21st kilometer and drove to the finish line to get some clothes he had left there. He didn't explain why he pumped his fists in apparent victory as he crossed the finish line or why he didn't immediately correct marathon officials when they named him the winner.

Take a Bite Out of Crime
In 1996 there were 1,102 reports of people being bitten by other people in New York City. If anyone assumes there must have been something in the water in 1996 and that those were isolated incidents, they'd be wrong. Every year in New York, approximately 1,600 people are bitten by other people. Apparently 1996 was a slow year.

Timing Is Everything
The last original *Peanuts* comic strip was published on February 13, 2000. This was slated to be *Peanuts* creator Charles M. Schulz's farewell strip. Ironically, Schulz died only hours before the morning paper carrying this comic strip was to be delivered.

It's a Bird! It's a Plane! It's...Avrocar?!?

Not all UFOs are alien spaceships. One top-secret program was contracted out by the U.S. military to an aircraft company in Canada.

Oh, the 1950s—a time of sock hops, drive-in movies, and the Cold War between America and the Soviet Union, when each superpower waged war against the other in the arenas of scientific technology, astronomy, and politics. It was also a time when discussion of life on other planets was rampant, fueled by the alleged crash of an alien spaceship near Roswell, New Mexico, in 1947.

Watch the Skies

Speculation abounded about the unidentified flying objects (UFOs) spotted nearly every week by everyone from farmers to airplane pilots. As time passed, government authorities began to wonder if the flying saucers were, in fact, part of a secret Russian program to create a new type of air force. Fearful that such a craft would upset the existing balance of power, the U.S. Air Force decided to produce its own saucer-shape ship.

In 1953, the military contacted Avro Aircraft Limited of Canada, an aircraft manufacturing company that operated in Malton, Ontario, between 1945 and 1962. Project Silverbug was initially proposed simply because the government wanted to find out if UFOs could be manufactured by humans. But before long, both the military and the scientific community were speculating about its potential. Intrigued by the idea, designers at Avro—led by British aeronautical engineer John Frost—began working on the VZ-9-AV Avrocar. The round craft would have been right at home in a scene from the classic science fiction film *The Day the Earth Stood Still*. Security for the project was so tight that it probably generated rumors that America was actually testing a captured alien spacecraft—speculation that remains alive and well even today.

Of This Earth

By 1958, the company had produced two prototypes, which were 18 feet in diameter and 3.5 feet tall. Constructed around a large triangle, the Avrocar was shaped like a disk, with a curved upper surface. It included an enclosed 124-blade turbo-rotor at the center of the triangle, which provided lifting power through an opening in the bottom of the craft. The turbo also powered the craft's controls. Although conceived as being able to carry two passengers, in reality a single pilot could barely fit inside the cramped space. The Avrocar was operated with a single control stick, which activated different panels around the ship. Airflow issued from a large center ring, which was controlled by the pilot to guide the craft either vertically or horizontally.

The military envisioned using the craft as "flying Jeeps" that would hover close to the ground and move at a maximum speed of 40 mph. But that, apparently, was only going to be the beginning. Avro had its own plans, which included not just commercial Avrocars, but also a family-size Avrowagon, an Avrotruck for larger loads, Avroangel to rush people to the hospital, and a military Avropelican, which, like a pelican hunting for fish, would conduct surveillance for submarines.

But Does It Fly?

The prototypes impressed the U.S. Army enough to award Avro a $2 million contract. Unfortunately, the Avrocar project was canceled when an economic downturn forced the company to temporarily close and restructure. When Avro Aircraft reopened, the original team of designers had dispersed. Further efforts to revive the project were unsuccessful, and repeated testing proved that the craft was inherently unstable. It soon became apparent that whatever UFOs were spotted overhead, it was unlikely that they came from this planet. Project Silverbug was abandoned when funding ran out in March 1961, but one of the two Avrocar prototypes is housed at the U.S. Army Transportation Museum in Fort Eustis, Virginia.

Say It Ain't So

Myth: Penguins, attempting to watch airplanes flying overhead, will fall over backwards in efforts to keep their eyes on the soaring sight.

Truth: One could easily envision the waddle-prone creatures toppling over onto their backs while excitedly eyeballing the whir of an airplane overhead. However, there is no truth at all to this silly penguin myth. Penguins, the nervous-nellies that they are, will typically run and hide from the frightening, loud noises of a plane in flight.

Myth: Drivers of red automobiles receive more speeding tickets than do drivers of any other color car.

Truth: Actually, white car owners typically receive the most tickets. Statistically, white cars make up a greater share of the car population, so the heightened instances of white car pullovers would make sense. Red car pullover rates, too, run proportional to the red car share of the car population. It is actually gray cars that, proportional to their share of the overall car population, are pulled over at surprisingly high rates.

Myth: Be careful of cats. They will suck the breath right out of babies!

Truth: As many cat owners can attest, some feline pets do seem inexplicably drawn to their owners' faces in the bedtime hours. Waking up with a cat-hat is commonplace for many kitty parents. However, no instances of cat-on-child suffocation have ever proven true. Still, cats have sometimes been blamed for crib death. In one such 2000 case, the death of an infant was initially blamed on a supposed baby-breath-sucking cat. The innocent cat was exonerated, however, when a pathologist eventually linked the sudden death to non-feline-related causes.

Myth: Poinsettias, the popular holiday flowers, are poisonous.

Truth: Allowing a supposedly toxic flower to become such a traditional component of the holiday season seems crazy, but this rumor persists, nonetheless. Perhaps it is due to the word *poinsettia*'s auditory resemblance to *poison,* or maybe it's because of a few toxic plants that are in the poinsettia family tree. Whatever the reason, the myth of the poisonous flower has sent many a protective mom into a Christmastime tizzy.

Chicago's Green Mill

*A little bar on Chicago's North Side holds a
century's worth of history and lore.*

Chicago may be one of only a few contemporary American cities
where drink specials run all day long and bars serve liquor until
5:00 A.M., but in the 1920s, Prohibition reigned supreme—well,
sort of. The city has plenty of stories from this era: Just consider Al
Capone, Eliot Ness, and the St. Valentine's Day Massacre. But there
are few landmarks that still resonate with Chicago's mob heyday like
the Green Mill jazz club.

In 1910, Tom Chamales bought the club and turned it
into one of Chicago's swankiest establishments. In the
Roaring Twenties, one of Al Capone's mobster
cronies, "Machine Gun" Jack McGurn,
became a co-owner after a manager
hired him to "persuade" a popular
Green Mill performer not to take
his act to a competitor (and in this
instance, *persuade* meant "slice
his throat and cut his tongue").

Throughout the decades, the club has drawn a diverse crowd of
music lovers, mob aficionados, and locals looking for decently priced
drinks. Everyone from Charlie Chaplin to Frank Sinatra has partied
here. They might even have sat at the famed table where Al Capone
once watched both entrances, lest he needed to make a quick
getaway through the secret door behind the bar, which opened to a
tunnel that led to a nearby building.

Crowds come and go, but good music remains the same. To this
day the Green Mill is the go-to spot for jazz on Chicago's North
Side. Harry Connick, Jr., Branford Marsalis, and Brazilian jazz gui-
tarist Paulinho Garcia have all graced its stage.

In the 1980s, the Green Mill started one of the first poetry-slam
nights in the country, Uptown Poetry Slam (named for the local Chicago neighborhood). The Uptown Poetry Slam is still popular at the
Green Mill today, along with, of course, a full calendar of jazz.

Merger Mayhem! Or: How to Fail in Business Without Really Trying

*As many businesses find out, what appears to be
two plus two doesn't always equal four.*

Some business mergers don't turn out to be as feasible in reality as
they may sound in theory. But these failures shouldn't come as a
complete surprise: According to financial experts, 50 to 80 percent
of all business mergers fail.

K-Mart Holdings Company and Sears Roebuck

This merger had financial experts scratching their heads from the
get-go. K-Mart, already bankrupt, paid $11 billion for Sears—which
had its own share of financial troubles—to form a bastion against
giant competitor Wal-Mart. The merger, which was finalized in
2005, spurred a layoff of more than 500 Sears employees.

Daimler and Chrysler

It was the largest corporate takeover of 1998: Daimler/Benz bought
the Chrysler Group for $38 billion, forming the world's fifth-largest
automotive company. However, the company was hard-pressed to
make a profit, and the merger eventually failed. Daimler announced
plans in 2007 to sell Chrysler to Cerberus Capital Management, and
the partnership was dissolved.

AOL and Time Warner

The announcement that Internet giant AOL was going to buy media
giant Time Warner in 2000 to become AOL Time Warner brought
out the best satirical work of the top political cartoonists. A victim
of the Internet business bust, the merger turned out to be such a
debacle that today, even though AOL takes in more money than
Yahoo!, Amazon, and eBay combined, its stock is practically worthless. The biggest loser in the merger was AOL: Most Time Warner
divisions are still performing well. It wasn't long before the company quietly stopped using AOL at the beginning of its name and
reverted to simply Time Warner.

Fast Facts

- *Soviet leader Joseph Stalin had a webbed left foot, and his left arm was shorter than his right.*

- *Known for his victories as a singles and doubles tennis player at the U.S. Open and Wimbledon during the 1910s and '20s, R. Norris Williams also gained fame as a survivor of the* Titanic *disaster.*

- *British troops experienced one of their worst defeats at the Battle of Isandlwana on January 22, 1879. Roughly 25,000 Zulu warriors attacked a British camp, killing about 1,300 soldiers and leaving only 55 survivors.*

- *A person's body weighs about 50 times what his or her brain weighs. People share that same weight/brain ratio with mice.*

- *Neil Armstrong, the first man to walk on the moon, and Gene Cernan, the last astronaut to stroll on Earth's nearest neighbor (so far), both graduated from Purdue University.*

- *When cart and chariot congestion became unmanageable in Rome, Julius Caesar forbade vehicles from the city during the daytime.*

- *Carnivorous plants usually eat insects, although some have been known to catch frogs and small mammals.*

- *McMurdo Station, the Antarctic scientific outpost that has a winter population of fewer than 200 people, also has the world's southernmost, and coldest, ATM.*

- *The first president to command a six-figure salary was Harry S. Truman, whose annual stipend was increased from a mere $75,000 to $100,000 in 1949.*

- *The wingspan of a jumbo jet is longer than the first flight of the Wright brothers.*

Music's Wackiest Families

Some musicians claim that their rock band is like a family.
But what happens when the family is a rock band?

The Jacksons

Once upon a time in Gary, Indiana, there lived a couple named Joseph and Katherine Jackson. He worked in a steel mill, and she was a salesclerk. The couple had nine children, six boys and three girls. The boys showed an unusual talent for music from an early age, and in the 1960s the five oldest brothers—Jackie, Tito, Jermaine, Marlon, and Michael—began touring together as the Jackson 5.

The Jackson 5 was one of the biggest musical acts of the early 1970s. As they grew older, the siblings began to pursue solo careers. Michael and Jermaine, along with their sisters Rebbie and Janet, have achieved success as solo artists. Michael and Janet Jackson have 23 number-one singles between them.

It wasn't until the early '90s that whispers about the Jackson family turned into shouts of media scrutiny. In 1991, La Toya released her book *La Toya: Growing Up in the Jackson Family,* in which she portrays her father as a physically and sexually abusive monster who controlled his children and their careers. In 1993, Michael was accused of sexual molestation, and during the ensuing media circus, more Jackson family secrets began to leak out. It is perhaps fortunate for the Jackson clan that Michael's increasingly outlandish antics siphon media attention away from their endless family feuds.

The Osmonds

While the Jackson family takes the cake in both controversy and reconstructive surgery, the Osmond clan wins in the less exciting—but more amusing—category of pure cheesiness. The nine Osmond children grew up in Utah and were raised in the Church of Jesus Christ of Latter-day Saints. Five of the Osmond brothers—Alan, Wayne, Merrill, Jay, and Donny—toured the country throughout the '60s and '70s as the Osmond Brothers. The two oldest brothers, Virl and Tom, are deaf and did not perform.

The most famous Osmond siblings are Donny and Marie. There is no entertainment medium unknown to the Osmonds, who have released records; written books; and appeared in television shows, movies, documentaries, and even Broadway plays. Keeping true to her Mormon faith, Marie once turned down the role of Sandy in *Grease* because she felt that the movie was immoral.

Through all the hoopla, the Osmond family has mostly managed to steer clear of Jackson-esque controversy. This is not to say there are no skeletons in this family's closet: A 2001 TV movie, *Inside the Osmonds,* revealed that there was high tension, jealousy, and artistic conflict throughout the Osmonds' careers. Yet there is no real scandal to be found here—all Osmond siblings approved of the movie (youngest brother Jimmy was a producer!), and they were happy for their family to be portrayed in this complex light.

The Osmonds rounded out their square image in 2007, when they staged a 50th anniversary reunion tour in Las Vegas. In November 2007, the family patriarch passed away—George Osmond was survived by 9 children, 55 grandchildren, and 48 great-grandchildren.

The Osbournes

This is an "Os" of a different kind. In the realm of demons, goblins, and ghouls, people may find the scariest of America's musician families: the Osbournes. Ozzy Osbourne married wife Sharon in 1981 after he was kicked out of the heavy-metal band Black Sabbath because of his heavy drug and alcohol use. Sharon proceeded to clean Ozzy up and single-handedly launch his solo career, despite the fact that the couple was known for their drunken antics throughout the 1980s.

Ozzy often spoke of demonic voices in his head that told him to do bad things, and in 1989, he finally took heed. Responding to the voices' insistence that Sharon "had to die," Ozzy tried to strangle his wife. He later claimed to have no memory of the incident, while Sharon explained that "he was totally insane from all the drink and drugs he was doing, and well, these things happen." Ozzy is also known for biting the heads off of various animals, and one hazy day he shot all of his cats.

Someone at MTV had a feeling that this family could be ratings gold. The first season of the reality show *The Osbournes* debuted in

2002, featuring Ozzy, Sharon, and two of their three teenage children, Kelly and Jack. Ozzy and Sharon's eldest child, Aimee, refused to participate. The show ran for three years and enjoyed the highest ratings in MTV history. In 2002, it won an Emmy for Outstanding Reality Program. When Sharon signed the contract for the show's second season, she stipulated that MTV supply a lifetime of therapy for the family's pets.

A Whole New Dimension

Not until *The Osbournes* premiered was the world so thoroughly exposed to the skewed family life of famed musicians. Previously, fans had to read memoirs to reveal the hidden secrets of their favorite singers; now they simply have to tune in. A recent batch of reality television series appears to have been made in the interest of presenting the "admirable" family lives of their idols to America's youth:

- From 2003 to 2005, MTV aired *Newlyweds: Nick and Jessica,* which focused on the marriage of young pop singers Jessica Simpson and Nick Lachey. The couple divorced in 2006.

- From 2005 to 2006, MTV aired *Meet the Barkers,* featuring ex-Blink 182 drummer Travis Barker and his wife, Shanna Moakler. The couple filed for divorce in 2006.

- In 2005, UPN aired *Britney and Kevin: Chaotic,* which chronicled the relationship of pop singer Britney Spears and aspiring rapper Kevin Federline. The couple divorced in 2007.

It seems that reality is the new unreality—reality TV has a penchant for capturing the most unreal of lives, and only with such programming could this fairy tale come full circle: In 2007, the Jackson family announced that they will host their own reality show, an *American Idol*–esque competition that will seek out music's next big family act.

- *Before lipstick cases were invented in about 1915, lipstick came wrapped in paper.*

- *The first electric vacuum cleaner was invented by a janitor in Canton, Ohio, in 1907.*

PALINDROMES

When you've got a word, phrase, or sentence that reads the same backward and forward, you've got a palindrome!

No, it is open on one position.

Swap God for a janitor? Rot in a jar of dog paws!

Are we not drawn onward, we few, drawn onward to new era?

Delia sailed as a sad Elias ailed.

gnu dung

Stab nail at ill Italian bats.

Lager, sir, is regal.

Sore was I ere I saw Eros.

Are we not pure? "No sir!" Panama's moody Noriega brags. "It is garbage!" Irony dooms a man; a prisoner up to new era.

Denim axes examined.

Ma is as selfless as I am.

Ed, I saw Harpo Marx ram Oprah W. aside.

Yawn a more Roman way!

"Some deer fees!" I say as I see free demos.

Ah, Satan sees Natasha.

But sad Eva saved a stub.

I prefer pi.

Kodak ad OK!

Amen, I call a cinema.

"My gym tasks are too lonely?" a Jay Leno looter asks at my gym.

A coup d'etat saved devastated Puoca.

Naomi, did I moan?

Was it a bar or a bat I saw?

The Golden Age of New York Publishing

The 1940s, 1950s, and 1960s were the golden years of America's publishing industry, and New York was the vital center of the book world. The great New York houses— Random House, Simon & Schuster, Doubleday, and Alfred A. Knopf—rose like temples of art in Manhattan.

Shortly after World War II, American readers entered a wonderland of books and literature. Back from the battlefields and factories of the war streamed writers eager to make their mark on a publishing industry revitalized by peace. Robert Penn Warren earned the 1947 Pulitzer Prize for Literature for *All the King's Men.* Also in 1946, John Hersey published *Hiroshima,* and Dr. Benjamin Spock invaded the nursery with *Baby and Child Care.*

The Postwar Boom

Readers haunted libraries and bookstores to see what new pronouncements of taste came from the giant publishers. Hopeful writers, like pilgrims, flocked to New York to try to join their congregations. Radio was pedestrian, television was in its infancy, and movies tried too hard to appeal to everyone—but books brought art and the craft of storytelling into every home.

Fresh from combat in the Philippines came a 25-year-old soldier named Norman Mailer, who became the enfant terrible of the book world with the 1948 release of his novel *The Naked and the Dead.* Emblematic of the Golden Age, Mailer was a boozer, brawler, and wild man; yet, he pioneered new forms of both fiction and nonfiction. In the profanity-shy world of American letters, he stayed true to the gritty world of GIs by coining the word *fug.*

Other novels that sprung forth from the war experience included James A. Michener's Pulitzer Prize–winning *Tales of the South Pacific,* Irwin Shaw's *The Young Lions,* John Hersey's *The Wall,* and Herman Wouk's *The Caine Mutiny.* On the nonfiction shelf were Dwight Eisenhower's *Crusade in Europe* and Samuel Eliot Morison's monumental 15-volume *United States Naval Operations in World War II.*

Changes in the 1950s

With the 1951 publication of J. D. Salinger's *The Catcher in the Rye* came the "Years of the Disaffected." Ray Bradbury's *The Martian Chronicles* and *Fahrenheit 451* heralded the birth of new forms of science fiction that replaced rockets and ray guns with troubling questions about human nature. The Beats—Jack Kerouac, Lawrence Ferlinghetti, Allen Ginsberg, William S. Burroughs—arrived, and in 1955 Mailer cofounded the newspaper *The Village Voice*.

By 1955, the United States had 8,420 public libraries, and the "Pyramids of Park Avenue" were doing their best to keep them stocked. Emerging literary titans, including Truman Capote, Gore Vidal, Grace Metalious, and Ayn Rand, were feted at lavish New York parties and had their exploits detailed in the newspapers.

From Vidal's *A Visit to a Small Planet* to Neville Shute's chilling *On the Beach* (both 1957), the Cold War infected writers, and science fiction flew high with the voices of Isaac Asimov, Philip K. Dick, Harlan Ellison, and Kurt Vonnegut.

Readers Become Distracted

By 1960, disparate forces began to put the squeeze on Park Avenue publishing. Television developed into a force for change and drew people away from their reading lamps. A booming resurgence of European publishing snatched up new authors and sent their works directly to American bookstores. In Russia, the complete works of Tolstoy were released in 90 volumes, and Boris Pasternak's *Dr. Zhivago* took the West by storm. In New York and throughout the country, authors could—and did—appear on television. Mailer carried out a celebrated and entertaining feud with Vidal on the talk shows. Mailer also made the news by stabbing (almost fatally) his then-wife at a drunken party in 1960.

Mailer was the poster child for unpredictable self-promotion. He had something to say about everything. He called poetry "a natural activity" and said that a poem is not written, but "a poem comes to one." Technology, on the other hand, was "insidious, debilitating, depressing." He never owned a typewriter, let alone a computer, and wrote 1,500 words a day with a pen. But in the 1960s, he pioneered a new form of nonfiction that combined events, autobiography, and commentary with his books *Presidential Papers, An American*

Dream, Why Are We in Vietnam?, Armies of the Night (1969 Pulitzer Prize and National Book Award winner), and *Miami and the Siege of Chicago.* He won a second Pulitzer for *The Executioner's Song* and died in 2007, an unrepentant bad boy.

Southern Gothic novelist and journalist Capote, fresh from the success of *Breakfast at Tiffany's* (1958), created the nonfiction novel with 1966's *In Cold Blood,* a success of monumental proportions. He planned the party of the century, the Black-and-White Ball, at the Plaza Hotel. He observed his multitude of friends and then wrote about their lives in the nonfiction *Answered Prayers.* When the first chapter of that work appeared in *Esquire,* many close friends shut him off completely. Devastated, he went into a spiral induced by drugs and alcohol and died at age 59, apparently forgetting his own advice: "Failure is the condiment that gives success its flavor."

During the Nixon years, the new writer was epitomized by Joan Didion. A journalist, essayist, and novelist with a BA in English from Berkeley, she wrote of life in 1960s California, a land of conspiracy theorists, paranoiacs, and sociopaths. By the time her nonfiction *Slouching Toward Bethlehem* came out in 1968, the great publishing houses were being quietly bought up by the same television networks and European publishers that had appeared at the beginning of the 1960s.

New York remains home to great publishers, editors, and writers, but the Golden Years shone with a radiance that will likely never be seen again.

- *All three of the Brontë sisters (Anne, Charlotte, and Emily) published their works under pen names.*

- *Never give up: Author John Creasy, who eventually had almost 600 mystery novels published, was turned down more than 700 times before his first novel was printed.*

- *Ink has been around almost 6,000 years. Ballpoint pens were invented less than 150 years ago.*

- *On average, nearly 500 new books are published each day.*

Fast Facts

- *A bolt of lightning is about as thick as your thumb. You can see it from so far away because of its luminescence.*

- *Warthogs can run fast—up to 35 mph. That's fast enough to whiz past a chicken, which can only run 9 mph.*

- *Sharks continually grow new teeth to replace ones lost in their search for food. The average shark tooth lasts about ten days, which might be why you never see shark dentists.*

- *The only product Elvis Presley ever promoted was Southern Made Donuts. He made a radio commercial for the snack food that aired during* Louisiana Hayride *on November 6, 1954.*

- *The sole golf course on the island of Tonga has only 15 holes.*

- *Time to rethink that new career? A person can't be a sumo wrestler unless he weighs more than 154 pounds and is taller than 5' 7".*

- *The first snowboard was called a* snurfer *and was made with two skis attached together.*

- *Police started collecting and using fingerprints as evidence in the late 1800s.*

- *During his nine-year reign as pope (beginning in 955), John XII was charged with multiple sexual acts and toasting the devil with wine. He was allegedly killed by a jealous husband.*

- *Fireworks were invented by the Chinese between 1,000 and 2,000 years ago.*

- *Former president William Jefferson Clinton was born William Jefferson Blythe III in Hope, Arkansas. The future politician's name was changed to Clinton when his mother married Roger Clinton when Bill was four years old.*

The Curse of the Lottery Winners

Though many lottery winners live happily ever after, there are those whose "good luck" was nothing more than a prelude to tragedy—proving that money is not always the solution to social and personal ills, and giving credence to the old adage, "Easy come, easy go."

- At age 77, New Yorker Clarence Kinder won $50,000 in the state lottery on a Thursday night—and died from a heart attack the following night.

- Only a few hours after Carl Atwood won $57,000 on the televised lottery program *Hoosier Millionaire*, the 73-year-old was fatally hit by a pickup truck while walking to the store where he bought his winning ticket.

- Jeffrey Dampier won $20 million in the lottery and became a Tampa popcorn entrepreneur. Dampier's generosity to his sister-in-law, Victoria Jackson—gifts, apartment rent—evidently wasn't enough: Jackson and her boyfriend kidnapped and murdered Dampier for his fortune. They were sentenced to life in prison.

- After collecting the first of his annual $1.24 million checks, Billy Bob Harrell—a down-on-his-luck Texan who hit the state jackpot for $31 million—began spending like there was no tomorrow. He picked up a ranch, a fashionable home—and a never-ending line of family, friends, and even strangers with their palms outstretched, dogging him day and night. The spending spiraled out of control for 20 months, until Harrell, who had had quite enough, locked himself in his bedroom and let a shotgun solve his dilemma.

- William "Bud" Post won $16.2 million in the Pennsylvania lottery in 1988. When he died of respiratory failure on January 15, 2006, Post was living on a $450 monthly disability check and was estranged from his family. Not only was his fortune wiped out, but he ended up deeply in debt, and he served a jail term for threatening a bill collector with a shotgun. At one point, Post filed for bankruptcy, came out of it with a million dollars to his name, and spent it all in short order.

HELLISH HEADLINES

Man Shoots Neighbor with Machete

Check with Doctors Before Getting Sick

Actor Sent to Jail for Not Finishing Sentence

Stud Tires Out

Gunfire in Sarajevo Threatens Cease-fire

Deaf Mute Gets New Hearing in Killing

Prisoner Serving 2,000-year Sentence Could Face More Time

Man Struck by Lightning Faces Battery Charge

Joint Committee Investigates Marijuana Use

Statistics Show that Teen Pregnancy Drops Off Significantly After Age 25

Squad Helps Dog Bite Victim

Idaho Group Organizes to Help Service Widows

Thugs Eat Then Rob Proprietor

Dealers Will Hear Car Talk at Noon

Soap and Water Still Cleans Well

Typhoon Rips Through Cemetery; Hundreds Dead

Hospitals Are Sued by 7 Foot Doctors

Meeting on Open Meetings Is Closed

Stolen Painting Found by Tree

Grammer Hotline Available

Mayor Says D.C. Is Safe Except for Murders

Bible Church's Focus Is the Bible

Legislator Wants Tougher Death Penalty

Steals Clock, Faces Time

Lack of Brains Hinders Research

The Moors Murderers: Britain's Most Hated Couple

A killing spree fascinated and horrified England in the 1960s. Saddleworth Moor had always had an ominous air to it, but tensions suddenly got much, much worse.

Burying a body in highly acidic soil is smart—the flesh decays faster, making it harder for police to tell exactly what happened to the victim. That's what Ian Brady and Myra Hindley were counting on when they buried their victims in an acidic grassy moor.

Normal and Abnormal Childhoods

Myra Hindley was born in 1942 just outside of Manchester. She was a normal, happy girl and even a popular babysitter among families in her neighborhood. At age 15, she left school. Three years later, she secured a job as a typist for a small chemical company. There she met Ian Brady, a 23-year-old stock clerk.

Born to a single mother, Brady was given to a nearby family at a young age when his mom, a waitress, could no longer afford to take care of him. In school, he was an angry loner who bullied younger children and tortured animals.

At the chemical company, Hindley became enamored with Brady, an intense young man fascinated with Nazis and capable of reading *Mein Kampf* in German. In her diary, Hindley gushed that she hoped he would love her, although Brady was decidedly distant. It wasn't until a year after they met that he asked her on a date—at the company's Christmas party.

An Off-kilter Romance

Brady's preoccupation with Nazism, torture philosophies, and sado-masochism didn't bother Hindley, and as the couple became closer, they began to photograph themselves in disturbing poses. It became evident that Brady had found a companion to help turn his twisted fantasies into reality: Between 1963 and 1965, the pair murdered five children and buried their bodies in the Saddleworth Moors, leading the gruesome acts to be called the *Moors Murders*.

The Murders Begin

Their first victim, 16-year-old Pauline Reade, was on her way to a dance on July 12, 1963, when a young woman offered her a ride. Assuming that it was okay to take a ride from a fellow female—Myra Hindley—Reade accepted. Along the way, Hindley suddenly pulled the car over to look for a missing glove; Reade helpfully joined Hindley in looking. Meanwhile, Brady had followed the car on his motorcycle. He snuck up behind Reade as she was looking for the glove and smashed her skull with a shovel. Reade's body was later found with her throat slashed so deeply that she was nearly decapitated. Unfortunately, hers wasn't nearly the grisliest death in the Moors Murders.

Four months later, on November 23, 1963, at a small-town market, Hindley asked 12-year-old John Kilbride to escort her home with some packages. He agreed. Brady was hidden in the backseat, and Kilbride became victim number two.

Keith Bennett had turned 12 only four days before June 16, 1964, when he encountered Hindley. Walking to his grandmother's house, he accepted a ride from Hindley, who again claimed to need help finding a glove. This time, instead of waiting in the car, she watched as Brady murdered the boy.

As the murderous couple stalked their fourth victim, their bloodlust swelled. On Boxing Day, an English holiday that falls on December 26, the couple lured ten-year-old Lesley Ann Downey to their home. Sadly, their youngest victim suffered the most gruesome and memorable fate. The couple took pornographic photos of the gagged child and recorded 16 minutes of audio of Downey crying, screaming, vomiting, and begging for her mother.

Expanding the Circle

But their treacherous ways reached a pinnacle when, perhaps bored with each other, they tried to get Hindley's 17-year-old brother-in-law, David Smith, in on the act. Like Brady, Smith was a hoodlum, not at all liked by Hindley's family. Smith and Brady had previously bonded by bragging about doing bad things, including murder. Until October 6, 1965, however, Smith assumed it was all a joke.

The couple invited Smith to their house, and he waited in the kitchen while Hindley went to fetch Brady. Upon hearing a scream, he ran to the living room to see Brady carrying an ax and what he perceived to be a life-size doll. It wasn't a doll, of course, but 17-year-old Edward Evans. Smith watched as Brady hacked the last bit of life out of the boy. Afraid that he would be next, Smith helped the couple clean up the mess as if nothing had happened. He waited, terrified, until early the next morning and then snuck out and went to the police.

Facing the Consequences

This wretched crime spree shook Great Britain. The trial of Myra Hindley and Ian Brady lasted 14 days, during which dozens of photos were submitted as evidence, including pictures of the couple in torturous sexual poses. Hindley claimed that she was unconscious when most of the photos were taken and that Brady had used them to blackmail her into abetting his crimes. That claim was quickly dismissed, as police investigators who examined the photos testified that she appeared to be fully aware of what was going on and even seemed to be enjoying herself.

At the time of the trial, the bodies of Lesley Ann Downey, John Kilbride, and Edward Evans had been discovered, all buried in the moor. Great Britain had just revoked the death penalty, so Ian Brady was sentenced to three sequential life sentences for the murders. Myra Hindley was charged with two of the murders as well as aiding and abetting and sentenced to life in prison.

The couple suffered miserably behind bars. After serving nearly 20 years, Brady was declared insane and committed to a mental hospital. Hindley was so viciously attacked that she had to have plastic surgery on her face. In the 1980s, the couple admitted to the murders of Pauline Reade and Keith Bennett and led police to Reade's grave. Hindley claimed remorse and appealed many times for her freedom. She received an open degree from a university, found God in prison, and even enlisted the help of a popular, devout Roman Catholic politician, Lord Longford, in her bid for release. But the high court of England denied her requests. Although she fought for her freedom up until her death in 2002, perhaps Hindley knew deep down that she'd never be free—she even called herself Britain's most hated woman. The BBC agreed and ran the quote, along with her infamous mug shot and jail photos, as her obituary.

He Said, She Said

There is nothing worse than a sharp image of a fuzzy concept.
—*Ansel Adams*

When the well's dry, we know the worth of the water.
—*Benjamin Franklin*

An intellectual snob is someone who can listen to the *William Tell Overture* and not think of The Lone Ranger.
—*Dan Rather*

A computer once beat me at chess, but it was no match for me at kickboxing.
—*Emo Philips*

I think men who have a pierced ear are better prepared for marriage. They've experienced pain and bought jewelry.
—*Rita Rudner*

All of the problems we face in the United States today can be traced to an unenlightened immigration policy on the part of the American Indian.
—*Pat Paulsen*

The only true wisdom is in knowing you know nothing.
—*Socrates*

Don't compromise yourself. You're all you've got.
—*Janis Joplin*

There is still no cure for the common birthday.
—*John Glenn*

The execs don't care what color you are. They care about how much money you make. Hollywood is not really black or white. It's green.
—*Will Smith*

Every man has a right to a Saturday night bath.
—*Lyndon B. Johnson*

The best way to keep one's word is not to give it.
—*Napoleon Bonaparte*

Start every day off with a smile and get it over with.
—*W. C. Fields*

John Kennedy Toole and
A Confederacy of Dunces

*When John Kennedy Toole committed suicide on March 26,
1969, he believed himself a failure. Only 31 years old,
Toole was depressed and frustrated over his lack of success
in the world of publishing. No one was interested in his
novel,* A Confederacy of Dunces. *Not yet, anyway.*

Who wanted to read about a fat glutton ranting and raving in the
streets of New Orleans? That was the question Toole had set for
himself by making such a figure the focus of his tour de force novel.
He was afraid that he knew the answer, and it wasn't a good one.
Despondent, Toole asphyxiated himself by running a garden hose
from the exhaust pipe through the window of his car. But Toole's
biggest fan, his mother, refused to give up on him, even after he'd
given up on himself.

Gimme Shelter

Thelma Agnes Ducoing Toole had always coddled and spoiled her
son. From the moment he was born on December 17, 1937, she
wrapped him in a cocoon of Southern domesticity and Roman
Catholicism. She kept little John indoors, discouraged him from
playing with other youngsters, and told everyone who would listen
that he was a literary genius who was going to make it big one day.
And indeed, her son showed a great deal of intellectual promise: At
only 16 years old, he wrote a novel called *The Neon Bible*. It seems
that Toole made no attempt at the time to find a publisher for this
work, but the seeds of his ambition had been sown.

After graduating from Tulane University, he earned a master's
degree at Columbia University and began preparing for his doctoral
studies. His plans were rudely interrupted by the draft in 1961, however, and Toole spent two years in the U.S. Army, teaching English
in Puerto Rico.

Upon leaving the army, Toole went to live with his parents in
New Orleans, but he was no longer the sheltered child he'd once
been. When not busy with his day job teaching at Dominican Col-

lege, he socialized with the colorful characters who hung around the French Quarter. These musicians, strippers, drunks, and food vendors inspired him to write his second novel, *A Confederacy of Dunces*.

An Unforgettable Protagonist

The main character in *A Confederacy of Dunces* is Ignatius J. Reilly, a man in some ways very much like Toole. Ignatius is obese and gluttonous, yet his intellectual genius leads him to feel superior to nearly everyone around him. Still living with his mother at age 30, he finds a way to blame all of his weaknesses and screw-ups on the fickle finger of fate. He is happy—as happy as someone like Ignatius can be—to spend his days writing a never-ending treatise about the evils of modernity, emotionally abusing his mother, and masturbating to memories of his dead dog. His lethargic bliss comes to an end, however, when his mother crashes their car and Ignatius is forced to find employment.

A Confederacy of Dunces is also filled with the kind of supporting characters that stay with the reader long after the novel is read: Irene Reilly, Ignatius's wine-swigging, long-suffering mother; Myrna "The Minx" Minkoff, a bohemian Jewish woman who antagonistically corresponds with Ignatius from New York; Angelo Mancuso, the incompetent police officer who tries to arrest Ignatius for vagrancy; and Darlene, a dumb-but-sweet stripper at Night of Joy, a nightclub in the French Quarter. These characters wind their way through the novel's many subplots, which are all masterfully tied together at the end of the book.

The Long, Sad Road to Publication

In 1966, *A Confederacy of Dunces* was rejected by Simon & Schuster. It's impossible to know just how much effort Toole put into getting it published or how many publishers he queried, but it's certain that his lack of success led to a deepening depression, severe migraine problems, and a crippling dependence on alcohol. Toole may also have been conflicted about his sexuality; friends and relatives disagree over whether he was gay. Toole left a note when he committed suicide, but his mother destroyed it and was later, at various times, either evasive or misleading as to what it said.

After Toole's suicide in 1969, the handwritten *Confederacy* manuscript sat, collecting dust in his mother's home as she tried unsuccessfully to find a publisher. Finally, in 1976, she persuaded Walker Percy, an acclaimed author and a professor at Loyola University New Orleans, to read her son's work. Percy was not enthused by the idea, but he ultimately acquiesced if only to get Mrs. Toole off his back. He fell in love with the novel, however, and his endorsement led to its publication by Louisiana State University Press. The first printing consisted of only 800 copies, but Thelma Toole had lived to see her son's fragile creation published. Shortly thereafter, to the surprise of virtually everyone, she also saw her son posthumously awarded the Pulitzer Prize for Fiction in 1981. She died three years later.

Is There a Curse on *Confederacy*?

A Confederacy of Dunces has sold more than 1.5 million copies in 18 languages, and first edition copies now sell for thousands of dollars. When it comes to being adapted for film, however, some think the novel is as cursed as its tragic author and its porcine protagonist. When *Confederacy* was still in galleys, someone at Louisiana State University Press sent it to Scott Kramer, a young executive at 20th Century Fox. Nearly three decades later, Kramer is still trying to get the picture made. Millions of dollars have been spent on the project's development, and through the years such big names as John Belushi, Drew Barrymore, Will Ferrell, Stephen Fry, Richard Pryor, Harold Ramis, Scott Rudin, and Steven Soderbergh have been attached to it. Currently optioned by Paramount (after much legal wrangling between Kramer and Soderbergh on one side and Rudin on the other), the film is on hold once again.

Some novels are simply unfilmable: *Lolita* has been adapted for the screen twice, but most critics and readers agree that neither version does the book justice. Perhaps, were a *Confederacy* movie ever actually made, it would elicit the same response. Perhaps its stalled development is a blessing in disguise. And, perhaps the world should just be grateful that the book itself—through a miracle of luck and maternal pride—was ever published at all.

SAY IT AIN'T SO

Myth: Elephants are afraid of mice.

Truth: Who hasn't come across an image of a great elephant cowering in fear from the mere sight of a skittering mouse? This myth couldn't be further from the truth, because elephants—among the most fearless of all animals—barely notice mice, much less fear them. On occasion, an elephant will encounter a noise it cannot identify, in which case, it might demonstrate some nervousness. However, the squeak of a mouse does not typically send an elephant running for the hills, as folklore might suggest.

Myth: Henry Kissinger was the last person in Harvard history to graduate with straight A's.

Truth: While former national security advisor, secretary of state, and Nobel Peace Prize laureate Henry Kissinger was, in fact, a stellar student, since his 1950 graduation a few Harvard alums have managed to pick up their diplomas with a stream of straight A's behind them. Besides, although Kissinger most certainly did graduate summa cum laude, his record of straight A's wasn't quite as perfect as the myth implies. It was apparently slightly tarnished by one pesky little B in a philosophy course.

Myth: Yreka, a small town in Siskiyou County near the Oregon border in northern California, was so named for a poorly made canvas sign at the town's bakeshop that transmitted the word *bakery* without the *b* and backward.

Truth: Mark Twain furthered this rumor in his autobiography, relaying the explanation as he had heard it. According to his understanding, soon after the town's settling, visitors to the small community saw a freshly painted bakery sign upon entering town. The *b* had not yet been painted on, so the sign appeared to read *yreka*. The community had not yet been named, so when the visitors began calling it by this odd name, the community supposedly picked up on it, too. In truth, the story of the bakery sign is just a clever legend. The name *Yreka* actually comes from a Native American word meaning "white mountain," after the nearby Mount Shasta.

A Cinematic Rebirth: Hollywood Grows Up in the '60s and '70s

Movie formulas had always served Hollywood studios well. Good guys wore white; bad guys wore black. The hero always walked (or rode) off into the sunset with the heroine in the end. The monster always wreaked havoc on the town, and there was always time during a crisis to break into song. But then it was time to grow up.

Hollywood had become quite rich and quite comfortable with its formulas of the 1930s, '40s, and '50s. But in the '60s, American culture began to change, and television provided big competition. Social, political, and cultural norms in America were turned upside down. The president was assassinated, draft cards were burned, and the generation gap became a chasm. Suddenly, the formula wasn't enough for audiences . . . or for filmmakers. From the ashes of these tumultuous times rose a rebirth of American cinema. A new class of movies—many with directors who were schooled in classrooms rather than on soundstages—dared to go where no celluloid had gone before.

Bonnie and Clyde

If any one film marked the beginning of this rebirth, it was *Bonnie and Clyde.* Director Arthur Penn redefined the "cops and robbers" genre in 1967 with this fairy tale about two outlaws. Crime became glamorous, as the tagline for the film claimed, "They're young . . . they're in love . . . they rob banks." The violence was loud and graphic, the action was relentless, and the ending was brutal. The characters of Bonnie Parker and Clyde Barrow, although portrayed as robbers and killers, became the standard for antiheroes in future films, including George Roy Hill's *Butch Cassidy and the*

Sundance Kid and Brian De Palma's *Scarface*. Nominated for ten Oscars and winner of two, *Bonnie and Clyde* opened the door for Hollywood's new cinema.

M*A*S*H

This 1970 film was set during the Korean War, but it might as well have been set against America's ongoing conflict in Vietnam. Director Robert Altman created the ultimate in antiestablishment and antiwar attitudes in the main characters—army surgeons required to patch up wounded soldiers so they could go back to the front to get injured again or killed. *M*A*S*H* portrayed undisciplined and cynical doctors who were forced into the military. The result was the darkest of black comedies, one that allowed Altman to write his own ticket as a cutting-edge director. He prolifically helmed several outstanding features in the five-year period following *M*A*S*H*, including *Brewster McCloud, McCabe & Mrs. Miller, The Long Goodbye, California Split,* and *Nashville.*

The Last Picture Show

Director Peter Bogdanovich moved into the future by way of the past in this 1971 feature. A film writer for *Esquire* magazine, he followed the examples of French New Wave directors and decided to make his own movies. *The Last Picture Show,* based on the novel by Larry McMurtry, depicts life in a small, dusty, lonely Texas town in the early 1950s as two friends finish their senior year of high school. Frank sexual situations and nudity placed the film at the forefront of early-'70s cinema, but lush black-and-white cinematography made it feel like a throwback to the '40s or '50s. In fact, it was the first mainstream black-and-white movie to come out since the mid-'60s, and it proved that such a limited color palette could be a viable artistic choice. Bogdanovich continued to make films, releasing two more commercial blockbusters in the next two years. *What's Up, Doc?* in 1972 recalled Hollywood's great screwball comedies of the 1930s, and 1973's *Paper Moon* was another evocative black-and-white movie, this time set during the Great Depression.

American Graffiti

A graduate of the USC School of Cinema-Television, director George Lucas indulged his interest in fast cars and first loves with

American Graffiti in 1973. Shot on a budget of less than one million dollars, the film eventually grossed $115 million, proving that this new breed of independent filmmaker could turn a profit for distributing studios. Somewhat autobiographic in nature, *American Graffiti* follows the adventures of Southern California teens on one night in 1962. Lucas later solidified his place in Hollywood history by becoming the creative force behind the immensely popular and successful *Star Wars* series.

The Godfather

A UCLA Film School alum, director Francis Ford Coppola cut his teeth working under low-budget producer Roger Corman in the 1960s. In 1972, Coppola took a best-selling novel by Mario Puzo and created a dark, sprawling saga of the Mafia in America, *The Godfather*. Gangsters in the movies had never been portrayed as three-dimensionally—or as brutally—as the Corleone family, which was headed by film icon Marlon Brando. Coppola's vision continued with 1974's *The Godfather: Part II*, which expanded the story and spanned a 60-year period. Both films were critical and box-office successes, but they are only part of Coppola's cinematic accomplishments, which also include 1974's *The Conversation* and 1979's *Apocalypse Now*.

Taxi Driver

Frequently called the greatest living American film director, Martin Scorsese graduated from the prestigious New York University Film School. Like many of his contemporaries, he drew heavily on his own experiences—in this case, growing up in the gritty neighborhoods of New York City. *Taxi Driver* teamed Scorsese with edgy actor Robert De Niro—one of their many pairings. Like other films of the era, *Taxi Driver* painted its lead character as an antihero. Loner Travis Bickle became a fully realized character, driving his cab through the foul streets of the Big Apple, stalking a presidential candidate, befriending a preteen prostitute (played by Jodie Foster), and murdering several unsavory individuals. The bloody violence and gritty real-life locations became trademarks for Scorsese, who went on to direct other stark and compelling films, including *Raging Bull, Goodfellas, Casino,* and *The Departed,* for which he won what many saw as a long-overdue Oscar for best director.

Where You'd Least Expect It

A stolen painting by Mexican artist Tamayo was retrieved from an unlikely place: the trash. Out on a stroll, Elizabeth Gibson spotted it nestled among some garbage. After finding the painting posted on a Web site four years later, Gibson received a share of the one million dollars it fetched at Sotheby's.

John Wilkes Booth's body is buried in a Baltimore cemetery, but his third, fourth, and fifth vertebrae can be found on display in the National Health and Medicine Museum in Washington, D.C. They were removed for investigation after he was shot and killed while on the run following Lincoln's assassination.

Normally on display at the Elvis After Dark Museum, a handgun once owned by the King was stolen during a ceremony on the 30th anniversary of his death. Soon thereafter, the missing gun was found stashed inside a mucky portable toilet only yards from where the gun's exhibit case sat.

Egypt, which receives less rainfall than most places on Earth, doesn't seem like the kind of place where you'd find sea creatures. Yet, it was there that geologists discovered the nearly complete skeleton of a Basilosaurus, a prehistoric whale. During the whale's lifetime, 40 million years ago, Egypt's Wadi Hitan desert was underwater.

Something missing from Neil Armstrong's famous moon-stepping speech was found years later by a computer programmer. Using software that detects nerve impulses, the missing word *a* was found, which changed Armstrong's statement, "one small step for man" to his intended, different meaning: "one small step for *a* man."

Femme nue couchée, a racy female nude painted by Gustave Courbet in the 19th century, turned up on a Slovakian doctor's wall in 2000, nearly six decades after it disappeared during World War II. It was believed to have been stolen by members of the Russian Red Army, but the country doctor claimed that he received the art in payment for services rendered.

The pathologist who performed Albert Einstein's autopsy, Dr. Thomas Harvey, kept a pretty major souvenir: Einstein's brain. Thirty years postmortem, the brain segments were found in the doctor's Kansas home, stored in a pair of mason jars.

Building the Colosseum

With recently deceased dictator Nero out of the picture, Rome's new ruler, Vespasian, sought to show the ravaged populace that he wasn't like his self-serving predecessor. He proved to be the ruler who could finally bring the people out of their long-lasting troubles—all it took was an architectural triumph designed to house 50,000 roaring Romans thirsty for an entertainingly gruesome battle.

During his reign as emperor in the first century A.D., Nero had repeatedly proved himself a ruthless ruler, stealing everything he could from the Roman people and killing anyone who got in his way. In the year between Nero's forced suicide and the rise of Vespasian (born Titus Flavius Vespasianus), three other emperors took brief turns ruling Rome, but Vespasian became the man who mattered. He chose to launch his reign with a monumental gesture meant to cause the people to forget Nero. He initiated construction of the most substantial arena of the time, a structure that became the cultural nucleus of Rome—and remained so for the next 450 years.

Putting a Bad Ruler Behind Them

During Nero's reign, which marked the end of the long-running and brutal Julio-Claudian dynasty, land and resources were absorbed into his extravagant estate, the Domus Aurea. Set in the heart of Rome, Nero's grandiose property featured a lake, a mansion with more than 300 rooms, and hundreds of acres of land. The opulent interior of the house showcased unrivaled luxuries, from expansively marbled floors to a slave-driven revolving dome ceiling that would intermittently release mists of perfume and flutters of rose petals over the frequent assemblages of partygoers. Ever the egotist, Nero commissioned a towering bronze statue in his own image, the *Collossus Neronis,* and ordered it to be erected at the palace steps to greet—or perhaps intimidate—visitors.

As an apt show of goodwill to the Roman people, Vespasian confiscated the land for his building project from Nero's lavish estate. The great Flavian Amphitheater eventually resided beside the lake Nero had built to complete his posh property. Historians suggest that it is from Nero's statue that the Flavian Amphitheater drew its eventual name, the Colosseum.

A Massive Undertaking

The arena was built with a multitude of materials and mirrored Greek architecture, despite the lack of experience the Romans had with such technology. Adapting to the task, the Romans used travertine stone to make up much of the exterior of the elliptical building; wooden floors covered in sand (which was good for absorbing blood) spread across the entirety of the interior. Tiers of seats allowed for massive seating capacity, and mazes beneath the main floor kept wild animals contained in preparation for events. Trapdoors to surprise gladiators, as well as a retractable roof to provide shade for patrons, completed the structure. Upon its opening, the Colosseum was the perfect meeting place for the Roman community.

The construction of the Colosseum lasted ten years and extended through two reigns. Upon Vespasian's death, his son Titus ascended to the position of emperor in A.D. 79 and sought to finalize the arena's creation. Titus brought thousands of slaves from Jerusalem to speed up completion of the arena, and the Romans celebrated in A.D. 80 with inaugural games that included the slaying of 9,000 wild animals, noonday executions, and gladiatorial brawls that usually ended in death. This introductory series marked the beginning of a 450-year stretch of ongoing community celebrations and the creation of traditional Roman-style entertainment.

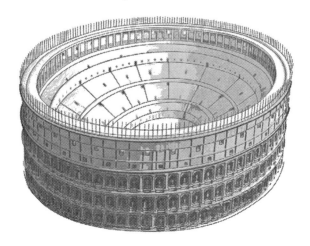

Fast Facts

- A shark's jaws are not attached to the rest of its skeleton; that great maw is held in place by muscles and ligaments.

- When the purportedly penny-pinching executives, or "Scotch bosses," at the Minnesota Mining and Manufacturing Company (3M) didn't put enough adhesive on their tape, people complained. They responded by putting better adhesive on their new product. The tape stuck—and so did the name.

- Twenty years after the disappearance of more than 100 English settlers from "The Lost Colony" on Roanoke Island, North Carolina, seven survivors were reported to be captives of the Iroquois in a village along the Neuse River.

- Of the 656 muscles in your body, it only takes about 2.5 percent of them to smile.

- Actor Tom Cruise was a wrestler in high school.

- Thomas Morgan and Elizabeth Caerleon were married for 81 years. When she died on January 19, 1891, their aggregate age was 209 years, 262 days.

- Shredded pieces of aluminum dropped by American planes during World War II to baffle enemy radar were called chaff.

- English men were once legally barred from witnessing childbirth.

- In Chico, California, bowling on the sidewalk is not only illegal, it is punishable by a fine. If you're wearing one of those silly bowling shirts, there may be possible imprisonment.

- President Zachary Taylor died in office in 1850 from gastroenteritis. The mysterious circumstances of his sudden death caused his descendants to exhume his body in 1991. Nothing unusual was discovered.

Craig Breedlove and the Spirit of America

*This driver made his claim on the title of the
fastest human being in the world.*

Craig Breedlove was an authentic American icon. Five-time holder
of the world land-speed record and innovator in the design and engineering of rocket cars, he was born in Southern California on March
23, 1937. Growing up in the car-crazy 1950s, Breedlove obtained
his first automobile at age 13. By 16, he was winning drag races with
his souped-up 1934 Ford Coupe. Using an alcohol-based fuel, he
pushed the vehicle to 154 miles per hour in the dry lake beds of the
Mojave Desert.

A job as a structural engineering technician at Douglas Aircraft
gave Breedlove an education in designing his own high-speed cars,
leading ultimately to the Spirit of America, a car designed with a
surplus military jet engine as its propulsion system. Affable and
handsome, Breedlove became a major celebrity, earning the heroic
nickname "Captain America." The Beach Boys even included a song
about him on their hit album *Little Deuce Coupe.*

Is It a Rocket or a Car?

Breedlove built the first version of his Spirit of America rocket car in
the early 1960s and tested it in Utah's Bonneville Salt Flats in 1962.
His goal was to reclaim the world land-speed record for the United
States, but poor handling led to failure. Undeterred, Breedlove
tinkered with the design, adding a more easily steered front wheel
and a new stabilizer, and tried again in 1963. This time the vehicle
worked perfectly. On August 5, 1963, at Bonneville, the Spirit of
America reached a speed of 407.45 mph to break the previous
record of 394.2 mph, set by English driver John Cobb in 1947.

This new record was not without controversy. Some claimed that
the vehicle, with its three-wheel design, was a motorcycle rather than
a car. Others said the fact that the wheels were jet-driven meant it
was neither car nor motorcycle. Regardless of how you pigeonhole
the Spirit, however, no vehicle had ever traveled that fast on land.

Not So Fast

As it turned out, Breedlove's was a short-lived record. In February 1964, fellow American Tom Green managed 413 mph at Bonneville. And just three months later, Art Arfons from Ohio hit 434 mph. After breaking Cobb's 16-year-old record, Breedlove saw his record fall to third place in less than a year. Not content to be outdone so quickly, he returned to Bonneville on October 13, 1964, and reclaimed the top spot with a 468 mph performance. For good measure, he tried again two days later and became the first person to go faster than 500 mph on Earth's surface, notching a mark of 526.28 mph. While the speed impressed the competition, not everything worked according to plan. Both drag chutes on the Spirit of America were lost, as well as the wheel brakes. Because of these failures, Breedlove cut through a row of telephone poles at 400 mph and hit a brine pond while still going 200. Although the car would never drive again, Breedlove swam to shore unscathed.

Taking the Lead

In what was becoming a land-speed-record derby, Breedlove's record was broken again less than two weeks later, when Arfons managed 536 mph. Breedlove was already working on a new Spirit of America, but Arfons's mark stood for just longer than a year. Then the competition got fierce: On November 2, 1965, the Spirit of America Sonic 1 hit 555 mph at Bonneville. Just five days later, Arfons reached 576. Breedlove returned to Bonneville eight days after Arfons notched his mark to reclaim the record with a speed of 600, making him the first person to hit 600 mph in a land vehicle. This record would stand for almost five years until Gary Gabelich notched 622 mph on October 23, 1970.

- *In 1698, Russia imposed a tax on beards.*

- *Roman charioteers had a short life span since race accidents usually resulted in serious injury or death. Gaius Appuleius, however, began racing at age 18 and retired at 42, winning 1,400 races.*

- *The Swiss Army used carrier pigeons to send messages until 1994 and bicycle units until 2003.*

The Times They Are A-Changin'

1941

January 23: In testimony before Congress, Charles Lindbergh recommends that the United States negotiate a neutrality pact with Adolf Hitler.

February 4: The United Service Organization (USO) is founded to entertain American troops.

February 11: Glenn Miller receives the first gold record, for one million sales of "Chattanooga Choo Choo."

February 15: Jazz bandleader Duke Ellington records "Take the A Train."

March 1: The first commercial FM radio station in the United States goes on the air in Nashville, Tennessee.

March 14: Bandleader Xavier Cugat and his orchestra record the hit "Babalu."

March 22: Washington state's Grand Coulee Dam goes into operation.

April 26: The Chicago Cubs is the first baseball team to install an organ in its stadium.

May 1: *Citizen Kane*, directed by its star, Orson Welles, premieres in New York City.

May 1: General Mills introduces the little round cereal known as Cheerios.

May 15: New York Yankee Joe DiMaggio begins a 56-game hitting streak.

July 1: The Bulova Watch Company pays nine dollars for the first TV commercial.

July 16: Joe DiMaggio goes three for four in his 56th straight game with a hit. His streak ends the next day against the Cleveland Indians.

September 1: Jews living in Germany are required to wear a yellow six-pointed star.

December 7: The Japanese attack the U.S. naval base at Pearl Harbor, Hawaii. The next day, the United States and Britain declare war on Japan.

December 21: Chicago Bears kicker Ray McLean makes the last drop-kick for an extra point in the NFL.

Legally Speaking

Every day, in addition to the thousands of people who deliberately and maliciously perform illegal acts, there are thousands more who inadvertently break laws and statutes that are outdated, outlandish, and somewhat amusing—but still on the books. These are America's forgotten laws. What's not so funny is that most are still enforceable.

- Kentucky's 100-year-old "Infidel" law effectively bans any non-Christian religious publication from public schools—and most public schools across the state have reinforced the ban in their policy manuals. One old Kentucky law that *should* be enforced is the statute that requires all residents of the state to bathe once a year.

- In Los Angeles, it's unlawful to bathe two babies in the same bathtub simultaneously.

- Maine has a law that bans the sale of cars on Sunday. (Does Detroit know about this?)

- You can go to jail for taking a bite out of someone else's hamburger in Oklahoma. You'll also be violating the law of the Sooner State if you make faces at a dog.

- In Boston, it's okay to kiss in public—as long as it isn't in front of a church or on Sunday: That's the day when all displays of public affection are against the law.

- If you're planning on going to a movie in Gary, Indiana, watch what you eat. It's illegal to go to a theater within four hours of eating garlic.

- It's illegal to tie a giraffe to a telephone pole in Atlanta.

- If you put a penny in your ear, you're in violation of Hawaiian law.

- Several states have laws that only allow sex between heterosexuals—and only in the missionary position.

- In Port Arthur, Texas, it's against the law to emit any obnoxious odor in an elevator.

Syllable Secrets: Etymology

February: Second month of the year; from Middle English *Februarie*, which derives through Old English *Februarius*, from Latin *Februa* (feast of purification)

Uncle: The brother of one's father or mother; from Latin *avunculus* (mother's brother), akin to Latin *avus* (grandfather)

Dream: A series of thoughts and images "seen" during sleep, or a strongly desired goal; Middle English *dreem*, which derives from Old English *drēam* (noise, joy) and Old Norse *draumr* (dream); akin to Old High German *troum* (dream)

Sauce: A condiment for food, usually a dressing or topping; from the Latin *salsa*, feminine of *salsus* (salted), past participle of *sallere* (to salt)

Jail: A place of confinement for people accused or convicted of crimes; from Middle English *jaiole*, which derives from Anglo-French *gaiole* or *jaiole*, which comes from Late Latin *caveola*, diminutive of Latin *cavea* (cage)

Beast: Four-footed mammal; from Latin *bestia*

Yawn: An involuntary reaction to tiredness or boredom, opening the mouth wide for an intake or expulsion of breath; from Middle English *yenen* or *yanen*, which derives from Old English *ginian*; akin to Old High German *ginēn* (to yawn), Latin *hiare*, Greek *chainein*

Phobia: Deep, sometimes irrational, fear attached to a place, action, or thing; comes from Greek *-phobos* (fearing), from *phobos* (flight), which itself derives from *phebesthai* (to flee)

Imbibe: To drink or absorb; from Middle English *enbiben*, which comes from Middle French *embiber*, deriving from Latin *imbibere* (to drink in), which is formed from *in-* + *bibere*, to drink

August: Eighth month of the year; from Latin *Augustus*, which comes from *Augustus* Caesar

Reflect: To think quietly and calmly, or in the case of a highly polished surface, to give back an image or likeness; from Latin *reflectere* (to bend back): *re-* + *flectere* (to bend)

Valachi Speaks

On June 22, 1962, in the federal penitentiary in Atlanta, Georgia, a man serving a sentence of 15 to 20 years for heroin trafficking picked up a steel pipe and murdered another convict. The killer was Joseph "Joe Cargo" Valachi; the intended victim was Joseph DiPalermo—but Valachi got the wrong man and killed another inmate, Joe Saupp. This mistake touched off one of the greatest criminal revelations in history.

Joe Valachi, a 59-year-old Mafia "soldier," was the first member of the Mafia to publicly acknowledge the reality of that criminal organization—making *La Cosa Nostra* (which means "this thing of ours") a household name. He opened the doors to expose an all-pervasive, wide-ranging conglomerate of crime families, the existence of which was repeatedly denied by J. Edgar Hoover and the FBI. By testifying against his own organization, Valachi violated *omerta,* the code of silence.

The Boss's Orders
Vito Genovese was the boss of New York's powerful Genovese crime family. Valachi had worked for the family for much of his life—primarily as a driver, but also as a hit man, enforcer, numbers runner, and drug pusher. When Valachi was on his way to prison after having been found guilty of some of these activities, Genovese believed the small-time operator had betrayed him to obtain a lighter sentence for himself. So Genovese put a $100,000 bounty on Valachi's head. He and Valachi were actually serving sentences in the same prison when Valachi killed Joe Saupp—mistaking him for Joseph DiPalermo, whom he thought had been assigned by Genovese to murder him. Whether or not Valachi had broken the code of silence and betrayed Genovese before the bounty was placed on his head, he certainly did it with a vengeance afterward.

But why did Valachi turn informer? The answer to that question isn't entirely clear. Most speculate that Valachi was afraid of a death sentence for killing Saupp and agreed to talk to the Feds in exchange for a lighter sentence.

The Cat Is Out of the Bag

Valachi was a barely literate, street-level miscreant whose knowledge of the workings of the organization was limited. However, when he was brought before John L. McClellan's Senate Permanent Investigations Subcommittee in October 1963, he began talking beyond his personal experience, relaying urban legends as truth, and painting a picture of the Mafia that was both fascinating and chilling.

All in all, Joe Valachi helped identify 317 members of the Mafia. His assistance gave Attorney General Robert Kennedy "a significant addition to the broad picture of organized crime." Unlike Hoover, Bobby Kennedy had no problem acknowledging the Mafia. (One theory about Hoover's denials is that they were a result of long-term Mafia blackmail regarding his homosexuality.)

Valachi's revelations ran the gamut from minor accuracies to babbling exaggerations, as well as from true to false, but the cat was out of the bag. Americans became fascinated with crime families, codes of honor, gang wars, hit killings, and how widely the Mafia calamari had stretched its tentacles. Very private criminals suddenly found their names splashed across headlines and blaring from televisions. During the next three years in the New York–New Jersey–Connecticut metropolitan area, more organized criminals were arrested and jailed than in the previous 30 years. Whatever safe conduct pass the Mafia may have held had expired.

On-screen and in Print

When journalist Peter Maas interviewed Valachi and came out with *The Valachi Papers,* the U.S. Department of Justice first encouraged but then tried to block its publication. Regardless, the book was released in 1968. This work soon became the basis of a movie that starred Charles Bronson as Joe Valachi. The novel *The Godfather* was published in 1969, and in the film *The Godfather: Part II,* the characters of Willie Cicci and Frank Pentangeli were reportedly inspired by Valachi.

The $100,000 bounty on the life of Joseph Valachi was never claimed. In 1966, Valachi unsuccessfully attempted to hang himself in his prison cell using an electrical cord. Five years later, he died of a heart attack at La Tuna Federal Correctional Institution in Texas. He had outlived his chief nemesis, Genovese, by two years.

HOW IT ALL BEGAN

The Little Black Dress

The "little black dress," aka LBD, is an essential part of any woman's wardrobe. The original LBD was made by famed Parisian couturier Coco Chanel. It was given its particularly functional name in a 1926 issue of *Vogue* magazine, which also referred to it as a "Ford"—recognizing that here was an item that could, and would, be reproduced endlessly through mechanical means, making it affordable to the masses. While expensive couture frocks were considerably different from cars coming off an assembly line, the association the *Vogue* writer was making came from a famous line in Henry Ford's autobiography: "Any customer can have a car painted any color that he wants so long as it is black."

The World's First Movie Premiere

In 1894, French chemists (and brothers) Louis Jean and August Marie Lumière saw Thomas Edison's miraculous Kinetoscope at a Parisian arcade. Unfortunately, because viewers peered into the device through small holes, watching movies through a Kinetoscope was limited to one person at a time. So the siblings had the idea to adapt a mechanism that was commonly used in sewing machines to invent a device that could both project *and* expose film, allowing a number of people to watch it at the same time. The Lumières got their patent in February 1895, and on December 28 of that year, they held the world's first public screening of a motion picture in the Grand Café in Paris on their Cinematographe. The cost of admission was one franc, for which the audience was entitled to see, among other films, *Workers Leaving the Lumière Factory, The Blacksmith at Work,* and *The Sprinkler Sprinkled.* As far as we know, there was no red carpet, preening starlets, or exchange of empty compliments involved.

"Clean as a Whistle"

Since when has the whistle been synonymous with cleanliness? Back in the prehistoric day when reeds were used to make whistling sounds, they had to be entirely dry and free of all debris in order to attain the desired tone.

The Boy Band Craze of the 1990s

All of a sudden in the '90s, it seemed that boy bands were everywhere. What was that about?

As with many such trends, the explosion of boy bands was fueled by money—and lots of it. In 1995, there were more than 20 million girls between the ages of 10 and 19 living in the United States; even discounting those with good taste in music, there was a lot of green on the line.

Boy bands tend to excite certain members of the preadolescent female population, while irritating just about everybody else. The official dividing line between "boy band" and "band that is made up of males" is blurry, as there have been bands with male members since the beginning of time. Doubtless the bards of yore were often young, attractive, stylishly dressed teenage boys. In the 1950s and 1960s, musical acts including the Temptations and the Monkees were rehearsed and prepackaged by music producers. The distinguishing factor of the 1990s boy band craze, however, seems to be the unparalleled extent of the commercialism coupled with the bands' sheer popularity.

The Basic Ingredients

The components of a successful boy band have been honed to a veritable art form: a generous helping of good looks; a dollop of fashion, dancing, and singing prowess; and a sprinkling of talent. Boy bands rarely write their own music, and their songs are molded into a formula so consistent that it can be difficult to distinguish one song from the next.

The most popular early boy band was New Kids on the Block from Boston, which was put together by boy band pioneer/music producer Maurice Starr. While New Kids on the Block were wildly successful in the late '80s, their popularity steadily declined in the early '90s.

Producer Lou Pearlman, seeking to replicate the success of the New Kids, staged auditions in his Orlando, Florida, mansion. By 1993, he had formed Backstreet Boys. Backstreet Boys hold the title of most successful boy band in history: Their popularity hit epic proportions with the 1999 release of *Millennium.* The first single from this album, "I Want It That Way," hit number one on the charts in more than 18 countries.

Next came 'N Sync, a group Pearlman formed in 1995 after observing the success of Backstreet Boys. 'N Sync's 2000 album, *No Strings Attached,* holds the record for most albums sold in a single year—9.9 million. This band's success seemed an eerie replica of the Backstreet Boys fad.

But boy bands aren't purely an American phenomenon—they have been popular the world over. In fact, England's Take That and Westlife are among the most successful boy bands in history, and Puerto Rico's Menudo experienced international success—and launched the career of Ricky Martin.

Coming Out Half-Baked

Despite the smashing success of the most popular boy bands, it's not all smiles and roses in the boy band universe. After a few years of gargantuan success, even the biggest boy bands decline in popularity, after which the best-looking members of the band pursue solo careers. Cases in point: Jordan Knight and Joey McIntyre of New Kids on the Block; Nick Carter and Brian Littrell of Backstreet Boys; Justin Timberlake and JC Chasez of 'N Sync; and Nick Lachey of 98 Degrees, all of whom put out albums on their own.

But most boy bands never even achieve stardom. The list of less successful boy bands is prodigious and includes such acts as 3T, 2Be3, 3 Deep, and B2K. And then for those that are successful, there are the legal battles. Backstreet Boys and 'N Sync both sued Pearlman in the late '90s for scamming them out of money. Pearlman went on to form moderate boy band successes LFO, Take 5, and O-Town. In May 2008, he pleaded guilty to fraud. Ex-boy band members have since accused Pearlman of sexual inappropriateness.

Many critics claim that the boy band phenomenon is officially over. While Backstreet Boys released a somewhat successful album in 2005, it came nowhere near their previous numbers—the craze has definitely abated. Pearlman is perhaps misguided in his repeated claim that the boy band phenomena will cease "when God stops making little girls."

Strange Justice

Doing It for the Kids

Basketball Town, a sports and recreational facility for kids in California, was forced to shut down as a result of $100,000 in legal fees because of a lawsuit filed by a wheelchair-bound man. The plaintiff claimed he couldn't attend a party on the mezzanine level there because it wasn't wheelchair accessible. Even the offer of a $35,000 wheelchair lift wasn't enough to mollify the plaintiff. The legal wrangling and countersuits led most to believe the only solution would be to close the facility.

Just Put It on His Tab

After several break-ins, a bar owner decided to set a trap, along with a warning sign around his windows, to convince wannabe burglars that it just wasn't worth it. But a drunken and drug-crazed robber tried anyway and set off the trap, electrocuting himself. The district attorney chose not to pursue murder charges, but the burglar's family sued the bar owner anyway. A jury awarded the family $150,000, but that amount was later cut in half when somebody realized that the burglar should have to take at least *some* of the responsibility.

What Does That *R* on the Gear Shift Mean Again?

After a night of hard drinking, a young woman accidentally backed her car off a dock. Although her passenger managed to get out and escape, the inebriated driver couldn't get out of her seat belt and didn't survive. The driver's parents sued the carmaker for making a seat belt their daughter couldn't operate underwater, even though her blood alcohol level was 0.17—almost twice the legal limit. A jury found the car company mostly responsible for the woman's fate and awarded her family $65 million. Cooler heads prevailed when an appeals court tossed the verdict out.

Staying on Track

After a woman was struck by a metropolitan subway train in a major city, she was awarded $14.1 million. While these dreadful events happen all the time, this one was a bit different. Further investigation by the city's police force revealed that the woman had been attempting suicide and was lying across the tracks when the train ran over her. The conductor was warned of the situation and slowed the train down but did not stop it. Yet, when the court learned of the suicide attempt, the ruling wasn't thrown out. It was instead reduced by 30 percent, to $9.9 million.

Professor W. I. Thomas and the Scandal of 1918

Trumped-up charges—devised with the intent of pulverizing nonconformists—are not a modern-day concoction. Just look back to the "Scandal of 1918" and its victim to catch a glimpse of manipulative politics at its most conniving.

Professor W. I. Thomas was a steadfast devotee of his two great loves: education and women. As a professor and prolific researcher, Thomas was deeply entrenched in his academic life. In his personal life, however, he was a sucker for the ladies. The combination of the two would prove to be his ruin.

An Unconventional Beginning
The son of a Methodist minister in a small Virginia farming community, William Isaac Thomas did not seem destined for academia. His ancestors stemmed from the Pennsylvania Dutch—so-called "plain people" who were more apt to drive a plow than to write a thesis. Thomas's love of learning was, at least in part, inspired by his father's insistence that he and his seven siblings be well educated. The family even moved from Virginia to Knoxville, Tennessee, the hub of the University of Tennessee, to ensure access to educational prospects.

Thomas began his voyage through academia at that university. Majoring in literature and classic languages, Thomas was awarded the University of Tennessee's first-ever doctoral degree. Upon graduation, he remained at the school and taught a wide array of classes: English, Greek, Latin, and German, just to name a few.

After studying for two years in Germany, Thomas accepted an English professorship at Oberlin College in Ohio, where he added sociology to his teaching repertoire. From there, he moved on to the University of Chicago, where he remained for nearly 25 years—until the Scandal of 1918 erupted.

Gossips Will Talk
Although Thomas was known as a womanizer, his escapades were mostly confined to episodes of overly friendly flirting rather than

true acts of philandering. A frequenter of the bohemian art scene and known for his splashy presence, Thomas stood apart from his more conservative university colleagues. He and his wife, Harriet, were social activists and antiwar pacifists during World War I. The academic culture of the time was not keen on such liberal leanings, so Thomas was unsurprisingly somewhat of a professional outcast.

The real trouble began when Thomas was found in a hotel with the young wife of an army officer. Enlisting the Mann Act, local authorities were able to pinpoint a supposed illegality and file charges against Thomas. Although those charges were later dropped, the damage had been done. The scandal served to ostracize Thomas from the academic community for the rest of his life.

The Mann Act was the brainchild of James Robert Mann, a conservative lawmaker. Its purpose was to control prostitution, but it was repeatedly used in a questionable manner by authorities. One particular loophole was used to terrorize silent film star Charlie Chaplin, boxing great Jack Johnson, and legendary architect Frank Lloyd Wright. The law, designed to obstruct abductions for sexual slavery, restricted women from crossing state lines for sexual activity. Thus, the Mann Act could make a mutually acceptable drive into another state with a female pal into a criminal an act of prostitution.

An Early Feminist?

Ironically, while Thomas was arrested for charges in line with the worst kind of female exploitation, his seminal work, *Sex and Society,* was quite feminist for its time. In it, Thomas called for a reevaluation of popular biological theories about the inferiority of women to men. Although many a modern-day woman might take offense at some of his specific language, Thomas was actually a maverick in finding more differences in intellect within the sexes than between them. Some boys are smart and others, not so much; the same holds true for girls. But, unlike the popular theory of the day, boys as a whole are not demonstrably smarter than girls. In fact, Thomas concluded that women might even hold the upper hand with their "superior cunning."

Thomas divorced his first wife, Harriet, after nearly 50 years of marriage. Soon thereafter, at age 72, he married his 36-year-old research assistant, Dorothy. It would seem that Thomas's reputation as a womanizer may not have been totally unearned after all.

Odd Beer Names

You're thirsty, so you decide to stop in your local pub for a drink. The "Menu of Indecision" is literally jam-packed with hundreds of beers. Some are recognizable, but most have names that make you chuckle aloud. Here's a short list of a few oddly named American and Canadian brands.

- Arrogant Bastard Ale
- Oliver's Hot Monkey Love
- Bourbon Barrel Lower da Boom
- Flying Frog Lager
- Satan's Pony Amber Ale
- Butt Monkey Chimp Chiller Ale
- Squatters Emigration Amber Ale
- San Quentin Breakout Stout
- Aroma Borealis Herbal Cream Ale
- Kill Ugly Radio
- Old Knucklehead
- Alley Kat Amber
- Money Shot Cream Ale
- Oatmeal Breakfast Stout
- 3 Stooges Beer
- Moose Drool
- Stone Double Dry Hopped Levitation Ale
- Demon Sweat Imperial Red
- Monk in the Trunk
- Dead Frog Ale
- Tongue Buckler
- Bitter American

America Goes to Kindergarten

Kindergarten—which literally means "children's garden"
in German—is now considered a normal transition
between home and full-time schooling for young children.
But initially, America was slow to warm to the idea.

Friedrich Froebel first conceived of kindergarten in 1840 as an introduction to art, mathematics, and natural history—a pre-education for children of all classes, as opposed to the custodial religious services that had been created for the offspring of the very poor. But after it became associated with radical feminist ideals in its German homeland and in Prussia, authorities became upset that women's nurturing skills might be translated into a wider commercial sphere, and kindergarten was soon banned.

You Can't Keep a Good Idea Down

German liberals in exile, however, exported the idea to other countries: Bertha Ronge took it to England, then her sister Margarethe Meyer Schurz opened the first American (even if it was German-speaking) kindergarten in Wisconsin in 1856. Elizabeth Palmer Peabody created the first English-speaking kindergarten three years later in Boston. She wrote many books about the topic and edited a kindergarten-related newsletter. But it was Susan Elizabeth Blow who established the first public kindergarten in 1873, Des Peres School in St. Louis. She taught children in the morning and gave seminars to teachers in the afternoon. By 1883, a mere ten years later, every St. Louis public school had a kindergarten, making the city a model for the nation.

The movement really garnered momentum after Commissioner of Education William Harris spoke to Congress on February 12, 1897, in support of public kindergartens: "The advantage to the community in utilizing the age from four to six in training the hand and eye; in developing the habits of cleanliness, politeness, self-control, urbanity, industry; in training the mind . . . will, I think, ultimately prevail in . . . the establishment of this beneficent institution in all the city school systems of our country."

Fast Facts

- *The first Ford automobiles featured engines made by Dodge. John and Horace Dodge built engines for the Ford Motor Company at their shop in Detroit.*

- *From the 14th to the 18th centuries, more than a hundred incidents of the Black Plague (each resulting in the death of thousands) paralyzed European cities. It was so contagious that merely touching a victim could lead to infection and death.*

- *In swimming competitions, there are four kinds of strokes: crawl, butterfly, backstroke, and breaststroke. Sorry, no dog-paddling allowed.*

- *In the National Basketball Association's first season, 1946–47, the top-paid player was Detroit's Tom King, who made $16,500. He also acted as the team's publicity manager and business director.*

- *It has been reported in* Ripley's Believe It or Not *that the toe tag from the corpse of Lee Harvey Oswald, President Kennedy's alleged assassin, sold at auction for $9,500.*

- *Michelangelo started his sculpture* Pietà *at age 22.*

- *The San Andreas Fault is slipping about two inches per year, which means that Los Angeles will be a suburb of San Francisco in 15 million years.*

- *During his 16th-century reign, Süleyman the Magnificent extended the Ottoman Empire from Algiers to the Austrian border.*

- Bibliophobia *is the fear of books.*

- *In 2005, three-and-a-half years after the company filed for bankruptcy, Polaroid chairman Jacques Nasser received $12.8 million for selling shares of the company. Meanwhile, 6,000 former employees each got $47 and lost their benefits.*

The Story of the Straitjacket

❖ ❖ ❖ ❖

The ancient word strait *has survived as an uncommon adjective, as in* straitlaced, *and as a noun, as in the Bering* Strait. *But the most common modern use of this word is as part of the compound* straitjacket.

Before progressive psychoanalysis and newer medications, doctors didn't know how to treat mentally ill patients, so they often restrained them in a jacketlike garment with overlong sleeves. The ends of the sleeves went far beyond a patient's hands, and they were secured to the patient's back, keeping his or her arms crossed close to the chest, restricting most arm movement. Many institutional straitjackets are made of canvas or duck cloth for material strength, but modern jackets intended as fetish wear or fashion items often use leather or PVC instead.

The establishment of asylums and the use of straitjackets gained momentum in the early 1800s. Doctors listed such things as religious excitement, sunstroke, and reading novels as possible causes for mental illness. They believed that patients had lost all power over their morals and that strict discipline was necessary to help patients regain self-control.

Get Me Out of Here

Escape artists have used straitjackets in their acts for years. Harry Houdini first thought of using the straitjacket in the early 1900s while touring an insane asylum in Canada. He amazed disbelievers by getting out of one in front of live audiences. Later, he turned it into a public spectacle by escaping as he hung upside-down, suspended from a towering skyscraper.

The Guinness Book of World Records reports that David Straitjacket escaped from a Posey straitjacket in 2005 in 81.24 seconds. This record was broken in succession by Jeremy Kelly and Ben Bradshaw. On July 4, 2007, Jonathan Edmiston, aka "Danger Nate," escaped from his Posey in an incredible time of 20.72 seconds.

And, for the record, the Posey *is* considered to be the most difficult commercially available straitjacket from which to escape.

The Graduate

Robert Redford and Doris Day were originally considered to play young Benjamin and the seductive Mrs. Robinson before those roles in this 1967 film went to Dustin Hoffman and Anne Bancroft instead. Director Mike Nichols showed great intuition in only his second feature film—great enough to win the Academy Award for Best Director. When Benjamin and Elaine hop the bus to end the film, they have no clue as to their future together or what they'll do next, and the actors weren't quite sure how to play the scene. Nichols was able to coax the appropriate "performance" from actors Hoffman and Katharine Ross by keeping the cameras running long after the shot was supposed to be over. As actors, they didn't have any idea what they were supposed to do next—perfectly reflecting the same predicament faced by their characters.

The Blob

This 1958 monster movie, featuring an oozing and growing mass of who-knows-what, was the first starring role for 28-year-old Steve McQueen, who played a character nearly ten years younger. His movie girlfriend, Aneta Corsaut, went on to play teacher Helen Crump in TV's *The Andy Griffith Show* during the 1960s. Composer Burt Bacharach and lyricist Mack David wrote the film's theme song, "Beware of the Blob." It became a Top 40 hit, reaching number 33 on the charts for "The Five Blobs." This vocal "group," however, was actually just one performer, Bernie Nee.

Raiders of the Lost Ark

Released in 1981, this action and adventure film started out with nail-biting scenes that would have made for a great climax in most other films. Director Steven Spielberg had Harrison Ford, as thrill-seeker and archeologist Indiana Jones, open the flick by narrowly escaping being flattened by an enormous rolling boulder. Another famous scene came about through the star's frustration rather than creativity. Jones encounters a sword-slinging villain, and the script originally called for the hero to engage in a gripping duel, with Jones finally winning by snapping the weapon away from his foe with his trusty whip. But Ford was extremely ill with food poisoning and didn't want to perform such an extended sequence. He quickly ended the threat by simply pulling his pistol and shooting the bad guy.

Stetson Kennedy: An Unsung Hero for Civil Rights

"Stetson was deeply involved in ways few, if any, white people were, and he did it in ways that are inspirational to us folks that grew up surrounded by a bunch of conformist racists."
—*Hodding Carter III, professor of public policy,*
University of North Carolina, Chapel Hill

Stetson Kennedy risked his life to infiltrate the Ku Klux Klan during the 1940s, a time when the Klan was extremely popular. The Ku Klux Klan, also known as the KKK, consists of members who deem anyone of anything other than white descent to be a threat to the United States. During that time, one important Klan duty was to "protect" white heritage by any means necessary, including murder, rape, burning crosses, and other vile activities.

An Activist Lifestyle

Born in Florida in 1916, Kennedy was a passionate writer with an interest in Southern and African American folklore. In 1937, at age 21, he left university to manage folklore, oral histories, and ethnic studies at the Works Progress Administration (WPA) Florida Writers' Project. Kennedy was always a human rights activist, and as a member of the NAACP, he believed in a live-and-let-live policy—so much so that he even ran for a spot in the Senate with that phrase as his platform.

After World War II, in response to what Kennedy saw as unchecked racism, he decided to infiltrate the Klan as John Perkins, an encyclopedia salesman, eventually working his way up to become a hit man in the organization. With the help of another Klan informant, he penned *I Rode with the Ku Klux Klan,* a gripping book that detailed murders, initiations, and other rituals. The work was published in 1954, and needless to say, the Klan was furious, even going so far as to put out a hit on Kennedy's life, offering $1,000 for every pound of his dead flesh.

Local law enforcement and the FBI were hardly moved by the book, but thankfully, the media couldn't get enough. Various newspapers published Kennedy's articles detailing his KKK activities. Minutes from KKK meetings were read on the radio, and the *Superman* radio program aired several episodes in which the Man of Steel fought the Klan and revealed their code words to thousands, if not millions, of listeners. This exposure made the Klan lose a lot of the mystique that had surrounded it, and it is believed that membership began to fade as a result.

Questions and Controversy

In the 1990s, *I Rode with the Ku Klux Klan* was rereleased as *The Klan Unmasked*. This time, however, it came under closer scrutiny, and Kennedy faced accusations of fabricating parts of his nonfiction book, claims that were renewed in the 21st century. Some writers argued that Kennedy had fictionalized part of the material and reported on the activities of a second infiltrator and informant as if he had experienced the events himself.

In his 90s, Kennedy claimed that he couldn't remember every detail but insists that he did, in fact, infiltrate the Klan. His friends and defenders, who included Studs Terkel and other scholarly and noted names, have argued that what his work has accomplished is far more important than the specifics of how he compiled it and whether or not he should have given more acknowledgment to other sources, especially considering that it happened more than 60 years ago.

"With half a dozen Stetson Kennedys," wrote Terkel, "we can transform our society into one of truth, grace and beauty."

- *Croesus, king of Lydia, attacked the Persians in 547 B.C. Before the campaign, the oracle of Delphi told him that he would destroy a great empire. The empire Croesus destroyed was his own.*

- *The eighth American president, Martin Van Buren, was the first president to be born a U.S. citizen. Those before him were born English citizens.*

- *More than 300,000 copies of* Uncle Tom's Cabin *were sold in America in its first year of publication. One million copies were sold in England in the first year.*

ANAGRAMS

An anagram is a word or phrase that exactly reproduces the letters in another word or phrase. The most interesting of them reflect or comment on the subject of the first.

astronomer—moon starer

circumstantial evidence—can ruin a selected victim

mother-in-law—woman Hitler

George W. Bush—He grew bogus.

slot machines—cash lost in 'em

William Shakespeare—I am a weakish speller.

animosity—is no amity

Justin Timberlake—I'm a jerk, but listen.

How the West Was Won—What we shot, we owns!

public relations—crap, built on lies

Emperor Octavian—captain over Rome

Elvis—lives

conversation—Voices rant on.

David Letterman—nerd amid late TV

Howard Stern—wonder trash

Stevie Wonder—er, doesn't view

semolina—is no meal

William Shatner—Will is earthman.

Madonna Louise Ciccone—occasional nude income

Osama bin Laden—a bad man (no lies)

Buffy the Vampire Slayer—Pithy female braves fury.

Cyndi Lauper—end up a lyric

the eyes—They see.

ARPANET: The Grandfather of the Internet

Rumors abound that ARPANET was designed as a communications network that would withstand nuclear attacks. That is simply not true. The creators of ARPANET weren't seeking invulnerability, but reliability—in order to fulfill one man's vision of an "inter-galactic" computer network. It was a crude beginning to the Internet, but it led to important technical developments that made today's Internet a reality.

On October 4, 1957, the Soviet Union launched the world's first human-made satellite, *Sputnik I,* into space. It was a clear message that Russian technology was more advanced than American technology. To amend this oversight, the Advanced Research Projects Agency (ARPA) was formed to fund technical research. The United States already had a substantial financial investment in computer tech—the initial purpose of ARPA was to figure out the best way to put that to use. Though it fell under the auspices of the U.S. Department of Defense (and was renamed *DARPA*), the research was never intended to be used solely for military purposes. Instead, the agency's purpose was to develop technology that would benefit civilization and the world in general.

Not Connected to Other Galaxies—Yet

The expert chosen to head ARPA's initial effort was Joseph "Lick" Licklider, a leading computer scientist. Lick had a vision of a worldwide communications network connected by computers, which he referred to as the "inter-galactic computer network." Lick departed ARPA in 1965, before his plan could be implemented, but he left a lasting impression on his successor, Bob Taylor.

Taylor selected a new leader for the system design team that would make Lick's vision a reality: Dr. Lawrence "Larry" G. Roberts, an MIT researcher. He became one of the four people most closely associated with the birth of the Internet. (The other three are Vinton Cerf, Leonard Kleinrock, and Robert Kahn.) Roberts had gained experience in computer linking while at MIT, having linked computers using the old-fashioned telephone method of circuit switching. The concept of packet switching was at first controversial, but it proved to be one of the key factors in linking multiple computers to form a network. The other important technical achievement was the use of small computers, known as interface message processors (IMPs), to store and handle the data packets.

By 1968, the concept for ARPANET was in place, and invitations to bid on the project were sent to 140 institutions; only 12 actually replied. The others apparently believed the concept to be impractical, even bizarre, and never bothered to bid. In the end, BBN Technologies—Licklider's former employer—got the nod.

A Hesitant Start

The first piece went to UCLA, thanks to the reputation of Professor Kleinrock, an expert in computer statistical analysis and measurement. The first IMP link was with Stanford Research Institute (SRI). The first message was sent on October 29, 1969, and was supervised by Kleinrock—it was an omen of things to come. The message was supposed to be *login,* but after two letters, the system crashed, and only *lo* was sent. About an hour later, the system was up and running again, and the full message was transmitted. By December 5, 1969, four IMPs were linked: UCLA, SRI, University of California at Santa Barbara, and the University of Utah. These IMP sites were chosen on the basis of their ability to research and implement the protocol that would allow for the continued growth of ARPANET.

ARPANET was no longer just a vision—it was a reality. The growth of ARPANET during the 1970s was phenomenal, as newer and better protocols were designed. In 1971, e-mail was born; in 1972, telnet was developed; and in 1973, file transfer protocol came into play.

By 1986, ARPANET had serious competition from the National Science Foundation Network (NSFNET), which became the true backbone of the Internet. ARPANET closed up shop in 1990. In 1991, NSFNET opened to the public, introducing the Internet we know today. Within four years, more than 50 million people had traveled the information superhighway. As of March 2008, worldwide Internet usage stood at 1.4 billion—and that's only the beginning. The Internet may not have solved all of the problems of the world, but it has managed to connect people around the world in ways they'd never previously imagined.

INSPIRE ME

Vitruvian Man

Never has the name of such a famous work of art remained as unknown as Leonardo da Vinci's masterpiece, *Vitruvian Man* (circa 1490). You may not know him by name, but *Vitruvian Man* is that drawing of a naked man, his arms and legs spread wide, standing inside both a circle and a square. His image is surrounded by what looks like scrawled gibberish, but which is actually Leonardo's penned explanation of the strange image, written backwards.

The drawing looks more like a page torn from a medieval medical textbook than a work of art, and that is just the point. Leonardo was inspired by the mathematical musings of Roman architect Vitruvius, who believed that the proportions of mankind's buildings should be based on the allegedly perfect proportions of man himself (the Romans weren't at all concerned with women). Here is the essence of Vitruvius' idea: The center of the human body is the navel. Stand a man with his arms and legs outstretched and draw a circle around him with the navel as the center. If you then draw a navel-centered square inside the circle, the tips of the fingers and toes will fit into the corners of the square while simultaneously touching the circumference of the circle.

Vitruvius made additional observations about man's proportions that have lived on forever in the form of playground bets: A palm is the width of four fingers, the length of a man's outspread arms is equal to his height, the length of the ear is one-third the length of the face—the list goes on. Vitruvius' claims don't measure up to reality, and one can only guess that he was referring to average measurements that are never realized in the body of a single person. Indeed, Leonardo's drawing reveals *Vitruvian Man*'s imperfections—in his drawing, the square and circle do not have the same center.

But Leonardo was less concerned with the accuracy of Vitruvius' mathematics than with the idea that there is an essential symmetry to the "human" (aka male) body. Leonardo did some measurements and calculations of his own before drawing his *Vitruvian Man*. The drawing is considered the perfect marriage of science and art. It is believed that Leonardo saw the square as a symbol for material existence and the circle as a symbol for spirituality. For Leonardo, the human body was an analogy for the workings of the universe.

The National Film Board of Canada

In Canada, it's a cherished institution. In the United States, it's a name that's usually mentioned only during broadcasts of the Academy Awards. But either way, it can affect the movies we see.

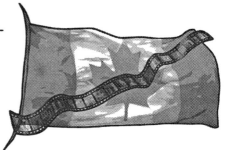

Canadians believe that the government should proudly support the arts. When it comes to movies, that's precisely the role of the National Film Board of Canada (NFB). Its mandate is "to produce and distribute audio-visual works which provoke discussion and debate on subjects of interest to Canadian audiences and foreign markets; which explore the creative potential of the audio-visual media; and which achieve recognition by Canadians and others for excellence, relevance, and innovation."

Early Canadian Films

Founded in 1918, the Canadian Government Motion Picture Bureau was the major Canadian film producer, but in 1938, the government invited noted British documentary filmmaker John Grierson to study Canadian production. The results of his report were included in the National Film Act of 1939, which established the National Film Board. Given the timing, it's hardly surprising that part of its initial thrust was to create propaganda films for World War II.

Getting Animated

When Norman McLaren joined the NFB in 1941, the board started to produce animated films. Working with American companies such as Disney, the NFB produced effective propaganda cartoons for the Allied war effort. McLaren, a pioneer in experimental animation, won an Oscar in 1952 for *Neighbours,* an antiwar cartoon short that popularized a new form of character movement known as pixilation.

In 2006, the 65th anniversary of NFB animation was marked with the release of a DVD boxed set of restored classics in tribute to the pioneer: *Norman McLaren—The Master's Edition.*

Dogged by Controversy

McLaren's antiwar stance was only the beginning of a tradition of controversy that has stayed with the NFB. In line with the NFB's independence, a 1950 revision of the Film Act removed any direct government interference into the board's operation and administration. However, the government found other ways to stifle controversy: In 1996, the board lost one-third of its operating budget, forcing layoffs and privatization.

American conservatives have also had a long-standing beef with the NFB that began after a number of productions rankled their sensibilities. *If You Love This Planet* (1982), which won the Academy Award for Best Documentary (Short Subject), was labeled "political propaganda" in the United States.

But not all controversy was outside of Canada. Paul Cowan's *The Kid Who Couldn't Miss* (1982), a film that stripped away some of the mystique of Canadian World War I flying hero Billy Bishop, caused a firestorm of anger and calls to cut funding to the NFB. Originally released as a documentary (and currently listed as a docudrama), the film provoked an answering movie, H. Clifford Chadderton's *The Billy Bishop Controversy,* to counter bias that Chadderton felt Cowan had included in his film.

But the NFB continued to embrace controversy. *Abortion: Stories from North and South* (1984) and *Out: Stories of Lesbian and Gay Youth in Canada* (1994) drew fire from religious groups and social conservatives.

Quality Wins the Day

Yet, the fact remains that NFB productions have been consistently recognized for their quality and artistic brilliance. Stuart Legg's 1941 *Churchill's Island* won the first-ever Best Documentary Academy Award. Eleven other NFB productions have won Oscars, including one in 2007 for *The Danish Poet.* In 1989, the NFB won an honorary Oscar in recognition of its 50th anniversary and its record of excellence in filmmaking. Through the years, the NFB has been honored with more than 5,000 film awards.

1924 Murder Mystery

*Who's at the heart of the cloaked-in-secrets demise of
Thomas Ince? Who, of the loads of lovelies and gallons
of gents on the infamous* Oneida *yacht that night, was
the killer? Curious minds demand to know.*

The night is November 15, 1924. The setting is the *Oneida* yacht.
The principal players are: Thomas H. Ince, Marion Davies, Charlie
Chaplin, and William Randolph Hearst.

The Facts

By 1924, William Randolph Hearst had built a huge newspaper empire;
he dabbled in filmmaking and politics; he owned the *Oneida*.
Thomas H. Ince was a prolific movie producer. Charlie Chaplin was
a star comedian. Marion Davies was an actor. The web of connections went like this: Hearst and Davies were lovers; Davies and
Chaplin were rumored to be lovers; Hearst and Ince were locked in
tense business negotiations; Ince was celebrating a birthday.

For Ince's birthday, Hearst planned a party on his yacht. It was
a lavish one—champagne all around. In the era of Prohibition, this
was not just extravagant, it was also illegal. But Hearst had ulterior
motives: He'd heard rumors that his mistress, Davies, was secretly
seeing Chaplin, and so he invited Chaplin to the party. The *Oneida*
set sail from San Pedro, California, headed to San Diego on Saturday, November 15.

An unfortunate but persistent fog settled over the events once
the cast of characters were onboard the yacht. What is known definitively is that Ince arrived at the party late, due to business, and that he
did not depart the yacht under his own power. Whether he was sick
or dead depends on which version you believe, but it's a fact that Ince
left the yacht on a stretcher on Sunday, November 16. What happened? Various scenarios have been put forward over the years.

- **Possibility 1: Hearst shoots Ince.** Hearst invites Chaplin to
  the party to observe his behavior around Davies and to verify their
  affair. After catching the two in a compromising position, he flies

off the handle, runs to his stateroom, grabs his gun, and comes back shooting. In this scenario, Ince tries to break up the trouble but gets shot by mistake.

- **Possibility 2: Hearst shoots Ince.** It's the same end result as possibility 1, but in this scenario, Davies and Ince are alone in the galley after Ince comes in to look for something to settle the queasiness caused by his notorious ulcers. Entering and seeing the two people together, Hearst assumes Chaplin—not Ince—is with Davies. He pulls his gun and shoots.

- **Possibility 3: Chaplin shoots Ince.** Chaplin, a week away from marrying a pregnant 16-year-old to avoid scandal and the law, is forlorn to the point where he considers suicide. While contemplating his gun, it accidentally goes off, and the bullet goes through the thin walls of the ship to hit Ince in the neighboring room.

- **Possibility 4: An assassin shoots Ince.** In this scenario, a hired assassin shoots Ince so Hearst can escape an unwanted business deal with the producer.

- **Possibility 5: Ince dies of natural causes.** Known for his shaky health, Ince succumbs to rabid indigestion and chronic heart problems. A development such as this would not surprise his friends and family.

Aftermath

Regardless of which of the various scenarios might actually be true, Ince was wheeled off Hearst's yacht. But what happened next?

That's not so clear, either. The facts of the aftermath of Ince's death are as hazy as the facts of the death itself. All reports agree that Ince did, in fact, die. There was no autopsy, and his body was cremated. After the cremation, Ince's wife, Nell, moved to Europe. But beyond those matters of record, there are simply conflicting stories.

The individuals involved had various reasons for wanting to protect themselves from whatever might have happened on the yacht. If an unlawful death did indeed take place, the motivation speaks for itself. But even if nothing untoward happened, Hearst was breaking the Prohibition laws. The damage an investigation could have caused was enough reason to make Hearst cover up any attention that could have come his way from Ince's death. As a result, he tried to hide all mention of any foul play. Although Hearst didn't own the *Los Angeles Times,* he was plenty powerful. Rumor has it that an early edition of the paper after Ince's death carried the screaming headline, "Movie Producer Shot on Hearst Yacht." By later in the day, the headline had disappeared.

For his part, Chaplin denied being on the *Oneida* in the first place. In his version of the story, he didn't attend the party for Ince at all. He did, however, claim to visit Ince—along with Hearst and Davies—later in the week. He also stated that Ince died two weeks after that visit. Most reports show that Ince was definitely dead within 48 hours of the yacht party.

Davies agreed that Chaplin was never aboard the *Oneida* that fateful night. In her version, Ince's wife called her the day after Ince left the yacht to inform her of Ince's death. Ince's doctor claimed that the producer didn't die until Tuesday, two days later.

So, what really happened? Who knows? Most of the people on the yacht never commented on their experience. Louella Parsons certainly didn't. The famed gossip columnist was reportedly aboard the *Oneida* that night (although she denied it as well). She had experienced some success writing for a Hearst newspaper, but shortly after this event, Hearst gave her a lifetime contract and wide syndication, allowing her to become a Hollywood power broker. Coincidence? No one can say for certain.

- *When the first atomic bomb was dropped in New Mexico in 1945, the flash could be seen throughout that state as well as in parts of Arizona and Texas.*

- *Catgut (the name of the product of which tennis racket strings are made) is made from the intestines of mostly livestock animals, but not cats.*

- *Barnacles, those critters that glue themselves to old boats and docks, have both male and female sex organs.*

- *In 1893, New Zealand was the first country in the world to grant women the right to vote.*

Where You'd Least Expect It

Leon Theremin, a Russian-born New York engineer of electronic musical instruments, returned to Russia in 1938 and went missing. Many years later, he was discovered, still in Russia. Apparently Stalin had deemed him a menace to Soviet security, so he had been "rehabilitating" Theremin in a Siberian labor camp.

A bear set to star in a television commercial seemed to have gotten a bit of stage fright. While filming an ad on the Scottish isle of Benbecula, Hercules was lost for nearly a month. He was ultimately found taking a leisurely swim after he had apparently returned to the wild.

One of only three pianos ever owned by Chopin resurfaced in recent years. A music professor fell onto the discovery while researching records about a famous piano maker. The newly found piano, which had been bought at auction by its owner of 20 years, is the only one of Chopin's three that still works.

The body of female Egyptian Pharaoh Hatshepsut, oft depicted in a gender-confusing fake beard, was lost for years before its eventual discovery in a tomb. Using a molar that had been found in a selection of Hatshepsut's embalmed body parts, scientists matched it to a not-yet-identified mummy.

As the first president of the United States, George Washington came into office without any tradition behind him. No one necessarily knew what would be significant and what would not. Washington thought it important to inaugurate his term with a speech. Years later, however, a historian deemed the speech insignificant and doled out the pages to interested parties. More than 200 years later, all but 7 of the 31 pages have been found, spread among various individuals.

Published in 1827 when the author was only 18, Edgar Allan Poe's *Tamerlane* could easily have been forgotten—and nearly was. In 1890, in a dime bin at a Boston bookstore, the first of only 12 currently known copies was discovered bearing not Poe's name but the byline "A Bostonian."

Football Is Football—Or Is It?

❖ ❖ ❖ ❖

Football, no matter where it's played, is derived from an impromptu sport developed at Rugby School in England back in 1823 and credited to William Webb Ellis. Today, it's played in different countries under varying rules, most notably in Canada, Australia, and America. But that's not to be confused with what Americans call soccer, *played as* football *throughout the world.*

Canadian Football Versus American Football

- The American football field is 100 yards long and 53⅓ yards wide. The Canadian field is larger—110 yards long and 65 yards wide.

- Canadian football places the goalposts on the goal line. American football places them behind the end zone.

- American teams are allowed 11 players on the field at one time. Canadian teams can use 12.

- On kickoff, American receivers can call a fair catch, downing the ball when they catch it. Canada has no such rule, but the kicking team must give the player catching the ball a five-yard buffer zone.

- Canadian players have to move more quickly between plays, having only 20 seconds on the play clock from the end of one play to when the ball is snapped for the next. American players have a luxurious 40 seconds to run a new play after the ball was downed on the previous one; if the clock was stopped between plays, they have 25 seconds from when it is restarted.

- American teams get a two-minute warning before the end of a half. The Canadian warning is three minutes.

- When lining up for a play, all offensive players in the Canadian backfield (except the quarterback) are allowed to be in motion. In American football, not so much—only one player can be in motion.

- American teams at the line of scrimmage are separated by only the length of the football. Canadian teams must line up a yard apart.

- If a Canadian team misses a field goal, the defensive team can run it out of the end zone; if the defense fails to do so, the kick is worth a point. When an American team muffs a field goal outside the 20-yard line, its opponent gets a first down at the same line of scrimmage.

Australian Rules Football

There is absolutely no similarity between Australian rules football (also known as *footy*) and American or Canadian football. These are just a few of the hundreds of differences in the Australian version:

- The football field (or *pitch*, as it's called) is an oval rather than a rectangle. It is 165 by 135 meters at its longest and widest points.

- There are 18 players from each team on the field at any given time. None wear any protective equipment—the uniform consists of shorts, sleeveless shirts, and studded *boats* (shoes).

- Players may either run with a ball or kick it, but they cannot pass it. If a player chooses to run with the ball, it must be bounced on the ground once every 15 meters (about 50 feet).

- A defender may not tackle a player below the waist or above the shoulders.

- There are two ways to score. A straight goal (six points) is scored when an attacking player kicks the ball over the goal line between the goalposts without touching a post or another player. If the ball strikes another player or a goalpost but still passes over the goal line, that's a *behind goal* worth one point.

- Any ballcarrier held firmly by a defender must get rid of the ball by kicking it or batting it with his hand. If that doesn't occur, the referee can award the defending team a free kick.

INSPIRE ME

"Amazing Grace"

"Amazing Grace" is a sweet song with a bittersweet backstory. Most people are familiar with the song, but how many know the story associated with it?

In 1748, British slave buyer and slave ship captain John Newton experienced a spiritual awakening. His ship encountered a vicious storm at sea, and the young captain, struck by the recognition of his own mortality, realized the error of his slave-trading ways. He accepted God into his heart. Legend has it that he turned his ship around, went back to Africa, and returned his slaves to their rightful land. He then penned "Amazing Grace" as testimony to the glory of divine grace and the moralizing effects of Christianity.

As is often the case, unfortunately, the truth is not as inspiring as the legend. In actuality, Newton continued to trade slaves for five years after his revelation, although he did finally quit the devil's work in 1754. He went on to become a priest in the Church of England in 1764. But it was not for another eight years, in 1772 and decades after his Christian conversion, that he wrote the classic hymn "Amazing Grace." Newton eventually became an outspoken abolitionist.

Despite the song's distinctly Christian theme, it has been inspirational to those outside the faith who have also taken up its message. The lyrics make it clear that the song is about a Christian God's grace, but the overarching idea is that faith brings happiness and can inspire goodness. It's therefore not altogether surprising that a Christian hymn written on the other side of the Atlantic is now an important song of the Cherokee Nation.

In 1838, President Andrew Jackson sent federal troops to Georgia, Tennessee, North Carolina, and Alabama to remove the Cherokee from their homes. This move was prompted by the discovery of gold in Cherokee territory.

The ensuing forced march to the West claimed the lives of approximately 5,000 Cherokee and is now referred to as the Trail of Tears. During the journey, the Cherokee sang "Amazing Grace" in their own language as a source of courage. The song remains popular among the Cherokee today.

John Myatt, Master Forger

When people hear the word forgery, *they usually think of money.*
But legal currency isn't the only thing that can be faked.

"Monet, Monet, Monet. Sometimes I get truly fed up doing Monet.
Bloody haystacks." John Myatt's humorous lament sounds curiously
Monty Pythonesque, until you realize that he can do Monet—and
Chagall, Klee, Le Corbusier, Ben Nicholson, and almost any other
painter you can name, great or obscure. Myatt, an artist of some
ability, was probably the world's greatest art forger. He took part
in an eight-year forgery scam in the 1980s and '90s that shook the
foundations of the art world.

Despite what one might expect, art forgery is not a victimless
crime. Many of Myatt's paintings—bought in good faith as the work
of renowned masters—went for extremely high sums. One "Gia-
cometti" sold at auction in New York for $300,000, and as many as
120 of his counterfeits are still out there, confusing and distressing
the art world. But Myatt never set out to break the law.

Initially, Myatt would paint an unknown work in the style of
one of the cubist, surrealist, or impressionist masters, and he seriously duplicated both style and subject. For a time, he gave them
to friends or sold them as acknowledged fakes. Then he ran afoul of
John Drewe.

The Scheme Begins
Drewe was a London-based collector who had bought a dozen
of Myatt's fakes over two years. Personable and charming, he
ingratiated himself with Myatt by posing as a rich aristocrat. But
one day he called and told Myatt that a cubist work the artist had
done in the style of Albert Gleizes had just sold at Christies for
£25,000 ($40,000)—as a genuine Gleizes. Drewe offered half of that
money to Myatt.

The struggling artist was poor and taking care of his two children. The lure of the money was irresistible. So the scheme developed that he would paint a "newly discovered" work by a famous
painter and pass it to Drewe, who would sell it and then pay Myatt

his cut—usually about 10 percent. It would take Myatt two or three months to turn out a fake, and he was only making about £13,000 a year (roughly $21,000)—hardly worthy of a master criminal.

One of the amazing things about this scam was Myatt's materials. Most art forgers take great pains to duplicate the exact pigments used by the original artists, but Myatt mixed cheap emulsion house paint with a lubricating gel to get the colors he needed. One benefit is that his mix dried faster than oil paints.

The Inside Man

But Drewe was just as much of a master forger, himself. The consummate con man, he inveigled his way into the art world through donations, talking his way into the archives of the Tate Gallery and learning every trick of *provenance*, the authentication of artwork. He faked letters from experts and, on one occasion, even inserted a phony catalog into the archives with pictures of Myatt's latest fakes as genuine.

But as the years went by, Myatt became increasingly worried about getting caught and going to prison, so at last he told Drewe he wanted out. Drewe refused to let him leave, and Myatt realized that his partner wasn't just in it for the money. He loved conning people.

The Jig Is Up

The scam was not to last, of course. Drewe's ex-wife went to the police with incriminating documents, and when the trail led to Myatt's cottage in Staffordshire, he confessed.

Myatt served four months of a yearlong sentence, and when he came out of prison, Detective Superintendent Jonathan Searle of the Metropolitan Police was waiting for him. Searle suggested that since Myatt was now infamous, many people would love to own a real John Myatt fake. As a result, Myatt and his second wife Rosemary set up a tidy business out of their cottage. His paintings regularly sell for as much as £45,000 ($72,000), and Hollywood has shown interest in a movie—about the real John Myatt.

• *For 47 days in 1961, New York's Museum of Modern Art displayed* Le Bateau, *a painting by French artist Henri Matisse, upside down. It was placed right side up as soon as the error was noticed.*

Fast Facts

- *Nintendo was first established in 1889 as a company specializing in the production of Japanese playing cards called* hanafuda. *That term literally translates as "flower cards."*

- *Not only was President Richard Nixon the first American president to visit both China and the Soviet Union, he was also the first to visit all 50 states while in office.*

- *In 2004, the University of Connecticut won both the men's and the women's NCAA basketball championships. It is the only school to ever do the double dip.*

- *Can you find the islet of Langerhans on a map? Probably not. It's actually the name of a part of the pancreas that produces hormones.*

- *President James Garfield was shot by an assassin in 1881. Six doctors attempted to treat the wounded president, but several probed the wound with their bare fingers, introducing fatal infection into his body.*

- *In 1997, University of Nebraska sophomore Jeremy Sonnenfeld became the first bowler to "knock 900" by rolling three perfect 300 games in a row in an official tournament.*

- *During the 76 years of his life, French King Louis XIV took only three baths, each of them reluctantly. He masked his odor with large amounts of perfume.*

- *The average person is 33 percent more likely to be killed by a collapsing sand structure than by a shark attack.*

- *The Suez Canal was closed in June 1967 during the Arab-Israeli Six Day War. The canal remained closed by an Egyptian blockade until its reopening in June 1975.*

Al Capone's Empire

❖ ❖ ❖ ❖

If you took three pushpins and stuck them into a map of the United States in the three places Al Capone spent most of his time, you'd have a triangle spanning New York, Chicago, and Florida. Considering the size of the globe, this triangle wouldn't look like much. And yet, Capone is one of the world's most notorious criminals.

New York

Alphonse Gabriel Capone was born on January 17, 1899, in Brooklyn, New York. He was the fourth son of Italian immigrants who moved to the area near the Navy Yard upon first arriving in the United States. By all accounts, Capone's childhood was a normal, if rather harsh, one. The neighborhood by the Brooklyn Navy Yard was tough. But soon, Capone's father moved the family to an apartment over his barbershop. The new neighborhood had a greater diversity of nationalities than the one in which they had previously lived. Capone was a typical child, hanging out with friends and doing fairly well in school. Or at least until he reached the sixth grade. The story is rather simple: a teacher hit him, he hit back, and he was expelled. Capone never returned to school.

Shortly after these events, the family moved again, and the new neighborhood would have quite an effect on the young Capone. He met the people who would have the most influence on him throughout his life. Johnny Torrio, the "gentleman gangster," taught him how to have what seemed like an outwardly respectable life while simultaneously conducting business in the numbers racket and brothels. Capone also met Frankie Yale, who was on the opposite end of the gangster spectrum from Torrio. Frankie was a muscle guy who used aggression and strong-arm tactics to build a successful criminal business. In the midst of all this lawless learning, Capone met Mae Coughlin, a middle-class Irishwoman. They had a son in 1918 and married shortly after.

Capone made an attempt to earn a legitimate living—moving to Baltimore after he was married and doing well as a bookkeeper. But when his father died in 1920, Capone followed Torrio to Chicago to start the career that would make him infamous.

Chicago

Torrio had taken over the underworld business in Chicago, and with the coming of Prohibition in 1920, he ended up controlling an empire that included brothels, speakeasies, and gambling clubs. Torrio brought Capone on board as partner. Capone moved his family into a house on Chicago's Far South Side. But after a reform-minded mayor was elected in the city, Torrio and Capone moved their base of operations southwest to suburban Cicero, where the pair essentially took over the town. Frank Capone, Al's brother, was installed as the front man of the Cicero city government and was fatally shot by Chicago police in 1924.

By this point, Capone had made a name for himself as a wealthy and powerful man. He was also a target. When gangland rival Dion O'Bannon was killed, Capone and Torrio easily took over O'Bannon's bootlegging territory—but they also set themselves up for a lifelong war with the remaining loyalists in O'Bannon's gang.

Capone and Torrio survived many assassination attempts. In 1925, when Hymie Weiss and Bugs Moran attempted to kill Torrio outside the crime boss's own home, Capone's partner finally decided to retire. He handed the empire over to Capone. Capone adapted to his role as the head honcho very easily. He actively cultivated a public persona, showing up at the opera, Chicago White Sox games, and charity events. He played politics with the smoothest politicians. And he dressed impeccably.

From 1925 to '29, Capone simultaneously polished his public persona and meted out violence to retain his superior gangland status. In New York in 1925, he orchestrated the Adonis Club Massacre, killing a rival gang leader and establishing his influence outside of Chicago. In 1926, he is believed to have had Billy McSwiggin, a public prosecutor, killed. When public perception turned against him, Capone stepped up his community involvement. He frequently told the press that his motto was "public service." In fact, because he provided jobs for hundreds of Italian immigrants through his bootlegging business, he genuinely considered himself a public servant. When it came to his employees, Capone could be generous to a fault. He also cultivated relationships with jazz musicians who appeared in his Cicero nightspot, The Cotton Club. In 1926, Capone organized a peace conference to try to stop the violence among gangs.

The crime boss was wildly successful in creating his public image—so successful, in fact, that he caught the attention of the president of the United States. After the St. Valentine's Day Massacre in Chicago in February 1929, in which seven members or associates of a rival gang were killed, the government initiated a focused attempt to put Capone behind bars. In 1930, Capone was listed as Public Enemy Number One. Knowing PR is everything, he was also running a soup kitchen that provided free meals. In 1931, he was convicted on multiple counts of tax evasion and was sentenced to 11 years behind bars. He was ultimately transferred to Alcatraz, where he was unable to use money or personal influence to carve out the kind of pampered life he expected to live while in prison.

Florida

Because of intense media scrutiny in Chicago, Capone bought an estate in Palm Island, Florida, in 1928. Though the residents of the town were chilly to his family's arrival, the Capones established a home and a retreat in this small community. It was to this estate that Capone would return when looking to avoid the glare of his public profile in Chicago, and it was at this estate that he eventually died. While in prison, Capone suffered from neurosyphilis and was confused and disoriented. He was released from prison in 1939 and had a brief stay in a Baltimore hospital, but he returned to Palm Island, where he slowly deteriorated until his death on January 25, 1947. The man who took the world by storm with his organized and brutal approach to crime was survived by his wife, son, and four grandchildren. Though he occupied only a small corner of the world, Al Capone left a huge mark on it.

- *In the 1970s, well diggers near the mausoleum of Chinese Emperor Qin Shi-Huangdi discovered buried statues. They found the terra-cotta army, 8,099 life-size figures created in 209 B.C. to serve their deceased emperor.*

- *Jimmy Carter was the first U.S. president born in a hospital.*

Syllable Secrets: Word Histories

Waif: In 1991, Kate Moss and other super-slim, young models (who, in turn, had been preceded by the aptly nicknamed '60s model Twiggy) were dubbed *waifs*, a term that dates all the way back to 1376. In its original meaning, the term denoted unclaimed property, flotsam, or even a stray animal or person. By 1784, it referred to someone, particularly a child, who had no home or community. Since children who have no one to look after them are naturally thin, the word stuck to refer to the physique of such people.

Zaftig (also zoftig): Now used to denote a woman who is overweight, back in 1935–40, this word of Yiddish origin (it comes from *zaftik*, which literally means "juicy," and it evolved from *zaft*—"juice"—and Middle High German's *saft*) was used to describe an attractive female with curves. Such a woman might also be described as buxom, or more understatedly, well proportioned. Feel free to make your own comments about how quickly popular tastes change.

Saccharine: This word does not refer to an actual sugar substitute, but it can be used literally or metaphorically to mean "overly sweet." (The artificial sweetener doesn't have an *e* at the end, but the word was first used in that form in 1885.) *Saccharine* was first recorded in the 17th century and actually means "of or like sugar." It is derived from the Latin *saccharum* (sugar), which came from the Greek *sakkharon*, although it is related to the Sanskrit *sarkara*, which referred to gravel or grit in the fourth century.

Nachos: The favorite mid-game snack of millions—sturdy corn chips slathered in melted cheese and an assortment of toppings—was (at least according to the *Dallas Morning News*) named for the man who invented it in 1943. Ignacio Anaya was a cook in Piedras Negras, a Mexican town near the U.S. border. *Anayas*, presumably, didn't have quite the same ring as nachos.

Bagel: Not unexpectedly, this word is of Yiddish origin (*beygl*, 1919), although there's a surprise in its roots—it's from the Middle High German *boug-* ("ring, bracelet"), related to *biogan* ("to bend"). One type of flattened bagel with sprinkled onion flakes is referred to as a *bialy*, a shortened form of Bialystok, a city in Poland. Bagels were considered somewhat exotic in parts of the United States until the 1970s and '80s, when they became mass produced and available throughout the country.

Great Singer-Songwriters of the 1990s Who Met an Early Demise

"It's better to burn out than to fade away."—Neil Young

Famous musicians who died tragically are like grown-up child stars who are now drug addicts—they're not hard to come by. But these three great musicians of the '90s stand out in popular memory for their rare musical talent, tumultuous lives, and too-early deaths.

Kurt Cobain

Kurt Cobain was the front man for the grunge-rock band Nirvana. In 1994, at age 27, Cobain died of a self-inflicted gunshot wound to the head. He had suffered from depression and substance abuse for years, and he ran away from a drug rehabilitation center days before his suicide. Conspiracy theories surrounding his death abound, but most see the close-range gunshot wound, previous suicide attempts, and suicide note as indications that Cobain died by his own hand.

Elliot Smith

Elliot Smith was known from a young age for prodigious musical talent, unstable moods, and proclivity for illegal substances. His songs are recognized for their poetic flow and achingly beautiful lyrics. In 2003, Smith was found dead from an apparently self-inflicted stab wound to the chest. Although he had attempted suicide before, the presence of his girlfriend when he died has left the circumstances in question. Smith's death has never officially been declared a suicide.

Jeff Buckley

Critical acclaim greeted Jeff Buckley's 1994 debut album, *Grace,* and the singer quickly developed a following. But in 1997, Buckley drowned in Wolf River Harbor, just off the Mississippi River in Memphis. A friend reported that Buckley had spontaneously decided to go for a swim without taking off his clothes or boots. The death was ruled an accidental drowning. While Cobain and Smith's deaths set off a cascade of conspiracy theories, Buckley's drowning resulted in an outpouring of tribute songs.

Strange Justice

The Fruit of the Suit
Back in 1893, in the case of *Nix* v. *Hedden,* the U.S. Supreme Court was called upon to solve a question that had plagued salad-eaters for centuries: Was the tomato a fruit or a vegetable? The decision was important because, at the time, imported vegetables were taxed while imported fruit was not. Chief Justice Melville Fuller and his associates ignored botanical evidence that established the tomato as a fruit—rather, they considered dictionary definitions and expert testimony. The result? The court unanimously found the tomato to be a veggie.

Yourself for the Defense
Under the Sixth Amendment to the U.S. Constitution, everyone accused of a crime is entitled to legal representation. If someone can't afford a lawyer, a public defender is appointed. The accused may choose to defend him- or herself—sometimes with less than successful results. In one such case, the defendant questioned the victim, asking, "Did you get a good look at my face when I took your purse?" The defendant was found guilty and sentenced to ten years in jail for robbery.

Turn the Other Cheek
A woman teaching catechism filed suit against her archdiocese after her pastor punched her. She sued the church for emotional distress, defamation, and battery following a disagreement on how she was teaching the lessons of the Lord to her grade-school-age students. When the archdiocese refused to acknowledge or investigate her complaint, the woman felt she had no alternative but to file the lawsuit. A jury found in her favor and awarded her nearly one million dollars for the assault. The guilty priest may have gotten off easy—he died three weeks into the trial.

Landlord Lands a Legal Lulu
An apartment landlord acknowledged that he had committed 70 out of more than 400 alleged building-code violations. The judge gave him a choice of sentences—he could either spend up to 17 years in jail and pay up to $21,000 in fines, or he could live in one of his own apartment buildings for two months. Seeking to demonstrate that the conditions in his buildings weren't as bad as they had been portrayed, he chose to live amid the rats and filth in an apartment that had no heat or functioning refrigerator. His first day in his new home? Christmas Eve.

He Said, She Said

The only place success comes before work is in the dictionary.
—*Vince Lombardi*

I think more people would be alive today if there were a death penalty.
—*Nancy Reagan*

One of the definitions of sanity is the ability to tell real from unreal. Soon we'll need a new definition.
—*Alvin Toffler*

Carpe per diem—seize the check.
—*Robin Williams*

Death is no more than passing from one room into another. But there's a difference for me, you know. Because in that other room I shall be able to see.
—*Helen Keller*

There is more stupidity than hydrogen in the universe, and it has a longer shelf life.
—*Frank Zappa*

Nobody will ever win the Battle of the Sexes. There's just too much fraternizing with the enemy.
—*Henry Kissinger*

I have bad reflexes. I was once run over by a car being pushed by two guys.
—*Woody Allen*

What's money? A man is a success if he gets up in the morning and gets to bed at night and in between does what he wants to do.
—*Bob Dylan*

Brains are an asset, if you hide them.
—*Mae West*

Quote me as saying I was misquoted.
—*Groucho Marx*

A vote is like a rifle: Its usefulness depends upon the character of the user.
—*Theodore Roosevelt*

The World of Voguing

When most people hear the word vogue, *they think of Madonna's hit 1990 song and music video of the same name. However, the song is actually based on a dance with a rich history and with moves far more complex than suggested by Madonna's call to "strike a pose, there's nothing to it."*

The Movement Begins

The roots of voguing may travel as far back as late 19th-century Chicago, where underground gay communities hosted elaborate drag balls. For the most part, these balls were only held on New Year's Eve and Halloween, when the participants could legitimize their drag. Other theories argue that voguing got its start in Harlem during the 1920s Harlem Renaissance, when black gays hosted costume balls.

Whatever the precise genealogy of voguing, it emerged as a distinct art form during the mid- to late-1970s, in the poor African American and Latino gay communities of Harlem. While the youths of Harlem were organizing themselves into gangs, the voguing community had a different idea. Instead of gangs, they formed voguing "houses." Each house was presided over by a "mother," and the different houses competed in voguing competitions called "balls."

Strike a Pose

The essence of voguing is that the performer flawlessly fuses together several diverse components of a dance, all while walking down a runway dressed up as a specific persona. The vogue dance varies from community to community, but it generally combines elements of jazz, gymnastics, bodybuilding, ballet, break-dancing, and karate. Complex hand and arm movements are incorporated as part of the "pose," which imitates traditional runway poses. The term voguing came as a reference to the fashion magazine *Vogue*.

Inseparable from the dance is the persona. Voguers are asked to perform in a given category, such as "businessman," "femme queen," or "school girl." Essential to the success of the performance is "realness"—the voguer must convincingly look and act like a businessman, for instance, from clothing to accessories to gesture. Voguers are rewarded with trophies and cash prizes.

Many voguers lived in poverty and made money illegally. They were often discriminated against for their sexual orientation and cast to society's edges. The different ballroom "houses" fostered a sense of community, and many voguers became skilled and devoted dancers. The underground ballroom scene had its own lingo, its own rules, and, above all else, its own dance.

The Underground Goes Overground

As the voguing movement became more popular, members of the Harlem houses would sometimes visit the midtown clubs of mainstream Manhattan. By the late 1980s, professional voguers were hired at trendy midtown hot spots, and some clubs hosted "vogue night" every week.

The process seemed complete in 1989 when the ballroom scene's most famous houses staged a competitive ball at a celebrity-studded AIDS fund-raising event in Manhattan. That same year, top voguers were sent to vogue down the Paris runways. A 1989 *Time* magazine article declared, "At the hottest clubs in Manhattan, on MTV and at Paris fashion shows, the ultra-hip are into voguing."

And then, in 1990, documentary filmmaker Jennie Livingston released *Paris Is Burning,* a documentary about underground ball culture that was seven years in the making. The film was critically acclaimed and spawned an avalanche of academic controversy that deserves a genre of its own.

Movie critics and academics alike were intrigued by the socially subversive nature of voguing as presented in Livingston's film. They argued that by dressing as movie stars and fashion models, the socially marginalized voguers were actually mocking the power given these roles by society. Others vehemently disagreed with this interpretation, pointing out that the vogue competitors did not mock but rather emulated and admired these roles, thus paying homage to the very power structures that kept them down. A central part of the ballroom philosophy was that one can feel beautiful by looking beautiful; by imitating power, one can have it—at least for those few shining moments out on the runway. Voguing was thus simultaneously an act of control and escapism. Venus Xtravaganza, one of the film's stars, expressed her desire to be a "spoiled, rich white girl."

Ironic Consequences

Voguing's 15 minutes of fame did embody a puzzling irony: An underground culture that sought to imitate the mainstream was made mainstream by a documentary that sought to represent the underground. Yet, once Madonna's song hit the airwaves and Livingston's movie graced the big screen, the media's new proprietorship of voguing quickly proved that, in fact, the voguers themselves could never hope to become the spoiled, rich white girls that they dressed up to be. Madonna made millions off her song, and so did MTV. Within two years of the release of *Paris Is Burning,* all but two of the subjects featured in the film sued for a portion of the film's profits. Their case was denied. Within five years of the film's release, five of those in the film were dead. Venus Xtravaganza, a prostitute, was murdered by one of her clients.

The fear that the documentary carnivorously absorbed voguing into the mainstream is arguably the least of the concerns of the voguing community itself. Ballroom houses continue to thrive, having sprung up in Los Angeles, Chicago, and even in Indiana and Kentucky. The ballroom community is alive and well, proving once again that subcultures continue to exist, even if they aren't featured on MTV.

- Smith *is the most common surname in the United States, Wales, England, and Scotland; and fifth in Ireland and Canada.* Schmidt *(a version of* Smith*) ranks second in commonality in Germany.*

- *Time zones in the United States were adopted in 1883 because standardized schedules—and identically set clocks—kept the trains punctual.*

- *The Lincoln penny was the first "portrait coin" regularly produced in the United States. No one knows for sure how many pennies are in circulation; estimates are that it's in the hundreds of billions.*

The Blair Witch Project

Made by two young filmmakers on the ridiculously small budget of $35,000, this 1999 film only brought in $1.5 million in its first week's box office—nothing to pay attention to. But the power of word-of-mouth and a compelling prerelease Web site eventually turned the largely improvised flick into a genuine blockbuster that grossed more than $140 million domestically in three months. A sequel in 2000, *Book of Shadows,* was not as successful, delivering less than 20 percent of the original's sales.

Goldfinger

The 1964 James Bond spy flick *Goldfinger* featured fast cars (including the sleek, gadget-filled Aston-Martin DB-5 and introducing the Ford Mustang to the public) and fast women. It also featured German actor Gert Frobe as master villain Auric Goldfinger—the "Man with the Midas Touch." He was also a man with a tin ear. Unable to speak English, Frobe tried to deliver his dialogue through phonetic pronunciation. The results were less than acceptable. Ultimately, the film's producers were forced to dub his entire spoken role with a voice actor named Michael Collins.

Masque of the Red Death

Director Roger Corman built his reputation in Hollywood by quickly making cheap and scary films that turned a profit. He produced and directed a series of movies in the 1960s based on the stories of Edgar Allan Poe and often starring horror regular Vincent Price. While shooting *Masque of the Red Death* in 1964, Corman became friendly with starlet Jane Asher. One day, she brought a friend to watch the production, and Corman told the young lad to "stick around and have lunch," not realizing that he was Jane's steady boyfriend—Paul McCartney from the Beatles.

Some Like It Hot

Considered among the greatest movie comedies of all time, this 1959 flick is the story of two Roaring Twenties jazz musicians who witness the St. Valentine's Day Massacre and escape by posing as female members of an all-girl band. There is a wonderful scene where all the attractive young girls show up at a posh hotel in Florida, drawing the attention of the elderly millionaires seated on the veranda. During one of the takes, director Billy Wilder noticed a *real* millionaire had pulled up a chair with the rest, not aware of the filming. The director quickly shooed him away.

The McDonald's Kingdom

In the restaurant industry, there is probably no greater success story than McDonald's. Supporters claim the introduction of the "take away meal" was a good thing, revolutionizing the way billions of people around the world eat. However, many would disagree and go as far as to say that this concept has ruined Americans' health and the fabric of the nation's culture. But few can debate the fact (no matter which side of the bun they're on) that McDonald's has become synonymous with fast food around the world.

Setting the Record Straight

If you thought Ray Kroc opened the first McDonald's, you'd be wrong. In 1940, two brothers, Dick and Maurice (Mac) McDonald, opened the first McDonald's on Route 66 in San Bernardino, California. As was common at the time, carhops served hungry teens with made-to-order food. But that all changed in 1948, when the McDonalds fired the carhops and implemented their innovative "Speedee Service System," a technique that streamlined the assembly process and became the benchmark for premade hamburgers. Additionally, this process allowed profits to soar... they could now sell hamburgers for 15 cents, or half what a dinner would cost.

In 1953, Dick and Mac decided to franchise their restaurant, and the second McDonald's opened in Phoenix, Arizona. It was the first Mickey D's to sport the famous golden arches. A year later, an entrepreneur and milkshake-mixer salesman named Ray Kroc visited. He was impressed with the McDonalds' enterprise, and he immediately joined their team. In 1955, he founded the current McDonald's Systems, Inc., and opened the ninth McDonald's restaurant in Des Plaines, Illinois. Six years later, Kroc bought the business from the McDonald brothers for $2.7 million. The poorly constructed deal stipulated that Dick and Mac could keep the original restaurant but somehow overlooked their right to remain a McDonald's franchise. Because of this error, Kroc opened a restaurant down the block from the original store, and within a short time he drove the brothers out of the hamburger business.

Two All-Beef Patties

Kroc's many marketing insights included Hamburger University—where the graduates are presented with bachelor's degrees in Hamburgerology—ads targeting families, and the introduction of Ronald McDonald and "McDonaldland." Feeling the need to adapt, the company altered the menu for the first time in 1963, adding the Filet-O-Fish (prompted by Catholics who didn't eat meat on Fridays), followed by such famous additions as the Big Mac and apple pie.

McDonald's spread like wildfire and, in 1967, the first McDonald's restaurant outside the United States opened in Richmond, British Columbia. Ten years later, McDonald's was operating on four continents. It completed its world domination in 1992 by opening an African restaurant in Casablanca, Morocco.

In 1974, along with Fred Hill of the Philadelphia Eagles, McDonald's founded the Ronald McDonald House, an organization that caters to families of critically ill children seeking medical treatment. As of 2008, there were 259 outlets.

Hold the Mayo

All has not gone smoothly for the Mc-empire over the past several years, however. In 2000, Eric Schlosser published *Fast Food Nation,* a critical commentary on fast food in general and McDonald's in particular. This was followed by several lawsuits: one on obesity (claiming McDonald's "lured" young children into their restaurant with their playgrounds) and others asserting various claims of damaged health due to saturated fats.

A huge sensation followed the 2004 release of the film *Supersize Me.* This documentary accused fast-food restaurants of ignoring America's escalating obesity crisis. Later that year, in response to the public's desire for healthier food, McDonald's did away with its super-size meals and implemented more chicken and fish options. In 2005, they added a range of salads and low-sugar drinks and agreed to put nutritional information on all their packaging.

In addition to its new health-conscious menu, McDonald's has also tightened its belt by closing several restaurants to compensate for occasionally sagging financial reports. But not much deters McDonald's, which, for the foreseeable future, remains the king of the world's fast-food empire.

The Times They Are A-Changin'

1951

January 18: The National Football League rules that guards, tackles, and centers are ineligible to catch a forward pass.

January 22: Future Cuban dictator Fidel Castro is ejected from a Winter League baseball game after beaning a batter.

January 27: Nuclear testing begins at the Frenchman Flats, Nevada, test site northwest of Las Vegas when a one-kiloton bomb is dropped.

January 29: Actor Elizabeth Taylor divorces her first husband, Conrad Hilton, Jr.

February 26: The 22nd Amendment to the U.S. Constitution is ratified, limiting the president to two terms in office.

March 12: The *Dennis the Menace* comic strip appears in U.S. newspapers for the first time.

April 17: Mickey Mantle gets his first hit in his first game for the New York Yankees.

May 25: Willie Mays goes without a hit in his first game for the New York Giants.

June 14: The U.S. Census Bureau begins using the first commercial computer, the UNIVAC 1.

June 25: CBS star Arthur Godfrey appears in the first color TV broadcast.

August 11: WCBS in New York City broadcasts the first baseball game in color between the Boston Braves and the Brooklyn Dodgers.

August 31: The first 33⅓ RPM album is introduced in Dusseldorf, Germany.

September 3: The TV soap opera *Search for Tomorrow* premieres on CBS. Each episode is 15 minutes long.

October 15: *I Love Lucy* premieres on CBS.

December 23: The first coast-to-coast football game is broadcast on the Dumont Television Network; the Los Angeles Rams beat the Cleveland Browns 24–17 in the NFL championship game.

History's Most Idiosyncratic VIPs

*High-level dignitaries should demonstrate dignified behavior—
and yet, the annals of history show a litany of idiosyncratic
elite. Whether it was a tendency toward eccentricity that
suited them to politics and social status or, rather, the
privileged position itself that drove them kooky, odd conduct
by high-powered bigwigs has always been around.*

His Royal Snobbery

Consider Charles Seymour, the sixth Duke of Somerset and Baron of Trowbridge. This historical figure is often referred to as the "Proud Duke," but a more fitting nickname might be the "Pompous Duke." Baron Thomas Babington Macaulay, a 19th-century poet and politician, once quipped that Seymour's "pride of birth and rank amounted almost to a disease." So snobbish was the duke that he wouldn't lower himself to the level of his servants by uttering even a single word to them. Instead, he enlisted sign language to communicate his needs and desires. He preferred not to mingle with the general masses, either—he had private homes built along his travel routes from Somerset to London so that he could remain isolated from lower-class travelers who used inns.

Hungarian Bloodletter

Countess Elizabeth Bathory of Hungary is another historical figure who displayed some notable eccentricities. Her odd behavior, however, was of a more criminal nature. A raven-haired beauty with smooth ivory skin, Bathory, along with a team of cohorts that included a dwarf named Ficzko, tricked hundreds of young maidens into her home, Cachtice Castle, enticing them with hopes of well-paid work, only to brutally torture and murder them. According to some accounts, the countess sought their virginal blood for rejuvenating baths. Apparently, skin care in 16th- and 17th-century Hungary wasn't up to snuff. Also known as the "Bloody Countess" for her particularly disturbing behavior, Bathory was imprisoned in a fortress and lived for four years trapped behind a wall of stones, with meals slipped to her through the cracks. She died behind those walls.

Slippery Cal

Calvin Coolidge, the 30th president of the United States, also had a strange personal grooming regimen. Thankfully, his product of choice was not the blood of young virgins, but the more easily accessible petroleum jelly. Coolidge was dubbed "Silent Cal" for his introverted disposition and tendency toward taciturnity. Alice Roosevelt Longworth, Theodore Roosevelt's eldest daughter, famously described Coolidge as looking "as if he had been weaned on a pickle." With that image in mind, consider Coolidge's strangest habit: In bed, whilst eating his typical morning breakfast of boiled wheat and rye, he enjoyed having his head massaged with Vaseline. Pair that odd picture with another of his strange eccentricities, his regular exercise routine—atop the electric horse that he kept in the White House—and you have one idiosyncratic national leader, indeed.

Dinner Goes to the Dogs

Another odd aristocrat, the eighth Earl of Bridgewater, Sir Francis Henry Egerton, was a lonely sort who nursed a peculiar penchant for a few of his prized possessions, namely his pet dogs and his enormous collection of shoes—he had a pair for each day of the year. Egerton, who lived in the late 18th and early 19th centuries, was known for hosting fantastic dinner parties in which he demanded only the finest decorum from his guests. Instead of hosting humans, though, his table was set for his brood of pet pups. Dressed in the most exquisite fashions of the day, and with first-rate, handmade leather shoes to rival his own, the dogs' necks were adorned with crisp linen napkins. If a dog deviated from what Egerton considered acceptable table manners, it was exiled to the kitchen for a lonely week of solitary meals.

Wearers Beware

Instead of requiring particular dress from his subjects, as his near-contemporary Egerton did with his dogs, idiosyncratic Czar Paul I of St. Petersburg strictly forbade specific articles of clothing for all of the inhabitants of his land. The czar associated round hats, sleeveless vests, pantaloons, laced shoes, and top boots with French revolutionaries, so he passed a law decreeing the wearing of these items unconstitutional. Hundreds of armed troops were unleashed on the streets to ambush those frocked hooligans, who were then stripped of the undesirable garb. One boot-wearing lawbreaker even watched as authorities snipped his too-tall boots down to shoe shape.

Crime and Punishment

Austrian Empress Maria Theresa was known for her exemplary and visionary leadership skills in the 1700s, but she also had a few strange tendencies on her rap sheet. After dealing with rumors of her own husband's supposed infidelities, Maria became staunch in her distaste for all indecent behaviors. The empress sought to weed out sinners by forming a task force to locate and punish adulterers, prostitutes, and other unseemly sorts. Prostitutes, for instance, were exiled to isolated regions of the country—creating, in essence, sinner suburbs. Stranger than these organized witch hunts, though, is the legend related to the birth of her daughter, Marie Antoinette. The empress seized the opportunity of her imminent labor to attend to another medical need. Since she was already in pain anyway, she figured she'd have her dentist pull out that pesky bad tooth. Now that's multitasking!

Written in the Stars

Some modern leaders have had a few eccentric habits, as well. Take Ronald Reagan, the 40th U.S. president. Early in their marriage, he and his wife Nancy developed a strong dependency on astrology, which guided them through many of his important leadership decisions. Feeling particularly vulnerable after a 1981 assassination attempt, the Reagans enlisted the help of famous astrologists to draw up the appropriate charts to see what the stars had in store for them, and then they used the charts to plan the president's calendar. The determinations they came to through the guidance of astrology affected the bombing of Libya, the invasion of Grenada, and the launch of the *Challenger.*

- *A conflict between French King Philip IV and Pope Boniface VIII led to the king's excommunication by Boniface. A month after Philip had the pope imprisoned for three days, Boniface died of a violent fever.*

Popular Hairstyles Through the Ages

Humans are the only animals to willingly and consciously cut their hair, and although this ability definitely has its perks, it's also been the source of many woes and bad decisions. Here are some of the more extreme, time-consuming, gravity-defying looks that have graced our crowns throughout the ages.

Mohawk

Originally worn in Native American cultures, the mohawk re-appeared sometime in the 1970s, along with the punk rock movement. At its most extreme, the mohawk, called the *mohican* in the UK, featured a stripe of hair sticking straight up and running down the middle of the head, with the sides of the head shaved. It made a statement about not giving in to social standards. However, with the metrosexual "fauxhawk" (small spike, not shaved on sides), the mohawk of today is much more watered-down.

Mullet

Also appearing sometime in the 1970s, the mullet soared to popularity in the '80s among rockers and rednecks. But the origins of the short-on-the-top-and-sides, long-and-free-in-the-back look are a bit mysterious. Some say that hockey players originated the 'do, and others think it's an offspring of rock 'n' roll (David Bowie was an early adopter)—but most agree that it should be retired.

Pompadour

In a pompadour, the hair is gelled back, giving it a sleek, wet look, and the front is pushed forward. The look is often associated with the 1950s, when it was worn by the likes of Elvis Presley and Johnny Cash. But Madame de Pompadour, a mistress to King Louis XV and a fashionista in her time, originally donned the look in the 1700s. The style is still worn by retro rockabilly types, including Brian Setzer.

Beehive

This is another style with origins that date back to the 18th century. During the outlandish wig phase, when the bigger and more extravagant the piece, the more money and social status it carried, 'hives were very popular. Women allegedly even used them to house trinkets, such as small caged birds. In the 1960s, the beehive surged in popularity, and today, the crown of the beehive queen belongs to cartoon character Marge Simpson, who sports a tall blue updo.

Afro

Birthed by the black pride movement, the afro represents a time when African Americans stopped applying harsh chemicals to achieve something close to Caucasian texture and style to their hair. In the 1960s, the afro was a political statement, but today it is worn as fashion. Anyone with extremely curly hair can also adopt the style.

Powdered Wigs

In the 18th century, hygiene was hardly what it is today, and head lice were a rampant problem, so wigs were worn to cover shaved heads. But powdered wigs themselves were hotbeds for lice, roaches, and other critters. Still, wigs were worn until the end of the 18th century, when an expensive tax on white powder made the trend die down.

- *Everyone in President Lyndon Baines Johnson's family had LBJ as their initials. His wife was nicknamed Lady Bird, and his daughters were Linda Bird and Lucy Baines. Even the family dog, Little Beagle Johnson, got in on the action.*

- *During the Battle of the Yellow Ford in 1598, the British suffered their worst defeat at the hands of Irish clansmen. Out of 4,000 English troops engaged, their casualties surpassed 1,500.*

- *Political enemies Thomas Jefferson and John Adams both died on July 4, 1826, the 50th anniversary of the Declaration of Independence.*

- *At the height of his power, Attila the Hun ruled an empire that extended through half of Europe to the steppes of Central Asia.*

- *Trampolines don't have to be all fun and games. NASA has used them to train astronauts for flight.*

- *America's first federal gasoline tax, one cent per gallon, was created on June 6, 1932. By 2008, the rate was 18.4 cents per gallon.*

- Kristallnacht, *also sometimes known as The Night of Broken Glass, began on November 9, 1938. German civilians joined Nazi storm troopers in ransacking more than 7,500 Jewish businesses, damaging more than 1,000 synagogues, and arresting 30,000 Jews.*

- A Robin Hood *in archery is when two arrows are shot into a target, and the second arrow splits the first.*

- *While hiding inside the Zamboni before the Carolina Hurricanes' first ever preseason game in 1997, team mascot Stormy had a major anxiety attack and had to be hospitalized.*

- *When his landing craft neared Anzio Beach during World War II, James Arness, later the star of* Gunsmoke, *was ordered off first. He was the tallest soldier on the craft, and his superiors wanted to see how deep the water was.*

- *The first weekly* New York Times *best-seller list appeared on August 9, 1942. The number-one best-selling novel was* And Now Tomorrow *by Rachel Field. It held the top spot for a week.*

- *The first electronic computer, ENIAC, was 80 feet long, weighed 30 tons, and had 17,000 tubes. Today's desktop model can store a million times more information.*

- *The body of Pope Formosus was exhumed in 897 and tried by his successor, Pope Stephen VI, on multiple religious charges. The cadaver was found guilty and thrown into the Tiber River.*

- *The U.S. Postal Service introduced zip codes in 1963.*

Great Ad Campaigns That Made Us Buy

There are a lot of people who want you to buy something, and when the advertising industry is on, the ads they come up with can sure be effective.

Could a simple soft drink unite those embroiled in a state of hostility? Bill Backer, an advertising representative for the Coca-Cola account, believed Coke could do just that when he brainstormed an anthem of peace to air alongside a pack of Coke-adoring pacifists. The song's lyrics—about the act of singing itself—insisted that buying a Coke would keep the world in perfect harmony. Sappy as the image may have been, Coca-Cola calculated that about 4,000 pieces of fan mail were sent the week the commercial debuted.

If a schmaltzy song can sell soda, perhaps an animated, life-size faux-food product could accomplish a similar trick. Enter Twinkie the Kid. This Hostess mascot was a cowboy by trade but was equally adept at saving sponge-cake-loving children from peril.

How Much Would That Cost?

In the 1990s, MasterCard claimed that so many special moments are "priceless"—but for those items that can be purchased, you should use your credit card. Combined visions—one part life's happy happenstance and one part purchased goods—all brought forth the same conclusion: Memories are invaluable, but you have to spend some dough to fuel them with consumer goods.

For those times when fast cash can't save the day, though, how about an intervening breath mint? Mentos, aka the "freshmaker," was up for almost any face-saving endeavor. Just ask that poor schmuck who sat on a freshly painted park bench in his neatly pressed suit. Thanks to the salvation of the roll of Mentos that he found in his pocket, he was able to see the bright side of his situation: a newly pin-striped suit, instead of ruined workday garb.

At least with a campaign such as the ever-evolving "Got Milk" onslaught, the product is actually used to hawk itself. Now, if only the ad industry didn't insist on doing so with that messy moo juice adorning the drinker's lips.

The Fashion Industry's Biggest Blunders

Fashion gives birth to red-hot ideas more quickly than most people can imagine. But these trends often depart as fast as they come, consigning racks of yesterday's brilliant inspirations to bargain-basement sale bins.

The turn of the 20th century gave women a break from various kinds of fashion torture. In China, woman finally stopped the crippling practice of binding their feet. In the West, women quit tightening their corsets to nearly dangerous levels. It was a big change from the popular fashion adage that had proclaimed, "Your waist should never be bigger than your age."

Deadly Styles
However, even if fashion became kinder, it never became less bizarre. The late 1800s saw men wearing highly starched necklines with pointy collars. Dubbed the *patricide,* this style got its name from the tale of a man who returned home from university. As the student embraced his father, the sharp, pointed collar cut the father's throat and killed him.

Tightness as a Virtue
Also coming into vogue about this time was the wool bathing suit. After swimming, if the wearer lay in the sun for too long, the suit grew tighter and tighter. Because of the easy availability of wool, however, this trend lasted much longer than one might expect.

Flapper dresses were all the rage in the Roaring Twenties, but little is remembered about Paul Poiret's "hobble skirts." Heavily influenced by Asian design and color, these skirts were made to fit so tightly that it was nearly impossible for a woman to move—let alone to climb a flight of stairs or run from a fire.

Flaunting Your Features
The 1940s featured big bands and swing and ushered in the cone-shape bra. But billionaire Howard Hughes, entrepreneur and lover

of cleavage, decided to take the point one step farther: To capitalize on actor Jane Russell's assets while making the movie *The Outlaw*, Hughes designed a cantilevered bra for her to wear. Subsequently, twin peaks in Alaska were named after her.

The 1950s were all about poodle skirts, saddle shoes, and pedal pushers. But the coonskin cap was one style that came and went quickly, much to the dismay of Davy Crockett fans everywhere.

Television and movies tried to influence fashion, but no fashion trend made quite as big a splash as Audrey Hepburn's classic A-style dress did in the movie *Roman Holiday*. Ryan O'Neal's "see-through" cheeks-exposing jeans in the movie *So Fine* might have showed off the garment industry's seamy side, but the public didn't buy them.

The Not-so-distant Past

The 1980s were a decade filled with fashion missteps—thankfully, paper clothes never caught fire, and green suede Robin Hood boots disappeared.

It's hard to imagine James Dean or John Wayne carrying a clutch, but the "man purse" came into style in dribs and drabs, much to the ridicule of John Q. Public. The grunge look and Euro-trash styles were easier for celebrities to wear than for normal folks, with low-riding pants "cracking up" more than a few people.

Debacles of the 21st century have included singer Björk's much-criticized "swan dress" at the Academy Awards. In terms of hairstyles, pink wigs rocketed and then fizzled, Billy Ray Cyrus tried to revive the mullet, and pink and purple hit the racks, and then went south. Feather earrings—which first made their debut in the '70s—tried to make a revival in 2000 but quickly faded out of sight.

For lots of spare change, everyone wanted to own a few pairs of Manolo Blahniks. But in 2001, Blahnik had to pull a line of razor-sharp three-inch titanium stiletto heels because they were so sharp that they cut through carpet, not to mention dancing partners' feet.

For centuries, only the well-heeled dwelled on fashion. For most people, clothes evolved from need and function, not style. But times are different, and as the saying goes, if you don't like the fashion now, just wait five minutes and it'll change.

Fumbling Felons

Reruns Are Always Annoying
In July 2006, a convenience store supervisor in Edinburgh, Scotland, conspired with a friend to rob his store of more than three thousand dollars and to beat him up for good measure. Their plan seemed foolproof. Police arrived at the store to find the safe open and the supervisor bleeding from repeated blows to the head and body. Upon further investigation, however, the security camera footage showed the supervisor opening the door on his day off and walking in with his friend. The 20-year-olds, known to gamble together, admitted to staging the whole thing.

Don't Drink and Mow
A Martinsburg, West Virginia, man was accused of drunk driving on his riding lawn mower in October 2007—a mile from his home. After an officer—still in his police car—asked the man to pull over, the man "sped" away on his mower. The officer then jumped out of his car, chased the mower on foot, and caught up to it after a short jog. The officer allegedly found a case of beer strapped to the front of the riding mower. When the driver refused a field sobriety test, the authorities held him on $7,500 bond.

Man of a Thousand Faces
A disguised man robbed a bank in Manchester, New Hampshire, in July 2007. That may not be so unusual, but unfortunately for him, the man had disguised himself as a tree. He walked into the bank with leaves and branches duct-taped to his face and body and demanded money. Despite his face being somewhat obscured, someone recognized the robber after seeing footage released from a bank security camera. An anonymous tip led police straight to the man later that night.

Always Know Your Customer
On September 19, 2007, in Charleston, West Virginia, a 19-year-old sent a text message to his friend asking if he "wanted to buy some reefer." The teen received a text message back saying simply "yes," and a meeting was arranged. What the young man didn't know was that his friend had changed his cell phone number and that the number to which he sent the text belonged to a state trooper. Oops. The teenager was charged with delivery of a controlled substance and possession with intent to deliver marijuana.

Transformation: The Christine Jorgensen Story

❖ ❖ ❖ ❖

Can experimental surgery truly lead to happiness?

"Ex-GI Becomes Blonde Beauty" screamed the front-page headline of the *New York Daily News* on December 1, 1952. In a country weary from the Korean War and jittery over the McCarthy hearings, it was just the sort of story everyone wanted to see. It announced that George William Jorgensen of the Bronx had received the first sex-change operation, which took place in Denmark. It wasn't precisely true, but it made for great copy.

This pioneering surgery had actually first been performed in the 1920s and early 1930s by Dr. Magnus Hirschfeld at the Institute of Sexual Science in Berlin. But then Hitler and the Nazis came along, and such surgery disappeared.

Jorgensen was among the first of the postwar transgendered people. The new element in Jorgensen's surgery was the use of artificial hormones to enhance the physical change. In Copenhagen, Jorgensen had his male sexual organs removed. Several years later, he—now she—received an artificial vagina when that procedure became available. Jorgensen's doctor, Christian Hamburger, then supervised her hormone therapy. Jorgensen chose the name "Christine" to honor the man who had made a woman out of her.

William Jorgensen had been a frail, introverted boy who avoided contact sports and ran from fights at Christopher Columbus High School. Upon his graduation in 1945, he was drafted and spent a hitch in the U.S. Army before receiving an honorable discharge. But he was not happy. He later reflected that he was "a woman trapped in a man's body," so he began to research the possibility of a sex change. He was on his way to Sweden to meet with doctors there when, during a stop in Copenhagen to visit friends, he learned about Dr. Hamburger.

A New Life

The press picked up on the sensationalism of the *New York Daily News* headline, and on her return to the United States two months later, Christine was met with media attention and curiosity. The notoriety could easily have been short-lived, but she was canny enough to stay in the public eye and build a career—both as a photographer-performer and as a spokesperson for transsexuality and transgendered people.

Jorgensen was usually a good sport in interviews, where she was inevitably confronted with jokes such as, "Christine went abroad and came back a broad." But an encounter with talk show host Dick Cavett didn't go nearly so well. Cavett was curious about romance in her life, so he asked about her "wife." He later insisted that he hadn't intended to insult her, but Christine got up and walked out. With no other guests scheduled that evening, Cavett found he had some time to fill. In reality, Christine was never married, though she was engaged to a man. When it was discovered that her birth certificate identified her as a male, the authorities refused to issue a marriage license.

Showbiz Beckons

Christine soon moved into the world of entertainment. Known for her candor and sharp wit, she toured college campuses on the same circuit as stand-up comedians. In an era when civil rights, women's rights, and gay rights took center stage, she was in the right place at the right time. She was the subject of a 1970 film, *The Christine Jorgensen Story,* and was the supposed inspiration for the movie *Glen or Glenda?*

Christine worked as an actor in summer stock and as a night-club entertainer, performing regularly at Freddy's Supper Club in Manhattan, where her repertoire included the song "I Enjoy Being a Girl." She recorded an album and eventually returned to Copenhagen to perform her act in 1984. In 1989, Christine said that she'd given the sexual revolution "a good swift kick in the pants." She died that same year, after a battle with bladder and lung cancers.

• *The ancient city of Babylon was thought to be impregnable. King Cyrus of Persia captured it, however, by reducing the amount of water flowing into the city and entering via the riverbed.*

• *A day on Mars lasts 39.5 minutes longer than a day on Earth.*

PALINDROMES

When you've got a word, phrase, or sentence that reads the same backward and forward, you've got a palindrome!

Ed, I spotted a clam in an animal cadet topside.

Ungate me, Vic, I've met a gnu.

No, Mel Gibson is a casino's big lemon.

party booby trap

Gateman sees name, garageman sees name tag.

Oh, who was it I saw? Oh, who?

Dogma: I am God.

Sex at my gym taxes.

Tulsa nightlife: filth, gin, a slut

Did Joe kill like O. J. did?

Sis, ask Costner to not rent socks "as is"!

laminate pet animal

never odd or even

Ma handed Edna ham.

Leno located a cadet: a colonel!

oozy rat in a sanitary zoo

Lana, can I sit on Otis in a canal?

Name is Orton, not Rosie, man!

Madam, I do get a mate. God, I'm Adam.

Flee to me, remote elf.

A new order began, a more Roman age bred Rowena.

E.T. is opposite.

No yarn in rayon?

Red Quagmire:
The Russo-Afghan War

*Americans cheered the early stages of modern Islamic
extremism when it focused on the enemies of the United States.
But the enemy of your enemy is not always your friend.*

In February 1979, the Islamic Revolution in Iran ousted the U.S.-
backed shah, setting the stage for the Hostage Crisis and the Iran-
Contra Scandal. On February 14, U.S. Ambassador to Afghanistan
Adolph Dubs was abducted and killed by Islamists. In March, a
peace treaty was signed between Egypt and Israel, which angered
the Soviet Union. And Muslim Afghans were threatening the pro-
Russian Afghan government. The situation was ripe for trouble.

Soviet Advances in Afghanistan

The Soviets had been sending arms and advisers to the Afghans for
60 years, and finally, an Afghan Communist government emerged.
Neither the Soviets nor the new government was about to let a
bunch of religious fanatics march in and take over.

Between April 1978 and December 1979, the government struck
back, arresting Islamic mullahs and their supporters and execut-
ing an estimated 27,000 people. The city of Herat rebelled, so the
government and its Russian allies flattened the city, killing another
24,000. More than half of the 90,000 soldiers in the Afghan army
deserted or joined the rebels. In no time, the United States and half
a dozen Islamic states were supporting those rebels—called *mujahideen.* The Soviets lost all patience at that point. Near Christmas
1979, the Red Army stormed into Afghanistan.

Massive Power Can't Always Carry the Day

In what became known as "The Soviet Vietnam," the 40th Army
spread out across the country and began hunting insurgents. Soviet
aircraft responded with air strikes. But 80 percent of the country
remained outside their control.

The Afghan people have been mountain fighters since the time
of Alexander the Great. They struck at the Russians and then melted

away. The Soviets called up reservists to supplement their troops. They deployed the Mi-24 Hind helicopter gunship, the best attack helicopter in existence at the time. Although the Russians won all of the major battles, they could never gain control of the countryside.

Building a Religious Resistance

The United States, Saudi Arabia, and Pakistan were busily supplying the rebels with weapons, which tipped the scale against the Russians. The Muslim world actively recruited foreign fighters to wage war against the infidel Soviets in Afghanistan. One, a young Saudi named Osama bin Laden, eventually evolved his unit into al-Qaeda.

The mujahideen paid great attention to sabotage, attacking power plants, pipelines, radio stations, public buildings, airports, hotels, and cinemas. They murdered anyone associated with the government and absolutely refused to back down.

Changes in the USSR

In 1982, hard-liner Leonid Brezhnev, general secretary of the Communist party of the Soviet Union (and thus political and governmental boss) died, and after two short-term successors, Mikhail Gorbachev took over. It soon became obvious that the Cold War was winding down; Gorbachev announced the Soviet withdrawal from Afghanistan. On February 15, 1989, the last soldiers left.

The Soviets had suffered hundreds of thousands killed and wounded. Material losses included hundreds of aircraft, helicopters, tanks, artillery pieces, and almost 12,000 trucks. Their army was wrecked, their economy ruined. The Soviet Union itself soon disappeared as more and more satellite states declared independence.

More than one million Afghans were killed, and five million fled to Pakistan. Cities were destroyed, and 10–16 million land mines were left scattered across the countryside. And worst of all, a civil war in Afghanistan still raged between the remnants of the Communist government and the mujahideen. The mujahideen took the upper hand in 1992, but when rural warlords continued to fight among themselves, a group of religious fundamentalist fighters called the Taliban rose up against them. By the end of 1996, the Taliban had taken control of the capital of Kabul and set up an Islamic state. The religious order it established evolved into a perfect breeding ground for the next holy war—led by Osama bin Laden and al-Qaeda.

The Beta Wars

When videotape recorders entered the consumer market,
formatting differences between Betamax and VHS didn't exactly
spark a shooting war, but in some quarters they could have.

On first hearing about high-definition television, comedian Paula
Poundstone said that she wasn't buying into another system until she
was certain that it was the *last* system. It was a complaint that most
Americans understood.

The question of media formatting goes back at least to the days
when the printing press replaced hand-lettered manuscripts, but it
became a matter of open, partisan warfare in 1975 when videotape
was introduced as a mass medium. Sony introduced the Betamax
video system, which was followed a year later by JVC's totally incom-
patible VHS. It was eight-tracks and cassette tapes all over again.

Quality Versus Price and Convenience

There is little disagreement that Sony's Betamax was a technically
superior system, but JVC's VHS (which stood for *Video Helical
Scan*) was marketed intensively. Its players were cheaper and easier
to make, and other manufacturers started to adopt the VHS format.
Additionally, Beta featured only one-hour tapes—not long enough to
record a movie—while VHS had two-hour tapes. By the time Beta
developed B-II (two-hour) and B-III (three-hour) formats, VHS had
a four-hour format. Eventually, Beta achieved five hours, and VHS
reached 10.6 hours.

In 1985, Sony introduced SuperBeta; JVC countered with
Super-VHS. As the systems tried to outdo each other, Beta was
never quite able to catch up. Major studios released fewer movies
on Beta. Then, in a 1989 episode of *Married . . . with Children,* the
Bundys were described as "the last family on earth with Beta." That
offhand comment was the kiss of death.

VHS ruled the roost. At least, that is, until DVDs came along.

• *In the typical American home, television sets outnumber the*
people living there.

Fast Facts

- Soviet gymnast Larissa Latynina won a record 18 Olympic medals. She competed in three Olympic Games, in 1956, 1960, and 1964.

- In 1674, King Louis XIV of France learned that a nine-year-old Irish boy had made fun of his bald head. He had the youth imprisoned in the Bastille, where he remained for 69 years.

- Although no one will ever know for sure, the surface of the sun is thought to be about 10,000° F.

- Marie Maynard Daily became the first African American woman to earn a Ph.D. in chemistry when she earned a doctorate from Columbia University in 1947.

- Portuguese explorer Pedro Álvares Cabral set out for the Americas with 13 ships in March 1500. He discovered Brazil a month and a half later, claiming it for Portugal.

- Tears kill bacteria that get into your eye.

- The Vermont Teddy Bear Company created and sold a product called the Crazy for You Bear in 2005. It came in a straitjacket with commitment papers.

- Nero's wife, Poppaea, regularly took a bath filled with the milk from 500 female asses to make her skin softer and whiter. When she was exiled from Rome, she was permitted only 50 asses.

- Chinese dialects are the second-most widely spoken language in Australia.

- The highest temperature ever recorded in the United States was 134° F at Greenland Ranch in Death Valley, California.

- The @ sign is believed to be at least six centuries old.

The Mysterious Death of Thelma Todd

Old Hollywood has more than its fill of secrets. Here's another one.

On December 16, 1935, at about 10:30 A.M., actor Thelma Todd was found dead behind the wheel of her Lincoln Phaeton convertible. Her maid, Mae Whitehead, had come to clean the luxurious apartment Todd lived in above her rollicking roadhouse, Thelma Todd's Sidewalk Café. The maid discovered Thelma in a nearby garage. Some sources claim the ignition of her car was still turned on and the garage door was opened a crack. An obvious suicide? Not quite.

Humble Beginnings

Thelma Todd was born in Lawrence, Massachusetts, on July 29, 1905 or 1906, depending on the source. She was an academically gifted girl who went on to attend college, but her mother pushed her to use her physical assets as well as her intellectual gifts. She made a name for herself in local beauty pageants, winning the title "Miss Massachusetts" in 1925. Though she did not take the top prize in the "Miss America" pageant, she was discovered by a talent agent and soon began appearing in the short one- and two-reel comedy films of producer/director Hal Roach.

Before Thelma knew it, she was starring with big names, including Gary Cooper and William Powell, and working at an exhausting pace on as many as 16 pictures a year. Her forte was comedy, however, and she found her biggest success as a sidekick to such legends as the Marx Brothers and Laurel and Hardy. Around Hollywood, she was known as "The Ice Cream Blonde" or "Hot Toddy" (a nickname she assigned to herself). But Thelma knew that fame was fleeting, and she decided to invest in a nightclub/restaurant with her sometimes boyfriend, director Roland West. The upscale gin joint became a favorite with Hollywood's hard-partying, fast set.

A Complicated Girl

To say that Thelma's love life was messy would be an understatement. Her marriage to playboy Pasquale "Pat" DiCicco (from 1932 to 1934) was a disaster, filled with domestic abuse. She turned to West after her divorce but was reportedly also seeing mobster Charles "Lucky" Luciano on the side. It was said that Luciano wanted a room at the Sidewalk Café for his gambling operation, and he was willing to go to great lengths to get it. The rumor was that even after he got Thelma hooked on amphetamines, she was still of sound enough mind to refuse. Supposedly, the couple got into a huge screaming match about the subject one night at another restaurant, The Brown Derby, and various threats were exchanged.

So, Who Did It?

All the romantic drama and hard living came to a head on the evening of December 14, 1935. Thelma had been invited to a party involving a good friend of hers, Ida Lupino, and she was driven there by her chauffeur, Ernest Peters. Unfortunately for Thelma, her ex-husband showed up with another woman and made a scene. After a nasty argument, DiCicco left with his date, and a drunken Thelma informed Lupino that there was a new man in her life, a rich businessman from San Francisco.

Thelma was dropped back at her apartment by Peters at around 3:30 A.M. on December 15. She apparently couldn't get into the building and instead retreated to the garage, perhaps to sleep there. She might have turned on the car for warmth, not paying attention to the carbon monoxide. The Los Angeles County determined the time of death had been between 5:00 and 8:00 A.M.

Making the circumstances even more mysterious is the fact that, although Thelma was determined to have died early on Sunday morning, December 15, her body was not found until Monday morning. There were uncorroborated reports that she had been seen during the day on Sunday in Beverly Hills. Is it possible that Thelma actually died 24 hours later than was reported?

The coroner's report listed carbon monoxide asphyxiation as the cause of death and ruled it a suicide, but Thelma's crazy life led many to dismiss that verdict. With so many intriguing suspects—the violent ex-husband, the jealous boyfriend, the ruthless gangster lover, and the mysterious out-of-town paramour—who could blame them? That initial report was reconsidered and overturned, with the ruling changed to accidental death, but some observers believe the incident was never investigated thoroughly.

HOW IT ALL BEGAN

Pirate Jewelry

One reason given for why pirates wore gold earrings is because no one could be assured of returning from a long, dangerous sea journey back in the bad old days. In case of accident—or an ill-fated sword battle—the hope was that these golden earrings would be taken from the corpse to pay for a decent burial.

"Happy Birthday to You"

This little number, performed innumerable times (and often off-key), seems to have been around forever. Yet, it was composed in the late 19th century in Louisville, Kentucky, by sisters Mildred and Patty Smith Hill. Mildred, a church organist and concert pianist, was considered an authority on what were then referred to as "Negro spirituals." Dr. Patty Smith Hill received many honors, including the title of professor emeritus at Columbia University. Mildred came up with the simple tune, and Patty added words. She titled the song "Good Morning to All" and published it in an 1893 book, *Song Stories for the Kindergarten.* It later evolved from a greeting into a celebration. The words to "Happy Birthday to You" were later added as a second verse, and after the song began appearing on stage, on radio, and in movies, a third Hill sister, Jessica, convinced a copyright court that the song belonged to her sisters.

"Mad as a Hatter"

The Mad Hatter was popularized in Lewis Carroll's *Alice's Adventures in Wonderland,* but Carroll did not coin the phrase. Making hats and madness had already been linked. During the early days of processing felt to use in hatmaking, the toxic substance mercury was used, which resulted in many industry workers developing mental or neurological disturbances. From this unfortunate situation, the phrase "mad as a hatter" came to indicate anyone who had gone insane.

"Crocodile Tears"

When someone is said to be crying "crocodile tears," they are feigning sorrow. This phrase actually does come from crocodiles, specifically a peculiarity in which crocodiles shed tears while eating. This is caused by food pressing against the roof of the animal's mouth, which activates the lachrymal glands that secrete tears. This makes crocodiles appear to be crying without really being sad at all.

Plato's Academy

❖ ❖ ❖ ❖

Many people may refer to the ancient philosopher Plato in only one context: As the inspiration for the term platonic love, *he unwittingly loaned his name to a description of love sans* carnality. *But his other gifts to humanity are infinitely more precious.*

Plato (c. 428–347 B.C.) had been a student of Socrates, a philosopher who wandered Athens, stopping to hold discussions about the conduct of life. Plato adopted Socrates' philosophy concerning virtuousness and the formation of a noble character, but after Socrates' death, he abandoned his original plans to become a politician. The older philosopher had angered the powerful rulers of the day with calls for virtuous behavior, so they sentenced him to execution via a poisonous drink of hemlock.

After Socrates was dead, Plato traveled for more than a decade, studying subjects including geometry, geology, astronomy, and religion in areas such as Italy and Egypt. Plato's writing picked up considerably after 400 B.C. He may be best known today for *The Republic,* which is written in a question-and-answer format suggesting dialogue. It is one of the most influential works of philosophy ever written, touching upon the great issues of life: wisdom, courage, justice, how an individual relates to him- or herself as well as society as a whole, what it means to live a "good life." Plato had a threefold theory of the structure of society, which he saw as divided into governing class, warriors, and workers. He held a similar theory about the soul, which he believed consisted of reason, spirit, and appetite. In Plato's view, an ideal government would have only philosophers as rulers.

The Concept of a University

Plato created his Academy around 387 B.C. on a site that was related to a mythological Athenian hero called *Akademos.* This became the basis for the word *academia.* Located just outside the city walls of Athens, the area contained a sacred grove of olive trees that may have been dedicated to Athena, the goddess of wisdom. Festivals, athletic events, and even funerals were held there.

Plato's Academy is considered to have been the first European university—it offered subjects including biology, mathematics, political theory, and, of course, philosophy. Perhaps most important, it sometimes advocated skeptical thinking and denied the possibility of ever attaining an absolute truth: Since people perceive everything through subjective senses, all they can strive for is a high degree of probability. The manner in which Plato ran the Academy and his ideas of what an educated citizen should be still exert a major influence on educational theory, logic, and legal philosophy today.

The Academy's Downfall

Plato remained associated with the Academy until his death, and it continued to flourish for centuries until it came into direct conflict with the Byzantine Emperor Justinian (c. A.D. 481–565). This emperor oversaw many positive accomplishments, such as the rewriting of Roman law, *Corpus Juris Civilis*, which still remains the basis for much contemporary civil law. But he was also devoted to the restoration of the Byzantine Empire, and he didn't mind using despotic force (such as the compulsory conversion of everyone to his form of Catholicism) to achieve his goals.

Anyone who didn't subscribe to Justinian's faith was either converted or hideously tortured to death. Justinian ordered Plato's Academy closed down—on the grounds that it was pagan in nature—and its property confiscated, beginning a surge of religiously justified seizures and destruction. Further, the emperor demanded the total erasure of Hellenism, which had given the world its first democratic constitutional reforms, dramatic tragedies about individual human dignities and rights (the Greeks were the first people on record to question the morality of slavery), and the Olympic Games—in all, the very concept of humanism.

FROM THE VAULTS OF HISTORY

Memory Is Fleeting
Winston Churchill is arguably the most famous person to serve as prime minister of Great Britain. It's rumored that he was born in a women's bathroom. When asked to corroborate that rumor, the quick-witted and master orator replied, "Although present on that occasion, I have no clear recollection of the events leading up to it."

Youthful Indiscretion
As everyone knows, popes are chosen by the College of Cardinals, not born to the office like royalty. They do not grow up being trained for the papacy, and some have had experiences that might contrast with their religious calling. Pope Pius II, for instance, was an accomplished writer. Among his works was *De duobus amantibus historia* (*A Tale of Two Lovers*)—considered an erotic book by 1444 standards.

The Brushstrokes of Fiction
Virginia Woolf, author of short stories, novels, and essays, such as *To the Lighthouse, Orlando, Mrs. Dalloway,* and "A Room of One's Own," did her writing while standing up at a sort of podium or stand-up desk. Woolf apparently wanted to emulate her sister Vanessa, a painter, who stood at an easel to create her artwork.

Do as I Say, Not as I Do
Benito Mussolini, dictatorial prime minister of Italy from 1922 to 1943, drafted thousands of men and sent them to war during World War II. Ironically, Mussolini was himself a draft dodger for two years in World War I.

Going to Extremes
Edgar Allan Poe, master American horror writer and poet, once attended the U.S. Military Academy at West Point under duress from his guardian, John Allan. Poe disliked West Point, and he pleaded with Allan to release him from the academy. He soon realized, however, that the only way out of West Point was to be court-martialed and dismissed. Poe decided to neglect his duties in hopes of such a resolution. It's even rumored that, after reading a bulletin regarding the dress code for a parade that stated only one type of belt should be worn, Poe decided to wear the white belt specified—with no other clothing except gloves. He didn't last a full year before being drummed out.

History of Taxidermy

❖ ❖ ❖ ❖

Want a rat torso, an evil eye, or a dried turkey head? How about an end table with the base made from an elephant's foot or a thermometer (it really works!) made from a freeze-dried deer foot? Before you decide to buy a mounted, two-headed calf at an auction, take a look at the process that got it there.

I'm Stuffed, Thank You

Taxidermy, Greek for "the arrangement or movement of the skin," is a general term that describes various procedures for creating lifelike models of animals that will last a long, long time—possibly even forever. The models, or representations of the animals, could include the actual skin, fur, feathers, or scales of the specimen, which is preserved and then mounted.

A quick search on the Internet will certainly reveal the odd, the bizarre, and many sideshow items, some of which are even for sale. The main focus of taxidermy, however, is the integrity of the final product, and getting the best results might require a far greater range of skills and crafts than simply stuffing and mounting. Those in the know consider it a precise art.

Take This Job and Stuff It

By the early 1800s, hunters began bringing in their trophies for preservation. The process usually began with an upholsterer skinning the creature. Then, the hide was removed and left outside to rot and self-bleach. Once this stage was complete, the tanner stuffed the hide with rags and cotton and then sewed the skin closed to replicate the live animal.

These rough methods of taxidermy are a far cry from modern-day processes. Today, professional taxidermists abundantly prefer the term *mounting* over *stuffing,* and rags and cotton have been replaced by synthetic materials.

They Don't Have to Sing for Their Supper

Dermestid beetles can be used to clean skulls and bones before mounting. As one might guess, these beetles clean by eating anything organic left on the bones, but at least they eliminate the need to use large cooking pots to boil the skulls clean. But wait, before you judge too harshly, it should be pointed out that this same method of turning the beetles loose is used by museums on delicate skulls and bones.

Cryptic as It May Sound

Freeze-drying is the preferred method for preserving pets. It can be done with reptiles, birds, and small mammals, such as cats, large mice, and some dog breeds. However, freeze-drying is expensive and time-consuming—larger specimens require up to six months in the freeze dryer.

But taxidermy can be even more creative than preserving animals. In crypto-taxidermy brand-new animals—dragons, jackalopes, unicorns—can be made. The subjects can also be extinct species, such as dinosaurs, dodo birds, or quaggas.

Some taxidermists have an impish side, as well. One popular practice places animals in human situations, building entire tableaux around them. This is called anthropomorphic taxidermy. Walter Potter has created a number of such works. *The Upper Ten,* or *Squirrels Club,* for example, features a group of squirrels relaxing at an upper-crust men's club. Another well-known work, *Bidibidobidiboo* by M. Cattelan, shows a suicidal squirrel dead at its kitchen table— definitely a conversation-starter in any home or business.

A new trend is the creation of entirely artificial mounts that do not contain any parts of the animal at all: for instance, re-creations of fish taken from pictures by catch-and-release anglers. This technique is called *reproduction taxidermy,* and although it is not traditional, it is definitely a more environmentally savvy method of preservation.

- *A cancerous tumor was discovered on President Grover Cleveland's upper palate in 1893. Successful surgery was performed on the presidential yacht in secrecy, out of fear of a market panic.*

- *President John Quincy Adams kept a pet alligator while in office.*

Curious Classifieds

Teeth extracted by the latest Methodists.

It takes many ingredients to make our burgers great but... "The secret ingredient is our people."

Stock up and save. Limit: one.

Widows made to order. Send us your specifications.

Tattoos... While you wait

For you alone! The bridal bed set...

Snowblower for sale... only used on snowy days

Braille dictionary for sale. Must see to appreciate!

Attorney at law; 10% off free consultation

"I love you only" Valentine cards: Now available in multipacks

Dog for sale: eats anything and is fond of children.

For rent: 6-room hated apartment

Mixing bowl set designed to please a cook with round bottom for efficient beating

The fact that those we have served return once again, and recommend us to their friends, is a high endorsement of the service we render. Village Funeral Home.

Joining nudist colony, must sell washer and dryer—$300

MOVING SALE: Wheelchair, hospital bed, deluxe sliding stair glide, and a motorcycle

LOST DIAPER BAG: With very sentimental items. In Taco Bell parking lot.

A superb and inexpensive restaurant. Fine food expertly served by waitresses in appetizing forms.

We build bodies that last a lifetime.

Christmas tag sale. Handmade gifts for the hard-to-find person.

Our bikinis are exciting. They are simply the tops.

Groundbreaking Scientific Theories (Part II)

As knowledge of the world becomes more complex, scientific breakthroughs become increasingly difficult to achieve. Here are a few examples of those who dared to see the future.

Discovery of Cell Nuclei

Here's a quick lesson in biology: The fundamental unit of any living organism is the cell. Some organisms, such as bacteria, algae, and amoebas, have only one cell. Others—people, for instance—have millions or billions of cells. Humans, plants, animals, bugs, and some single-celled organisms all have one thing in common, though: Each one of our cells has a nucleus. Robert Brown, a Scottish botanist, was the first to make this outstanding discovery.

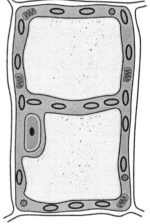

Born in 1773, Brown studied medicine at the University of Edinburgh. Shortly after his graduation, he worked for five years as an army surgeon. Best known for traveling to distant lands and discovering hundreds of new plant species, Brown rose to prominence as a leading expert in botanic research. In 1831, while studying how herbs and orchids become fertilized, he noticed that each plant cell he studied had a structure in common. Brown decided to call this the *nucleus* of the cell, after the Latin word meaning "kernel," or "little nut."

Brown wasn't the first to see the nucleus of a cell. That credit went to the guy who perfected the microscope, Dutch scientist Antonie van Leeuwenhoek. Brown, however, was the first to recognize its significance, noting that the cell nucleus was found in every cell of the plants he studied. His observations, research, and theories brought him much notoriety and fortune until his death in 1858.

Genetics According to Mendel

Do you know why a person might have her mom's red hair and not her dad's blonde hair? How about why someone has hazel eyes like Grandpa, even though Mom and Dad both have dark brown eyes? An Austrian-born geneticist named Johann Mendel, or Gregor Johann Mendel—the name by which he's more widely known—started to figure it out. Before Mendel, scientists didn't quite know how traits were passed from one generation to the next. There were several theories floating around, but most relied heavily on guesswork and didn't follow disciplined scientific methods to form their conclusions. Mendel changed that.

Mendel was born in 1822, the second of three children. He took an early interest in beekeeping and gardening, which guided his studies later in life. After joining a monastery and becoming a monk, Johann took the name Gregor and began studying the genetic variations of plants. He focused on the ordinary garden pea. After rigorous experimentation—on about 29,000 peas—and countless statistical and mathematical conclusions, Mendel discovered that peas pass their genetic traits to their offspring in a very specific way. How long would it take to count 29,000 peas, perform experiments, watch them grow, take notes on observations, and write a book about it? That's dedication!

Like most groundbreaking science throughout history, Mendel's theories weren't widely accepted when he published his work. In fact, his theories all but faded into history after his death in 1884. However, some 20 years later, other scientists discovered Mendel's work and replicated his experiments. Suddenly, everyone flocked to his ideas. Mendel's discovery became known as "Mendel's Laws of Inheritance" and laid the foundation for modern genetics and new experimentation with genes.

Vitamins According to Funk

What's the deal with food packaging listing all the important vitamins the food contains? Even something as sugary-good and delicious as breakfast cereal contains several "essential vitamins." What are these things? Let's turn the time machine back to 1911 and focus on a Polish biochemist by the name of Casimir Funk, the pioneer of vitamins.

The first part of the word *vitamin* comes from the Latin word for "life"; Funk knew that it would represent these life-giving, ammonia-based chemical compounds that he had discovered. These compounds can prevent diseases, help keep the body working in tip-top condition, and encourage healthy growth. Vitamins are essential for all multicelled life-forms to grow healthy and strong.

In Japan, it was discovered that a disease called *beriberi,* which attacks the nervous system, the heart, and the digestive system, was less likely to be contracted by those who ate lots of brown rice. No one knew why. Funk began experimenting by feeding rice to two groups of pigeons. He fed one group rice with its outer coating still on, and the other group rice with its coating removed. Funk discovered that the pigeons that ate the rice with the coating removed contracted beriberi, while the others remained healthy. After concentrating the nutrients he found in the coating of the rice, he labeled this concentration a *vitamine* in 1911.

Funk published a paper on his findings in 1912. His work was well received, especially by those suffering from beriberi and other diseases caused by vitamin deficiencies. He wasn't the only one to publish research on these nutrients at the time, but his was the most thorough and widely accepted.

The Discovery of DNA Structure by Watson and Crick

Deoxyribonucleic acid—DNA for short—contains a living organism's genetic information. Although scientists have known about DNA since the 1860s, no one knew what DNA structure looked like. Imagine trying to find your way around a building without knowing anything about its appearance, inside or outside. You might know it's made of brick, concrete, steel, and glass, but what shape does it take? Where are the stairs and the elevator? James Watson and Francis Crick wanted to answer those very same questions about DNA—the building blocks of life.

Watson and Crick were molecular biologists from the United States and Great Britain, respectively. In the 1950s, they built their first model of DNA from metal and wire at Cambridge University in England. But they weren't the only scientists on the hunt for the elusive DNA structure. Finding it would bring fame and fortune to the person or persons who discovered it. Watson and Crick gath-

ered information from all over the place. They attended lectures, read scientific papers, looked at X-rays, and did their own experiments before deciding that building a model was the best way to approach the challenge. Unfortunately, their model failed. It failed so badly that the head of their department told them to cease all DNA research. But the pair couldn't let it go.

A breakthrough came in 1953 when a competing scientist, also frustrated in trying to discover the structure of DNA, shared his work (and his partner's, without her knowledge) with Watson and Crick. The new insight caused them to take a huge leap in thought. It had been widely accepted that DNA probably had two chains or strands that wrapped around themselves like a staircase. This is the double helix. Watson and Crick theorized that one side of the chain wound upward and the other side downward, with matching chemicals (base pairs) holding the two helices together. Discovering how the four base pair chemicals—adenine with thymine and cytosine with guanine—fit together was the final piece in unlocking the mystery. We now know, of course, that the structure of DNA is one of the most important discoveries of the last 100 years. It has influenced everything from medication and foods to technology and health. In 1962, Watson, Crick, and Maurice Wilkins (the scientist who shared the work of his partner, Rosalind Franklin) won the Nobel Prize for Physiology/Medicine. Franklin did not receive the Nobel Prize, but only because the award is reserved for the living—she had died four years earlier.

- *The mountain retreat of Masada was seized by Jewish revolutionaries escaping from the Romans in A.D. 70. Romans captured the fortress in A.D. 73 but found all 936 defenders dead.*

- *President John Quincy Adams regularly swam nude in the Potomac River at 5:00 A.M. He took his last swim on his 79th birthday.*

- *About one million Union soldiers in the Civil War were under the age of 19. More than 800,000 were only 16 or 17 years old.*

Stage Names, Real Names

❖ ❖ ❖ ❖

To make it big in the music business, a performer needs a catchy name. Just look at the list below, where the stage name is followed by the real name, and ask yourself: Would you be more likely to buy a record from the fabulous Queen Latifah or one by someone named Dana Owens?

- Dido: Florian Cloud De Bounevialle Armstrong
- MC Hammer: Stanley Kirk Burrell
- Snoop Dogg: Calvin Broadus
- Chubby Checker: Ernest Evans
- C. C. Deville: Bruce Anthony Johanssen
- Pink: Alecia Moore
- 50 Cent: Curtis Jackson
- Gene Simmons: Chaim Witz
- Elvis Costello: Declan Patrick McManus
- Slash: Saul Hudson
- Moby: Richard Melville Hall
- Liberace: Wladziu Lee Valentino
- Freddie Mercury: Frederick Farookh Bulsara
- Busta Rhymes: Trevor Tahiem Smith
- Shania Twain: Eileen Regina Edwards
- Sting: Gordon Matthew Sumner
- Bono: Paul David Hewson
- Seal: Henry Olusegun Olumide Samuel
- Shakira: Shakira Isabel Mebarak Ripoll

Fast Facts

- The Vatican city-state in Rome was established in 1929 and is the world's smallest independent country, at about 110 acres.

- Most pictures of German Kaiser Wilhelm II show him holding something to mask the fact that he had a withered arm.

- Umami is a Japanese word meaning "savory." This taste, commonly found in meat, cheese, mushrooms, or broth, was identified by Professor Kikunae Ikeda of Japan in 1908. Some people consider it a fifth basic taste, joining sweet, sour, salty, and bitter.

- Sea horses are the only animal species in which males can give birth.

- The original source of the Hearst family fortune was gold, which was discovered by George Hearst in California. Late in his life, he also served as a Democratic senator from that state.

- There are 27 bones in that appendage at the end of your arm. Now give yourself a hand!

- During World War I, Herman Göring took over as the commander of the "Flying Circus" after original commander Manfred von Richthofen—the Red Baron—and his replacement were killed. Göring later became commander of the German Luftwaffe during Word War II.

- Can you spell that for me, please? People who fear the number 666 suffer from hexakosioihexekontahexaphobia.

- Ramses II of Egypt had an impressive number of children. The latest studies suggest the pharaoh had as many as 50 sons and 53 daughters.

- More than 29 years after the Japanese surrendered in World War II, Lieutenant Onoda Hiro was discovered in the Philippines. He refused to surrender until ordered to by his commanding officer.

The Most Watched City on Earth

If you ever get that feeling that there's a pair of eyes on you, try walking around in the shoes of a Londoner.

The people of London, England, are photographed 300 times a day by closed-circuit television cameras (CCTVs). The UK is home to an estimated five million surveillance cameras: 1 for every 12 citizens.

Big Brother Is Watching—and Listening and Talking

It seems the CCTVs are dissatisfied with merely watching; now some of them talk, too. The mysterious men and women behind the camera wait until a Londoner does something naughty and then politely chastise the offending party. For example, a woman who leaves a bottle on a park bench will suddenly hear a voice from above, asking her to throw it away.

No, this is not a scene from a science-fiction novel—a handful of such cameras have already been installed, and there are more to come. Police have also started putting cameras in their helmets.

The surveillance shenanigans don't stop there. Radio Frequency Identification Technology (RFID), which uses radio waves to detect small implanted chips, is already used in English passports and in the travel cards Londoners swipe when using public transit. With these chips, people can easily be tracked. Experts fear that the technology will soon be used to monitor purchases and employees. They may even be implanted in all citizens. RFID chips are commonly implanted in European pets.

Government officials and the corporations that produce these technologies claim that surveillance is in the interest of security. During the 1990s, the English Home Office, which is involved in law enforcement, spent 78 percent of its budget on CCTVs. Many studies have shown that these cameras do not actually reduce crime. However, studies *have* found that adding more streetlights reduces crime by 20 percent. If only there was a larger profit margin in lightbulbs.

The Man from S.E.X.: Alfred Kinsey and His Institute for Sex Research

Proper folks never mentioned it. It was best kept under the covers, with the lights off. If there was a problem, it was never solved. "It" was sex.

In the 20th century, American society's view on sex was basically the same as it had been in the 19th century... and the 18th century, as well. Heavily influenced by religious tenets and conventions, sex was for procreation only, not pleasure. The common belief held that it was dirty; something about which civilized people never spoke. It was kept locked tight, packed away, and zipped up. Then along came Alfred Kinsey.

Setting the Scene

The eldest of three, Kinsey was born in Hoboken, New Jersey, in 1894, to devout Methodist parents who forbade any discussion or thoughts of sex. This, combined with a sickly childhood, may have contributed to Kinsey's interest in his future profession. He joined the Boy Scouts and quickly became an Eagle Scout. This exposure to the outdoors eventually led to his fascination with gall wasps—they became the subject of his doctoral thesis. He ultimately amassed a collection of more than five million specimens, which was later donated to the American Museum of Natural History in New York.

Gifted with a keen interest in biology, Kinsey graduated magna cum laude from Bowdoin College in Maine, with degrees in biology and psychology. Continuing at Harvard University, he earned his doctorate in 1919 and joined the faculty of Indiana University as an assistant professor of zoology. He wrote a textbook on the subject, which was widely adopted by high schools across the country.

Foreplay

Clara "Mac" McMillen was a recent graduate of Indiana University when she met Dr. Kinsey. They were married within a year, although the start of their relationship was anything but ideal. Honeymooning by hiking and camping through the White Mountains of New

Hampshire led to an unconsummated beginning. There is some question as to the cause—some suggest the less-than-romantic environment of howling winds and a lean-to tent, while others point to some physical issues that made the act inherently difficult. Many believe that this experience was only one of the many factors that led to Kinsey's ultimate research.

The professor quickly realized that many people shared the same difficulties and frustrations about sex as he faced with Mac. What's more, Kinsey was angered at the total lack of scientific information that could explain the phenomenon of sex and all its variations. No one had ever made a serious study of human sexuality as something that wasn't dirty and unmentionable—until Kinsey.

By the late 1930s, Kinsey offered a course on marriage (a not-so-subtle substitution for "sexual behavior") at the university. Working without notes (although he did have explicit slides), Kinsey addressed the anatomy and mechanics of sex, the acts of love and self-satisfaction, and the resulting pleasure from the natural biological activities of humans. The reaction was overwhelmingly positive, yet Kinsey needed more from those who took his work seriously. He had a few questions that he still wanted to ask.

Doing the Deed

Kinsey and his staff began a systematic process of interviewing men—more than 5,000 of them. Using codes to ensure confidentiality, the surveys were clinical and to the point. They began with 12 basic demographic questions to identify the respondent: age, race, education level, occupation, and the like. The interview then moved to 350 queries based on sexual data—specific questions concerning likes, dislikes, techniques, partners (even for those with nonhuman interests), variety, and frequency of occurrences. One assumption that Kinsey's team made was that "everyone had done everything." Questions never asked, "Have you ever... ?" Rather, they began, "When did you first... ?" Their results were amazing.

Respondents talked freely about sex—sex with wives, partners (paid or not), lovers, themselves. But Kinsey also broke ground in areas never dreamed of, such as adolescent memories, along with the most unpleasant subjects—sex with children or animals, bodily functions. The mass of information he compiled was beyond anything previously attempted.

Kinsey's research also took on the subject of homosexuality. Author Gore Vidal once observed that Americans believed that "homosexuality was a form of mental disease, confined for the most part to interior decorators and ballet dancers." But it wasn't just Americans in general. Until 1973, the American Psychiatric Association classified homosexuality as a mental disorder. Kinsey's inquests refuted that notion, showing that more than a third of males had taken part in a homosexual experience at least once and that 8 percent were "exclusively homosexual" for at least three years at some point in their lives. He even pointed out that, biologically speaking, almost every animal species exhibited some sort of homosexual behavior. Kinsey's interest in the subject may have been due to his own bisexuality.

Climax

Kinsey founded the Institute for Sex Research at Indiana University in 1948 to further his investigations. The next year he published his findings in a landmark book, *Sexual Behavior in the Human Male.* Within six months, more than 150,000 copies had been sold, and the book was translated into French and Italian. If people didn't want to *hear* about such things, they certainly seemed ready to *read* about them. Known as the *Kinsey Report,* the book ruffled the feathers of more than a few: Kinsey found himself accused of being party to a Communist plot on one end of the spectrum and chastised for largely ignoring the emotional elements of sex on the other. Kinsey took no payment from the book sales, instead contributing his profits to the institute for further research.

By 1953, Kinsey and his team had interviewed nearly 6,000 females and issued *Sexual Behavior in the Human Female.* A Gallup poll reported that people, by a two-to-one margin, believed the *Kinsey Reports* were "a good thing" to have available. Of course, church groups responded with rage: Billy Graham denounced the book (without actually reading it), saying it was "impossible to estimate the damage . . . to the deteriorating morals of America."

Much of this criticism was deserved—Kinsey's samples didn't accurately reflect the makeup of the country—and he readily admitted this. Yet, his work clearly changed society's views of human sexuality, laying the foundation for the sexual revolution of the '60s. Researchers Masters and Johnson furthered this work in the '70s, leading to a new posture surrounding "the birds and bees" in America.

He Said, She Said

Opportunity is missed by most people because it is dressed in overalls and looks like work.

—Thomas A. Edison

Music should strike fire from the heart of man, and bring tears from the eyes of woman.

—Ludwig van Beethoven

Middle age is when you've met so many people that every new person you meet reminds you of someone else.

—Ogden Nash

If slaughterhouses had glass walls, everyone would be a vegetarian.

—Paul McCartney

I've done the calculation and your chances of winning the lottery are identical whether you play or not.

—Fran Lebowitz

There is nothing so annoying as to have two people talking when you're busy interrupting.

—Mark Twain

I think we agree, the past is over.

—George W. Bush

True terror is to wake up one morning and discover that your high school class is running the country.

—Kurt Vonnegut, Jr.

Money is better than poverty, if only for financial reasons.

—Woody Allen

Laziness may appear attractive, but work gives satisfaction.

—Anne Frank

A hero is no braver than an ordinary man, but he is braver five minutes longer.

—Ralph Waldo Emerson

A celebrity is anyone who looks like he spends more than two hours working on his hair.

—Steve Martin

They Helped Kill Lincoln: Booth's Coconspirators

John Wilkes Booth is well known for his assassination of President Abraham Lincoln at Ford's Theatre on April 14, 1865, but the rather lengthy list of his coconspirators has not been quite so memorable.

A popular Shakespearean stage actor who traveled the country performing, John Wilkes Booth could have kept busy enjoying his notoriety and fame. Instead, inspired by the secession of the Southern states that set off the Civil War, he was firmly entrenched in his racist beliefs and loyalty to the Confederacy. Once Lincoln freed the slaves in the rebelling states, a conviction took hold in Booth's mind branding the abolitionist president his archenemy. Dead set on bringing down Lincoln and preserving the Confederacy and the institution of slavery, Booth began to plot his attack. Initially, he planned to kidnap Lincoln and then ransom him for captive Confederate soldiers, but the conspiracy evolved, of course, into the first presidential assassination in U.S. history.

The Accomplices

Booth, who was charismatic and persuasive, had no trouble forming a gang of like-minded conspirators. Samuel Arnold, George Atzerodt, David Herold, Lewis Powell, John Surratt, and Michael O'Laughlen all joined with Booth to design various plots that would achieve victory for the South and cause trouble for Lincoln and his backers.

Meeting regularly at a boardinghouse run by Mary Surratt, the mother of one of the conspirators, the club decided to kidnap Lincoln in early 1865. They would simply snatch him from his box at a play and then ransom him for a few imprisoned Confederate soldiers. It would be a twofold victory, as they would cause grievance for their nemesis and bring the Confederacy closer to victory. Their plan was thwarted, though, when Lincoln failed to appear at the scheduled event. Similar plans were hatched, but for various reasons, none of the kidnapping plots came to fruition. Frustrated with his inability to capture Lincoln and spurred by Lincoln's continued attempts to dismantle the system of slavery, Booth determined that kidnapping was simply not enough: Lincoln must die!

Arnold, John Surratt, and O'Laughlen later swore that they knew nothing of the plot to commit murder, but Atzerodt, Herold, and Powell most certainly did. They each had their own assigned roles in the grand assassination plot, unsuccessful though they were in carrying out those parts. Atzerodt was slated to assassinate Vice President Andrew Johnson, while Powell and Herold were scheduled to kill Secretary of State William Seward. All three assassinations were planned for the same time on the evening of April 14.

Going into Action

Only Booth found complete success in the mission, however. Atzerodt apparently backed down from his assignment in fear. Powell cut a path of carnage through the Seward mansion, stabbing the secretary of state in the face and neck and wounding two of Seward's sons, a daughter, a soldier guarding Seward, and a messenger, although no one was killed. Herold had been with Powell but ran away when the mission didn't seem to be going smoothly. Booth shot Lincoln in the back of the head. The president died on the morning of April 15.

Booth immediately fled the scene, injuring a leg in his mad dash. He met up with Herold, and the pair was on the run for two weeks before finally being discovered on a small farm. The fugitives were holed up in a barn—Herold surrendered, but when Booth refused to do the same, soldiers set the barn on fire. In the ensuing melee, Booth was shot in the neck; he died a few hours later. Atzerodt, Herold, and Powell were hanged for their crimes, as was one more purported coconspirator, Mary Surratt. She ran the boardinghouse in which much of this plot was hatched, a plot which definitely included her son at various times. Her specific involvement and knowledge of the affair, however, has frequently been challenged.

The rest of the original coconspirators, as well as others with suspicious acquaintance to the group, were sentenced to jail time for their involvement.

say It Ain't So

Myth: Suck on a penny to beat a breathalyzer test.

Truth: Pennies have no magical control over boozy breath. From the early '80s on, pennies have been made mostly of zinc with a thin copper exterior. Neither zinc nor copper has any known power to ward off the long arm of the law.

Myth: Turkeys are so stupid they will drown themselves while admiring a downpour of rain.

Truth: Perhaps Thanksgiving Day enthusiasts invented this lamebrained myth to make themselves feel better about rampant feasting on dim-witted turkeys once a year, but there is no truth to this odd idea. Turkeys, although never seen working their way through a tricky crossword puzzle, are no more mentally challenged than any other bird. Besides, turkeys are not even physically capable of staring up at the falling rain as described in this myth. Turkeys' eyes are set on opposite sides of their noggins so, at best, were they so mesmerized by the rain, only one eye at a time could view its fall.

Myth: Geraldo Rivera changed his name from the more Anglo Jerry Rivers to draw in Latino fans.

Truth: Although calling talk show icon Geraldo Rivera a journalist might, according to some, be a misnomer, calling him Mr. Rivera is not. His grandparents came from Puerto Rico and brought the Rivera surname with them. Born Gerald Rivera to a Latin dad and a Jewish mom, Geraldo's only name change came with the addition of a somewhat subtle o, not a full-fledged switch from Jerry Rivers as has oft been claimed.

Myth: Opossums swing upside down on trees, hanging only by their tails.

Truth: Opossums, the only North American marsupial, do not hang from trees by their tails, but they are extremely adept tree crawlers. The sturdy tail provides leverage in scaling trees and—thanks to a pair of opposable thumbs on their hind feet—opossums can easily grasp branches and such for optimal scrambling. However, erase the image of upside-down, dangling opossums, because tail swinging isn't the norm.

Frederick Law Olmsted and Central Park

*Because Central Park is a staple of New York City and an
outstanding example of what a public park should be, it's
hard to believe there was ever a time when Central Park
didn't exist. It's also hard to remember that its creation
was the result of one man with a marvelous vision.*

New York City's Central Park is one of the most famous parks in the
world. It often makes cameo appearances in books and movies and
has long been the model of a restful retreat for harried urbanites.

We Want Green

By 1850, the outcry from citizens in New York City had reached an
all-time high—people clamored for the creation of a large, central
park to alleviate the crowded conditions of the rapidly growing city.
A series of influential essays by Andrew Jackson Downing, a landscape designer, were published in *The Horticulturist*. Editorials in
the *Evening Post* insisted that the subject of a public park should be
brought to the forefront of civic discussion. In that year's mayoral
election, both candidates included the creation of a public park in
their campaign platforms. When Ambrose C. Kingsland was elected
mayor of New York in 1851, he recommended that the Common
Council set aside funds to purchase property for the park. The land
for Central Park, in the area between the city and the village of Harlem, was bought in 1853.

Bridges, Metaphorical and Literal

In 1857, New York City held a design competition to create the lay-
out of the park. Officials were looking for a design that would rival
parks in London and Paris. The winners of the competition were
Frederick Law Olmsted and Calvert Vaux, who together created the
Greensward Plan: a park that would contain separate circulation systems so that park users were not exposed to crosstown traffic. Pedestrians, horseback riders, and carriages followed their own series of
paths throughout the park; thoroughfares were concealed by densely

planted shrub walls. A potpourri of bridges was installed throughout the park—not one was identical to another.

Culturally, Central Park was an example of an idyllic design that welcomed people from all classes. At the time, the concept of a public park being open to everyone was not the self-evident idea that it is today. Olmsted's social consciousness led him to envision a green space that would be accessible to all citizens.

Portrait of the Artist

Olmsted was named the architect in chief of the Central Park project. As such, he was able to bring his vision of social equality to one of the largest parks in the country. A public park, he felt, should provide a restful place for those who did not have the means to vacation at country houses in other states.

Before falling victim to the allure of designing parks, Olmsted led a varied life—traveling throughout the American South from 1852 to 1857, writing essays about slavery's impact on Southern culture for the *New York Daily Times;* sailing to England and hiking more than 300 miles; cofounding *The Nation.*

At the end of his life, Olmsted was known for much more than just Central Park. He left behind a wealth of letters and writings, and he is considered the pioneer of landscape architecture in the United States. In fact, he was the driving force behind the majority of urban parks throughout the country. He designed the grounds for the 1893 Columbian Exposition in Chicago; the grounds that surround the U.S. Capitol; and even the grounds for McLean Hospital in Belmont, Massachusetts, where he died on August 28, 1903.

HOW IT ALL BEGAN

The Umbrella
The idea of carrying paper or fabric on a canelike stick above one's head originated in Mesopotamia circa 1400 B.C.—but the contraption was intended to protect the skin from sunlight, not rain. The umbrella became waterproof through the ingenuity of Roman women, who oiled their paper sunshades. Parasols remained feminine accessories until the latter part of the 18th century in Europe; men simply wore hats and let their clothes get ruined. It was (surprise!) an Englishman who finally made the umbrella butch enough for the gents. Jonas Hanway accomplished this through no small amount of ridicule when, in 1750, he decided to carry one outdoors, rain or shine. He was purposely splashed with mud by passing carriages, hollered at by hooligans, and snubbed by one-time business associates. Fortunately, Hanway was already rich, so he could afford his little obsession. Slowly but surely, other men realized that by making a one-time investment, they could save on ordering coaches at the first droplets of a storm. For a time, umbrellas even carried Hanway's name. To this day, however, nobody has invented a surefire method of remembering where one has *left* one's umbrella.

The Piggy Bank
The most popular animal associated with coin savings banks is the pig, but not because of its cute belly or natural propensity for hoarding. No, many years ago, European dishes and cookware were created from a dense orange clay called *pygg*. When housewives began tossing spare change into an earthenware jar of this type, it became known as a *pygg* bank; and when a 19th-century British potter was asked to make such a bank, he misunderstood and shaped it like the farm animal instead. Everyone thought the porcine bank was so adorable that it caught on, and it has stayed the same ever since.

"It's Greek to Me"
This phrase, used by someone to indicate that he or she doesn't understand a word of what's being said, is really a quotation from the first act of William Shakespeare's *Julius Caesar*. The character Casca, one of the plotters who participates in Caesar's assassination, describes overhearing Cicero, who actually *was* speaking in Greek in order to deter eavesdroppers. The ploy obviously worked.

Doomed Cults and Social Experiments

❖ ❖ ❖ ❖

On the upside, cults have the possibility of offering people acceptance and a sense of community when they would not otherwise have it. On the downside, if you join a cult, you could die.

The People's Temple

The Leader: Jim Jones started his People's Temple with the idea that social justice should be available to all—even the marginalized, the poor, and minorities. He established a commune outside San Francisco in 1965 with about 80 people. Jones capitalized on the rising tide of activism in the 1960s, recruiting affluent, Northern California hippies to help the working-class families who were already members of the People's Temple. The People's Temple helped the poorer members of their group navigate the confusing social welfare system. The Temple opened a church in an impoverished section of San Francisco that provided a number of social services, such as free blood pressure testing, free sickle-cell anemia testing, and free child care for working families.

The Turning Point: Not all was as it appeared inside the People's Temple. A perfect storm of complaints from disaffected members, media reports that questioned the Temple's treatment of current members, and an IRS investigation led Jones to move the People's Temple to Guyana, on the northern tip of South America. In the summer and fall of 1977, the People's Temple started what was supposed to be a utopian agricultural society, which they called Jonestown.

The Demise: In November 1978, U.S. Representative Leo Ryan of San Francisco led a fact-finding mission in response to constituents' concerns that members of the Temple were being kept in Guyana against their will. He offered to help anyone who wanted to leave. A few members joined him, but as the congressional party was waiting on a landing strip for transportation, attackers drove out of the jungle and shot at them. Ryan and four others were killed.

Apparently worried about the closer scrutiny all this could bring, on November 18, Jones ordered his followers to commit "revolutionary suicide" by drinking Fla-Vor-Aid laced with cyanide. More than 900 members of the People's Temple died.

The Family

The Leader: Charles Manson was worried about pollution and the damage it would do to the environment. Unfortunately, he manifested his concern by brainwashing teenagers and sending them on murder sprees. Manson had a hard life—spent mostly in juvenile halls, jail, and institutions. He finally ended up in San Francisco, surrounded by young women, most of whom were emotionally unstable and in love with him. With a group of these girls, he headed south to Los Angeles.

The Turning Point: After moving into the Spahn Ranch north of LA, where Manson and his followers survived by scavenging food discarded from grocery stores, he started to polish what he considered his philosophy—an Armageddon in which race wars, what he called *Helter Skelter,* would break out. According to this philosophy, Manson would, coincidentally, be the one who would guide the war's aftermath and therefore rule the world.

Reportedly in an attempt to spark these race wars, the Manson Family staged a series of mass murders, most famously those of Sharon Tate and her guests on August 9, 1969. Because of orders from Manson, four members of the Family killed Tate and her three friends. They did it, according to Susan Atkins, one of the murderers, to shock the world.

The Demise: Bragging to others about their murder sprees ultimately ended up undoing the Family. Friends of Manson eventually told police details of the murders. But the problem wasn't exactly finding the culprits, the problem was proving that members of the Family were responsible for the murders Manson ordered them to perform. Ultimately, a grand jury took only 20 minutes to hand down indictments in the cases against members of the Family.

Branch Davidians

The Leader: David Koresh joined the Branch Davidians in 1981. The group had been in existence since 1955, having broken off from the Davidian Seventh-Day Adventists, which itself was a group that split with the Seventh-Day Adventist church more than 20 years before that. Koresh was amiable and flamboyant, easygoing and intelligent. After a face-off with the son of the leader of the Branch Davidians, Koresh ultimately ended up as the group's leader and spiritual guide. As all serious cult leaders know, it was important not only to establish himself as the lord, but also to impress upon his flock the impending apocalypse and the absolute necessity of following the rules he created.

The Turning Point: Koresh stockpiled weapons in anticipation of inevitable attacks. He taught his followers that they should prepare for the end. He questioned their loyalty and expected them to kill themselves for the cause. On February 28, 1993, the end began. Based on reports of illegal arms sales, child abuse, and polygamy, federal agents raided the Mount Carmel Center near Waco, Texas, setting off a gunfight that ultimately set up a 51-day siege of the Branch Davidian compound.

The Demise: On April 19, 1993, federal agents, in an attempt to force the Davidians out, launched tear gas into the compound. Koresh and the Davidians, none too happy themselves, began shooting. The agents injected more gas, and the give-and-take continued for several hours. About six hours after the gassing began, fires erupted inside the compound. Accusations were made as to which side was responsible for the fires, but later investigations concluded that they had been set by the Branch Davidians. This was followed by more gunfire in the compound, and agents on the scene reportedly believed the Davidians were either killing themselves or shooting one another. Firefighters came to the scene but were not allowed to combat the flames for some time out of fear of gunfire. After the smoke cleared, 75 people within the compound were found dead. Koresh was identified by dental records; he had been killed by a gunshot to the head.

- *Switzerland has four official languages: German, French, Italian, and Romansch.*

- *The first man to win Wales's annual Man Versus Horse race was Huw Lobb in 2004, the race's 25th year. He earned the £25,000 prize, until then the biggest unclaimed prize in British athletics.*

Fumbling Felons

When You're Hungry, You're Hungry

In Appleton, Wisconsin, a burglar reportedly entered an unlocked apartment but didn't steal any of the "valuables" within. No, this thief had a particular goal in mind and took six eggs, a container of beef ravioli, a pizza, a can of peaches, and a Hot Pocket (chicken-and-broccoli variety). The October 2007 crime apparently occurred sometime between 8:30 A.M. and 12:30 P.M.—prime snacking hours!

Taking the Credit

In Britain, two 18-year-olds were arrested for vandalizing a children's campsite. They apparently broke into the facility late one night, smashed plates and dishes, and discharged fire extinguishers. One of the boys decided to write his name in black permanent marker on the wall, boasting that he "was here!" The two wrote the name of their gang, as well. Police simply entered the vandal's name into the computer system for all the information they needed. The boys were quickly arrested. As punishment, they were fined and ordered to perform community service.

The Lap of Luxury

In an attempt to help pay for her and her boyfriend's drug-dealing debts, a woman in Providence, Rhode Island, rented a limo and attempted to rob a bank. The woman hired the driver to take her to the airport, but she asked him to stop at a bank's drive-through lane, where she got out of the limo and handed a teller a note. The note demanded money and claimed that there were two bombs inside the bank. In response, the teller hit the panic button. The would-be bank robber immediately got back in the car without any money, and the limo driver pulled off, unaware of what had occurred. Police eventually arrested the woman and charged her with attempted bank robbery.

It Works in the Movies

In Silver Springs Shores, Florida, a man was charged with commercial burglary, possessing tools for burglary, and felony criminal mischief. The enterprising criminal had a plan to break into a drugstore by removing an air-conditioning cover and gaining access to the air vent. He was going to crawl through it to get into the store, but instead he got stuck until the store opened the next day—ten hours later! In his defense, the man claimed he "heard a cat" and was trying to "chase" it.

Who Was Roget?

*If there ever was any truth in the saying "The best
things happen when you least expect them," then the
story of Peter Mark Roget might just illustrate that point
perfectly. And if it doesn't illustrate it, then it may well
demonstrate, exemplify, or even illuminate that point.*

Monologophobians, Unite

Using the same word more than once can be an effective technique,
or it can plunge the thought into an unwanted abyss. The world
may never know if Dr. Peter Mark Roget suffered from *monologo-phobia,* the obsessive fear of using the same word twice, but he did
spend his life compiling a classed catalog of words to facilitate the
expression of his ideas. His thesaurus, he claimed, would "help to
supply my own deficiencies." Roget's definition of *deficiencies* might
conflict with most, since he was an accomplished scientist, physi-cian, and inventor before he became one of the world's most famous
lexicographers.

Birth, Genesis, Nativity, Nascency, the Stork...

Roget was born in 1779 and became a physician at age 19. As a
young doctor, he influenced the discovery of laughing gas as an
anesthetic and published important papers on tuberculosis, epilepsy,
and the medical care of prisoners. As a scientist, he invented a log
log slide rule to determine roots and powers of numbers (which was
used for more than 150 years—until the invention of the calculator)
and began a series of experiments about the human optic system
that would later aid the development of the modern camera.

While watching the wheels of a carriage through the blinds of a
window, he realized that the image of an object is retained on the
retina for about one-sixteenth of a second after the object has gone
out of view, a point he subsequently proved. This startling conclu-sion helped lay the groundwork for a shutter-and-aperture device he
developed, an early prototype for the camera.

Amazingly, Roget also helped with the creation of the London
sewage system and was an expert on bees, Dante, and the kalei-

doscope. Achievements none too bad for a man who considered himself deficient!

The Logic and the Idea

It was only when Roget was 70 that he began putting together his first thesaurus (he borrowed the Greek word for "treasure house"), which would later bear his name. Roget's system, compiled from lists he had been saving most of his life, instituted a brand-new principle that arranged words and phrases according to their meanings rather than their spellings.

The thesaurus, now nearly 160 years in print, has sold more than 30 million copies worldwide and has become an institution of the English language. Despite critics' complaints that this reference book plunges people into "a state of linguistic and intellectual mediocrity" in which language is "decayed, disarranged, and unlovely," Roget set out to create a tool that would offer words that could express every aspect of a particular idea rather than merely to list potential alternative choices. He also believed that people often just forgot the precise word they wanted and that his book would help them remember.

"A Rose by Any Other Name"

• In 1852, Roget's first thesaurus contained 15,000 words; the sixth edition, published 149 years later in 2001, includes a whopping 325,000 words and phrases.

• Anyone can use the name *Roget* on their thesaurus, but only HarperCollins has trademark-protected *Roget's International Thesaurus.*

• New editions of the thesaurus are greeted by the press and public as a mirror of the times in which we live. The 1980s brought into vogue such terms as *acid rain, creative accounting, insider trading, Cabbage Patch dolls,* and *bag lady.* The '90s ushered in new terms such as *eating disorder, Tamagotchi, double whammy, zero tolerance, air kissing, focus group, spin doctor, Prozac, road rage,* and *bad hair day.*

• The 21st century is bringing into play such phrases as *Ashtanga yoga* and *WAP phones.*

Syllable Secrets: Word Histories

Gadget: Originating in 1886 (although it may date back to the 1850s), *gadget* was sailors' slang for any small mechanical thing for which they had no name. It possibly originated much earlier than this time with the French *gâchette* ("trigger of a mechanism").

Teenager: This word dates back only to 1941, although the word *teen-age* was first used in 1921. *Teen* was used as a noun to describe a not-quite-adult person in 1818. *Teenaged*, though, comes from 1952. The latest spin-off is *tween* (although usually used solely to describe girls be*tween* childhood and adolescence, a formidable marketing target). More interesting, perhaps, is the now-archaic Middle English meaning of the word *tene:* "misery; grief."

Android: Popularized in the 1950s by science fiction writers, the word that means "automaton resembling a human being" actually goes back to 1727 (fr. the Greek *andro-*, "human," + *eides*, "form"). Also known as a *replicant* (from *replica*, or "exact copy") in the 1982 film *Blade Runner* (which was adapted from the novel *Do Androids Dream of Electric Sheep?* by Philip K. Dick), and a *mecha* (mechanical person) in the film *Artificial Intelligence: A.I.* (2001).

Cesarian: A 1903 shortened, Americanized version of the term *caesarian section* (first used in 1615), an operation that was supposedly named after Caius Julius *Caesar*, who had to be delivered of his mother surgically (legend traces his name to the Latin *caesus*, from *caedere*, which means "to cut"). This detail of Caesar's birth, however, may not be entirely accurate, as such operations in ancient times were inevitably fatal to the mother, and history shows that Caesar's mother did not die in childbirth. This is an awkward detail that everybody seems to have conveniently forgotten, as the name stuck.

Magazine: The original meaning (from the Arabic *makhzan*, or "storehouse") was altered by 1583 to that of a "place where goods, particularly military ammunition and supplies, are stored." In fact, the word is still used to denote a metal receptacle for bullets inserted into certain types of automatic weapons. The most common current definition of *magazine*, though, that of a "periodical journal," dates back to the publication of the very first example of such a printed work, 1731's *Gentleman's Magazine.* The name was probably derived from the publication's being a "storehouse" of information.

Philippa Schuyler: Biracial Prodigy

"You were an accident" are words a child should never hear from a parent. But it could be worse: "You were an experiment in hybrid vigor and miscegenation." That's exactly what Philippa Schuyler found out, and it rocked her coddled, heralded young life.

Born on August 2, 1931, Philippa Schuyler made headlines in African American newspapers across the United States. Her parents, famed Harlem journalist George Schuyler and Josephine Cogdell, a white Texan from a wealthy family, were proud socialists who firmly believed in hybrid vigor. They thought that babies born of black-and-white couples would have the best characteristics of both parents and their races. Through this idea, George and Josephine believed they had found the obvious answer to all of America's racial problems.

Promise Fulfilled

And from an early age, their daughter seemed to prove them right. Philippa was precocious from the start, learning to read and write by two-and-a-half and playing Mozart by age four. Josephine played doctor/nutritionist with Philippa's health. She believed firmly in a raw diet, so her daughter never ate anything that was cooked. Most modern raw foodists are vegan; Josephine included raw meat in Philippa's diet as well. The mother believed that liver and brains (washed under hot water) were the most nutritious. Besides raw flesh, they ate cod liver oil, wheat germ, and lots of fruit. Sugar, tobacco, and alcohol weren't even allowed into their home, and Philippa never got sick.

There's no question the Schuylers loved Philippa, but what's not known is whether George and Josephine loved each other. He was often away, traveling and writing to maintain their tony Harlem address, while Josephine threw herself into her daughter's development, bringing in private tutors and keeping painstakingly intricate scrapbooks. When Philippa did attend school, she was advanced compared to the other students, but being of mixed race, she didn't feel like she fit in.

Philippa began touring as a concert pianist at age 11, performing for foreign nobility and dignitaries alike. Although popular in the United States (thanks mostly to her father's writing), her most notable fan was New York Mayor Fiorello La Guardia, who declared June 19, 1940, to be Philippa Duke Schuyler Day.

More Questions than Answers

By age 13, Philippa had written more than 100 compositions and seemed to be on an unstoppable route to becoming a famous pianist. But as she got older, her identity and race became an issue, and she was not the commodity she once was. When she saw those developmental scrapbooks, Philippa was appalled. She felt that she was nothing more than a science experiment, not knowing what her own personality was or what was programmed into her.

In adulthood, Philippa took after her father and became a journalist (writing in several languages for various publications), lecturer, and activist. Disdained in America, she toured the world again, this time lecturing instead of playing piano, and all the while going through an identity crisis. She decided that she liked Latin America's lax attitudes toward race and eventually began using the alias Felipa Monterro y Schuyler, posing as a woman of Spanish descent. Unlucky in love, Philippa continued to throw herself into her work. She eventually ended up in Vietnam, covering the war there.

At age 35, in 1967, Philippa drowned when a helicopter she was on, transferring children from an orphanage in a war zone, crashed. Her intelligence has been recognized at the Philippa Schuyler Middle School for the Gifted and Talented. Students at this advanced school in Brooklyn go through a rigorous curriculum, enhanced with a strong homeschool connection, much like its namesake. Even the motto, "To Whom Much Is Given, Much Is Required," is reminiscent of the troubled intellect of Philippa Schuyler.

- *Watch your head! There could be more than 100,000 pieces of debris, unused probes, defunct satellites, and assorted manufactured items orbiting in space right now.*

- *Flying birds lose their feathers bilaterally so they don't become unbalanced when taking off or flying.*

Behind the TV Shows of Our Times

Password
In the world of TV game shows, *Password* was legend. With more than 2,500 episodes aired in the '60s and '70s, the game teamed a celebrity with a contestant, who competed against another such team to recognize words by giving only one-word clues. Play passed back and forth until someone guessed the correct word. Points went down as clues accumulated. It sometimes made strategic sense to pass the first clue to the other team rather than play it oneself. Host Allen Ludden started the show by saying, "Hi, doll." The story was often told of a large mannequin posed in front of his TV at home, assuring him that there would always be at least one face watching him every day. In reality, his greeting was directed to his mother-in-law—actor Betty White's mom. Ludden met White when she was a celebrity panelist on the show.

Turn-On
With the enormous success of *Rowan & Martin's Laugh-In* on NBC in 1968, copycat shows were sure to follow. *Turn-On* was a fast-paced ABC comedy also produced by *Laugh-In* producers George Schlatter and Ed Friendly. Success was not forthcoming for *Turn-On,* however—it was almost immediately canceled when ABC executives recognized that it was full of double entendres and secret implications. (It has even been rumored that the suits canceled the show before the first episode was over.) While the country was relaxing its moral values, it clearly wasn't ready to see a pregnant woman singing "I Got Rhythm" or a Catholic nun primping for a date. Some stations dumped the show during its first commercial break. Guest-hosted by Tim Conway, *Turn-On* is one of the shortest-running TV series ever broadcast.

Head of the Family
Comedian Carl Reiner was fresh from a successful run as a writer and second-banana performer on Sid Caesar's *Your Show of Shows* in the 1950s. Deciding to write a comedy show about a father and husband in the TV business, he starred in the pilot that broadcast as *Head of the Family* in the summer of 1960. It bombed badly, and friend and producer Sheldon Leonard knew why—Reiner was all wrong for the lead. They recast the show, and the failed *Head of the Family* became immensely popular as *The Dick Van Dyke Show* in 1961.

Loving *Lolita:* The Scandal of Naughty Nabokov

The name "Lolita" has become synonymous with any sexy, underage lass with a come-hither look. The story of Humbert Humbert, a grown man who develops lusty designs on a 12-year-old girl, raised eyebrows and concerns when it was published in 1955. Critics and the public alike wondered, "Where does literature end and pornography begin?"

The Author

Russian-born Vladimir Nabokov fled his homeland with his family after the 1917 Russian Revolution. He attended school in England and took up writing novels and poetry in Paris in the late 1930s. Nabokov and his family fled again, this time to the United States in 1940, as the Nazis began their assault on Europe. The author took up residency at Wellesley College near Boston, where he gained notoriety as a brilliant writer and lecturer, as well as an expert butterfly collector. Nabokov became a U.S. citizen in 1945 and continued as a collegiate professor at Harvard and Cornell. While traveling in Oregon, he wrote his greatest, and most controversial, novel.

The Book

Lolita follows a college professor who has a perverse preoccupation with adolescent girls. Settling in New England, he is smitten with Dolores (whom Humbert calls "Lolita"), the 12-year-old daughter of his widowed landlord. He is so enamored of Lolita that he marries her mother just to be close to his "stepdaughter." But his wife dies, leaving Humbert to care for Lolita. She takes up with a potential rival named Clare Quilty and distances herself from Humbert. Some years pass before Humbert hears from Lolita, now married and pregnant at 17 years old. Humbert trades his fortune to Lolita for the name of her former paramour. He finds Quilty, shoots him dead, and winds up imprisoned for murder. While waiting for the trial, he writes a book called *Lolita* and then dies. At the close of the novel, Lolita dies in childbirth.

The Reaction

Despite Nabokov's literary reputation, no U.S. publisher would touch *Lolita*. The subject of pedophilia, no matter how well-written, was taboo in the United States in the mid-1950s. A publisher in Paris finally put out 5,000 copies in 1955; they quickly and quietly sold out. A London reviewer noted that it was one of the best books of the year, prompting a competitor to claim that *Lolita* was "the filthiest book I have ever read" and "sheer unrestrained pornography." These declarations led to the book being banned in England and France. When it was finally published in the United States in 1958, there was praise for the writing style but condemnation for the subject. Yet the controversy made it a best seller—the first novel since *Gone with the Wind* to sell more than 100,000 copies in its first three weeks.

Many public libraries banned the book from their shelves, and the *Chicago Tribune* refused even to review it. The *New York Times* called the book "highbrow pornography." Nabokov eventually wrote the screenplay for Stanley Kubrick's 1962 cinematic version of *Lolita*. Years before the establishment of the MPAA rating system, it was recommended for "persons over 18 years of age"; film posters asked, "How did they ever make a movie of *Lolita*?" (To start with, they made her 14 years old rather than 12.)

The Aftermath

Lolita eventually became regarded as one of the greatest works in 20th-century American literature. Its success allowed Nabokov to move with his family to Switzerland, where he continued to write and chase butterflies. Before his death in 1977, Nabokov stated that he was most proud of writing *Lolita*. He once noted, "I am probably responsible for the odd fact that people don't seem to name their daughters Lolita any more. I have heard of young female poodles being given that name since 1956, but of no human beings."

- *The cost of a 30-second TV commercial during the first Super Bowl in 1967 was $42,000. In 2007, the price had skyrocketed to $2.6 million.*

- *Fleas can flee (by jumping up to 200 times their own length), but they can't fly.*

Fast Facts

- *Queen Elizabeth I of England was the daughter of Anne Boleyn and King Henry VIII. Declared illegitimate following her parents' annulment, she nonetheless remained a legal heir to the throne.*

- *Argea Tissies aced the number-two hole at the Italian Seniors Open in 1978. Five years later, on the same date, on the same hole, she did it again.*

- *In the third century B.C., King Pyrrhus of Epirus defeated Roman troops by sending elephants onto the battlefield. The Romans panicked when they saw the gigantic animals approaching.*

- *Nicholas Sparks, author of* The Notebook, Message in a Bottle, *and other novels, was a successful track-and-field athlete at the University of Notre Dame. As of 2008, he and his teammates still held the school record for the 800-meter relay.*

- *Thomas Selfridge was the first person killed in a powered, fixed-wing aircraft. On September 17, 1908, his plane, piloted by Orville Wright, crashed after takeoff.*

- *The Black Plague claimed more than 100,000 lives in London from 1665 to 1666. It was believed at the time that animals spread the disease, so 40,000 dogs and 200,000 cats were killed.*

- *Julie Krone, one of the most successful female jockeys of all time, was the first woman to win a Triple Crown race, capturing the 1993 Belmont Stakes aboard Colonial Affair.*

- *William Lear of Lear Jet fame is also known for developing the 8-track cartridge, an entertainment staple in cars, pickup trucks, and big rigs during the 1970s.*

- *Former Beatle Paul McCartney has lent his name to a Polish school that teaches English by playing the music of the Beatles and McCartney.*

Lulu: Idol of Germany

From Hollywood "It Girl" to heyday has-been in less than five years—this was the fate cast by Hollywood studio bosses, who were unable to reel in the rebellious and outspoken Louise Brooks. But the "girl in the black helmet," whose trademark shiny black bob has since been copied by everywoman and starlet alike, didn't prove so easy to throw aside.

Louise Brooks, born Mary Louise Brooks to an attorney father and artistically eccentric mother in Kansas in 1906, picked up her contentious temperament early. The philosophy, if that's not too formal a term for it, of the Brooks household was every child for herself. Mother Myra Brooks was known to sit back and laugh as her "squalling brats" took to fisticuffs to settle their disputes. Fighting, it seemed, was in Louise's blood. She started her serious performing career at age 15 as a dancer in the prestigious Denishawn troupe but was later released because of her truculent tendencies. This dismissal marked an early indication of the turbulent path her Hollywood career would take.

A Hit in Hollywood

Despite her belligerent reputation, or perhaps partly because of it, the burgeoning movie industry took note of the young and talented Brooks, casting her in a slew of silent films. She was popular with the public and quickly became the premiere on-screen darling of Paramount. Offscreen, though, her bosses might have described her as anything but darling.

Only a couple of years into her film career, Louise was already at the top of the silent film heap; but, like F. Scott Fitzgerald's description of his wife, Zelda, Louise, too, thought of herself as a failed social creature. This weakness was her undoing. Unable—or at least unwilling—to comply with societal niceties, Louise was revered for her beauty, as well as for a charisma that translated effervescently to the big screen, but her talents were overshadowed by her unabashed honesty. Although Paramount capitalized on her acting aptitude (and Hollywood men on her sexual liberty), Louise irrecoverably cut ties with Paramount when executives reneged on one too many offers.

Europe Beckons

While on leave from Hollywood, Louise was quickly snatched up by German Expressionist filmmaker G. W. Pabst and was cast as Lulu in *Pandora's Box*. This now-infamous character was a sexually charged vaudevillian whose amorous exploits included the first-ever on-screen depiction of lesbian relations. Finally, a genre that seemed fitting to Louise's sexually charged and controversial nature! On the heels of *Pandora's Box* came *Diary of a Lost Girl,* another Pabst-directed exposé on society's sexual underbelly and social conduct. In this film, Louise's character, Thymiane, suffers through rape, the birth of her illegitimate child, the death of said child, and eventually, prostitution.

No Chance for a Comeback

Upon her return to Hollywood in 1930, Louise fell victim to the cold-hearted punishment of blacklisting. Unhappy with Paramount, she had refused to participate in sound editing for *The Canary Murder Case.* Thus, the film showcased Louise's role as "The Canary" with another songbird, Margaret Livingston, on vocals. Because her prior films had all been silent, Paramount was able to claim that Louise's melodious voice was inept for singing in talkies, a low blow that further solidified her downhill reputation. From then on, Louise moved from roles in which she was critically ignored to low-budget films to an embarrassing final role in a John Wayne Western.

Louise never made it back to her short-lived Hollywood high point. She did, however, make a blaring reappearance late in life through a writing career in which she brutally dissected the heartless world of cinema. In Louise's own words, the character of Lulu "dropped dead in an acute attack of indigestion" after devouring her "sex victims." It appears that fickle Hollywood had chewed up and spit out young Louise in much the same fashion.

• *Originally, the 1976 Winter Games were awarded to Denver, but voters did not want to take on the expense of hosting the event and so declined the offer.*

The Times They Are A-Changin'

1961

January 4: The longest recorded labor strike ends after 33 years when Danish barbers' assistants go back to work.

January 15: The Supremes sign a contract with Motown Records.

January 25: President John F. Kennedy holds the first nationally televised live presidential news conference.

January 31: NASA's Ham becomes the first chimpanzee to shoot into space when it is launched 157 miles into space aboard a Mercury-Redstone 2 rocket.

March 21: The Beatles make their first evening appearance at the Cavern Club in Liverpool, England.

March 29: The 23rd Amendment is ratified, allowing residents of Washington, D.C., to vote for president.

May 5: Astronaut Alan Shepard becomes the first American in space aboard *Freedom 7.*

May 25: President Kennedy announces the goal of putting a man on the moon before the end of the decade.

August 13: Construction begins on the Berlin Wall, which separates communist East Berlin from West Berlin and ratchets up the Cold War.

September 15: Hurricane Carla hits the Texas and Louisiana coasts with winds of 170 mph.

September 26: Roger Maris hits home run number 60, tying Babe Ruth's single-season record. He will break that record on October 1.

October 3: *The Dick Van Dyke Show* debuts on CBS.

December 14: Jimmy Dean's "Big Bad John" becomes the first country song to earn a gold record.

December 22: James Davis of Livingston, Tennessee, becomes the first American soldier to die in Vietnam.

December 31: The Beach Boys perform under that name for the first time.

Bram Stoker and Henry Irving: Close Friendship or Unrequited Love?

Was actor Henry Irving the inspiration for Bram Stoker's famed novel Dracula, *and were their personal issues revealed in the book? Maybe, but sometimes a stake is just a stake.*

Bram Stoker, best known for his macabre masterpiece *Dracula*, spent much of his life as the manager of Sir Henry Irving, one of the most famous British actors of the 19th century. It is clear the two had a deep friendship, but the precise nature of their relationship has long been contested. Some say Irving was dominant and abusive in his veritable lordship over Stoker, suggesting that the sinister Dracula character was inspired by Stoker's secret hatred for his boss. Others contend that Stoker was a homosexual who siphoned his unrequited romantic feelings into sexually charged novels.

The Man Who Met His Idol

Stoker was born in Dublin, Ireland, on November 8, 1847. A sickly child, he barely left his bed until age seven. Yet, by the time he was a student at Trinity College Dublin, he was a star athlete and president of the philosophical society. Postgraduate employment saw him working for about ten years in the Irish Civil Service. Office drudgery didn't dampen Stoker's spirits, though—during this period, he wrote his first book, reviewed the theater for local newspapers, and became obsessed with Irving.

Then, in 1876, Stoker met his idol. Irving was acting in Dublin, and Stoker's review of his performance was so enthusiastic that Irving wanted to meet his admirer. The fateful meeting is recounted with great detail in Stoker's book *Personal Reminiscences of Henry Irving,* which he published in 1906, after Irving's death. At an early gathering, Irving recited a poem, and Stoker proceeded to "burst into something like hysterics." Irving was also overcome with emotion and left the room, returning with a photograph of himself on which he had written, "My dear friend Stoker, God bless you! God bless you!" Stoker remembered, "Soul had looked into soul! From that hour began a friendship as profound, as close, as lasting as can be between two men."

But every spring love has its winter season. Literary historians have argued that the Irving-Stoker relationship was codependent and emotionally abusive. Irving was a world-famous actor; Stoker was an unknown novelist. Since age 18, Irving had traveled all over Great Britain, playing roles large and small. His big break finally came in 1874, when he played the title character in *Hamlet* at the famed Lyceum Theatre in London. His acting style was mesmeric and unique—instead of the loud bantering and over-dramatic gestures to which theater audiences of the period were accustomed, Irving played his parts with quiet, refined dignity. In 1878, Irving became the manager of the Lyceum Theatre, and he recruited his new friend Stoker as his personal manager.

Stoker worked for Irving until Irving's death in 1905. During this period, the Lyceum flourished, and Stoker accompanied Irving on frequent tours abroad. While Stoker sang nothing but songs of praise for his comrade in *Personal Reminiscences of Henry Irving,* some who knew both men claimed that Irving was domineering and prone to dark moods. Stoker, however, did claim some success of his own while working for Irving. *Dracula* was published to moderate response and praise in 1897. The hypothesis that Dracula is loosely based on Irving is purely speculative, even though a few writers have made compelling cases. Stoker biographer Barbara Belford has claimed that *Dracula* is "bristling with repression and apprehension of homosexuality, devouring women, and rejecting mothers." Literary critic Phyllis Roth wrote that the character of Dracula "acts out the repressed fantasies of the others."

The Art of Repression

Although some may be reading a bit too much between Stoker's lines on that count, there is convincing evidence that he was a closeted homosexual. In his youth, Stoker idolized and corresponded with American poet Walt Whitman, who was famous for his liberal attitude toward homosexuality. In one letter to Whitman, Stoker declared, "I would like to call you comrade and talk to you as men who are not poets do not often talk.... I know I would not be long ashamed to be natural before you... you have shaken off the shackles and your wings are free. I have the shackles on my shoulders still—but I have no wings."

A Wilde Situation

Some also believe that Stoker had a complex relationship with the openly homosexual playwright Oscar Wilde. In 1878, Stoker married the notoriously beautiful Florence Balcombe, who only a short time prior had been the beloved girlfriend of a young Oscar Wilde. There is little surviving documentation of the relationship between Wilde and Stoker, but historians argue the two men kept up icy social relations throughout their life and that Wilde was jealous of Stoker's marriage.

And then there was the famous Wilde sodomy trial of 1895, which resulted in Wilde spending two years in prison. Since *Dracula* was published in 1897, some historians have proposed that Stoker wrote the novel during the trial and funneled his complex feelings about homosexuality into the overly sexual book. But recent discoveries of Stoker's working notes on *Dracula* reveal that he began planning the book five years before Wilde's trial.

What is clear is that Stoker was one of the only artists in Wilde's circle who did not vocally come to his defense during the trials. Essays Stoker wrote on censorship suggest that he was morally opposed to "loose" sexual codes, feeling instead that writers should censor their work so as not to propagate immorality. In "The Censorship of Stage Plays," Stoker wrote that "we do not allow to the human what we overlook in other animals. Hence arise such words... [as] *reticence, taste,* and the whole illuminative terminology based on higher thought and ambition for the worthy advance of mankind."

Thus, while Stoker may have been in love with Irving, it seems unlikely that he ever acted on his feelings, despite conjectures about the late-night sessions the two frequently held at the Lyceum Theatre. Whatever the sexual overtones of their relationship, Stoker held a deep love for Irving. Whatever the inspiration for the delectably sexual *Dracula,* it is a novel that has lived for more than a century in the popular imagination.

HELLISH HEADLINES

Men Recommend More Clubs for Wives

If Strike Isn't Settled Quickly It May Last Awhile

Tiger Woods Plays with His Own Balls, Nike Says

Red Tape Holds Up New Bridges

Kicking Baby Considered to Be Healthy

Include Your Children When Baking Cookies

Condom Faults Could Lead to Dating Policy

Yellow Snow Studied to Test Nutrition

Babies Are What the Mother Eats

Local Man Has Longest Horns in Texas

Cancer Society Honors Marlboro Man

Clinton Apologizes to Syphilis Victims

Teacher Strikes Idle Kids

Nicaragua Sets Goal to Wipe Out Literacy

Some Pieces of Rock Hudson Sold at Auction

Stiff Opposition Expected to Casketless Funeral Plan

Neighbors Said Sniper Not Very Neighborly

Deaf College Opens Doors to Hearing

Endfield Couple Slain: Police Suspect Homicide

Here's How You Can Lick Doberman's Leg Sores

Local High School Dropouts Cut in Half

Organ Festival Ends in Smashing Climax

Lawmen from Mexico Barbecue Guests

Lung Cancer in Women Mushrooms

Study Reveals Those Without Insurance Die More Often

Good Foreign Policies, Happy Endings

In some circles, diplomacy and foreign policy may be thought of as negative terms, but when they're effective, great things can happen.

In today's world, it seems as though the overriding philosophy is "every country for itself": protecting the resources of the land, the people, and the country as a whole. Taking care of one's own surely isn't all bad, but whatever happened to goodwill? Yes, altruism, clearly, is less of a priority—taking its place is a bombastic ethnocentrism that is eroding that old-fashioned optimistic ideal of humanity. But for all the pessimism involving foreign relations in the last century, the U.S. government is still slipping in some good deeds here and there.

USAID

There's USAID, a foreign assistance agency with roots that go back to World War II. The organization was founded on the belief that, in order to achieve democracy and a global free market, the entire world must develop sustainable economic growth. In Brazil, for instance, where youth unemployment is high and electrical power availability is low, USAID found a way to address the problems together for a better outcome. Between 10 and 20 million poor Brazilians lack access to power grids, so USAID recruited groups of unemployed 16- to 24-year-olds to participate in their training program. In learning how to utilize renewable energy sources and rely less on the nation's power grid, young people who would have otherwise faltered in the job market now have marketable skills. Additionally, a more ecologically sound energy sector is emerging in Brazil as a result.

The World Bank

The World Bank, established in 1944 to encourage postwar global rebuilding, is doing its part, too. Once a mere lending institution, it has evolved into an elaborate consortium set to alleviate the pressures of worldwide poverty. With this goal in mind, the World Bank, unlike typical financial institutions, provides more than just monetary assistance to those in need. A World Bank program in Bolivia, the Bolivia Land for Agricultural Development Project, began in late 2007 to bring land to poor farmers by providing them with revolving credit and then finding third parties to match funds. Ongoing technical assistance and monitoring is also given through the World Bank to ensure success for the previously landless farmers.

The Peace Corps

Initiated by President John F. Kennedy and established in 1961, the Peace Corps was built with the intent of bringing peace to the world through volunteer service. A lofty goal, for sure, but through the many participants in its history and the programs pressed forth by them, it is a goal that can be met. Take the Kenyan Sign Language project: In 2002, while already in Kenya providing volunteer service to the community through the Peace Corps, a group noticed the lack of aid for hearing-impaired Kenyans. Few written materials in Kenyan Sign Language existed. Due to lack of funding, Kenyans with hearing impairments were neglected at schools, and in some cases, even their own family members had difficulty communicating with them. During a period of roughly 18 months, the Peace Corps created a software program to fill in this gap. Once finished, they worked with donor organizations to get the computers that the Kenyans needed to run the program.

Food for Peace

Helping out on the food front is Food for Peace, a USAID program put together during the Eisenhower administration, which funnels U.S. food overseas to fight malnutrition and starvation worldwide, while encouraging global agricultural development. In Zimbabwe, a country with a staggeringly high unemployment rate of roughly 80 percent in 2007 and ever-worsening drought conditions, the people rely heavily on staple foods, such as grains. These are inexpensive and relatively easy to grow. With the ongoing economic deterioration of the land, the poor people in urban areas of Zimbabwe have suffered greatly. By bringing sorghum, a nutritionally sound grass cereal, into the area for farming and trade, Food for Peace has helped citizens of Bulawayo (Zimbabwe's second-largest city) establish a model for consumer trade while providing sustenance to its people. Better yet, sorghum suits the dry climate of the region much better than the corn that was previously planted there.

The Carter Center

Another do-good group, the Carter Center—created in 1982 by former President Jimmy Carter and his wife, Rosalynn—was established in an effort to improve human existence the world over. With projects in 72 countries, the organization is making a difference. For example, in Chad—a country with ongoing internal unrest and poor economic development—*dracunculiasis,* or guinea worm disease, plagued the region (and the intestines of its people) for years. The Carter Center took on the challenge in 1986 and seriously arrested the pandemic by 1998 through water-safety education and assistance with larvicidal treatments.

Operation Provide Hope

Since 1992, Operation Provide Hope, a U.S. State Department program, has been donating medical supplies to the former Soviet Union. The incentive was initially established to help the region segue into a freer democratic state. In addition to the supplies, the program has built medical facilities and trained local people to make the facilities sustainable. In this region, prior to Operation Provide Hope, even a minor infection could turn into a major problem. Since implementation of the program, though, the line between life and death has become more distinct.

Clearly, while one hand of a government tends to its own flock, the other hand can still lend help to those in need of a good deed.

- *Bunny Austin was the first man to ever wear shorts at Wimbledon, and Yvon Petra was the last champion to wear long trousers.*

- *In February 1979, agents of the U.S. Drug Enforcement Administration arrested five brokers, four clerks, and three others for selling cocaine on the floor of the Chicago Board Options Exchange.*

- *Judy Scheindlin, better known as Judge Judy, makes $25 million per year. Supreme Court Justice Ruth Bader Ginsburg, who sits on the nation's highest court, earns $190,100.*

- *Lucy Harris became the first woman drafted by an NBA team when the New Orleans Jazz selected the Delta State star in 1977.*

Strange Justice

She'll Drink to That

A woman employed by a drug and alcohol treatment center as a teacher for recovering abusers was fired after her third conviction for drunk driving. She sued the center for wrongful termination, claiming she hadn't corrupted any students and her ability to teach hadn't been affected (even if the same thing couldn't be said for her driving). The state's education chief upheld the firing, citing a zero-tolerance statute. The state courts agreed, leaving her (it's hoped) not too high and dry.

What a Drag

Two young men headed out on a Friday night for a beer-filled evening of fun. They took things a little too far by hurling empty bottles at a woman in her car. Caught by the police, they were found guilty of criminal damage, fined $250, and given a choice of spending two months in jail or walking through downtown for one hour dressed as women. The men chose to don dresses and wigs.

Piercings Get to the Point

The big retailer hired a young lady, knowing she had four ear piercings and several tattoos. Within several years, however, the woman had joined a religious group that encouraged body piercing, and she had her eyebrow pierced. Since the retailer had a policy against facial piercings, the employee was terminated. The Equal Employment Opportunity Commission found she had been discriminated against, and she filed a $2 million claim against her former employer. But the District Court and Court of Appeals denied the claim of discrimination, leaving the woman's claim as full of holes as her ears.

Gimme an *S*! Gimme a *U*! Gimme an *E*!

Nearly 100 high school cheerleaders decided to file a suit against their district administrators after that organization banned many of their cheerleading moves and routines—including pyramids, mounts, and tumbling—as "dangerous and unnecessary." The girls claimed that grounding their activities was like asking a football team to stop tackling. In protest, the cheerleaders tossed around cardboard cutouts of themselves at that season's football games. A judge went along with the kids, issuing an injunction against the ban and leaving the cheerleaders jumping for joy.

Famous Simply for Being Famous

Today's 24-hour news cycle, and the machinery of fame that accompanies it, demands constant feeding. Some people achieve fame by actually accomplishing something. Other people achieve fame because... well, they just do.

One tried-and-true method of achieving celebrity without really having to do anything is to be born into the right circumstances. The United States, with no aristocracy of its own, has always been deeply fascinated by those who have won life's lottery without even trying—that is, those born into fabulous wealth.

Brenda Frazier

Socialite Brenda Diana Duff Frazier (1921–82) became famous when she appeared as a debutante on a 1938 cover of *Life* magazine, which went on sale when the country was still grappling with the Great Depression. Frazier, a banking and grain heiress, was an attractive teenager at 17 and a has-been by 29. No particular scandal marked her decline; rather, she became a recluse, addicted to drugs and alcohol. Unwittingly, she set another trend by suffering from anorexia and bulimia long before those eating disorders became household words.

Barbara Hutton

The sad-eyed heir of the Woolworth five-and-dime retail fortune, Barbara Hutton (1912–79) came to be known as the "Poor Little Rich Girl." Her mother committed suicide when Barbara was six, and the lonely only child was abandoned by her father and raised by a series of relatives and nannies. Hutton inherited almost $50 million at age 21 and went on to wed seven times—primarily coupling with abusive fortune hunters, playboys, and dubious European "royalty." Her 1942 marriage to debonair film star Cary Grant led the press to cynically dub them "Cash and Cary," although Grant was the only one of Hutton's mates who never took any money from her (they divorced in 1945). As Hutton grew older and more disappointed in life, she was reportedly often seen intoxicated, bestowing expensive gifts on younger men. Devastated by the death of her only child, Lance Reventlow, in a 1972 plane crash, Hutton died of a heart attack seven years later. She reportedly left an estate worth only $3,000.

Gloria Vanderbilt

Born in 1924 into a grand old American fortune—her paternal great-great-grandfather, Cornelius Vanderbilt, "The Commodore," made his money in railroads—Gloria Vanderbilt didn't necessarily have the best that money could buy. Her father died when she was just 15 months old, and her mother (known as "Big Gloria") controlled the child's four-million-dollar trust fund but lacked maternal instincts. Big Gloria much preferred gadding about with a decadent set of international high society.

Gertrude Vanderbilt Whitney, scion of the Whitney fortune and the sister of Little Gloria's father, sued for custody in a 1934 court case that riveted the nation with its lurid details (women sleeping until mid-afternoon, seen in bed together, and so on). After sculptor/philanthropist Whitney was granted custody, she left Gloria pretty much to her own devices, which included marrying very old men quite early in life. After a string of high-profile romances and poor-choice weddings, her fourth and final marriage to Wyatt Cooper was actually happy, producing two sons (in addition to two sons she had from a previous marriage). This was not to last, however, when her husband died during open-heart surgery at age 50, and their son Carter committed suicide in front of his mother by jumping from a high-rise apartment window. Vanderbilt's surviving son from this marriage, Anderson Cooper, is a successful CNN reporter/anchor. Gloria Vanderbilt, an accomplished collage and watercolor artist, made a fortune of her own by licensing her name to lines of accessories and clothing, most notably denim jeans, in the 1970s and '80s.

Edie Sedgwick

A cousin of actor Kyra Sedgwick, Edie Sedgwick (1943–71) was descended from a family that could trace its roots back to the American Revolution. Unfortunately, while the family possessed the requisite wealth and bloodlines, it also hid some very dark secrets, including madness, suicide, and alleged incest. A vivacious, photogenic charmer, art student Edie had already been institutionalized before she came to New York City and met Andy Warhol, who re-imagined the stylish waif as a "superstar" in a Faustian bargain that served them both—for a while. Edie's name and connections got her into *Vogue;* editor Diana Vreeland declared Edie the "It Girl" of the early 1960s. Sedgwick bleached her cropped hair silver to match Warhol's wig and flittered through glittering nights before a series of bad love affairs and a serious drug addiction sent her speeding back home to California. Although she tried her best to get clean and happy, Sedgwick's demons caught up with her. However, she remains a fashion icon decades after her untimely passing.

Paris Hilton

All of this brings us to the latest installment in the famous-for-nothing game: Paris Hilton, who has made herself a cottage industry through her family name and hotel fortune, a relentless pursuit of publicity, an Internet-peddled sex video, and a starring role in a reality television series. Paris's underwear-free dances on club tables, affairs with other heirs, tiny accessories such as dogs and "frenemies," and total self-absorption have already held the world's interest far beyond any reasonable sell-by date. The fact that Hilton finally served prison time for one of several infractions after a DUI arrest incited glee in many quarters.

So it is and will ever be, because much of the pleasure derived from watching the antics of the rich and useless is enjoying their inevitable falls from grace. We want to be them (or at least have what they've got) even as we despise them; we want them to be punished for being given everything and then wasting it. As the *New York Times* reviewer of a Brenda Frazier biography noted, the delight that we peons take in miseries visited upon the high-born "serves the democratic desire for simultaneous admiration of and revenge on those who have done nothing to merit their money and fame."

- *The last NASCAR driver to be convicted of running moonshine was Buddy Arrington, who got nabbed peddling the homemade stuff in the hills of southern Virginia in 1969.*

- *Eyelash curlers were invented in 1923. Waterproof mascara— made partially of turpentine—was invented a few years later.*

He Said, She Said

If we worked on the assumption that what is accepted as true really is true, then there would be little hope for advance.
—*Wilbur Wright*

Nothing is work unless you'd rather be doing something else.
—*George Halas*

A hospital bed is a parked taxi with the meter running.
—*Groucho Marx*

Without music, life would be an error. The German imagines even God singing songs.
—*Friedrich Nietzsche*

It is an open question whether any behavior based on fear of eternal punishment can be regarded as ethical or should be regarded as merely cowardly.
—*Margaret Mead*

Never pick a fight with an ugly person, they've got nothing to lose.
—*Robin Williams*

It's a recession when your neighbor loses his job; it's a depression when you lose your own.
—*Harry S. Truman*

The best you can get is an even break.
—*Franklin P. Adams*

I saw the angel in the marble and carved until I set him free.
—*Michelangelo*

The first time I see a jogger smiling, I'll consider it.
—*Joan Rivers*

He who joyfully marches to music in rank and file has already earned my contempt. He has been given a large brain by mistake, since for him the spinal cord would suffice.
—*Albert Einstein*

When someone does something good, applaud! You will make two people happy.
—*Samuel Goldwyn*

Robert Manry and *Tinkerbelle*

Robert Manry boarded the tiny vessel Tinkerbelle *and crossed the Atlantic Ocean in what, at the time, was the smallest boat ever to have made it across those vast seas. He suggested he wanted to keep himself "aware of his lowly place in the universe." Ironically, the voyage that raised his humble status also caused the downfall of his family's happiness.*

Robert Manry was born in Landour, India, in the Himalayan Mountains, in June 1918. As a child, he savored his first sailing experience alongside his father. His fire for a nautical adventure was fueled by a German sailor who spoke to his high school class and told of his own exciting adventures. Between a seemingly idyllic childhood and a comfortable adulthood that took him to Cleveland, Ohio, as a copy editor for the *Plain Dealer,* Manry studied for a semester in China; served in Austria, France, and Germany during World War II; and earned a political science degree from Antioch College. Not until he had a family of his own, complete with a son and daughter, did he again tap into his inner sailor.

The Pull of the Sea

In 1958, at age 40, Manry purchased his prized possession, a used 13.5-foot sailboat named *Tinkerbelle* that was nearly as old as he was. Manry devoted his energies to *Tinkerbelle* in an effort to restore its seaworthiness. The vessel earned a place on every family vacation, and it eventually became the craft that transported him on his famous voyage. That ultimate trip was not, however, a goal he had set upon when purchasing the tiny boat. Those plans unfolded after a seemingly innocuous invitation from a friend to join him on his own voyage in a boat nearly twice the size of *Tinkerbelle.* The friend backed out, but the adventure bug had bitten Manry. He told only his family of his plans before deciding to sail the Atlantic alone in 1965.

Packed for almost any possibility, Manry depended on Dexedrine to keep himself awake and aware. Days on the seas, of course, took their toll. At times, he was overcome with hallucinations that forced him to lose consciousness. Vicious nightmares of harm to his family ravaged him during those times; dramatic weight loss and dangerous storms affected him during his waking hours. But Manry and the small but mighty *Tinkerbelle* continued on their way.

At the end of his 78-day journey, Manry was flabbergasted by the fanfare that awaited him. Back at home, his voyage had topped such national news stories as the growing war in Vietnam. Awaiting him at his destination of Falmouth, England, was a huge celebration that even included his family, who were flown over by the *Plain Dealer.*

Consequences

Alas, the story does not end with the happiness of a goal accomplished. The years that followed were not filled with the excitement and joy of fame; instead, a sickening series of events, at least partially caused by the *Tinkerbelle* voyage, devastated the Manry family. Victims of an onslaught of media attention that surrounded the now-famous clan, the Manry children spiraled downward. The entire Manry family took to bickering in unease over the constant glare of the limelight. In a freak automobile accident, Manry's wife was killed not quite four years after the voyage; Manry himself died of a heart attack only five-and-a-half years after his adventure. The Manry kids, still teenagers and still suffering the inadvertent consequences of the famous voyage, were left parentless. Douglas Manry eventually was homeless for a time, sleeping in the very park named after his famous father. But he and his sister Robin forever remembered the seemingly proud summer that their dad made history for the toll it took on their once-tranquil household.

- *The cymbal company Zildjian, founded in Constantinople in 1623, opened its first American factory in 1927. It is the oldest business with operations in the United States.*

- *Abram C. Pheil was the first airline passenger on a commercial flight. Pheil paid five dollars to fly in Florida from St. Petersburg to Tampa on January 1, 1914.*

- *Highly groomed lawns such as are seen today only became popular in the early part of the 20th century.*

FROM THE VAULTS OF HISTORY

Endings and Beginnings
The last public execution by burning at the stake happened at Newgate Prison in England in 1786. Phoebe Harrius was tried and sentenced for counterfeiting coins, which was considered high treason at the time. The first execution using a gas chamber took place on February 8, 1924, in Nevada. Gee Jon was executed for murdering a rival gang member.

Wedded Bliss
On December 14, 867, Pope Adrian II became the last Catholic pope to have a wife. Adrian had been married before ascending to the papacy, but he apparently refused to take the vow of celibacy or give up his wife before accepting the position.

If Everybody Else Jumped into a Volcano...
Kiyoko Matsumoto, a student at an all-girls school in Japan, started a new trend on February 11, 1933. She committed suicide by jumping into the center of Mount Mihara, a volcano on the island of Oshima, near Tokyo, Japan. Within the year, more than 900 other people had followed her example.

The Mother Road
Before the U.S. interstate system was developed, it wasn't always easy to get from one part of the country to another. One road, however, which wound from Chicago to Los Angeles, became the stuff of legend. Route 66 was established by Congress in 1926 and traversed Illinois, Missouri, the corner of Kansas, Oklahoma, the Texas panhandle, New Mexico, Arizona, and Southern California. In his Depression-era novel *The Grapes of Wrath,* John Steinbeck dubbed it "The Mother Road." Route 66 inspired many to look west for their fortune and was also the subject of a song performed by everyone from Nat King Cole to the Rolling Stones to Depeche Mode. Get your kicks on Route 66!

Gone for the Ages
In 1681, the last-known dodo, a flightless bird native only to the island of Mauritius in the Indian Ocean, died. In 1507—not even two centuries earlier—the Portuguese were the first Europeans to discover the exotic bird. Its speedy decline and extinction was due to humans and the feral dogs, pigs, rats, and monkeys they brought with them to the island.

The Great Piano Con

Lauded late in life as a great piano virtuoso, British pianist Joyce Hatto produced the largest collection of recorded piano pieces in the history of music production. But were they hers?

Joyce Hatto was known as an extraordinary pianist. Her recorded repertoire available in the UK grew to more than 100 CDs and included some of the most difficult piano pieces around. What was truly amazing is that she somehow managed to record this music while suffering the effects of cancer and dealing with the usual wear and tear of an aging body. How did she do it? Perhaps her penchant for plagiarism helped. As it turned out, the majority of her works were stolen from other artists' recordings and then reproduced as her own!

Having enjoyed a full, albeit rather insignificant, career as a concert pianist, Hatto abandoned her stage show in 1976 to focus on her advancing disease. On the cusp of 50, she had only a few recorded numbers under her belt. However, that soon changed, as she spent her remaining years prolifically, but as it turned out, falsely, adding to that collection.

The CD Deluge Begins

That Hatto's husband, William Barrington-Coupe, ran the Concert Artists Recordings label under which her recordings were released undoubtedly helped to assist in the harmonious heist. His music-business acumen provided both the technological savvy to engineer the pieces that had been previously released by other pianists and the means to unleash the forged works on an unsuspecting public.

Of course, the scam couldn't last forever. Internet rumors began surfacing in 2005, but *Gramophone,* a monthly music magazine in London, wasn't able to definitively break the news of the deception until February 2007, about eight months after Hatto's death. In fact, her death at age 77 may have actually been an impetus for the discovery.

After Hatto's passing, her celebrity fire burned hotter than ever. Beloved by a small fan base during her life, Hatto-mania came out in full force upon her death. Some even deemed her one of the great pianists of modern times. But with that superstar status came a renewed flurry of suspicions surrounding the likelihood of a woman of her age and ailing health being able to produce such a copious collection. *Gramophone* issued a summons for anyone who knew of any fraudulence. Months passed with no evidence, until a reader finally contacted the magazine to reveal his strange findings. As it turned out, this man's computer actually discovered the deceit.

The Con Revealed

Popping in a purported CD of Hatto hits, the reader's computer identified that a particular ditty was not a work of Hatto but one by little-known pianist Lazlo Simon. The reader immediately contacted *Gramophone* with his discovery. Based on his report, *Gramophone* sent the recordings to a sound engineer, who put music science to the test, comparing sound waves from Hatto's ostensible recording of Liszt's 12 Transcendental Studies to Simon's version. An identical match was uncovered! After that, more and more tested pieces attributed to Hatto were found to belong to other musicians.

Hatto and husband were able to manage the ruse by utilizing music technology to recycle others' recordings and reproduce them as Hatto's own; by that same technology, the deceptive duo was discovered. So, how could the pair not foresee that music science would reveal them, even as they used its wizardry themselves? Barrington-Coupe has not, as of yet, produced a viable answer.

Although he denied any wrongdoing at first, Barrington-Coupe eventually confessed to the fraud, defending his actions by insisting that Hatto knew nothing of the scheme and he had made very little money on it. He further claimed that the whole plot was inspired by nothing more than his love for his ailing wife and his attempt to make her feel appreciated by the music community during her final years. An assertion such as this can neither be proved nor disproved, but *Gramophone* pointed out that Barrington-Coupe continued to sell the false CDs after she had died.

Fast Facts

- *A person eating a big meal might swallow more than 200 times.*

- *The ancient city of Babylon was located on the modern-day site of Al Hillah, Iraq. Babylon was said to have been surrounded by a wall 100 feet wide, 300 feet high, and 56 miles in length.*

- *The largest American corporation named for an owner's daughter is Sara Lee. Founder Charles Lubin first named a cheesecake for his daughter in 1949.*

- *American interstate highways going east and west have even numbers. North-and-south highways are given odd numbers.*

- *The Hunza, an ethnic group in northwest Kashmir, have not experienced cancer, coronary heart disease, or ulcers. Many of the men and women live to age 100.*

- *To conserve fuel during World War II, King George VI of England ordered that no more than five inches of lukewarm water could be used to take baths in Buckingham Palace.*

- *A normal person's bladder holds about 16 ounces of urine. They'll feel the need to "go" when it's about three-quarters full.*

- *Theodore Roosevelt was shot as he campaigned for the presidency in 1912. The bullet hit him in the chest but not before passing through his glasses' case and the speech he had folded in his pocket. Roosevelt received a superficial wound and finished his speech before going to the hospital for treatment 90 minutes later.*

- *During steel magnate Charles M. Schwab's tenure as president of the American Society of Mechanical Engineers in the 1920s and '30s, the society lost $215,000. When Schwab and the council couldn't remember the details while under oath, New York Supreme Court Justice William Black ruled that "Rip Van Winkling" was not a defense.*

Marian Anderson at the Met

❖ ❖ ❖ ❖

Imagine today's popular singers, with all the post-production and computer-aided technology they have at their disposal, moving a crowd of thousands to tears by the sheer sound of their voices. It seems improbable, but from 1915 to 1965, opera singer Marian Anderson did just that.

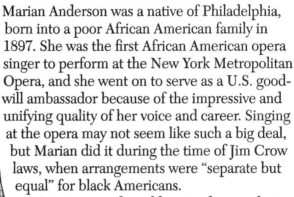

Marian Anderson was a native of Philadelphia, born into a poor African American family in 1897. She was the first African American opera singer to perform at the New York Metropolitan Opera, and she went on to serve as a U.S. goodwill ambassador because of the impressive and unifying quality of her voice and career. Singing at the opera may not seem like such a big deal, but Marian did it during the time of Jim Crow laws, when arrangements were "separate but equal" for black Americans.

Marian sang for sold-out audiences, but she often had to stay at the homes of fans because African Americans weren't allowed in many hotels; if she was allowed to stay at a hotel, she had to use the freight elevator to get to her room. She would have never been able to receive formal voice training to learn arias and *leiders* if kind musicians hadn't recognized her talent and tutored her for free (or, in the case of her church, donated money toward her education)—"reputable" music schools wouldn't have looked past the color of her skin.

International Success

Thankfully, Marian was not afraid to travel; going to Europe truly allowed her to shine. Opera fans adored her, the press raved about her, and she was treated like a celebrity while selling out shows throughout the continent. In 1936, she was even invited to perform in Nazi Germany—until her "hosts" confirmed that she wasn't 100-percent white.

After touring in Europe, Marian had a chance to be a superstar in the United States. However, she faced racial adversity again when the Daughters of the American Revolution (DAR) refused to allow her to perform in Constitution Hall, which the organization owned. Controversy raged, leading First Lady Eleanor Roosevelt to resign from the DAR and help set up a dramatic and historic free concert performed to a mixed-race crowd at the base of the Lincoln Memorial.

Conquering the Met

Never one to comment on the injustice surrounding her career or the state of the country, Marian continued to focus on her voice and touring. In 1954, at age 57, she was finally invited to perform as the gypsy Ulrica in the opera *Un Ballo in Maschero* at the New York Metropolitan Opera.

In a review of her performance, one reporter wrote, "There were those who wished the night had happened ten years earlier when the contralto was at her peak." He wasn't alone; many reporters expressed their wonderment as to why Marian was just getting a chance to perform at the Met 20 years after she became a superstar.

Her popularity peaked at this time, but Marian jumped at the chance to serve as a U.S. emissary with the United Nations when a big fan of hers, President Dwight Eisenhower, invited her to do so. Throughout Marian's diplomatic tour of the world, America's racial policies were addressed by foreign citizens, who wondered how she could represent a country in which she herself could not be entirely free. Marian simply explained in her calm way that she was very saddened by the situation.

Today, it's hard to imagine what life was actually like for Marian Anderson; we take for granted many things she never got to experience. Marian may not have been as visible as Martin Luther King, Jr., but her faith, family support, talent, elegance, and silent contribution to civil rights causes made her an icon.

- *The unlikely Jamaican bobsled team, which provided plenty of laughs by placing last in the 1986 Winter Olympics, finished ahead of the USA sled team at the 1994 games.*

- *A new American citizen is born about every 11 seconds.*

Where You'd Least Expect It

A bug collection put together by the famous 19th-century scientist Alfred Wallace was found in 2005 by his grandson—hidden in the family attic. Along with Charles Darwin, Wallace theorized about evolution by natural selection. Having put together numerous biological collections, Wallace was financially forced to sell them off one by one to support his family, but his grandson reported that he'd held on to some of his favorite specimens.

Rusty, an eight-year-old poodle-Maltese mix from Sydney, Australia, was missing for two months before he was found—2,000 miles away! A positive confirmation was made with the tracking microchip in his skin, but no one knows how he traveled so far when his paws showed no wear and tear.

According to German news reports, a man was investigated for fraud after exchanging a potato-filled computer for a new one. His complaints of the missing computer innards might have worked had he not come back a second time with another spud-packed computer complaining of the same problem.

A novel detailing an actual botched raid of Cuba in 1851 was lost for a century and a half before finally turning up in the spotlight. The book was penned under a pseudonym by 22-year-old Lucy Petway Holcombe, a Southern belle intent on changing the U.S. policy on Spanish rule over Cuba. Holcombe later married Francis W. Pickens, who served as governor of South Carolina during the Civil War. She became known as Queen of the Confederacy.

Robert Frost wrote a poem for John F. Kennedy's presidential inauguration, but he couldn't read it through the sun's glare at the actual ceremony. So, he recited another poem from memory, instead. The poem he originally wrote, though, was the first item to adorn the wall of JFK's presidential office. Surprising, then, that it was found years later haphazardly stashed in someone's home.

Stolen in the 1970s, a stash of 500 tapes with unreleased Beatles' recordings was recovered in 2003 by London police who were on the trail of illegal bootlegs circulating the city. The officers' hunt led them to Holland, where they discovered a major piracy operation in full swing, along with the missing tapes.

What's New in Voodoo?

❖ ❖ ❖ ❖

New Orleans is famous for many things, one of them being the voodoo shops competing to sell you a spell or two.

Not surprisingly, New Orleans boasts at least four shops that specialize in voodoo paraphernalia, along with an honest-to-goodness voodoo museum. Its Creole heritage provides some qualification for New Orleans to bill itself as the voodoo capital of the world. Whether you're a believer in spells, love potions, and zombies or not, the items carried by these quaint shops are well worth the visit. It's an opportunity to inhale the essence that makes New Orleans unique among American cities.

Details, Details
The word *voodoo* is derived from the Fon word *voudoun* (spirit). Erzuli's, Bloody Mary's, Reverend Zombie's, and Voodoo Authentica are all voodoo shops located in the famed French Quarter of New Orleans. These shops offer a variety of items unique to the uninitiated, such as potion oils, gris-gris (lucky mojo bags), voodoo dolls, jujus (blessed objects that ward off evil), ritual kits (everything you need to perform your own voodoo ritual for less than $50), voodoo candles, handmade crafts, incense, jewelry (including chicken-foot fetishes and gator-tooth necklaces), voodoo spells, spiritual guidance, voo beanies, African power dolls, spiritual goat's milk soaps, T-shirts, and much more. You can even have a hex removed if someone was mean enough to lay one on you, or join a class to learn how to make your own voodoo doll.

Most of the shops also feature ghostly tours, which usually include a visit to the grave of Marie Laveau, one of the world's better-known voodoo queens and a popular woman in New Orleans history. So, the next time you're in New Orleans, don't be a zombie—drop into one of the city's unique voodoo shops and visit for a spell, especially during Voodoofest, which takes place every Halloween.

Artists United! The History of United Artists Corporation

❖ ❖ ❖ ❖

It was a curious quartet of Hollywood superstars: One was a swashbuckling leading man, another was known as "America's Sweetheart," a third called himself the "Little Tramp," and the fourth was considered the father of epic filmmaking. Together, they formed the first production company run by creative talent rather than by studio moneymakers.

Bucking the System

Hollywood stars Douglas Fairbanks, Mary Pickford, Charlie Chaplin, and William S. Hart did their part for the World War I effort by traveling the country and selling Liberty Bonds. Behind the scenes, they discussed how much they disliked the studio executives who ruled their lives. Even though they were big stars, the four felt that they were slaves to the decisions of others.

The idea of forming their own distribution company developed, and in 1919, they founded United Artists. Although Hart declined to join, groundbreaking director D. W. Griffith took his place. The team's ambitious plan was to release five top-quality films every year. These pioneers were unique in Hollywood: They had no actual shooting studio, nor did they maintain any performers under contract.

Mary Pickford

Douglas Fairbanks

Charlie Chaplin

D. W. Griffith

Fairbanks and Pickford: United Artists, Indeed

Douglas Fairbanks was a successful star in romantic comedies when he met the diminutive Mary Pickford at a party in 1916. At age 24, she had already starred in nearly 200 films. Although married to others, the couple began an affair that eventually culminated in their marriage in 1920. They purchased a sprawling hunting lodge in Beverly Hills and renovated it into a 22-room mansion they called *Pickfair*. Fairbanks and Pickford separated in 1933 and divorced three years later.

Charlie Chaplin: Genius at Work

The derbied comic came to Hollywood in 1913, having established his talents at Chicago's Essanay Film Studios. Although he had near-complete creative control in producing his comedies, per the terms of a contract with Mutual Films worth nearly $700,000 per year, he still sought more independence. His greatest silent comedies, including *The Gold Rush*, were made for United Artists.

D. W. Griffith: Master Storyteller

David Wark Griffith began making short films in 1908—and within five years, he had directed more than 450! This laid the foundation for his first masterpiece in 1915, *Birth of a Nation*. At more than three hours, the film established a new standard for feature films. Although Griffith's association with United Artists was interrupted when he returned to the studio system for a few years in the mid-1920s, United Artists produced his blockbuster films including *Way Down East* and *Orphans of the Storm,* both starring Lillian Gish.

Coming Together

The first years were difficult, as United Artists' plan to produce five films a year was overambitious and resulted in a low-quality product. Producer Joseph Schenck was tapped to run United Artists in 1924, and he brought top-notch stars with him, including his wife, Norma Talmadge, and stone-faced comedian Buster Keaton. Soon, Schenck was able to attract megastars Rudolph Valentino and John Barry-more as well. He also started a separate company to build first-rate movie theaters, where the films of United Artists could be shown.

Falling Apart

By the 1930s, United Artists had established itself as a major player in Hollywood. But internal dissension and a shortage of good films resulted in the loss of an amazing $65,000 per week for the corporation by the end of the 1940s. Two enterprising attorneys salvaged the fading film company in the 1950s, leading to banner decades in the '60s and '70s with fan favorites such as the James Bond and Rocky series.

Fumbling Felons

Three Times Is No Charm
In December 2005, an unmasked man in Frisco, Texas, attempted to break into three different ATM machines at three different locations with an ax! The machines are apparently built to withstand such an attack. Meanwhile, security cameras at each of the locations captured the incidents on tape. Television news quickly broadcast the footage, and the man, who saw how easily he'd be recognized, turned himself in shortly afterward. His bond was set for $20,000—for each ATM.

There's Nothing Like a Good Disguise
In Ashland, Kentucky, a man tried to rob a liquor store with his face completely wrapped in gray duct tape. Claiming to have a knife, the man threatened to harm the clerk if she didn't give him the money out of the cash register. The clerk complied, but as the robber tried to leave, the store manager pulled out a wooden club and chased him into the parking lot. Several employees joined in and tackled the robber. During a later interview, the suspect—who's since been indicted—claimed that he wasn't the robber, that he had no memory of entering the store, and that he couldn't remember police removing the duct tape.

Driving Through Adversity
A 40-year-old man with no arms and one leg received five years in prison in New Port Richey, Florida, for felony driving. The man once held a valid license, but it had been suspended several times in the previous 20 years. He had previously spent three years in prison for other offenses, such as habitually driving without a license and kicking a state trooper. (Details on *how* he kicked a state trooper were not forthcoming.)

Going to the Dogs
A woman and two men attempted to steal copper wiring and pipes from an abandoned nursing home in Gainesville, Georgia, in July 2007. The trio apparently ignored signs declaring that the property was owned by the Gainesville police department. And it wasn't just police property—it was a K-9 training facility (also clearly marked). Police dog handlers arrived and discovered the thieves, who dropped their tools and took off running. Naturally, the handlers released the entire K-9 unit to go after them. One thief ended up with a superficial dog bite on the buttocks. All were caught and charged with burglary.

Adam Clayton Powell, Jr.: The Harlem Cat

Known for his catchphrase "Keep the faith, baby," the U.S. representative from Harlem was a flashy and enigmatic politician who helped usher in the civil rights era.

Born in Connecticut in 1908 and raised in Harlem, Adam Clayton Powell, Jr., spent his youth reconciling the teachings of his minister father with the much different messages he received in speakeasies and through jazz music. After Powell flunked out of New York's City College, his father pressured him into attending Colgate University in upstate New York, where he earned his bachelor's degree. That was quickly followed up with a masters in religious education from Columbia University in 1931.

While at Columbia, Powell began to feel outrage at the plight of fellow African Americans. Operating a food bank and organizing literacy classes, he built a reputation throughout Harlem for his generosity and commitment to decrying the racism that was so rampant in New York City. But for all his successes, his efforts were often met with stiff opposition.

Organizing the Community

Frustrated by the persistent refusal of many shops and industries to hire African American workers, Powell started to encourage people to use their money as a force for change. His "Don't buy where you can't work" campaign rocked the status quo, and many white-owned businesses realized that their economic viability depended on changing their hiring practices.

Powell's reputation for activism and community service, as well as his great personal charm, led to a stint on the New York City Council. It didn't take long, however, before he was flummoxed by what he perceived as a lack of real power to effect change at city hall and decided to run for the United States Congress. On January 3, 1945, he began a 22-year career in the House of Representatives. The people of the district of Harlem had elected a tireless advocate for equal rights.

Using His Political Muscle

In an era when public use of racial slurs was common even on the Capitol floor, Powell was unlike anything the predominantly white House of Representatives had ever seen. He was a snappy dresser, confident and hungry to make the country a better place. One of only two African Americans in the House, he stormed into Washington eager to rock the boat, giving little thought to the status quo and diving into the legislative process with gusto. He railed against Congress for not doing more to eliminate the horrible practice of lynching African Americans, which was still pervasive in the Deep South and Midwest. When he felt his colleagues in Congress were dragging their feet or snubbing his efforts, he criticized them in public.

Ushering in Civil Rights

Powell learned early about the power of the dollar, and he continued to leverage that power in Congress. He frequently used what came to be known as the "Powell Amendment," a rider attached to federal legislation requiring all recipients of federal funding to stop discriminatory practices. This paved the way for racial integration in public schools and helped spark the broader civil rights movement. Powell continued to gain power and influence in Congress as chairman of the House Education and Labor Committee, a position he was elected to in 1961. He helped enact the great social programs of the time, including antipoverty initiatives and federal minimum wage laws.

Powell's relentless agitation in Congress frustrated and outraged many of his colleagues. Despite his dedication to the worthy causes of civil rights and the eradication of poverty, Powell was hardly a man without flaws. He had large tastes, and his reckless ways eventually caught up with him. In 1967, he was expelled from the House for questionable behavior with female staffers and controversy surrounding his wife's congressional paychecks. However, he regained his seat in the House in 1969 after taking his case to the Supreme Court. Unfortunately for Powell, the people of Harlem had had enough, and he lost his bid for reelection the next year.

Through success and failure, Powell never ceased to be a thorn in the side of those who would perpetuate racism or turn a blind eye to it. He succumbed to prostate cancer on April 4, 1972.

He Said, She Said

All labor that uplifts humanity has dignity and importance and should be undertaken with painstaking excellence.

—*Martin Luther King, Jr.*

Never miss a good chance to shut up.

—*Will Rogers*

Never go to bed mad. Stay up and fight.

—*Phyllis Diller*

It is amazing how much can be accomplished if no one cares who gets the credit.

—*John Wooden*

Those who do not feel pain seldom think that it is felt.

—*Dr. Samuel Johnson*

Don't tell people how to do things, tell them what to do and let them surprise you with their results.

—*George S. Patton*

A word to the wise ain't necessary—it's the stupid ones that need the advice.

—*Bill Cosby*

We believe that if men have the talent to invent new machines that put men out of work, they have the talent to put those men back to work.

—*John F. Kennedy*

I am thankful for laughter, except when milk comes out of my nose.

—*Woody Allen*

Where lipstick is concerned, the important thing is not color, but to accept God's final word on where your lips end.

—*Jerry Seinfeld*

Sometimes I wonder if men and women really suit each other. Perhaps they should live next door and just visit now and then.

—*Katharine Hepburn*

Beware of the man who works hard to learn something, learns it, and finds himself no wiser than before.

—*Kurt Vonnegut, Jr.*

Who Downed the Red Baron? The Mystery of Manfred von Richthofen

*He was the most successful flying ace of World War I—
the conflict that introduced the airplane as a weapon of
war. Yet, his demise has been credited to a number of
likely opponents, both in the sky and on the ground.*

A Precious Little Prussian

Manfred von Richthofen was born in Silesia, Prussia (now part of
Poland), in May 1892. Coming from a family steeped in nobility, the
young von Richthofen decided he would follow in his father's footsteps and become a career soldier. At 11 years old, he enrolled in the
cadet corps and, upon completion, became a member of a Prussian
cavalry unit.

Up, Up, and Away

The Germans were at the
forefront in using aircraft as
offensive weapons against
the British, French, and Russians during World War I. Von
Richthofen was recruited into
a flying unit as an "observer"—
the second occupant of a two-seat
plane who would direct the pilot over areas to gather intelligence.
By 1915, von Richthofen decided to become a pilot himself, having
already downed an enemy aircraft as an observer.

The young and green pilot joined a prestigious flying squad, one
of the premier German *jagdstaffeln*—literally "hunting squadrons."
In late 1916, von Richthofen's aggressive style brought him face-to-
face with Britain's greatest fighter pilot, Major Lanoe Hawker. After
a spirited battle in the sky, the German brought Hawker down in a
tailspin, killing him. Von Richthofen called Hawker "a brave man
and a sportsman." He later mounted the machine gun from the British plane over the door of his family home as a tribute to Hawker.
The bold flying ace often showed a great deal of respect and affin-

ity for his foes, once referring to his English dogfight opponents as "waltzing partners." Yet, he remained ruthless, even carrying with him a photograph of an Allied pilot he had viciously blown apart.

Creating an Identity

Von Richthofen quickly became the most feared, and respected, pilot in the skies. As he sought faster and more nimble aircraft, he decided he needed to be instantly recognizable. He ordered his plane to be painted bright red, with the German Iron Cross emblazoned on the fuselage. The "Red Baron" was born.

The End—But at Whose Hands?

By the spring of 1918, the Red Baron had shot down an amazing 80 Allied airplanes. This feat earned him the distinguished "Blue Max" award, and he assembled his own squadron of crack-shot pilots known as "the Flying Circus." But the celebrated pilot was not without his failures.

Von Richthofen suffered a head wound during an air battle in July 1917, which may have left an open wound exposing a small portion of his skull until his death. There are theories that this injury resulted in brain damage—if so, it would have caused the Red Baron to make some serious errors in judgment that may have led to his death on April 21, 1918.

On that day, von Richthofen was embroiled in a deadly dogfight with British Royal Air Force Sopwith Camels. As the Red Baron trained his machine-gun sights on a young pilot, enemy fire came seemingly from nowhere, striking his red Fokker. Von Richthofen crashed in an area of France occupied by Australian and Canadian allies. He was buried with full military honors by a respectful British Royal Air Force (RAF).

However, questions remain to this day as to who exactly killed von Richthofen. He suffered a fatal bullet wound through his chest. The RAF credited one of their pilots, but another story tells of Canadian soldiers who pounced on the plane crash and literally murdered the Red Baron. Still other tales claim von Richthofen was shot from the ground by rifle or machine-gun fire as he flew overhead.

The answer remains lost, perhaps forever. But there is no question as to the identity of the greatest flying ace of the First World War. That honor belongs to the Red Baron.

Fast Facts

- *Mariner 9 was the first successful Mars orbiter, transmitting more than 7,000 images of the Red Planet and providing exploratory information to lay the groundwork for later missions to find frozen water beneath the ice caps.*

- *The first radio commercial aired on WEAF in New York on August 28, 1922. It was a ten-minute advertisement for the Queensboro Real Estate Corporation.*

- *In the early- to mid-1800s, a trip by Conestoga wagon from Philadelphia to Pittsburgh—a distance of about 300 miles—took roughly three weeks.*

- *Following Walter Raleigh's beheading in 1618, his head was embalmed and given to his widow. She willed it to her son, Carew, who kept it until his death. It was buried with him.*

- *The world's smallest submarine was built by Pierre Poulin and made its dive to qualify for the record on June 26, 2005, in Memphremagog Lake, near Magog, Quebec, Canada. Submarines are measured by displacement, and its displacement was 1,367 pounds (620 kilograms).*

- *During a 60-year life span, an average tree will produce nearly two tons of leaves to be raked.*

- *Confederate volunteers in the Civil War were paid $11 per month in 1861. Their pay was increased to $18 per month by 1864, but by then the currency was almost worthless.*

- *The only father-son combination to hit back-to-back home runs in the same major league baseball game was Ken Griffey, Sr., and his son, Ken Griffey, Jr., who did it while playing for the Seattle Mariners in 1990.*

- *The highest temperature ever recorded in Antarctica was 59° F.*

Photographs That Steal Your Soul

Does life imitate art, or does art imitate life? This is one of those chicken-and-egg questions that resists an easy answer. But if you want proof that art exposes the otherwise concealed aspects of life, look no further than the photographs of Diane Arbus.

Reality Bites

When modern cultures first make contact with traditional cultures, it often isn't the guns or bombs or mysterious command of fire (in lighters) that most frightens the indigenous people. It's the photographs. Anthropologists have been told time and again by members of emerging cultures that a person's soul is stolen by the camera and transposed into the photograph. This may sound strange, but what if there's something to it? One of the most controversial photographers in history, Diane Arbus, has often been accused of maliciously freezing her subjects in poses they never would have wanted the world to see. She laid bare their innermost souls, unveiling a version of reality that people would prefer to keep cloaked.

From High Society to Underworld

Diane (pronounced *Dee-ann*) Arbus was born in 1923 as Diane Nemerov, daughter of a wealthy Manhattan department store owner. Diane always felt self-conscious about her wealth and was more interested in black-and-white images than the silver spoon. After spending many years shooting commercial photographs for various New York City magazines, she became known in the 1960s for her meticulously crafted black-and-white portraits. She loved to capture individuals who were on the fringes of society: little people, giants, circus freaks, transvestites, the mentally insane, and the physically handicapped. In the last two years of her life, she photographed the inhabitants of New Jersey institutions for the mentally retarded.

Some charged Arbus with voyeurism, while others questioned whether her disabled subjects had the authority to allow her to take their picture. Arbus's photographs are undeniably eerie and powerful. They capture individuals in less than flattering poses. Susan Sontag accused Arbus of "suggesting a world in which everybody is

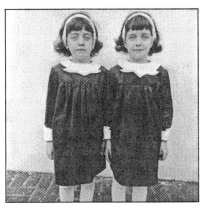

alien, hopelessly isolated, immobilized in mechanical, crippled identities and relationships." In an artistic medium capable of capturing reality, some felt that Arbus unfairly and even immorally captured only its bleakest aspects.

One of Arbus's most famous photographs features seven-year-old identical twins dressed alike. There is something ghostly about the image, with one twin slightly frowning and the other smiling, just as slightly. Years later, the girls' father told the *Washington Post,* "We thought it was the worst likeness of the twins we'd ever seen." That comment goes to the heart of Arbus's art: She was not interested in immediate likenesses but in deeper, more universal truths.

But Arbus didn't reserve her talents for the so-called freaks of society. She also photographed middle-class families, journalists, artists, and movie stars. She revealed the hidden ugliness and pain behind even the most illustrious of her subjects. This may well be why famous people tended to dislike her portraits of them. Arbus once photographed the legendary Mae West. Arbus's husband, Allan Arbus, later revealed, "Mae West hated the pictures. Because they were truthful." Journalist and author Norman Mailer took one look at Arbus's picture of him and proclaimed that "giving a camera to Diane Arbus is like putting a live grenade in the hands of a child."

Although Arbus's critics lament her exploitation of the world's outcasts, Arbus herself never treated her subjects as outsiders or considered them repulsive. She spent hours getting to know her subjects before she would begin a shoot, preferring to photograph them in their own homes, among their own possessions. Of the "freaks" that she photographed, Arbus observed that "most people go through life dreading they'll have a traumatic experience. Freaks were born with their trauma.... They're aristocrats." Arbus may have photographed what the world didn't want to see, and she succeeded in capturing what is usually hidden. Arbus committed suicide in 1971 at age 48.

🎼 Behind the Songs of Our Times

"All You Need Is Love" (1967)

As a reaction to the escalating Vietnam War, the Beatles performed "All You Need Is Love" as the British contribution to the *Our World* TV broadcast of June 25, 1967. It was the first show broadcast live by satellite around the world. Scores of invited friends (as well as recording and TV technicians) took part in the song. As more than 400 million viewers watched, the Beatles delivered their message of peace and love. Within two months, the song was number one on the Top 40 charts.

"Palisades Park" (1962)

America knows him as the host of TV's wacky *The Gong Show* and the creator of memorable shows such as *The Newlywed Game* and *The Dating Game*. But few people know that Chuck Barris penned a Top Ten pop song in the early 1960s. "Palisades Park" reached number three on the charts for singer Freddy Cannon in 1962. It was actually the B-side to the intended hit song, "June, July and August," but a Michigan radio station played "Palisades Park" by mistake. It took off and became a hit.

"Runaround Sue" (1961)

Doo-wop singer Dion learned his craft singing on the street corners of the Bronx. A recording artist with a long and diverse career, Dion struck gold with "Runaround Sue" in 1961. Even though Dion was married to a woman named Sue, she was *not* the subject of the song. When written with Ernie Maresca, the subject was actually named "Roberta," but "Sue" just fit better. Dion claims the song was penned in a school yard, creating riffs that could carry lyrics they made up on the spot.

"Gonna Fly Now" (Theme from *Rocky*) (1976)

The movie *Rocky* earned Oscar gold in 1976 as Best Picture. The theme, "Gonna Fly Now," hit the top of the charts that same year—but was almost knocked out in the first round. Composer Bill Conti and lyricist Carol Connors attended a prerelease screening of the film with director John Avildsen, writer and star Sylvester Stallone, and other invited guests. At the end of the screening, writer Ray Bradbury told Avildsen that he had an Academy Award–winning film on his hands—if he'd just get rid of the theme song that had been written and performed by Stallone's brother, Frank. The director enlisted Conti and Connors to whip something up, and Bradbury's hunch became fact.

Celebrities' Real Names

Many celebrities have catchy names that strike your interest and imagination. But you didn't think they were born with them, did you?

- Anna Nicole Smith—Vickie Lynn Hogan
- Whoopi Goldberg—Caryn Johnson
- Twiggy—Lesley Hornby
- Jack Palance—Volodymir Ivanovich Palahnuik
- Winona Ryder—Winona Laura Horowitz
- Carmen Electra—Tara Patrick
- Vin Diesel—Mark Vincent
- Brigitte Bardot—Camille Javal
- Charlton Heston—John Charles Carter
- Woody Allen—Allen Stewart Konigsberg
- Rita Hayworth—Margarita Carmen Cansino
- Gene Wilder—Jerome Silberman
- Elle Macpherson—Eleanor Gow
- Raquel Welch—Jo Raquel Tejada
- Harry Houdini—Ehrich Weiss
- Jennifer Aniston—Jennifer Anastassakis
- John Cleese—John Cheese
- Hulk Hogan—Terry Bollea
- Natalie Portman—Natalie Hershlag
- Nicolas Cage—Nicolas Coppola
- Ralph Lauren—Ralph Lipschitz

ʃyllable ʃecretʃ: Etymology

Little: Something small or tiny in size; from Middle English *littel*, which comes from Old English *lȳtel*; akin to Old High German *luzzil*

Wolf: A large, predatory canid (related to the domesticated canine, or dog) living and hunting with others of its kind (packs); from Old English *wulf*; akin to Old High German *wolf*, Latin *lupus*, and Greek *lykos*

Envy: Coveting something or someone unavailable and feeling resentment as a result; the Middle English *envie* comes from Old French, which in turn derives from Latin *invidia*, which comes from *invidus* (envious) and from *invidere* (to look askance at, or envy), from the combination *in-* + *videre* (to see)

October: The tenth month of year, but formerly the eighth month of the early Roman calendar; Middle English *Octobre* came from Old English and Old French: Old English *October*, from Latin *octo* (eight), and Old French, from Latin *October*

Immature: Not fully grown, or (in the case of an adult) behaving in a manner more like a child; derives from Latin *immaturus*, which comes from *in-* + *maturus* (mature)

Logic: Deductive reasoning; the Middle French *logique*, comes from Latin *logica*, from Greek *logike*, which is the feminine of *logikos*, which comes from *logos* (reason)

Doubt: Distrust or suspicion that causes problems in decision making; an alternate of Middle English *douten*, which derives from Old French *douter* (to doubt), which in turn comes from Latin *dubitare*; akin to Latin *dubius* (dubious)

Toe: Usually five to each foot on a human; Middle English *to*, which comes from Old English *tā*, and akin to Old High German *zēha* (toe)

Masculine: Characteristic of the male; from Latin *masculinus*, which comes from *masculus*, which itself derives from *mas* (male)

Feminine: Uniquely related to the female; Middle French *feminin*, from Latin *femininus*, which comes from *femina* (woman)

Hate: Intense feeling of hostility and aversion; Old English *hete*, akin to Old High German *haz* (hate) and Greek *kēdos* (care)

The Hitler Diaries Hoax

Adolf Hitler was an ambitious politician, but when it came to writing, he could be pretty darn lazy. After the success of Mein Kampf, *the first volume of which was published in 1925 and the second in 1926, he seemed content to rest on his laurels, even if those laurels were in a cozy cell in Landsberg prison. Surely such a significant figure would leave behind a greater written legacy than that. This literary lethargy would eventually make historians very cranky—and very gullible.*

The Roots of the Hoax

Though Hitler did halfheartedly pen a 200-page sequel to *Mein Kampf* in 1928, he grew bored with the project and never bothered to have it published. In fact, only two copies existed, and those were kept under lock and key by Hitler's order. This manuscript was discovered by American troops in 1945, but though authenticated by several of Hitler's associates, it was considered to be both an inflammatory piece of Nazi propaganda and a dull rehash of *Mein Kampf.* For these reasons, the book was never published widely.

Hitler was literally a "dictator," relying on secretaries to take down his ideas and plans. Often, even Hitler's most grandiose and terrible commands—such as the one to destroy European Jewry—were given only verbally. Historians were also frustrated by the dearth of personal correspondence that could be linked to Hitler. His mistress, Eva Braun, was not the brightest woman to ever walk the face of the earth, and their letters have not been found.

Fertile Ground for a Fake

This lack of primary-source material is what made the Hitler diaries hoax such a success at first. A staff reporter at West Germany's *Stern* magazine, Gerd Heidemann, fell for the ruse hook, line, and sinker, and saw the publication of the diaries as a way of advancing his stalled career in journalism. He convinced his editors at *Stern* that the journals were real, and they paid 9.3 million marks (about 6 million U.S. dollars at that time) for the first serial rights. On April 25, 1983, *Stern* hit the streets with a sensational cover story: "Hitler's Diary

Discovered." Media outlets around the world were more than happy to follow *Stern's* lead, and the *New York Times, Newsweek,* and the London *Sunday Times* all immediately jumped on the huge story.

The editors at *Stern* certainly should have been more wary of Heidemann's story, as he was obsessed with Hitler and the Third Reich. He had a passion for acquiring Nazi collectibles of almost any sort, even emptying his bank account to buy Hermann Göring's dilapi-dated private yacht. However, Heidemann's enthusiasm was so contagious, and the demand for all things Hitler so great, that it seems his superiors simply couldn't resist. But from whom had Heidemann obtained the diaries? And where had they been all these decades?

Fabricating the Führer

Konrad Kujau had started forging documents as a youth in East Germany, but he really hit his stride after defecting to West Germany and setting up an antiquities store in Stuttgart. Kujau was brazen and seemingly fearless in his work. He made and sold "genuine" Nazi items that sound ludicrous now and should have raised alarms for his clients then: Who could believe, for example, that Hitler had once written an opera? Yet his customers wanted to believe, and as long as Kujau shunned publicity, he was able to make a nice living off their ignorance and inexperience. After all, these were private collectors who wanted to hold onto their purchases as investments. But Kujau got greedy, and maybe just a little hungry for fame. Enter *Stern* reporter Heidemann, sniffing for a story.

In 1981, Kujau showed Heidemann 62 volumes of what he claimed were Hitler's diaries, dated from 1932 to 1945. Heidemann was astonished and asked Kujau about their history; how had such important documents remained hidden and unknown for so many years? Kujau was ready with a plausible-sounding (to Heidemann, at least) explanation: Nazi flunkies had tried to fly Hitler's personal belongings, including the diaries, out of Berlin, but the plane had been shot down and crashed in Dresden, its cargo surviving without any major damage. Conveniently for Kujau, Dresden was now behind the Iron Curtain, so his claim of obtaining the volumes one at a time from an East German general could not easily be confirmed or disproved. But if anyone longed to believe, it was Heidemann.

Media Circus

The publication of the diaries was an international bombshell, with historians, journalists, politicians, and antiquities dealers lining up to take sides in the media. Some historians immediately pointed out Hitler's aversion to writing in longhand, but others, such as the esteemed British World War II expert Hugh Trevor-Roper, declared the diaries to be authentic. On the day the story was published, *Stern* held a press conference in which Trevor-Roper, along with German historians Eberhard Jackel and Gerhard Weinberg, vouched for the documents. It would be a mistake all three would grievously regret.

The media uproar only intensified when, less than two weeks later, it was revealed beyond any question that the Hitler diaries were forged. Not only were the paper and ink modern, but the volumes were full of events and times that did not jibe with Hitler's known activities and whereabouts. Kujau was so careless in his fakery that he didn't even bother to get the monogram on the title page right: It read *FH* rather than *AH*. Some observers pointed out that the German letters *F* and *A* are quite similar, but surely as a German himself, Kujau would have known the difference. The best guess is that the diaries were sloppily prepared for his usual type of client—a dullish foreigner who wouldn't ask too many questions—and that Heidemann's arrival on the scene turned what might have been just another smooth and profitable transaction into a worldwide scandal.

Off to the Clink

Heidemann was arrested and tried for fraud, and Kujau was arrested and tried for forgery. Both men wound up serving more than four years in prison. Kujau reveled in his celebrity after his release, appearing on talk shows and selling paintings as "genuine Kujau fakes." But although Kujau tried to treat his crime as a lighthearted joke, it should be noted that had he not been unmasked, the diaries could have done real damage. Perhaps most serious—the document claimed that Hitler had no knowledge of the Holocaust.

- *The first of two volumes of* Mein Kampf (My Struggle)—*written in prison by Adolf Hitler*—*were transcribed by his fellow inmate and future deputy, Rudolf Hess.*

America's First Skyscraper

Chicago's Home Insurance Building certainly earned the grandiose nickname "the father of the skyscraper" when its creation set off the trend toward today's array of sky-climbing constructs, but the long-gone structure would be dwarfed in today's modern landscape.

Completed in 1885, William LeBaron Jenney's architectural innovation was the first ever building to feature a structural steel frame. It was initially erected at what is today a diminutive ten stories tall, or about 138 feet. Even with two additional stories tacked on five years later, the structure known as "America's First Skyscraper" would, at 180 feet, still be tiny when compared to Chicago's current skyscraper giant, the Sears Tower, which boasts a rooftop height of approximately 1,450 feet. Stack up eight Home Insurance Buildings, and the Sears Tower would still soar overhead.

Vertical Construction

Modeled in classic Chicago School architectural styling, the Home Insurance Building led the burgeoning trend toward the upward urban sprawl that now defines major U.S. cities: Prior to its creation, architects had only plotted building growth in a horizontal fashion. But with this new breed of building, the future of business architecture was all upward. After all, why rely on mere land, when the sky's the limit?

Torn down in 1931—fewer than 50 years after its construction—the Home Insurance Building was replaced just three years later by the still-standing, 45-story LaSalle National Bank Building, which was originally called the Field Building. The Home Insurance Building had served its purpose, and the city was ready to ring in the next round of architectural advancements. And just as the Home Insurance Building initiated a new era in architecture, the replacement structure was significant for its own gateway effect: It capitalized on the architectural trend of the time by capturing the magniloquence of the Art Deco movement. But as significant as the Field Building may have been, it didn't break new ground in the same way as the Home Insurance Building had.

FROM THE VAULTS OF HISTORY

Strike a Pose
The daguerreotype was an early, although now obsolete, photographic process invented in 1837. Not long after that, in 1843, Antoinette de Correvont opened up a portrait studio in Munich, Germany, becoming the first female photographer.

Starting a Trend
On October 6, 1866, Frank Sparks, with brothers Simeon and William Reno, pulled off the first train robbery in U.S. history. The trio boarded the eastbound Ohio & Mississippi train at the Seymour, Indiana, depot. Brandishing guns and wearing masks, the criminals emptied one safe and pushed the other out the window to pick up later. The robbers got away with $12,000. The three were later arrested but never stood trial.

That's Gotta Hurt!
Captain Jonathan Walker (no relation to the liquor) was the last person to be branded as punishment for a crime in the United States. He was convicted of aiding seven slaves in their attempt to escape from Florida to the Bahamas in 1844. Walker was branded on the palm of his right hand with the letters *SS*, signifying "Slave Stealer." In his poem "The Branded Hand" two years later, John Greenleaf Whittier suggested that it might instead mean something else:

> "Then lift that manly right-hand, bold ploughman of the wave!
> Its branded palm shall prophesy, 'Salvation to the Slave!'"

A Car for the Common Folk
Ferdinand Porsche is the name behind the luxurious Porsche sports car. But he also created the first Volkswagen. The name *Volkswagen* literally means "people's car." The idea came from the suggestion of Adolf Hitler, who wanted a car for regular people that could carry five passengers, travel at speeds of 65 mph, and be affordable. The concept for the VW Beetle was born.

Of Mouse and Man
Walt Disney introduced the world to Mickey Mouse in 1928. He got the idea after watching some mice while he was working. This is somewhat surprising, considering the fact that Disney suffered from *murophobia*—fear of mice.

Mutiny on the *Potemkin*

At the beginning of 1905, the Russian empire was in a state of flux. The populace churned with discontent, and the autocratic power of Czar Nicholas II was in danger of collapse. At the time, the average worker in the Russian industrial complex labored a punishing 11-hour workday, with the slight break of a 10-hour workday on Saturday. Worker safety was not a high priority; conditions were extremely poor. Unrest was spreading throughout Russia.

STRIKE!

In January 1905, four members of the Assembly of Russian Workers were unfairly dismissed from their jobs at the Putilov Iron Works in St. Petersburg, resulting in a general strike. The strike was organized by Father George Gapon, the founder of the labor union and a Russian Orthodox priest. Eventually, more than 100,000 people refused to return to work. Within a week, business and daily life in St. Petersburg had ground to a halt—the city had no electricity or gas to stand against the brutal Russian winter, no newspapers were being printed, and public areas were closed.

Gapon decided to make a personal appeal to the czar. On January 22, having received 135,000 signatures on a petition demanding a shorter workday, increased wages, and better working conditions, he led a large group of unarmed workers and their wives and children to present the petition to Czar Nicholas II. As the crowd neared the palace, the police and the czar's Cossack soldiers opened fire, killing and wounding scores of laborers and their families. The incident would come to be known as Bloody Sunday.

The exact number of casualties is unknown. The official count produced by the government listed 96 killed and 300 injured, but labor groups claimed that up to 4,000 had been killed or wounded. Lenin would later comment that, on the day after the violence, "St. Petersburg looked like a city just conquered by an enemy." News of Bloody Sunday spread throughout the Russian Empire, exacerbating the already strained relationship between the czar's government and the populace. Labor unions went on strike in response to the news; renters attacked their property owners and refused to pay their rents.

In addition to the strain of Bloody Sunday, the Russian Empire had been locked in bitter conflict with the Japanese regarding Manchuria and Korea since February 1904. The relatively younger and inexperienced Japanese army had gained a number of decisive victories over the Russians, and by the middle of 1905, the Russian navy was devastated and broken. The conflict culminated in May 1905 with the Battle of Tsushima, which left the Baltic Sea and Eastern fleets destroyed; only the Black Sea Fleet remained.

Unrest at Sea

In June 1905, morale in the Black Sea Fleet was at an all-time low. The Central Committee of the Social Democratic Organization of the Black Sea Fleet was planning a simultaneous uprising on all ships to occur sometime in the autumn. Aboard the *Potemkin,* one of the most advanced ships in the fleet, trouble was brewing. Weeks of poor food and cruel treatment at the hands of the ship's officers had created resentment among the enlisted men. However, the *Potemkin* was isolated from the rest of the fleet on artillery drill orders at Tendra Island in the Black Sea, and the crew was unaware of the planned fleetwide mutiny.

Discontent among the crew came to a boil when the ship took on meat containing maggots. The crew complained and refused to eat the putrid meat. The ship's medical officer pronounced the meat suitable for consumption, claiming the maggots were dead and would cause no harm. A borscht was made from the rotten meat. The crew protested, refusing to eat the borscht, and purchased food from the ship's store, instead. When the second in command of the ship, Ippolit Giliarovsky, became aware of this, he ordered 12 of the men who had refused to eat the stew be executed at random.

As men were chosen and armed marines prepared to fire, a sailor named Afanasy Matushenko, who served as the ship's torpedo quartermaster, spoke up. "Comrades," he said, "don't forget your oath! Don't shoot at our own men!"

The marines did not fire. Instead, acting on Matushenko's orders, the sailors took up arms against the officers who had oppressed them. In moments, seven officers lay dead. Some accounts suggest that Matushenko was the one who shot Giliarovsky. The medical officer who had declared the meat suitable for human consumption was also killed in the uprising. One sailor, Grigory Vakulinchuk, was mortally wounded. The bodies of the officers were thrown overboard, and the officers who had not been killed in the mutiny were driven overboard themselves.

Arriving in Odessa

That evening, the *Potemkin* arrived at the port of Odessa, where a general strike was already under way. The authorities in the port city refused to refuel and resupply the ship, but they did allow Vakulinchuk's body to be brought ashore. The following day, his funeral procession became a political event, with many of the striking populace turning out to support the crew of the *Potemkin*. Some accounts of the event report that police and soldiers opened fire on the crowd, killing as many as 2,000. The *Potemkin* left port.

Showdown

Two squadrons of the Black Sea fleet were dispatched to apprehend the *Potemkin*. The joint squadron gathered at Tendra Island and bore down on the mutinous ship. However, placing faith in their comrades among the squadron, the *Potemkin* sailed straight into and through the line of ships and emerged on the other side unscathed.

The *Potemkin* sailed to the Romanian port of Constanta, where the crew attempted to restock. The authorities, however, refused to resupply the ship. Desperately in need of fuel and food, the ship sailed for the Russian port of Theodosia but received a similarly cold reception there. Eventually, it returned to Constanta, where the *Potemkin* surrendered to Romanian authorities on July 8, 1905.

Although the crew of the *Potemkin* did not succeed in defeating the czarist regime, a revolutionary seed had been planted in the Russian navy. Sailors were involved in mutinies up to and after the decisive revolution of 1917. Lenin would later write that the *Potemkin* uprising had been the first attempt at creating "the nucleus of a revolutionary military force."

The *Potemkin* mutiny is also notable for the film it inspired. Sergei Eisenstein's *The Battleship Potemkin* is widely regarded as one of the most influential films of all time. It is most famous for the sequence on the Odessa steps; this confrontation forms the climax of Eisenstein's film. That scene has been re-created in homage by several filmmakers, most notably by director Brian De Palma in the film *The Untouchables* and Francis Ford Coppola in *The Godfather.*

Fast Facts

- *An individual dollar bill weighs a gram, as does a five dollar bill. A 20, a 50, and a 100 dollar bill are likewise one gram in weight.*

- *A bank in Vernal, Utah, was built from bricks delivered by the U.S. Postal Service in 1916. The builders discovered that it was cheaper to mail them than to ship them from Salt Lake City.*

- *The Museum of the Royal College of Surgeons of England acquired two sections of Napoleon's intestine in 1841. The specimens were destroyed during the Battle of Britain in World War II.*

- *Over an entire lifetime, the average person sheds more than 40 pounds of skin.*

- *Deke Slayton, the only astronaut of the Mercury Seven not to fly in the Mercury program, finally escaped Earth's gravitational pull as a member of the Apollo-Soyuz project.*

- *In 1964, archeologists discovered one of the earliest known battle sites near the northern border of Sudan. The skeletons of 59 people—dating from 13,000 years ago and pierced by numerous arrowheads—were found.*

- *Sports you don't see at the Olympics any more: golf, lacrosse, croquet, waterskiing, powerboating, and rugby. Each of these were official events at one time or another.*

- *Prince Albert, who would later become King George VI of England, played doubles at Wimbledon with partner Louis Grieg. His parents, King George V and Queen Mary, were there to watch the match.*

- *Empress Elizabeth of Austria was assassinated in Geneva by Italian anarchist Luigi Lucheni in 1898. When asked why he committed the act, Lucheni stated, "I wanted to kill a royal. It did not matter which one."*

MTV: Cultural Monolith

Screaming out of about a half-million television sets on August 1, 1981, was something most people hadn't seen before: an entire cable channel dedicated to broadcasting music videos. The channel was named, aptly, Music Television, or MTV.

Using a montage of images from the *Apollo 11* moon landing, MTV kicked off its birthday at 12:01 A.M. with the introduction, "Ladies and gentlemen, rock and roll." The first video played? "Video Killed the Radio Star" by the Buggles. The format of the first days of MTV was similar to Top 40 radio at the time—hosts introduced song after song, but instead of playing a song on the radio, the hosts played a video on cable. The first hosts, called VJs—video jockeys—were Nina Blackwood, Mark Goodman, Alan Hunter, J. J. Jackson, and Martha Quinn.

The Evolution

Early programming at MTV consisted almost entirely of videos made for cheap or cut together from other sources, such as concerts. As MTV started to stake its claim in popular culture, however, videos started to become more slick and developed. Record companies soon realized the marketing potential that came with having a video on MTV, so they began to finance the creation of individual artists' videos. Videos became more elaborate and highly stylized, oftentimes including story lines and character development. Many directors who would later find success directing feature films started their careers directing music videos. Many rock groups who were just starting out hit it big with videos that ultimately gained a huge following among the MTV audience. Eventually, programming at MTV branched out into award shows, animated shows, and reality shows, gradually moving away from music videos.

In the mid-1980s, Viacom bought MTV (among other channels) and created MTV Networks. Shows hosted by VJs slowly lost airtime in lieu of more conventionally formatted programs. Programs such as *MTV News* and *MTV Unplugged*, which featured acoustic performances, were worked into the lineup. In the early 1990s, more animated shows, including *Beavis and Butthead* and *Celebrity Deathmatch*, were introduced. By 2001, reality programming, such as *MTV's Fear* and *The Osbournes*, was placed onto the schedule. Almost all of MTV's music programming had been moved to other channels. In addition, the network had launched channels across the globe, taking over airwaves in Europe and Japan, India and Australia.

The Youth

MTV's audience has always been a young group—people between 12 and 24 years old.

The *MTV Generation* became a term to define those growing up in the 1980s. But as that generation aged, the channel continued to change its programming and identity to match the interests of the next group of 12–24-year-olds. As a result, videos were gradually replaced with reality shows. Series such as *The Real World* and *Road Rules* became staples in MTV's rotation. But as MTV continued to gain popularity and became a huge dictator of taste for the youth generation, it also came under fire for its impact on culture.

Groups such as the Parents Television Council and the American Family Association have criticized MTV frequently, arguing that the channel advocates inappropriate behavior and lacks moral responsibility for its careless programming targeted at kids. Of course, MTV hasn't always been its own best advocate, as seen in controversies such as the 2004 MTV-produced Super Bowl halftime show, in which Justin Timberlake tore off part of Janet Jackson's wardrobe and exposed her (pierced) breast; as well as MTV's problematic coverage in July 2005 of the Live 8 benefit concert, when the network cut to commercials during live performances and MTV's hosts repeatedly referred to the show by anything but its actual name. Given that they were broadcasting the show to the very fans who wanted to see the Live 8 bands they were interrupting, this may have marked a milestone in cultural politics, where the typically liberal youth culture was just as annoyed with the channel as the conservative groups were.

Social Activism

While full recovery from such snafus is probably unlikely, MTV has tried to respond to criticism about its programming. The network has a long history of promoting social, political, and environmental activism in young people. During election years, the network has invited presidential candidates to discuss their platforms. MTV has also initiated annual campaigns addressing a variety of issues affecting the youth culture—hate crimes, drug use, violence. In addition, MTV started branching out into various social activities, most notably the Rock the Vote campaign, which encouraged young people to vote.

The Meaning

MTV's effect on popular culture has been enormous. Some call it a reflection of what's happening in the youth culture today, but others say it dictates what is happening now and what will happen in the future. Still, MTV—for all its bravado regarding its youth and flexibility—has stayed the course like any solid corporation. Its mission has always been to appeal to youth culture. So, while the gradual decline in the airing of music videos may be bemoaned by older viewers who enjoyed them during MTV's infancy, the young people in the 21st century want reality shows about rich people who live in Southern California. The target demographic has stayed the same, but the people in that demographic have changed.

One critique the network can't seem to dodge, though, is its effect on the music industry itself. First, MTV has a tendency to remember only its own history as opposed to musical history in general. Older artists influential in the creation of genres and styles are oddly left out of the MTV world, despite the fact that so many artists on MTV are quite obviously in debt to them. Second, by playing only those artists who fit into a prescribed image and are backed by big money from music companies, the network has had the net effect of aiding the consolidation of the music industry and narrowing the choices to which consumers are exposed. As it was in 1981, MTV is still screaming out from televisions around the world. But now, the network is doing so in a highly stylized, profit-making way—and doing so from *billions* of television sets around the world.

The Times They Are A-Changin'

1971

January 1: Cigarette commercials are banned from American television.

January 5: The Harlem Globetrotters lose to the New Jersey Reds, 100–99, ending a 2,495-game winning streak.

January 12: *All in the Family* debuts on CBS and airs the first toilet flush on TV.

January 25: Charles Manson and his female followers are convicted of the Tate-LaBianca murders.

February 9: Leroy "Satchel" Paige becomes the first player from the Negro Leagues to be elected to the National Baseball Hall of Fame in Cooperstown, New York.

February 14: President Richard Nixon installs his secret taping system in the White House.

March 8: Joe Frazier beats Muhammad Ali in 15 rounds at Madison Square Garden, retaining the heavyweight boxing title.

March 29: First Lieutenant William L. Calley, Jr., is found guilty of the massacre at My Lai during the Vietnam War.

April 23: The Rolling Stones release "Brown Sugar."

April 24: An estimated 200,000 Vietnam War protesters march on Washington, D.C.

June 30: The 26th Amendment is ratified when Ohio becomes the 38th state to approve a voting age of 18.

July 1: The state of Washington becomes the first in the nation to ban sex discrimination.

October 1: Walt Disney World opens in Orlando, Florida.

November 24: A man calling himself D. B. Cooper hijacks a Northwest Orient Airlines plane and parachutes from it—carrying $200,000 in ransom money—to get away.

November 27: Don McLean's "American Pie," a song more than eight minutes long, first enters the pop charts.

Vlad the Impaler:
The Original Dracula

Most people are aware of Bram Stoker's Dracula *and the many cultural reincarnations that the title character has gone through. But the fictional character of Dracula was based on a human being far more frightening than his fictional avatar.*

Background

The late 1300s and early 1400s were a dramatic time in the area now known as Romania. Three sovereign states—Transylvania, Moldavia, and Wallachia—held fast to their independence against the Ottoman Empire. Wallachia was an elective monarchy, with much political backstabbing between the royal family and the *boyars*, the land-owning nobles.

Vlad III, known after his death as Vlad the Impaler, was born in the latter half of 1431 in the citadel of Sighisoara, Transylvania. His family was living in exile when he was born, ousted from their native Wallachia by pro-Turkish boyars. He was the son of a military governor who himself was a knight in the Order of the Dragon, a fraternity established to uphold Christian beliefs and fight Muslim Turks. Vlad II was also known as Vlad Dracul—*Dracul* meaning *devil* in Romanian. The *a* at the end of Dracul means "son of."

The throne of Wallachia was tossed from person to person, much like a hot potato, but with a lot more bloodshed. In 1436, Vlad Dracul took over the throne of Wallachia, but two years after that, he formed an alliance with the dreaded Turks, betraying his oath to the Order of the Dragon. He was assassinated in 1447 for his treachery.

Unfortunately for Vlad the Impaler, while his father was negotiating deals with the sultan of the Ottoman Empire, he traded his sons as collateral for his loyalty. While in captivity, Vlad the Impaler was frequently beaten and tortured.

Battleground

Released by the Turks after his father was killed, Vlad the Impaler showed up in Wallachia and defeated the boyars who had taken over the throne. He ruled for a brief time during 1448, but Vlad was quickly kicked out when the man who assassinated his father appointed someone else to fill the kingly duties. Vlad the Impaler bided his time, and in 1456, he not only took back the throne of Wallachia but also killed his father's murderer. He ruled Wallachia until 1462, but he was not a happy monarch.

Vlad the Impaler had a habit of killing huge numbers of people—slaves who didn't work hard enough, weak people who he felt were wasting space in his kingdom, and of course, criminals—you *really* did not want to be a criminal in Vlad's kingdom. Mostly, as might be guessed from his nickname, Vlad liked impaling people and then perching them in circles around town, an example of what would happen if citizens stepped out of line. In addition, he was rumored to drink the blood of those he had killed. On the upside, however, the crime rate in Wallachia was impressively low.

Breakdown

In 1461, Vlad the Impaler took on the Turks but was run out of Wallachia the next year. He lost the throne to Sultan Mehmed II's army and eventually sought refuge in Transylvania. The sultan installed Vlad's brother Radu on the throne of Wallachia. Once again, Vlad the Impaler was not happy. In 1476, with help from his Transylvanian pals, he launched a campaign to take back the throne of Wallachia, and he succeeded, impaling up a storm along the way. The Turks retaliated, and even though Vlad tried to organize an army to fight them, he couldn't raise a battalion large enough to defeat the Turks permanently. In his final battle, Vlad was killed, though the manner of his death is unknown. Some say that he was mistakenly killed by his own army, while others say that he was killed and decapitated by the Turks. One thing is known, however: Unlike the hundreds of thousands he killed, Vlad the Impaler was never one of the impalees.

- *Rafael Trujillo, the dictator of the Dominican Republic during the middle of the 20th century, created the Christopher Columbus medal. The first recipient, however, died of tetanus after being stuck by Trujillo as the leader pinned the medal on him.*

- *Moscow has a museum dedicated to cats.*

HOW IT ALL BEGAN

Playing Cards

Playing cards have been a tradition in China for millennia, but their present markings date back to 14th-century France. The four suits represent the major classes of society at that time. Hearts are taken from the shield, translating to nobility and the church; the spear-tip shape of spades stands in for the military; clubs are clover, meant to represent rural peasantry, and diamonds are similar to the tiles then associated with retail shops and were therefore intended to signify the middle class.

Diamond Engagement Rings

Although many give credit to the South African De Beers diamond cartel for popularizing the jewel as "the" gemstone for a ring given in anticipation of marriage, this practice began well before the 15th century. The earliest record may be a wedding document from Venice, Italy, dated 1503, listing "one marrying ring having diamond" as belonging to a Mary of Modina. The citizens of this famously canal-laced city were reportedly the first to recognize the enduring hardness of the diamond, as well as the fact that judicious cutting and polishing would reveal a rainbow of twinkling light. Cost and rarity limited wide distribution, but diamonds quickly caught on among the status conscious, and by the 17th century, every noblewoman (or woman who wanted to be seen as such) was clamoring for a diamond in her betrothal ring.

Influenza

Whereas some illnesses are named after the person who discovered them, *influenza* derives from a superstition among Romans in the mid-1700s, when the first viral outbreak was recorded in their city. The citizens believed that the stars in heaven could sway contagion, and so the Italian word for "influence" continues to identify this disease.

"Spittin' Image"

Early Americans used the phrase "spirit and image" to describe a relative, particularly a child, who resembled another family member in disposition and appearance. It was used so frequently in the South that it soon became a phonetic contraction, while still maintaining its original meaning.

Riots at *Rite of Spring*

Ah, the ballet. The grace. The beauty. The fistfights?

When Igor Stravinsky's *Rite of Spring* premiered at the Théâtre des Champs-Élysées in Paris on May 29, 1913, spectators—so displeased with the discordant nature of the music, the experimental choreography, and the nontraditional costume of the cast—exploded into a full-blown riot.

Although Stravinsky was well-known for his diverse styling, the pre-Modernist audience apparently didn't have any hint of what was to come. Classical ballet, which most people were accustomed to, is tulle and temperance, not sexuality, barbarism, and bassoon. From the start, the audience in attendance at *Rite of Spring* was turned off by the innovations of all the major components: music, dance, story, and costume. The catcalls that erupted moments after the ballet began were a testament to their hatred of the whole darned thing!

What Part *Did* They Like?

The music, composed by Stravinsky, was riddled with a cacophony of new sounds and rhythms. Where typical scores felt light and even springlike themselves, the music in *Rite of Spring* was bumpy, angular, and full of haphazard staccatos.

Reflecting the music, the dance moves, choreographed by Vaslav Nijinsky, featured jerky twists and pelvic thrusts more indicative of Elvis than of a graceful ballet. The dancers' arms and legs flailed wildly in angles depicting the primitive movements of fertility rites in pagan Russia. Struck by the incongruity between this performance and the ballet they thought they knew, the audience hissed with such furor that the performers couldn't hear one another.

The story of *Rite of Spring* includes, in addition to the dance of fertility, an abduction, a virgin sacrifice, and paganism. A tad bit racier than *Swan Lake* and, apparently, an overload to the genteel sensibilities of the audience.

In the spirit of the story, the costumes reflected the tribal culture in which it was set. Thus, the dancers were adorned in heavy woolen smocks, decorated with geometrics, which created a furnacelike effect for the mocked and—now sweating—performers. Their elaborately painted faces peering out at the audience topped off the atrocity of the sacrificial ritual to the god of spring uncomfortably unfolding before them.

Intermission at Last

Even with the intermission intervention of the Paris police, the spectators were still so overloaded by the ballet's brashness that their rioting carried on through the entire performance.

Stravinsky hid backstage embarrassed, perplexed, and angered by the reception. In later reflection, Stravinsky would blame the premiere's failure, in part, on Nijinsky's mistranslation of the music, suggesting he was a fine dancer but had been overwhelmed by the choreographic task he'd been handed.

Over the Years

Rite of Spring ran through its scheduled performances without further uproar. The Nijinsky choreography has since been lost, but similar angular dance moves have replaced them in the continued versions performed as a mainstay by troupes worldwide. In addition, the music was used in the Disney classic *Fantasia* to enhance the depiction of the cosmos creation, a true homage to Stravinsky's intent for the music to portray life in its most primitive form.

Stravinsky never attempted such audience-accosting innovation again, continuing his career without evidence of such bizarre scandal. Though Stravinsky might have given up his visionary take on the future of music, his *Rite of Spring* score had already done its magic. Musicologists consider it one of the great masterpieces of the 20th century. Stravinsky successfully achieved his goal of a harmonious juxtaposition of rhythm, pitch, and—somehow—dissonance.

It seems that *Rite of Spring*'s premiere audience was cultured enough to enjoy the theater, but they just weren't quite ready for the vanguard styling of forward-thinking Stravinsky. And it shrunk them down to a caterwauling crowd of crybabies.

- *Men's vocal cords are longer than are women's vocal cords. That extra length makes them vibrate more slowly, and that's why men usually have deeper voices.*

Fumbling Felons

Keep Your Pants On

A police officer in Spokane, Washington, took her van to the dealership for servicing. Later that day, a witness reported a naked man driving by repeatedly and pleasuring himself in a van. Turns out it was the officer's van. After the witness provided the plate number, police found the van back at the dealership—where the naked driver worked. He had apparently gone on a 16-mile test-drive! The man was charged and jailed for taking a motor vehicle without permission as well as for lewd conduct.

A Successful Robber *Must* Be Taken Seriously

A man in Inwood, West Virginia, attempted to rob a store with a gun-shape cigarette lighter. He disguised himself by wearing a pair of blue women's panties over his face. The store clerk, not surprisingly, thought it was a joke and refused to give up any money. Realizing that his plan was falling apart, the man hopped into a Jeep and fled into the night. Within a matter of minutes, the police stopped a vehicle matching the description given by the clerk. After searching the driver and the area, they found the pistol-shaped lighter and recovered the blue underwear nearby. Unlike the clerk, the police didn't treat the matter as a joke.

In the Driver's Seat

Apparently suffering from a powerful craving, a six-year-old boy in Colorado attempted to drive to Applebee's. He grabbed his grandmother's keys and placed his booster seat in the driver's seat. Although he managed to start the car, he couldn't get it out of reverse. The child backed up about 47 feet, crossing the street and hitting the curb. The car continued rolling an additional 29 feet before taking out a transformer and communications box. Fortunately, no one was injured. But it's still a mystery to investigators how the boy reached the gas pedal.

The Immovable ATM

In Milwaukee, three men tried to steal an ATM from a gas station. They smashed their SUV through the mostly glass wall where the ATM stood and then yanked on the machine. Discovering that it was bolted to the floor, they decided to wrap a rope around the ATM and tie it to the truck's bumper. But although the driver gunned the accelerator, the ATM refused to budge. They soon gave up completely. The ATM, although badly scratched, still stands where it always did, and it still works.

Women Break the Atmosphere Ceiling

The first U.S. astronauts were the renowned Mercury Seven. But they were followed fairly quickly by the Mercury 13. Never heard of them? Here's the lowdown on women in the U.S. space program.

In 1960, Dr. William R. Lovelace II, who helped develop the training regimen for NASA's male astronauts, decided he would extend the system of NASA fitness tests to women. He invited Geraldyn "Jerrie" Cobb, an accomplished pilot, to take them; she passed easily. Then, with financing from world-famous pilot Jacqueline Cochran (who didn't participate herself because she was considered too old), he brought together a group of 13 women—the First Lady Astronaut Trainees, or FLATs. The 13 were Cobb, Myrtle Cagle, sisters Jan and Marion Dietrich, Wally Funk, Jane Hart, Jean Hixson, Gene Nora Stumbough, Irene Leverton, Bernice Steadman, Sarah Gorelick, Jerri Sloan, and Rhea Hurrle.

The Not-So-Friendly Skies

The 13 were serious about becoming astronauts, but they ran into a wall of bureaucratic prejudice. (This was two years before the Civil Rights Act of 1964.) One of the most significant was NASA's requirement that astronauts have engineering degrees and be graduates of military jet test-piloting programs that were only open to men. NASA wasn't about to bend those rules. Some officials appeared sympathetic to the women's argument, but behind closed doors, it was a different story. At the bottom of a letter on the subject, Vice President Lyndon Johnson wrote, "Let's stop this now."

In 1963, Russian cosmonaut Valentina Tereshkova became the first woman in space. No female astronauts were selected until 1978.

A New Generation

The new astronaut recruits in 1978 were called NASA Group 8. Their selection had been based on two directives. NASA needed personnel for space shuttles—pilots, engineers, and scientist astronauts—but there was also a need to create a diverse astronaut corps, so NASA recruited women and minorities. Out of 8,079 applicants in all, a mere 208 were given tests and interviewed. On January 16, 1978, the 35 members of NASA Group 8 were formally announced. Of those, six were women, three were African American, and one was Asian American. These new astronaut candidates were nicknamed the "Thirty-Five New Guys" (or TFNG, an acronym that has a less respectable military meaning, as well).

The women of Group 8 were all officially mission specialist astronauts, as opposed to their male counterparts, many of whom were pilot astronauts. This raised a few eyebrows because of a general belief that women tended to have faster reflexes than men—science fiction authors had been writing about female space pilots for decades. The women of Group 8 left their mark on NASA:

- Dr. Sally Ride, a physician, was the first American woman to go into space, on June 18, 1983.

- Dr. Shannon Lucid was a biochemist who at one time held the record for the longest mission by a woman—188 days—serving on the *Mir* space station.

- Dr. Kathy Sullivan, a geologist, was the first American woman to walk in space.

- Dr. Judith Resnick, an engineer, died in 1986 aboard *Challenger.* Three other Group 8 astronauts—Ronald McNair, Ellison Onizuka, and Dick Scobee—died with her.

- Dr. Margaret Rhea Seddon, physician, participated in two Spacelab missions aboard the space shuttle *Columbia* focusing on the study of biology and life sciences.

- Dr. Anna Fisher, a physician, participated in the first space salvage mission in 1984, bringing back satellites from space. Her second scheduled space mission was canceled after the *Challenger* tragedy.

Mission specialist requirements are a bachelor's degree in engineering, physical sciences, biological sciences, or mathematics, and at least three years of related experience or an advanced degree. The physical requirements are as follows: vision of minimum 20/150 uncorrected, but 20/20 corrected; maximum sitting blood pressure of 140/90; and height between 150 and 193 cm.

Women Gain Influence

Women have gone on to play a major role in the American space program. Astronaut Dr. Kathryn Thornton, aboard the *Discovery* on a secret mission in November 1989, became the first woman to fly on a military flight. In 1992, Dr. Mae Jemison became the first African American woman in space. In 1995, Eileen Collins became the first woman to pilot a shuttle. In 1999, she became the first female space shuttle commander.

In 1996, Group 8 alum Lucid spent six months aboard the Russian space station *Mir*. Susan Helms became the first female crew member of the International Space Station in 2001. And in 2002, biochemist Dr. Peggy Whitson became the station's first resident science officer. On August 16, 2002, she spent four hours and 25 minutes on a space walk installing micrometeoroid shielding for the space station.

On a more somber note, teacher Christa McAuliffe, selected from among 11,000 applicants to receive training as a mission specialist, died along with Resnick and the rest of the *Challenger* crew on January 28, 1986, when the shuttle exploded during liftoff. And on February 1, 2003, Dr. Kalpana Chawla and Dr. Laurel Clark were aboard the shuttle *Columbia* when it broke up over Texas. The entire crew of seven died.

Of the original six female astronauts, Ride (two flights; 344 space hours) founded her own company, Sally Ride Science, to motivate girls and young women to pursue careers in science, math, and technology; she has also written science books for children. After serving as NASA's chief scientist at the Washington, D.C., headquarters, Lucid (five flights; 5,354 space hours) has resumed duties at the Johnson Space Center in Houston. Seddon (three flights; 722 space hours) retired from NASA in 1997 and moved to the Vanderbilt Medical Group in Nashville, Tennessee. Sullivan (three flights; 532 space hours) went on to serve as president and CEO of the Center of Science & Industry in Columbus, Ohio. Fisher (one flight; 192 space hours) was assigned to the Shuttle Branch while awaiting assignment either as a space shuttle crew member or aboard the International Space Station. After her death aboard the *Challenger*, Resnick (two flights; 144 space hours) was posthumously awarded the Congressional Space Medal of Honor.

He Said, She Said

It takes a great deal of courage to stand up to your enemies, but even more to stand up to your friends.
—*J. K. Rowling*

Why does the air force need expensive new bombers? Have the people we've been bombing over the years been complaining?
—*George Corley Wallace*

A politician will do anything to keep his job—even become a patriot.
—*William Randolph Hearst*

Women should be obscene and not heard.
—*Groucho Marx*

Nerves provide me with energy. They work for me. It's when I don't have them, when I feel at ease, that I get worried.
—*Mike Nichols*

When angry, count four; when very angry, swear.
—*Mark Twain*

The path of least resistance is the path of the loser.
—*H. G. Wells*

Once a woman has forgiven her man, she must not reheat his sins for breakfast.
—*Marlene Dietrich*

A conscience cannot prevent sin. It only prevents you from enjoying it.
—*Harry Hershfield*

We have just enough religion to make us hate, but not enough to make us love one another.
—*Jonathan Swift*

I can't reconcile my gross habits with my net income.
—*Errol Flynn*

Scoundrels are always sociable.
—*Arthur Schopenhauer*

Thinking is a momentary dismissal of irrelevancies.
—*R. Buckminster Fuller*

The Real Origin of the Barbie Doll

❖ ❖ ❖ ❖

*It didn't take long for the Barbie doll to become not only
an iconic toy, but a symbol of adult style and ambition,
as well. Where exactly did Barbie come from?*

When Barbie appeared in 1959, she was the first adult-styled plaything for young girls. Previously, girls were offered stuffed animals
and vinyl baby dolls, presumably meant to evoke their maternal
instinct. But Barbie was a creature to which a young girl could
aspire—albeit one that was, er, rather statuesque.

German Influences

Before Barbie, there was a doll called Bild Lilli, a provocative copy
of a cartoon character in the German newspaper *Bild*. Clad only
in a short skirt and tight sweater, Bild Lilli was sold to grown men
through tobacco shops and bars.

Ruth Handler, the genius behind Barbie, instinctively understood that young girls wanted to enter the adult world years before
their time. Handler had noticed her own daughter, Barbara, assign-
ing her paper dolls grown-up roles while playing
with them. When Handler spotted Bild Lilli
in Europe during a family vacation, she recognized the doll's possible commercial potential
and purchased several examples, each in a different outfit.

Barbie's earliest appearance, although toned
down from Bild Lilli, still owed much to her forerunner: She was pale, with pouty red lips and
heavily made-up eyes that cast a knowing
sidelong glance, not to mention her absurd
measurements (which, on a human counter-
part, would equal 38"-18"-32"). Barbie was also
a protofeminist icon, holding at least 95 different
careers. Her original job description, as "a teenage
model dressed in the latest style" (even though she
looked at least a decade older), later evolved into

nonspecific "career girl," with astronaut, ballerina, doctor, pilot, attorney, paleontologist, and presidential candidate versions.

The Barbie Empire Grows

Millions of baby-boom children grew up imagining themselves as Barbie, who went on to acquire boyfriend Ken, close friend Midge, little sister Skipper, and a wardrobe that any Hollywood star would envy. Actually, "acquire" could have been Barbie's middle name (although it was really *Millicent*). She needed *everything*. At first, it was just a trunk to hold her irresistibly detailed clothes and teeny accessories. Then came furniture and a beach house, accessed via luxury cars (pink Cadillac, red Porsche). Her features and hair softened; her other friends (Stacey, a British pal; and Christie, her African American girlfriend) came and went; and, after the longest engagement in history, she finally dumped Ken (named after Handler's son). Just like real life, only writ small.

During the past half-century, Barbie has reflected both fashion and social history. Charlotte Johnson, who originally dressed the doll, took her job seriously, interpreting the most important clothing trends of each successive era. Barbie also inspired top designers, including Armani, Christian Dior, Dolce & Gabbana, John Galliano, Gucci, Alexander McQueen, and Vivienne Westwood, to create exclusive originals for her; Philip Treacy designed her hats, and Manolo Blahnik her shoes.

The Decline of the Barbie Era

But what was once shocking has now become rather staid. What excites little girls nowadays is the hypersexualized, even more cartoony-looking Bratz, who come off as even poorer role models. In comparison, Barbie looks square and has accordingly lost market share. Her future seems to be more as a nostalgic collectible for adults—a complete collection of early Barbies, plus friends and outfits, was auctioned for record prices at the venerable Christies in late 2006; a single doll, Barbie in Midnight Red, sold for $17,000. In order to retain value, collectors keep limited editions in their original boxes.

In an odd way, Barbie has come full circle: From her sordid, bar-hopping start as Bild Lilli, Barbie has once again become a toy for grown-ups only.

Fast Facts

- *Jim Clark, winner of 25 Grand Prix races, was the first driver to win the Indianapolis 500 driving a car with the engine in the rear.*

- *A group of iguanas is called a* mess. *A group of raccoons is a* gaze. *A group of hippos is called a* bloat.

- *Thomas Eagleton, George McGovern's first Democratic running mate in the 1972 presidential election, resigned from the ticket when it was learned he had previously received electroshock therapy for depression.*

- *When parts of Skylab, the first U.S. space station, crashed to Earth near the town of Esperance, Australia, the municipality fined the United States $400 for littering.*

- *The last composition that Mozart wrote was meant for a funeral.*

- *About five years after his surrender at Appomattox Court House, Virginia, Confederate General Robert E. Lee died of pneumonia. His last words were reportedly, "Strike the tent."*

- *Consultant William Fried, speaking to a group of eighth-graders at a 2005 career day, listed stripper and exotic dancer among occupations that can earn six-figure salaries (depending on bust size).*

- *The mutineers of the HMS Bounty settled on the uninhabited Pacific island of Pitcairn in 1789 to escape punishment for their act. Fifty islanders, almost all descendants of the mutineers, reside on the island in modern times.*

- *Mice can squeeze into a building through a hole the diameter of a pencil. They can also crawl straight up a pipe, inside or out.*

- *While an officer in the South Pacific during World War II, future president Richard Nixon set up a hamburger stand to provide sandwiches and Australian beer to returning flight crews.*

Entrepreneurs of Death: The Story of the Brownsville Boys

Following the rise of the National Crime Syndicate, or what people now call the Mafia, a group of enterprising killers formed an enforcement arm that the press dubbed "Murder, Incorporated." Officially, they were known as "The Combination" or "The Brownsville Boys," since many of them came from Brooklyn's Brownsville area.

The Combination began their mayhem-for-money operation around 1930 following the formation of the National Crime Syndicate. Until their demise in the mid-1940s, they enforced the rules of organized crime through fear, intimidation, and murder. Most of the group's members were Jewish and Italian gangsters from Brooklyn; remorseless and bloodthirsty, murder for money was their stock-in-trade. The number of murders committed during their bloody reign is unknown even today, but estimates put the total at more than a thousand from coast to coast. The title "Murder, Incorporated" was the invention of a fearless *New York World-Telegram* police reporter named Harry Feeney; the name stuck.

Filling a Need

The formation of the group was the brainchild of mob overlords Johnny Torrio and "Lucky" Luciano. The most high-profile assassination credited to the enterprise was the murder of gang lord Dutch Schultz, who defied the syndicate's orders to abandon a plan to assassinate New York crime-buster Thomas Dewey. The job went to one of the Combination's top-echelon gunsels, Charles "Charlie the Bug" Workman, whose bloody prowess ranked alongside such Murder, Inc., elite as Louis "Lepke" Buchalter, the man who issued the orders; Albert Anastasia, the lord high executioner; Abe "Kid Twist" Reles, whose eventual capitulation led to the group's downfall; Louis Capone (no relation to Al); Frank Abbandando; Harry "Pittsburg Phil" Strauss, an expert with an ice pick; Martin "Buggsy" Goldstein; Harry "Happy" Maione, leader of the Italian faction; Emanuel "Mendy" Weiss, who is rumored to have never committed murder on the Sabbath; Johnny Dio; Albert "Allie" Tannenbaum; Irving "Knadles" Nitzberg, who twice beat a death sentence when his convictions were overturned; Vito "Socko" Gurino; Jacob Drucker; Philip "Little Farvel" Cohen; and Sholom Bernstein, who like many of his cohorts turned against his mentors to save his own life. It was an era of infamy unequaled in mob lore.

Loose Lips

Though many of the rank and file of Murder, Inc., appeared to enjoy killing, Reles, a former soda jerk, killed only as a matter of business. Known as "Kid Twist," Reles may not have been as bloodthirsty as some of his contemporaries, but he was cursed with a huge ego and a big mouth, and he wasn't shy about doing his bragging in front of cops, judges, the press, or the public at large. The little man with the big mouth would eventually lead to the unraveling of the Combination and greatly weaken the power of the National Crime Syndicate. When an informant fingered Reles and "Buggsy" Goldstein for the murder of a small-time hood, both men turned themselves in, believing they could beat the rap just as they had a dozen times before, but this one was ironclad. Reles sang loud and clear, implicating his peers and bosses in more than 80 murders and sending several of them to the electric chair, including the untouchable Buchalter. He also revealed the internal secret structure of the National Syndicate. Reles was in protective custody when he "fell" to his death from a hotel room on November 12, 1941, while surrounded by police. By the mid-1940s, Murder, Inc., was a thing of the past, and the National Crime Syndicate was in decline. When it came to singing like a canary, only Joe Valachi would surpass the performance of Reles, once the most trusted member of the Brownsville Boys.

- *When Wayne Gretzky retired, the National Hockey League retired his number. The last player to wear number 99 before him was Toronto's Wilf Paiement, who sported hockey's most famous double digit during the 1981–82 season.*

- *Baseball's only designated pinch-runner, Herb Washington swiped 28 bases and scored 29 runs for Oakland in 1974, but he never batted or played in the field.*

☐ Behind the TV Shows of Our Times

You're in the Picture

Jackie Gleason was often referred to as "The Great One." He had secured his place in TV history by playing always-trying-but-never-winning bus driver Ralph Kramden on *The Honeymooners* series in the 1950s. In January 1961, Gleason offered a game show to TV audiences called *You're in the Picture,* in which celebrities stuck their heads through holes in prepainted pictures and had to guess the scene in which they were now involved. Gleason was the MC, egging them on. The premise doesn't sound promising, but it was actually much worse. With the abominable show ditched after its only airing, the network had a hole in its schedule. Gleason returned to the same time slot the following week and made an on-air apology—which many viewers said was much funnier and more appealing than *You're in the Picture.*

Life with Lucy

In the early days of TV, Lucille Ball distinguished herself as the "Queen of Comedy" on her hit show, *I Love Lucy.* Red-haired and wild-eyed, she defined female physical comedy, while engaging in a never-ending war of words with her Cuban bandleader husband, Ricky Ricardo—played by her real-life mate, Desi Arnaz. From that time on she was never far away from the small screen. But, apparently, the 35 years since her *I Love Lucy* debut made a difference. In 1986, Lucy bombed in an embarrassing comedy series called *Life with Lucy.* At 75, with a voice hoarsened by a lifetime of cigarette smoking, she struggled through eight episodes as a doting grandmother before ABC canceled the show.

Gunsmoke

Long before the days of reality shows, television was loaded with Westerns. Big, sprawling sagas of American expansion into the West, they were full of cowboys, Indians (before they were called *Native Americans*), horses, and gunfights. Like many early TV shows, *Gunsmoke* had previously appeared on the radio. It featured Marshal Matt Dillon, sworn to uphold law and order in Dodge City. When the TV show premiered in 1955, it featured a new actor as Dillon. Few people knew James Arness, who was replacing William Conrad from the radio. To introduce Arness to audiences, *Gunsmoke* producers chose the biggest Western star they could find—"The Duke" himself, John Wayne.

Italian City-states:
Art, Commerce, and Intrigue

The city streets are alive with traffic. As wealthy residents move through the crowd, attended by anxious servants, homeless war veterans beg for spare change by the side of the road. Vendors hawk their wares, bargaining with harried homemakers, each side determined to get the most for their money before they finally agree on a price. The smell, the noise, the confusion—sounds like a typical day in New York or any other 21st-century city, right? In fact, this was a typical day in 15th-century Florence or Venice or any one of the countless city-states that once occupied most of Italy.

Some time after the fall of the Roman Empire in the fifth century, the country now known as Italy dissolved into individual communities called city-states. Devastated by long years of war and disease, each city remained a self-governing body that for generations did not bow to a centralized government. Most of them evolved into powerful entities that, by the 14th century, influenced many cultures of the Western world.

Life at the Top

The city-states were usually run by wealthy aristocrats—sometimes the same family remained in power for generations. But that was no guarantee things would run smoothly. Family members could be killed or exiled when another relative attempted to usurp more wealth or power. Many leaders employed diplomacy, caution, and a taste tester to make sure their food wasn't poisoned. When negotiations broke down, a dose of arsenic was a favorite bargaining tool—it often cast the deciding vote as to who would remain in charge.

Science and the Arts Flourish

Florence is widely considered the birthplace of the Renaissance, a period known for the study of humanist philosophy and new schools of art. Humanism, which would affect religious beliefs throughout Europe, was a concept from the ancient Greeks that stated human life was valuable not just in relation to God but in general. The rebirth of this idea generated changes in art—which had long been used almost exclusively for religious images—and supported disciplines such as astronomy and science. For many years, Florence was ruled by Lorenzo de'Medici, a patron of the arts who encouraged the work of some of the greatest thinkers and artists of the day, including Leonardo da Vinci, Michelangelo Buonarroti, and Sandro Botticelli.

Venice, on the Adriatic Sea, was one of the wealthiest cities in all of Europe by the late 13th century. The city-state was ruled by a great council, whose upper echelon chose a "Council of Ten." From their ranks, one member was chosen to serve as "Il Doge" (the duke), the ceremonial head of the city. Known internationally for its handcrafted Murano glassware, Venice was also a major shipping port that imported and sold goods from both the Eastern and Western worlds. The government practiced relative religious tolerance at a time when torture and killing were commonly used elsewhere by the Catholic Church to weed out nonbelievers.

Rigid Roles

Like the residents of many other city-states, the people of Florence and Venice lived in an unbreakable caste system, where few ever changed their social position. Although some historians today believe that the opposite was true because the people lived so closely together, on the whole, the working class did not socialize with the nobility. The contained surroundings did offer one benefit to the workers, however. Although they often struggled to pay their taxes and feed their families, the poor and the working class were exposed to humanist philosophies and had the opportunity to enjoy public displays of art. The standard of living for aristocrats would seem primitive by modern standards, but Italy's city-states contained palaces filled with gold tableware and beautiful artwork as well as residents who dressed in silk and satin. Women—no matter what their social standing—had few, if any, legal rights. Their life choices were limited to either marrying or becoming nuns in the Catholic Church.

Today, there are faster communications and methods of transportation, as well as lightning-quick technology. And yet, not much has changed from the days when people believed disease was caused by demons. The rich still build palatial homes and spend money; many of the poor are still homeless; and anyone who has ever been to New York or any other major city knows that the noise is everywhere.

Syllable Secrets: Word Histories

Boomer: The phrase *Baby Boom* was coined in 1941, four years before the most iconic one in American history to date; the derivative *baby boomer,* to describe a member of that spike in birthrates, was first recorded in 1974. Now the even shorter term *boomer* (as cited in the *New York Times,* October 27, 2007) connotes someone born during the period 1946–64. So-called *shadow boomers* entered the world from 1958–64, and the children of the boomers—1982–94—have been dubbed *echo boomers.*

-gate: A suffix now attached to indicate any scandal, especially one politically motivated, this term immortalizes the Watergate building complex in Washington, D.C., where the Democratic Party's headquarters was burglarized in June 1972 by a "dirty-tricks" group linked to Richard Nixon's White House. Other examples include Koreagate, Irangate, and Monicagate. Now, it seems, any controversy at all can get saddled with its own "gate." For example, when talk show host Ellen Degeneres had a problem giving away a rescue-group dog named Iggy—*Us* magazine wrote about IggyGate.

ASAP: Derived from World War II army slang, this acronym for "as soon as possible" entered the language in 1955.

Lovebird: This figurative description of a human lover dates back to 1911, but it's taken from the 1595 definition for a "small species of West African parrot, noted for the remarkable attention mating pairs pay to one another." Aww.

Ugly: This word was derived from the original *uglike* (c. 1250, to be "frightful or horrible in appearance"), which in turn came from Old Norse *uggligr* ("dreadful, fearful"). The meaning was slightly softened (if you can call it that) to "very unpleasant to look at" around 1375.

Junk: What meant "worthless stuff" in 1338, became a verb meaning "to throw away as trash" in 1916. *Junkie* ("drug addict") arrived in 1923, but *junk* for "narcotic" is thought to date back further, although no one seems precisely sure. *Junk mail* arrived in 1954; *junk food* in 1973.

Zeitgeist: This word dates back to 1845 and literally means the "spirit of the age"; it is used as a description of an era's general moral, intellectual, and cultural climate. It comes from combining two German words: *zeit* ("time") and *geist* ("spirit" or "ghost").

Hemingway's Cats

The great American author and proverbial "man's man"
Ernest Hemingway was a big fan of bullfighting, boxing,
and hunting—and also of cats. Ever since he was given
Snowball, a six-toed feline (known as a polydactyl*) by a*
ship's captain in the 1930s, Hemingway allowed cats to
multiply with abandon in his Key West, Florida, home.

In 2003, the Hemingway Home and Museum, where the writer lived
and worked for ten years on novels including *To Have and Have*
Not and short stories such as "The Snows of Kilimanjaro," became
embroiled in a dispute over its nearly 60 resident felines. All of these
cats are descendants of Snowball, and they all carry the gene for
polydactylism; only half, however, have extra toes.

Just Trying to Help

The legal battle began after the local
Society for the Prevention of Cruelty to Animals (SPCA) cited animal
welfare legislation requiring any business employing animals in acts or advertisements to have a special license. The
Hemingway cats, many named after literary
and entertainment celebrities (such as Audrey
Hepburn, Emily Dickinson, Simone de Beauvoir, and Charlie Chaplin), are featured on the museum's Web site and are a huge tourist
attraction, but they do not exactly perform, per se. The museum
faced huge fines and confiscation of the cats by the Department of
Agriculture if it didn't cage the furry creatures. A local animal shelter official thought she was doing a good deed by taking the cats in
to be neutered; the museum fought to stop her, saying she had left
almost no cats able to continue Snowball's bloodline.

The hard-fought battle of the little-six-toed-guy against the big-
bad-government made its way through the courts, ending with a
2007 victory for the beleaguered and bewhiskered: The cats still freely
roam the grounds, and the tourists keep coming to enjoy the cats.

How Dry I Am:
The Saga of Owens Valley

*At the beginning of the 20th century, Los Angeles was a
bustling city of only 250,000. Any development to which
it might aspire in the future, however, was dependent on
one simple but important commodity: water. How it got
the water it needed remains controversial today.*

Rainfall in the city of Los Angeles was insufficient to keep the
watersheds full enough to accommodate the city's rapid growth.
New residents were migrating west to take advantage of the climate,
but the city couldn't sustain the expansion—it *was* a desert, after all.
In 1913, the Los Angeles Department of Water and Power, under
the direction of Superintendent William Mulholland, completed
construction on a 220-mile-long aqueduct, which diverted water
from the Owens River in eastern California. This enraged residents
of Owens Valley, a small agricultural community near the Nevada
border, and led to one of the longest and fiercest water wars in U.S.
history.

Life-giving Water
There's no doubt that the water from the Owens River not only
spurred the growth of Los Angeles, it also turned the arid lands of
the San Fernando Valley into a virtual oasis, sending property values
soaring and making fat cats out of favored politicians, bankers, and
realtors—all cronies of Los Angeles Mayor Frederick Eaton. Like the
mayor himself, all of them invested on the basis of privileged insider
information. Although Eaton promised Owens Valley residents that
the water would only be for domestic use in Los Angeles proper, the
original aqueduct flow was ultimately diverted to the San Fernando
Valley for agricultural irrigation. The subterfuge led Owens Valley
residents to claim that the water rights had been obtained through
deception, and the peaceful farming valley became a hotbed of
violence. Sections of the water system were sabotaged; farmers who
sold their property to Los Angeles at allegedly subpar rates were
considered traitors, pitting neighbor against neighbor.

Livelihoods Lost

Los Angeles obtained a large portion of water rights from Owens Valley farmers, but the demand from San Fernando Valley investors was so great and so much water was diverted that the once-fertile Owens Valley was fast becoming the Sahara of the Western world. In the meantime, the formerly arid San Fernando Valley was becoming a lush paradise. In 1924, Owens Lake, into which the river once flowed, dried up, and a group of armed farmers used dynamite on the Alabama Gates spillway section of the aqueduct, releasing water back into the Owens River. The desperate farmers tried everything from violence to lawsuits—all to no avail. By 1928, 90 percent of the water rights belonged to Los Angeles; agriculture in Owens Valley came to a halt.

In 1970, a second aqueduct was completed. Lack of an environmental impact report led to the overuse of groundwater, which dried out springs and seeps. Vegetation that depended on underground water began disappearing—a loss that caused further devastation to Owens Valley. Inyo County sued Los Angeles, but the water continued to flow while Los Angeles filed brief environmental impact reports that the courts ultimately found inadequate. In 1991 and 1997, agreements were signed between Inyo County and Los Angeles that called for the rewatering of the Owens River by 2003. But once again, Los Angeles was remiss in its promise. New lawsuits were filed, new agreements were reached, and deadlines were revised (and missed again), but on December 6, 2006, Los Angeles Mayor Antonio Villaraigosa finally opened a valve sending a flow of water back to the Owens River. Unfortunately, the rate of underground pumping of Owens Valley water far exceeds the rate of replenishment, and the degradation and biodiversity of Owens Valley land continues to be a major controversy. Under deteriorating climactic conditions, reversing desertification can be very difficult, but the Los Angeles Department of Water and Power has made a strong commitment to restoring the Owens Valley watershed and can even boast of several small successes in restoring the ecosystem.

The longest water war in U.S. history—one that inspired the motion picture *Chinatown*—may finally be at an end; though for some Owens Valley residents, especially descendants of the original farmers, a little enmity may exist until the land is restored.

Strange Justice

Sax Player Socks It to Band Director

A first-year high school student who played baritone saxophone for his school's marching band was excited when the band was selected to perform for a national tournament parade on New Year's Day. The day after the parade didn't go quite as well, however, when the band's director grabbed the student, shook him by the shoulders, and swore at him for wearing orange socks instead of the required white. The student sued the band director and school district for emotional distress, seeking $150,000 in damages. He collected to the tune of $25,000.

A Whale of a Lawsuit

A lonely drifter may have decided to share his despair by taking a moonlight swim with a five-ton killer whale in a marine attraction. Found dead the next morning, the man hadn't died from attack—the coroner determined the cause of death was drowning and hypothermia from the 52°F water. No matter, the man's parents sued the marine attraction for several million dollars, claiming the park had been negligent in failing to post warnings not to enter the whale's tank and falsely portraying it as "huggable." Realizing their folly, the parents dropped the suit a month later.

Watch Your Steps, Doc

A physician was taking a jog through a condominium complex when he tried to pass under a staircase. Misjudging the height of the staircase, he cracked his head and fell, suffering a broken ankle and a nasty cut on his forehead that needed 60 stitches. He filed suit against the building's management for $25,000 in medical costs and another $250,000 in lost income, claiming the staircase was not up to code. The management argued that the steps *were* up to code and the area wasn't meant for pedestrians anyway. The parties settled out of court for $20,000.

But Was the Garage Big Enough?

A 70-year-old mentally impaired man believed a salesperson at the local car dealership was just being a good friend, so incredibly, he bought 18 cars from him in a mere 14 months. The man's guardian found out and filed a complaint with the state attorney's office who, in turn, filed a claim against the dealership for deceptive practices. The dealership admitted no wrongdoing, but it did settle the claim for $50,000 and a new car. It also paid $15,000 in fines and $17,000 in legal fees.

What the Heck Is a Gaffer?

You plunked your hard-earned money down at the box office.
You grabbed a bucket of popcorn and a soft drink. You found a
comfortable seat, away from the chattering groups of teenagers.
You were thoroughly entertained for two hours and are ready to
head home to scrape the gum from your shoes. As the closing credits
roll, you have just one question: "What the heck is a gaffer?"

The world of professional filmmaking employs thousands of people
in highly skilled positions—many of which are a mystery to the general moviegoing public. Here's a cheat sheet:

Gaffer: This is the chief lighting person—the man or woman who
follows the design drawings from the lighting director—placing all
lights, colored gels, and other rigging gear.

Production Designer: This role is key in developing the overall
appearance of the picture. The production designer usually has a
background in art. He or she works with the director, cinematographer, set designer, costume designer, and anyone else involved
with creating the visual "look" of a film.

Key Grip: People who move and arrange major set pieces, cameras, dollies, and who work with the lighting crew are called *grips.*
The key grip is the supervisor of the grips and works with the
cinematographer to make the set look like it should.

Best Boy: This role (which can belong to a man or woman) belongs
to the second-in-command for the key grip, helping to get the
movie set in shape for shooting.

Set Dresser: A living room set, for example, might have a ceiling
and three walls, two doors, and two windows. But what about the
drapes? What about the chairs, sofa, end tables, lamps, pictures on
the walls, doorknobs, or the 1,001 other things that make a movie
set believable? The set dresser makes sure all of those items are in
their proper places before the director yells, "Action!"

Armorer: Any film that features gunplay needs an armorer. This
person ensures that all prop weapons used are accurate and historically correct. More important, the armorer is charged with the duty
of ensuring the guns and weapons are safely stored and handled.

Second Unit Director: Every film includes scenes that don't require the main performers or main action. Crowd scenes and shots that introduce a location or show travel are usually filmed by a secondary crew, or the "second unit." The second unit director manages the shooting of these elements.

Boom Operator: Ever since the silent era ended, sound has been an important part of the film industry. And if you've got sound, you need to have someone operating the microphones. The *boom* refers to the boom microphone, which is often at the end of a long pole. It can pick up sounds by hanging above the actors, just out of camera range.

Foley Artist: A young woman walks slowly down a dark alley, followed by a sinister stranger—all to the sound of crisp, crackling footsteps. These sounds, and many, many others, often need to be enhanced or re-created. The Foley artist watches the finished scene on a screen and mimics the footsteps to make sounds that are recorded to replace the original sounds. This process gets its name from James Foley, an early filmmaker who used this technique.

Craft Service: Like the army, a film crew travels on its stomach. As such, craft service is responsible for providing beverages and snacks on a movie set or location. They also clean up after the crew has gone home.

ADR Editor: Among the alphabet soup of film jargon is *ADR*—Automatic Dialogue Replacement (which isn't really automatic). Many factors can make the recorded sound from a scene unusable. The performers record their lines again while watching the completed action on a screen—a process called *looping*—and then the ADR editor splices the new audio into the scenes.

Unit Publicist: This person is part of the publicity department that goes out on location during the filming. The unit publicist assembles press kits, sets up media interviews, and works to keep peace with the local residents.

Trouble for the Prince of Noir

Robert Mitchum was the original offscreen bad boy—before James Dean ever appeared on the scene. He defined cool before Hollywood knew the hip meaning of the word. He was rugged, handsome, and jaunty. A hobo turned actor, he was the antithesis of the typical screen hero—and he was on his way to becoming a star, primarily in film noir. Then it happened: A drug bust with a busty blonde, and Mitchum was in the headlines in a way he never intended. Perversely, this incident accelerated his stardom.

In August 1948, Hollywood tabloids were emblazoned with headlines proclaiming the scandalous drug bust of actor Robert Mitchum, in the company of 20-year-old aspiring actress Lila Leeds, for possession of marijuana. This was the era of marijuana frenzy. The government was at war with cannabis users, and propaganda, entrapment, blatant lies, and excessive punishments were just a few of the weapons they used. Mitchum was the perfect whipping boy. The actor was no stranger to pot and hashish, having experimented with both as early as 1936 when he was a 16-year-old hobo riding the rails. He was also a fugitive from the law, having escaped from a Georgia chain gang after being arrested for vagrancy in Savannah at age 16. Despite hiring Hollywood's hottest defense attorney, Jerry Geisler, Mitchum was found guilty and sentenced to 60 days on a prison farm. His "I don't give a damn" smirk when sentence was pronounced would define the attitude of the '50s drug culture that burst upon the scene as the decade ended.

A Career Ruined?

When Mitchum was sentenced, he was earning $3,000 a week—a princely sum at the time. He had also been nominated for an Academy Award for *The Story of G.I. Joe* (his only nomination), was married to his childhood sweetheart Dorothy Spence, and had signed a seven-year contract with RKO studios. When the tabloids ran a picture of prisoner 91234 swabbing the jail corridors in prison attire, the actor anticipated it would be "the bitter end" to his career and marriage. In reality, the publicity would have the opposite effect.

With the exception of becoming a small embarrassment to the studio and the cancellation of a speech Mitchum was scheduled to deliver to a youth group, the actor's offscreen bad-boy persona had little negative effect on his career or personal life. If anything, it only added to his counterculture, tough guy, antihero image.

Great PR

While Mitchum served his 60-day sentence on the honor farm (which he described as "Palm Springs without the riff-raff"), RKO released the already-completed film *Rachel and the Stranger.* Not only did movie audiences stand and cheer when Mitchum appeared on the screen, the low-budget movie also became the studio's most successful film of the year.

In 1950, another judge reviewed Mitchum's conviction and reversed the earlier court decision. The arrest smelled of entrapment: Leeds's Laurel Canyon bungalow had been bugged by two overly ambitious narcotic agents. The judge changed Mitchum's plea to not guilty and expunged the records of the actor's conviction—not that Mitchum appeared to care one way or the other. By then, he was a bona fide Hollywood star.

A Long and Successful Livelihood

Mitchum enjoyed an illustrious career, making more than 70 films, some to critical acclaim. He also enjoyed success as a songwriter and singer, with three songs making it onto the best-seller charts. His marriage remained intact for 57 years, possibly a Hollywood record. He earned a star on the Hollywood Walk of Fame along with several other prestigious industry awards. Not a bad lifetime achievement for a pot-smoking vagabond fugitive from a chain gang. Often seen with a cigarette dangling from his sensual lips, Mitchum died of lung cancer and emphysema on July 1, 1997, at his home in Santa Barbara, California.

- *Aztec Emperor Montezuma is said to have drunk 50 goblets of chocolate, flavored with chili peppers, every day.*

- *Depending on her size—and therefore her age—a lobster can lay 75,000 eggs or more.*

Fast Facts

- *For couples who last this long, the traditional gift for a 70th wedding anniversary is platinum.*

- *Joseph Jakobs, a German spy caught on English soil during World War II, was the last person to be executed in the Tower of London. He went before a firing squad on August 14, 1941.*

- *The world's first telephone book was published in New Haven, Connecticut, in February 1878. It had 50 names in it.*

- *Wild West legend Bill Hickok was holding two pair—aces and eights—when he was killed playing poker. These cards are now known as a "Dead Man's Hand."*

- *Daniel Boone's parents were Quakers. Boone was one of 11 children; he and his wife, Rebecca, had 10 kids of their own.*

- *Herod the Great was identified in the New Testament Gospel of Matthew as having massacred all boys up to two years old in Bethlehem. There is no historical evidence of such a slaughter.*

- *Catnip is a mint plant that contains* nepetalactone, *a chemical that makes cats happy and excited. They're the only animals that catnip affects this way.*

- *On his first shift in his first National Hockey League game, Pittsburgh Penguin Mario Lemieux stole the puck from Boston Bruins defenseman Ray Bourque and scored his first goal on his first shot.*

- *As little as 50 milligrams of pure nicotine can kill a 150-pound adult.*

- *Although the official cause of Joseph Stalin's death was a cerebral hemorrhage, it is believed he was assassinated. The Soviet Politburo waited more than a day to seek help for the dying Stalin.*

- *There are 2.5 million rivets holding the Eiffel Tower together.*

The New Technology Culture

Wait! Don't buy that new gadget yet—there might just be an even newer version of it coming tomorrow. Versions 2.0 and beyond of products show up in what seems to be a continuous loop, especially now that technology has become a pervasive element in most people's everyday lives. But what's the point of buying a newer version of something you already have?

Necessity

A quick check of history and culture tells us that some things demand improvement. Take, for example, refrigeration. In its initial stages, refrigeration essentially involved the use of ice and snow to cool food down to a temperature at which it could be kept safely and wouldn't spoil. Later, the first cellars were developed: Holes in the ground were lined with wood or straw and packed with snow and ice. Eventually, machines were developed to cool food. But these used toxic gases, and leaking refrigerators caused fatal accidents. Researchers tried to find a different way to refrigerate, ultimately settling on the use of Freon, which became standard for almost all home kitchens. Unfortunately, the chlorofluorocarbons were destroying the ozone layer, so further developments in refrigeration were necessary.

The same process goes for medicines or vehicles. Medical research is constantly coming up with new versions of old antidotes, building both on the need for new solutions and the availability of technology to research and develop them. The bicycle was invented because Karl von Drais wanted to find an alternative to the horse during a time when crop failure was causing starvation and death. The needs of a culture or society often demand that kind of improvement of old methods, which often leads to the discovery of completely new devices or processes.

Desire

Of course, some versions of technology, machines, and vehicles are improved upon even without a desperate need. Because, let's face it, sometimes people just want cooler products. For instance, the iPod, Apple's portable media player, was regenerated through quite a number of versions just to perfect its usability. Developed initially to compete against the big and clunky or the small and mostly useless digital music players on the market, Apple concocted a cool-looking device that fit a ton of music in its user's pocket. Subsequent improvements included an upgraded interface, upgraded technology, and upgraded storage. Were these really necessary to make it more user-friendly? Did customers really need a touch-sensitive wheel when a scroll wheel performed precisely the same function? Maybe, maybe not. But it can't be denied that consumers jumped at the newer versions, so more than likely, Apple would have been hard-pressed to come up with any reason *not* to improve their product.

Competition

Whether society needs or demands a new and improved product is sometimes incidental to the fact that companies are going to offer their "new and improved" products no matter what. Especially with technology—video game consoles, iPods, cell phones, even household appliances, cars, and televisions—improvements come fast and furious, at rates that may seem mind-boggling to the individual consumer. Many companies need to get ahead of their competition in the marketplace, so it's out with the old and in with the new before the old actually has time to age. Some companies even follow an itinerary of planned obsolescence for their devices, targeting a certain life span for the product and then coming out with a new version. Sometimes they'll even go so far as to stop providing technical support for older models. Proponents believe this stimulates economic involvement in a market economy. Skeptics say it's a cheesy way to scam consumers and it also creates waste that affects the environment. Regardless, as the old adage says, "The more things change, the more things stay the same."

ANAGRAMS

An anagram is a word or phrase that exactly reproduces the letters in another word or phrase. The most interesting of them reflect or comment on the subject of the first.

a decimal point—I'm a dot in place.

Margaret Thatcher—that great charmer

the hurricanes—these churn air

Statue of Liberty—built to stay free

Leonardo da Vinci—did color in a nave

"To be or not to be: that is the question; whether 'tis nobler in the mind to suffer the slings and arrows of outrageous fortune"—In one of the Bard's best-thought-of tragedies, our insistent hero, Hamlet, queries on two fronts about how life turns rotten.

war on terrorism—swarm into error

schoolmaster—the classroom

Princess Diana—end is a car spin

Marilyn Monroe—in lore, my Norma

payment received—every cent paid me

summer, autumn, winter, spring—"Time's running past," we murmur.

Madonna Louise Ciccone—one cool dance musician

Presbyterian—best in prayer

President Bush of the USA—a fresh one, but he's stupid

snooze alarms—Alas! No more Z's!

Victoria, England's Queen—governs a nice, quiet land

Jennifer Aniston—fine in torn jeans

the American Dream—Meet a dear, rich man.

the terrorist Osama bin Laden—Arab monster is no idle threat.

Mark Twain—am rank wit

The Cleveland Gas Explosion

❖ ❖ ❖ ❖

In 1942, the East Ohio Gas Company constructed a tank farm for liquefied natural gas (LNG) near Lake Erie. Placed in a mixed-use section of Cleveland, Ohio, it provided natural gas to local war industries. In 1944, however, one of these tanks ruptured, setting in motion a chain of events that would cause massive loss of life and property.

On the afternoon of October 20, 1944, a leak developed in a storage tank holding more than 650 million gallons of liquefied natural gas. The winds blowing off Lake Erie pushed the white vapor into the Cleveland sewer system, where the gas mixed with air and became explosive. The blast created a fireball towering more than half a mile high—it was visible more than seven miles away. Jets of flame blasted out of the sewer, propelling manhole covers into the air. Later, a manhole cover from the affected area would be found several miles away.

All Clear—Or Not

After the first explosion, area residents assumed that the incident had been handled by the fire department and returned to their homes. Unfortunately, not much later, a second storage tank exploded. Pockets of natural gas persisted in the sewer system and exploded throughout the afternoon, trapping residents in their homes and businesses. The full chain of events resulted in an inferno that engulfed more than a square mile and caused the evacuation of more than 10,000 people, leaving almost 700 homeless.

The cost of the resulting fires in terms of casualties and property damage was staggering: The incident claimed 130 lives, including 55 employees of the East Ohio Gas Company. More than 200 people were injured. Two factories and 79 homes were destroyed. Property losses also included more than 200 automobiles and tractors, as well as damage to streets and underground utility installations. In addition to the physical structures destroyed by the fire, many residents kept significant amounts of cash, as well as stock and bond certificates, in their homes, all of which were lost to the fire. In total, the losses of property were estimated somewhere between the present-day equivalent of $80 and $172 million.

Corner-cutting Causes

Because the United States was in the midst of World War II, the public initially suspected that the explosion was the work of a German saboteur. However, the subsequent investigation determined that the nickel content of the steel LNG tank had been the primary cause of the leak. Nickel is added to steel to increase its strength. During the war, however, rationing for various metals was in effect, and the tank was constructed of steel that had too small an amount of nickel. The temperatures required for LNG storage, generally between $-120°$ and $-170°$ C, made the steel composing the tank very brittle. Today, the standard nickel content for steel used in LNG applications is nearly three times what was in the steel of the leaking tank. Additionally, the tanks at the East Ohio storage facility lacked a means of secondary containment in case of leakage. That's required today for all above-ground LNG storage tanks.

It may seem incredible, but the Cleveland gas explosion involved a fairly small amount of LNG by present-day standards. Today's LNG tankers can safely carry more than 20 times the amount of gas involved in the Cleveland explosion.

- *While president, Lyndon Johnson had his gallbladder and a stone from his ureter removed. During a post-surgery press conference, Johnson lifted his pajama top to show his 12-inch scar.*

- *Former Texas Governor John Connally raised $11 million in his run for the Republican nomination for president in 1980. Connally wound up with only one delegate to the Republican convention.*

- *The rocks at the bottom of the ocean are much younger than the rocks that make up the seven continents.*

INSPIRE ME

To the Lighthouse

Virginia Woolf's modernist masterpiece *To the Lighthouse* was certainly inspired by a vast ocean of influences. But the primary influence behind the novel's second part, entitled *Time Passes,* was good old-fashioned competition—literati style.

Woolf belonged to a wildly talented but intellectually snobbish group of English modernist writers, which included James Joyce, Katherine Mansfield, D. H. Lawrence, and E. M. Forster, all of whom sought to stretch language to its limits by representing reality as it is really experienced. One of the hallmarks of modernist literature is a technique called *disjointed time.* Time, as humans experience it, is illogical. Sometimes a single moment feels like a lifetime, while several years seem to pass in the blink of an eye. How can a writer use language to accurately capture this peculiarity of the human experience?

Virginia Woolf's diaries reveal that she was in competition with other modernists to depict the experience of time. Mansfield often experimented with time, and Woolf deemed her "the only writer I have ever been jealous of." Woolf was determined to take up the ultimate challenge: To represent the passage of time in the absence of humans. While other modernist writers succeeded in highlighting the paradoxical lengthiness of short periods of time—James Joyce's epic novel *Ulysses* takes place during a single day—Woolf sought to alternate the human experience of time with time as it really passes. Woolf once wrote, "The real novelist can somehow convey both sorts of being....I have never been able to do both."

But eventually she succeeded. *To the Lighthouse* is composed of three sections. The first covers one day in the life of a family. The third covers another day in the life of the same family. But the second section, *Time Passes,* represents the ten years that elapse between these two days. The section takes place inside a house that gradually decays in the absence of its previous inhabitants. There is no plot or action in the traditional sense. Yet the section is unexpectedly beautiful and captivating. Only by contrasting "human time" with "real time" could Woolf successfully reveal the magnificence and strangeness of time as we know it. Or, in the words of Woolf herself: "Suddenly one hears a clock tick. We who had been immersed in this world became aware of another. It is painful."

International Opera House

A thick black line runs across the center of the Haskell Free Library's reading room and on the floor above, under the seats of the opera house upstairs. But this isn't any old line. It's the United States–Canada border, which happens to slice straight through this neoclassical, three-story building.

Walk through the library's front door, and you are officially in Derby Line, Vermont. But when you check out books—your choice of English or French—you must do so in Stanstead, Quebec. If you are upstairs watching a show in the opera house, you will probably be sitting in the United States, but you would be applauding performers onstage in Canada.

A Vision of Unity

The Haskell Free Library and Opera House was built in 1904 by American sawmill owner Carlos Haskell and his Canadian wife, Martha Stewart Haskell. Mrs. Haskell, the wealthy granddaughter of one of Derby's founding families, was born in Canada, lived in the United States, and had business interests in both. The couple's idea was that by building this institution across the border, it could be used by people of both countries, and the profits from the opera house would support the operation of the library.

When the Haskells passed away, the family donated the building to the towns of Derby Line and Rock Island, Quebec (which later became Stanstead). It is run by a private international board of four Americans and three Canadians that governs both the building and its facilities. Registered in 1976 on the National Register of Historic Places for Orleans County in Vermont, the Haskell Free Library and Opera House is also on the list of provincial heritage buildings in Quebec. Modeled after the former Boston Opera House, this unique structure boasts painted scenes of Venice on its drop curtains in the opera hall and two-foot-thick walls made with granite from Stanstead.

The 400-seat theater has its drawbacks, though. There's no orchestra pit, incendiary special effects are not allowed, and the dressing rooms are tiny. There's also no air-conditioning, and the wooden chairs are hard—unless, of course, you pay 50 cents to rent one of the pink sofa cushions offered by the ushers.

Split Personality

Keith Beadle, one of the trustees, grew up using the library. He tells the media that running a building straddling two countries can often be a logistical problem, reporting that maintenance issues are particularly difficult. Most work must be done by hiring companies from both sides of the border or the tradespeople will be working illegally at least part of the time. However, in a recent renovation, Canadian immigration agreed to let American workers make some improvements as long as they came in through the front door (on the American side). However, when the American crews were up on the roof, they were on the Canadian side, and labor unions wanted to fine the contractor $8,000. They later resolved the dispute amicably.

The Sign of the Times

The turn-of-the-century building has always been a point of pride between the two communities. Many townsfolk have grown up and married, much like Carlos and Martha Haskell, and share relatives on both sides of the border.

But recent world events are pressing down hard on these two small towns. American border officials, part of the Department of Homeland Security, have new stricter regulations as they guard the frontier into Canada in the streets linking Derby Line and Stanstead. What worries the locals is that authorities may tighten the loose agreements the two villages share that allow them to come and go from the library without reporting to customs, even if they cross the border one or more times while inside.

But in the meantime, kids still hop back and forth over the black line, and tourists still take pictures of themselves straddling the border, with one foot inside Canada and one inside the United States.

- *When full, the average person's stomach can hold half to three-quarters of a gallon of food.*

- *Salt itself has no smell.*

He Said, She Said

Happiness is your dentist telling you it won't hurt and then having him catch his hand in the drill.

—*Johnny Carson*

I think your whole life shows in your face, and you should be proud of that.

—*Lauren Bacall*

Our greatest responsibility is to be good ancestors.

—*Dr. Jonas Salk*

We all have ability. The difference is how we use it.

—*Stevie Wonder*

You can't wring your hands and roll up your sleeves at the same time.

—*Pat Schroeder*

The most savage controversies are those about matters as to which there is no good evidence either way.

—*Bertrand Russell*

Patriotism means to stand by the country. It does not mean to stand by the president.

—*Theodore Roosevelt*

Remind people that profit is the difference between revenue and expense. This makes you look smart.

—*Scott Adams*

Cross-country skiing is great if you live in a small country.

—*Steven Wright*

If I weren't earning $3 million a year to dunk a basketball, most people on the street would run in the other direction if they saw me coming.

—*Charles Barkley*

The reason grandparents and grandchildren get along so well is that they have a common enemy.

—*Sam Levenson*

My most important piece of advice to all you would-be writers: when you write, try to leave out all the parts readers skip.

—*Elmore Leonard*

Way Out West? The Making of
The Great Train Robbery

At the turn of the 20th century, movie viewing had yet to become a group activity. Short film clips were displayed in parlors, known as nickelodeons, on individual viewers called Kinetoscopes and Vitascopes. Customers stood in line to be thrilled by such seemingly mundane scenes as a train pulling into a station or a man and a woman kissing.

Prolific inventor Thomas Edison produced these clips in a studio called Black Maria, in the exotic moviemaking locale of West Orange, New Jersey. Edison's camera operator, Edwin S. Porter, had a greater vision for movies. Believing the clips could tell complete stories, he produced and directed America's first "feature film"—albeit a brief 12 minutes in length—1903's *The Great Train Robbery*.

A Flurry of Firsts

Porter was the first to use location shooting. He was also the first to have one location stand in for another, using the northern New Jersey woods as a substitute for the Wild West. He was also the first to use a method of dynamic editing called *cross-cutting,* in which the viewer's attention is focused on two separate but simultaneous scenes of action. In addition, Porter found a way to move the bulky camera so that it was mobile rather than stationary.

Most important, this film's story has a beginning, middle, and end. Bandits stop a train, rob its passengers, and make their escape on horseback. A posse takes chase and guns the bandits down. Porter based the story on an 1896 stage play of the same name and the real-life adventures of outlaws Butch Cassidy and the Sundance Kid, who robbed a Wyoming train in 1899.

The director obviously knew the potential impact that moving pictures could have—he finished *The Great Train Robbery* with a scene of a thug firing his pistol right into the camera, causing startled viewers to duck and recoil in surprise.

It wouldn't be the last time that happened in the movies.

The Extremely Wild Blue Yonder of Howard Hughes

Howard Hughes has been called many things: gifted, eccentric, reckless, crazy. The brilliant billionaire made his fortune in media and aviation, but his life was tempered by bizarre personal habits and activities.

A Little Texan

Born in a Houston, Texas, suburb in 1905, Howard Robard Hughes, Jr., was the son of an entrepreneurial oil baron father and a domineering mother. His father pioneered a revolutionary oil drill bit and made a fortune with the Hughes Tool Company. His mother, fearing sickness for her son, rushed the boy to the doctor at the slightest hint of illness. If residents of the neighborhood suffered from bouts of colds or flu, she would bundle Howard off to a safe distance until the maladies passed. A fear of germs would plague Howard all of his life.

At age 14, Hughes took his first flying lessons, which triggered his lifelong love affair with the great blue yonder. He showed an interest and proficiency in math and engineering, briefly attending classes at Caltech in California and Rice University in Texas. His parents' unexpected deaths in the early 1920s left Howard rich and alone before his 20th birthday.

California, Here He Comes

As gifted as Hughes was with engineering, his true dream was to produce movies in Hollywood. He married a young woman named Ella Rice, and the newlyweds moved to Los Angeles.

But Hughes's wealth didn't necessarily guarantee success. His first film production, *Swell Hogan*, was so bad that it was never released, despite his investment of $60,000. His next two films, comedies called *Everybody's Acting* and *Two Arabian Knights,* were moderate successes that lead to his first epic production: *Hell's Angels* (1930). At nearly $4 million, it was by far the most expensive movie made up to that time, and it was loaded with Hughes's favorite subject—airplanes. Although he was pleased with the final product itself, the film had another cost—Rice divorced Hughes. She couldn't deal with his propensity to work up to 36 straight hours at a time and felt completely shut out of his life.

Thereafter, Hughes, ever the tall and handsome Texan, spent time with many Hollywood beauties. At one point or another, he was seen in the company of Katharine Hepburn, Bette Davis, Carole Lombard, Ava Gardner, Ginger Rogers, Terry Moore (an Oscar nominee for *Come Back, Little Sheba*), and Jean Peters (who appeared in *Viva Zapata!* and *Niagara*)—eventually marrying the last in 1957 (the couple divorced in 1971). While he was never romantically involved with Jane Russell, he did design a special bra to emphasize her already ample assets in the 1943 film, *The Outlaw.*

Up, Up, and Away

Howard Hughes's only full-time companion was aviation. Despite being a self-educated pilot and engineer, he designed and built record-setting airplanes. His H-1 Racer cracked the airspeed barrier of 352 miles per hour in 1935 with Hughes, of course, at the controls. Within two years, he set the transcontinental speed record—flying from Los Angeles to New York City in just under seven-and-a-half hours. While evidence indicates that the Japanese Zero, German Focke-Wulf, and American Hellcat fighter planes were heavily influenced by the Racer's design, Hughes was unable to secure a military contract to build the plane.

Hughes did, however, design the XF-11 spy plane; the U.S. Army Air Forces ordered 100 of them, only to cancel the request when the war ended. On the very first test flight, Hughes crashed the prototype, destroying several homes in the Beverly Hills area and seriously injuring himself. A broken collarbone, numerous fractured ribs, a collapsed lung, and multiple third-degree burns kept him bedridden for five weeks. Not liking the hospital bed, he called his engineers at Hughes Aircraft and designed a special one over the phone.

Another proposed contribution to the Second World War effort was Hughes's Hercules H-4 cargo plane. With a wingspan of more than 300 feet and a height of nearly 80 feet, the eight-engine seaplane would be the largest ever built. Although nicknamed the "Spruce Goose," the H-4 was actually built from birch wood, as metal was extremely hard to come by during the war. Like the XF-11, the Hercules was canceled when the war ended, but Hughes did take it out for a test spin in November 1947. The enormous "flying boat" lifted off for nearly a mile, coasting at 135 miles per hour a mere 70 feet above the waters of Long Beach, California. It was the only time the Spruce Goose would fly.

A Restless Tenant

During his career, Hughes had owned Trans World Airlines (TWA), as well as RKO, a prominent movie studio. But as Hughes reached age 60, he began to shun his businesses and live in opulent and luxurious hotels in America, Central America, and the Caribbean. Locating himself in the top-floor penthouse, he would often buy the hotel that rested below his feet. In Las Vegas, Hughes lived in constant fear of radiation from nearby nuclear experiments—going so far as to offer one million dollars to President Lyndon Johnson in 1968 if he would stop the atomic tests.

By now, Hughes's germ phobia—along with a longtime addiction to codeine and other painkillers—had led to bizarre habits and rituals. Since the late 1950s, his diet had consisted mostly of fresh whole milk, chocolate bars with almonds, pecans, and bottled water. Unless traveling, he spent his time stark naked in darkened rooms, declining to meet with anyone except his closest aides. He refused to touch anything unless he used a tissue as a barrier between his hands and the object. By 1970, his health had deteriorated so much that the six-foot, four-inch tall Hughes weighed less than 100 pounds. His hair and beard were long, shaggy, and gray, and the nails on his fingers and toes were inches long. He ordered his urine to be saved, stored in capped containers on shelves.

When Hughes died of kidney failure in April 1976, he was aboard a private plane en route to his hometown of Houston.

- *Golfer Arnold Palmer once hooked one into the fork of a tree. He climbed up, hammered the ball out with a 1-iron, chipped, and putted for par on the hole.*

- *Garlic was once thought to be best suited for medicinal purposes and had no place in the kitchen.*

- *Roy Rogers proposed to Dale Evans while both were on horseback.*

WHO KNEW?

Deep-Sea Mail Delivery
Apparently, tourists and the people of the Japanese coastal town of Susami, Wakayama, love the water very much. The town has the world's deepest post office box, which sits 32 feet below the ocean's surface. Special waterproof plastic postcards are sold, and mail is placed inside the post box by using special plastic bags. Workers collect mail daily, and the box has been known to hold more than 200 pieces at busy times.

Modern-Day Flying Machines
The Flugtag, an annual race sponsored by the energy drink Red Bull and held in many countries, has been around since 1991. In German, the word *Flugtag* literally means "flight day" but is translated as "airshow." Contestants build zany, often rickety, homemade flying machines and plunge them off a pier into water, attempting to "fly" the farthest. The events often attract up to 300,000 spectators annually. As of the 2007 contests, the record for farthest flight is 195 feet set in Austria in 2000. The U.S. Flugtag record, set in Nashville, Tennessee, in 2007, is 155 feet.

How Hot Is Hot?
The scoville scale measures the piquancy (hotness) of chili peppers. For instance, jalapeños measure around 10,000 scoville heat units (shu). Tabasco sauce rates between 2,500 and 5,000 shu. The chocolate brown habanero pepper rates a mouth-scorching 301,000 shu. However, the world's hottest pepper, crowned by Guinness World Records in fall 2006, is the Bhut Jolokia. It has been measured at a tongue-melting 1,001,304 shu! Mouth masochists, enjoy!

It Only Looks Like It's Floating
The heaviest manufactured mobile object ever made is the Troll Offshore Gas Platform, which sits just off the coast of Norway in the North Sea. Without the added weight of water sitting on this massive structure, it boasts a dry weight of 656,000 metric tons! Standing 1,210 feet tall, it was made with enough concrete to pour the foundations for 215,000 average homes. One hundred thousand tons of steel were used for its construction—approximately 15 Eiffel Towers.

American Women Get the Vote

Between 1818 and 1820, Fanny Wright, a feminist from Scotland, lectured throughout the United States on such topics as voting rights for women, birth control, and equality between the sexes in education and marriage laws. Little did she know that it would take another 100 years for American women to achieve the right to vote on these issues.

The Beginning

To be technical, Margaret Brent, a landowner in Maryland, was the very first woman in the United States to call for voting rights. In 1647, Brent insisted on two votes in the colonial assembly—one for herself and one for the man for whom she held power of attorney. The governor rejected her request.

Then there was Abigail Adams. In 1776, she wrote to her husband, John, asking him to remember the ladies in the new code of laws he was drafting. She was summarily dismissed.

Almost half a century later, Fanny Wright showed up from Scotland. Although she recognized the gender inequities in the United States, she still fell in love with the country and became a naturalized citizen in 1825.

It wasn't until the 1840s, however, that the feminist ball really got rolling. Because progress was achieved in fits and spurts, women's suffrage eventually took the good part of a century after that to come to fruition.

The Middle

Before the Civil War, the women's suffrage movement and abolition organizations focused on many of the same issues. The two movements were closely linked in action and deed, specifically at the World Anti-Slavery Convention in London in 1840. However, female delegates to the convention, among them Lucretia Mott and Elizabeth Cady Stanton, were not allowed to participate in the activities because of their gender. London is a long way to travel to sit in the back of a room and be silent. Stanton and Mott resolved to organize a convention to discuss the rights of women.

The convention was finally held in 1848 in Seneca Falls, New York. Stanton presented her *Declaration of Sentiments,* the first formal action by women in the United States to advocate civil rights and suffrage.

Two groups formed at the end of the 1860s: the National Woman Suffrage Association (NWSA) and the American Woman Suffrage Association (AWSA). The NWSA, led by Susan B. Anthony and Stanton, worked to change voting laws on the federal level by way of an amendment to the U.S. Constitution. The AWSA, led by Lucy Stone and Julia Ward Howe, worked to change the laws on the state level. The two groups were united in 1890 and renamed the National American Woman Suffrage Association.

The End

In 1916, Alice Paul formed the National Woman's Party (NWP). Based on the idea that action, not words, would achieve the suffragists' mission, the NWP staged Silent Sentinels outside the White House during which NWP members held banners and signs that goaded the president. When World War I came along, many assumed the Silent Sentinels would end. Instead, the protesters incorporated the current events into their messages and were ultimately arrested. Once the public got wind of the horrendous treatment the women were subjected to in jail, the public tide turned in their favor. In 1917, President Woodrow Wilson announced his support for a suffrage amendment. In the summer of 1920, Tennessee ratified the 19th Amendment—the 36th state to do so—and in August of that year, women gained the right to vote. It had certainly been a long time coming.

- *With a vote of 169 to 0, the delegates to South Carolina's constitutional convention voted to secede from the United States on December 20, 1860. Ten Southern states would follow.*

Things to Do at *Carnaval*

Carnaval, *thought to come from the Latin* carne *and* vale, *which literally translates to "goodbye meat," is a four-day pre-Lent party held throughout Brazil with dancing, music, and elaborate* destaques *(costumes).*

Those lucky enough to experience *Carnaval* should be sure to add the following to their to-do list:

Enjoy the taste of fresh *acai*: This wonder berry is just beginning to be touted by the health conscious in the rest of the world for its amazing antioxidants, omegas, and nutrients. Brazilians have enjoyed the chocolate and tart berry taste of *acai* for years. It's usually mixed with guarana, an energy-boosting berry. The taste is unusual for first-timers, but after a few rounds of this power-packed combo, they have energy to spare.

Join a samba school: Samba, the sexy hip-shaking moves that pulse through *Carnaval,* is taken seriously in Brazil. Those thousands of dancers aren't just drunk locals, they're part of various samba schools throughout Rio de Janeiro. The point of all the over-the-top costumes, singing, and displays is to win votes. The parade in the Sambodromo arena is actually a competition, and schools practice year-round to be crowned winner of *Carnaval.*

For much-needed financial support, schools let in a few outsiders to learn the samba and the school's theme song. While no one expects an outsider to be a *passissta* (the best dancers and often the most scantily clad), the schools are being judged throughout the chaos, and one misplaced feather or sloppy hip shake could cost vital points. Visitors should bring their A-game if they hope to participate in the true spirit and intensity of *Carnaval.*

Skip Rio and do *Carnaval* in Bahia: Brazil's strong African roots are most present in the region of Bahia. Here, *Carnaval* takes place in Salvador. The dancing is just as zesty, but costuming is less significant, and the music is performed by bands atop slowly moving trucks. Depending on whom you ask, many consider this to be the best *Carnaval* celebration in all of Brazil.

Fast Facts

- The silhouette of a dribbling basketball player on the National Basketball Association's logo is an image of former Los Angeles Lakers great Jerry West.

- Two men attempted to kill President Harry Truman at the Blair House in 1950. They failed, but one White House police officer and one of the assassins were killed. Two other White House police and the second assassin were wounded, but each recovered. Truman later commuted the death sentence of the second assassin.

- For about 1,500 years—from A.D. 393 until 1894—there were no Olympic Games. The games were reintroduced by Frenchman Pierre de Coubertin in an effort to encourage global peace.

- The remains of a giant ape, perhaps ten feet tall and weighing 1,000 pounds, were found in a cave in China. It's believed the beast lived 300,000 years ago.

- Actor Paul Newman attempted to enlist in the Naval Air Corps during World War II, but he was discovered to be color-blind. He instead served in the U.S. Navy in the South Pacific.

- Of all the planets in the sun's solar system, Venus is the only one that rotates clockwise.

- Radio station WLTO in Lexington, Kentucky, ran a contest to "win 100 grand." When the winner went to claim her prize, she received a Nestlé's 100 Grand candy bar. She sued for $100,000.

- Pope John XXI (1276–77) had been in office less than a year before the ceiling on a new wing of his palace collapsed on him while he slept. He died six days later.

- Stella Walsh, who won the women's 100-meter dash at the 1932 Olympics, was killed in 1980. During her autopsy, doctors discovered that she was really a he.

Magnetic Hill Phenomenon

It has taken researchers hundreds of years to finally solve the mystery of magnetic hills, or spook hills, as they're often called. This phenomenon, found all over the world, describes places where objects—including cars in neutral gear—move uphill on a slightly sloping road, seemingly defying gravity.

Moncton, in New Brunswick, Canada, lays claim to one of the more famous magnetic hills, called, appropriately, Magnetic Hill. Over the years, it has also been called Fool's Hill and Magic Hill. Since the location made headlines in 1931, hundreds of thousands of tourists have flocked there to witness this phenomenon for themselves.

Go Figure

Much to the dismay of paranormal believers, people in science once assumed that a magnetic anomaly caused this event. But advanced physics has concluded this phenomenon is due "to the visual anchoring of the sloping surface to a gravity-relative eye level whose perceived direction is biased by sloping surroundings." In nonscientific jargon, all that says is that it's an optical illusion.

Papers published in the journal of the Association of Psychological Science supported this conclusion based on a series of experiments done with models. They found that if the horizon cannot be seen or is not level then people may be fooled by objects that they expect to be vertical but aren't. False perspective is also a culprit; think, for example, of a line of poles on the horizon that seem to get larger or smaller depending on distance.

Engineers with plumb lines, one made of iron and one made of stone, demonstrated that a slope appearing to go uphill might in reality be going downhill. A good topographical map may also be sufficient to show which way the land is really sloping.

I Know a Place

Other notable magnetic hills can be found in Wisconsin, Pennsylvania, California, Florida, Barbados, Scotland, Australia, Italy, Greece, and South Korea.

Rock Around the Block

The sound of pop-rock music has always been influenced by certain regions of the country or world. Major music centers such as New York, Los Angeles, London, Philadelphia, San Francisco, Chicago, and Nashville have always been primary influences for the distinct sounds associated with the pop-rock culture. From time to time, however, savvy record producers and music promoters cast their eyes toward areas not normally associated with music influence.

It's been well established that rock music began with the Memphis sound—a combination of blues, country, and gospel first known as rockabilly, then rock 'n' roll, and finally simply as rock. It was Memphis that spawned the career of the King of Rock 'n' Roll and set the stage for the emergence and acceptance of just about every musical genre that followed, from R&B to grunge. Elvis popularized rock 'n' roll, and his importance in pop culture should never be underestimated. Still, it's important not to forget the designers of his sound—the people behind the scenes, such as Sam Phillips and Chips Moman, who revived the sagging career of the King. Almost every musical genre since the advent of rock is reflective of a certain regional style and sound.

Detroit, Michigan

The Motown sound, prevalent from 1960 to the mid-'70s, was a designer sound orchestrated by Detroit record shop owner Berry Gordy, Jr., but executed by some of the most technically adept musicians, songwriters, and arrangers ever assembled. Motown was a unique blending of pop, R&B, and gospel-style call-and-response harmony supported by strings, brass, tambourines, and the innovative percussion sound of two drummers. The Motown sound produced the most consistent number of chart-topping records until the disco craze of the mid-'70s. (More than two-thirds of all Motown records produced during that period ended up on the top 50 best-seller charts.) The Motown sound faded from the pop scene when Gordy became interested in producing films and moved his operation west. In 1988, Gordy sold Motown to MCA for $61 million.

Though the Motown sound has been frequently referred to as the Detroit sound, in reality there was another distinct style with that name that included performers the likes of Mitch Ryder, Bob Seger, the Amboy Dukes, and Grand Funk Railroad.

Asheville, North Carolina

When people think of Asheville, North Carolina, what usually comes to mind are the Great Smoky Mountains and the scenic Blue Ridge Parkway, but Asheville is also a major player in influencing certain pop-rock sounds. Once an economically depressed area, Asheville has risen from the ashes to earn the title "Soho of the South," after the trendy Manhattan art district, thanks to its lively, flashy cultural arts community. Asheville is a regional stronghold of live music venues, recording facilities, and exceptionally talented regional music groups and performers, including Warren Haynes (23rd on *Rolling Stone*'s list of the 100 Top Guitarists and a member of the Allman Brothers Band), Grammy-winner David Holt, Toubab Krewe, and Afromotive. The scene in Asheville is quite diverse, ranging from West African rock rhythms popular in the mid-'70s to moog-heavy techno to punk, indie-rock, classic Southern rock, and bluegrass. It's also one of the largest and friendliest gay and lesbian areas outside of San Francisco.

Athens, Georgia

A vibrant music scene has been thriving in Athens since the early 1900s, when the historic Morton Theatre was a haven for traveling musicians playing a new type of music called jazz. The more recent Athens style, a combination of new wave, pop-rock, and alternative rock, went national in the late '70s with the launching of the B-52's, whose quirky, sometimes spoken-word style made them a national favorite. In the '80s, R.E.M. became one of the world's most popular rock bands. Athens, much like Asheville, has an active live music scene; two hot spots made *Paste Magazine*'s list of America's 40 top live music venues.

Seattle, Washington

The name *grunge* quickly became associated with the music coming out of Seattle in the late '80s and early '90s. That was due to the "grungy" discordant and distorted guitar sounds, not to mention the unkempt appearance and thrift store duds of most band members. Grunge musicians scorned theatrics to concentrate instead on straight-ahead, high-energy music performances. Regional groups such as Nirvana, Soundgarden, Pearl Jam, and Alice in Chains—many of which recorded for local label Sub Pop—burst on the national scene making grunge the most popular alternative-rock sound in the country. By the mid-'90s, grunge was beginning to fade, and many of the groups were disbanding. The suicide of Nirvana's Kurt Cobain hastened the process, though Nirvana's albums continue to enjoy brisk sales today.

Manchester, England

Regional innovation and decentralization is what keeps rock music fresh, new, and exciting. There's no telling where the next genre of alternative rock will spring from. The Manchester sound of the late '80s and early '90s is a good example. Sometimes called *Madchester* or *baggy,* after the loose-fitting clothing worn by exponents and fans, it was a combination of punk-rock, rave culture, and northern soul that became the strongest regional influence to come out of England since the Liverpool sound of the '60s. It brought international prominence to such groups as the Stone Roses, whose debut album topped the list of greatest British albums of all time in the music paper *NME;* Happy Mondays; Inspiral Carpets; James; and 808 State.

Minneapolis, Minnesota

Minneapolis's influence goes back to the early '60s when the first recording studio in the state, Kay Bank, started producing hit records such as "Surfin' Bird" by the Trashmen. The Minneapolis sound, per se, is a funky mix of disco and R&B, in the manner of its most prominent exponent, Prince, the architect of the Minneapolis sound. But what really makes the Twin Cities area unique is its diversity of musical genre, from the folk rock sounds of Bob Dylan and the Jayhawks to the hip-hop sounds of Atmosphere, with a side trip into post-punk with the Replacements, Husker Du, and Soul Asylum. And there's been everything in between, including a fast-growing, live electronic dance music scene, a nationally renowned symphony orchestra, some of the nation's most talented and innovative studio musicians, and even *A Prairie Home Companion.*

The Times They Are A-Changin'

1981

January 20: Iran frees 52 Americans who have been held hostage there for 444 days.

March 2: Howard Stern begins broadcasts on WWDC in Washington, D.C.

March 6: Walter Cronkite signs off for the last time as anchor of the *CBS Evening News,* to be replaced on March 9 by Dan Rather.

March 30: President Ronald Reagan is shot and wounded by John W. Hinckley III.

April 4: Henry Cisneros becomes the first Mexican-American mayor of a U.S. city when he is elected in San Antonio.

April 11: Actress Valerie Bertinelli marries rocker Eddie Van Halen.

April 24: The IBM PC is introduced.

May 13: Pope John Paul II is shot and seriously wounded by Mehmet Ali Agca in St. Peter's Square.

June 12: *Raiders of the Lost Ark,* starring Harrison Ford, premieres.

July 7: Sandra Day O'Connor is nominated as the first female justice on the Supreme Court. She will be confirmed by the Senate 99–0 the following day.

July 29: In the most watched royal wedding ever, Prince Charles of England weds Lady Diana Spencer

August 5: President Ronald Reagan fires more than 11,000 striking air traffic controllers.

September 7: *The People's Court* with Judge Wapner premieres.

September 19: Paul Simon and Art Garfunkel reunite for a concert in Central Park.

October 22: The U.S. national debt passes the one-trillion-dollar mark for the first time.

December 11: In his 61st and final fight, Muhammad Ali loses to Trevor Berbick.

California, Sinclair, and EPIC

It was 1934, and the Depression that had started in 1929 was still dragging on despite President Franklin Roosevelt's programs to bring economic relief. California was suffering no more or no less than the rest of the nation, but California author Upton Sinclair was ready with a remedy that could make all the difference.

Upton Sinclair knew a little something about wealth and poverty. Born in 1878 into an extremely poor family, he spent periods of time living with wealthy grandparents. He would later say that witnessing these two extremes turned him into a socialist.

Success in Writing

Sinclair funded his college education by selling stories and articles, and he was soon supplying his parents with regular income. After reading such authors as Jack London and Frank Norris, he formed the Intercollegiate Socialist Society along with London, Clarence Darrow, and Florence Kelley. In 1904, Fred Warren, editor of *Appeal to Reason,* commissioned Sinclair to write a novel about the Chicago meat-packing industry: *The Jungle.*

After President Theodore Roosevelt read *The Jungle,* he ordered an investigation of industry practices. He told Sinclair that, while he disapproved of his advocacy of socialism, "radical action must be taken to do away with the efforts of arrogant and selfish greed on the part of the capitalist." These contradictory sentiments, of course, illuminate Sinclair's problem. Right-thinking Americans were taught to be suspicious of socialism, lumping it in with Bolshevism and bomb-throwing anarchists. Sinclair would have to overcome the label if he was going to affect change.

Failed Political Career

Sinclair split with the Socialist party over American involvement in World War I, but in 1926, he rejoined the party to run for governor of California. He was trounced. But he ran again in 1934—this time as a Democrat—touting a program called End Poverty in California (EPIC).

"The meaning of our movement to End Poverty In California and its polling the largest vote ever cast in a California primary," he wrote, "is that our people have reached the saturation point as regards suffering. . . . We have one-and-a-quarter million persons dependent upon public charity, and probably as many more who are able to get only one or two days' work a week or who are dependent on relatives and friends. That is too heavy a burden of suffering for any civilized community to carry."

Sinclair planned to fund EPIC with an ad valorem tax on property assessed above $100,000 (which Sinclair argued was really worth $250,000). This, of course, raised the ire of the corporations and the rich—they closed ranks behind Republican Frank Merriam, who painted Sinclair as a radical. Sinclair lost the race, but he did manage to win 879,537 votes against Merriam's 1,138,620.

Later, in a letter to prominent Socialist Norman Thomas, Sinclair wrote: "The American People will take Socialism, but they won't take the label. . . . I think we simply have to realize the fact that our enemies have succeeded in spreading the Big Lie. There is no use attacking by a frontal attack, it is much better to outflank them." Although Sinclair was convinced that the substance of his policies was acceptable to the public, he never found a way to persuade people to consider them.

- *The Stanley Cup, hockey's Holy Grail, was once left behind in a photographer's studio. The housekeeper filled it with dirt and turned it into a geranium pot.*

- *In the 50 years between 1850 and 1900, the population of New York City grew by almost 500 percent.*

- *Although giraffes have no vocal cords, they aren't exactly all neck and no noise. They have been known to bleat, bellow, snort, snore, moan, cough, and hiss.*

- *Marcel Renault, a cofounder of the Renault car company, was one of the first drivers to die during competition when he was killed during the 1903 Paris-Madrid race.*

The Wacky World of Car Art

Recycling isn't just for plastics. Some artistic-minded folks have found a crafty way to funnel old cars into new modes of creative expression: car art.

Carhenge
Crafted in 1987, *Carhenge* stands as an exact proportional replica to the famed Stonehenge in England. Car for car to stone for stone, the measurements match up with precision. A total of 38 automobiles make up this tributary structure near Alliance, Nebraska. With some cars positioned upright, their trunks buried deep underground, and others settled into various contorted angles, this Stonehenge clone is complete with its coating of stone-gray paint.

Cadillac Ranch
Cadillac Ranch, located just off Route 66 in Amarillo, Texas, features a row of ten Golden Age Cadillacs buried in the ground with only their back halves sticking up. What can be seen of the cars above ground is spray-painted in various ever-changing shades of graffiti. The cars are periodically repainted by the sculpture's keepers, but visitor contributions of paint are strongly encouraged.

The *Spindle*
In 1989, a 40-foot spike was erected in a parking lot in Berwyn, Illinois, onto which eight cars were threaded in a towering vertical row. The *Spindle,* sometimes referred to as the car-kabob, was dismantled in May 2008 to make way for the construction of a new building, but it was reported that negotiations began almost immediately to rebuild it in a new location.

Cartopia
For those lovers of car art who want function with their form, there are also annual celebrations of art cars. One such event, *Cartopia,* held in Berwyn, Illinois, provides a showcase for the country's coolest art cars, complete with a parade. Hundreds of art cars zoom through town to show off the talents of their owners.

Former Day Jobs

❖ ❖ ❖ ❖

*Not everybody started at the top of their profession—in
fact, pretty much no one did. Here's what a few people
were up to before they became household names.*

- Actor Rock Hudson, cartoon tycoon Walt Disney, and crooner
  Bing Crosby worked for the post office: Hudson as a letter carrier,
  Disney as an *assistant* letter carrier, and Crosby as a postal clerk.

- Legendary lover Casanova founded the French state lottery.

- Actor/director Clint Eastwood was a firefighter, lumberjack, steel-
  mill furnace stoker, and lifeguard, so he comes by those craggy,
  manly good looks honestly.

- Speaking of craggy good looks, actor Robert Mitchum was a
  heavyweight boxer, and actor Lee Marvin was a plumber and a
  U.S. Marine.

- Singer Rod Stewart was a grave digger.

- Actor Harrison Ford was, famously, a carpenter, who installed
  kitchens and such for moguls who would later pay him much more
  handsomely for his theatrical labors.

- Actor/sex symbol Jayne Mansfield was a concert pianist and violinist before she became what some people labeled "the poor man's
  Marilyn Monroe."

- Actor Dustin Hoffman was once a janitor, but even that had to be
  easier than his other job, that of attendant in a mental hospital.

- Actor Greta Garbo toiled as a latherer in a men's barbershop.

- Actor Al Pacino was variously employed as a theater usher, porter,
  and superintendent of an office building.

- Actor Audrey Hepburn secretly worked with the Dutch Resistance
  as a youngster during World War II and also performed as a ballet
  dancer.

It Only Cost a Dime:
The Golden Age of Comics

*Cartoons and comic strips had appeared in newspapers
and magazines since the 1800s, and a few clever packagers
reprinted them in booklets in the early 20th century. But by
the late 1930s—as America finally emerged from its economic
woes—the "Golden Age of Comics" was dawning. This
heyday of comic publishing lasted into the early 1950s.*

Up in the Sky

In 1934, National Allied Publications became the first publisher
to create an all-original comic book, called *More Fun,* avoiding the
common practice of reprinting newspaper comic strips. They later
created *Adventure Comics,* which would run for more than 45 years.
In 1937, National started a comic book called *Detective Comics,*
often abbreviated as "DC Comics"; this eventually became the
company's name.

One of DC Comics' first series, *Action Comics,* debuted in June
1938. It featured something new and different—a groundbreaking
hero. Written and drawn by high school pals Jerry Siegel and Joe
Shuster, this *super* hero was called (logically) Superman. Clad in
blue tights and a red cape and boots, Superman was superbly strong
and jumped one-eighth of a mile in a bound (it would be a little
while before he actually flew). He came to Earth as a baby from the
doomed planet Krypton, and as he grew into adulthood, he hid his
real identity as mild-mannered Clark Kent and fought for "truth,
justice, and the American way."

Young readers ate it up—they had never seen anything like
Superman before.

Enter the Caped Crusader and More

Detective Comics featured whodunits with exotic crimesolvers such
as Ching-Lung and Slam Bradley. A most mysterious crimefighter
first appeared in the May 1939 edition of *Detective Comics,* issue
27. Drawn by Bob Kane, he was called The Batman. The dark and

hooded hero had no real superpowers like DC's other popular character, but he could swing and glide through the night as he captured crooks. DC was two-for-two in successful superheroes. The company's triumphs continued into the 1940s, with crusading characters such as the Flash, Green Lantern, Hawkman, Green Arrow, Aquaman, and Wonder Woman. With such success, imitations were bound to appear.

Timely Comics (which would eventually become Marvel Comics) soon had their own stable of superheroes, many of whom fought the foes of World War II. Characters such as Captain America, the Sub-Mariner, and the Human Torch (not to be confused with the Fantastic Four comic character of the 1960s) tangled with the Red Skull and even Adolf Hitler himself.

Look—It's Lawsuit Man!

While these characters were unique and posed no apparent threat of infringement to DC, other comic publishers were not so lucky. One competitor, Fawcett Comics, introduced a caped superhero in 1940 called Captain Marvel. This star of *Whiz Comics* drew a cease-and-desist order from DC in 1941, but the legal case would be drawn out until the close of the Golden Age. There were trials and appeals, but just before beginning another long, arduous process in a retrial, Fawcett settled with DC in 1952; the company paid Superman's owners $400,000 and agreed to cease all publication of Captain Marvel. Ironically, *Whiz Comics* had consistently outsold *Action Comics* and *Superman* in the 1940s. Other characters, such as Fox Feature Syndicate's Wonder Man and Fawcett's Master Man, had already felt the sting of DC's legal eagles.

The Also-rans

Many other Golden Age comics were published by such companies as Dell Comics (which featured animated characters from Disney, Warner Brothers, and MGM), Quality Comics (with titles such as *Plastic Man, Police Comics,* and *Blackhawk*), and Archie Comics (with *Pep Comics* and *Archie*).

- *In 1984, scientists crossbred a sheep with a goat and created—wait for it—a* geep. *It looked like a goat wearing an angora sweater.*

Fumbling Felons

Keep It to Yourself

A 60-year-old man in Duisburg, Germany, decided to appeal his court conviction for streaking at a girls' soccer match. Perhaps believing it might help his case, the man stripped off all his clothes in the courtroom when the jury adjourned for deliberation. Needless to say, new charges were immediately filed.

Don't Display Your Own Evidence

An Italian university student was arrested in 2007 for marijuana charges after dropping his cell phone. Apparently, the student had taken a picture of himself in front of a marijuana plant and then inexplicably used that picture as a screen saver on his phone. That wasn't so bad, until he lost the phone. A retiree found it and turned it over to the police. Upon seeing the picture, police called the student in, where he promptly broke down and confessed to everything, including the location of his crop. He was immediately arrested.

The Internet Knows Everything

Two burglars broke into an indoor amusement center in Colorado Springs, Colorado. Police suspect that they had inside help, as the felons had keys, pass codes, and combinations. What they didn't have, however, was information about the safes—which took them more than 75 minutes to open. Security footage showed them fumbling with the dials. In an attempt to obscure the lens of a security camera, the bungling duo sprayed it with WD-40 lubricant, which cleaned the lens instead. Eventually, one of the burglars left the room. Police later checked a computer in a nearby office and found that the thief had performed Google searches for "how to open a safe" and "how to crack a safe." It must have helped. The two easily opened the safes after that, escaping with cash, a laptop computer, and a PlayStation, totaling more than $12,000.

Take Your Name Tag with You

In June 2007, a man who was admitted to a Newark, New Jersey, hospital was arrested for vandalizing the hospital's helicopter. He apparently left the emergency room and walked onto the helipad. Perhaps searching for drugs, the man entered the helicopter and ransacked it. Damages were estimated around $55,000. The vandal, however, left behind his grocery store name tag in the helicopter. Police swiftly arrested him.

The Curse of the Boy King

The discovery of King Tut's tomb in 1922 is said to be the most important find ever in the field of Egyptology. But was there anything to the story of a curse that led to the death of the interlopers who dared disturb the resting place of the boy king? Or was that just an urban legend?

In November 1922, English archaeologist Howard Carter announced one of the world's greatest archaeological finds: the resting place of Tutankhamen, Egypt's fabled boy king. At nine years old, he was the youngest pharaoh ever to rule the ancient land of the Nile. The tomb, discovered in the Valley of the Kings, was amazingly intact; it was one of the few Egyptian tombs to have escaped grave robbers. The furnishings and treasures were dazzling. In fact, the golden death mask that adorned the sarcophagus is purported to be the most renowned example of Egyptian art.

The boy king, who reigned from 1355 to 1344 B.C., was only 19 years old when he died. Until recently, the cause of his death was a mystery to historians. Many believed Tut had been murdered, but a recent CT scan of the mummy conducted by a team of researchers dispelled that possibility. According to experts, his death may have been from an infection that occurred as the result of a broken leg.

The Curse That Won't Die

Another mystery surrounding the boy king is the alleged curse on anyone disturbing his resting place. That rumor can be traced back to the press. In 1923, shortly after the tomb was discovered, the man who endowed the expedition to locate Tut's tomb, Lord Carnarvon, was bitten on the cheek by a mosquito and died from a resulting infection. This was not an ominous event in itself, but when the lights of Cairo went out at the exact moment of his death, the press had a field day, and an urban legend was born. The legend continues to this day, especially each time Tut goes on tour.

Life in the Trenches

Although trench warfare can be traced back to the Battle of the Trench in A.D. 627 and was employed during the American Civil War, it reached its zenith during World War I, when life in the trenches produced death in record numbers on both sides of no-man's-land.

The advanced weaponry of World War I rendered direct frontal warfare a dangerous—even suicidal—proposition, so troops began employing trench warfare. These static defenses were earthen forts where soldiers could defend their perimeters and be deployed to outflank the enemy. Everything in between was referred to as no-man's-land because any attempt to cross it was lethal. The distance between trenches was typically 100 to 300 yards; the depth of the trenches was generally 8 to 16 feet.

Stuck

Because the armies couldn't advance and refused to retreat, these fortifications were inhabited far longer than anyone expected. They literally became hellholes of pestilence. Trenches frequently filled with waist-deep water, and temperatures often hovered at 0° F. Rations were in short supply. Decaying corpses presented a continual health hazard—not to mention an ungodly stench—as did overflowing latrines. This was before the time of antibiotics, and the slightest wound could result in death. The wounded often suffered agonizing pain for weeks before they could be taken to a hospital; in the meantime, rats the size of cats fed on their festering wounds. Many soldiers contracted lice, which led to painful trench fever. A lack of dental hygiene led to gingivitis, which is still known as trench mouth.

Unrelenting artillery barrages caused even hardened veterans to suffer from shell shock, known today as post-traumatic stress disorder. Desperation and near madness drove some soldiers to wound themselves in an effort to be sent to the hospital, where they would frequently die from lack of adequate medical attention and supplies. To this day, skeletal remains of World War I soldiers are still being uncovered at construction sites that were once part of the Western Front. Trench warfare was one of the true horrors of war.

HELLISH HEADLINES

Traffic Dead Rise Slowly

War Dims Hope for Peace

Circumcisions Cause Crybabies

New Study of Obesity Looks for Larger Test Group

Drunk Gets Nine Months in Violin Case

Lawyer Says Client Is Not That Guilty

Hirohito's Body Moved

Scientists Note Progress in Herpes Battle; Ear Plugs Recommended

Woman Off to Jail for Sex with Boys

N.J. Judge to Rule on Nude Beach

Hitler, Nazi Papers Found in Attic

British Left Waffles on Falkland Islands

Iraqi Head Seeks Arms

Ban on Soliciting Dead in Trotwood

Survivor of Siamese Twins Joins Parents

Rest of the Year May Not Follow January

Sadness Is No. 1 Reason Men and Women Cry

Something Went Wrong in Jet Crash, Expert Says

Kids Make Nutritious Snacks

British Union Finds Dwarfs in Short Supply

Dead Cats Protest

Collegians Are Turning to Vegetables

Two Convicts Evade Noose, Jury Hung

Death Causes Loneliness, Feeling of Isolation

Half of U.S. High Schools Require Some Study for Graduation

The Hundred Years' War— in Five Minutes

Although the name would suggest otherwise, the Hundred Years' War was not actually one drawn-out, century-long fight. Rather, it was a period of time containing multiple episodes of conflict.

Beginning in 1337 and ending in 1453, the ongoing trouble between England and France persisted through 116 years with unsuccessful attempts at peace, truces, and treaties between battles. Only in hindsight did historians combine these events under the descriptive title of the Hundred Years' War.

More than 400 years before the start of the Hundred Years' War, the region of France now known as Normandy welcomed a handful of Scandinavians. A century and a half later, with offspring of those feisty Vikings in tow, the Normans seized control of England and made it their own. Although settled comfortably into England, the Normans would maintain control over regions of France; however, with nationals from each region intermingling across country lines, ownership of and control over various regions became hazy. The question of who could claim rights to the different areas soon led to fierce bickering. These battles between France and England revved up until the 14th century, when the Hundred Years' War officially began.

First Things First

The first phase of the Hundred Years War, often called the Edwardian War (1337–60), was instigated by a saga comparable to the Shakespearean struggle between the Montagues and Capulets: The son of King Edward I of England married the daughter of King Philip IV of France, and their mixed-breed child was in line to claim the French throne. But nobles of the land would not hear of someone they considered a mutt running their country, so they required that the royal ancestral lineage be paternal. All the while, control of France's Gascony and Calais regions was in dispute, and this monarchal twist only added to the tension. Ultimately, the English were the victors. The nobles of France, in a tizzy over their questionable leadership in the crown, couldn't unify their vast resources and relinquished control of huge swaths of land. The French became awash in national disenchantment.

Take Two
Although a peace treaty had been agreed upon, the two countries still couldn't get along. They were ready to fight again, so the second phase of the Hundred Years' War, called the Caroline War (1369–89), began. Spies aided France in learning England's fighting methods. Armed with this knowledge, the French soldiers were better mobilized with the hand-to-hand combat tools that had brought England victory in the first phase of the Hundred Years' War. This time, the win went to France. Once again, a truce was signed.

At It Again
The truce didn't last, and the Lancastrian War (1415–29) broke the peace as England attacked. Outnumbered, the English engaged their previous tactics and caught France off guard. The French succumbed to defeat. They refused to accept terms, however, so the truce was left up in the air. The Lancastrian War dragged on until Joan of Arc came forward to claim that she was destined to lead France to triumph over England. She did, in fact, win many a great victory, but her efforts didn't end the fighting, and she suffered execution at the hands of the English. Nonetheless, Joan of Arc's reign did segue into France's eventual victory soon after her death.

All's Well That Ends Well?
Although it had appeared England would be the final victor in this series of wars, at the last minute, Philip the Good of Burgundy pulled his troops from England and turned things around for France. Additionally, France finally one-upped England's weaponry advantage with its new super stash of heavy artillery, mobile cannons. Although England dominated 100 years earlier with longbows, the new technology made them seem crude by comparison.

In the end, France earned back the majority of the land it had lost, with England retaining the city of Calais for roughly another century. Both countries learned the meaning of loyalty to homeland, and once again, during the final stretch of their century-long fight, their differences were settled with a treaty.

Fast Facts

- *The first Avon lady was Mrs. P.F.E. Albee of Winchester, New Hampshire, who went door-to-door selling Little Dot Perfume. An Albee Barbie doll was issued in 1997.*

- *The gluteus maximus, the muscle that makes up the buttocks, is the biggest muscle in the body.*

- *British geologist William Buckland was known for his ability to eat anything, including rodents and insects. When presented with the heart of French King Louis XIV, he gobbled it up without hesitation.*

- *In May 1861, a gold piece worth a dollar in the Union was worth $1.10 in Confederate currency. By war's end, that same piece of gold—still a Union dollar—was worth $60 in the Confederacy.*

- *Pianos come in 12 different sizes, ranging from the relatively tiny spinet (at about three feet in length) to the concert grand piano (nine feet long or more).*

- *While walking on the moon during the Apollo 14 mission, astronaut Alan B. Shepard became the first galactic golfer, driving a pair of dimpled domes into space.*

- *First Lady Eleanor Roosevelt was forced to carry a pistol in her purse after receiving a number of threatening letters during the Great Depression.*

- *More men than women are left-handed. Some psychologists have noted that lefties are more often found in creative fields.*

- *Immortalized in bronze by cowboy sculptor Tex Wheeler, renowned racehorse Seabiscuit took one look at his likeness and tried to take a bite out of the sculptor's $25,000 portrait.*

- *In 1955, nearly one in three American homes lacked full indoor plumbing.*

Bob Jones University Ahead: Keep to the Right

A school with a heritage of more than 80 years, Bob Jones University (BJU) has based its existence on religious fundamentalist principles. With "stricter than strict" school rules and a "holier than thou" attitude, BJU, located in Greenville, South Carolina, has earned its self-developed slogan, "The World's Most Unusual University."

Genesis

Born in 1883 in Alabama, Bob Jones, Sr., came from an extremely religious family. Jones led his first congregation at age 13 and became a licensed preacher within two years. By the 1920s, his ministry was second in size only to that of evangelist Billy Sunday. He soon realized the best way to spread the word was through the establishment of his own institute of higher learning.

Bob Jones College opened in Panama City, Florida, in time for the 1927–28 school year, though the Great Depression—combined with defaulted student payments—led to the school's bankruptcy in 1933. Not to be deterred, Jones found a deserted Methodist school in Cleveland, Tennessee, and continued his educational ministry there, also opening an elementary and high school known as "Bob Jones Academy." In 1947, physical expansion was no longer possible at the Tennessee campus, so the school moved to its present location in Greenville, South Carolina, where the college became a university.

Revelations

Jones's fundamentalist preaching in the academic setting embraced separatism—the university's religious teachings were to be kept separate from all other faiths. For example, Bob Jones, Jr., successor to his father's ministry, criticized the Roman Catholic Church, claiming that Catholicism was "not another Christian denomination" but rather "a satanic counterfeit." He also taught that "all popes are demon possessed."

Bob Jones University embraced racial segregation until 1971, when it allowed married African Americans to attend. Like many in the Deep South, the elder Jones believed in "separate but equal" opportunity, hoping to build "a school just like BJU, here in the South for the colored people." Exclusion of African American students was based on the fear that they might seek to date white students and possibly intermarry, creating a world Bob Jones, Sr., believed would be fit for the Antichrist. In 1975, however, the prospect of losing valuable tax exemptions led BJU to allow students of any race (married or not) to attend. Still, a prohibition on interracial dating remained in effect until 2000.

In keeping with its separatist stance, BJU avoided accreditation for many years, giving graduates of the school credentials that carried little weight in their search for a career in the outside world. Only recently has the school gained accreditation among Christian school organizations.

Judges

Students at BJU are not "typical" undergrads. You won't find them wearing personal mp3 players, T-shirts, or flip-flops around campus, nor will you see them sporting pierced navels or tattoos. School codes at Bob Jones University include curfews (that mandate "lights out" at midnight); no televisions (except for video game use), VCRs, or DVD players; and no jazz, country, rock, rap, or Christian contemporary music. Students living in residence halls are prohibited from going to movie theaters. Dress codes forbid facial hair and slippers, and men may only wear hats indoors at athletic facilities. Women are not allowed to wear shorts outside of their dorms, and "all dresses, skirts, pants, and shirts must be loose-fitting."

Bob Jones University continues to deliver 19th-century ideology in the 21st century, akin to trying to use a telegraph to connect to the Internet. Comparing his school to other institutions, Bob Jones III once stated, "All education is brainwashing. We wash with the pure water of God's Word, and they wash with the polluted waters of the New Age."

Unusual university? Indeed.

- *The first successful organ transplant was performed in December 1954 by surgeon Joseph Murray, who switched a kidney from one brother into his identical twin.*

He Said, She Said

I will never be an old man. To me, old age is always 15 years older than I am.

—*Francis Bacon*

I don't know who my grandfather was; I'm much more concerned to know what his grandson will be.

—*Abraham Lincoln*

Success is the ability to go from failure to failure without losing your enthusiasm.

—*Sir Winston Churchill*

I can resist everything except temptation.

—*Oscar Wilde*

The emotional, sexual, and psychological stereotyping of females begins when the doctor says, "It's a girl."

—*Shirley Chisholm*

I find it rather easy to portray a businessman. Being bland, rather cruel, and incompetent comes naturally to me.

—*John Cleese*

It is not enough to succeed. Others must fail.

—*Gore Vidal*

Sure there are dishonest men in local government. But there are dishonest men in national government too.

—*Richard M. Nixon*

Like the measles, love is most dangerous when it comes late in life.

—*Lord Byron*

I took a speed-reading course and read *War and Peace* in 20 minutes. It involves Russia.

—*Woody Allen*

A husband is what's left of a man after the nerve is extracted.

—*Helen Rowland*

Show me a good loser, and I'll show you a loser.

—*Vince Lombardi*

Love on the Set: The Bergman-Rossellini Scandal

It didn't take much to rock the staid conventions of society shortly after the end of World War II. A movie director and his leading lady found that out the hard way.

It began with a fan letter sent in 1949. "I saw your films ... and enjoyed them very much," the letter began. It was addressed to Italian film director Roberto Rossellini and written by none other than actor Ingrid Bergman, who wrote it after seeing Rossellini's movie *Open City*. Bergman's letter also suggested that he direct her in a film. Their resulting collaboration was 1950's *Stromboli*. That movie, however, was eclipsed by the controversy that swirled around the couple when it became known that the married Bergman was having a baby by Rossellini, who was also married. The ensuing scandal engulfed Bergman in a scarlet torrent of hatred so vitriolic that she would find herself branded on the floor of the U.S. Senate as "a horrible example of womanhood and a powerful influence for evil."

A Hollywood Success Story

Since taking America by storm in 1939's *Intermezzo*, the talented Swedish-born Bergman had costarred with Humphrey Bogart in *Casablanca*, been menaced by Charles Boyer in *Gaslight* (her first Oscar-winning role), and been romanced on-screen by Cary Grant, Gary Cooper, and Gregory Peck. Audiences loved her in strong but pious parts such as the nun in *The Bells of St. Mary's*. In fact, Bergman had been Hollywood's top box-office female draw three years in a row. To the public, the beautiful actor with the sunny smile had it all: a fabulous career, an adoring husband, and a devoted daughter. But privately, Bergman's marriage had entered rocky shoals, and she was looking for new acting challenges after the failure of her pet film project, *Joan of Arc*. Consequently, the idea of working with Rossellini—the director being hailed for his mastery of what would come to be called Italian neorealist cinema—was appealing. Bergman later admitted, "I think that deep down I was in love with Roberto from the moment I saw *Open City*."

On Location

Stromboli was filmed on location in Italy, and rumors of an affair between Bergman and Rossellini soon reached America. During filming, Bergman received a letter from Joseph Breen, head of America's stentorian Production Code office—which enforced morality in motion pictures—asking her to deny rumors of the affair. Instead, on December 13, 1949, this woman who had played a nun and other saintly figures admitted she was carrying Rossellini's love child. A firestorm of negative publicity followed the announcement.

Bergman was reproached by Roman Catholic priests and received thousands of letters denouncing her—she was warned not to return to America. On February 2, 1950, Bergman and Rossellini's son, Robertino, or Robin, was born. Less than two weeks later, *Stromboli* was released in the United States to disastrous reviews and very little business.

The Storm Grows

The scandal reached critical mass (and the height of lunacy) on March 14, when Senator Edwin C. Johnson railed against Bergman on the Senate floor. Johnson proposed a bill that would protect America from the licentious scourge that film stars of questionable "moral turpitude" such as Bergman threatened. He suggested future misconduct could be avoided if actors were required to be licensed, with the license being revoked for salacious behavior. Though this idea was met with derision, Bergman's career in Hollywood was all but dead.

After divorcing their spouses, Bergman and Rossellini wed in Mexico on May 24, 1950. The couple continued to make films together in Italy and had twin girls Isabella (who went on to her own film stardom) and Isotta Ingrid in 1952. By the time Bergman was hired to star in *Anastasia* in 1956, America was ready to forgive her, and the actor was rewarded with both the New York Film Critics Award and her second Best Actress Oscar. By that point, her marriage to Rossellini—tested by financial problems and the director's affair while making a film in India—was nearing an end.

Bergman would go on to another marriage and further acclaim in her career, but she was always quick to point to the importance of her relationship with Rossellini, and the two remained devoted. Bergman died on her birthday in 1982 of breast cancer.

Strange Justice

He Wants "Be Kind to Criminals Week"

The man broke into a house, tied up the terrified tenants, and even shot two of them (permanently blinding one) before fleeing. One of the victims wriggled free and dialed 911. Cops gave chase and, when the armed offender refused to stop, they shot him. He subsequently pleaded guilty to a long list of felonies. Then he sued the police for using excessive force in capturing him. A jury awarded the crook $184,000, but the trial judge and court of appeals both threw the claim out the window.

She Let Her Fingers Do the Walking

Troubled by the unsightly bulge around her midsection, a woman decided to get liposuction. Consulting her local phone book, she chose a physician—not bothering to determine whether the doctor was board certified in plastic surgery. In fact, the doctor she selected was actually a dermatologist. That, however, didn't stop him from performing the surgery. When the botched procedure left scars across her belly, she sued—the phone book company, blaming them for not noting whether the doctor was properly licensed in cosmetic surgery. A jury found in her favor, awarding $1.2 million to her and an additional $375,000 to her husband for loss of spousal services.

Now Don't Blow a Fuse

A young lady was sure she had uncovered a conspiracy that threatened all of humankind: The U.S. government was preparing to reinstate slavery around the world. She knew this because, of course, she was a cyborg, and being a cyborg allowed her to discover these threats telepathically. She sued two former U.S. presidents, a presidential candidate, and many top-level government agencies. It was suggested that the judge established a new world record in the fastest case dismissal of all time.

What—No Tip?

A tourist in a West Coast city was accosted by a mugger, who grabbed her purse and ran. A cabbie witnessed the whole thing and chased down the thug, pinning him to a wall and courageously making a citizen's arrest. The mugger didn't like the rough treatment (his leg had been broken), so he sued the cabbie and the taxi company for using excessive force. A jury gave the ruffian more than $24,000 for injuries suffered in the commission of the crime, but a judge later overturned the verdict.

Who Shot JFK? Conspiracy Theories

*Conspiracy theories are a favorite American pastime, right up
there with alien abductions and Elvis sightings. Perhaps no
conspiracy theories are more popular than the ones involving
that afternoon in Dallas—November 22, 1963—when the
United States lost a president. John F. Kennedy's life and
death have reached out to encompass everyone from Marilyn
Monroe to Fidel Castro, Sam Giancana to J. Edgar Hoover.*

- **The single-shooter theory:** This is the one the Warren Commission settled on—that Lee Harvey Oswald (and *only* Lee Harvey Oswald), firing his Mannlicher-Carcano rifle from the window of the Texas Book Depository, killed the president in Dealey Plaza. But this is the official finding, and where's the excitement in that?

- **The two-shooter theory:** A second shooter on the nearby grassy knoll fired at the same time as Oswald. His bullets hit Texas Governor John Connally and struck President Kennedy from the front. This theory arose after U.S. Marine sharpshooters at Quantico tried to duplicate the single-shooter theory but found it was impossible for all the shots to have come from the Book Depository.

- **The LBJ theory:** Lyndon Johnson's mistress, Madeleine Brown, said that the vice president met with powerful Texans the night before the killing. She claimed he told her, "After tomorrow those goddamn Kennedys will never embarrass me again—that's no threat—that's a promise." Jack Ruby also implicated LBJ, as did E. Howard Hunt, just before his death.

- **The CIA theory:** After Kennedy forced Allen Dulles to resign as head of the CIA following the Bay of Pigs fiasco, the CIA, resenting Kennedy's interference, took its revenge on the president. They'd had plenty of practice helping plotters take out Patrice Lumumba of the Congo, Rafael Trujillo of the Dominican Republic, and President Ngo Dinh Diem of Vietnam.

- **The Cuban exiles theory:** Reflecting more bitterness over the Bay of Pigs, the powerful Cuban exile community in the United

States was eager to see Kennedy dead and said so. However, this probably played no part in the assassination.

- **The J. Edgar Hoover and the Mafia theory:** The Mafia was said to have been blackmailing Hoover about his homosexuality for ages. The theory goes that when Attorney General Robert Kennedy began to legally pursue Jimmy Hoffa and Mafia bosses in Chicago, Tampa, and New Orleans, they sent Hoover after JFK as payback.

- **The Organized crime theory:** Chicago Mafia boss Sam Giancana, who supposedly shared the affections of Marilyn Monroe with both JFK and RFK—using Frank Sinatra as a go-between—felt betrayed when RFK went after the mob. After all, hadn't they fixed JFK's 1960 election? This theory is a tabloid favorite.

- **The Soviet theory:** High-ranking Soviet defector Ion Pacepa said that Soviet intelligence chiefs believed that the KGB had orchestrated the Dallas killing. But they were probably just bragging.

- **The Roscoe White theory:** According to White's son, this Dallas police officer was part of a three-man assassination team. The junior White, however, gives no indication of the reasons behind the plot.

- **The Saul theory:** A professional hit man was paid $50,000 to kill Kennedy by a group of very powerful, unknown men. He was also supposed to kill Oswald. Clearly, this theory isn't thick with details.

- **The Castro theory:** Supposedly the Cuban government contracted Oswald to kill Kennedy, telling him that there was an escape plan. There wasn't.

- **The Israeli theory:** Angry with JFK for pressuring them not to develop nuclear weapons and/or for employing ex-Nazis in the space program, the Israelis supposedly conspired in his assassination.

- **The Federal Reserve theory:** Kennedy issued Executive Order 11110, enabling the U.S Treasury to print silver certificates in an attempt to drain the silver reserves. It is theorized that such a development would severely limit the economic power of the Federal Reserve. Could this have played into his assassination?

People will probably still be spinning these theories in a hundred years. But then, everyone needs a hobby.

Alien

Directed by Ridley Scott, 1979's *Alien* was considered a "haunted house in deep space" film. The nightmarish creature, designed by imaginative artist H. R. Giger, was played by seven-foot-tall Bolaji Badejo. On the spaceship *Nostromo*, space traveler Kane, played by John Hurt, was infested by the alien and, to the utter shock of fellow crew members, his body ruptured. A baby alien puppet burst from Hurt's chest, spewing blood and guts across the faces of the unsuspecting actors in the scene. Veronica Cartwright's reaction of total shock was totally real.

Fargo

This compelling and quirky 1996 story about a kidnapping gone wrong came from the Coen Brothers. Set in frigid North Dakota and Minnesota, the film offered stellar performances from Frances McDormand, William H. Macy, and Steve Buscemi, among others. Opening titles indicate that *Fargo* is "a true story (that) took place in Minnesota in 1987." Interviews quoted the creators claiming the movie was "pretty close" to the facts. But news media reports offered no accounts of similar events, revealing this claim to be another practical joke from those crazy Coens.

The Fly

This 1958 horror film started as a short story that first appeared in *Playboy* magazine. Author James Clavell wrote the subsequent screenplay. Vincent Price liked to tell the story of how he and fellow actor Herbert Marshall nearly collapsed with laughter as they tried to shoot the scene in the garden where they are searching for the fly while a squeaky voice cried, "Help me! Help me!" They finally got through an acceptable take by turning almost back-to-back and not looking at each other.

The Godfather

The title role in this sprawling story of organized crime was one of the most coveted in Hollywood history. Imagine any of the following as the gruff and crafty Vito Corleone—Frank Sinatra, Anthony Quinn, Ernest Borgnine, TV stars David Jansen (*The Fugitive*) and Vince Edwards (*Ben Casey*), entertainer Danny Thomas, and even aging crooner Rudy Vallee. They all sought the part, but writer Mario Puzo and director Francis Ford Coppola could only foresee two actors as the Don—Laurence Olivier or Marlon Brando. Brando got the nod—and an Oscar (which he refused).

The Famed Canadian Group of Seven

A lot of things come in sevens: sins, dwarfs, colors in a rainbow, days in a week. Perhaps less known is that painters also come in sevens—namely, the seven Canadian landscape painters who formed the appropriately named Group of Seven in 1919.

Claiming a National Art Form

Members of the Group of Seven met in 1912 and 1913 as regular patrons of the Toronto Arts and Letters Club. They were all landscape painters who shared the sentiment that Canadian landscape art should be stylistically distinct from the Impressionist European landscapes popular at the time. The Seven's art was indeed strongly influenced by Impressionism, but there were several departures, such as the use of bold, vivid color; strong symbolism; and an altogether sharper and more potent feel.

The group went on excursions together to nearby hubs of pristine wilderness. One of their favorite destinations was Algonquin Park, where in 1917 one of the painters, Tom Thomson, died mysteriously in a canoeing accident. Were it not for his untimely death, the painters would surely have been known as the Group of Eight—they were not named until 1919, two years after Thomson's death. The Group of Seven consisted of Franklin Carmichael, Lawren Harris, A. Y. Jackson, Frank Johnston, Arthur Lismer, J.E.H. MacDonald, and Frederick Varley.

The group's first exhibition was held in 1920 at the Toronto Art Gallery. During the next decade, they traveled throughout Canada, painting landscapes and popularizing their art. Two members of the group, Jackson and Harris, made annual trips to the Arctic. Over the years, the group lost and gained members, making their name obsolete. In 1931, they officially disbanded, and the Canadian Group of Painters was formed.

The Legacy of the Seven

The Group of Seven was successful in instituting a uniquely Canadian school of art. Many of the group's members went on to teach at various institutions, and they all enjoyed prestige throughout their careers. They served as mentors and inspirations for subsequent generations of artists.

The most salient display of the group's legacy is the McMichael Canadian Art Collection, located just north of Toronto. The wealthy McMichael family collected the group's work, and in the 1960s they donated the entirety of their collection to the Province of Ontario, along with their large rural property. The McMichaels mandated that the museum must hold only works by the original Group of Seven or their contemporaries. Six members of the Group of Seven are buried in a small graveyard on the museum grounds.

A series of legal battles sprung up after the museum hosted modern artists whose work did not reflect the artistic tradition established by the Seven. The museum changed hands a few times, and its original vision was lost, but in 2004 a court ordered that the museum's original mandate be upheld. The museum is now home to works by the Seven and their followers, as well as art by Canadian aborigines.

Canadian Controversy

The Group of Seven has sparked much controversy among art historians. The Seven thought that Canada needed to have its own landscape art because, well, Canada has its own landscape: The often rough and jagged features of the land don't mesh well with Impressionism, which was founded in the more pastoral landscapes of Northern Europe.

The criticism is that the Seven's landscapes symbolically robbed Canadian aborigines of their proper claim to the land. The Seven wanted Canadian painters to paint their own land with a sense of ownership and pride; yet their paintings never included images of the indigenous structures that are found throughout the Canadian wild. This criticism lends more weight to the famed Seven quote that "the great purpose of landscape art is to make us at home in our own country." A tenuous compromise to this debate is found in the McMichael Canadian Art Collection's display of aboriginal art.

- *The Baby Ruth candy bar was not named for baseball slugger Babe Ruth but actually for President Grover Cleveland's daughter Ruth.*

The Truth About Monopoly

When the nation was in the depths of the Great Depression, people needed a distraction. If they couldn't corner the stock market in the real world, why not become property moguls on the game board?

Monopoly is as American as apple pie or Norman Rockwell. Yet, the story of how the most commercially successful board game came to be is a rather sordid tale. Apparently, despite information perpetuated for some 40 years by the game's manufacturer, "creator" Charles Darrow was not its true inventor at all. Darrow actually passed off Elizabeth Magie Phillips's concept as his own invention.

Fun for Landlords

On January 5, 1904, Phillips, aka Lizzie J. Magie, received a patent for The Landlord's Game. It was based on economist Henry George's belief that landowners should be charged a single federal tax to extend equality to renters, from whom landlords were, in George's opinion, disproportionately profiting. Magie created an educational game, demonstrating how a single tax would control land speculation.

Except for the fact that properties were rented rather than purchased, The Landlord's Game was suspiciously identical to Parker Brothers' Monopoly, which premiered almost 30 years later. Through the years, The Landlord's Game was passed through communities, evolving along the way. It picked up the name Monopoly despite Magie's intention for the game to be a teaching tool *against* the very idea of monopolies. The Atlantic City–inspired properties were also incorporated. This well-documented chain of events led to Charles Darrow, who learned the game at a hotel in Pennsylvania.

Enthralled, Darrow produced his own copies of the game and subsequently patented and sold "his" idea to Parker Brothers. The company conveniently forgot its refusal to buy the same game (under its old name) from Magie years earlier but promptly covered those tracks. It slyly bought out Magie's patent for a paltry $500, paid off at least three other "inventors" who had versions circulating, and cranked up its propaganda machine. Monopoly has sold in excess of 250 million copies.

Say It Ain't So

Myth: The word *news* was created by joining the cardinal directions of north, east, west and south.

Truth: Although this myth would be a tidy fit, unfortunately there is no truth to it. Describing current events as *news* is simply revealing what is going on that is new. Pluralize the word *new,* and plain and simple, you get news.

Myth: So grateful for their success in online dating, a couple from Romania chose the name *Yahoo* for their newborn son.

Truth: In many parts of the world, parents traditionally choose names in honor of ancestors or events. Sometimes, as would be the case in this mythical instance, names even recall a serendipitous occurrence such as finding love online. In this example, though, a baby named *Yahoo* turned out to be the result of a fabricating news reporter, not Internet-loving parents.

Myth: Dr. Benjamin Spock, the renowned child-care expert and author of several books, was father to a son who took his own life.

Truth: The now deceased Dr. Spock fathered two sons during his first marriage. Both sons, Michael and John, were successful in their chosen professions (in the museum and construction fields, respectively) and outlived their father, who died in 1998. Sadly, however, this rumor may have been based on the fact that Spock's grandson *did* kill himself. On Christmas Day, 1983, Peter Spock, the son of Michael, plummeted to his death from atop the Boston Children's Museum. He was only 22 years old.

Myth: Nine months after 9/11, hospitals around the country experienced an unusual surge of births.

Truth: Although the phenomenon of "blackout babies" has been well documented in other periods of devastation, couples were apparently *not* sticking close to home base, engaging in activities that are most often conducted with the lights off, in the time soon after the September 11 attacks.

Roles That Animals Have Played for Humans

Animals have been kept by humans for companionship, utility, and pleasure since prehistoric times. But the role of pets has evolved in the past few hundred years.

Animal Stars

Animals have been amusing people since the entertainment business began. Circuses have wowed audiences for hundreds of years, and Wild West shows have been a key attraction since the mid-1800s.

Starting in the 1950s, animals were introduced in television series, forever changing the way people related to their pets. *Fury* and *My Friend Flicka* showcased horses' relationships with their owners. Fury could kneel, limp, and knock boxes out of people's hands...and even smile for the camera! Mr. Ed refused to talk to anyone but his owner, but he'd count by pawing the ground the appropriate number of beats for anyone. A large black bear named Bruno costarred with Clint Howard on *Gentle Ben;* the bear slept with its trainer and drank Coca Cola as a treat.

It's been written that Suzy the dolphin, better known as Flipper, once saved TV producer Ivan Tors from drowning. Tors produced a number of shows, among them, *Gentle Ben.* That show and *Flipper* reportedly filmed near each other; supposedly, Bruno and Suzy were friendly.

But perhaps the most famous animal star to date was Lassie. A two-time Emmy winner, Lassie—whose original name was Pal—was owned by trainers Rudd and Frank Weatherwax. This honey-colored collie became a symbol of love, trust, and heroism after appearing in movies and debuting in the TV series (also called *Lassie*) in 1954.

During the course of an incredible 588 episodes, Lassie was transformed from a television star into a cultural icon. The Weatherwax brothers occasionally bred Lassie, whose descendants now number in the hundreds.

Beautiful, Brave, and Smart

Some animals exhibit great feats of bravery, often saving their owners from fire, danger, or medical trauma. Dogs have been known to alert neighbors when their owners become impaired or unconscious, wake people when they smell smoke, or save the inhabitants of the house from dangerous intruders.

Guide dogs provide invaluable service, too. Educated from puppyhood, these canines undergo rigorous training in guide-dog schools; only the very talented and those with special abilities graduate to become workers for the visually impaired. Recently, several organizations have begun training guide dogs to warn diabetics before they have seizures due to dangerously low blood-sugar levels. These dogs can detect a chemical imbalance while the person is sleeping; they then wake the person so he or she can immediately inject insulin. Now that's quite a nose.

I Wanna Be Like...

Some people prefer coming home to a pet with eight sticky legs, one that's scaly and poisonous, or one that can swing from room to room. Hollywood celebrities have encouraged the exotic pet trend, and John D. Consumer quickly picked up the habit faster than a case of lice. Monkeys, chinchillas, kangaroos, tarantulas, rodents, eagles, pythons, iguanas, and tropical fish top the list of animals that are sold in the United States; some are legally imported, some not. Demand for exotic pets is booming, but buyers beware: The CDC reports that most imported animals arrive with minimal screening and no quarantine, making zoonotic diseases (those that jump to humans) accountable for three-quarters of all emerging infectious threats.

So, whether they take their pets to Capitol Hill (as several politicians do), bring them to their medical offices (some dentists and doctors claim that animals help relieve the stress of procedures for many patients), or stick their heads in a lion's mouth, people will always have a strong relationship to animals ... real *and* fictional.

PALINDROMES

When you've got a word, phrase, or sentence that reads the same backward and forward, you've got a palindrome!

Marge lets Norah see Sharon's telegram.

Reviled did I live, said I, as evil I did deliver.

Stella won no wallets.

Vanna, wanna V?

Let O'Hara gain an inn in a Niagara hotel.

Egad! No bondage!

Step on no pets!

Yo! Bottoms up, U.S. motto, boy!

"Deliver My Band's DNA," by Mr. Evil Ed.

A Santa dog lived as a devil god at NASA.

a car, a man, a maraca

A prewar dresser drawer, Pa!

Ah, Satan, shall a devil deliver Hannah? Reviled lived Allah's Natasha!

Dennis, no misfit can act if Simon sinned.

Did I draw Della too tall, Edward? I did!

Evil Tim must at summit live.

Wontons? Not now.

Too far, Edna, we wander afoot.

Sycamore has a hero: Macy's.

So, Ida, adios!

Sh! Tom sees moths.

Oy! Oy! A tonsil is not a yo-yo!

"Not New York," Roy went on.

"To the Shores of Tripoli": America's First Foreign War

❖ ❖ ❖ ❖

Ever wonder why the U.S. Marines will fight their country's battles "to the shores of Tripoli"? Here's the answer.

On November 26, 1804, William Eaton, acting as an agent for the U.S. government, disembarked from the brig USS *Argus* at Rosetta, Egypt, to find Hamet Karamanli, the former ruler of Tripoli and leader of the Barbary pirates. A few years earlier, Hamet had been deposed in a coup and ultimately replaced by his brother Yusuf Karamanli. Eaton wanted Hamet to become the ostensible leader of an expedition to overthrow Yusuf, whose pirates had captured the frigate USS *Philadelphia* and its crew. The small U.S. Mediterranean Squadron was spread too thin, and the ships could never fight their way past the hundreds of guns guarding the port of Tripoli, so the town had to be taken by land. And Eaton needed to produce an army to do that.

Unsafe at Sea

For hundreds of years Britain, France, and Spain had been paying protection money to the Barbary pirates to leave their ships alone. The United States, now independent from Britain and no longer under its system of payments, became fair game. In 1785, after the merchant ships *Maria* and *Dauphin* were captured by swift pirate raiders, America suddenly became aware that there was a problem. American preachers and journalists thundered about "dark-skinned monsters holding Americans as slaves" (conveniently ignoring the fact that Americans held many thousand slaves of their own). Captured sailors of all nations wound up in the dungeons of Tripoli, Tunis, and Algiers, including Miguel de Cervantes, author of *Don Quixote*, who spent five years as a Barbary captive in the late 16th century.

Secretary of State Thomas Jefferson thought the United States had but three choices: Pay tribute to the pirates like the European countries (which he didn't favor); forbid American vessels to sail in the Mediterranean (which he couldn't enforce); or go to war (which he preferred). But in this case, Jefferson's preferences weren't taken into account. Instead, Congress allocated $40,000 to ransom the captives and $100,000 a year in payment. Apparently the pirates thought they could do better raiding, because they refused the offer.

Representative Robert Goodloe Harper made a stirring promise to spend "millions for defense, but not one cent for tribute," and Congress authorized $688,888.82 for the construction of six frigates, but an agreement on tribute was reached nonetheless. America would pay the pirates a large ransom (more than a million dollars) and yearly tribute. It was expensive and embarrassing, but cheaper than a full-scale war. America had a rich merchant fleet to protect.

This Means War

By 1797, John Adams had become president and all of the American captives had either died in prison or been released. For four years there was relative peace. Then, near the end of Adams's term, Yusuf Karamanli decided that the Americans weren't paying enough and declared war on the United States. That was fine with most Americans, who were fed up with paying tribute. Jefferson became president in 1801, and he saw America's fight with the Barbary pirates as a test of the young nation's mettle. He sent a six-ship squadron to the Mediterranean under Commodore Edward Preble.

Those six ships had to patrol more than 1,200 miles of coastline, a nearly impossible task. This was made more difficult when the frigate *Philadelphia* ran aground off Tripoli and was captured in October 1803. Something had to be done—such a warship could not be left in the hands of pirates.

On the night of February 16, 1804, Lieutenant Stephen Decatur led a raiding party, armed with cutlasses and tomahawks, into Tripoli harbor in small boats. He and his crew annihilated the Tripolitan prize crew and burned the *Philadelphia*—a feat that Britain's Admiral Nelson called "the most daring act of the age." But the biggest problem remained—the crew of the *Philadelphia* and Americans from other ships were still in the dungeons of Tripoli.

The American captives couldn't just wait out the war. While those with exploitable talents were treated well, most were tortured and forced to do hard labor. A favorite method of torture was the bastinado, where a captive was beaten on the soles of his feet, a tremendously painful punishment. Men were dying, committing suicide, or "going Turk" (converting to Islam and fighting for Yusuf).

Rescue Party

Back in Egypt, Eaton managed to scrape together 90 of Hamet's followers, joined by 50 Greek mercenary soldiers, 20 Italian gunners, and a fire-eating Englishman named Farquhar. About 300 Bedouin Arab cavalry completed the local contingent.

Eaton wanted to include 100 U.S. Marines from the fleet, now commanded by Captain Samuel Barron, but Barron refused. In the end, the only Americans who took part were Eaton, Lieutenant Presley O'Bannon of the marines with a sergeant and a few enlisted soldiers, and Midshipman Pascal Paoli Peck, U.S. Navy. So the sum total of marines going to "the shores of Tripoli" was ten.

On March 5, 1805, the expedition set off across the desert. Lacking most necessary equipment (such as water bottles) they stumbled into Bomba on April 15. They had been 25 days without meat and 15 days without bread. For two days, they'd eaten nothing at all. Smoke signals brought the USS *Argus,* which had ample provisions and one of two promised cannons.

The Battle of Derna

They set off for Derna, arriving on April 26. When an attempt to negotiate with the governor of the town brought the response "your head or mine," Eaton attacked. After some hours, during which his force took casualties and had its one cannon put out of action, Eaton decided on an all-out assault. Brandishing a sword and leading his force, Eaton swept through the barricades and took the town. Resistance collapsed, and the governor took refuge within his harem. It wasn't Tripoli, but it was close enough. Yusuf agreed to release American captives and leave American ships alone. The war was over.

In addition to the "Shores of Tripoli," there is one other lasting legacy of the Tripolitan War. To this day, when a marine officer is commissioned, he proudly receives a Mameluke saber like the one presented to the valiant Lieutenant O'Bannon by Hamet Karamanli.

Fast Facts

- *In the tenth century, the Grand Vizier of Persia, Abdul Kassem Ismael, carried 117,000 books with him as he traveled. It took 400 camels to carry the volumes.*

- *The average person loses as many as 40,000 dead skin cells every minute.*

- *In 1966, radio pioneer Gordon McLendon bought KGLA-FM in Los Angeles, changed the call letters to KADS-FM, and aired only commercials. He returned the station to "regular programming" in 1967.*

- *The first time an instant replay was seen on TV was during an Army-Navy football game on December 7, 1963. CBS director Tony Verna masterminded the idea.*

- *Candy bars in the early part of the 20th century included Chicken Dinner and Chick-O-Stick (neither of which contained chicken) and Baby Lobster bar (which was seafood-free).*

- *More than 25 percent of all the gold in the world is held in a vault in New York City. It's owned by 122 countries and organizations that buy, sell, and trade it there.*

- *The father of antiseptic surgery was Joseph Lister, a British doctor who treated kings and queens. Two postage stamps have been issued in the United Kingdom to honor his accomplishments.*

- *After Mexican army officers looted a French pastry restaurant in Mexico City in 1838, a brief war broke out between France and Mexico when Mexico failed to pay 600,000 pesos to cover the damages.*

- *Players who ran the floor in the first professional basketball league, which was formed in 1898, were paid $2.50 for home games and $1.25 for road matches.*

The IRA and Sinn Féin

The Irish Republican Army (IRA) and its political body, Sinn Féin, are two of the most controversial institutions in Ireland. Deciphering their history is like trying to trace the lineages of the old European monarchies—there are countless crossbreedings, divergences, and circuitously snaking twists along the way.

Back to the Beginning

The English infiltration of Ireland began in A.D. 1170, when the Normans, who had already colonized England, decided to make Ireland a part of their kingdom. In the following centuries, the Irish increasingly adopted the customs, system of government, and language of their English neighbors. For the Irish clans that continued to rule and practice their customs, English dominion was a constant threat.

Since the northern tip of Ireland is the farthest from England, the population there retained a culture distinct from the southern areas of the island. But in the early 1600s, Queen Elizabeth I established the Plantation of Ulster in Northern Ireland, and colonists from England, Scotland, and Wales flooded the land. The native Irish Catholics in Ulster were forced to the margins of society.

Thus began the sectarian struggle in Northern Ireland that continued for centuries. The largely Protestant descendants of the colonization of Ulster fought—militarily, culturally, ideologically—with the largely Catholic descendants of the area's original inhabitants. It was within this inflammatory context that the IRA and Sinn Féin emerged.

The Early Days of Sinn Féin and the IRA

According to Irish political lingo, those who seek a united Ireland free from English rule are called *nationalists,* while those who desire continued political allegiance with England are called *unionists.* Sinn Féin was founded as a political party in 1905 by a nationalist who wanted Ireland to establish its own monarchy. During this same period, a group of young revolutionary nationalists sought to establish a socialist democracy in Ireland. They built up an army and staged the famous Easter Rising of 1916. Although the rebellion was quickly suppressed, supporters of the nationalist movement formed the Irish Republican Army in the following years. The political party Sinn Féin had been mistakenly credited with the Easter Rising, so from that point on, it was considered the political arm of the IRA.

The Irish War of Independence, which consisted of bloody guerrilla warfare between England and the IRA, was fought between 1919 and 1921. The Anglo-Irish treaty of 1922 officially liberated the southern 26 counties of Ireland from English rule but kept the 6 counties of Northern Ireland under English control. Sinn Féin negotiated the treaty, but some party members were none too happy with the decision to divide Ireland. When the agreement was ratified, many members of Sinn Féin defected, taking with them the anti-treaty contingent of the IRA.

Civil war ensued. The pro-treaty forces in Ireland, assisted by the English, won the war. The Irish Free State (now the Republic of Ireland) gained its independence, while Northern Ireland remained part of the United Kingdom.

Schism in the Party

After the end of the civil war, Sinn Féin split. Some members founded the new Free State's political parties, while those opposing the government became a radical political party that would not participate in the parliament. The IRA became a fringe paramilitary group, also consisting of those who refused to accept the existence of the Free State or acknowledge that Northern Ireland was part of the United Kingdom. During the 1940s, '50s, and '60s, the IRA carried out attacks on police stations in Northern Ireland and staged political assassinations and intermittent bombings.

During the 1960s, many members of Sinn Féin adopted a more Marxist outlook. They began to denounce the bloody tactics of the IRA. At the same time, violence and rioting continued in Northern Ireland, where nationalists and Catholics protested the civil rights abuses that were practiced against them by Protestants and unionists.

In an attempt to abstain from violence, the IRA failed to protect the Catholic communities of Northern Ireland and the group splintered. The Official IRA and the Official Sinn Féin favored a peaceful approach to securing a united Ireland. The Provisional IRA and Provisional Sinn Féin, however, believed that violence was the answer. They also continued to abstain from parliamentary politics. The Official Sinn Féin has since morphed into other Irish leftist parties, such as the Labour Party and the Workers Party. The IRA and Sinn Féin of today are descendants of the Provisional IRA and Sinn Féin.

The Troubled Pathway to Peace

In 1972, British paratroopers killed 14 unarmed demonstrators in what became known as the Bloody Sunday massacre. In the aftermath of this event, IRA membership dramatically increased. The IRA became a clandestine operation with a complex and ambiguous network of terrorist cells, while Sinn Féin sought to establish itself as a legitimate political party. The British government suppressed the IRA and its sympathizers: During the '70s and '80s, thousands of political prisoners were arrested. Meanwhile, the IRA terrorized communities in Northern Ireland, murdering or torturing civilians suspected of being informants. They also started bombing England.

The popularity of Sinn Féin was jeopardized by the unpopularity of the IRA. Most nationalists in Northern Ireland, while sympathetic to the IRA, preferred a peaceful approach to negotiations with England. In 1986, Sinn Féin leader Gerry Adams sought to bring the party into mainstream politics, while a group led by Ruairí Ó Brádaigh refused to do so until a united, free Ireland was established. The latter group broke off to form the radical Republican Sinn Féin.

Progress at Last

Adams's Sinn Féin is now a major player in Irish politics. In 1997, an IRA cease-fire was declared. In 1998, the monumental Belfast Agreement paved the way for self-determination for Northern Ireland. Yet the implementation of the agreement remains troubled. One provision was that the IRA decommission all of its weapons, and indeed this qualification has been met. Sinn Féin denies any connection with violence instigated by those claiming affiliation with the IRA, but allegations have been made against top Sinn Féin officials regarding their continued involvement. Moreover, some Sinn Féin officials have been accused of being double agents for the UK.

As for the IRA, violence continues under the auspices of newly created fringe groups such as the "Real IRA." Sinn Féin's connection with the IRA remains ambiguous, yet its popularity has grown substantially due to its involvement in the peace process and its support of reforms in areas such as health care and minority rights. Sinn Féin is now the largest nationalist party in Ireland.

More Odd Beer Names

❖ ❖ ❖ ❖

*Here's another helping of some of those oddly
named American and Canadian brands.*

- Polygamy Porter
- Flying Dog In-Heat Wheat Hefeweizen
- Ruination
- Dead Guy Ale (with a label that glows in the dark)
- White Dog Cafe Leg Lifter Lager
- Cave Creek Chili Beer
- Doggy Style Classic Pale Ale
- Cold Cock Winter Porter
- Dixie Crimson Voodoo Ale
- Sweaty Betty Blonde Wheat

- Stinky Hippie
- Blood of 1,000 Corpses
- Horse You Rode in On
- Hoppin' to Heaven India Pale Ale
- Otay Buckwheat Ale
- Crop Circle Extraterrestri-Ale Amber Ale
- Kilt Lifter Scotch Ale
- Tire Biter Ale
- Bard's Tale Beer
- Mothership Wit

He Said, She Said

It is sad to grow old but nice to ripen.

—Brigitte Bardot

Heredity is a splendid phenomenon that relieves us of responsibility for our shortcomings.

—Doug Larson

I think patriotism is like charity—it begins at home.

—Henry James

Women who seek to be equal with men lack ambition.

—Timothy Leary

Beautiful young people are accidents of nature, but beautiful old people are works of art.

—Eleanor Roosevelt

I am not the only person who uses his computer mainly for the purpose of diddling with his computer.

—Dave Barry

Marriage can be viewed as the waiting room for death.

—Mike Myers

The shower is the greatest invention. I don't like to take a bath. I don't like to wash my face in the water I've been sitting in.

—Lewis Grizzard

He was a self-made man who owed his lack of success to nobody.

—Joseph Heller

Time rushes toward us with its hospital tray of infinitely varied narcotics, even while it is preparing us for its inevitably fatal operation.

—Tennessee Williams

Fear is the foundation of most governments.

—John Adams

Love is an irresistible desire to be irresistibly desired.

—Robert Frost

Wit has truth in it; wisecracking is simply calisthenics with words.

—Dorothy Parker

Crime and Funishment: When Mobsters Screw Up

Not everything goes off without a hitch. In fact, it rarely does. Here are some examples of some of the most-botched crime jobs in history.

Organized crime is serious business. After all, it usually involves violence, weapons, other people's money, the law, and prison. With those pieces loose on the chessboard, it's really easy to mess up. Take the two New York mobsters who agreed to do a little job: hit Al Capone. They had a nice trip on the Twentieth Century Limited, but in Chicago they were met at the train, taken someplace quiet, and beaten to death. Pieces of them were sent back with a note: "Don't send boys to do a man's job."

Don't Mess with the Wrong Guy

There's also the mistake of not knowing who you're dealing with. Faced with debts in his electrical business, Florida businessperson George Bynum borrowed $50,000 from a mob loan shark. He was able to make $2,500 payments on the interest, but he couldn't pay off the principal, so he decided to go into the crime business himself. He tipped off a burglary gang about a house that he had wired, in exchange for a cut of the take. The burglars broke in, but the home owner was there, and they beat him up. The owner was Anthony "Nino" Gaggi, a Gambino family mobster.

Gaggi found out that Bynum had planned the burglary. On July 13, 1976, John Holland called Bynum from the Ocean Shore Motel and pitched a lucrative wiring contract. When Bynum arrived at the motel, Gaggi and some friends were waiting, and that was the last anyone heard from Bynum.

If You're Laying Low, *Lay Low!*

Often the bungling of criminals is much more humorous. Enrico "Kiko" Frigerio was a Swiss citizen, and when the famed Pizza Connection—a scheme to push heroin through pizza parlors in New York—was broken by the FBI in 1984, he fled to Switzerland. Frigerio stayed there for years, until a documentary film crew decided to do a movie about his life. As technical advisor, he decided to give them a tour of his old New York haunts, but when he stepped off a plane onto U.S. soil, he was immediately arrested. Frigerio hadn't realized that he was still under indictment. Oops!

A Continuing Comedy of Errors

Jimmy Breslin once wrote a comic novel called *The Gang That Couldn't Shoot Straight.* He must have been thinking about New Jersey's DeCavalcante crime family, the only one never given a seat on the Mafia's ruling commission. Vincent "Vinnie Ocean" Palermo ruled the DeCavalcante family like a bad Marx Brothers movie. Once, Palermo's men were given a supply of free cell phones—supplied by the FBI to tap their conversations. Another time, Palermo put a .357 Magnum to the head of a boat mechanic to force him to admit that he'd ruined the motor on Palermo's speedboat. "I was so mad, I bit his nose," Palermo said.

Then there was the time that Palermo and the missus went on vacation, and he decided to hide the family jewelry—$700,000 worth—in the bottom of a trash bag. "My wife took the garbage out for the first time in 20 years, and that was the end of the jewelry."

Finally, in 1999, Palermo was arrested and agreed to turn informant in exchange for leniency in sentencing. He helped to put away such stalwarts as Frankie the Beast, Anthony Soft-Shoes, and Frank the Painter. Palermo himself admitted to four murders, including that of newspaper editor Frank Weiss. He said that it was a good career move: "I shot him twice in the head. They made me a captain." He will not be missed.

- *When he was 39, President Franklin Roosevelt suffered from polio, which left him paralyzed from the waist down. Of more than 35,000 photos of Roosevelt, only two show him in a wheelchair.*

Fumbling Felons

Sometimes You Just Need a Hug

Crime scenes can often be confusing places, with victims and onlookers in a state of shock, not sure quite what has happened. But some crimes have a stronger sense of surreality than others. One early summer night, a man crashed the patio of a private party at a Capitol Hill home in Washington, D.C. He held a gun to the head of a 14-year-old guest and demanded money, or he would "start shooting!" The remaining five guests froze for what they later said seemed like minutes; everyone looked at each other in shock. Finally, one guest suggested to the gunman, "Why don't you have a glass of wine with us?" The robber agreed, took a sip, and replied, "Damn, that's good wine." He proceeded to take another sip, then ate some Camembert cheese that was on the table. Looking around, he put away his gun and apologized. "I think I may have come to the wrong house.... I'm sorry.... Can I get a hug?" One by one, the guests took turns giving him a hug. The gunman mumbled to himself, "That's really good wine," then asked for a group hug. With arms outstretched, the guests complied. Apparently satisfied, the would-be robber left the patio and walked off with a wine glass full of the expensive wine. The guests—unsure of what exactly had just happened—simply walked in the house, locked the door, and stared at each other in silence. One guest called the police, and when the officers arrived, they found the empty crystal wine glass sitting in the alley behind the home—unbroken. No fingerprints were found. Nothing was stolen. There were no reports of an arrest.

Driving Lessons Not Included

Two car thieves envisioned pulling a "gone in 60 seconds" type robbery. Their heist, however, took a little longer. With their eyes on a red Ford GT, the criminals busted into a California car dealership and pillaged offices until they found the key safe. After busting it open, they hopped in the sporty number, turned the ignition, and listened to the quiet of a dead engine. Thinking quickly, the pair jump-started the car from a battery charger and again they were off—until they reached the locked gates outside. They grabbed the keys to a Lincoln Navigator and smashed down the gates. Apparently, the criminals never learned how to handle the 550-horsepower monster. The Ford GT was found only a few miles away with $30,000 in damage.

Marilyn Monroe Copycats

Depending on your age, when you think of a Marilyn Monroe imitator, you may picture a drag queen or even an early-1990s Anna Nicole Smith. But Marilyn copycats go back to the 1950s, when the actress was still alive and working.

During Marilyn Monroe's heyday, men and women alike couldn't get enough of the star. Her movies entertained, her personal life made headlines, and her sex appeal shook a modest America to its core.

Monroe had a production contract with 20th Century Fox, and the company struck gold with her. There was certainly unmet demand for more sexy starlets like her—so much so, in fact, that other studios took notice, scrambling to sign the next Marilyn Monroe. The bustier, the better—performing talent wasn't always a deciding factor.

Monroe may quickly have been typecast as a sexpot or a good-time gal, but she was no idiot. She was fully aware of the copycat phenomenon. "These girls who try to be me, I guess the studios put them up to it, or they get the ideas themselves. But gee, they haven't got it. You can make a lot of gags about it like they haven't got the foreground or else they haven't the background."

Of course, none of the copycats had the same success as Monroe, and many faded into obscurity after B-movie stardom. Marilyn Monroe's real story is pretty hard to beat, but here are the stories of some of the more notable Marilyn knockoffs.

Jayne Mansfield

Probably the most successful blonde in the faux-Marilyn bunch, Jayne Mansfield was credited as not only being a buxom beauty but also as having actual acting chops. One thing she definitely had a knack for was PR, and undoubtedly, if she were still alive today, she would be no stranger to *Entertainment Tonight* or TMZ.com.

Born Vera Jayne Palmer, Mansfield kept the last name from her first marriage—to Paul Mansfield at age 16—because she liked the sound of it. Throughout her career, she claimed that her IQ was an impressive 163, but that was hardly a selling point—she was more famous for being the first big-name actress to appear nude on the silver screen. Obviously comfortable with her body, Mansfield had more than one public "wardrobe malfunction." Those, along with her much-publicized love life, led to an amazing 2,500 photographs in newspapers during a few months in 1956 and 1957.

Of her three marriages, her most famous was to Mr. Universe 1955, Mickey Hargitay. The couple enjoyed sharing the spotlight and making babies—they had three children, including daughter Mariska, star of the popular TV show *Law and Order: Special Victims Unit.*

Press came easy to Mansfield, but movie roles did not. She found much success working the nightclub circuit, making $35,000 a week at her peak. En route to one gig, however, Mansfield, her manager (and lover), and the three Hargitay kids were in a terrible accident. Their car slammed into the back of a semitrailer, peeling the top off and instantly killing the adults in the front seat. The children survived with little physical harm, and Mansfield again made headlines, as pictures of the gruesome crash scene made their way into newspapers around the country.

Mamie Van Doren

Along with Monroe and Mansfield, Mamie Van Doren rounded out what was affectionately called the "Three Ms." What she lacked in fame and IQ, Van Doren made up in sheer sex appeal. Born Joan Lucille Olander, she seemed fully aware of her copycat status—her stage name, taken from the noted intellectual Van Doren family, was a stab at Mansfield's claimed IQ. She milked the role, signing a contract with Universal Studios to star in typecast roles as the thrill-seeking bad girl. And Van Doren didn't let something as trivial as a meaningful acting career stop her from having fun. She oozed sexuality; in the 1980s, a book detailing trysts with many Hollywood leading men brought her back into the spotlight.

Keeping up with the times and technology, Van Doren keeps her (admittedly, mostly geriatric) fans on the edge of their computer seats via her Web site, which features vintage and modern photos of the star and her blog. She's also got a MySpace page. One recent venture is Mamietage, a custom-blend red wine.

Sheree North

While considered a talented actress and an even more talented dancer, Sheree North's potential was never fully realized, as 20th Century Fox used her mostly to threaten Marilyn Monroe when she got out of line (although Monroe was hardly moved). North's biggest break came when Monroe turned down a part in *How to Be Very, Very Popular.* When the heyday of the blonde bombshell began to fade, North slipped into obscurity and resurfaced years later in numerous television roles on shows including *The Golden Girls* and *Magnum, P.I.* Her most famous modern gig, undoubtedly, was as Babs Kramer, Kramer's mother on *Seinfeld.* She revealed his first name, Cosmo, to fans. In 2005, she died of unspecified complications from surgery.

Diana Dors

Known as the "English Marilyn Monroe," Diana Dors was the curvaceous leading lady of the UK in the '50s and '60s. Despite being overshadowed by the living legend that was Monroe, Dors actually appeared in her first film in 1947, the same year Marilyn first flitted across the silver screen.

Born Diana Mary Fluck, Dors changed her surname to that of her maternal grandmother at the suggestion of her first director—he feared that *Fluck* would lend itself to crude suggestions. An early bloomer, she first appeared as a pinup at age 13. Dors signed her first film contract at 17 and later found herself in the limelight as the sexy siren in films such as *Yield to the Night* and *Lady Godiva Rides Again.*

As a rising star, she flitted from man to man until she married Dennis Hamilton in 1951. With a focus on PR, he helped propel her to stardom; he may have been the impetus behind her purchase of a Rolls-Royce, a prop that allegedly enabled her to raise her fee for appearing in a review from £25 to £40 a week. The couple was already separated when Hamilton died in 1959. Dors married twice more, to Richard Dawson and Alan Lake, who committed suicide months after Dors's 1984 death from cancer.

Marshall Field: A Chicago Institution

❖ ❖ ❖ ❖

*It's hard to imagine what Chicago would be like
today if Marshall Field hadn't lived there.*

Aside from the legendary flagship store that bore his name for
125 years, Marshall Field's credits to the city of Chicago include:
the Field Museum, the Museum of Science and Industry, the John
G. Shedd Aquarium, and the University of Chicago. That's quite an
influence to wield over a single city, all due to Field's generosity and
philanthropy.

The Man Behind the Legendary Clock

Born in Conway, Massachusetts, Field moved to Chicago when he
was 21 and started working at a dry-goods merchant. Within ten
years, he became a senior partner at his own establishment, Field,
Palmer, Leiter & Co. In 1881, Field bought out his business partners and changed the store's name to Marshall Field and Company.

Field changed the face of shopping to reflect the extravagance
of the gilded age in the late 1800s. Returns accepted and refunds
issued with a smile are just a couple of the ideas that he established.

The department store café developed after a clerk shared her
lunch with a tired shopper. Immediately, Field thought of opening a
tearoom so shoppers wouldn't have to leave to eat. Traditional dishes
join new favorites today at the Walnut Room.

Field's also started the first bridal registry and revolving credit
and was the first store to use escalators. Marshall Field's book
department pioneered the concept of the book signing, and Christmas at Field's became legendary, with its downtown windows filled
with sparkling animated displays. The phrases "Give the lady what
she wants" and "The customer is always right" are slogans attributed
to Field and his colleague, Harry Gordon Selfridge.

An Era Ends

In 2005, Federated Department Stores acquired Marshall Field's and
changed the name in 2006 to Macy's Department Store. His name
may be gone, but Field's legacy in the retail business will carry on.

The Times They Are A-Changin'

1991

January 12: The U.S. Congress passes a resolution authorizing the use of military force to liberate Kuwait from Iraq. Operation Desert Storm will begin on January 17.

February 1: South African President F. W. de Klerk announces he will repeal all of the country's apartheid laws.

February 4: Major League Baseball officially bans Pete Rose from being elected to the Hall of Fame.

February 8: Pitcher Roger Clemens signs a contract with the Boston Red Sox for $5,380,250 per year, a record at the time.

March 3: Four Los Angeles police officers are captured on amateur video beating Rodney King.

April 1: The U.S. Supreme Court rules that race is not a valid reason to bar jurors from serving.

April 17: The Dow Jones average closes above 3,000 for the first time.

April 22: Johnny Carson announces he will retire from *The Tonight Show.*

June 12: Boris Yeltsin is elected President of Russia, which is still a Soviet republic.

July 22: In Milwaukee, Jeffrey Dahmer is arrested after the remains of 11 men and boys are found in his apartment.

August 15: Paul Simon's free concert in Central Park is attended by 750,000 people.

October 6: Elizabeth Taylor marries for the eighth time, this time to Larry Fortensky.

October 7: Law professor Anita Hill accuses Supreme Court nominee Clarence Thomas of making sexually inappropriate comments. The Senate confirms Thomas to the Supreme Court on October 15.

November 17: Fox TV airs the first network condom commercial.

December 21: Actor Jane Fonda marries millionaire and CNN founder Ted Turner.

Groundbreaking Scientific Theories (Part III)

In more recent years, science has continued to lead the way in helping society understand its surroundings. Here are a few more examples of those who took giant leaps in logic.

New Radioactive Elements Discovered by the Curie Duo

In 1896, a physicist named Antoine Henri Becquerel accidentally discovered the phenomenon of radioactivity. No one quite knew what it meant. But two years later, Marie Curie and her husband, Pierre, discovered radium, an element so radioactive that it actually glows in the dark! That same year, they also discovered polonium, naming it after the country where Marie was born—Poland.

Through their experiments, Marie and Pierre Curie began to discover the properties of radiation and new elements. This was quite dangerous, even if they didn't know it. Radio-activity can be harmful, even fatal, after prolonged exposure without proper shielding from its rays. Back then, however, the discovery of radiation was so recent that no one knew it was dangerous, not even the Curies. Their laboratory conditions were considered primitive, even by the standards of the early 1900s. The scientists handled the radioactive substances without protective equip-ment, often carrying it in their pockets, keeping it next to their bed at night, and holding it with their bare hands! In fact, the original notebooks used by the Curies are so contaminated by radiation that they must be kept in a sealed lead vault at the Bibliothèque Nationale in Paris. They are so dangerous that anyone wishing to view them must sign a waiver releasing the authorities of any liability for exposure to radioactivity. The radium that infects them has a half-life of about 1,600 years, so in the 37th century, they'll be only half as radioactive as they are now. It will be quite some time before they are safe to handle without protective equipment.

In 1903, the Curies, along with Becquerel, won the Nobel Prize in Physics for their research on radiation. Sadly, weakened by his exposure to radiation, Pierre died three years later, at the age of 46, in a traffic accident—it was rumored that he was not strong enough to dodge the vehicle that hit him. Marie went on to receive a second Nobel Prize in Chemistry (for the discovery of radium and polonium) in 1911. She died in 1934 of leukemia—presumably caused by her prolonged exposure to radiation. She was 66.

The Atomic Structure According to Rutherford

You can feel this book in your hands, right? It's made of paper and ink, right? Well, not exactly. It's made of millions and millions of atoms. Atoms are so tiny they can't be seen with the naked eye, but everything—and that means *everything*—is made up of atoms. The weird thing is that atoms are made up of mostly nothing but empty space. That was proved by a physicist named Ernest Rutherford.

Born in New Zealand in 1871, Rutherford was the fourth of 12 children. Voracious for scientific knowledge and understanding, he studied and taught at a number of universities around the world, including Cambridge University in England and McGill University in Canada. In 1909, Rutherford discovered that atoms were similar to the solar system, in that they have a nucleus with various particles orbiting around it. With that discovery, however, Rutherford came to believe that most of an atom is just empty space. This disputed the ruling theory at the time, which was that atoms were like "plum pudding." Scientists presumed that an atom had the same consistency throughout except for the electrons positioned like plums within the atom.

When Rutherford bombarded a thin piece of gold foil with alpha particles (a weak type of radiation), a small percentage of the alpha particles scattered at extremely wide angles. The physicist described the result "as if you fired a fifteen-inch shell at a piece of tissue paper and it came back and hit you." The reflected alpha particles were colliding with the previously unknown, positively charged nucleus. His theory was that the atom consisted of a tightly packed nucleus, a lot of empty space, and a few negatively charged particles orbiting around it. Rutherford's theory became the foundation for understanding the nature of the atom and nuclear physics. He died at age 66 in 1937.

Nuclear Fission According to Hahn

They say curiosity killed the cat, but satisfaction brought him back. If you applied that principle to a physicist, what would you get? A Nobel Prize in Chemistry—just what physicist Otto Hahn received in 1944.

When Italian physicist Enrico Fermi created several radioactive elements by bombarding the heaviest natural element, uranium, with neutrons, Hahn became keenly interested. He wanted to understand how uranium could turn into two or more different elements.

Born in Germany in 1879, Hahn studied chemistry at the University of Marburg. After graduating and conducting research at several universities, Hahn returned to Germany to further his studies. Along the way, he discovered several radioactive elements and made many discoveries. Prior to winning the Nobel Prize in 1944, Hahn had been nominated as early as 1914 for discovering a radioactive element called mesothorium 1. His greatest discovery, however, came in 1938.

In collaboration with Lise Meitner and Fritz Strassman, Hahn successfully split the nucleus of a uranium atom and discovered that some of its mass was converted to energy. The rest was divided into two lighter nuclei. The physicists called this process fission. The implications astounded their fellow scientists, who believed that the energy created from splitting a uranium atom could cause a chain reaction that would, in turn, split other uranium atoms. They further theorized that this energy could be harnessed and put to use. This particularly interested the Nazi German government, which forced many scientists to research the theory in an attempt to create a new kind of weapon—an atomic bomb. Hahn is credited with being the "founder of the atomic age." He died in 1968.

The Mondo Movie Craze

*This movie trend in the 1960s was all about celebrating
excess for its own sake. How far would they go?*

With a warning that reads in part: "The duty of the chronicler is
not to sweeten the truth but to report it objectively," *Mondo Cane*
(*A Dog's World*), the first mainstream "shockumentary," unspooled
before thrill-seeking American audiences in 1963. The film promised to "enter a hundred incredible worlds where the camera has
never gone before" and presented a loosely strung travelogue of
outrageous rites, repulsive rituals, and downright bizarre behavior.

More, More, More

A combination of archival footage and staged sequences shot in
grainy documentary style to appear authentic, *Mondo Cane* featured
a wide range of shocking footage—including mass animal slaughter,
a group of religious women tongue-bathing parish steps, a visit to a
pet cemetery, diners feasting on cooked insects, a match in which
two natives conk each other on the head with logs, and plenty of topless African women. The 108-minute film, underscored by sardonic
narration, weaves back and forth between the "primitive" and the
"civilized" world. The outrageousness is further accentuated by the
inclusion of a perky song titled "More" that is endlessly repeated
(the song garnered an Oscar nomination for Best Song in 1963).

Mondo Cane was cowritten and directed by Paolo Cavara and
Gualtiero Jacopeti. The word *mondo* quickly became a euphemism
for "extreme." The movie was so popular around the world that it
started a trend of similar films throughout the 1960s. Each subsequent *mondo* release attempted to top the previous one. Titles
included *Mondo Macabro, Mondo Mod, Mondo Exotica,* and *Mondo
Topless.* By the time *Mondo Bizarro* was released in 1966, the footage in the films was almost all staged. The genre petered out by
the end of the decade, but a resurgence of the genre occurred in
the late 1970s with the *Faces of Death* series, whose hallmark was
explicit and gory sequences. The influence of the *mondo* films can
be seen in recent reality TV shows such as *Fear Factor* and *Survivor.*

Fast Facts

- A metal mechanical bank from the early 1900s dubbed *Shoot the Chute* and featuring the comic strip character Buster Brown—in working order without scratches and dents—is worth $30,000 or more to collectors.

- The Communist leader of Romania, Nicolae Ceausescu—known as "the giant of the Carpathians"—banned the game Scrabble because he felt it was too intellectual. He also believed that baseball was subversive.

- The average child will require 8,000 diaper changes before he or she is potty trained.

- President William Howard Taft was so obese that he used a reinforced steel chair while dining.

- The manner and site of execution of those imprisoned in the Tower of London was primarily dependent on the station of the condemned. Nobles such as Anne Boleyn were beheaded in private.

- The biggest type of spider in the world is the goliath bird-eating spider, a dinner-plate-size behemoth native to parts of South America.

- According to legend, trainers put a goat in a racehorse's stall to keep the horse calm. If the goat was stolen, it was called "getting one's goat."

- Albert Woolson, a Union drummer boy during the American Civil War, died on August 2, 1956, at 108 years old. He was the last surviving veteran of the war.

- On August 21, 1975, Rick and Paul Reuschel of the 1975 Chicago Cubs combined to pitch a shutout, becoming the first brotherly duo to pull off such a feat.

Star-crossed Lovers:
Sylvia Plath and Ted Hughes

An icon to troubled teenage girls everywhere, poet
Sylvia Plath killed herself and became immortal.

She was a young American studying at England's Cambridge University on a Fulbright scholarship. He was an aspiring poet from a remote British mining town who had variously worked as a zoo attendant, a night guard, and a gardener. When they first met at a party in 1956, she bit so deeply into his cheek that she drew blood; he tore off her headband to ensure that they would meet again. They wed four months later, and that union—or rather, its shocking denouement—has been a fixture of gossip and literature ever since.

The Players

She was Sylvia Plath; he, Ted Hughes. They ultimately had two children (a girl born in 1960, a boy in 1962) during a tempestuous marriage that ended circa 1962, after he left her for Assia Wevill, a married family friend. But Wevill was more of a symptom than a cause.

When Hughes's book *The Hawk in the Rain* was published shortly after his marriage to Plath, he was hailed as one of the most important poets of his generation. Plath had been a precocious poet herself, first published at age 8, and much praised at Smith College. At the time of her marriage, however, her work was not gaining recognition, despite manic bursts in the wee hours that could produce two or three poems at a time. On top of professional angst, Plath suffered through raging arguments, crying babies, and Hughes's infidelity.

Plath's Final Statement

On February 11, 1963, 30-year-old Plath put milk and bread at her children's bedsides. She sealed her flat's kitchen with wet rags, put her head into the oven upon a neatly folded cloth, and turned on the gas. With this action, Plath became forever enshrined in the pantheon of brilliant-but-victimized women. It was a drastic final solution seen as a fabulous career move by Plath's contemporary, poet Anne Sexton: *"That* death was mine." As Sexton foresaw, Plath was celebrated as an unsung heroine by the burgeoning women's liberation movement, despite her delight in household chores such as washing and ironing (mundane domestic acts she deemed "celestial" in letters to her mother) and her willing subjugation to a "genius" husband, which made her feel "very feminine and admiring." Nonetheless, Plath came to be viewed by many young women as a protofeminist who had hoped in vain to have it all: an adoring husband, marvelous children, *and* a glamorous career.

Acclaim Too Late

Some of Plath's final poems appeared in the American magazine *Encounter* to great acclaim eight months after her death. Her poetry was also splashed across *Time* magazine, and her slightly fictionalized autobiography-as-novel, *The Bell Jar*—which among other things described her shock treatment for depression and a previous suicide attempt—caused a sensation when published in the United States in 1971 (it had been released under a pseudonym in England a month before her death). Plath's collected works, edited by Hughes, won her a posthumous Pulitzer Prize and helped make her one of the world's best-selling female poets.

But as the executor of Plath's estate, Hughes exercised what some saw as a jealous control over his late wife's writings, and he was even suspected of doctoring them as he saw fit. That he claimed to have destroyed some of her journal material (because, reportedly, it might hurt the children's feelings) was proof to many of his complicity in his wife's death. Hughes's bad reputation became writ in stone in 1969 when Wevill duplicated Plath's suicide-by-oven, taking their four-year-old daughter, Shura, with her. Yet Hughes declined to defend himself, even as crowds jeered him as a killer, and Plath's Yorkshire grave perpetually had his name chipped off by her angry fans. However, ongoing resentment toward Hughes failed to prevent his 1984 appointment to the esteemed post of Britain's Poet Laureate.

Another Point of View

Hughes finally told his side of the story in the 1998 book *Birthday Letters,* which was mostly written in the form of letters to Plath on each of her birthdays since her suicide. He claimed that she would push him away only to plead for his return, in a seemingly endless cycle of rejection and need. Worse, nothing he did was ever enough to exorcise the ghost of Plath's father, who died when Sylvia was only ten (this has the ring of truth, as Plath's most famous poem is the furious "Daddy"). As one of Hughes's friends summed up: "Long before he walked out of the house to be with someone else, it was already pretty clear that Plath had left him for her father," adding that Hughes had been at least as much a victim as Plath ever was. "His story has dovetailed with a particular moment in feminist thinking, a surge of political correctness and the tendency of people to read poems as life transcripts.... [The book] makes you feel that he never stopped loving her."

The case for rehabilitating Hughes's battered image was also helped by recent critical reappraisals of the situation. A professor and biographer of both Anne Sexton and Plath declared that "depression [had] killed" the latter, while another pundit announced that "the very source of Sylvia Plath's creative energy was her self-destructiveness." Even Plath's own mother sadly wrote: "Her physical energies had been depleted by illness, anxiety and overwork...some darker day than usual had temporarily made it seem impossible to pursue." Indeed, until recently, no one seems to have considered postpartum depression as a factor; after all, Plath's son was scarcely more than a year old at the time of her death.

As for Hughes, although he may have found a measure of contentment in a second marriage while ushering his children by Plath into adulthood, any sympathy that may have been engendered by *Birthday Letters* came too little, too late: Almost simultaneously with its publication, Hughes died at age 68.

- *English King Henry VIII ordered a cook be boiled to death in one of his own pots for poisoning 17 people in the household of the Bishop of Rochester.*

- *An average American will spend a little more than ten years watching TV. Of that, not quite one-third will be commercials.*

- *Abraham Lincoln had a five-dollar Confederate bill in his pocket when he was shot by John Wilkes Booth.*

Curious Classifieds

This is the model home for your future. It was panned by *Better Homes and Gardens*.

The hotel has bowling alleys, tennis courts, comfortable beds, and other athletic facilities.

Full-size mattress. Royal Tonic, 20-year warranty. Like new. Slight urine smell. $40.

For a successful affair, it's the Empire Hotel.

Tickle Me Elmo. New in box. Hardly tickled. $700.

Free dinner with any pest control job

Tired of cleaning yourself? Let me do it.

For sale—Diamonds, $20; microscopes, $15.

Girl wanted to assist magician in cutting-off-head illusion. Blue Cross and salary.

Wanted: chambermaid in rectory. Love in, $200 a month. References required.

The most romantic love songs of the '50s: including "16 Tons" by Tennessee Ernie Ford

Will swap white satin wedding gown (worn once) for 50 pounds fresh Gravy Train.

Modular sofas. Only $299. For rest or fore play.

Used tombstone, perfect for someone named Homer HendelBergen-Heinzel. One only.

Save regularly in our bank. You'll never reget it.

Springmaid sheets are known as America's favorite playground.

Valentine's Day Sale: Ty-D-Bol blue toss-ins.

Wanted: Unmarried girls to pick fruit and produce at night.

Illiterate? Write today for free help.

Used cars: Why go elsewhere to be cheated? Come here first!

No Regrets: The Life of American Poet Hart Crane

I am not ready for repentance;
Nor to match regrets. For the moth
Bends no more than the still
Imploring flame.

At first glance, the opening words of "Legend"—an early poem by Hart Crane—could almost be read as a challenge. Review the lines again, and the sadness that permeates them offers a glimpse into the troubled psyche of a young man who apparently felt more than just a little out of step with the rest of the world. In some ways, they might almost be considered the suicide note he never left when, at age 32, he leaped from the deck of a steamship into the Gulf of Mexico.

Although he died young, Crane succeeded in his life's goal of being remembered as a poet. While the amount of work he produced may have been small in comparison to others, students of American literature have expressed new interest in both his life and his writing in recent years—in Crane's case, the two were virtually inseparable. While every artist's work is influenced by his lifestyle, in many respects Hart Crane seemed to embody both the best and the worst aspects of his generation.

Understanding the Man

Harold Hart Crane was born on July 21, 1899, in the village of Garrettsville, Ohio, a tiny 2.5-square-mile town that today is home to a little more than 2,000 residents. His love of words was evident at an early age, but his father, a successful businessman, tried to turn Hart's attention toward more practical matters. When he wasn't focused on trying to change his son, the elder Crane was busy fighting with his wife, a devout Christian Scientist. As a result, Crane spent much of his childhood at his grandparents' home in Cleveland.

The aspiring writer discovered at an early age that he was homosexual—not something readily accepted by the world at that time. Crane felt that this was just another aspect of his personality that set him apart. Although he tried to comply with his father's wishes to fit in, after his parents divorced in 1916, he dropped out of school and fled to New York. Still determined to be a poet, Crane devoured the work of other wordsmiths in an effort to learn his craft. Although he lived in a garret and was forced to sell ads for poetry magazines to support himself, he knew that he was among kindred spirits. He spent every spare moment at the home of Margaret Anderson, founder and editor of *The Little Review,* who first recognized the talent of Ezra Pound and Robert Frost.

Testing the Waters

Crane grew discouraged when his own work went unappreciated— and climbed aboard an emotional roller coaster that he rode for the rest of his short life. He returned to Cleveland in 1922, where he spent his days writing advertising slogans. In his spare time, he wrote "My Grandmother's Love Letters," a charming poem that was soon accepted by a literary magazine. Encouraged, Crane returned to New York, where he relied on the generosity of friends, including playwright Eugene O'Neill and photographer Walker Evans, for necessities such as food and rent. Finally free of mundane concerns, he focused on his work. A year later, Crane completed "For the Marriage of Faustus and Helen," his first major poem.

Unlike some of his contemporaries who were breaking away from traditional forms, Crane didn't use free verse. He modeled his work on that composed by classic authors such as John Donne and modern poets such as Walt Whitman. His stanzas were rich with obscure imagery that at the same time evoked a sense of immediacy. Although the average reader may not have always been able to easily understand him, Crane was seeking new ways to use formal language to describe the frenetic fury of the Jazz Age.

Building a Reputation

Crane moved into a boardinghouse overlooking the Brooklyn Bridge, a view that would become as much an inspiration for him as it had for so many other artists and writers. His work started to appear in significant literary magazines, and he attracted a small audience that seemed to appreciate his poems. Although his personal life seemed filled with a growing sense of alienation, he was attempting to create a landscape of hope with his words. He played the role of social outcast to the hilt, however—besides flaunting his sexuality, he was frequently drunk and violent and was sometimes beaten up by the partners he chose for one-night stands.

His first volume of poems, *White Buildings*, was published in 1926. It contained some of his best work, including erotic poems that he collectively titled *Voyages*. This success convinced Crane that it was time for him to follow in Whitman's footsteps by creating an epic poem about American life, using the Brooklyn Bridge as his focal point. Published in 1930, *The Bridge* was not well received, and that sent Crane into another downward emotional spiral. His drinking grew worse, and he spent his nights prowling waterfront bars trying to pick up men.

In an effort to escape his demons, Crane began to travel. After receiving a Guggenheim Fellowship in 1931, he went to Mexico, where he had an affair—reputedly his first heterosexual affair—with Peggy Cowley, the wife of his friend, Malcolm Cowley.

The End Comes

Crane's voice was stilled a short time later when, just before noon on April 27, 1932, he threw himself off of the steamship carrying him back to New York from Mexico. Since his body vanished beneath the waves and was never recovered, his life is commemorated by a marker on his father's tombstone in Garrettsville that reads simply "Harold Hart Crane 1899–1932 Lost at Sea," and by a handful of poems, which proclaim that Crane lived by his own standards.

- *When Napoleon III of France withdrew his forces from Mexico in the 1860s, it marked the end of French support for Emperor Maximilian I. Sentenced to death on June 19, 1867, Maximilian requested that his executioners aim for his heart.*

- *Politicians avoiding military service in times of war are not a new phenomenon. President Grover Cleveland used the legal option of paying a replacement to serve in the Civil War after he was drafted in 1863.*

- *During the English Civil War, Arthur Aston lost his leg in a fall from a horse in 1644. Oliver Cromwell's troops used Aston's wooden leg to beat him to death in 1649.*

HOW IT ALL BEGAN

The First Decapitation Machine

Execution by removing a person's head from his or her body was all the rage a few hundred years ago. Axes were unreliable, so executioners were always looking for a better way to perform the task. The world's first machine developed for this purpose was the Halifax gibbet, used in its British birthplace since 1286. It differed from the later French guillotine in that it had a huge horizontal ax blade, whereas the guillotine had a slimmer profile and a blade whose leading edge was at a 45-degree angle.

The guillotine was allegedly invented in 1792 by Joseph-Ignace Guillotin. In reality, he simply proposed the idea. The actual design was by a Parisian surgeon, Dr. Antoine Lewis. The prototype was built in 1792 by piano-maker Tobias Schmidt and first used that year on a highwayman named Nicholas-Jacques Pelletier. The crowd, accustomed to the entertainment value offered by a hanging body jerking around in its death dance, found this swift method of execution lacking and lustily called for the return of the gallows. There's just no pleasing some people.

"Up for Grabs"

This phrase, meaning that something is available to anyone who wants it, is a fairly recent expression, dating back to the Great Depression, when restaurants saved every scrap of excess food. The leftovers were put into bags and set at the end of the counter, where any person in need could take one without suffering the indignity of having to beg.

The Original *Sopranos*

As a secret society in medieval Sicily, the Mafia came into being as a means of overthrowing foreign invaders (small private armies were then called *mafie*). By the 18th and 19th centuries, these brutal groups were in a position to extort cash from previous clients. Assassins would leave a signature black handprint at murder scenes, but that practice was discontinued once the science of fingerprinting was developed in 1858. After World War II, the Mafia left its native rural strongholds to migrate in great numbers to the New World, where it came to rule over organized crime for decades. Ironically, the world's most famous gangster—Al Capone—was never declared "Capo di Tutti Capi" (Boss of All Bosses) by the mob; as a descendant of a Naples bloodline, and therefore not Sicilian by birth, he could never be considered completely trustworthy.

Lights, Camera, Technicolor!

❖ ❖ ❖ ❖

*Moving pictures were astonishing to the audiences
who first saw them. It wasn't too hard to get used to
seeing them in black and white. But when movies went
to color, all of a sudden, that was like real life.*

Tripping the Shutter

The marvel of moving pictures was first demonstrated by Californian
Eadweard Muybridge, who set up a series of 24 still cameras at a
racetrack in Palo Alto, California, in 1878. The shutter of each camera was connected to a string; as the horse galloped by, the strings
were tripped, and each camera captured an image. Muybridge
fashioned a crude process to project the images in sequence, demonstrating his process to an art society in San Francisco in 1880.

Inventor Thomas Edison set up a lab in West Orange, New Jersey, and patented a 35mm motion picture camera called the Kineto-
graph in 1891. The novelty of moving pictures quickly became big
business in the entertainment world at the turn of the 20th century.
Edison hired Edwin S. Porter, a camera technician, in 1900. Porter quickly realized that entire stories could be told with film, and
he proceeded to do just that. Other major film studios opened in
Chicago but, by the mid-teens, inclement weather and labor issues
there drove filmmakers to sunny Southern California.

Problems Persist

As the film industry continued to grow, several issues remained. The
cinema was silent and images were black-and-white—hardly realistic.
During the 1920s, feature films were usually accompanied by live
piano or organ music, improvised by the theater musician as action
unfolded on the screen. Some studios tried to increase the visual
experience by hand-tinting certain scenes in various washes of color.

Color movies had been tried with limited success in England.
Known as Kinemacolor, the process involved special cameras and
projectors that used black-and-white film with two colored filters.
But the result was questionable, producing fringed and haloed
effects that distracted from the projected image. Even so, more than

50 American films were produced with the Kinemacolor process by the late teens.

The Color of Money

Technicolor picked up where Kinemacolor left off. Three chemical and mechanical experts named Kalmus, Comstock, and Wescott recognized the need for a realistic color film stock and created the Technicolor Company in 1915 (taking *Tech* from their alma mater, Massachusetts Institute of Technology). Their two-color dye process gained limited use for some sequences in epics from the 1920s, including *The Phantom of the Opera, The Ten Commandments, King of Kings,* and *Ben-Hur.* By 1933, the two-color process had reached talking pictures with *The Mystery of the Wax Museum.*

Still, Technicolor was garish and didn't look real. Kalmus convinced Walt Disney to try a new, refined three-color Technicolor process on his animated short *Flowers and Trees.* The result was a breathtaking success: an Academy Award for Disney and a contract to produce all future Disney films in Technicolor (which remained in force until the Hollywood Technicolor plant closed in 1975).

The new Technicolor process used a series of filters, prisms, and lenses to create three films: a red, blue, and green record. The three were then combined, and the result was a three-strip print. The success of this film stock was not lost on Hollywood, as budgets were increased to allow for color productions. While black-and-white features, such as *Citizen Kane, Casablanca,* and *Treasure of Sierra Madre,* became classics from the 1930s and '40s, Technicolor became part of the visual story for such '30s blockbuster films as *Robin Hood, The Wizard of Oz,* and *Gone with the Wind.*

Aging Somewhat Gracefully

By the 1950s, television had taken a large bite out of moviegoing America. To fight back, Hollywood tried gimmicks such as wide screens (CinemaScope and VistaVision, for example) and three-dimensional projection (3-D). Technicolor continued to thrive and was used for 3-D features including *House of Wax* and *Dial M for Murder.* But by the 1970s, the costs for Technicolor prints had become very high, and the dye process was too slow to serve the country's theaters with enough prints. *The Godfather* and *The Godfather: Part II* were among the last films to use the Technicolor process.

Strange Justice

A Heart Attack Waiting to Happen

The lady weighed more than 300 pounds. She smoked more than a pack of cigarettes a day, and she had high blood pressure, high cholesterol, and a family history of coronary artery disease. It was no surprise, then, when she had a heart attack. Well, maybe it was to her. She sued her doctors and the U.S. government for one million dollars—claiming they didn't do enough to help her to change her destructive lifestyle. Apparently, they didn't yell loudly enough or stuff enough medication down her throat to make a difference. The jury is still out on whether she'll collect.

Got Milk?

As a boy, he had done what Mom always said—"Be sure to drink your milk every day." But, as a grown man, he suffered a mild stroke and was sure his lifetime "addiction" to milk was to blame. So he sued the state's dairy commission, along with the grocery chain where he bought most of the milk. The man's claim sought punitive damages, as well as warning labels for "dangerous" dairy products and a fund to care for other suffering addicts with "a cow on their back." The judge quickly dismissed the suit, calling the whole affair "udderly ridiculous."

Give the Lady a Hand

Everyone thought she was a sweet little old lady. But the granny turned into a tiger when she brought a lawsuit against the inventor of a popular device that controls electrical appliances by the clapping of hands. She received the gadget as a holiday gift, but when the lady repeatedly clapped her hands, the only reaction she got was inflamed arthritis. During the trial, it was discovered that the woman had set the sensitivity control too low to react to her claps. The court "handed" down a swift dismissal.

A Shocking Verdict

The view from the top of the rocks was breathtaking. Having trekked to the summit of the national park's tallest peak, the man enjoyed the vista with no notice of the approaching storm clouds. Without any warning, he was blasted by the swift crackle of a lightning bolt. When he recovered, he sued the park service, believing they were negligent in not posting warnings or instructions about the dangers of lightning strikes. The court didn't go along with that theory and struck the claim down like... well, like a bolt of lightning.

The Real-life Explorers Who Made *King Kong*

Long before Jurassic Park, The Blob, *or even* Godzilla *terrorized big-screen audiences, a prehistoric gorilla by the name of Kong served up its own enormous case of king-size quivers to the moviegoing masses.*

Monkeys are a mainstay of zoos today, but in the early 20th century, when Merian C. Cooper's original *King Kong* came out, few zoos held displays of the entertaining and excitable creatures. Capitalizing on that void and incorporating his own anthropological background, Cooper coupled with fellow filmmaker and friend Ernest B. Schoedsack to parlay their nature documentary into a feature film. Little did they know at the time how their "creature feature epic," the first of its kind, would change the landscape of cinematic and pop culture.

Thrilling Adventure

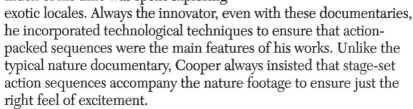

Cooper lived an exciting life before creating one of the most adventurous epics of all time. As a U.S. Army officer and bomber pilot in World War I, he traveled the globe and was a prisoner of war. His initial filmmaking career was devoted to creating nature documentaries for Paramount Pictures. As such, much of his time was spent exploring exotic locales. Always the innovator, even with these documentaries, he incorporated technological techniques to ensure that action-packed sequences were the main features of his works. Unlike the typical nature documentary, Cooper always insisted that stage-set action sequences accompany the nature footage to ensure just the right feel of excitement.

Schoedsack, too, was an ardent fan of technological advancements in filmmaking. Schoedsack and Cooper met while both were providing military service in Ukraine. Upon their return to the United States, they forged a working relationship that combined their mutual interests in nature, adventure, and filmmaking innovations. Their initial collaborations continued their previously established work in the documentary genre, but their united efforts on *King Kong* put Cooper and Schoedsack on the cinematic map.

It's All in the Script

From the start, the filming of *King Kong* was riddled with odd and unexpected roadblocks. The original scriptwriter commissioned by Cooper fell ill and died before producing a workable text. Even though scriptwriter Edgar Wallace is credited as a writer on the film, Cooper; Shoedsack's wife, Ruth Rose; and James Ashmore Creelman were forced to quickly rework the entire script to get it done in time for production. Creelman was hired to reconstruct Wallace's unedited draft to Cooper's liking. Although Creelman's changes were pleasing to the perfectionist Cooper, he still thought that the script lacked snap. Thus, Rose was asked to jump into the screenwriting process. Cooper was pleased with her adjustments but, of course, felt compelled to imprint his own voice, as well.

Another marked change in the film's production revolved around its name. *King Kong* went through several name changes before its release. The movie went by *Kong, King Ape, The Beast, The Ape,* and *The Eighth Wonder* before finally being released as *King Kong.* In fact, even as press release packets were being sent out in anticipation of the release, the film was referred to as *The Eighth Wonder.* Only one known pamphlet—which brought $11,000 at auction in 2005—exists with this designation.

Pushing Film Technique Forward

Several technologically innovative methods were employed in *King Kong*'s production. One technique, stop-motion, was a new trick in which objects were filmed at different locations and positions in many frames to mimic movement. This animation method was utilized to create special effects involving the film's prehistoric creatures—dinosaurs and the ape himself. By today's standards, the choppiness of the technique might appear hokey, but at the time, stop-motion was a cutting-edge means to meet the movie's needs.

Another method employed, rear-projection, was combined with the magic of stop-motion to create the illusion that Kong was tromping through scenes alongside the live actors. To achieve rear-projection, a camera projects a previously recorded background onto the scene's backdrop while live action takes place in front of it. This technique was not a first choice—in fact, multiple alternate routes were explored fully. However, just as filming was scheduled to start, an advanced version of rear-projection was discovered, and Cooper jumped on the innovation.

Although some have suggested that Kong was, at times, portrayed by a man in an ape suit, all scenes with the prehistoric beast were made utilizing stop-motion, rear-projection, and other special effects with one of the four Kong models crafted in various sizes. Although the differing dimensions could not produce a consistently accurate Kong, whether the gigantic ape terrorized at 18 feet or the 24 feet he appeared to be while menacing Manhattan, each rendition was produced by a miniature model made from crude materials including aluminum, rubber, and wire.

Boffo Box Office

King Kong, released in 1933, had the biggest opening weekend of its time. It became the highest-grossing film of the year and the fifth of the entire decade. Not bad considering that 1933 was, by many accounts, the lowest point of the Great Depression. The film's great success brought the production company that carried it, RKO (Radio-Keith-Orpheum), back from the brink of bankruptcy.

Critics and the public were in love with the mammoth gorilla. In fact, the film was so popular that it was rereleased three more times in the next 20 years. But with each new showing, the strong arm of censorship took its toll. Through the years, various images deemed too horrifying were cut out, piece by piece. For instance, scenes featuring the giant gorilla taking a few nibbles of a New Yorker and causing a person to plummet to his death were removed. By modern standards, these scenes might seem fairly tame, but such gruesomeness was uncommon then. In 1971, however, the original film was pieced back together and rereleased, yet again, in its entire form.

Since *King Kong* popped into pop culture, countless monster movies have been created, including those manufactured during the great giant monster genre surge in the 1950s. But it was the great Kong and the technological ambitiousness of its creators, Cooper and Schoedsack, that set the stage for the special effects and terrifying monsters that scare audiences right out of their seats today.

He Said, She Said

Taxes are what we pay for civilized society.
—*Oliver Wendell Holmes, Jr.*

Those who have succeeded at anything and don't mention luck are kidding themselves.
—*Larry King*

Why does Sea World have a seafood restaurant? I'm halfway through my fishburger and I realize, oh my God, I could be eating a slow learner.
—*Lynda Montgomery*

If your ship doesn't come in, swim out to it.
—*Jonathan Winters*

I have a theory that the truth is never told during the nine-to-five hours.
—*Hunter S. Thompson*

Ninety-eight percent of the adults in this country are decent, hardworking, honest Americans. It's the other lousy two percent that get all the publicity. But then, we elected them.
—*Lily Tomlin*

If there is a 50–50 chance that something can go wrong, then nine times out of ten it will.
—*Paul Harvey*

I intend to live forever. So far, so good.
—*Steven Wright*

Marriage is nature's way of keeping us from fighting with strangers.
—*Alan King*

Life is a moderately good play with a badly written third act.
—*Truman Capote*

In America, anyone can become president. That's the problem.
—*George Carlin*

Doing nothing is better than being busy doing nothing.
—*Lao Tzu*

The best time to make friends is before you need them.
—*Ethel Barrymore*

America from Ghost-to-Ghost

Although Americans have been chasing ghosts for centuries, today there is a glut of books, movies, television shows, and paranormal research societies that offer insight into the unknown.

No matter where people are in the United States, chances are good that they'll find a number of legends attached to their hometown. The trappings of the tales may be different, but you can find something throughout the country.

The East Coast

Take New York City, for instance. The city is world-renowned for Broadway and the theater. Not as well known are the stories of ghosts treading the boards.

At the Belasco Theatre on 44th Street, there's at least one person who's no longer on the program but still shows up for every curtain call. This theater has reportedly been haunted for decades by the ghost of former owner David Belasco, who had the neo-Georgian playhouse built in 1907. Originally known as the Stuyvesant, Belasco renamed the theater three years after it opened. Once one of the most important men on Broadway, Belasco was so passionate about the theater that he has continued to attend opening night performances since his death in 1931. Sometimes, his spirit is accompanied by that of a woman known simply as the "Blue Lady."

The New Amsterdam Theater on West 42nd Street is said to be haunted by the ghost of a *Ziegfeld Follies* chorus singer. Despondent over her bad marriage, Olive Thomas apparently committed suicide in the place where she was happiest. Dressed in her green beaded stage costume and headpiece, she wanders through the building after the final curtain call, carrying a blue glass bottle of pills.

The internationally known Palace Theatre on Broadway is said to be home to more than 100 spirits, including singer Judy Garland, who apparently still hovers by the stage door—perhaps waiting for her fans. However, there's one ghost that no one wants to encounter: the acrobat who broke his neck onstage. The story goes that anyone who sees him will die soon afterward.

The West Coast

Travel west to California and you'll find a haunted site that is open to the public and annually attracts more than a million visitors. Alcatraz, the forbidding facility that sits on a barren, rocky island, became known as America's most famous—or infamous—maximum-security prison between 1934 and 1963. During that time, it served as the home of notorious criminals, such as Al Capone and George "Machine Gun" Kelly. Maybe a few of them still haven't left.

Visitors have reported the presence of cold spots as they enter the cell house through double steel doors. A metal door in C Block, which had been welded shut, leads to a utility corridor that is reportedly haunted by three convicts who were killed during a 1946 escape attempt. Over the years, prison guards allegedly reported eerie sounds, including crying and moaning from empty cells. Phantom figures were seen walking the corridors late at night.

One of the most psychically disturbed areas at Alcatraz is "the Hole," the place where prisoners who broke the rules were punished. Cell 14D, one of the underground four-by-eight-foot cells, is noticeably colder than the others. A supernatural presence is believed to have existed there for more than 60 years, since the night an inmate screamed that a ghost with glowing eyes was locked inside the cell with him. While the guards had always joked about a phantom haunting that part of the jail, no one was laughing when they opened the cell the next morning to find the inmate dead, with hand marks on his neck.

Although the cause of death was listed as strangulation, no earthly or unearthly source was ever discovered that could have caused the inmate's death. What happened the following day was equally upsetting. During roll call, the guards discovered that one extra convict kept appearing in line—the same man who had died the night before. As the guards and the other inmates watched, he vanished before their eyes. Like the evil that may have murdered him that fatal night, his ghost reportedly is still imprisoned in the Hole.

Down South

But if there is one spot that can be considered the capital of America's supernatural world, it's New Orleans, Louisiana. Even skeptics change their minds after a visit to the fascinating world of the French Quarter.

What lurks there, aside from the beautiful centuries-old buildings, the music, and the nightlife? Take a "ghost tour" of this part of the city and find out. First settled by the French in the early 18th century, the Quarter has been home to a host of memorable characters who apparently refuse to leave even after death. Marie Laveaux, the voodoo queen who captivated the city in the early 19th century, is reportedly buried in St. Louis No. 2 Cemetery, but her spirit is said to linger close by. Many people believe that Laveaux will answer the prayers of anyone who leaves an offering at her grave.

At the heart of the French Quarter stands the elegant three-story mansion that once belonged to Louis and Delphine LaLaurie, an attractive, popular couple who lived there in the 1830s. They enjoyed hosting lavish parties, but one night a fire broke out, and guests were shocked to discover a number of terrified slaves chained in a secret room. It seemed that the LaLauries also enjoyed torturing and conducting medical experiments on their servants, who in some cases had been held captive for years. Infuriated local residents were ready to lynch the couple when they learned of the abuse, but Louis and Delphine managed to slip away. The ghosts of their victims are said to still wander the house—reenacting the most terrible moments of their lives.

If the thought of coming face-to-face with a few ghosts isn't too alarming, then visit some of these locations and others like them, some of which may be located close to home. Just remember, people can shut off the television or put down the scary book—it's not quite that easy to walk away from the real thing.

- *King Mithridates VI of Pontus on the Black Sea made himself invulnerable to poison by taking small doses on a regular basis. Still, when he tried to poison himself to escape the Romans, it did not work.*

- King Kong *has often been reported to have been Adolf Hitler's favorite movie.*

- *While county sheriff in Buffalo, New York, future president Grover Cleveland earned the nickname "Buffalo's Hangman" after personally springing the trap on two murderers sentenced to hang.*

Fast Facts

- *The first FAX machine was patented in 1843 by a Scottish inventor named Alexander Bain, 33 years before Alexander Graham Bell demonstrated the telephone.*

- *In 1963, the first artificial heart was patented by Paul Winchell, better known as the Grammy-winning voice of Tigger from Disney's* Winnie the Pooh *cartoons.*

- *The Seven Years' War, which began in 1756, pitted Great Britain, Prussia, and Hanover against Sweden, Russia, Austria, France, and Saxony. It's referred to as the French and Indian War in the United States. Winston Churchill called it the First World War.*

- *James Connolly of the United States won the first gold medal of the modern Olympic Games, finishing on top in the hop-step-jump competition.*

- *There are 600 to 800 kernels of corn on the average cob, and all corn cobs have an even number of rows.*

- *President Gerald Ford was a male model in his youth. His work appeared in both* Life *and* Cosmopolitan *magazines.*

- *The rubber band was patented in 1845, a year after Charles Goodrich discovered vulcanization.*

- *Liberty Island, the location of the Statue of Liberty, was called Bedloe's Island until President Eisenhower approved the name change in 1956.*

- *Cal Hubbard is the only person inducted into three different sports halls of fame: baseball, college football, and pro football.*

- *People share their mattress and pillow with up to ten million dust mites, each of which is about a hundredth of an inch long.*

Bettie Page: The Queen of Curves

❖ ❖ ❖ ❖

Dark and sometimes moody, mysterious and captivating, Bettie Page had a sunny smile that would melt butter. Whatever happened to this pinup who disappeared at the height of her notoriety?

Bettie Page, the sexy queen of pinups, easily transitioned from sweet to sultry to dark. The 2005 movie *The Notorious Bettie Page,* starring indie darling Gretchen Mol, only begins to skim the surface of her complex life. Page disappeared from the limelight at her peak, leaving many fans, fanzines, fan clubs, and products behind.

Many young women have tried to copy those signature bangs (to the dismay of their unforgiving foreheads), and a body like hers is less appreciated in the modern day. A waist that small with hips that shapely? Most of today's stars seem more intent on achieving the skin-and-bones "waif" look.

The Girl's Got Range

From 1950 to 1957, Bettie Page ruled everything from simple, girl-next-door swimsuit spreads to taboo bondage films. The films eventually earned Page a subpoena from the U.S. government.

In his book, *The Real Bettie Page,* Richard Foster calls her "a swinging fifties chick who looks like the girl next door, yet tells you she knows the score. She winks, tosses back her famous gleaming black bangs, and flashes you her killer come-hither smile. Her curves entice, entrance, and devastate. She's a leggy, torpedo-chested weapon aimed at your heart.... She's bikinis and lace. She's cotton candy and a ride on the Tilt-a-Whirl at Coney Island."

But Foster's love for the Dark Angel, as Bettie Page is sometimes called, led him to the awful truth—that after her queen-of-curves years, Page's life spiraled downward, until she ended up in a mental institution after being convicted of attempted murder.

Humble Beginnings

Betty Mae Page, born in Tennessee in 1923, was the second of Edna and Roy Page's six children. Roy, a mechanic, couldn't find work during the Great Depression. Add Roy's supposedly insatiable sexual appetite—he sexually abused Bettie and impregnated a 15-year-old neighbor—and Edna's cold shoulder toward her children, and the result is a perfectly dysfunctional family pie.

Page was a good student and active in school—but she wasn't involved with boys. She was a typical goodie-goodie, raised as a faithful Christian by her devout, God-fearing mother, who didn't allow her to date. She escaped her oppressive upbringing by envisioning herself as a movie star. A few years after graduating from college, Page decided to follow her dream and moved to New York.

Between boyfriends, secretarial jobs, and small modeling gigs, Page met Jerry Tibbs on the beach at Coney Island in October 1950. Tibbs, an African American police officer from Harlem with a passion for photography, immediately asked Page if she'd ever thought about modeling. She agreed to let him shoot her. Tibbs showed Page tricks of the trade, doing her makeup and giving her tissues to stuff her bra. Eventually, he realized that her hairstyle—a simple part down the middle—was taking away from her beauty on camera. With a quick snip, the Bettie Page bangs arrived.

In Front of the Camera

Tibbs introduced Page to photographer Cass Carr, and her modeling career began to take off. In 1952, Page met Irving Klaw, the man who would turn the Queen of Curves into the Dark Angel. Klaw ran a successful mail-order business and photo shop in New York, selling stills and head shots from famous movies. But his bread and butter was earned from bondage photos. Klaw shot photographs of girls being spanked, tied up, and wearing six-inch heels with black lingerie. Today, you'll see racier displays in a Victoria's Secret ad, but this was the 1950s, and Page's carefree photos inspired sexually repressed Americans all around the country.

Klaw, along with his business partner and sister, Paula, took Page in like family. She enjoyed modeling but never gave up on her dream of being an actress, and spent her prosperous $75-per-day modeling payments on acting classes.

By 1955, Page was at her peak, gracing the pages of the January issue of *Playboy* in her most famous pose—wearing only a Santa hat and a naughty smile. But by 1957, Page was burned out on show business. She moved to Florida, rekindled a relationship with an old flame, and got married in 1958.

A Slow Slide

By New Year's Eve of that same year, however, the relationship fizzled. Frustrated, financially unstable, and brokenhearted, Page spent the night crying along the roads of Key West. She felt hopeless—and that's when she spotted a church. Page turned her life over to God, quit modeling, and spun into religious fervor. She spent the next few years in various Bible camps and schools; she wanted to be a missionary. But Page was a bit too fanatical, even for Baptist ministers. Her classmates and instructors began to see that her zeal was becoming frightening and dark; they speculated that Page, now pushing 40, wasn't well.

During the next few years, Page committed several violent acts. She pulled a gun on a missionary at a Bible camp, and later, she attacked and stabbed an elderly woman and her husband, from whom she rented a trailer in California. Page was diagnosed with paranoid schizophrenia and sentenced to a mental hospital.

However, because of good behavior, she was released early. Through a roommate service, she moved into the home of Leonie Haddad. After a few months of living together, Page heard Haddad on the phone with the agency asking for a new roommate and she snapped, stabbing Haddad 12 times.

Page went on trial for attempted murder in 1983 and spent seven years in a mental institution before being released on good behavior. Older, heavier, and with no money—even with all of those Bettie Page products swarming the globe—she became a recluse.

With her likeness on everything from posters to dioramas, Bettie Page is as popular now as she was in the 1950s. For women, Page represents the ultimate example of body confidence. She was comfortable posing in a leopard-print bathing suit as well as posing nude in a park. Through every wink and grin, she seems to be secretly speaking to young women about the power of curves—an important message today in a time when many female celebrities are diminishing before the public's very eyes.

Presto! Change-o! Wham-O!

*In 1948, young business owners Richard Knerr and Arthur
"Spud" Melin developed a slingshot specifically designed
to hurl bits of meat into the air to feed hawks and falcons.
Their new company's name was a stroke of onomatopoeia—
Wham-O was the sound the slingshot made.*

Whirling Disks

Californian Fred Morrison fashioned a small plastic disc toy he
called the Pluto Platter, noting America's fascination with flying saucers. In 1955, Knerr and Melin saw the plaything and purchased the
design. But Knerr wasn't pleased with the name. While traveling the
East Coast, he noted the recent closing of the Frisbie Baking Company. He had heard stories of pie-plate tossing as a sport at nearby
Yale University in the 1920s. The idea intrigued him and he quickly
changed the Pluto Platter to Frisbee.

Loop the Hoop

In 1957, a visiting Australian told of native children who exercised by
twirling bamboo hoops around their waists like Hula dancers. The
concept was not lost on Knerr and Melin. Using a tough but light-
weight plastic, they fashioned a large hoop, and the Hula-Hoop was
born. At a cost of $1.98 each, Americans purchased 25 million hoops
in the first four months of 1958. Worldwide sales topped 100 million
by the end of the year, when the fad died as quickly as it had started.

Bouncing into History

In late 1964, chemist Norman Stingley concocted a synthetic rubber
compound that had a lot of bounce to the ounce. His employer saw
no commercial potential, but Wham-O picked up Stingley's idea,
creating the Super Ball. At just under two inches in diameter, the
Super Ball was no ordinary orb: Once the ball bounced, it continued
to bounce...and bounce...and bounce.

Wham-O also made its name by creating crazy toys such as the
Slip-N-Slide, Monster Magnet, Silly String, and the Air Blaster—
guaranteed to blow out a candle (and someone's hearing) at 20 feet.

The Bard vs. Bacon: Who Wrote Shakespeare?

"What's in a name? That which we call a rose, by any other name, would smell as sweet." But would that which we call prose, by any other name, read as neat?

The quote above was penned by William Shakespeare—or was it? Many scholars have raised doubts as to whether he really wrote some of the finest words in Western literature. Did other writers actually do the deed? Both sides believe they have the evidence to prove their point.

Meet Bill

William Shakespeare was born in Stratford-upon-Avon, England, in April 1564—the exact date is unknown. This and many other details of his life are vague, which has fueled the rampant speculation about authorship. It is generally accepted that he was the first in his family to read and write, although the extent of his education has been widely questioned. His father was involved in local politics, so it is likely that Shakespeare attended school until his early teens to study Latin and literature. At age 18, Shakespeare married Anne Hathaway, who was eight years older than he was and three months pregnant with their first child, Susanna. Twins Hamnet and Judith were born two years later.

The Bard's life story seems to disappear into the mist for more than seven years at this point, resurfacing in 1592, when he became involved in London theater. As a playwright and actor, he founded a performing troupe that was soon part of the court of King James I. Shakespeare retired in 1613, returning to his hometown with some wealth. He died in 1616 and was laid to rest in the Holy Trinity Church of Stratford-upon-Avon.

The Play's the Thing

While Shakespeare's plays were performed during his lifetime, they were not collected and published in book form until seven years after his death; *The First Folio* contained 36 of his theatrical works. Editors John Heminge and Henry Condell categorized the plays as tragedies, comedies, and histories. Many of Shakespeare's works, such as *Hamlet* and *King Lear,* were based on writings of former playwrights or even of Shakespeare's contemporaries—a common practice of the time. He also penned more than 150 sonnets, which often focused on love or beauty.

The diversity of this amazing body of work is what leads many to wonder whether Shakespeare had the education or ability to write it all. Certainly, they insist, others with better backgrounds and academic credentials were more likely to have actually written such great and timeless works of literature. Furthermore, they say, many of the plays displayed the acumen of a well-traveled writer— something Shakespeare was most likely not—someone who had a great knowledge of foreign languages, geography, and local customs. Who could have written such worldly plays?

Bringing Home the Bacon

Francis Bacon was born into a royal London family in 1561. Fragile as a young child, Bacon was schooled at home. He spent three years at Trinity College at Cambridge and traveled to Paris at age 15. Bacon became a lawyer and a member of the British Parliament in 1584. He soon joined the court of Queen Elizabeth and was knighted by King James I in 1603. Bacon eventually ascended to the positions of solicitor general and attorney general of the British government. He died of bronchitis in 1626.

Bacon is best remembered for his part in developing the scientific method, a process of systematic investigation. This standard prescribes defining a question, performing diligent research about the subject, forming a hypothesis, experimenting and collecting data, analyzing the results, and developing a conclusion. The progression has become commonplace in all types of scientific work, from grade school projects to research labs, and is still used today. But the multitalented Bacon was also a writer and essayist who once observed that "knowledge is power." His works include *Novum*

Organum, Astrologia Sana, and *Meditationes Sacrae.* But could the man who penned these works be diverse and capable enough to also write *Much Ado About Nothing, Romeo and Juliet,* and words such as "If music be the food of love, play on"?

Something Is Rotten in the State of... Authorship

Speculation about the origin of Shakespeare's work began in the mid-1800s, as writers and scholars sought to demystify the works of the Bard. By the early 1900s, even the great American humorist Mark Twain had weighed in and questioned the authenticity of Shakespeare's plays and sonnets, albeit in his own way. In *Is Shakespeare Dead?*, Twain parodied those intellectuals who tried to discredit the man from Stratford-upon-Avon. The satiric piece questioned how biographers could write such detailed stories about their subject when so little solid information existed in the first place. But Twain also raised the question of whether Shakespeare could even write.

Similarities between the writings of Shakespeare and Bacon are abundant, and perhaps a bit too coincidental. For example, Shakespeare's *Hamlet* offers, "To thine own self be true, ... Thou canst not then be false to any man." In *Essay of Wisdom,* Bacon wrote, "Be so true to thyself as thou be not false to others." Plagiarism? Who can really say? In *Julius Caesar,* Shakespeare wrote, "Cowards die many times before their deaths." In Bacon's *Essay of Friendship,* he offered, "Men have their time, and die many times." Coincidence? Sure, maybe. The Bard wrote, "Tomorrow, and tomorrow, and tomorrow/Creeps in this petty pace from day to day" in *Macbeth.* Bacon observed in *Religious Meditations,* "The Spanish have a proverb, 'To-morrow, to-morrow; and when to-morrow comes, tomorrow.'" Is it possible that Shakespeare knew of the same Spanish proverb? Certainly. While other similarities and questions proliferate, enough disbelief and lack of concrete evidence remain to thrill the world's doubting Thomases.

Parting Is Such Sweet Sorrow

Amid the swirl of controversy, most academics are convinced that Shakespeare himself wrote the plays and sonnets that made him famous. Of course, that conviction has done little to discourage those who have their doubts.

Fumbling Felons

Be Prepared

A man decided to rob a safe in an Illinois post office. After realizing that his personal safe-cracking tools weren't up to the job, he decided to burglarize a nearby grain elevator for larger, more powerful tools. When he failed to find the necessary equipment there, he burglarized a house close by but still found nothing useful. Continuing on his way, he burglarized the Town Hall—still nothing. He even burglarized a local church—dead end. He returned to the post office but soon realized he had cut himself at some point, leaving blood across the post office floor. Concerned about being identified by the DNA, the would-be safe-cracker burned the post office down. Unfortunately, even that wasn't enough to cover his tracks. Police cracked the crime through the footprints he left in the new-fallen snow from one crime scene to the next. Remarkably, there had been a way the burglar could have avoided all this trouble—he had apparently failed to notice the note stuck to the front of the safe revealing the combination.

There's No Place Like Home

A robber in Salisbury, North Carolina, was arrested but quickly escaped custody, eluding police by running through the woods. It quickly turned into a full-out manhunt, with the help of search dogs and a police helicopter, but officers simply could not find the fugitive. The search spread out beyond the woods. Despite the fact that this trick never worked for preschoolers or during a game of peek-a-boo past the age of one, police found the man hiding at his home in his own bed. Apparently it doesn't work for escaped prisoners, either.

Stay Alert!

As gas prices skyrocketed, it's no wonder a man in Muncie, Indiana, attempted to siphon gasoline from a gas station's underground tank. The clever thief installed a 55-gallon tank with a battery-operated pump inside his white van. One night, he attached a hose to that pump and tank and plunged the other end into a gas station's tank under the pavement. He would have been fine if he hadn't fallen asleep. The next morning, the gas station manager saw the van parked on the lot and immediately called police. When officers opened the van, they found the man next to the tank and pump—still sleeping. The authorities charged him with theft and possession of a firearm without a permit.

A New Land

It took a little more than 40 years, but the Inuit of Canada
finally saw their dream come true. Their new territory
was the biggest change to the map of North America
since Alaska and Hawaii became U.S. states in 1959.

On April 1, 1999, the Canadian territory of Nunavut was born.
Nunavut (the word means "our land" in Inuktitut) spans the eastern half of Canada's rugged northland. Roughly the size of Western
Europe, it is the least populated and largest of the territories of
Canada, with fewer than 30 isolated towns scattered across its vast
region. The capital, Iqaluit (formally Frobisher Bay), is home to
5,000 people, or almost 20 percent of the territory's population.

Nunavut is the first full-fledged political region in North America
governed by aboriginal peoples. Though its new boundaries were
created in 1993 when the Nunavut Land Claims Agreement Act
was officially passed, it took five more years to properly abolish the
previous Northwest Territorial districts and set up a working government. The 19 members of the unicameral Legislative Assembly do
not belong to political parties, and the legislature works on a consen-
sus model. The head of the government, the premier of Nunavut, is
elected by the members of the Legislative Assembly.

Baby, It's Cold Outside

Documents reveal that the Inuit have lived in this area for more
than 4,000 years. With the average winter temperature hovering
around $-22°$ F, the aboriginal peoples have adapted superbly to
their environment. They rely on animals—fish, sea mammals, and
those on land—for almost all their needs: food, shelter, clothing, and
more. Their fortunes have risen and fallen over the centuries, but
their success was once based on trading furs and letting whalers hunt
the Arctic waters for bowhead whales to harvest their oil and baleen.

When Europeans landed on their shores, the Inuit helped the
ill-equipped foreigners survive the harsh conditions of the Arctic
by serving as hunters, interpreters, and guides. They traded their
services for guns, cloth, metal, tools, alcohol, and tobacco. But by

the 1920s, things took a turn for the worse: Exploration was nearly complete, fur prices were fluctuating, and bowhead whales were rare. Sadly, the Inuit had been decimated by many new diseases that the Europeans brought with them from their home countries.

Nearly a century later, however, Canada's Inuit have proven resilient as ever, continuing to flourish and grow. As a community, they make a point to meld traditional ways as smoothly as possible with modern technology; as individuals, they tend to stay close to home and Mother Nature.

Pejoratively Speaking

The Inuit, or Eskimos, make up 85 percent of the 30,000 people living in these vast regions of tundra, pine forests, and ice fields in and around the Arctic Circle. It has become politically incorrect to call the Inuit *Eskimos,* although all Inuit in Canada and Greenland are Eskimos (not all of the Yupik and Inupiat in Alaska are). For some reason, a false but widely held belief is that the word *Eskimo* means "eaters of raw meat." Etymologists at the Smithsonian Institute say that the word *Eskimo* means "snowshoe netters." Linguists from the Innu-Montagnais (the language from which the word originates) reported in 1978 that the word *Eskimo* means "people who speak a different language."

You Can Call Me Al

A funny thing happened when Nunavut officially became a new territory. The remaining Northwest Territories decided that perhaps they should also change their name to stay more in touch with *their* culture and identity. So the premier asked the deputy premier to draw up a list of possibilities for the next session of the legislative assembly. Pranksters, however, hijacked the process, with "Bob" becoming the second-most-popular choice. Since then, the debate has faded somewhat.

- *Red is the most popular color for flags around the world, followed by white and then blue.*

- *Confederate General Robert E. Lee never earned a single demerit while a student at West Point.*

The World of Toys for Grown-ups

❖ ❖ ❖ ❖

Toys have gone from basic to high tech—now there are electronic games, foldable exercise bicycles, electronic cars, and even programmable puppets. Some adults never grow out of their toy fixations—the toys are just more expensive.

The Best, Only, and Unexpected

For fewer than 500 smackers, Hammacher Schlemmer, America's longest-running catalog, will sell you a handheld Instant Star and Constellation Finder, a self-sustaining Ecosphere, a backpack bicycle, or a foldable exercise bike. An interesting item in the 2005 catalog: Schlemmer offered a $50,000 remote-control toy called Robby the Robot. Modeled on the classic 1956 film *Forbidden Planet*, Robby moves, makes sounds, and does everything but the dishes.

By Land or by Sea

The Saleen S7 supercar might not be the most expensive auto out there (it costs about $400,000), but it's certainly unique. Its aerodynamic features create so much downforce that even if you drove the S7 upside down at 160 mph on a roller-coaster track, the car wouldn't lose its contact with the driving surface—or so they say.

Meanwhile, you could buy a $350,000 Seawind 300C state-of-the-art amphibian aircraft. These are built to order, so don't expect immediate delivery, but a $9,000 deposit will guarantee you a boat that can ride at 190 mph or 165 knots. It comfortably seats two adults and three kids.

Tried and True

Clifford Berryman's Bevo Teddy Bear—based on the cartoon that inspired the term "teddy bear"—sold with other stuffed animals for $25,560 at auction. Bevo first appeared in the *Washington Post* in 1902. In perfect condition, poor Bevo has never been played with.

If all this is out of your price range, for a mere $7,500, you can order a hand-tooled Monopoly set. Its leather-bound board comes embossed in gold or silver, and it includes figurines of pewter, sterling silver, or silver-gilt.

He Said, She Said

Maturity is only a short break in adolescence.

—Jules Feiffer

The only disability in life is a bad attitude.

—Scott Hamilton

Love doesn't make the world go round. Love is what makes the ride worthwhile.

—Franklin P. Jones

I've been on so many blind dates I should get a free dog.

—Wendy Liebman

Experience is the name everyone gives to his mistakes.

—Oscar Wilde

A wise man will make more opportunities than he finds.

—Sir Francis Bacon

If you want to know what God thinks of money, just look at the people he gave it to.

—Dorothy Parker

Good manners can replace morals. It may be years before anyone knows if what you are doing is right. But if what you are doing is nice, it will be immediately evident.

—P. J. O'Rourke

You can only be young once but you can be immature forever.

—Dave Barry

If you can count your money, you don't have a billion dollars.

—J. Paul Getty

People do not seem to realize that their opinion of the world is also a confession of character.

—Ralph Waldo Emerson

I don't like nostalgia unless it's mine.

—Lou Reed

There's a difference between a philosophy and a bumper sticker.

—Charles M. Schulz

Walt Disney: FBI Man or Mouse?

❖ ❖ ❖ ❖

As the creator of the cutest cartoon mouse in the world, Walt Disney carefully protected and shielded the rodent and his friends from anything that could put their world in a bad light. But it seems that Disney, whose entertainment empire was as pure as Snow White, may have protected and shielded other facets of his life from public view—ones that might have darkened his squeaky-clean image.

Young Walter

Walt Disney was born in Chicago on December 5, 1901, to parents Elias and Flora. His father was a farmer and carpenter, running the household with an overly firm hand. Walt and his siblings, working the Disney land near Kansas City, often found themselves on the receiving end of a strap as their 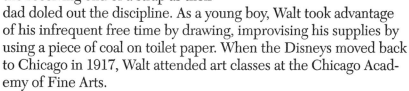 dad doled out the discipline. As a young boy, Walt took advantage of his infrequent free time by drawing, improvising his supplies by using a piece of coal on toilet paper. When the Disneys moved back to Chicago in 1917, Walt attended art classes at the Chicago Academy of Fine Arts.

Armed with forged birth records, Walt joined the American Red Cross Ambulance Corps and entered World War I in 1918, just before it ended. He returned to Kansas City, where two of his brothers continued to run the Disney farm. Although he was rejected as a cartoonist for the *Kansas City Star,* Walt soon began to create animated film ads for movie theaters, working with a young Ub Iwerks, who eventually became an important member of Disney Studios.

In 1922, Disney started Laugh-O-Gram Films, producing short cartoons based on fairy tales. But the business closed within a year, and Walt headed to Hollywood, intent on directing feature films. Finding no work as a director, he revisited the world of film animation. With emotional and financial support from his brother Roy,

Walt slowly began to make a name for Disney Brothers Studios on the West Coast. The company introduced "Oswald the Lucky Rabbit" in 1927 but lost the popular character the next year to a different company. Disney was left in the position of having to create another cute and clever cartoon animal.

The Tale of the Mouse

According to Disney, the Kansas City office of Laugh-O-Gram Films was rampant with mice. One mouse was a particular favorite of Walt. This rodent became the inspiration for Disney's next cartoon character. Working with Iwerks, and borrowing copiously from their former meal ticket Oswald, Disney Studios produced *Steamboat Willie* in November 1928. With a voice provided by Disney himself, Mickey Mouse quickly became a hit in movie theaters. The animated star introduced additional Disney icons, including girlfriend Minnie Mouse, the always-exasperated Donald Duck, faithful hound Pluto, and dim-but-devoted pal Goofy. Disney's cartoons won every Animated Short Subject Academy Award during the 1930s.

A Dark Side of Disney

As Disney Studios moved into animated feature films (which everyone said would never work), Walt began to wield the power he'd gained as one of Hollywood's most prominent producers. What's more, his strict upbringing and harsh bouts of discipline had left him with a suspicious, ultraconservative mind-set. Bad language by employees in the presence of women resulted in immediate discharge—no matter the inconvenience. Disney was prone to creating a double standard between himself and his employees. For example, although Walt kept his dashing mustache for most of his life, all other Disney workers were prohibited from wearing any facial hair. While he considered his artists and animators "family," he treated them in the same way Elias Disney had treated his family—unfairly. Promised bonuses turned into layoffs. Higher-paid artists resorted to giving their assistants raises out of their own pockets. By 1941, Disney's animators went on strike, supported by the Screen Cartoonists Guild. Walt was convinced, and stated publicly, that the strike was the result of Communist agitators infiltrating Hollywood. Settled after five weeks, the Guild won on all counts, and the "Disney family" became cynically known as the "Mouse Factory."

An Even Darker Side

Disney was suspected of being a Nazi sympathizer; he often attended American Nazi Party meetings before the beginning of World War II. When prominent German filmmaker Leni Riefenstahl tried to screen her films for Hollywood studios, only Disney agreed to meet her. Yet, when World War II began, Disney projected a strictly all-American image and became closely allied with J. Edgar Hoover and the FBI.

According to more than 500 pages of FBI files, Disney was recruited by Hoover in late 1940 to be an informant, flagging potential Communist sympathizers among Hollywood stars and executives. In September 1947, Disney was called by the House Un-American Activities Committee to testify on Communist influence in the motion picture industry. He fingered several of his former artists as Reds, again blaming much of the 1941 labor strike on their efforts. He also identified the League of Women Voters as a Communist-fronted organization. Later that evening, his wife pointed out that he meant the League of Women Shoppers, a consumer group that had supported the Guild strike. Disney's testimony contributed to the "Hollywood Blacklist," which included anyone in the industry even remotely suspected of Communist affiliation. The list resulted in many damaged or lost careers, as well as a number of suicides in the cinematic community. Included in the turmoil was Charlie Chaplin, whom Disney referred to as "the little Commie."

The FBI rewarded Walt Disney for his efforts by naming him "SAC—Special Agent in Charge" in 1954, just as he was about to open his first magical amusement park, Disneyland. Disney and Hoover continued to be pen pals into the 1960s; the FBI made script "suggestions" for *Moon Pilot,* a Disney comedy that initially spoofed the abilities of the Bureau. The bumbling FBI agents in the screenplay became generic government agents before the film's release.

After a lifetime of chain-smoking, Disney developed lung cancer and died in December 1966. His plans for Disney World in Florida had just begun—the park didn't open until 1971. Upon his passing, many remembered the man as kindly "Uncle Walt," while others saw him as the perfect father for a mouse—since he had always seemed to be a bit of a rat.

Fast Facts

- *The Chinese are credited with inventing paper. The earliest form, made from hemp, was created in Shaanxi between 206 B.C. and A.D. 24. Cai Lun improved the paper-making process in A.D. 105.*

- *Lloyds of London paid out $3,019,400 in insurance claims to the families of the victims who perished in the* Titanic *disaster.*

- *One eyebrow can include as many as 550 hairs.*

- *Keelhauling was a punishment inflicted on sailors up until the middle of the 19th century. The victim would be pulled under the bow of a ship, which often resulted in drowning.*

- *The Sony Corporation was originally known as* Totsuken, *but the company changed its name because, rightly so, it was felt that* Sony *would be easier to pronounce.*

- *The White House has 35 bathrooms.*

- *The Chicago Cubs sued newspaper carrier Mark Guthrie in 2004 to get back the $301,000 they mistakenly paid him instead of actual Cubs' pitcher Mark Guthrie.*

- *A manhole cover weighs more than 80 pounds.*

- *England's King George III was declared insane in 1811. Studies of his hair have discovered high levels of arsenic, which contributed to, if not necessarily outright caused, his mental illness.*

- *The first American president to be photographed was John Quincy Adams.*

- *In October 1916, Margaret Sanger opened the first birth-control clinic in the United States. Nine days later, it was raided and Sanger was jailed for 30 days.*

The Wives of Henry VIII

❖ ❖ ❖ ❖

England's Henry VIII is famous for having six wives. But how much do you know about those ladies themselves?

A true Renaissance man and child of privilege, Henry VIII spent his youth enjoying life's finer pursuits, learning about music, languages, the arts, sports, poetry, and architecture. During these years, he also picked up a penchant for vice, earning a steadfast reputation as a gambler and, most notably, a womanizer. Although Henry was second in line to succeed his father as King of England and Lord of Ireland, his elder brother's death left the position open. Henry took over the monarchy just shy of his 18th birthday, but he was more interested in entertainment than politics. The new king took a few years to get settled into the business of running England, but he was quickly thrust into his first marriage. Undeserved as his lecherous reputation might be— monarchs were expected to play the part of the playboy—Henry certainly did run up quite a collection of wives: a total of six by the time of his death in 1547 at age 55.

Catherine of Aragon

Marriage to wife number one, Catherine of Aragon, was an arrangement pushed by her father, King Ferdinand II of Spain, and Henry's own father, Henry VII. Catherine had been married to Henry's older brother Arthur for only a few months, and upon his passing, Henry was betrothed to the widow. In this way, the fathers were guaranteeing an ongoing union between England and Spain. It took Henry nearly a quarter of a century to end this marriage of convenience, but he was finally granted an annulment on the grounds that Catherine had once been married to his brother. The pope refused to grant this annulment, so Henry arranged to receive it from the archbishop of Canterbury. This severely damaged Henry's—and England's—

relationship with the Roman Catholic Church. Three years later, Henry closed Catholic monasteries and abbeys.

Anne Boleyn

Anne Boleyn, marchioness of Pembroke, was a lady-in-waiting who became the other woman. Anne was an English noble, educated in France, who provided reputable servitude to Queen Catherine. During her period of personal assistance, Anne and Henry began their affair, with Henry proposing marriage roughly six years prior to his annulment from Catherine. An argument has been made that the pair did not consummate their affair until Henry's annulment was final (although others claim she was pregnant when she married). According to the theory, Anne was not so moralistic that she wouldn't engage with a married man—she had simply seen the fate that befell her sister Mary when she carried on with Henry. When Mary Boleyn finally gave in and consummated *her* affair with the king, she was rewarded with a pink slip and sent packing. It turns out that Mary was the luckier of the two, being simply sent away. Anne, on the other hand, after failing to produce a male heir, was beheaded on trumped-up charges of adultery and witchcraft.

Jane Seymour

Apparently, Henry viewed his wives' ladies-in-waiting as his own personal marriage buffet. Upon Queen Anne's passing, he plucked his third wife, Jane Seymour, from Anne's group of attendants. Of course, it has been suggested that Henry's interest in Jane was the true reason he had Anne killed—not the six fingers he accused her of having (which was seen as the mark of the devil). Unfortunately, Jane only lasted a year as Henry's wife. Although she finally brought Henry a legitimate male heir, Edward, Jane succumbed to a fever caused from complications of childbirth.

Anne of Cleves

On the market yet again, Henry once more tried his hand at an arranged marriage. Following his chancellor's advice, Henry agreed to marry Anne of Cleves for her family's advantageous political ties to both the Catholic Church and the Protestant Reformation. With the nuptials already scheduled, Henry was said to have voiced his misgivings upon finally meeting his bride-to-be. Although striking in personality, Anne was not as agreeable in appearance as the king had hoped: He likened Anne's visage to that of a horse. Although he followed through with the vows, Anne—dubbed "Flanders Mare" by Henry—was released from her role as queen through an annulment. But at least she got a generous settlement for her troubles.

Catherine Howard

The tables were turned on the adulterous King Henry by his fifth wife, Catherine Howard, a woman who was known to engage in illicit affairs of her own. Even before settling down with the king, Catherine—who was Anne Boleyn's first cousin—was intimately involved with many men about town. Soon after they were wed, the king discovered that his bride was still sowing her oats with other suitors. Apparently, what's good for the gander was most certainly not good for the goose, for Henry said, "Off with her head!" and Catherine was no more.

Catherine Parr

Henry's sixth and final wife, Catherine Parr, was famous for her own lengthy list of marriages. With two marriages before Henry and one after, Catherine holds the record for the most-married queen in English history. She is also the only one of Henry's six brides to make it out of her marriage alive and without an annulment. Only four years after their wedding, Henry died at age 55 from obesity-related complications. Catherine escaped the fates of Henry's first five wives and survived as a widow free to marry one last time—to Thomas Seymour, Jane Seymour's brother.

- *Almost 25 percent of the settlers of the 13 colonies remained loyal to England during the American Revolution. Benjamin Franklin's son, William, remained true to the crown and never spoke to his father again.*

- *Shah Jahan, Mughal emperor of the Indian subcontinent, began construction of the Taj Mahal in 1631 as a mausoleum for his third wife, Mumtaz Mahal. She died giving birth to their 14th child.*

- *Horses are born without teeth.*

ANAGRAMS

An anagram is a word or phrase that exactly reproduces the letters in another word or phrase. The most interesting of them reflect or comment on the subject of the first.

the United States of America—Attaineth its cause: Freedom!

Clint Eastwood—lies down to act

Marilyn Monroe—I marry loon men.

Harry Potter—try hero part

Academy Awards—saw drama decay

Thomas Alva Edison—Aha! Ions made volts.

Lee Harvey Oswald—revealed who slay

Chairman Mao—I am on a march.

Marilyn Manson—Manly man? No sir!

Adolf Hitler—do real filth

Agatha Christie—Rich hag is at tea.

Oscar Wilde—I lace words.

Paul McCartney—Pay Mr. Clean cut.

Elvis Costello—voice sells lot

Robin Williams—I warm billions.

Ronald Wilson Reagan—no darlings, no ERA law

Arnold Schwarzenegger—He's grown large n' crazed.

Christopher Reeve—script: he ever hero

Jackie Gleason—angelic as joke

Steve Martin—I'm star event.

Sean Connery—on any screen

Elvis Aaron Presley—earns lovely praise

Tony Blair, P.M.—I'm Tory, plan B.

The Zoot Suit Riots

A volatile mix of hot summer nights, angry sailors, and ethnic tension in Southern California during World War II could only lead to an explosion.

The country was abuzz with wartime pressure and a fresh surge of racial tension in 1943. World War II was in full swing, and Los Angeles was flooded with sailors. They spilled out of local naval bases into a city already filled to the brim. Added to the heap of an overpopulated city came the self-described *pachucos* (a word that has its origins in a slang term for residents of El Paso, Texas). Pachucos, decked out in distinctive full zoot-suit garb and ducktail 'dos, had been seen around town for years and had fostered a reputation for stirring up trouble. It didn't seem to matter that this "trouble" was often the product of an anti-Latino bias that circulated through the streets of LA among residents and law enforcement officials alike. With the addition of so many military personnel to the city, the blend of diversity and testosterone proved to be violent.

An Unfamiliar Culture

Prior to their Los Angeles experience with Mexican Americans, the era's military personnel typically possessed little experience with the flamboyantly represented Latino culture they now found in their midst. The hue of pachucos' skin differentiated them from the white masses, but their telltale garb really jabbed at the restless forces. The ostentatious jewelry, prominently wide-brimmed hats, and elaborately tapered pants earmarked the pachucos as the "trouble-making" Zoot Suiters.

Despite the pachucos' cartoonish costumes, many Los Angelinos believed that there were good reasons for the masses to fear their presence. With their infiltration of Los Angeles came a rash of gang activity, and a mysterious but much-publicized gang-related death made headlines in 1942. These events served to perpetuate the public cries of the zoot-suit-menace mania that was already striking the area. All this racially laced trepidation came to a head in the summer of 1943.

The Mob Attacks

Based on claims of a pachuco-prompted altercation, a group of sailors initiated retaliation on a grand and vindictive scale. On June 3, 1943, a group of sailors embarked on an incursion into the barrios of East LA. Armed with belts, clubs, and chains, the assemblage was out for blood.

Although pachucos were typically clad in zoot suits, not all zoot-suit-adorned Mexican Americans were part of the pachuco group. That made no difference to the sailors, however. No Latino male was safe. Zoot-suit wearers were the initial targets, but soon the sailors found any East LA resident fair game. Zoot suit or not, any Mexican American man who crossed the mob's path was made victim of the angry onslaught. Worse yet, women were raped, and even the occasional African American and Filipino American to happen onto the scene was attacked by the mob.

But Who's Responsible?

To add insult to injury, at the end of the days-long attack, a collective of mostly Mexican Americans was charged with the illegalities. While hundreds of Mexican Americans were arrested, a mere nine sailors were taken into custody. Of those nine, only one was deemed guilty—and just of a small-time crime.

The *Los Angeles Times* marked its approval of this discrimination with a headline that declared "Zoot Suiters Learn Lesson in Fight with Servicemen." The implication of the article was that the menacing Mexicans were simply out of control. The national press picked up the story and reported a similar version of the tale in other cities. In outrage, or perhaps in a frenzy of the racially tense excitement overtaking the nation, copycat riots emerged across the United States. In response to the fracas, the U.S. military ordered all personnel to keep away from the streets of Los Angeles in an effort to settle the unrest. Of course, in one last jab at the pachucos, an ordinance was passed in Los Angeles that declared the wearing of zoot suits illegal.

- *The five types of discharge from U.S. military service are honorable, general (under honorable conditions), other than honorable, bad conduct, and dishonorable.*

Behind the Songs of Our Times

"Bette Davis Eyes" (1981)

Singer Kim Carnes's number one hit, "Bette Davis Eyes," never once described exactly what kind of eyes it was talking about. Regardless, the Oscar-winning Bette Davis herself acknowledged the song's success, writing letters to all involved in appreciation of the opportunity to become a "part of modern times." Her grandson now looked up to and respected the former star of films including *Jezebel* and *All About Eve*. When "Bette Davis Eyes" won Grammys for Song of the Year and Record of the Year, Carnes, along with the songwriters, received roses and congratulations from Davis.

"Save the Last Dance for Me" (1960)

Jerome "Doc Pomus" Felder was a famous songwriter of the 1950s and '60s, and in conjunction with his partner, Mort Shuman, he wrote—among dozens of hits—"Viva Las Vegas" and "Little Sister," both recorded by Elvis Presley. He also wrote "Save the Last Dance for Me," most notably recorded by the Drifters (and said to be one of the 25 most popular songs ever recorded). Crippled by polio as a child, Pomus had to use crutches (and later, a wheelchair) throughout most of his life. At his wedding, he arranged for his brother, equally famous divorce attorney Raoul Felder, to act as his stand-in for the traditional first dance with the bride. According to a member of Doc's family, when relatives went through his effects after his death, they discovered an invitation from the wedding, embossed with the names of Doc and his wife. When they turned the invitation over, they found the jottings of what became the hit—reminding a woman that, although she might dance with other suitors, she should always keep in mind the man who would take her home at evening's end.

"Yesterday" (1965)

Among the many hit Beatles songs, "Yesterday" stands out for several reasons. Released in the fall of 1965, it was the first single to feature only one Beatle—Paul—on it, as the other three are not found anywhere on the recording. It also has the distinction of being the most rerecorded song in pop music—more than 3,000 cover versions have been produced by other artists over the years. Like many composers, Paul McCartney wrote the tune first, then the lyrics later. As such, "Yesterday" was called "Scrambled Eggs" until Paul finished the words.

Unbelievable Beliefs

❖ ❖ ❖ ❖

*Faith is a very personal experience, and by definition,
it is not based on fact. Over the centuries, people have
expressed their faith in a variety of unique philosophies.*

The Hollow Earth Theory
In the early 19th century, John Cleves Symmes promoted the Hollow Earth Theory, which stated that the planet was actually several populated worlds nesting inside one another. Symmes's ideas influenced Cyrus Teed, who developed Koreshan Unity, a religion based on the theory. For about 100 years, Koreshan Unity drew thousands of followers worldwide. The Hollow Earth Theory was revived during World War II, when some authors theorized that the Nazis actually came from an underground civilization. More recently, Kevin and Matthew Taylor spent 12 years investigating the idea; they wrote a book about their findings, *The Land of No Horizon*.

The Millerites
William Miller, a farmer in northern New York, founded a doomsday cult in the 1800s. Studying the Bible convinced Miller that humanity was due for damnation. He began preaching this message in the early 1830s. His first prediction was that Jesus Christ would "come again to the earth, cleanse, purify and take possession of the same" between March 1843 and March 1844. When a comet appeared early in 1843, a number of his followers killed themselves, believing the end was near. However, when his prophecy didn't come to pass and the world survived, Miller stood by his message but became reluctant to set actual dates. Some of his followers took it upon themselves to announce October 22, 1844, as the big day, and Miller reluctantly agreed. This date came to be known as The Great Disappointment. Regardless, Miller and his followers established a basis on which the Seventh-Day Adventist Church was later founded.

The Raelian Movement
A belief in unidentified flying objects has haunted humanity for generations, with thousands claiming to have had direct contact

with alien beings from other worlds. Claude Vorilhon, a French race car driver and onetime musician, asserted that he was visited by an extraterrestrial in 1973. It was a life-altering experience for him that caused him to change his name to Rael and found the Raelian Church. Rael's religion proclaims that the *Elohim* ("those who came from the sky") created everything on Earth. Although many turn a skeptical eye toward Vorilhon, whose faith also preaches free love, the Raelian Movement is said to include as many as 65,000 members worldwide.

The Vampire Church

With offices located throughout the United States, Canada, and Australia, the Vampire Church provides the initiated and the curious with an opportunity to learn more about vampirism. However, don't expect to find much about the "undead," as vampires have been portrayed in stories since Bram Stoker wrote *Dracula* in 1897. Instead, the church offers insight into vampirism as a physical condition that sometimes requires unusual energy resources, such as blood. In addition, it explains the difference between psychic vampires and elemental vampires. According to the church's Web site, "The Vampire Church continues to grow as more true vampires find the haven they so seek with others of this condition and the knowledge and experience of others here."

The Church of Euthanasia

"Save the Planet—Kill Yourself." These words are the battle cry of the Church of Euthanasia, which was established by Boston resident Chris Korda in 1992. Korda, a musician, had a dream one night about an alien who warned her that Earth was in serious danger. The extraterrestrial, which Korda dubbed "The Being," stressed the importance of protecting the planet's environment through population control. As a result of the encounter, Korda established the Church of Euthanasia, which supports suicide, abortion, and sodomy (defined as any sex act that is not intended for procreation). According to the church's Web site, members are vegetarian, but they "support cannibalism for those who insist on eating flesh." Although it reportedly has only about 100 members in the Boston area, the church claims that thousands worldwide have visited its Web site and been exposed to its message.

The Times They Are A-Changin'

2001

January 8: A Southeast Asian ox called a *gaur* is born, becoming the first endangered species to be cloned.

February 12: The *NEAR Shoemaker* spacecraft becomes the first Earth vessel to land on an asteroid, 433 Eros.

February 18: NASCAR driver Dale Earnhardt is killed instantly in a crash on the last lap of the Daytona 500.

March 23: The Russian space station *Mir* crashes into the Pacific Ocean after a controlled reentry.

April 1: A Chinese fighter jet bumps a U.S. surveillance aircraft, forcing the American aircraft to make an emergency landing in China, where the crew is detained for 12 days.

April 28: After paying $20 million to become the first space tourist, Dennis Tito flies in a Russian capsule to the International Space Station.

June 11: Timothy McVeigh is executed for the 1995 Oklahoma City bombing.

July 2: Robert Tools receives the world's first self-contained artificial heart.

September 11: Nearly 3,000 people are killed when terrorists crash four hijacked planes into the World Trade Center in New York City, the Pentagon in Washington, D.C., and a field in Pennsylvania.

September 18: Letters containing anthrax, a poison, are mailed from Princeton, New Jersey, to ABC News, CBS News, NBC News, the *New York Post,* and the *National Enquirer.*

October 5: San Francisco Giants slugger Barry Bonds hits his 71st and 72nd home runs of the year, breaking the single-season home run record held by Mark McGwire.

November 22: Pope John Paul II sends the first papal e-mail from a computer in his Vatican office.

December 2: Enron files for Chapter 11 bankruptcy protection, becoming the largest business collapse in U.S. history up to that date.

Dynamite! The Life and Times of Alfred Nobel

It was a legacy that was hard to live down. But Alfred B. Nobel—inventor of the explosive dynamite—took what many considered to be a negative and used it to give back to humanity. Nobel's story is one of lifelong learning and perseverance, as well as isolation and loneliness.

The Initial Spark

Alfred Nobel was born in Stockholm, Sweden, in 1833, the son of Immanuel and Andriette Nobel. His father was a natural-born inventor who received three mechanical patents at the young age of 24. Yet, due to a series of financial disasters, Nobel was born into a family mired in bankruptcy. Frail and sickly, he excelled in academics during a brief stint in grade school. The family moved to St. Petersburg, Russia, when Nobel was only nine years old. He showed an amazing facility with languages, eventually becoming fluent in five: Swedish, Russian, French, English, and German.

Nobel's formal education concluded with a series of tutors, including a chemistry professor named Ninin who introduced a teenage Nobel to the volatile liquid nitroglycerine. Discovered by Italian chemist Ascanio Sobrero in 1847, the oily and highly unstable fluid was extremely sensitive to shock, making it a dangerous explosive. Sobrero was convinced that the substance could never be tamed. But Nobel's father had become an expert in manufacturing armaments, such as land and sea mines, so Nobel's interest in nitro served the family business as well.

The end of the Crimean War sent the Nobel and Sons munitions company into bankruptcy. Returning to Stockholm, Nobel and his three brothers formed a new company, appropriately named Brothers

Nobel, and continued working with nitroglycerine. The Swedish military showed great interest in the brothers' efforts, so a demonstration was arranged. Nobel filled an iron barrel with half gunpowder and half nitro and urged everyone to step back. The result was a bit *too* successful—a thundering explosion rocked the area, prompting the military to deem the mixture much too risky. They immediately ceased all further contact with the Brothers Nobel.

Stockholm Becomes a Boomtown

Nobel became obsessed with calming the wild nitroglycerine, working nonstop for days at a time. By 1863, he succeeded in igniting a mixture of gunpowder and nitro by means of a fuse. The triumph resulted in new manufacturing plants in Sweden, Germany, and Norway, although his efforts were not without disaster.

In the fall of 1864, Nobel's younger brother Emil was mixing chemicals at the plant in Stockholm. More than 40 gallons of nitroglycerine were stored there, so when a tremendous explosion rocked the area, it literally blew its six victims, including Emil, to pieces. For safety's sake, Nobel moved his experiments to a barge in Bockholm Bay, Sweden.

A Flash of Ingenuity

In an 1889 letter, Nobel noted his greatest invention by writing, "I prepared and detonated the first dynamite charge . . . in November 1863," although most sources note the patent date of 1867. Nobel finally calmed nitro by mixing it with kieselguhr—a chalky mineral made mostly of silica. The result was a paste that could be safely handled and rolled into paper tubes. He called his new creation *dynamite,* from the Greek word for "power." Dynamite became a safe means of removing large amounts of earth for mining and tunneling, as well as construction. Establishing worldwide manufacturing and distribution of dynamite, Nobel became wealthy and successful.

But there was a problem with this new invention: When it was stored, the nitro would slowly leak from the dynamite, once again resulting in an unstable and dangerous liquid. Nobel studied the problem and came up with the solution in 1876. He mixed nitro with wood pulp and other minerals, creating a compound Nobel called blasting gelatin. When ignited with a separate detonator, it became an even better method for excavation.

The Final Blast

Nobel knew that his invention would not only be used for constructive purposes. A substance as devastating as dynamite would also be used for violence and crime. Nobel had no wish to be remembered solely as the inventor of dynamite—after all, he amassed more than 350 patents in his career, many in the field of synthetic materials. He also wrote a tragic play, *Nemesis,* late in his life.

An incorrectly placed obituary in an 1888 French newspaper prematurely told of Nobel's passing, referring to him as "the merchant of death." Such a sobriquet did not suit Nobel. In fragile and failing health, he wrote a will in November 1895; the will stipulated that his fortune be used to establish a fund for making annual awards to individuals who "shall have conferred the greatest benefit on mankind." Five prizes would be given, one each in the fields of chemistry, physics, medicine, literature, and peace—"the best work for fraternity between the nations, for the abolition or reduction of standing armies, and for the holding and promotion of peace." (A sixth prize, for economics, was established in 1969.) Nobel, satisfied that he had left the world with a sense of hope and promise, died on December 10, 1896, following a stroke.

Prize Winners

The first Nobel Prizes were given in 1901. In the time since, U.S. presidents Teddy Roosevelt, Woodrow Wilson, and Jimmy Carter have received the peace prize, along with other notables including Mother Teresa, Albert Schweitzer, the Dalai Lama, Mikhail Gorbachev, Al Gore, and Martin Luther King, Jr. Winners in literature include Rudyard Kipling, George Bernard Shaw, Sinclair Lewis, Eugene O'Neill, Pearl S. Buck, William Faulkner, Winston Churchill, Ernest Hemingway, Boris Pasternak, John Steinbeck, Jean-Paul Sartre, and Toni Morrison. Recipients in the sciences and medicine include Marie Curie (twice; as well as daughter Irene, some 24 years later), Linus Pauling, Frederick Sanger (twice), Wilhelm Roentgen, Guglielmo Marconi, Max Planck, Albert Einstein, Niels Bohr (as well as son Aage, 53 years later), Enrico Fermi, and Ivan Pavlov. Recipients in economics include Milton Friedman and James Tobin. Those who many believe *should* have won a Nobel Prize but never did include Thomas Edison, Nikola Tesla, Mohandas Gandhi (nominated five times), Robert Oppenheimer, and Dmitry Mendeleyev.

Fast Facts

- Bill Gates's first business was Traff-O-Data, a company that developed machines to record the number of vehicles passing selected road points.

- The stripes on a tiger's face are used for identification, since no two tigers sport the same stripe pattern.

- In 1939, a group of Soviet meteorologists who studied Arctic temperatures over a decade concluded that the world's temperature was slowly rising and predicted global warming.

- Temperature variations on Earth's moon can range from 280° F during the daytime to −400° F at night.

- English Queen Elizabeth I felt she had a homely face and had all mirrors removed from her palace and forbade any artist from drawing her likeness except "especial cunning painters."

- Erich Alfred Hartmann, "The Black Devil" of the German Luftwaffe during World War II, flew more than 1,400 combat missions and scored 352 aerial victories, the most of any German pilot.

- Only three men—Dan Reeves, Mike Ditka, and Tony Dungy— have appeared in the Super Bowl as a player, an assistant coach, and a head coach.

- Nero attempted to kill his mother, Agrippina, four times before his guards stabbed her to death. Before she died, she requested to be stabbed in the womb, where Nero was conceived.

- Brain surgery is often performed with the patient awake. Since the brain has no nerves, the patient doesn't feel any pain.

- In the last month of his life, Vincent van Gogh completed a painting a day.

The Unlikely Art Career of Grandma Moses

Late bloomers, take heart: You haven't missed your chance. That's one of the most significant lessons to be learned from the incredible life of Anna Mary Robertson Moses (1860–1961), known to the world as "Grandma" Moses.

She was born before Abraham Lincoln took office, and when she died, President Kennedy offered tribute: "Both her work and her life helped our nation renew its pioneer heritage and recall its roots in the countryside and on the frontier. All Americans mourn her loss." Grandma Moses was one of the most successful, famous artists in her home country, and possibly the best-known American artist in Europe. Featured on radio, on television, and in magazines, Moses was the first artist to become a media superstar, and the influence of her unique, naive, folk-art style continues to this day. Indeed, it would not be outlandish to say that Grandma Moses was, and remains, the most famous female artist of all time.

Unexpected Success

It all started in 1938, when a New York City art collector drove through Moses's hometown of Hoosick Falls, New York, and spied her paintings in a drugstore. He bought them all, and then he found her at home, where he snapped up all of her remaining work. The following year, she was represented in an exhibition of contemporary unknown painters at the Museum of Modern Art in New York. And the year after that, "What a Farmwife Painted" opened at New York's Galerie St. Etienne. The exhibition stopped people in their tracks— and not only because the artist first began to paint seriously when she was 76 years old (due to arthritis, which made her forfeit her beloved embroidery). It was her subject matter, the nostalgic remembrance of things past, in what appeared to be a much simpler time: ordinary farm activities, such as maple sugaring or making candles, soap, and apple butter. But it was also the charming optimism, luminous color, and realism that emanated from the canvases, which then cost three to five dollars. These paintings were later reproduced on everything from ceramic plates to greeting cards.

Not All as Easy as It Seemed

But Grandma Moses's life was no rose garden. She was indeed a farmwife, with all that entailed, and a "hired girl" before that. At 12, she left school and home, where she had four sisters and five brothers, to go to work. At 27, she married the hired hand on the farm where she did the housework, and they had ten children, five of whom died as infants. Grandma Moses eventually outlived her husband and all of her children, but she did enjoy her 9 grandchildren and more than 30 great-grandchildren.

Grandma Moses painted more than 1,000 pictures, including 25 after her 100th birthday. The paintings have increased dramatically in value: Today her smallest works begin at $15,000, whereas a large oil painting can command in excess of $100,000.

In 2001, the Galerie St. Etienne created a traveling exhibition entitled "Grandma Moses in the 21st Century." It earned rave reviews from the public and critics, including the *New York Observer*'s notoriously tough Hilton Kramer, who gushed: "Grandma Moses is back, and she's enchanting."

Grandma Moses was a tough old gal, but her basic philosophy was one that remains relevant: "I look back on my life like a good day's work; it was done and I feel satisfied with it. I was happy and contented, I knew nothing better and made the best out of what life offered. And life is what we make it, always has been, always will be."

- *The average person uses just over three-quarters of a ton of wood each year in housing, paper goods, and other products that use it as an ingredient.*

- *The first auto race in the United States took place in Evanston, Illinois, on November 28, 1895. Frank Duryea beat three gas-fueled and two electric cars to win.*

- *According to lore, after the first Duke of Monmouth was beheaded in 1685, he was discovered to be lacking an official portrait. So his body was disinterred, his head sewn back on, and his portrait painted.*

Hot-rodding Heats Up

Victorious American GIs returned from World War II ready to kick up their heels. They had fought hard, and once they got back, they wanted to play hard. They had money to burn, having saved their military pay for the day when the war would be over. For many, the mechanical skills they had honed during the conflict prepared them for the perfect pastime—hot-rodding.

Excess cash, combined with the first automobiles to be manufactured in the country in five years, created a boom in new car sales across the United States. But instead of merely junking their old sedans, people began to tinker under the hood and chop the bodies of these beaters.

Southern California Is Ground Zero

The term *hot rod* most likely derived from *hot roadster,* and that's exactly what these cars were. These supercharged flying flivvers cropped up from coast to coast. But the center of this new diversion was Southern California, where warm weather and open land combined to make the perfect spot for racing.

The area north of Los Angeles, near the towns of Glendale, Pasadena, and Burbank, was covered with dry lake beds. The miles of barren land became the meeting place for gearheads and their thundering machines. Abandoned military airport runways were also natural racetrack straightaways, giving hot rods the chance to flex their metallic muscles in exciting drag races.

The phenomenon was not lost on people such as Wally Parks, who founded the National Hot Rod Association (NHRA) in 1951; the organization focused on safety and innovation. Magazines such as *Hot Rod* (which premiered in 1948) also supported action that was based on quality and care.

Unable to contain the growing craze, southern California gave up its hold on hot-rodding as it spread across the country. But areas such as the Midwest and New England were short on dry lake beds, so hot rods took to the streets of America, forcing police officers to chase down these speedsters.

WHO KNEW?

"Taking the Odds" Doesn't Mean You Always Win

The car used as a time machine in the *Back to the Future* movies was a De Lorean. Its inventor, John De Lorean, manufactured 9,000 cars in 1981. On the verge of success, the entrepreneur appeared in an ad for Cutty Sark alcohol that same year. Its tagline read, "One out of every 100 new businesses succeeds. Here's to those who take the odds." The De Lorean plant closed in 1982. Ouch!

Reach Out and Touch Someone

On December 11, 2004, more than five million people joined hands to form a human chain 652.4 miles (1,050 kilometers) long. It snaked from Teknaf to Tentulia in Bangladesh. Organizers, who billed the event as a human wall, were protesting against the ruling political party at the time. The chain averaged 7,664 people per mile.

Free-falling

Are there any bungee jumpers out there who enjoy the experience but find it's over far too quickly? They should visit the Sky Jump at the Macau Tower Convention and Entertainment Center in Macau, off the east coast of China. The ride starts on the 61st floor of the building—764 feet above the ground—and drops riders in a controlled descent for 17 to 20 seconds. Not a pure bungee jump, the Sky Jump offers a "decelerator descent" ride, which features a second cable to guide the direction of the fall rather than simply a free-swinging bungee cord.

He's Got a Basketball Jones

Despite standing at a petite height somewhere around 5'2" (minus the heels), artist extraordinaire Prince Rogers Nelson, or just simply Prince, is an excellent basketball player. In fact, he was well-known for his exceptional ball-handling ability and speed in high school.

Football Firsts

On February 4, 2007, Tony Dungy of the Indianapolis Colts and Lovie Smith of the Chicago Bears made football history. Super Bowl XLI marked the first time an African American appeared as the head coach of a football team in that event. It doesn't matter which one was present on the sidelines first. Both were present at the start of the game, so they share the designation of "first."

Military Blunders 101

❖ ❖ ❖ ❖

Many of military history's biggest blunders have resulted from inexperience, negligence, diplomatic indifference, incompetence, lack of discipline, overconfidence, or poor information. Some would be laughable, if they hadn't resulted in the loss of human lives.

The Battle of Karansebes (1788)

What was meant to be a decisive engagement against the Ottoman Empire during the Russo-Turkish War turned out to be a self-destructive defeat. Two contingents of the Austrian army—one scouting the enemy, the other setting up camp—converged; each thought the other was the enemy, and a battle ensued. The scouting party had been imbibing a little schnapps, and discipline fell apart. The Austrians killed 10,000 of their own troops while the enemy was still a two-day march away.

Pearl Harbor (December 7, 1941)

This battle is considered to be a double blunder: one each for the Americans and the Japanese. Though the debate continues to this day as to whether America had advance warning of the attack, many historians say both U.S. and British authorities should have known an attack was imminent and chose to ignore it so America would enter the war in Europe. The Japanese, on the other hand, may have surprised American forces, but they came up short on their two main objectives. They did not destroy the American fleet, because aircraft carriers were on maneuvers and not in port on the day of the attack. They also missed the oil refineries, which, despite damage and loss of lives, remained untouched. The attack was also meant to crush America's morale, but it had just the opposite effect: It spurred American patriotism as never before in history. Japanese Admiral Yamamoto expressed it best when he suggested: "I'm afraid we have awakened a sleeping giant and filled it with terrible resolve."

Hitler Declares War on the United States (1941)

Even the mighty führer blundered big time when he declared war on the United States immediately following the sneak attack on

Pearl Harbor. He walked right into President Franklin Roosevelt's web. The president had been waiting for a reason to enter the war in Europe. With the addition of the United States, the combined Allied forces were a little too much for Hitler, who just might have achieved his objective of dominance if he'd played the right card at the right time.

The Bay of Pigs Invasions (both of them)

Yes, there were two. The first one was in August 1851, when former Spanish officer and Cuban sympathizer Narciso López recruited a band of American mercenaries and landed at the Bahía de Cochinos (Bay of Pigs) to engage Spanish forces. The invaders were handily defeated and most were executed, including López and Colonel William Crittenden, nephew of American Attorney General John Crittenden. According to experts, the attack was a tactical error. The Bay of Pigs is too easily defended against an invasion from the sea.

Although President Kennedy voluntarily took the heat for the failure of the second Bay of Pigs debacle (which consisted of CIA-trained Cuban exiles, who expected but never received American support), the reason for the second failure was much the same as the first: The Bay of Pigs can be defended much too easily. In this case, however, contrary to the expectations of the Cuban exiles, many in the local population took up arms against the invaders who were there to liberate them. Fidel Castro was still a popular hero to many.

The Spanish-American War (1898)

SNAFU and *FUBAR* are both acronyms that originated in the military—Situation Normal All Fouled Up and Fouled Up Beyond All Recognition. At the start of the Spanish-American War, General William Rufus Shafter's troops were issued woolen winter uniforms. The tropical climate in Cuba took a greater toll on the troops than the fighting did—even the 375-pound Shafter was a victim of heat prostration. Additionally, the troopship set to transport the Rough Riders to Cuba was not large enough to carry the troops and their horses. Only one man was mounted in the "cavalry" charge up San Juan Hill: Lieutenant Colonel Theodore Roosevelt, who was allowed to bring his favorite horse, Little Texas. The other horses were left behind. The Rough Riders became the "Tough Trekkers" when they hoofed it up the hill.

Custer's Last Stand (The Battle of Little Bighorn, 1876)

No list of military blunders would be complete without this infamous cavalry catastrophe. It was mostly Custer's impatience and arrogance that caused the massacre of the Seventh Cavalry unit he led into battle. Custer's scouts also underestimated the size of the enemy force, an amalgamation of Cheyenne, Arapaho, and Sioux, consisting of nearly 2,000 warriors. Custer's force numbered 263. If he'd waited a little longer, Custer would have linked up with the rest of his command and had a fighting chance.

The Charge of the Light Brigade (The Battle of Balaklava, 1854)

This is another obvious choice. The Battle of Balaklava was one of the key engagements of the Crimean War. Major General Cardigan misunderstood the orders of his superior commander, Lieutenant General Raglan, and led his 670-strong cavalry unit to attack a Russian artillery bastion of more than 5,000. They went at it head-on, resulting in the deaths of 118 attackers (127 more were wounded). Cardigan survived long enough to become a field marshal—and have a sweater named after him. The battle itself was considered indecisive.

Invasion of Russia (1812 and 1941)

Perhaps the best known tactical errors involve Russia; both Napoleon and Adolf Hitler were helped to defeat by their unwise attacks on its vast, cold expanse. In Napoleon's case, his foolhardy 1812 invasion was foiled by strategic Russian retreats and the onset of the bitter winter. This failure was the beginning of the end for Napoleon, who ultimately abdicated the French throne in 1814.

Not learning from Napoleon's mistake, however, Hitler invaded the USSR in 1941, violating the 1939 nonaggression pact between Nazi Germany and Russia and exposing the Third Reich to a two-front war. The element of surprise and superior German equipment brought early success to Hitler's forces, but delays brought his army face-to-face with the brutal Russian winter. Mother Nature decimated the German troops, proving that the "master race" was no match for its biting cold.

Weird Fetishes

Although most people give the word fetish *a sexual connotation,
the dictionary also describes a fetish as "any object or idea
eliciting unquestioning reverence, respect, or devotion."
Since that covers a wide range of territory, here are just a
few of the more interesting fetishes reported of late.*

- A Tennessee man complained that his home had been burgled; among other things stolen were more than 300 tongue rings.

- A British machinist with bad earaches was found to have a pregnant spider living in his ear. He told a reporter that he had grown fond of the spider and intended to keep it as a pet.

- A 12-year-old Michigan boy has had an obsession with vacuum cleaners since infancy, when, according to his mother, he was mesmerized by the whirring noise. The boy enjoys vacuuming so much that he does the house up to five times a day with one of the 165 vacuum cleaners in his collection. Said a teacher, "It's not that he doesn't like recess, it's just that he prefers to stay in and clean."

- A Canadian woman *really* likes her daily newspaper. She not only reads it, but she eats it in strips and has done so for the past seven years—because it tastes good. Her only problem occurred when she developed a blockage of her esophagus, whereupon doctors found a ball of paper. After removing it, her doctors said that aside from the obstruction, eating newspaper is not bad for your health.

- In Detroit, a man was arrested for the seventh time—this time for stealing a mannequin outfitted in a French maid's uniform. The arrest came days after he was released for his sixth offense: stealing a mannequin with bobbed hair wearing a pink dress.

- One London woman walks around all day dressed as a beekeeper. She said she must do this because of her "electrical sensitivity." The veil keeps away the incapacitating waves from appliances, including cell phones and refrigerators. Her house windows have silver gauze shades, and the wallpaper has a tinfoil lining.

Christian Dior: From Frumpy Frocks to Flowing Fashion

Today, it seems like everything that can be done with fashion, pretty much has been done. Shapes, fabrics, cuts—people have worn and/or shunned it all. Even the sometimes alarming club-kid looks of the 1990s barely raise eyebrows today. But imagine what it must have been like before all those doors were opened.

In the 1950s, modern fashion and classic looks were just beginning to take shape. Surely it was exciting, after the rationing of everything from butter to stockings during World War II, for women to wear a beautiful, billowing dress, soft to the touch and conjuring images of a fashionable beauty the world had never seen before.

One might think that women everywhere would've tripped over themselves to make this look their own, but many were indignant: How dare an unknown designer waste luxurious fabrics creating elaborate dresses and suits while everyone else was mending old items and rationing?

The designer, of course, was Christian Dior, and one of his bedrock principles was that he did not compromise fashion for responsibility.

Great Ambitions

Born in Granville in the Normandy region of France in 1905, Dior was an unassuming, average-looking man who wouldn't even compromise with his beloved family. His father, a fertilizer manufacturer, hoped that Christian would go into the family business, but the young man had no desire for that lifestyle. Instead, Dior pursued a career in the arts, and in 1938 he landed a job as an assistant to designer Robert Piquet. But World War II loomed, and just one year later, Dior was off to fight.

Surviving the war, Dior returned home. The fighting had ravaged France, but the economy was slowly rebuilding; Dior knew he'd have to act soon to make his mark in the fashion industry. He approached fabric magnate Marcel Broussac with an idea that would

---

reinvent fashion—goodbye to the fabric shortage and stiff textiles, hello to accentuated curves and attention to detail.

On February 12, 1947, with backing from Broussac, Dior debuted his Corelle line, a new, refreshing, uplifting look. Shoulder pads were gone, hems were lengthened, waists were slimmed, and dresses flowed. Dior wanted to free women from the repressive styles that had accompanied them to the fields and industrial jobs they worked while the men were away fighting. He wanted to turn them back into "flower women." He accomplished this goal with suit jackets that tucked in at the waist and expanded at the hips, creating an inverted bellflower shape. As *Harper's Bazaar* editor Carmel Snow said, "It's quite a revelation, dear Christian. Your dresses have a new look."

New Look, Old Reactions

At first, middle-class women were appalled by the New Look, as the Corelle line came to be known. It seemed so extravagant, so wasteful. But Hollywood and the wealthy embraced the style. Stars Ava Gardner, Rita Hayworth, and Marlene Dietrich wore Dior creations to movie premieres to create the epitome of celebrity glamour. England's Princess Margaret wore them in private—the king forbade her and her sister, Princess Elizabeth, to wear such illustrious garments in public when common people were still participating in fabric rationing.

Dior Surprises Again

The New Look changed fashion, yet as Dior got bored and times changed, the designer did a complete overhaul and introduced the Flat Look. Think Audrey Hepburn, in simple, skinny black pants and matching cardigans, with flat shoes. Dresses went from detailed and flowing to boxy flat sheets, accentuating and complementing nothing about the woman's body. The same people who had jeered the New Look couldn't believe that Dior was trying to hide the female form.

But of course, Dior didn't let the critics shake him; the Flat Look, like the New Look before it, eventually caught on. Dior's reputation was solidified in the fashion industry, and he began to make deals to produce ties and cosmetics. Unfortunately, Dior died of a heart attack in 1957. Today, Dior is still a coveted name among young fashionistas and classic beauties all over the globe.

He Said, She Said

I have as much authority as the Pope. I just don't have as many people who believe it.

—*George Carlin*

Old age is like a plane flying through a storm. Once you're aboard, there's nothing you can do.

—*Golda Meir*

Everyone has a talent; what is rare is the courage to follow the talent to the dark place where it leads.

—*Erica Jong*

Majority rule only works if you're also considering individual rights. Because you can't have five wolves and one sheep voting on what to have for supper.

—*Larry Flynt*

We can lick gravity, but sometimes the paperwork is overwhelming.

—*Wernher von Braun*

The only valid censorship of ideas is the right of people not to listen.

—*Tommy Smothers*

Growth demands a temporary surrender of security.

—*Gail Sheehy*

A book is a version of the world. If you do not like it, ignore it; or offer your own version in return.

—*Salman Rushdie*

A business that makes nothing but money is a poor business.

—*Henry Ford*

I eat at this German-Chinese restaurant and the food is delicious. The only problem is that an hour later you're hungry for power.

—*Dick Cavett*

We rarely confide in those who are better than we are.

—*Albert Camus*

Vegetarian—that's an old Indian word meaning "lousy hunter."

—*Andy Rooney*

World's Most Unusual Museums

*A list of every hyper-specific museum in the world could fill
(and no doubt has filled) a book of its own, but perhaps this
random sampling might fuel some interesting vacation ideas.*

Beatles for Sale

Anywhere with even the slightest Beatles connection has tried to
cash in on the fame of the Fab Four, and although the most authentic sites are naturally in Liverpool, American fans need not despair.
The Hard Day's Nite [*sic*] B&B & Beatles Mini-Museum in Benton,
Illinois, is a house once owned by George Harrison's sister Louise
and boasts a room used by George himself. Louise answered thousands of fan letters from here. Off the mainland, the Kauai Country
Inn, the only Beatles museum in Hawaii, is also a organic farm with
an "extensive 40-year collection . . . including a Mini Cooper 'S' car
registered by [manager] Brian Epstein . . . and many other interesting items." It's also conveniently located near the Waialua River's
"Fern Grotto," used as a location in Elvis Presley's *Blue Hawaii*.

Elvis Has Left the Building

Speaking of the King, aside from the obvious tour of Graceland and
a visit to the Tupelo, Mississippi, shotgun shack (complete with gift
shop and chapel) where he and his twin, Jesse Garon, were born,
there's the "world's largest private collection of Elvis memorabilia" in
Pigeon Forge, Tennessee. Where else can you see items such as EP's
1967 "Honeymoon" Cadillac; the headboard from his Hollywood
bedroom, and artifacts from his last tour, including Prell shampoo
and Crest toothpaste?

The Peanut Gallery

Elvis's favorite sandwich was fried peanut butter, bacon, and banana;
and while we couldn't divine a shrine to pork, there *is* a First Peanut
Museum (in Waverly, Virginia), with myriad peanut memorabilia.
It competes against the Agrirama Peanut Museum in Tifton, Georgia,
which depicts "the dramatic transition from the horse and mule days
to mechanized farming." Neither of these should be confused with

the Charles M. Schulz Museum and Research Center in California's Santa Rosa, devoted to the man who created the comic strip *Peanuts.*

Gone Bananas

Top this off by visiting the International Banana Club Museum in Hesperia, California. The *Guinness Book of World Records* declared that this was the world's largest collection devoted to a single fruit. Established in 1976, it spent 32 years in Altadena, California, before moving to its present location. You'll find banana lamps, gold-plated bananas, banana trees, banana body spray, and even a Banana Club golf putter.

There's No Such Thing as Too Much Cheese

Still peckish? Consider the Netherlands' Kaasmuseum (Cheese Museum), located in Alkmaar in a 14th-century chapel. No buxom maids a-churning, just mechanisms for making and weighing the finished product; visit the outdoor cheese market Fridays from 10:00 A.M. to noon. (Alkmaar also has its own Fab Four museum.) Then there is the chocolate museum in Barcelona (which features entire dioramas, including bullfights, sculpted out of the sweet stuff) and one in Cologne (the 13,000-square-foot Schokoladenmuseum has its own greenhouse to support cacao plants). But don't forget the Burlingame, California, Pez Museum, which has every dispenser ever made—including a rare counterfeit one of Adolf Hitler.

Medical Mayhem

If that's not enough to kill an appetite, there's New York's Burns Archive, which houses photos of people with nightmarish medical conditions, and the Lizzie Borden B&B in Falls River, Massachusetts, site of two grisly ax murders, complete with obligatory gift shop. Or there's the possibility of Philadelphia's Mütter's Museum, "home to a plethora of what were once quaintly referred to as freaks," including a full-body cast of Chang and Eng, the original Siamese twins; a soap woman (buried in chemicals that turned her to, yes, soap); body tissue from presidential assassin John Wilkes Booth; and a giant colon. And don't forget the Cockroach Hall of Fame in Plano, Texas, which features dead insects dressed as celebrities, such as Liberoache and Marilyn Monroach (complete with blonde hair and white dress).

Fast Facts

- George Washington had only one tooth left by the time he was elected president. It is believed his loss of teeth was due to a mercury oxide treatment for malaria and smallpox.

- Dates, statistics, and other factual memories (such as trivia) are stored in the front left side of the brain.

- The iconic Disneyland castle that's so familiar was modeled on Neuschwanstein Castle, a real-life German castle built by King Ludwig II in the late 1860s and '70s.

- The Spirit of Ecstasy is the name of the sculpture on the hood of a Rolls-Royce.

- In 1988, the U.S. Patent Office awarded a patent to Harvard University for developing a genetically engineered mouse, the first patent ever awarded for an animal.

- The Battle of Long Island was the largest battle fought during the American Revolution. In August and September 1776, British troops drove the Continental Army first from Long Island and then Manhattan.

- A fully loaded semitrailer can weigh more than 40 tons. An average car with passengers weighs around one-and-a-half tons.

- The official U.S. presidential theme song is "Hail to the Chief." The music was originally written for verses of Sir Walter Scott's poem "The Lady of the Lake" in 1810.

- In 1999, the Houston Astros signed a 30-year, $100 million stadium-naming-rights deal with Enron. In 2001, they paid $2 million just to drop the name.

- Shaking hands spreads more germs than kissing does.

Love in the Time of Art: The Complex Affair of Frida Kahlo and Diego Rivera

❖ ❖ ❖ ❖

Even a typical, run-of-the-mill love affair is prone to ups and downs. But the relationship between artists Frida Kahlo and Diego Rivera gives the typical love story a run for its money. Jealousy, disloyalty, and short tempers along with a hefty dose of adultery, bisexuality, physical disability, artistic genius, and fame all play a part in one of the most fascinating love stories of modern times.

Meet the Girl

Frida Kahlo was born in 1907 in Coyoacan, Mexico, a small town near Mexico City. Kahlo contracted polio at age six; as a result, her right leg and foot were thin and stunted, a deformity that embarrassed her through childhood. At age 15, Kahlo enrolled in the National Preparatory School in Mexico City, where she became known for her personality and academic ability. In 1925, Kahlo was on the brink of graduating when she was seriously injured in a bus accident. She was bedridden for several months and sustained injuries to her back, pelvic bone, and spinal column that would affect her for the rest of her life.

But great pain can bring great fortune, as it was during this time that Kahlo began to paint. Although she had received little formal training, Kahlo proved to have natural skill. She continued as an artist even after physically recovering from the accident.

Meet the Boy

Diego Rivera was born in 1886 in the small town of Guanajuato, Mexico. He began his formal artistic training at age 10, and by 20 he was a successful artist. During his 20s, he traveled internationally. He became known as a huge (six feet tall, 300 pounds), outspoken, womanizing, politically liberal, and morally questionable example of a man.

Rivera was also known for political influence in his art. In the early 1920s, the liberal Mexican government decided to reclaim the indigenous heritage of pre-Columbian Mexico. The minister of education appointed artists to adorn public buildings with murals depicting the lives of contemporary Amerindians and telling ancient stories of the past. In 1921, Rivera began the first of his murals, in the auditorium at the National Preparatory School in Mexico City.

Girl Meets Boy

Even the most ardent cynics can't deny that the meeting of Kahlo and Rivera was hopelessly romantic. Kahlo was a student at the National Preparatory School when Rivera painted his mural. She admired Rivera because he continued to paint his controversial mural despite the right-wing students who rioted against him. She hid in the back of the auditorium to watch him paint.

Years later, Kahlo encountered Rivera at a party held by a mutual friend. At one point during the party, the boisterous Rivera took out a pistol and shot the phonograph. Kahlo was intrigued.

Soon after, Kahlo learned that Rivera was creating a new mural at the Ministry of Education in Mexico City. She gathered up some of her own paintings, boarded a bus, and walked right up to Rivera while he was painting. She showed him her work, and asked what he thought. He told her that she had talent, and thus bloomed the beginning of their relationship.

They were married in 1929; Kahlo was 22 and Rivera, 42.

Boy Hurts Girl, Girl Hurts Boy

It's no surprise that this relationship was headed for stormy waters. In 1930, Rivera was commissioned to paint in San Francisco, and Kahlo came along for a sojourn in the States. During this period, she developed her own art but was known as Rivera's young wife. Kahlo believed in recapturing her indigenous heritage and dressed in bright colors, large jewelry, and flowing skirts. Rivera shared Kahlo's cultural views but nonetheless dressed in European suits.

This tension between the theory and practice of the couple's radical views was a recurring theme in their relationship. Kahlo once boasted, "I was a member of the Party before I met Diego and I think I am a better Communist than he is or ever will be." While they both denounced capitalism, Rivera admired the industrial progress of the West and hoped to reconcile it with Communism. This belief got him in trouble in 1933 when he included a depiction of Stalin in a mural he painted in New York City's Rockefeller Center. The mural was supposed to pay homage to the possibilities of industrial progress, and John D. Rockefeller himself insisted that Rivera paint out Stalin. When Rivera refused, the mural was destroyed.

Girl Paints Her Reality

Kahlo, meanwhile, hated the United States and what she considered its advanced state of social decay. Her unhappiness inspired some of her best work. Her beautiful, dreamlike landscapes reflect a sense of personal anguish and divided identity. She also used imagery and symbolism to make political and sociocultural statements. Her works have been called surrealist, although Kahlo rejected this designation, explaining, "I never painted dreams... I painted my own reality."

After the Rockefeller debacle, Rivera and Kahlo moved back to Mexico. Rivera's repeated infidelities strained their relationship, but in 1934, Frida discovered that Rivera was having an affair with her younger sister. This ruptured their marriage, and things would never be the same—Kahlo initiated various love affairs with both men and women. Her most notorious lover was Leon Trotsky.

Kahlo and Rivera's relationship continued to deteriorate, and they divorced in 1939. Seemingly unable to be happy together or apart, they remarried in 1941.

Boy Loses Girl

Throughout the 1940s, Kahlo's career took off, while Rivera's stagnated. But this decade also marked a decline in her health. Kahlo underwent several operations on her back and leg, but each operation only did more damage. However, Kahlo's fierce spirit and inextinguishable love for Rivera never diminished. Less than two weeks before her death, the couple took part in a demonstration against the American intervention in Guatemala—despite protests from her doctors.

Kahlo died on July 13, 1954. Her body was taken to the foyer of the Palacio de Bellas Artes in Mexico City. Rivera sat by her side the whole night, refusing to believe that she was dead. For better or worse, Rivera had been an unending inspiration to Kahlo's art, and it seems that Kahlo was as integral to Rivera's spirit. Rivera's health steadily declined after his wife's death, and he passed away in 1957.

Index

Browning, Robert, 155
Brownsville Boys, 403–4
Brudenell, James, 88
Buchanan, James, 117
Buckland, William, 453
Buckley, Jeff, 272
Buffett, Warren, 138
Bug collections, 361
Burt, Harry, 48
Bush, George H. W., 194
Bush, George W., 181
Butch Cassidy and the Sundance Kid, 225–26
Buttafuoco, Joey, 58
Buttafuoco, Mary Jo, 58
Byron, George Gordon (Lord Byron), 157–58

C
Cabral, Pedro Álvares, 298
Cadillac Ranch, 443
Cameron, James, 41–43
Camp Hero, 52–53
Canada
  Artists, 463–64
  Avrocar, 201–2
  Football, 262–63
  Gander, Newfoundland, 83–85
  Group of Seven, 463–64
  Ice Hotel, 171
  Magnetic hills, 436
  National Film Board, 256–57
  9/11, 83–85
  Nunavut, 519–20
  robberies, 15–17
  Stopwatch Gang, the, 15–17
  U.S. Border, 424–25
Cancer treatment, 112
Candy (Southern and Hoffenberg), 23–26
Candy bars, 473
Cantat, Bertrand, 60
Capone, Al, 204, 268–70, 479
Capote, Truman, 213
Captain Marvel, 446
Car art, 443
Carbonari, 165
Carbonated drinks, 103
Carhenge, 443
Carnaval, 434

Carnes, Kim, 533
Carnivorous plants, 206
Car racing, 402, 442, 542
Carrier pigeons, 233
Carroll, Lewis. *See* Dodgson, Charles Lutwidge.
Carter, Howard, 448
Carter, Jimmy, 194, 270, 347
Carter Center, 347
Cartopia, 443
Casablanca, 131
Casanova, 444
Castro, Fidel, 128–30, 546
Catch Me If You Can, 199
Catgut, 260
Catherine of Aragon, 527–28
Catnip, 417
Cats, 194, 203, 391, 409, 417
Cavett, Dick, 293
Ceausescu, Nicolae, 491
Celebrities, 312, 375, 444. *See also specific persons.*
Celestial objects, 169, 293, 298, 435, 540
Cell nuclei, 308
Cell phones, 57, 159
Central Park, 322–23
Cernan, Gene, 206
Chamales, Tom, 204
Chamberlain, Neville, 181
Chaplin, Charlie, 244, 258–60, 363–64
Charge of the Light Brigade, 88, 547
Charles, Ezzard, 193
Charles V (emperor of Rome), 179
Chawla, Kalpana, 398
Cherokee Nation, 264
Chiang Kai-Shek, 181
Chicago, Illinois, 204, 380
Chicago Cubs, 526
Chickens, 214
Childbirth, 231
Child pornography, 57
Chili peppers, 102, 431
China, 45–47, 179–81
Chinatown, 411
Chinese language, 298
Chinese Revolutionary Alliance, 166
Chinese United League, 166
Chiropractors, 138
Chopin, Frédéric, 99, 261

Dench, Judi, 154
De Niro, Robert, 131
Deodorant, 33
De Palma, Brian, 226, 384
Desbois, Jacques, 171
Detroit, Michigan, 437–38
Diamonds, 57, 392
Diapers, 82, 491
Dickinson, Emily, 124–26
Dick Van Dyke Show, The, 334
Didion, Joan, 213
Dillinger, John, 34–36, 113
Diners Club credit card, 49
Dion, 374
Dior, Christian, 549–50
Diplomatic blunders, 179–81
Disney, Walt, 381, 444, 523–25
Disneyland, 525, 554
Ditka, Mike, 540
Ditko, Steve, 38–39
Divorce, 139
DNA, 103, 310–11
Dodge, John and Horace, 247
Dodgson, Charles Lutwidge, 114–16
Dodo birds, 355
Dogon people, 37
Dogs, 87, 169, 361
Domino tournament, 200
Dors, Diana, 484
Dracula (films), 190
Dracula (novel), 341–43, 390–91
Drewe, John, 265–66
Drug busts, 347
Duncan, Kenne, 176
Dungy, Tony, 540
Duryea, Frank, 542
Dust mites, 510
Duyser, Diane, 163

E
Eagleton, Thomas, 402
Eastwood, Clint, 444
Eaton, William, 470–72
EC Comics, 69–71
Edible dinnerware, 37
Edison, Thomas, 28, 196, 427, 500
Egerton, Sir Francis Henry, 283
Eiffel Tower, 417
Einstein, Albert, 228
Eisenhower, Dwight D., 138, 181

Eisenstein, Sergei, 384
Eldridge, USS, 52–53
Electrocution, 28
Elephants, 28, 224, 337
Eliot, T. S., 183–84
Elizabeth (empress of Austria), 385
Elizabeth I (queen of England), 51, 337, 540
E-mail, 94
English language, 138
Enron, 132–34, 554
EPIC (End Poverty in California), 441–42
Eros magazine, 141
Etymology, 22, 65, 77, 135, 189, 236, 271, 331, 376, 408, 466
Evans, Dale, 430
Everest, Mount, 194
Executions, 355, 417, 499
Exotic dancers, 402

F
Fairbanks, Douglas, 363–64
Family, the, (cult), 326
Fantastic Four, The, 39
Fargo, 462
Farrow, Mia, 96–97
Fashion
    blunders, 289–90
    Christian Dior, 549–50
    hairstyles, 285–86
    little black dress, 239
    swimsuits, 185
    underarm hair, 194
Fast Food Nation (Schlosser), 280
Fastow, Andrew, 133
Fawcett Comics, 446
FAX machines, 510
Federal Reserve, 461
Felder, Jerome "Doc Pomus," 533
Fenians, 165–66
Ferdinand, Franz, 165
Fetishes, 548
Field, Marshall, 485
Field, Rachel, 287
Film production. *See also specific films.*
    Canadian, 256–57
    Ed Wood films, 175–77
    French New Wave Cinema, 29–30
    history, 239, 427

Hunza, 358
Hutton, Barbara, 349–50

I
Ice cream, 48, 65
Ice hotels, 170–71
Idioms, 94, 142, 159, 239, 301, 324, 392, 491, 499
If I Knew Then (Fisher), 58
Incan Empire, 26
Ince, Thomas H., 258–60
Income, 80
Independent, The (newspaper), 196
Indian Railways, 168
Influenza, 392
Ink, 213
Internet addiction, 57
Internet development, 254
Interstate highways, 88, 358
Inuit, 519–20
iPods, 138
Irish Republican Army (IRA), 474–76
I Rode with the Ku Klux Klan (Kennedy), 250–51
Irving, Henry, 341–43
Isandlwana, Battle of, 206
Islet of Langerhans, 267
Ismael, Abdul Kassem, 473
Israel, 461
Is Shakespeare Dead? (Twain), 517
Italian city-states, 406–7
"I Want It That Way," 241

J
Jackrabbit Parole (Reid), 16–17
Jackson, Janet, 207
Jackson, La Toya, 207
Jackson, Michael, 44, 207
Jackson 5, 207
Jamaican bobsled team, 360
Japan, 37, 45–47
Jebb, Gladwyn, 79
Jefferson, Thomas, 286, 471
Jemison, Mae, 398
Jenner, Edward, 120
Jewelry, 177
Joan of Arc, 138
Jobs, Steve, 173
John XII (pope), 214
John XXI (pope), 435

John Paul II (pope), 200
Johnson, Edwin C., 458
Johnson, Jack, 244
Johnson, Lyndon B., 286, 422, 460
Johnson, Thomas H., 126
Johnson, Tor, 176
Johnston, James A., 151
Jones, Bob, Jr., 454–55
Jones, Bob, Sr., 454–55
Jones, Jim, 325–26
Jorgensen, Christine, 292–93
Judge Judy, 347
Jumbo jets, 206
Justinian (Byzantine emperor), 303

K
Kahlo, Frida, 555–57
Kane, Bob, 445
Kangaroos, 154
Kaplan, Fanya, 117
Karamanli, Hamet, 470–72
Karamanli, Yusuf, 470–72
Karansebes, Battle of, 545
Keelhauling, 526
Kefauver, Estes, 71
Kennedy, John F., 128–29, 361, 460–61, 546
Kennedy, Robert, 238
Kennedy, Stetson, 250–51
Kentucky Derby, 117
Khrushchev, Nikita, 181
Kidd, William (Captain Kidd), 143
Kindergarten, 246
Kinetoscope, 239, 427
King, Tom, 247
King Kong, 503–5, 509
Kingsford, E. G., 196
King Tut. *See* Tutankhamen.
Kinsey, Alfred, 315–17
Kinsey Reports, 317
Kirby, Jack, 38–39
Kissinger, Henry, 187, 224
Klan Unmasked, The (Kennedy), 251
Klaw, Irving, 512
Klug, Chris, 194
K-Mart, 205
Knerr, Richard, 514
Knights of Columbus, 168
Korea, 45–47
Koresh, David, 326–27

Marathon runners, 200
Marciano, Rocky, 192–93
Maria Theresa (empress of Austria), 284
Marie Antoinette, 284
Marijuana, 169
Marshall, George C., 181
Marshall Field and Company, 485
Marvel Comics, 38–39, 446
Marvin, Lee, 444
Marx, Karl, 49
Masada, 311
M°A°S°H, 226
Mason, Tom, 177
Masque of the Red Death, 278
Mathematics, 82
Mathis, Johnny, 103
Matisse, Henri, 266
Maximilian I (emperor of Mexico), 498
Mazatecan language, 49
McAuliffe, Christa, 398
McCartney, Paul, 81, 278, 337, 533
McDonald, Dick and Maurice, 279
McDonald's restaurants, 279–80
McFarland, Richard, 59
McFarland, Susan, 59
McGivney, Michael, 168
McGurn, Jack "Machine Gun," 204
McKinley, William, 20
McLaren, Norman, 256–57
McLendon, Gordon, 473
Meet the Barkers, 209
Mein Kampf (Hitler), 377, 379
Melford, George, 190
Melin, Arthur "Spud," 514
Mendel, Gregor Johann, 309
Mensa, 111
Mergers, 88, 205
Message in a bottle, 197
Meteorites, 61
Mexico, 473
Mice, 402, 554
Michelangelo, 247
Mickey Mouse, 381, 524
Military blunders, 545–47
Military discharges, 532
Millerites, 534
Mineral cures, 118–19
Ming dynasty, 179–80
Minneapolis, Minnesota, 439
Mitchell, Patrick "Paddy" Michael, 15–16

Mitchum, Robert, 415–16, 444
Mithridates VI (king of Pontus), 509
Mondo Cane, 490
Mongol empire, 37
Monmouth, Duke of, 542
Monopoly (game), 465
Monroe, Marilyn, 185, 482–84
Montauk, New York, 52–53
Montezuma, 416
Moore, Archie, 193
Moors murders, 217–19
Morgan, Henry, 144
Morgus the Magnificent, 137
Morris, Lee, 151
Moses, Anna Mary Robertson "Grandma," 541–42
Mott, Lucretia, 432
Mountain Dew, 154
Mourning, 80
Movies. See film production; *specific films.*
Mozart, Wolfgang Amadeus, 402
MTV, 386–88
Murray, Joseph, 455
Museums, 228, 552–53
Musgrave, Susan, 16–17
Music. *See also specific artists or songs.*
    boy bands, 240–41
    classical, 98–99
    family bands, 207–9
    hit songs, 44, 174, 374, 533
    loud, arrests for, 106
    pop-rock, 437–39
    scandals, 356–57
    stage names, 312
Mussolini, Benito, 20, 181, 304
Muybridge, Eadweard, 500
Myatt, John, 265–66
My Friend Flicka, 467

N
Nabokov, Vladimir, 23, 335–36
Napoleon Bonaparte, 385, 547
Napoleon III (emperor of France), 498
NASCAR, 351
Nash, John, 198
National Enquirer, 95
National Film Board of Canada, 256–57
Nauru, island of, 37
Nazi war criminals, 72–74, 109

Peter Pan, 199
Petra, Yvon, 347
Pheil, Abram C., 354
Philadelphia, USS, 470–71
Philip IV (king of France), 284
Phillips, Elizabeth Magie. *See* Magie, Lizzie J.
Phosphate mining, 37
Photography, 138, 372–73, 381, 526
Pianos, 261, 453
Picasso, Pablo, 146–47
Pickford, Mary, 363–64
Piggy banks, 324
Pig War, 188
Pilate, Pontius, 179
Piltdown Man, 26
Pink Panther movie series, 113
Pirates, 143–44, 301, 470–72
Pius II (pope), 304
Pius XII (pope), 74
Plan 9 from Outer Space, 175–77
Plath, Sylvia, 492–94
Plato's Academy, 302–3
Playing cards, 392
Plimpton, George, 185
Plumbing, indoor, 453
Poe, Edgar Allan, 261, 304
Poinsettias, 203
Poker, 417
Polaroid, 247
Pope, Generoso, 95
Popsicle Corporation, 48
Porsche, Ferdinand, 381
Porter, Edwin S., 427, 500
Portugal, 33
Potemkin mutiny, 382–84
Powell, Adam Clayton, Jr., 366–67
Powell, Lewis, 319–20
Presidents, U.S., 80, 194, 206. *See also specific presidents.*
Presley, Elvis, 214, 228, 552
Previn, Soon-Yi, 96–97
Prince (Prince Rogers Nelson), 544
Proietti, Monica "Machine Gun Molly," 76
Project Silverbug, 201–2
Protests, 544
Publishing industry, 211–13
Pulitzer, Joseph, 19–20
Puzo, Mario, 227, 462

Q

Quebec, 171
Quotations, 86, 220, 274, 318, 352, 368, 399, 426, 456, 478, 506, 522, 551

R

Rachel and the Stranger, 416
Radar, 52–53
Radio, 49, 371, 435, 473
Radioactive elements, 487–88
Raelian Church, 534–35
Raging Bull, 131
Raiders of the Lost Ark, 249
Railroads, 277
Raleigh, Walter, 371
Ramses II (pharaoh of Egypt), 313
Reagan, Ronald, 194, 284
Recorde, Robert, 82
Recording Industry Association of America, 169
Red Baron. *See* Von Richthofen, Manfred.
Reeves, Dan, 540
Reid, Stephen, 15–17
Reles, Abe "Kid Twist," 403–4
Religious simulacra, 162–63
Rembrandt, 148
Renault, Marcel, 442
Reno, Nevada, 139
Resnais, Alain, 29–30
Resnick, Judith, 397–98
Reuschel, Rick and Paul, 491
Revolutionary organizations, 165–66
Revolutions, 80
Ride, Sally, 397–98
Riley, Jim, 154
Rite of Spring, 393–94
Rivera, Diego, 555–57
Rivera, Geraldo, 321
Roberts, Lawrence "Larry" G., 253–54
Rockefeller, John D., 194
Rogers, Roy, 430
Rogers, William, 188
Roget, Peter Mark, 329–30
Roget's Thesaurus, 329–30
Rolls-Royce, 484, 554
Romania, 181
Rome, ancient, 206, 233
Roosevelt, Eleanor, 453
Roosevelt, Franklin D., 78, 82, 480, 546

Contributing Writers

Tom DeMichael is the co-author of *The Groovy Side of the '60s* and *The Best American History Quiz* and is a frequent contributor to Armchair Readers™. He holds a degree in American history and has authored several titles on that subject.

Rhonda Markowitz lives in Manhattan. She is co-author of *The Groovy Side of the '60s;* and author of "Folk, Pop, Mods and Rockers, 1960–1966," part of *The Greenwood Encyclopedia of Rock History* and (under the pseudonym Ron D. Brown) *Clint Black: A Better Man.* A reporter and producer for MTV News from 1990 through 1998, she won a Peabody Award for excellence in journalism.

Lexi M. Schuh is a wife, mother, and writer. In her free time she enjoys running, reading, and honing her vegetarian cooking skills.

Robert Norris is a 50-year veteran of the communications industry. Proverbially speaking, he has seen it from all sides: broadcast journalist, advertising executive, voice specialist, actor, and freelance writer.

Bryant Smith—writer, educator, performer, graphic designer—was born and raised in Chicago. His writing has been published in several journals, including the "Hip-Hop: Music and Culture" edition of Johns Hopkins University's *Callaloo.* His first book of poetry and short stories is forthcoming.

Richard Mueller is a screenwriter, novelist, and military historian who lives in Los Angeles. He has previously written for *Armchair Reader™: Civil War.* His work often appears in *The Magazine of Fantasy & Science Fiction,* and his episode of *Married... with Children* has just been remade in Russia and Hungary.

Katherine Don is a freelance writer who hails from a Chicago suburb and currently lives in Wrigleyville. When not typing away at her laptop, she volunteers for nonprofit organizations that deal with healthcare and penal system reform, researches for her book-in-progress, and hones her skills for world domination—or, at the very least, graduate school.

Kimberly Morris is a writer and an editor whose work has appeared in *New City, No Touching, Toasted Cheese, Jargon Magazine, Sleepwalk,* and *Hair Trigger.* Kim is the Supervisor of Story Development at 2nd Story, a hybrid performance series of storytelling and music, where she co-curates the Red Kiva performance series and is editor-in-chief of *2D,* a publication of stories and visual art.

Colleen Delegan, ex ad company creative director, currently divides her time between Chicago, Europe, and Asia. She has written pilots for NBC, CBS, and ABC. Her book *Three Thousand Coffees in Vienna* was published in 2004.

Maya Henderson is a Chicago-based writer who, in addition to researching articles on crazy pin-up girls, likes to write about alternative health/wellness, yoga, and music for a slew of local publications.

Paul Seaburn is the head writer for the family comedy *Taylor's Attic,* a humor writer for numerous publications, and a teacher of creative thinking techniques using comedy. His work has appeared in *Armchair Reader™: The Extraordinary Book of Lists, Toasts for Any Occasion,* and *50 Uses for Your Cat,* among many others.

James Duplacey has written more than 50 books on sport and culture, including *The Love of Hockey; Muhammad Ali: Athlete, Activist, Ambassador; Images of Glory; Hockey's Book of Firsts; The Ultimate Prize;* and *Jesse Ventura: From the Square Ring to Political Circle.* He is also a contributor to *Armchair Reader™: The Book of Incredible Information.*

Martin Graham has contributed to a number of books, including *Armchair Reader™: Civil War, The Civil War Chronicle, The World War II Chronicle,* and *The Blue & the Gray.* He has also written articles for *World War II, The Civil War Times,* and *Blue & Gray* magazines.

Terri Schlichenmeyer writes the book review column "The Bookworm Sez." She lives on a hill in Wisconsin with two dogs and 11,000 books.

Patricia Martinelli is a veteran freelance writer who has written books and articles about everything from crime to the supernatural.

Kelly Wittmann has published four children's educational books and has been co-editor of three adult trade books. She lives in Chicago.

Paul Morie works as a software engineer in Charleston, South Carolina.

Eric Peterson is the writer of *Roadside Americana* and has contributed to *Armchair Reader™: The Book of Incredible Information* and *Amazing Places to Go in North America.* He has also written numerous Frommer's guidebooks and writes about travel and other topics for such publications as *ColoradoBiz, Delta Sky,* and the *New York Daily News.*

Richard Knight, Jr., is a Chicago-based writer who has written extensively for the *Chicago Tribune* and the *Chicago Reader.* He is also the film critic for *Windy City Times.* He has published two collections of his film writing.

Hope you enjoyed this Armchair Reader™

You'll find the rest of the collection quite exciting.
Please look for these titles wherever books are sold.

ARMCHAIR
•READER™•

Weird, Scary & Unusual Stories & Facts

The Book of Incredible Information

The Amazing Book of History

The Extraordinary Book of Lists

Civil War • World War II

Grand Slam Baseball

Coming Attractions
The Book of Myths and Misconceptions
The Origins of Everything

Visit us at *www.armchairreader.com*
to learn all about our other great books from
West Side Publishing, or just to let us know
what your thoughts are about our books.
We love to hear from all our readers.

WEST
SIDE
PUBLISHING